Exploring Premium Media Site

Improve your grade with hands-on tools and resources!

- Master *Key Terms* to expand your vocabulary.
- Prepare for exams by taking practice quizzes in the *Online Chapter Review*.
- Download *Student Data Files* for the applications projects in each chapter.

And for even more tools, you can access the following Premium Resources using your Access Code. Register now to get the most out of *Exploring!*

- *Hands-On Exercise Videos* accompany each Hands-On Exercise in the chapter. These videos demonstrate both how to accomplish individual skills as well as why they are important.*
- *Soft Skills Videos* are necessary to complete the Soft Skills Beyond the Classroom Exercise, and introduce students to important professional skills.*

*Access code required for these premium resources

Your Access Code is:

Note: If there is no silver foil covering the access code, it may already have been redeemed, and therefore may no longer be valid. In that case, you can purchase online access using a major credit card or PayPal account. To do so, go to **www.pearsonhighered.com/exploring**, select your book cover, click on "Buy Access" and follow the on-screen instructions.

To Register:

- To start you will need a valid email address and this access code.
- Go to **www.pearsonhighered.com/exploring** and scroll to find your text book.
- Once you've selected your text, on the Home Page, click the link to access the Student Premium Content.
- Click the Register button and follow the on-screen instructions.
- After you register, you can sign in any time via the log-in area on the same screen.

System Requirements

Windows 7 Ultimate Edition; IE 8
Windows Vista Ultimate Edition SP1; IE 8
Windows XP Professional SP3; IE 7
Windows XP Professional SP3; Firefox 3.6.4
Mac OS 10.5.7; Firefox 3.6.4
Mac OS 10.6; Safari 5

Technical Support

h   ersoned.custhelp.com

D1530018

ex·ploring)
SERIES

1. Investigating in a systematic way: examining. 2. Searching into or ranging over for the purpose of discovery.

Microsoft®

Word 2013

COMPREHENSIVE

Series Editor Mary Anne Poatsy

Hogan | Lau

Series Created by Dr. Robert T. Grauer

PEARSON

Boston   Columbus   Indianapolis   New York   San Francisco   Upper Saddle River
Amsterdam   Cape Town   Dubai   London   Madrid   Milan   Munich   Paris   Montréal   Toronto
Delhi   Mexico City   São Paulo   Sydney   Hong Kong   Seoul   Singapore   Taipei   Tokyo

Editor in Chief: Michael Payne
Senior Editor: Samantha McAfee Lewis
Editorial Project Manager: Keri Rand
Product Development Manager: Laura Burgess
Development Editor: Vonda Keator
Editorial Assistant: Laura Karahalis
Director of Marketing: Maggie Moylan Leen
Marketing Manager: Brad Forrester
Marketing Coordinator: Susan Osterlitz
Marketing Assistant: Darshika Vyas
Managing Editor: Camille Trentacoste
Production Project Manager: Ilene Kahn
Senior Operations Specialist: Maura Zaldivar
Senior Art Director: Jonathan Boylan
Interior Design: Studio Montage
Cover Design: Studio Montage
Cover Photos: Supri Suharjoto/Shutterstock, wavebreakmedia/Shutterstock, Terry Chan/Shutterstock, Csaba Peterdi/Shutterstock
Associate Director of Design: Blair Brown
Digital Media Editor: Eric Hakanson
Director of Media Development: Taylor Ragan
Media Project Manager, Production: Renata Butera
Full Service Project Management: Andrea Stefanowicz/PreMediaGlobal
Composition: PreMediaGlobal

Credits and acknowledgments borrowed from other sources and reproduced, with permission, in this textbook appear on the appropriate page within text.

PEARSON

ISBN 10: 0-13-341222-9
ISBN 13: 978-0-13-341222-2

Dedications

For my husband, Ted, who unselfishly continues to take on more than his share to support me throughout the process; and for my children, Laura, Carolyn, and Teddy, whose encouragement and love have been inspiring.

Mary Anne Poatsy

I dedicate this work to my wonderful family—my husband, Paul, and my daughters, Jenn and Alli. You have made this adventure possible with your support, encouragement, and love. You inspire me!

Lynn Hogan

I dedicate this book to my only child, Catherine Shen, who taught me that there is another wonderful life outside of my work. My life has been more fulfilling and exciting with her in it. I also dedicate this book to the loving memory of my dog, Harry, who was by my side, through thick and thin, for 16 years. I miss him dearly every day.

Linda K. Lau

About the Authors

Mary Anne Poatsy, Series Editor

Mary Anne is a senior faculty member at Montgomery County Community College, teaching various computer application and concepts courses in face-to-face and online environments. She holds a B.A. in Psychology and Education from Mount Holyoke College and an M.B.A. in Finance from Northwestern University's Kellogg Graduate School of Management.

Mary Anne has more than 12 years of educational experience. She is currently adjunct faculty at Gwynedd-Mercy College and Montgomery County Community College. She has also taught at Bucks County Community College and Muhlenberg College, as well as conducted personal training. Before teaching, she was Vice President at Shearson Lehman in the Municipal Bond Investment Banking Department.

Lynn Hogan, Word Author

Lynn Hogan teaches at the University of North Alabama, providing instruction in the area of computer applications. With over 30 years of educational experience at the community college and university level, Lynn has taught applications, programming, and concepts courses in both online and classroom environments. She received an M.B.A. from the University of North Alabama and a Ph.D. from the University of Alabama.

Lynn is a co-author of *Practical Computing* and has served on the authoring team of *Your Office* as well as the *Exploring Office 2010* series. She resides in Alabama with her husband and two daughters.

Dr. Linda K. Lau, Word Author

Since 1994, Dr. Linda K. Lau is an associate professor of Management Information Systems (MIS) at the College of Business and Economics, Longwood University, located in Farmville, Virginia. She received the Outstanding Academic Advisor Award in 2006. Besides teaching and advising, Linda has authored and co-authored several journal and conference articles, edited two books, and sits on numerous editorial boards. Her current research interest focuses on campus ethics, hybrid/online learning, and e-commerce.

Linda earned her Ph.D. from Rensselaer Polytechnic Institute in 1993, and her MBA and Bachelor of Science from Illinois State University in 1987 and 1986, respectively. In her younger days, Linda worked as a flight attendant for Singapore International Airlines for six years before coming to America to pursue her academic dream. She also worked as a financial consultant with Salomon Smith Barney from 1999–2000 before returning to the academic world.

Linda resides in Farmville and Richmond with her family.

Rebecca Lawson, Office Fundamentals Author

Rebecca Lawson is a professor in the Computer Information Technologies program at Lansing Community College. She coordinates the curriculum, develops the instructional materials, and teaches for the E-Business curriculum. She also serves as the Online Faculty Coordinator at the Center for Teaching Excellence at LCC. In that role, she develops and facilitates online workshops for faculty learning to teach online. Her major areas of interest include online curriculum quality assurance, the review and development of printed and online instructional materials, the assessment of computer and Internet literacy skill levels to facilitate student retention, and the use of social networking tools to support learning in blended and online learning environments.

Dr. Robert T. Grauer, Creator of the Exploring Series

Bob Grauer is an Associate Professor in the Department of Computer Information Systems at the University of Miami, where he is a multiple winner of the Outstanding Teaching Award in the School of Business, most recently in 2009. He has written numerous COBOL texts and is the vision behind the Exploring Office series, with more than three million books in print. His work has been translated into three foreign languages and is used in all aspects of higher education at both national and international levels. Bob Grauer has consulted for several major corporations including IBM and American Express. He received his Ph.D. in Operations Research in 1972 from the Polytechnic Institute of Brooklyn.

Brief Contents

Contents

Microsoft Office 2013

Microsoft Office Word 2013

■ CHAPTER SIX Time Saving Tools: Using Templates, Multiple Documents, and Themes — 375

■ CHAPTER SEVEN Document Automation: Forms, Macros, and Security — 427

■ CHAPTER EIGHT Word and the Internet: Web Page Creation and Enhancement, and Blogs — 483

Application Capstone Exercises

Acknowledgments

The Exploring team would like to acknowledge and thank all the reviewers who helped us throughout the years by providing us with their invaluable comments, suggestions, and constructive criticism.

We'd like to especially thank our Focus Group attendees and User Diary Reviewers for this edition:

Stephen Z. Jourdan
Auburn University at Montgomery

Ann Rovetto
Horry-Georgetown Technical College

Jacqueline D. Lawson
Henry Ford Community College

Diane L. Smith
Henry Ford Community College

Sven Aelterman
Troy University

Suzanne M. Jeska
County College of Morris

Susan N. Dozier
Tidewater Community College

Robert G. Phipps Jr.
West Virginia University

Mike Michaelson
Palomar College

Mary Beth Tarver
Northwestern State University

Alexandre C. Probst
Colorado Christian University

Phil Nielson
Salt Lake Community College

Carolyn Barren
Macomb Community College

Sue A. McCrory
Missouri State University

Lucy Parakhovnik
California State University, Northridge

Jakie Brown Jr.
Stevenson University

Craig J. Peterson
American InterContinental University

Terry Ray Rigsby
Hill College

Biswadip Ghosh
Metropolitan State University of Denver

Cheryl Sypniewski
Macomb Community College

Lynn Keane
University of South Carolina

Sheila Gionfriddo
Luzerne College

Dick Hewer
Ferris State College

Carolyn Borne
Louisiana State University

Sumathy Chandrashekar
Salisbury University

Laura Marcoulides
Fullerton College

Don Riggs
SUNY Schenectady County Community College

Gary McFall
Purdue University

James Powers
University of Southern Indiana

James Brown
Central Washington University

Brian Powell
West Virginia University

Sherry Lenhart
Terra Community College

Chen Zhang
Bryant University

Nikia Robinson
Indian River State University

Jill Young
Southeast Missouri State University

Debra Hoffman
Southeast Missouri State University

Tommy Lu
Delaware Technical Community College

Mimi Spain
Southern Maine Community College

We'd like to thank everyone who has been involved in reviewing and providing their feedback, including for our previous editions:

Adriana Lumpkin
Midland College

Alan S. Abrahams
Virginia Tech

Ali Berrached
University of Houston–Downtown

Allen Alexander
Delaware Technical & Community College

Andrea Marchese
Maritime College, State University of New York

Andrew Blitz
Broward College; Edison State College

Angel Norman
University of Tennessee, Knoxville

Angela Clark
University of South Alabama

Ann Rovetto
Horry-Georgetown Technical College

Astrid Todd
Guilford Technical Community College

Audrey Gillant
Maritime College, State University of New York

Barbara Stover
Marion Technical College

Barbara Tollinger
Sinclair Community College

Ben Brahim Taha
Auburn University

Beverly Amer
Northern Arizona University

Beverly Fite
Amarillo College

Bonita Volker
Tidewater Community College

Bonnie Homan
San Francisco State University

Brad West
Sinclair Community College

Brian Powell
West Virginia University

Carol Buser
Owens Community College

Carol Roberts
University of Maine

Carolyn Barren
Macomb Community College

Cathy Poyner
Truman State University

Charles Hodgson
Delgado Community College

Cheri Higgins
Illinois State University

Cheryl Hinds
Norfolk State University

Chris Robinson
Northwest State Community College

Cindy Herbert
Metropolitan Community College–Longview

Dana Hooper
University of Alabama

Dana Johnson
North Dakota State University

Daniela Marghitu
Auburn University

David Noel
University of Central Oklahoma

David Pulis
Maritime College, State University of New York

David Thornton
Jacksonville State University

Dawn Medlin
Appalachian State University

Debby Keen
University of Kentucky

Debra Chapman
University of South Alabama

Derrick Huang
Florida Atlantic University

Diana Baran
Henry Ford Community College

Diane Cassidy
The University of North Carolina at Charlotte

Diane Smith
Henry Ford Community College

Don Danner
San Francisco State University

Don Hoggan
Solano College

Doncho Petkov
Eastern Connecticut State University

Donna Ehrhart
State University of New York at Brockport

Elaine Crable
Xavier University

Elizabeth Duett
Delgado Community College

Erhan Uskup
Houston Community College–Northwest

Eric Martin
University of Tennessee

Erika Nadas
Wilbur Wright College

Floyd Winters
Manatee Community College

Frank Lucente
Westmoreland County Community College

G. Jan Wilms
Union University

Gail Cope
Sinclair Community College

Gary DeLorenzo
California University of Pennsylvania

Gary Garrison
Belmont University

George Cassidy
Sussex County Community College

Gerald Braun
Xavier University

Gerald Burgess
Western New Mexico University

Gladys Swindler
Fort Hays State University

Heith Hennel
Valencia Community College

Henry Rudzinski
Central Connecticut State University

Irene Joos
La Roche College

Iwona Rusin
Baker College; Davenport University

J. Roberto Guzman
San Diego Mesa College

Jan Wilms
Union University

Jane Stam
Onondaga Community College

Janet Bringhurst
Utah State University

Jeanette Dix
Ivy Tech Community College

Jennifer Day
Sinclair Community College

Jill Canine
Ivy Tech Community College

Jim Chaffee
The University of Iowa Tippie College of Business

Joanne Lazirko
University of Wisconsin–Milwaukee

Jodi Milliner
Kansas State University

John Hollenbeck
Blue Ridge Community College

John Seydel
Arkansas State University

Judith A. Scheeren
Westmoreland County Community College

Judith Brown
The University of Memphis

Juliana Cypert
Tarrant County College

Kamaljeet Sanghera
George Mason University

Karen Priestly
Northern Virginia Community College

Karen Ravan
Spartanburg Community College

Kathleen Brenan
Ashland University

Ken Busbee
Houston Community College

Kent Foster
Winthrop University

Kevin Anderson
Solano Community College

Kim Wright
The University of Alabama

Kristen Hockman
University of Missouri–Columbia

Kristi Smith
Allegany College of Maryland

Laura McManamon
University of Dayton

Leanne Chun
Leeward Community College

Lee McClain
Western Washington University

Linda D. Collins
Mesa Community College

Linda Johnsonius
Murray State University

Linda Lau
Longwood University

Linda Theus
Jackson State Community College

Linda Williams
Marion Technical College

Lisa Miller
University of Central Oklahoma

Lister Horn
Pensacola Junior College

Lixin Tao
Pace University

Loraine Miller
Cayuga Community College

Lori Kielty
Central Florida Community College

Lorna Wells
Salt Lake Community College

Lorraine Sauchin
Duquesne University

Lucy Parakhovnik (Parker)
California State University, Northridge

Lynn Mancini
Delaware Technical Community College

Mackinzee Escamilla
South Plains College

Marcia Welch
Highline Community College

Margaret McManus
Northwest Florida State College

Margaret Warrick
Allan Hancock College

Marilyn Hibbert
Salt Lake Community College

Mark Choman
Luzerne County Community College

Mary Duncan
University of Missouri–St. Louis

Melissa Nemeth
Indiana University-Purdue University
Indianapolis

Melody Alexander
Ball State University

Michael Douglas
University of Arkansas at Little Rock

Michael Dunklebarger
Alamance Community College

Michael G. Skaff
College of the Sequoias

Michele Budnovitch
Pennsylvania College of Technology

Mike Jochen
East Stroudsburg University

Mike Scroggins
Missouri State University

Muhammed Badamas
Morgan State University

NaLisa Brown
University of the Ozarks

Nancy Grant
Community College of Allegheny
County–South Campus

Nanette Lareau
University of Arkansas Community
College–Morrilton

Pam Brune
Chattanooga State Community College

Pam Uhlenkamp
Iowa Central Community College

Patrick Smith
Marshall Community and Technical College

Paul Addison
Ivy Tech Community College

Paula Ruby
Arkansas State University

Peggy Burrus
Red Rocks Community College

Peter Ross
SUNY Albany

Philip H. Nielson
Salt Lake Community College

Ralph Hooper
University of Alabama

Ranette Halverson
Midwestern State University

Richard Blamer
John Carroll University

Richard Cacace
Pensacola Junior College

Richard Hewer
Ferris State University

Rob Murray
Ivy Tech Community College

Robert Dušek
Northern Virginia Community College

Robert Sindt
Johnson County Community College

Robert Warren
Delgado Community College

Rocky Belcher
Sinclair Community College

Roger Pick
University of Missouri at Kansas City

Ronnie Creel
Troy University

Rosalie Westerberg
Clover Park Technical College

Ruth Neal
Navarro College

Sandra Thomas
Troy University

Sheila Gionfriddo
Luzerne County Community College

Sherrie Geitgey
Northwest State Community College

Sophia Wilberscheid
Indian River State College

Sophie Lee
California State University,
Long Beach

Stacy Johnson
Iowa Central Community College

Stephanie Kramer
Northwest State Community College

Stephen Jourdan
Auburn University Montgomery

Steven Schwarz
Raritan Valley Community College

Sue McCrory
Missouri State University

Susan Fuschetto
Cerritos College

Susan Medlin
UNC Charlotte

Suzan Spitzberg
Oakton Community College

Sven Aelterman
Troy University

Sylvia Brown
Midland College

Tanya Patrick
Clackamas Community College

Terri Holly
Indian River State College

Thomas Rienzo
Western Michigan University

Tina Johnson
Midwestern State University

Tommy Lu
Delaware Technical and Community College

Troy S. Cash
NorthWest Arkansas Community College

Vicki Robertson
Southwest Tennessee Community

Weifeng Chen
California University of Pennsylvania

Wes Anthony
Houston Community College

William Ayen
University of Colorado at Colorado Springs

Wilma Andrews
Virginia Commonwealth University

Yvonne Galusha
University of Iowa

Special thanks to our development and technical team:

Barbara Stover

Cheryl Slavick

Elizabeth Lockley

Heather Hetzler

Jennifer Lynn

Joyce Nielsen

Linda Pogue

Lisa Bucki

Lori Damanti

Mara Zebest

Susan Fry

Preface

The Exploring Series and You

Exploring is Pearson's Office Application series that requires students like you to think "beyond the point and click." In this edition, we have worked to restructure the Exploring experience around the way you, today's modern student, actually use your resources.

The goal of Exploring is, as it has always been, to go further than teaching just the steps to accomplish a task—the series provides the theoretical foundation for you to understand when and why to apply a skill.

As a result, you achieve a deeper understanding of each application and can apply this critical thinking beyond Office and the classroom.

You are practical students, focused on what you need to do to be successful in this course and beyond, and want to be as efficient as possible. Exploring has evolved to meet you where you are and help you achieve success efficiently. Pearson has paid attention to the habits of students today, how you get information, how you are motivated to do well in class, and what your future goals look like. We asked you and your peers for acceptance of new tools we designed to address these points, and you responded with a resounding "YES!"

Here Is What We Learned About You

You are goal-oriented. You want a good grade in this course—so we rethought how Exploring works so that you can learn the how and why behind the skills in this course to be successful now. You also want to be successful in your future career—so we used motivating case studies to show relevance of these skills to your future careers and incorporated Soft Skills, Collaboration, and Analysis Cases in this edition to set you up for success in the future.

You read, prepare, and study differently than students used to. You use textbooks like a tool—you want to easily identify what you need to know and learn it efficiently. We have added key features such as Step Icons, Hands-On Exercise Videos, and tracked everything via page numbers that allow you to navigate the content efficiently, making the concepts accessible and creating a map to success for you to follow.

You go to college now with a different set of skills than students did five years ago. The new edition of Exploring moves you beyond the basics of the software at a faster pace, without sacrificing coverage of the fundamental skills that you need to know. This ensures that you will be engaged from page 1 to the end of the book.

You and your peers have diverse learning styles. With this in mind, we broadened our definition of "student resources" to include Compass, an online skill database; movable Student Reference cards; Hands-On Exercise videos to provide a secondary lecture-like option of review; Soft Skills exercises to illustrate important non-technical skills; and the most powerful online homework and assessment tool around with a direct 1:1 content match with the Exploring Series, MyITLab. Exploring will be accessible to all students, regardless of learning style.

Providing You with a Map to Success to Move Beyond the Point and Click

All of these changes and additions will provide you with an easy and efficient path to follow to be successful in this course, regardless of your learning style or any existing knowledge you have at the outset. Our goal is to keep you more engaged in both the hands-on and conceptual sides, helping you to achieve a higher level of understanding that will guarantee you success in this course and in your future career. In addition to the vision and experience of the series creator, Robert T. Grauer, we have assembled a tremendously talented team of Office Applications authors who have devoted themselves to teaching you the ins and outs of Microsoft Word, Excel, Access, and PowerPoint. Led in this edition by series editor Mary Anne Poatsy, the whole team is equally dedicated to providing you with a **map to success** to support the Exploring mission of **moving you beyond the point and click**.

Key Features

- **White Pages/Yellow Pages** clearly distinguish the theory (white pages) from the skills covered in the Hands-On Exercises (yellow pages) so students always know what they are supposed to be doing.

- **Enhanced Objective Mapping** enables students to follow a directed path through each chapter, from the objectives list at the chapter opener through the exercises in the end of chapter.
  - **Objectives List:** This provides a simple list of key objectives covered in the chapter. This includes page numbers so students can skip between objectives where they feel they need the most help.
  - **Step Icons:** These icons appear in the white pages and reference the step numbers in the Hands-On Exercises, providing a correlation between the two so students can easily find conceptual help when they are working hands-on and need a refresher.
  - **Quick Concepts Check:** A series of questions that appear briefly at the end of each white page section. These questions cover the most essential concepts in the white pages required for students to be successful in working the Hands-On Exercises. Page numbers are included for easy reference to help students locate the answers.
  - **Chapter Objectives Review:** Appears toward the end of the chapter and reviews all important concepts throughout the chapter. Newly designed in an easy-to-read bulleted format.

- **Key Terms Matching:** A new exercise that requires students to match key terms to their definitions. This requires students to work actively with this important vocabulary and prove conceptual understanding.

- **Case Study** presents a scenario for the chapter, creating a story that ties the Hands-On Exercises together.

Watch the Video for this Hands-On Exercise!

- **Hands-On Exercise Videos** are tied to each Hands-On Exercise and walk students through the steps of the exercise while weaving in conceptual information related to the Case Study and the objectives as a whole.

- **End-of-Chapter Exercises** offer instructors several options for assessment. Each chapter has approximately 12–15 exercises ranging from multiple choice questions to open-ended projects. Newly included in this is a Key Terms Matching exercise of approximately 20 questions, as well as a Collaboration Case and Soft Skills Case for every chapter.

ANALYSIS CASE
CREATIVE CASE

- **Enhanced Mid-Level Exercises** include a **Creative Case** (for PowerPoint and Word), which allows students some flexibility and creativity, not being bound by a definitive solution, and an **Analysis Case** (for Excel and Access), which requires students to interpret the data they are using to answer an analytic question, as well as **Discover Steps**, which encourage students to use Help or to problem-solve to accomplish a task.

MyITLab®
HOE1 Training

MyITLab®
Grader

- **MyITLab** provides an auto-graded homework, tutorial, and assessment solution that is built to match the book content exactly. Every Hands-On Exercise is available as a simulation training. Every Capstone Exercise and most Mid-Level Exercises are available as live-in-the-application Grader projects. Icons are included throughout the text to denote which exercises are included.

Instructor Resources

The Instructor's Resource Center, available at www.pearsonhighered.com, includes the following:

- **Instructor Manual** provides an overview of all available resources as well as student data and solution files for every exercise.

- **Solution Files with Scorecards** assist with grading the Hands-On Exercises and end-of-chapter exercises.

- **Prepared Exams** allow instructors to assess all skills covered in a chapter with a single project.

- **Rubrics** for Mid-Level Creative Cases and Beyond the Classroom Cases in Microsoft® Word format enable instructors to customize the assignments for their classes.

- **PowerPoint® Presentations** with notes for each chapter are included for out-of-class study or review.

- **Lesson Plans** provide a detailed blueprint to achieve chapter learning objectives and outcomes.

- **Objectives Lists** map chapter objectives to Hands-On Exercises and end-of-chapter exercises.

- **Multiple Choice and Key Terms Matching Answer Keys**

- **Test Bank** provides objective-based questions for every chapter.

- **Grader Projects** textual versions of auto-graded assignments for Grader.

- **Additional Projects** provide more assignment options for instructors.

- **Syllabus Templates**

- **Scripted Lectures** offer an in-class lecture guide for instructors to mirror the Hands-On Exercises.

- **Assignment Sheet**

- **File Guide**

Student Resources

Companion Web Site

www.pearsonhighered.com/exploring offers expanded IT resources and self-student tools for students to use for each chapter, including:

- Online Chapter Review
- Web Resources
- Glossary
- Student Data Files
- Chapter Objectives Review

In addition, the Companion Web Site is now the site for Premium Media, including the videos for the Exploring Series:

- Hands-On Exercise Videos*
- Audio PPTs*

*Access code required for these premium resources.

Student Reference Cards

A two-sided card for each application provides students with a visual summary of information and tips specific to each application.

Office

Office Fundamentals and File Management

CHAPTER 1

Taking the First Step

Andresr/Shutterstock

CASE STUDY | Spotted Begonia Art Gallery

You are an administrative assistant for Spotted Begonia, a local art gallery. The gallery deals in local artists' work, including fiber art, oil paintings, watercolors, prints, pottery, and metal sculptures. The gallery holds four seasonal showings throughout the year. Much of the art is on consignment, but there are a few permanent collections. Occasionally, the gallery exchanges these collections with other galleries across the country. The gallery does a lot of community outreach and tries to help local artists develop a network of clients and supporters. Local schools are invited to bring students to the gallery for enrichment programs. Considered a major contributor to the local economy, the gallery has received both public and private funding through federal and private grants.

As the administrative assistant for Spotted Begonia, you are responsible for overseeing the production of documents, spreadsheets, newspaper articles, and presentations that will be used to increase public awareness of the gallery. Other clerical assistants who are familiar with Microsoft Office will prepare the promotional materials, and you will proofread, make necessary corrections, adjust page layouts, save and print documents, and identify appropriate templates to simplify tasks. Your experience with Microsoft Office 2013 is limited, but you know that certain fundamental tasks that are common to Word, Excel, and PowerPoint will help you accomplish your oversight task. You are excited to get started with your work!

Windows 8.1.1 Startup

You use computers for many activities for work, school, or pleasure. You probably have never thought too much about what makes a computer function and allows you to do so many things with it. But all of those activities would not be possible without an operating system running on the computer. An *operating system* is software that directs computer activities such as checking all components, managing system resources, and communicating with application software. *Windows 8.1.1* is a Microsoft operating system released in April 2014 and is available on laptops, desktops, and tablet computers.

The *Start screen* is what you see after starting your computer and entering your username and password. It is where you start all of your computing activities. See Figure 1.1 to see a typical Start screen.

FIGURE 1.1 Typical Start Screen Components and Charms

In this section, you will explore the Start screen and its components in more detail. You will also learn how to log in with your Microsoft account and access the desktop.

Logging In with Your Microsoft Account

Although you can log in to Windows 8.1.1 as a local network user, you can also log in using a Microsoft account. When you have a Microsoft account, you can sign in to any Windows 8.1.1 computer and you will be able to access the saved settings associated with your Microsoft account. That means the computer will have the same familiar look that you are used to seeing. Your Microsoft account will allow you to be automatically signed in to all of the apps and services that use a Microsoft account as the authentication. You can also save your sign-in credentials for other Web sites that you frequently visit.

Logging in with your Microsoft account not only provides all of the benefits just listed, but also provides additional benefits such as being connected to all of Microsoft's resources on the Internet. These resources include a free Outlook account and access to cloud storage at OneDrive. *Cloud storage* is a technology used to store files and to work with programs that are stored in a central location on the Internet. *OneDrive* is an app used to store, access, and share files and folders. It is accessible using an installed desktop app or as cloud storage using a Web address. Files and folders in either location can be synced. For Office 2013 applications, OneDrive is the default location for saving files. Documents saved in OneDrive are accessible from any computer that has an Internet connection. As long as the document has been saved in OneDrive, the most recent version of the document will be accessible from any computer connected to the Internet. OneDrive allows you to collaborate with others. You can easily share your documents with others or add Reply Comments next to the text that you are discussing together. You can work with others on the same document simultaneously.

STEP 1 》 You can create a Microsoft account at any time by going to live.com. You simply work through the Sign-up form to set up your account by creating a username from your e-mail address and creating a password. After filling in the form, you will be automatically signed in to Outlook and sent to your Outlook Inbox. If you already have a Microsoft account, you can just go ahead and log in to Outlook. See Figure 1.2 to see the Sign-up page at live.com.

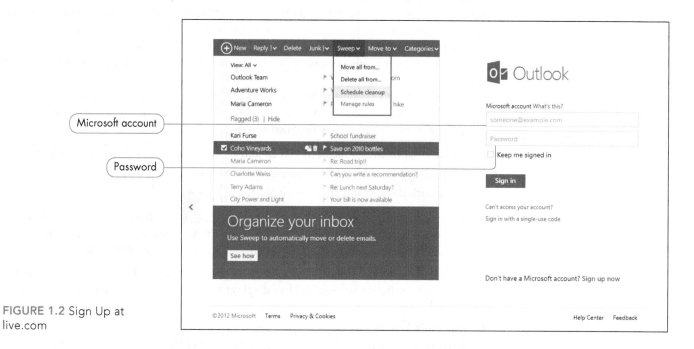

FIGURE 1.2 Sign Up at live.com

Identifying the Start Screen Components

The first thing you will notice when you turn on a computer running Windows 8.1.1 is that the Start screen has a new sleek, clean look and large readable type (refer to Figure 1.1). The user is identified in the top-right corner of the screen. You can click the user's name to access settings such as locking or signing out of the account. You can also change the picture associated with the account here.

You will notice that the Start screen is made up of several colorful block images called *tiles*. When you click a tile, you will be taken to a program, file, folder, or other *Windows 8.1.1 app*. Windows 8.1.1 apps are applications specifically designed to run in the Start screen interface of Windows 8.1.1. Some Windows 8.1.1 apps, such as desktop, Mail, and OneDrive, are already installed and ready to use. Others can be downloaded from the Windows Store. The default apps are brightly colored. Tiles for programs that run on the traditional Windows desktop are smaller and more transparent. The look of the tiles is customizable, but all tiles include the name of the app or program. Depending on the number of apps that you have installed, as you move your mouse to the bottom of the screen, you will see a horizontal scroll bar display. This can be used to access any app that does not display within the initial view of the Start screen.

STEP 2 》 The traditional Start button is not present in Windows 8.1.1. Instead, the *Charms* are available (refer to Figure 1.1). The Charms are made up of five icons that provide similar functionality to the Start button found in previous versions of Windows. The icons are Search, Share, Start, Devices, and Settings. Using the Charms, you can search for files and applications, share information with others within an application that is running, or return to the Start screen. You can also control devices that are connected to your computer or modify various settings depending on which application is running when accessing the Setting icon. To display the Charms, point to the top-right or bottom-right corners of the screen. Refer to Figure 1.1 to view the Start screen components and the Charms.

Interacting with the Start Screen

To interact with any tile on the Start screen (refer to Figure 1.1), simply click it. If you have signed in with your Microsoft account, you will automatically be able to access any of the Internet-enabled programs. For example, if you click Mail, you will go straight to your Outlook Inbox. If you right-click a tile, you will see several contextual options displayed. For example, the option to unpin the tile from the Start screen displays. To return to the Start screen from the desktop, point your mouse in the bottom-left corner of the screen. Pointing your mouse to the top-left corner reveals the open applications or programs that you have been accessing during this session. You can also use Charms to navigate back to the Start screen.

You may want to set up the Start screen so that programs and apps that you use most frequently are readily available. It is very easy to add tiles to or remove tiles from the Start screen. To add a tile, first display the Start screen.

1. Locate a blank area of the Start screen and right-click to display the *All apps* icon.
2. Click *All apps* and locate the desired new app that you want to add.
3. Right-click the app and click *Pin to Start*. The app is added to the Start screen.

The new app's tile is added at the end of your apps. You can move tiles by dragging the tile to the desired location. You can remove a tile from the Start screen by right-clicking the tile and clicking *Unpin from Start*. You can also group the tiles and name the groups:

1. To create a new group of tiles, drag a tile to the space to the left or right of an existing tile group. A light gray vertical bar displays to indicate where the new group will be located.
2. Add more tiles to this new group as needed.
3. To name the group, right-click any blank area of the Start screen and click Name groups. Type in the space provided to name a group. If a name is not entered for a group, the horizontal Name group bar disappears.

Accessing the Desktop

Although the Start screen is easy to use, you may want to access the more familiar desktop that you used in previous versions of Windows. The Desktop tile is available on the Start screen. Click the tile to bring up the desktop. Alternatively, you can be pushed to the desktop when you click other tiles such as Word. In Windows 8.1.1, the desktop is simplified to accommodate use on mobile devices where screen space is limited. However, on a laptop or desktop computer, you may want to have more features readily available. The familiar Notification area is displayed in the bottom-right corner. You will see the Windows Start screen, File Explorer, and Internet Explorer icons. See Figure 1.3 to locate these desktop components.

Taskbar

File Explorer

Internet Explorer

FIGURE 1.3 Desktop Components

STEP 3 >>

You can add more toolbars, such as the Address bar, to the taskbar by right-clicking the taskbar, pointing to Toolbars, and then selecting Address. The Address bar can be used to locate Web sites using the URL or to perform a keyword search to locate Web sites about a specific topic. You can also add programs such as the *Snipping Tool*. The Snipping Tool is a Windows 8.1.1 accessory program that allows you to capture, or *snip*, a screen display so that you can save, annotate, or share it. You can remove all of the icons displayed on the taskbar by right-clicking the icon you want to remove and selecting *Unpin this program from taskbar*.

TIP | Using the Snipping Tool

The Snipping Tool can be used to take all sizes and shapes of snips of the displayed screen. Options include Free-form Snip, Rectangle Snip, Window Snip, and Full-screen Snip. You can save your snip in several formats, such as PNG, GIF, JPEG, or Single file HTML. In addition, you can use a pen or highlighter to mark up your snips. This option is available after taking a snip and is located under the Tools menu in the Snipping Tool dialog box.

You can return to the Start screen by clicking the Start screen icon on the taskbar.

Quick Concepts

1. Logging in to Windows 8.1.1 with your Microsoft account provides access to Internet resources. What are some benefits of logging in this way? *p. 2*

2. OneDrive allows you to collaborate with others. How might you use this service? *p. 3*

3. What is the Start screen, and how is it different from the desktop? *p. 3*

4. The desktop has been a feature of previous Windows operating systems. How is the Windows 8.1.1 desktop different from previous versions? *p. 4*

Hands-On Exercises

1 Windows 8.1.1 Startup

The Spotted Begonia Art Gallery has just hired several new clerical assistants to help you develop promotional materials for the various activities coming up throughout the year. It will be necessary to have a central storage space where you can save the documents and presentations for retrieval from any location. You will also need to be able to collaborate with others on the documents by sharing them and adding comments. To begin, you will get a Microsoft account. Then you will access the desktop and pin a toolbar and a Windows 8.1.1 accessory program to the taskbar.

Skills covered: Log In with Your Microsoft Account • Identify the Start Screen Components and Interact with the Start Screen • Access the Desktop

STEP 1 ›› LOG IN WITH YOUR MICROSOFT ACCOUNT

You want to sign up for a Microsoft account so you can store documents and share them with others using the resources available with a Microsoft account, such as OneDrive. Refer to Figure 1.4 as you complete Step 1.

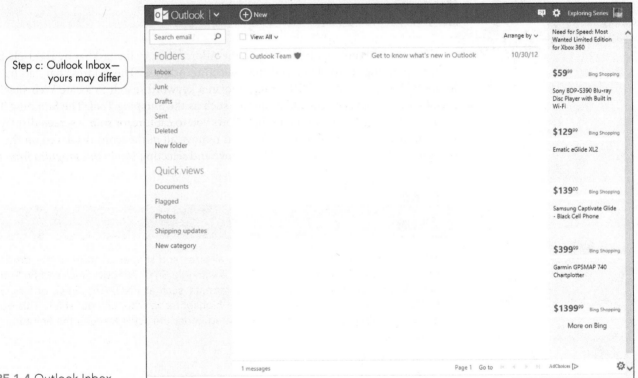

FIGURE 1.4 Outlook Inbox

a. Start your computer and enter your local username and password. On the Start screen, click the **Internet Explorer tile**. Click in the **Address bar** at the bottom of the screen. Type **live.com** and press **Enter**.

Internet Explorer displays, and you are taken to the Sign-up page for Outlook. This is where you can create a username and password for your Microsoft account.

> **TROUBLESHOOTING:** If you already have a Microsoft account, you can skip Step 1 and continue with Step 2. If someone else was already signed in at your computer, you can locate your username and click it to begin to log in.

b. Click the **Sign up now** link at the bottom of the screen. Fill in all text boxes and make all menu selections on the screen. Scroll down as needed. Type the **CAPTCHA code** carefully.

CAPTCHA is a scrambled code used with online forms to prevent mass sign-ups. It helps to ensure that a real person is requesting the account. You can choose not to accept e-mail with promotional offers by clicking the check box near the bottom of the screen to remove the check.

> **TROUBLESHOOTING:** You may want to write down your username and password so that you do not forget it the next time you want to log in with your Microsoft account. Keep this information in a safe and confidential location.

c. Click **I accept**. Your screen should display similarly to Figure 1.4.

Your Microsoft account is created, and you are taken to your Outlook Inbox.

d. Keep Internet Explorer open if you plan to continue using Outlook. Otherwise, sign out of Outlook and close Internet Explorer.

STEP 2 ❯❯ IDENTIFY THE START SCREEN COMPONENTS AND INTERACT WITH THE START SCREEN

You decide to explore the Start screen components. Then you use the Desktop tile on the Start screen to access the desktop. Refer to Figure 1.5 as you complete Step 2.

Step d: Display the Windows 8.1.1 desktop

FIGURE 1.5 Desktop

a. Point to the top-right corner to display the Charms. Click the **Start screen charm**.

Because you finished on the desktop after completing Step 1, clicking the Start screen charm takes you to the Start screen.

> **TROUBLESHOOTING:** If you skipped Step 1, log in to Windows with your username and password to display the Start screen.

b. Point to the bottom of the Start screen to display the horizontal scroll bar. Drag the scroll bar to the right to view all of the tiles available. Then drag the scrollbar back to the left to its original position.

Many components of the Start screen do not display until they are needed. This saves screen space on mobile devices. In this case, the horizontal scroll bar is hidden until needed.

c. Point to the bottom-right corner of the screen to display the Charms.

The Charms will display whenever you point to the top-right or bottom-right corners of the screen, regardless of the application you are using.

d. Locate and click the **Desktop tile**. See Figure 1.5.

STEP 3 ≫ ACCESS THE DESKTOP

You would like to add some components to make the desktop easier to use. You customize the desktop by adding the Address toolbar and the Snipping Tool to the taskbar. Refer to Figure 1.6 as you complete Step 3.

Step d: Snipping Tool

Step a: Address bar

Step e: Snipping Tool added to the taskbar

FIGURE 1.6 Taskbar with Address Bar and Snipping Tool

a. Locate and right-click the taskbar. Point to *Toolbars* and select **Address**.

The Address bar now displays on the right side of the taskbar.

b. Point to the top-right corner of the screen to display the Charms. Click the **Search charm**.

The Search pane displays on the right. The Search pane is organized into categories that you may want to search. For whatever category is selected, the relevant content is displayed.

TIP | Viewing Dialog Box Components

In Windows 8.1.1, many dialog boxes have been changed to panes. This is in keeping with the sleek, clean look of Windows 8.1.1. Even though the look is different, the functionality remains the same.

c. Type **Sn** in the **Search box**. Below the search box, the results listed display everything that begins with Sn.

d. Click the **Snipping Tool app** in the results list.

The Snipping Tool app displays on the desktop and the Snipping Tool icon displays on the taskbar.

e. Right-click the **Snipping Tool icon** on the taskbar. Click **Pin this program to taskbar**. See Figure 1.6.

The Snipping Tool and the Address bar will now be part of your taskbar.

TROUBLESHOOTING: If you are in a lab and cannot keep these changes, you can remove the Snipping Tool icon from the taskbar. Right-click the icon and click *Unpin this program from taskbar*. You can remove the Address bar by right-clicking the taskbar, pointing to Toolbars, and then clicking Address to remove the check mark.

---

f. Click the **Snipping Tool icon**. Click the **New arrow** in the Snipping Tool on the desktop. Click **Full-screen Snip**.

A snip of your desktop displays in the Snipping Tool program.

g. Click **File** and click **Save As**. Navigate to the location where you are saving your student files. Name your file **f01h1Desktop_LastFirst** using your own last name and first name. Check to see that *Portable Network Graphic file (PNG)* displays in the *Save as type* box. Click **Save**.

You have created your first snip. Snips can be used to show what is on your screen. Notice the Snipping Tool app does not display in your snip. When you save files, use your last and first names. For example, as the Office Fundamentals author, I would name my document *f01h1Desktop_LawsonRebecca*.

TROUBLESHOOTING: If PNG does not display in the *Save as type* box, click the arrow on the right side of the box and select *Portable Network Graphic file (PNG)*.

---

h. Close the Snipping Tool. Submit the file based on your instructor's directions.

i. Shut down your computer if you are ready to stop working. Point to the top-right corner to display the Charms. Click the **Settings charm**, click the **Power icon**, and then click **Shut down**. Otherwise, leave your computer turned on for the next Hands-On Exercise.

Files and Folders

Most activities that you perform using a computer produce some type of output. That output could be games, music, or the display of digital photographs. Perhaps you use a computer at work to produce reports, financial worksheets, or schedules. All of those items are considered computer *files*. Files include electronic data such as documents, databases, slide shows, and worksheets. Even digital photographs, music, videos, and Web pages are saved as files.

You use software to create and save files. For example, when you type a document on a computer, you first open a word processor such as Microsoft Word. In order to access files later, you must save them to a computer storage medium such as a hard drive or flash drive, or in the cloud at OneDrive. And just as you would probably organize a filing cabinet into a system of folders, you can organize storage media by *folders* that you name and into which you place data files. That way, you can easily retrieve the files later. Windows 8.1.1 provides tools that enable you to create folders and to save files in ways that make locating them simple.

In this section, you will learn to use File Explorer to manage folders and files.

Using File Explorer

File Explorer is an app that you can use to create and manage folders and files. The sole purpose of a computer folder is to provide a labeled storage location for related files so that you can easily organize and retrieve items. A folder structure can occur across several levels, so you can create folders within other folders—called *subfolders*—arranged according to purpose. Windows 8.1.1 uses the concept of libraries, which are folders that gather files from different locations and display the files as if they were all saved in a single folder, regardless of where they are physically stored. Using File Explorer, you can manage folders, work with libraries, and view favorites (areas or folders that are frequently accessed).

Understand and Customize the Interface

You can access File Explorer in any of the following ways:

- Click the File Explorer icon from the taskbar on the desktop.
- Click File Explorer from the Start screen.
- Display the Charms (refer to Figure 1.1) and click the Search charm. Type F in the Search box and in the results list on the left, click File Explorer.

Figure 1.7 shows the File Explorer interface containing several areas. Some of those areas are described in Table 1.1.

FIGURE 1.7 File Explorer Interface

TABLE 1.1   File Explorer Interface

Navigation Pane	The Navigation Pane contains five areas: Favorites, Libraries, Homegroup, Computer, and Network. Click an item in the Navigation Pane to display contents and to manage files that are housed within a selected folder.
Back, Forward, and Up Buttons	Use these buttons to visit previously opened folders or libraries. Use the Up button to open the parent folder for the current location.
Ribbon	The Ribbon includes tabs and commands that are relevant to the currently selected item. If you are working with a music file, the Ribbon commands might include one for burning to a CD, whereas if you have selected a document, the Ribbon would enable you to open or share the file.
Address bar	The Address bar enables you to navigate to other folders or libraries.
Content pane	The Content pane shows the contents of the currently selected folder or library.
Search box	Find files and folders by typing descriptive text in the Search box. Windows immediately begins a search after you type the first character, further narrowing results as you type.
Details pane	The Details pane shows properties that are associated with a selected file. Common properties include information such as the author name and the date the file was last modified. This pane does not display by default but can display after clicking the View tab.
Preview pane	The Preview pane provides a snapshot of a selected file's contents. You can see file contents before actually opening the file. The Preview pane does not show the contents of a selected folder. This pane does not display by default but can display after clicking the View tab.

File Explorer has a Ribbon like all the Office applications. As you work with File Explorer, you might want to customize the view. The file and folder icons might be too small for ease of identification, or you might want additional details about displayed files and folders. Modifying the view is easy. To make icons larger or to provide additional detail, click the View tab (refer to Figure 1.7) and select from the views provided in the Layout group. If you want additional detail, such as file type and size, click Details. You can also change the size of icons by selecting Small, Medium, Large, or Extra Large icons. The List view shows the file names without added detail, whereas Tiles and Content views are useful to show file thumbnails (small pictures describing file contents) and varying levels of detail regarding file locations. To show or hide File Explorer panes, click the View tab and select the pane to hide or show in the Panes group. You can widen or narrow panes by dragging a border when the mouse changes to a double-headed arrow.

Work with Groups on the Navigation Pane

The *Navigation Pane* provides ready access to computer resources, folders, files, and networked peripherals such as printers. It is divided into five areas: Favorites, Libraries, Homegroup, Computer, and Network. Each of those components provides a unique way to organize contents. In Figure 1.8, the currently selected area is Computer.

Earlier, we used the analogy of computer folders to folders in a filing cabinet. Just as you would title folders in a filing cabinet according to their contents, computer folders are also titled according to content. Folders are physically located on storage media such as a hard drive or flash drive. You can also organize folders into *libraries*, which are collections of files from different locations that are displayed as a single virtual folder. For example, the Pictures library includes files from the My Pictures folder and from the Public Pictures folder, both of which are physically housed on the hard drive. Although the library content comes from two separate folders, the contents are displayed as a single virtual folder.

Windows 8.1.1 includes several libraries that contain default folders or devices. For example, the Documents library includes the My Documents and Public Documents folders, but you can add subfolders if you wish so that they are also housed within the Documents library. To add a folder to a library, right-click the library, point to New, and then select Folder. You can name the folder at this point by typing the folder name. To remove a folder from the Documents library, open File Explorer, right-click the folder, and then select Delete.

The Computer area provides access to specific storage locations, such as a hard drive, CD/DVD drives, and removable media drives, including a flash drive. Files and folders housed on those storage media are accessible when you click Computer. For example, click drive C, shown under Computer in the Navigation Pane, to view its contents in the Content pane on the right. If you simply want to see the subfolders of the hard drive, click the arrow to the left of drive C to expand the view, showing all subfolders. The arrow is filled in and pointing down. Click the arrow again to collapse the view, removing subfolder detail. The arrow is open and pointing right. It is important to understand that clicking the arrow—as opposed to clicking the folder or area name—does not actually select an area or folder. It merely displays additional levels contained within the area. Clicking the folder or area, however, does select the item. Figure 1.8 illustrates the difference between clicking the folder or area name in the Navigation Pane and clicking the arrow to the left.

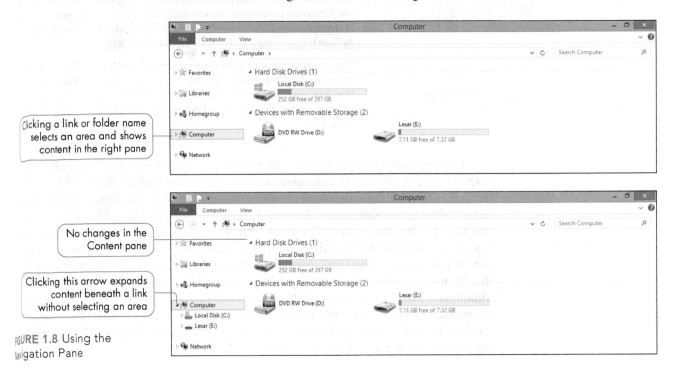

Clicking a link or folder name selects an area and shows content in the right pane

No changes in the Content pane

Clicking this arrow expands content beneath a link without selecting an area

FIGURE 1.8 Using the Navigation Pane

To locate a folder using File Explorer:

1. Click the correct drive in the Navigation Pane (or double-click the drive in the Content pane).
2. Continue navigating through the folder structure until you find the folder that you want.
3. Click the folder in the Navigation Pane (or double-click the folder in the Content pane) to view its contents.

The Favorites area contains frequently accessed folders and recent searches. You can drag a folder, saved search, library, or disk drive to the Favorites area. To remove a favorite, simply right-click the favorite and select Remove. You cannot add files or Web sites as favorites.

Homegroup is a Windows 8.1.1 feature that enables you to share resources on a home network. You can easily share music, pictures, videos, and libraries with other people in your home through a homegroup. It is password protected, so you do not have to worry about privacy.

Windows 8.1.1 makes creating a home network easy, sharing access to the Internet and peripheral devices such as printers and scanners. The Network area provides quick access to those devices, enabling you to see the contents of network computers.

Working with Folders and Files

As you work with software to create a file, such as when you type a report using Microsoft Word, your primary concern will be saving the file so that you can retrieve it later if necessary. If you have created an appropriate and well-named folder structure, you can save the file in a location that is easy to find later.

Create a Folder

You can create a folder a couple of different ways. You can use File Explorer to create a folder structure, providing appropriate names and placing the folders in a well-organized hierarchy. You can also create a folder from within a software application at the time that you need it. Although it would be wonderful to always plan ahead, most often you will find the need for a folder at the same time that you have created a file. The two methods of creating a folder are described next.

STEP 1 › Suppose you are beginning a new college semester and are taking four classes. To organize your assignments, you plan to create four folders on a flash drive, one for each class. After connecting the flash drive and closing any subsequent dialog box (unless the dialog box is warning of a problem with the drive), open File Explorer. Click Computer in the Navigation Pane. Click the removable (flash) drive in the Navigation Pane or double-click it in the Content pane. You can also create a folder on the hard drive in the same manner, by clicking drive C instead of the removable drive. Click the Home tab on the Ribbon. Click *New folder* in the New group. Type the new folder name, such as Biology, and press Enter. Repeat the process to create additional folders.

Undoubtedly, you will occasionally find that you have just created a file but have no appropriate folder in which to save the file. You might have just finished the slide show for your speech class but have forgotten first to create a speech folder for your assignments. Now what do you do? As you save the file, a process that is discussed later in this chapter, you can click Browse to bring up the Save As dialog box. Navigate to the drive where you want to store your file. Click *New folder* (see Figure 1.9), type the new folder name, and then double-click to save the name and open the new folder. After indicating the file name, click Save.

Click here to create a new folder

FIGURE 1.9 Create a Folder

OneDrive makes it easy to access your folders and files from any Internet-connected computer or mobile device. You can create new folders and organize existing folders just as you would when you use File Explorer. Other tasks that can be performed at OneDrive include opening, renaming, and deleting folders and files. To create a new folder at OneDrive, you can simply click the OneDrive tile on the Start screen. By default, you will see three items: Documents, Pictures, and Public Shared. You can right-click any of these three items to access icons for creating a new folder or to upload files. Once files and folders are added or created here, you can access them from any computer with Internet access at onedrive.live.com. Similarly, you can create folders or upload files and folders at OneDrive and then access them using the OneDrive tile on your Start screen.

Open, Rename, and Delete Folders and Files

You have learned that folders can be created in File Explorer but files are more commonly created in other ways, such as within a software package. File Explorer can create a new file, and you can use it to open, rename, and delete files just as you use it for folders.

Using the Navigation Pane, you can locate and select a folder containing a file that you want to open. For example, you might want to open the speech slide show so that you can practice before giving a presentation to the class. Open File Explorer and navigate to the speech folder. In your storage location, the file will display in the Content pane. Double-click the file. The program that is associated with the file will open the file. For example, if you have the PowerPoint program associated with that file type on your computer, then PowerPoint will open the file. To open a folder and display the contents, just click the folder in the Navigation Pane or double-click it in the Content pane.

STEP 3» At times, you may want to give a different name to a file or folder than the one that you originally gave it. Or perhaps you made a typographical mistake when you entered the name. In these situations, you should rename the file or folder. In File Explorer, move through the folder structure to find the folder or file. Right-click the name and select Rename. Type the new name and press Enter. You can also rename an item when you click the name twice— but much more slowly than a double-click. Type the new name and press Enter. Finally, you can click a file or folder once to select it, click the Home tab, and then select Rename in the Organize group. Type the new name and press Enter.

It is much easier to delete a folder or file than it is to recover it if you remove it by mistake. Therefore, be very careful when deleting items so that you are sure of your intentions before proceeding. When you delete a folder, all subfolders and all files within the folder are also removed. If you are certain you want to remove a folder or file, the process is simple. Right-click the item, click Delete, and then click Yes if asked to confirm removal to the Recycle Bin. Items are placed in the Recycle Bin only if you are deleting them from a hard drive. Files and folders deleted from a removable storage medium, such as a flash drive, are immediately and permanently deleted, with no easy method of retrieval. You can also delete an item (file or folder) when you click to select the item, click the Home tab, and then click Delete in the Organize group.

Save a File

STEP 2» As you create or modify a project such as a document, presentation, or worksheet, you will most likely want to continue the project at another time or keep it for later reference. You need to save it to a storage medium such as a hard drive, CD, flash drive, or in the cloud with OneDrive. When you save a file, you will be working within a software package. Therefore, you must follow the procedure dictated by that software to save the file. Office 2013 allows you to save your project to OneDrive or to a location on your computer.

The first time that you save a file, you must indicate where the file should be saved, and you must assign a file name. Of course, you will want to save the file in an appropriately named folder so that you can find it easily later. Thereafter, you can quickly save the file with the same settings, or you can change one or more of those settings, perhaps saving the file to a different storage device as a backup copy. Figure 1.10 shows a typical Save As pane for Office 2013 that enables you to select a location before saving the file.

Save to OneDrive

Save to your computer

Browse to a desired location

FIGURE 1.10 Save a File

Selecting, Copying, and Moving Multiple Files and Folders

You will want to select folders and files when you need to rename, delete, copy, or paste them, or open files and folders so that you can view the contents. Click a file or folder to *select* it; double-click a file or folder (in the Content pane) to *open* it. To apply an operation to several files at once, such as deleting or moving them, you will want to select all of them.

Select Multiple Files and Folders

You can select several files and folders, regardless of whether they are adjacent to each other in the file list. Suppose that your digital pictures are contained in the Pictures folder. You might want to delete some of the pictures because you want to clear up some hard drive space. To select pictures in the Pictures folder, open File Explorer and click the Pictures library. Locate the desired pictures in the Content pane. To select the adjacent pictures, select the first picture, press and hold Shift, and then click the last picture. All consecutive picture files will be highlighted, indicating that they are selected. At that point, you can delete, copy, or move the selected pictures at the same time.

If the files or folders to be selected are not adjacent, click the first item. Press and hold Ctrl while you click all desired files or folders, releasing Ctrl only when you have finished selecting the files or folders.

To select all items in a folder or disk drive, use File Explorer to navigate to the desired folder. Open the folder, press and hold Ctrl, and then press A on the keyboard. You can also click the Home tab, and in the Select group, click *Select all* to select all items.

In Windows 8.1.1, it is easy to make multiple selections, even if the items are not adjacent. Open File Explorer and select your drive or folder. Click the View tab and select Item check boxes in the Show/Hide group. As you move the mouse pointer along the left side of files and folders, a check box displays. Click in the check box to select the file. If you want to quickly select all items in the folder, click the check box that displays in the Name column heading.

Copy and Move Files and Folders

When you copy or move a folder, you move both the folder and any files that it contains. You can move or copy a folder or file to another location on the same drive or to another drive. If your purpose is to make a *backup*, or copy, of an important file or folder, you will probably want to copy it to another drive. It can be helpful to have backup copies saved in the cloud at OneDrive as well.

STEP 4 »   To move or copy an item in File Explorer, select the item. If you want to copy or move multiple items, follow the directions in the previous section to select them all at once. Right-click the item(s) and select either Cut or Copy on the shortcut menu. In the Navigation Pane, locate the destination drive or folder, right-click the destination drive or folder, and then click Paste.

Quick Concepts

1. The File Explorer interface has several panes. Name them and identify their characteristics. *p. 11*

2. After creating a file, such as a PowerPoint presentation, you want to save it. However, as you begin to save the file, you realize that you have not yet created a folder in which to place the file. Is it possible to create a folder as you are saving the file? If so, how? *p. 13*

3. What should you consider when deleting files or folders from a removable storage medium such as a flash drive? *p. 14*

4. Office 2013 enables you to save files to OneDrive or your computer. Why might it be helpful to save a file in both locations? *p. 14*

5. You want to delete several files, but the files are not consecutively listed in File Explorer. How would you select and delete them? *p. 15*

Hands-On Exercises

Watch the Video
for this Hands-
On Exercise!

MyITLab®
HOE2 Training

2 Files and Folders

You will soon begin to collect files from volunteers who are preparing promotional and record-keeping material for the Spotted Begonia Art Gallery. It is important that you save the files in appropriately named folders so that you can easily access them later. You can create folders on a hard drive, flash drive, or at OneDrive. You will select the drive on which you plan to save the various files. As you create a short document, you will save it in one of the folders. You will then make a backup copy of the folder structure, including all files, so that you do not run the risk of losing the material if the drive is damaged or misplaced.

Skills covered: Create Folders and Subfolders • Create and Save a File • Rename and Delete a Folder • Open and Copy a File

STEP 1 ⟩⟩ CREATE FOLDERS AND SUBFOLDERS

You decide to create a folder titled *Artists* and then subdivide it into subfolders that will help categorize the artists' artwork promotional files as well as for general record keeping for the art gallery. Refer to Figure 1.11 as you complete Step 1.

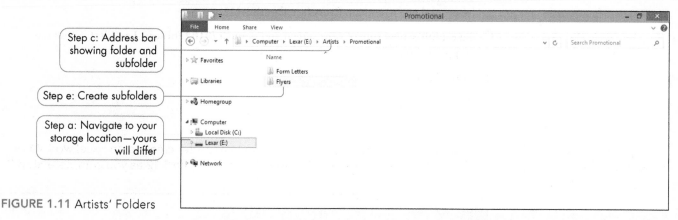

FIGURE 1.11 Artists' Folders

a. Navigate to the location where you are storing your files. If storing on your computer or a flash drive, navigate to the desktop. Click **File Explorer** on the taskbar and maximize the window. Click the **VIEW tab** and click to display the **Preview pane**, if necessary.

A removable drive is shown in Figure 1.11 and is titled *Lexar (E:)*, describing the drive manufacturer and the drive letter. Your storage area will be designated in a different manner, perhaps also identified by manufacturer (or perhaps you are saving your files on OneDrive). The storage area identification is likely to be different because the configuration of disk drives on your computer is unique.

> **TROUBLESHOOTING:** If you do not have a flash drive, you can use the hard drive. In the next step, simply click drive C in the Navigation Pane instead of the removable drive. You can also create and save folders and files at OneDrive.

b. Click the removable drive in the Navigation Pane (or click **drive C** if you are using the hard drive). Click the **HOME tab**, click **New folder** in the New group, type **Artists**, and then press **Enter**.

You create a folder where you can organize subfolders and files for the artists and their promotional materials and general record-keeping files.

> **TROUBLESHOOTING:** If the folder you create is called *New folder* instead of *Artists*, you probably clicked away from the folder before typing the name, so that it received the default name. To rename it, right-click the folder, click Rename, type the correct name, and then press Enter.

c. Double-click the **Artists folder** in the Content pane. The Address bar at the top of the File Explorer window should show that it is the currently selected folder. Click the **HOME tab**, click **New folder** in the New group, type **Promotional**, and then press **Enter**.

You decide to create subfolders of the *Artists* folder to contain promotional material, presentations, and office records.

d. Check the Address bar to make sure *Artists* is still the current folder. Using the same technique, create a new folder named **Presentations** and create a new folder named **Office Records**.

You create two more subfolders, appropriately named.

e. Double-click the **Promotional folder** in the Navigation Pane. Right-click in a blank area, point to *New*, and then click **Folder**. Type **Form Letters** and press **Enter**. Using the same technique, create a new folder named **Flyers** and press **Enter**.

To subdivide the promotional material further, you create two subfolders, one to hold form letters and one to contain flyers (see Figure 1.11).

f. Take a full-screen snip of your screen and name it **f01h2Folders_LastFirst**. Close the Snipping Tool.

g. Close File Explorer.

STEP 2 ≫ CREATE AND SAVE A FILE

To keep everything organized, you assign volunteers to take care of certain tasks. After creating an Excel worksheet listing those responsibilities, you will save it in the Office Records folder. Refer to Figure 1.12 as you complete Step 2.

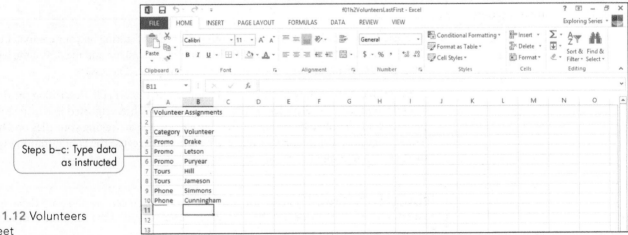

FIGURE 1.12 Volunteers Worksheet

Steps b–c: Type data as instructed

a. Navigate to the Start screen. Scroll across the tiles and click **Excel 2013**. If necessary, use the Search charm to locate Excel.

You use Excel 2013 to create the Volunteers worksheet.

b. Click **Blank workbook** in the Excel 2013 window that displays. Type **Volunteer Assignments** in **cell A1**. Press **Enter** twice.

Cell A3 is the active cell, as indicated by a green box that surrounds the cell.

c. Type **Category**. Press **Tab** to make the next cell to the right the active cell and type **Volunteer**. Press **Enter**. Complete the remaining cells of the worksheet as shown in Figure 1.12.

> **TROUBLESHOOTING:** If you make a mistake, click in the cell and retype the entry.

d. Click the **FILE tab** and click **Save**.

The Save As pane displays. The Save As pane is where you determine the location where your file will be saved, either your Computer or OneDrive.

e. Click **Browse** to display the Save As dialog box. Scroll down if necessary and click **Computer** or the location where you are saving your files in the Navigation Pane. In the Content pane, locate the Artists folder that you created in Step 1 and double-click to open the folder. Double-click **Office Records**. Click in the **File name box** and type **f01h2Volunteers_LastFirst**. Click **Save**. Refer to Figure 1.12.

The file is now saved as *f01h2Volunteers_LastFirst*. The workbook is saved in the Office Records subfolder of the Artists folder. You can check the title bar of the workbook to confirm the file has been saved with the correct name.

f. Click the **Close (X) button** in the top-right corner of the Excel window to close Excel.

STEP 3 ≫ RENAME AND DELETE A FOLDER

As often happens, you find that the folder structure you created is not exactly what you need. You will remove the Flyers folder and the Form Letters folder and will rename the Promotional folder to better describe the contents. Refer to Figure 1.13 as you complete Step 3.

Step d: Current folder structure

FIGURE 1.13 Artists Folder Structure

a. Navigate to the desktop, if necessary. Click **File Explorer** on the taskbar. Click the location where you are saving your files. Double-click the **Artists folder** in the Content pane.

b. Click the **Promotional folder** to select it.

> **TROUBLESHOOTING:** If you double-click the folder instead of using a single-click, the folder will open and you will see its title in the Address bar. To return to the correct view, click Artists in the Address bar.

c. Click the **HOME tab**. In the Organize group, click **Rename**, type **Promotional Print**, and then press **Enter**.

Because the folder will be used to organize all of the printed promotional material, you decide to rename the folder to better reflect the contents.

d. Double-click the **Promotional Print folder**. Click **Flyers**. Press and hold **Shift** and click **Form Letters**. Both folders should be selected (highlighted). Right-click either folder and click **Delete**. If asked to confirm the deletion, click **Yes**. Click **Artists** in the Address bar.

Your screen should appear as shown in Figure 1.13. You decide that dividing the promotional material into flyers and form letters is not necessary, so you deleted both folders.

e. Take a full-screen snip of your screen and name it **f01h2Artists_LastFirst**. Close the Snipping Tool.

f. Leave File Explorer open for the next step.

STEP 4 ≫ OPEN AND COPY A FILE

You hope to recruit more volunteers to work with the Spotted Begonia Art Gallery. The Volunteers worksheet will be a handy way to keep up with people and assignments, and as the list grows, knowing exactly where the file is saved will be important for easy access. You will modify the Volunteers worksheet and make a backup copy of the folder hierarchy. Refer to Figure 1.14 as you complete Step 4.

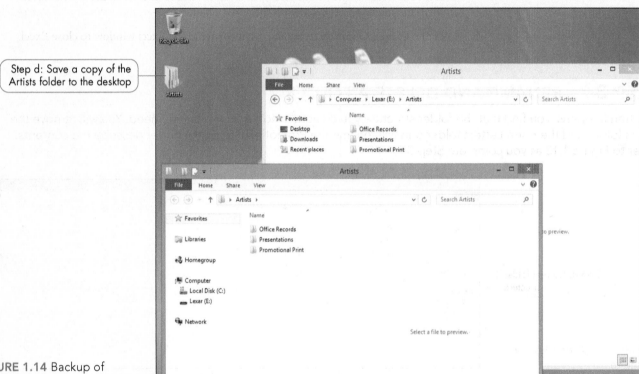

Step d: Save a copy of the Artists folder to the desktop

FIGURE 1.14 Backup of Artists Folder

a. Double-click the **Office Records folder**. Double-click *f01h2Volunteers_LastFirst*. Save the file with the new name **f01h2Stp4Volunteers_LastFirst** in the same location.

Because the file was created with Excel, that program opens, and the Volunteers worksheet is displayed.

b. Click **cell A11**, if necessary, and type **Office**. Press **Tab**, type **Adams**, and then press **Enter**. Click the **FILE tab** and click **Save**. The file is automatically saved in the same location with the same file name as before. Close Excel.

A neighbor, Sarah Adams, has volunteered to help in the office. You record that information on the worksheet and save the updated file in the Office Records folder.

c. Click the location where you save files in the Navigation pane in File Explorer so that the Artists folder displays in the Content pane. Right-click the **Artists folder** and click **Copy**.

d. Right-click **Desktop** in the Favorites group on the Navigation Pane and click **Paste**. Close File Explorer. If any other windows are open, close them also.

You made a copy of the Artists folder on the desktop.

e. Double-click the **Artists folder** on the desktop. Double-click the **Office Records folder**. Verify that the *f01h2Stp4Volunteers_LastFirst* worksheet displays in the folder. Take a full-screen snip of your screen and name it **f01h2Backup_LastFirst**. Close the Snipping Tool and close File Explorer.

f. Right-click the **Artists folder** on the desktop, select **Delete**, and then click **Yes** if asked to confirm the deletion.

You deleted the Artists folder from the desktop of the computer because you may be working in a computer lab and want to leave the computer as you found it. You may also want to empty the Recycle Bin.

g. Submit your files based on your instructor's directions.

Microsoft Office Software

Organizations around the world rely heavily on *Microsoft Office* software to produce documents, spreadsheets, presentations, and databases. Microsoft Office is a productivity software suite including a set of software applications, each one specializing in a particular type of output. You can use *Word* to produce all sorts of documents, including memos, newsletters, forms, tables, and brochures. *Excel* makes it easy to organize records, financial transactions, and business information in the form of worksheets. With *PowerPoint*, you can create dynamic presentations to inform groups and persuade audiences. *Access* is relational database software that enables you to record and link data, query databases, and create forms and reports.

You will sometimes find that you need to use two or more Office applications to produce your intended output. You might, for example, find that a Word document you are preparing for your investment club should also include a summary of stock performance. You can use Excel to prepare the summary and then incorporate the worksheet in the Word document. Similarly, you can integrate Word tables and Excel charts into a PowerPoint presentation. The choice of which software applications to use really depends on what type of output you are producing. Table 1.2 describes the major tasks of these four primary applications in Microsoft Office.

TABLE 1.2 Microsoft Office Software	
Office 2013 Product	**Application Characteristics**
Word 2013	Word processing software used with text to create, edit, and format documents such as letters, memos, reports, brochures, resumes, and flyers.
Excel 2013	Spreadsheet software used to store quantitative data and to perform accurate and rapid calculations with results ranging from simple budgets to financial analyses and statistical analyses.
PowerPoint 2013	Presentation graphics software used to create slide shows for presentation by a speaker, to be published as part of a Web site, or to run as a stand-alone application on a computer kiosk.
Access 2013	Relational database software used to store data and convert it into information. Database software is used primarily for decision making by businesses that compile data from multiple records stored in tables to produce informative reports.

As you become familiar with Microsoft Office, you will find that although each software application produces a specific type of output, all applications share common features. Such commonality gives a similar feel to each software application so that learning and working with Microsoft Office software products is easy. In this section, you will identify features common to Microsoft Office software, including such interface components as the Ribbon, the Backstage view, and the Quick Access Toolbar. You will also learn how to get help with an application.

Identifying Common Interface Components

As you work with Microsoft Office, you will find that each application shares a similar *user interface*. The user interface is the screen display through which you communicate with the software. Word, Excel, PowerPoint, and Access share common interface elements, as shown in Figure 1.15. One of the feature options includes the availability of templates as well as new and improved themes when each application is opened. A *template* is a predesigned file that incorporates formatting elements, such as a theme and layouts, and may include content that can be modified. A *theme* is a collection of design choices that includes colors, fonts, and special effects used to give a consistent look to a document, workbook, or presentation. As you can imagine, becoming familiar with one application's interface makes it that much easier to work with other Office software.

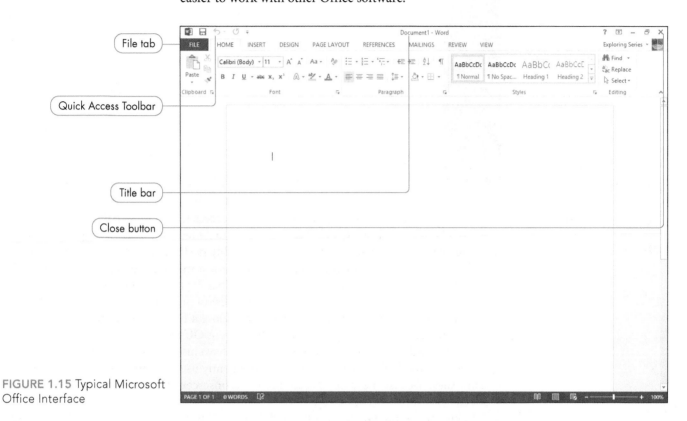

FIGURE 1.15 Typical Microsoft Office Interface

Use the Backstage View and the Quick Access Toolbar

The *Backstage view* is a component of Office 2013 that provides a concise collection of commands related to an open file. Using the Backstage view, you can find out information such as protection, permissions, versions, and properties. A file's properties include the author, file size, permissions, and date modified. You can create a new document or open, save, print, share, export, or close. The *Quick Access Toolbar*, located at the top-left corner of any Office application window, provides fast access to commonly executed tasks such as saving a file and undoing recent actions. The *title bar* identifies the current file name and the application in which you are working. It also includes control buttons that enable you to minimize, maximize, restore down, or close the application window (see Figure 1.15).

You access the Backstage view by clicking the File tab. When you click the File tab, you will see the Backstage view (see Figure 1.16). Primarily focusing on file activities such as opening, closing, saving, printing, and beginning new files, the Backstage view also includes options for customizing program settings, signing in to your Office account, and exiting the program. It displays a file's properties, providing important information on file permission and sharing options. When you click the File tab, the Backstage view will occupy the entire application window, hiding the file with which you might be working. For example, suppose that as you are typing a report you need to check the document's properties. Click the File tab to display a Backstage view similar to that shown in Figure 1.16. You can return to the application—in this case, Word—in a couple of ways. Either click the Back arrow in the top-left corner or press Esc on the keyboard.

Back arrow

Properties

FIGURE 1.16 The Backstage View

STEP 4》

The Quick Access Toolbar provides one-click access to common activities, as shown in Figure 1.17. By default, the Quick Access Toolbar includes buttons for saving a file and for undoing or redoing recent actions. You will probably perform an action countless times in an Office application and then realize that you made a mistake. You can recover from the mistake by clicking Undo on the Quick Access Toolbar. If you click the arrow beside Undo—known as the Undo arrow—you can select from a list of previous actions in order of occurrence. The Undo list is not maintained when you close a file or exit the application, so you can erase an action that took place during the current Office session only. Similar to Undo, you can also Redo (or Replace) an action that you have just undone. You can customize the Quick Access Toolbar to include buttons for frequently used commands such as printing or opening files. Because the Quick Access Toolbar is onscreen at all times, the most commonly accessed tasks are just a click away.

To customize the Quick Access Toolbar, click Customize Quick Access Toolbar (see Figure 1.17) and select from a list of commands. You can also click More Commands near the bottom of the menu options. If a command that you want to include on the toolbar is not on the list, you can right-click the command on the Ribbon and click *Add* to *Quick Access Toolbar*. Similarly, remove a command from the Quick Access Toolbar by right-clicking the icon on the Quick Access Toolbar and clicking *Remove from Quick Access Toolbar*. If you want to display the Quick Access Toolbar beneath the Ribbon, click Customize Quick Access Toolbar (see Figure 1.17) and click *Show Below the Ribbon*.

Undo

Repeat (or Redo)

Customize Quick Access Toolbar

FIGURE 1.17 Quick Access Toolbar

Familiarize Yourself with the Ribbon

The *Ribbon* is the command center of Office applications. It is the long bar located just beneath the title bar, containing tabs, groups, and commands. Each *tab* is designed to appear much like a tab on a file folder, with the active tab highlighted. The File tab is always a darker shade than the other tabs and a different color depending on the application. Remember that clicking the File tab opens the Backstage view. Other tabs on the Ribbon enable you to modify a file. The active tab in Figure 1.18 is the Home tab.

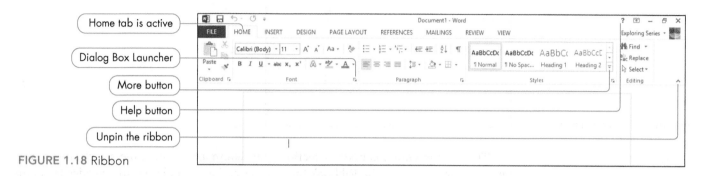

Home tab is active

Dialog Box Launcher

More button

Help button

Unpin the ribbon

FIGURE 1.18 Ribbon

When you click a tab, the Ribbon displays several task-oriented *groups*, with each group containing related *commands*. A group is a subset of a tab that organizes similar tasks together. A command is a button or area within a group that you click to perform tasks. Microsoft Office is designed to provide the most functionality possible with the fewest clicks. For that reason, the Home tab, displayed when you first open an Office software application, contains groups and commands that are most commonly used. For example, because you will often want to change the way text is displayed, the Home tab in each Office application includes a Font group with activities related to modifying text. Similarly, other tabs contain groups of related actions, or commands, many of which are unique to the particular Office application.

Because Word, PowerPoint, Excel, and Access all share a similar Ribbon structure, you will be able to move at ease among those applications. Although the specific tabs, groups, and commands vary among the Office programs, the way in which you use the Ribbon and the descriptive nature of tab titles is the same regardless of which program you are working with. For example, if you want to insert a chart in Excel, a header in Word, or a shape in PowerPoint, you will click the Insert tab in any of those programs. The first thing that you should do as you begin to work with an Office application is to study the Ribbon. Take a look at all tabs and their contents. That way, you will have a good idea of where to find specific commands and how the Ribbon with which you are currently working differs from one that you might have used previously in another application.

If you are working with a large project, you might want to maximize your workspace by temporarily hiding the Ribbon. You can hide the Ribbon in several ways. Double-click the active tab to hide the Ribbon and double-click any tab to redisplay it. You can click *Unpin the ribbon* (see Figure 1.18), located at the right side of the Ribbon, and click any tab to redisplay the Ribbon.

The Ribbon provides quick access to common activities such as changing number or text formats or aligning data or text. Some actions, however, do not display on the Ribbon because they are not so common but are related to commands displayed on the Ribbon. For example, you might want to change the background of a PowerPoint slide to include a picture. In that case, you will need to work with a *dialog box* that provides access to more precise, but less frequently used, commands. Figure 1.19 shows the Font dialog box in Word, for example. Some commands display a dialog box when they are clicked. Other Ribbon groups include a *Dialog Box Launcher* that, when clicked, opens a corresponding dialog box (refer to Figure 1.18).

Dialog box Help button

FIGURE 1.19 Dialog Box

The Ribbon contains many selections and commands, but some selections are too numerous to include in the Ribbon's limited space. For example, Word provides far more text styles than it can easily display at once, so additional styles are available in a *gallery*. A gallery also provides a choice of Excel chart styles and PowerPoint transitions. Figure 1.20 shows an example of a PowerPoint Themes gallery. Most often, you can display a gallery of additional choices by clicking the More button (refer to Figure 1.18) that is found in some Ribbon selections.

Themes gallery

FIGURE 1.20 PowerPoint Themes Gallery

STEP 3 ›

When editing a document, worksheet, or presentation, it is helpful to see the results of formatting changes before you make final selections. The feature that displays a preview of the results of a selection is called *Live Preview*. You might, for example, be considering changing the font color of a selection in a document or worksheet. As you place the mouse pointer over a color selection in a Ribbon gallery or group, the selected text will temporarily display the color to which you are pointing. Similarly, you can get a preview of how color designs would display on PowerPoint slides by pointing to specific themes in the PowerPoint Themes group and noting the effect on a displayed slide. When you click the item, such as the font color, the selection is applied. Live Preview is available in various Ribbon selections among the Office applications.

Office applications also make it easy for you to work with objects such as pictures, shapes, charts, and tables. When you include such objects in a project, they are considered separate components that you can manage independently. To work with an object, you must click to select it. When you select an object, the Ribbon is modified to include one or more *contextual tabs* that contain groups of commands related to the selected object. Figure 1.21 shows a contextual tab related to a selected SmartArt object in a Word document. When you click outside the selected object, the contextual tab disappears.

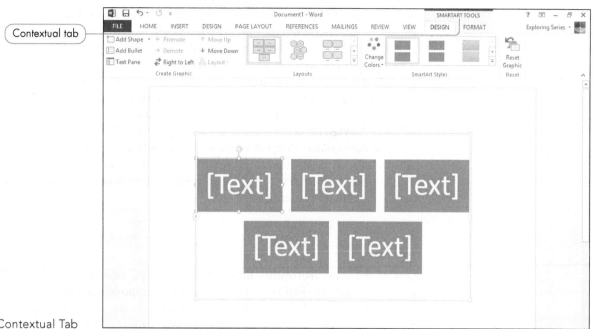

Contextual tab

FIGURE 1.21 Contextual Tab

TIP Using Keyboard Shortcuts

You might find that you prefer to use keyboard shortcuts, which are keyboard equivalents for software commands, when they are available. Universal keyboard shortcuts include Ctrl+C (copy), Ctrl+X (cut), Ctrl+V (paste), and Ctrl+Z (undo). To move to the beginning of a Word document, to cell A1 in Excel, or to the first PowerPoint slide, press Ctrl+Home. To move to the end of those items, press Ctrl+End. Press Alt to display keyboard shortcuts, called a **Key Tip**, for items on the Ribbon and Quick Access Toolbar. You can press the letter or number corresponding to Ribbon items to invoke the action from the keyboard. Press Alt again to remove the Key Tips.

Use the Status Bar

The *status bar* is located at the bottom of the program window and contains information relative to the open file. It also includes tools for changing the view of the file and for changing the zoom size of onscreen file contents. Contents of the status bar are unique to each specific application. When you work with Word, the status bar informs you of the number of pages and words in an open document. The Excel status bar displays summary information, such as average and sum, of selected cells. The PowerPoint status bar shows the slide number, total slides in the presentation, and the applied theme. It also provides access to notes and comments.

STEP 3 »

Regardless of the application in which you are working, the status bar includes view buttons and a Zoom slider. You can also use the View tab on the Ribbon to change the current view or zoom level of an open file. The status bar's view buttons (see Figure 1.22) enable you to change the *view* of the open file. When creating a document, you might find it helpful to change the view. You might, for example, view a PowerPoint slide presentation with multiple slides displayed (Slide Sorter view) or with only one slide in large size (Normal view). In Word, you could view a document in Print Layout view (showing margins, headers, and footers), Web Layout view, or Read Mode.

PAGE 1 OF 1   0 WORDS   100%

FIGURE 1.22 Word Status Bar

Additional views are available in the View tab. Word's Print Layout view is useful when you want to see both the document text and such features as margins and page breaks. Web Layout view is useful to see what the page would look like on the Internet. The Read Mode view provides a clean look that displays just the content without the Ribbon or margins. It is ideal for use on a tablet where the screen may be smaller than on a laptop or computer. PowerPoint, Excel, and Access also provide view options, although they are unique to the application. The most common view options are accessible from *View shortcuts* on the status bar of each application. As you learn more about Office applications, you will become aware of the views that are specific to each application.

STEP 1 ▶

The ***Zoom slider*** always displays at the far right side of the status bar. You can drag the tab along the slider in either direction to increase or decrease the magnification of the file. Be aware, however, that changing the size of text onscreen does not change the font size when the file is printed or saved.

Getting Office Help

One of the most frustrating things about learning new software is determining how to complete a task. Thankfully, Microsoft includes comprehensive help in Office so that you are less likely to feel such frustration. As you work with any Office application, you can access help online as well as within the current software installation. Help is available through a short description that displays when you rest the mouse pointer on a command. Additionally, you can get help related to a currently open dialog box by clicking the question mark in the top-right corner of the dialog box, or when you click Help in the top-right corner of the application.

Use Office Help

STEP 2 ▶

To access the comprehensive library of Office Help, click the Help button, displayed as a question mark on the far right side of the Ribbon (refer to Figure 1.18). The Help window provides assistance with the current application as well as a direct link to online resources and technical support. Figure 1.23 shows the Help window that displays when you click the Help button while in Excel. For general information on broad topics, click a link in the window. However, if you are having difficulty with a specific task, it might be easier to simply type the request in the Search online help box. Suppose you are seeking help with using the Goal Seek feature in Excel. Simply type *Goal Seek* or a phrase such as *find specific result by changing variables* in the Search box and press Enter (or click the magnifying glass on the right). Then select from displayed results for more information on the topic.

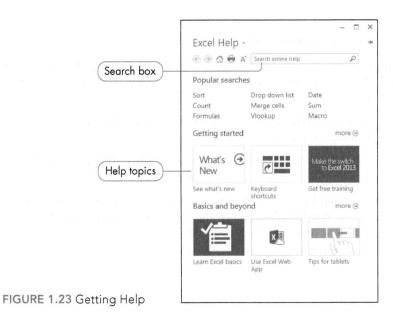

FIGURE 1.23 Getting Help

Use Enhanced ScreenTips

For quick summary information on the purpose of a command button, place the mouse pointer over the button. An *Enhanced ScreenTip* displays, giving the purpose of the command, short descriptive text, and a keyboard shortcut if applicable. Some ScreenTips include a suggestion for pressing F1 for additional help. The Enhanced ScreenTip in Figure 1.24 provides context-sensitive assistance.

FIGURE 1.24 Enhanced ScreenTip

Get Help with Dialog Boxes

Getting help while you are working with a dialog box is easy. Simply click the Help button that displays as a question mark in the top-right corner of the dialog box (refer to Figure 1.19). The subsequent Help window will offer suggestions relevant to your task.

1. How do you access the Backstage view, and what can you do there? ***p. 23***

2. What is the purpose of the Quick Access Toolbar? Suppose you often engage in an activity such as printing. What steps would you take to add that command to the Quick Access Toolbar? ***pp. 23–24***

3. The Ribbon is an important interface component of Office applications. What can you do with it? How is it organized? Is it always visible? ***pp. 25–27***

4. Occasionally, the Ribbon is modified to include a contextual tab. Define a contextual tab and give an example of when a contextual tab is displayed. ***p. 27***

5. After using Word to develop a research paper, you learn that the margins you used are incorrect. You plan to use Word's built-in Help feature to obtain information on how to change margins. Explain the process of obtaining help on the topic. ***pp. 28–29***

Hands-On Exercises

3 Microsoft Office Software

As the administrative assistant for the Spotted Begonia Art Gallery, you need to get the staff started on a proposed schedule of gallery showings worksheet. Although you do not have access to information on all of the artists and their preferred media, you want to provide a suggested format for a worksheet to keep up with showings as they get booked. You will use Excel to begin design of the worksheet.

Skills covered: Open an Office Application, Get Enhanced ScreenTip Help, and Use the Zoom Slider • Get Help and Use the Backstage View • Change the View and Use Live Preview • Use the Quick Access Toolbar and Explore PowerPoint Views

STEP 1 » OPEN AN OFFICE APPLICATION, GET ENHANCED SCREENTIP HELP, AND USE THE ZOOM SLIDER

Because you will use Excel to create the gallery showings worksheet, you will open the application. You will familiarize yourself with items on the Ribbon by getting Enhanced ScreenTip Help. For a better view of worksheet data, you will use the Zoom slider to magnify cell contents. Refer to Figure 1.25 as you complete Step 1.

FIGURE 1.25 Gallery Showings Worksheet

a. Navigate to the Start screen. Scroll across the tiles, if necessary, and click **Excel 2013**. Click **Blank workbook** in the Excel 2013 window that displays.

   You have opened Microsoft Excel because it is the program in which the gallery showings worksheet will be created.

b. Type **Date** in **cell A1**. As you type, the text appears in the current worksheet cell. Press **Tab** and type **Artist**. Press **Tab** and type **Media Used**. Press **Enter**. See Figure 1.25.

   The worksheet that you create is only a beginning. Your staff will later suggest additional columns of data that can better summarize the upcoming gallery showings.

c. Hover the mouse pointer over any command on the Ribbon and note the Enhanced ScreenTip that displays, informing you of the purpose of the command. Explore other commands and identify their purpose.

d. Click the **PAGE LAYOUT tab**, click **Orientation** in the Page Setup group, and then select **Landscape**.

   The PAGE LAYOUT tab is also found in Word, enabling you to change margins, orientation, and other page settings. Although you will not see much difference in the Excel screen display after you change the orientation to landscape, the worksheet will be oriented so that it is wider than it is tall when printed.

e. Drag the tab on the Zoom slider, located at the far right side of the status bar, to 190% to temporarily magnify the text. Take a full-screen snip of your screen and name it **f01h3Showings_LastFirst**.

f. Click the **VIEW tab** and click **100%** in the Zoom group to return the view to its original size.

When you change the zoom, you do not change the text size that will be printed or saved. The change merely magnifies or decreases the view while you work with the file.

g. Keep the workbook open for the next step in this exercise. Submit the file based on your instructor's directions.

STEP 2 ►► GET HELP AND USE THE BACKSTAGE VIEW

Because you are not an Excel expert, you occasionally rely on the Help feature to provide information on tasks. You need assistance with saving a worksheet, previewing it before printing, and printing the worksheet. From what you learn, you will find that the Backstage view enables you to accomplish all of those tasks. Refer to Figure 1.26 as you complete Step 2.

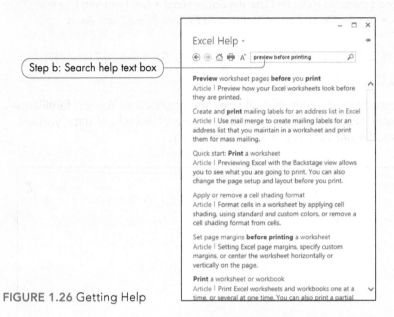

FIGURE 1.26 Getting Help

a. Click **Help**, which is the question mark in the top-right corner of the Ribbon.

The Help dialog box displays.

TIP | Using Shortcuts to Access Help

You can discover alternative ways to access Help. For example, the ScreenTip that displays as you point to the Help button suggests that you could press the F1 key.

b. Click in the **Search online help text box** at the top of the Help dialog box. Type **preview before printing** and press **Enter** (see Figure 1.26). In the Excel Help window, click **Preview worksheet pages before you print**. Read about how to preview a worksheet before printing. From what you read, can you identify a keyboard shortcut for previewing worksheets? Click the **Close (X) button**.

Before you print the worksheet, you would like to see how it will look when printed. You used Help to find information on previewing before printing.

c. Click the **FILE tab** and click **Print**.

Having used Office Help to learn how to preview before printing, you follow the directions to view the worksheet as it will look when printed. The preview of the worksheet displays on the right. To print the worksheet, you would click Print. However, you can first select any print options, such as the number of copies, from the Backstage view.

d. Click the **Back arrow** on the top left of the screen. Click **Help**. Excel Help presents several links related to the worksheet. Explore any that look interesting. Return to previous Help windows by clicking **Back** at the top-left side of the Help window. Close the Help dialog box.

e. Click the **HOME tab**. Point to *Bold* in the Font group.

You will find that, along with Excel, Word and PowerPoint also include formatting features in the Font group, such as Bold and Italic. When the Enhanced ScreenTip appears, identify the shortcut key combination that could be used to bold a selected text item. It is indicated as Ctrl plus the letter B.

f. Click the **Close (X) button** in the top-right corner of the Excel window to close both the workbook and the Excel program. When asked whether you want to save changes, click **Don't Save**.

You decide not to print or save the worksheet right now because you did not change anything during this step.

STEP 3 ≫ CHANGE THE VIEW AND USE LIVE PREVIEW

It is important that the documents you prepare or approve are error free and as attractive as possible. Before printing, you will change the view to get a better idea of how the document will look when printed. In addition, you will use Live Preview to experiment with font settings before actually applying them. Refer to Figure 1.27 as you complete Step 3.

FIGURE 1.27 Word Views

a. Navigate to the Start screen. Scroll across the tiles, if necessary, and click **Word 2013**. Click **Blank document**.

You have opened a blank Word document. You plan to familiarize yourself with the program for later reference.

b. Type your first and last names and press **Enter**. Drag to select your name.

Your name should be highlighted, indicating that it is selected. You have selected your name because you want to experiment with using Word to change the way text looks.

c. Click the **Font Size arrow** in the Font group. If you need help locating Font Size, check for an Enhanced ScreenTip. Place the mouse pointer over any number in the list, but do not click. As you move to different font sizes, notice the size of your name changes. The feature you are using is called Live Preview. Click **16** in the list to change the font size of your name.

d. Click any white space to deselect your name. Click **Read Mode** in the *View shortcuts* group on the status bar to change the view (see Figure 1.27). Click **Print Layout** to return to the original view.

e. Save the file as **f01h3Read_LastFirst** and click the **Close (X) button** to close the Word program. Submit the file based on your instructor's directions.

STEP 4 ≫ USE THE QUICK ACCESS TOOLBAR AND EXPLORE POWERPOINT VIEWS

In your position as administrative assistant, you will be asked to review documents, presentations, and worksheets. It is important that you explore each application to familiarize yourself with operations and commonalities. Specifically, you know that the Quick Access Toolbar is common to all applications and that you can place commonly used commands there to streamline processes. Also, learning to change views will enable you to see the project in different ways for various purposes. Refer to Figure 1.28 as you complete Step 4.

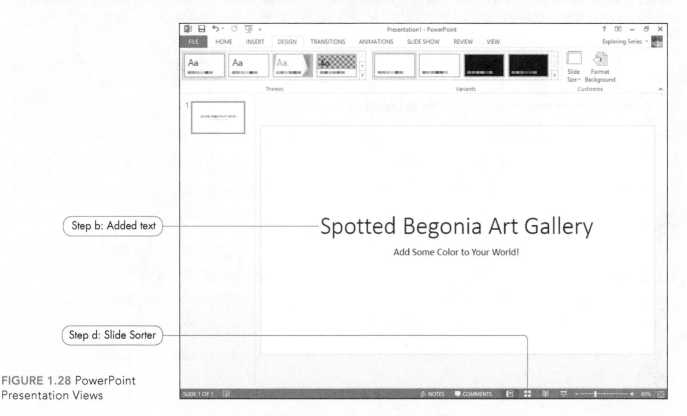

FIGURE 1.28 PowerPoint Presentation Views

a. Navigate to the Start screen. Scroll across the tiles, if necessary, and click **PowerPoint 2013**. Click **Blank Presentation**.

You have opened PowerPoint. A blank presentation displays.

b. Click **Click to add title** and type **Spotted Begonia Art Gallery**. Click in the bottom, subtitle box and type **Add Some Color to Your World!** Click the bottom-right corner of the slide to deselect the subtitle. Your PowerPoint presentation should look like that shown in Figure 1.28.

c. Click **Undo** two times on the Quick Access Toolbar.

The subtitle on the current slide is selected and removed because those are the most recent actions.

> **TROUBLESHOOTING:** If all of the subtitle text is not removed after two clicks, you should continue clicking until it is removed.

d. Click **Slide Sorter** in the *View shortcuts* group on the status bar.

The Slide Sorter view shows thumbnails of all slides in a presentation. Because this presentation has only one slide, you see a small version of one slide.

e. Move the mouse pointer to any button on the Quick Access Toolbar and hold it steady. See the tip giving the button name and the shortcut key combination, if any. Move to another button and see the description.

The Quick Access Toolbar has at least three buttons: Save, Undo, and Redo. In addition, a small arrow is included at the far-right side. If you hold the mouse pointer steady on the arrow, you will see the ScreenTip Customize Quick Access Toolbar.

f. Click **Customize Quick Access Toolbar** and select **New**. The New button is added to the toolbar. The New button enables you to quickly create a new presentation (also called a document).

g. Right-click **New** and click **Remove from Quick Access Toolbar**. The button is removed from the Quick Access Toolbar.

You can customize the Quick Access Toolbar by adding and removing items.

h. Click **Normal** in the *View shortcuts* group on the status bar.

The presentation returns to the original view in which the slide displays full size.

i. Click **Slide Show** in the *View shortcuts* group on the status bar.

The presentation is shown in Slide Show view, which is the way it will be presented to audiences.

j. Press **Esc** to end the presentation.

k. Save the presentation as **f01h3Views_LastFirst** and click the **Close (X) button** to close the PowerPoint program. Submit the presentation based on your instructor's directions.

The Backstage View Tasks

When you work with Microsoft Office files, you will often want to open previously saved files, create new ones, print items, and save and close files. You will also find it necessary to indicate options, or preferences, for settings. For example, you might want a spelling check to occur automatically, or you might prefer to initiate a spelling check only occasionally. Because those tasks are applicable to each software application within the Office 2013 suite, they are accomplished through a common area in the Office interface—the Backstage view. Open the Backstage view by clicking the File tab. Figure 1.29 shows the area that displays when you click the File tab in PowerPoint. The Backstage view also enables you to exit the application and to identify file information, such as the author or date created.

In this section, you will explore the Backstage view, learning to create, open, close, and print files.

FIGURE 1.29 The Backstage View

Opening a File

When working with an Office application, you can begin by opening an existing file that has already been saved to a storage medium, or you can begin work on a new file. Both actions are available when you click the File tab. When you first open an application within the Office 2013 suite, you will need to decide which template you want to work with before you can begin working on a new file. You can also open a project that you previously saved to a disk.

Create a New File

After opening an Office application, such as Word, Excel, or PowerPoint, you will be presented with template choices. Click *Blank document* to start a new blank document. The word *document* is sometimes used generically to refer to any Office file, including a Word document, an Excel worksheet, or a PowerPoint presentation. Perhaps you are already working with a document in an Office application but want to create a new file. Simply click the File tab and click New. Click *Blank document* (or *Blank presentation* or *Blank workbook*, depending on the specific application).

Open a File Using the Open Dialog Box

STEP 1 >> You may choose to open a previously saved file, such as when you work with the data files for this book or when you want to access any previously created file. You will work with the Open dialog box, as shown in Figure 1.30. The Open dialog box displays after you click Open from the File tab. You will click Computer and the folder or drive where your document is stored.

If it is not listed under Recent Folders, you can browse for it. Using the Navigation Pane, you will make your way to the file to be opened. Double-click the file or click the file name once and click Open. Most likely, the file will be located within a folder that is appropriately named to make it easy to find related files. Obviously, if you are not well acquainted with the file's location and file name, the process of opening a file could become quite cumbersome. However, if you have created a well-designed system of folders, as you learned to do in the "Files and Folders" section of this chapter, you will know exactly where to find the file.

FIGURE 1.30 Open Dialog Box

Open a File Using the Recent Documents List

STEP 3 >>

You will often work with a file, save it, and then continue the project at a later time. Office simplifies the task of reopening the file by providing a Recent Documents list with links to your most recently opened files (see Figure 1.31). To access the list, click the File tab, click Open, and then select Recent Documents. Click any file listed in the Recent Documents list to open that document. The list constantly changes to reflect only the most recently opened files, so if it has been quite some time since you worked with a particular file, you might have to work with the Open dialog box instead of the Recent Documents list.

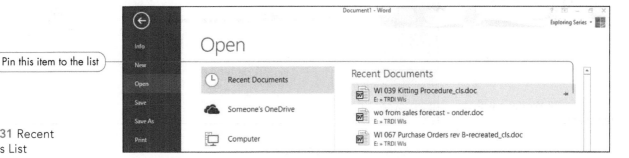

FIGURE 1.31 Recent Documents List

> ### TIP Keeping Files on the Recent Documents List
>
> The Recent Documents list displays a limited list of only the most recently opened files. You might, however, want to keep a particular file in the list regardless of how recently it was opened. In Figure 1.31, note the *Pin this item to the list* icon displays to the right of each file. Click the icon to pin the file to the list. At that point, you will always have access to the file by clicking the File tab and selecting the file from the Recent Documents list. The pushpin of the "permanent" file will change direction so that it appears to be inserted, indicating that it is a pinned item. If later you want to remove the file from the list, click the inserted pushpin, changing its direction and allowing the file to be bumped off the list when other, more recently opened, files take its place.

Open a File from the Templates List

You do not need to create a new file if you can access a predesigned file that meets your needs or one that you can modify fairly quickly to complete your project. Office provides templates, making them available when you click the File tab and New (see Figure 1.32). The Templates list is comprised of template groups available within the current Office installation on your computer. The Search box can be used to locate other templates that are available from Office.com. When you click one of the Suggested searches, you are presented with additional choices.

For example, you might want to prepare a home budget. After opening a blank worksheet in Excel, click the File tab and click New. From the template categories, you could click Budget from the *Suggested searches* list, scroll down until you find the right template, such as Family Budget, and then click Create to display the associated worksheet (or simply double-click Family Budget). If a Help window displays along with the worksheet template, click to close it or explore Help to learn more about the template. If you know only a little bit about Excel, you could then make a few changes so that the worksheet would accurately represent your family's financial situation. The budget would be prepared much more quickly than if you began the project with a blank workbook, designing it yourself.

Templates available from Office.com

Templates available in a typical Office installation

FIGURE 1.32 Working with Templates

Printing a File

There will be occasions when you will want to print an Office project. Before printing, you should preview the file to get an idea of how it will look when printed. That way, if there are obvious problems with the page setup, you can correct them before wasting paper on something that is not correct. When you are ready to print, you can select from various print options, including the number of copies and the specific pages to print. If you know that the page setup is correct and that there are no unique print settings to select, you can simply print the project without adjusting any print settings.

STEP 2

It is a good idea to take a look at how your document will appear before you print it. The Print Preview feature of Office enables you to do just that. In the Print pane, you will see all items, including any headers, footers, graphics, and special formatting. To view a project before printing, click the File tab and click Print. The subsequent Backstage view shows the file preview on the right, with print settings located in the center of the Backstage screen. Figure 1.33 shows a typical Backstage Print view.

Print Preview

Print

Print Settings

Zoom to Page

Show Margins

FIGURE 1.33 Backstage Print View

To show the margins of the document, click Show Margins (see Figure 1.33). To increase the size of the file preview, click *Zoom to Page* (see Figure 1.33). Both are found on the bottom-right corner of the preview. Remember that increasing the font size by adjusting the zoom applies to the current display only; it does not actually increase the font size when the document is printed or saved. To return the preview to its original view, click *Zoom to Page* once more.

Other options in the Backstage Print view vary depending on the application in which you are working. Regardless of the Office application, you will be able to access Settings options from the Backstage view, including page orientation (landscape or portrait), margins, and paper size. You will find a more detailed explanation of those settings in the "Page Layout Tab Tasks" section later in this chapter. To print a file, click Print (see Figure 1.33).

The Backstage Print view shown in Figure 1.33 is very similar across all Office applications. However, you will find slight variations specific to each application. For example, PowerPoint's Backstage Print view includes options for printing slides and handouts in various configurations and colors, whereas Excel's focuses on worksheet selections and Word's includes document options. Regardless of software, the manner of working with the Backstage view print options remains consistent.

Closing a File and Application

Although you can have several documents open at one time, limiting the number of open files is a good idea. Office applications have no problem keeping up with multiple open files, but you can easily become overwhelmed with them. When you are done with an open project, you will need to close it.

You can easily close any files that you no longer need. With the desired file on the screen, click the FILE tab and click the Close (X) button. Respond to any prompt that might display suggesting that you save the file. The application remains open, but the selected file is closed. To close the application, click the Close (X) button in the top-right corner.

TIP | Closing an Application

When you close an application, all open files within the application are also closed. You will be prompted to save any files before they are closed. A quick way to close an application is to click the X in the top-right corner of the application window.

Quick Concepts

1. You want to continue to work with a PowerPoint presentation that you worked with yesterday, but cannot remember where you saved the presentation on your hard drive. How can you open a file that you recently worked with? *p. 37*

2. As part of your job search, you plan to develop a resume. However, you find it difficult to determine the right style for your resume, and wish you could begin with a predesigned document that you could modify. Is that possible with Word? If so, what steps would you take to locate a predesigned resume? *p. 38*

3. Closing a file is not the same as closing an application, such as closing Excel. What is the difference? *p. 39*

Hands-On Exercises

Watch the Video
for this Hands-
On Exercise!

MyITLab®
HOE4 Training

4 The Backstage View Tasks

Projects related to the Spotted Begonia Art Gallery's functions have begun to come in for your review and approval. You have received an informational flyer to be distributed to schools and supporting organizations around the city. It contains a new logo along with descriptive text. Another task on your agenda is to keep the project moving according to schedule. You will identify a calendar template to print and distribute. You will explore printing options, and you will save the flyer and the calendar as directed by your instructor.

Skills covered: Open and Save a File • Preview and Print a File • Open a File from the Recent Documents List and Open a Template

STEP 1 ›› OPEN AND SAVE A FILE

You have asked your staff to develop a flyer that can be used to promote the Spotted Begonia Art Gallery. You will open a Word document that may be used for the flyer, and you will save the document to a disk drive. Refer to Figure 1.34 as you complete Step 1.

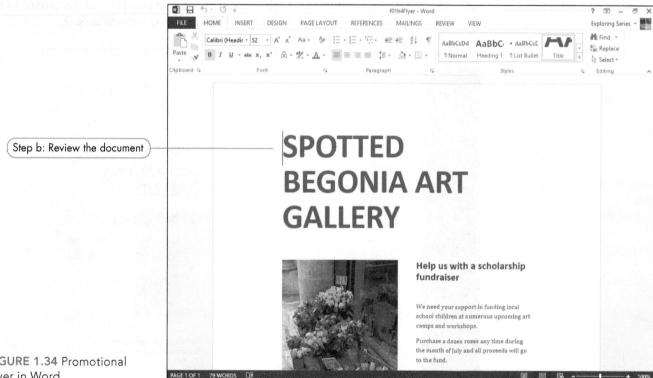

Step b: Review the document

FIGURE 1.34 Promotional Flyer in Word

a. Navigate to the Start screen. Scroll across the tiles, if necessary, and click **Word 2013**. Click **Open Other Documents** at the bottom-left corner of the Word 2013 window.

You have opened Microsoft Word because it is the program in which the promotional flyer is saved.

b. Click **Computer** and click **Browse**. Navigate to the location of your student files. Double-click *f01h4Flyer* to open the file shown in Figure 1.34. Familiarize yourself with the document. Then, if necessary, click **Read Mode** in the *View shortcuts* group on the Status bar to change to that view. Read through the document.

The graphic and the flyer are submitted for your approval. A paragraph next to the graphic will serve as the launching point for an information blitz and the beginning of the fundraising drive.

TIP Using Read Mode

Read Mode displays the document. If the document is large enough, multiple screens may display. You can use the arrows found on the middle edges of the document to navigate and view the entire document.

c. Click **Print Layout** on the Status bar to change to that view. Click the **FILE tab** and click **Save As**.

You choose the Save As command because you know that it enables you to indicate the location to which the file should be saved, as well as the file name.

d. Click **Browse**, navigate to the drive where you save your files, and then double-click the **Artists folder** you created earlier. Double-click **Office Records**, click in the **File name box**, type **f01h4Flyer_LastFirst**, and then click **Save**.

STEP 2 ›› PREVIEW AND PRINT A FILE

You approve of the flyer, so you will print the document for future reference. You will first preview the document as it will appear when printed. Then you will print the document. Refer to Figure 1.35 as you complete Step 2.

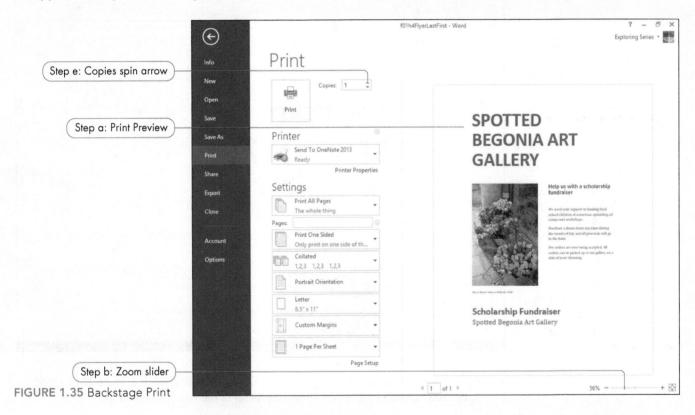

FIGURE 1.35 Backstage Print

a. Click the **FILE tab** and click **Print**.

Figure 1.35 shows the flyer preview. It is always a good idea to check the way a file will look when printed before actually printing it.

b. Drag the **Zoom slider** to increase the document view. Click **Zoom to Page** to return to the original size.

c. Click **Portrait Orientation** in the Print settings area in the center of the screen. Click **Landscape Orientation** to show the flyer in a wider and shorter view.

d. Click **Landscape Orientation** and click **Portrait Orientation** to return to the original view.

You decide that the flyer is more attractive in portrait orientation, so you return to that setting.

e. Click the **Copies spin arrow** repeatedly to increase the copies to **5**.

You will need to print five copies of the flyer to distribute to the office assistants for their review.

f. Click **Close** on the left side of the screen. When asked, click **Don't Save** so that changes to the file are not saved. Keep Word open for the next step.

STEP 3 ≫ OPEN A FILE FROM THE RECENT DOCUMENTS LIST AND OPEN A TEMPLATE

A large part of your responsibility is proofreading Spotted Begonia Art Gallery material. You will correct an error by adding a phone number in the promotional flyer. You must also keep the staff on task, so you will identify a calendar template on which to list tasks and deadlines. Refer to Figure 1.36 as you complete Step 3.

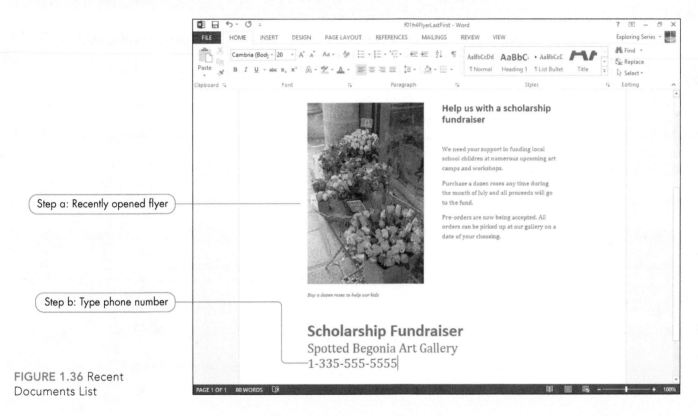

FIGURE 1.36 Recent Documents List

a. Click the **FILE tab**, click **Recent Documents** if necessary, and then click **f01h4Flyer_LastFirst** in the **Recent Documents list**.

> **TROUBLESHOOTING:** If the file opens in Read Mode, use the status bar to change to the Print Layout view.

b. Press **Ctrl+End** to move the insertion point to the end of the document and press **Enter**. Type **1-335-555-5555**.

Figure 1.36 shows the phone number correction.

c. Click **Save** on the Quick Access Toolbar, click the **FILE tab**, and then click **Close**.

When you click Save on the Quick Access Toolbar, the document is saved in the same location with the same file name as was indicated in the previous save.

d. Click the **FILE tab** and click **New**. Click **Calendar** from the list of the *Suggested searches* category just beneath the *Search online templates* box.

Office.com provides a wide range of calendar choices. You will select one that is appealing and that will help you keep projects on track.

e. Click a calendar of your choice from the gallery and click **Create**. Respond to and close any windows that may open.

The calendar that you selected opens in Word.

TROUBLESHOOTING: It is possible to select a template that is not certified by Microsoft. In that case, you might have to confirm your acceptance of settings before you click Download.

---

f. Click **Save** on the Quick Access Toolbar. If necessary, navigate to your Office Records subfolder (a subfolder of Artists) on the drive where you are saving your student files. Save the document as **f01h4Calendar_LastFirst**. Because this is the first time to save the calendar file, the Save button on the Quick Access Toolbar opens a dialog box in which you must indicate the location of the file and the file name.

g. Click **Save** and exit Word. Submit your files based on your instructor's directions.

Home Tab Tasks

You will find that you will repeat some tasks often, whether in Word, Excel, or PowerPoint. You will frequently want to change the format of numbers or words, selecting a different *font* or changing font size or color. A font is a complete set of characters, both upper- and lowercase letters, numbers, punctuation marks, and special symbols, with the same design including size, spacing, and shape. You might also need to change the alignment of text or worksheet cells. Undoubtedly, you will find a reason to copy or cut items and paste them elsewhere in the document, presentation, or worksheet. And you might want to modify file contents by finding and replacing text. All of those tasks, and more, are found on the Home tab of the Ribbon in Word, Excel, and PowerPoint. The Access interface is unique, sharing little with other Office applications, so this section will not address Access.

In this section, you will explore the Home tab, learning to format text, copy and paste items, and find and replace words or phrases. Figure 1.37 shows Home tab groups and tasks in the various applications. Note the differences and similarities between the groups.

FIGURE 1.37 Home Tab in Word, PowerPoint, and Excel

Selecting and Editing Text

After creating a document, worksheet, or presentation, you will probably want to make some changes. You might prefer to center a title, or maybe you think that certain budget worksheet totals should be formatted as currency. You can change the font so that typed characters are larger or in a different style. You might even want to underline text to add emphasis. In all Office applications, the Home tab provides tools for selecting and editing text. You can also use the Mini toolbar for making quick changes to selected text.

Select Text to Edit

Before making any changes to existing text or numbers, you must first select the characters. A general rule that you should commit to memory is "Select, then do." A foolproof way to select text or numbers is to place the mouse pointer before the first character of the text you want to select, and then drag to highlight the intended selection. Before you drag, be sure that the mouse pointer takes on the shape of the letter *I*, called the *I-bar*. Although other methods for selecting exist, if you remember only one way, it should be the click-and-drag method. If your attempted selection falls short of highlighting the intended area, or perhaps highlights too much, simply click outside the selection and try again.

Sometimes it can be difficult to precisely select a small amount of text, such as a single character or a single word. Other times, the task can be overwhelming, such as when selecting an entire 550-page document. Shortcut methods for making selections in Word and PowerPoint are shown in Table 1.3. When working with Excel, you will more often need to select multiple cells. Simply drag the intended selection, usually when the mouse pointer displays as a large white plus sign. The shortcuts shown in Table 1.3 are primarily applicable to Word and PowerPoint.

TABLE 1.3 Shortcut Selection in Word and PowerPoint

Item Selected	Action
One word	Double-click the word.
One line of text	Place the mouse pointer at the left of the line, in the margin area. When the mouse changes to a right-pointing arrow, click to select the line.
One sentence	Press and hold Ctrl while you click in the sentence to select.
One paragraph	Triple-click in the paragraph.
One character to the left of the insertion point	Press and hold Shift while you press the left arrow on the keyboard.
One character to the right of the insertion point	Press and hold Shift while you press the right arrow on the keyboard.
Entire document	Press and hold Ctrl while you press A on the keyboard.

After having selected a string of characters, such as a number, word, sentence, or document, you can do more than simply format the selection. Suppose you have selected a word. If you begin to type another word, the newly typed word will immediately replace the selected word. With an item selected, you can press Delete to remove the selection. You will learn later in this chapter that you can also find, replace, copy, move, and paste selected text.

Use the Mini Toolbar

STEP 3 >>

You have learned that you can always use commands on the Ribbon to change selected text within a document, worksheet, or presentation. All it takes is locating the desired command on the Home tab and clicking to select it. Although using the Home tab to perform commands is simple enough, an item called the *Mini toolbar* provides an even faster way to accomplish some of the same formatting changes. When you select any amount of text within a worksheet, document, or presentation, you can move the mouse pointer only slightly within the selection to display the Mini toolbar (see Figure 1.38). The Mini toolbar provides access to the most common formatting selections, such as adding bold or italic, or changing font type or color. Unlike the Quick Access Toolbar, the Mini toolbar is not customizable, which means that you cannot add or remove options from the toolbar.

Mini toolbar

FIGURE 1.38 Mini Toolbar

The Mini toolbar will display only when text is selected. The closer the mouse pointer is to the Mini toolbar, the darker the toolbar becomes. As you move the mouse pointer away from the Mini toolbar, it becomes almost transparent. Make any selections from the Mini toolbar by clicking the corresponding button. To temporarily remove the Mini toolbar from view, press Esc.

If you want to permanently disable the Mini toolbar so that it does not display in any open file when text is selected, click the FILE tab and click Options. As shown in Figure 1.39, click General, if necessary. Deselect the *Show Mini Toolbar on selection* setting by clicking the check box to the left of the setting and clicking OK.

General

Click to disable the Mini toolbar

FIGURE 1.39 Disabling the Mini Toolbar

Apply Font Attributes

The way characters appear onscreen, including qualities such as size, spacing, and shape, is determined by the font. Each Office application has a default font, which is the font that will be in effect unless you change it. Other font attributes include boldfacing, italicizing, and font color, all of which can be applied to selected text. Some formatting changes, such as Bold and Italic, are called *toggle* commands. They act somewhat like light switches that you can turn on and off. For example, after having selected a word that you want to add bold to, click Bold in the Font group of the Home tab to turn the setting "on." If, at a later time, you want to remove bold from the word, select it again and click Bold. This time, the button turns "off" the bold formatting.

Change the Font

All applications within the Office suite provide a set of fonts from which you can choose. If you prefer a font other than the default, or if you want to apply a different font to a section of your project for added emphasis or interest, you can easily make the change by selecting a font from within the Font group on the Home tab. You can also change the font by selecting from the Mini toolbar, although that works only if you have first selected text.

Change the Font Size, Color, and Attributes

STEP 2 ▶ At times, you will want to make the font size larger or smaller, change the font color, underline selected text, or apply other font attributes. For example, if you are creating a handout for a special event, you may want to apply a different font to emphasize key information such as dates and times. Because such changes are commonplace, Office places those formatting commands in many convenient places within each Office application.

You can find the most common formatting commands in the Font group on the Home tab. As noted earlier, Word, Excel, and PowerPoint all share very similar Font groups that provide access to tasks related to changing the character font (refer to Figure 1.37). Remember that you can place the mouse pointer over any command icon to view a summary of the icon's purpose, so although the icons might at first appear cryptic, you can use the mouse pointer to quickly determine the purpose and applicability to your desired text change. You can also find a subset of those commands plus a few additional choices on the Mini toolbar.

If the font change that you plan to make is not included as a choice on either the Home tab or the Mini toolbar, you can probably find what you are looking for in the Font dialog box. Click the Dialog Box Launcher in the bottom-right corner of the Font group. Figure 1.40 shows a sample Font dialog box. Because the Font dialog box provides many formatting choices in one window, you can make several changes at once. Depending on the application, the contents of the Font dialog box vary slightly, but the purpose is consistent—providing access to choices related to modifying characters.

FIGURE 1.40 Font Dialog Box

Using the Clipboard Group Commands

On occasion, you will want to move or copy a selection from one area to another. Suppose that you have included text on a PowerPoint slide that you believe would be more appropriate on a different slide. Or perhaps an Excel formula should be copied from one cell to another because both cells should be totaled in the same manner. You can easily move the slide text or copy the Excel formula by using options found in the Clipboard group on the Home tab. The Office **Clipboard** is an area of memory reserved to temporarily hold selections that have been **cut** or **copied** and allows you to paste the selections. To cut means to remove a selection from the original location and place it in the Office Clipboard. To copy means to duplicate a selection from the original location and place a copy in the Office Clipboard. Although the Clipboard can hold up to 24 items at one time, the usual procedure is to **paste** the cut or copied selection to its final destination fairly quickly. To paste means to place a cut or copied selection into another location. When the computer is shut down or loses power, the contents of the Clipboard are erased, so it is important to finalize the paste procedure during the current session.

The Clipboard group enables you not only to copy and cut text and objects but also to copy formatting. Perhaps you have applied a font style to a major heading of a report and you realize that the same formatting should be applied to other headings. Especially if the heading includes multiple formatting features, you will save a great deal of time by copying the entire set of formatting options to the other headings. In so doing, you will ensure the consistency of formatting for all headings because they will appear exactly alike. Using the Clipboard group's **Format Painter**, you can quickly and easily copy all formatting from one area to another in Word, PowerPoint, and Excel.

In Office, you can usually accomplish the same task in several ways. Although the Ribbon provides ample access to formatting and Clipboard commands (such as Format Painter, Cut, Copy, and Paste), you might find it convenient to access the same commands on a **shortcut menu**. Right-click a selected item or text to open a shortcut menu such as the one shown in Figure 1.41. A shortcut menu is also called a *context menu* because the contents of the menu vary depending on the location at which you right-clicked.

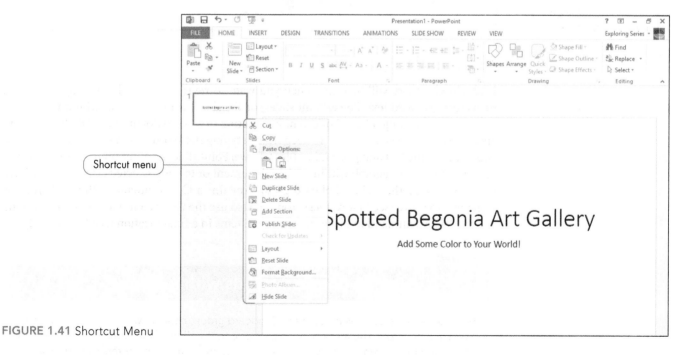

Shortcut menu

FIGURE 1.41 Shortcut Menu

Copy Formats with the Format Painter

STEP 3 > As described earlier, the Format Painter makes it easy to copy formatting features from one selection to another. You will find the Format Painter command conveniently located in the Clipboard group of the Home tab (see Figure 1.42). To copy a format, you must first select the text containing the desired format. If you want to copy the format to only one other selection, *single-click* Format Painter. If, however, you plan to copy the same format to multiple areas, *double-click* Format Painter. As you move the mouse pointer, you will find that it has the appearance of a paintbrush with an attached I-bar. Select the area to which the copied format should be applied. If you single-clicked Format Painter to copy the format to one other selection, Format Painter turns off once the formatting has been applied. If you double-clicked Format Painter to copy the format to multiple locations, continue selecting text in various locations to apply the format. Then, to turn off Format Painter, click Format Painter again or press Esc.

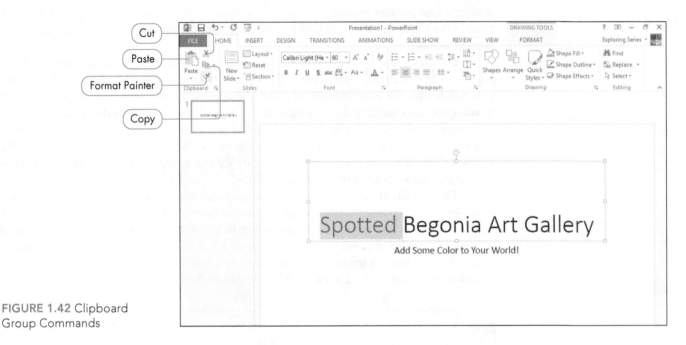

FIGURE 1.42 Clipboard Group Commands

Move and Copy Text

Undoubtedly, there will be times when you want to revise a project by moving or copying items such as Word text, PowerPoint slides, or Excel cell contents, either within the current application or among others. For example, a section of a Word document might be appropriate as PowerPoint slide content. To keep from retyping the Word text in the PowerPoint slide, you can copy the text and paste it in a blank PowerPoint slide. At other times, it might be necessary to move a paragraph within a Word document or to copy selected cells from one Excel worksheet to another. The Clipboard group contains a Cut command with which you can select text to move (see Figure 1.42). You can also use the Copy command to duplicate items and the Paste command to place cut or copied items in a final location (see Figure 1.42).

TIP | Using Ribbon Commands with Arrows

Some commands, such as Paste in the Clipboard group, contain two parts: the main command and an arrow. The arrow may be below or to the right of the command, depending on the command, window size, or screen resolution. Instructions in the *Exploring* series use the command name to instruct you to click the main command to perform the default action (e.g., Click Paste). Instructions include the word *arrow* when you need to select the arrow to access an additional option (e.g., Click the Paste arrow).

STEP 1》

The first step in moving or copying text is to select the text. Then do the following:

1. Click the appropriate icon in the Clipboard group either to cut or copy the selection. Remember that cut or copied text is actually placed in the Clipboard, remaining there even after you paste it to another location. It is important to note that you can paste the same item multiple times, because it will remain in the Clipboard until you power down your computer or until the Clipboard exceeds 24 items.
2. Click the location where you want the cut or copied text to be placed. The location can be in the current file or in another open file within any Office application.
3. Click Paste in the Clipboard group on the HOME tab.

In addition to using the Clipboard group icons, you can also cut, copy, and paste in any of the ways listed in Table 1.4.

TABLE 1.4   Cut, Copy, and Paste Options

Command	Actions
Cut	• Click Cut in Clipboard group. • Right-click selection and select Cut. • Press Ctrl+X.
Copy	• Click Copy in Clipboard group. • Right-click selection and select Copy. • Press Ctrl+C.
Paste	• Click in destination location and select Paste in Clipboard group. • Right-click in destination location and select Paste. • Click in destination location and press Ctrl+V. • Click the Clipboard Dialog Box Launcher to open the Clipboard task pane. Click in destination location. With the Clipboard task pane open, click the arrow beside the intended selection and select Paste.

Use the Office Clipboard

When you cut or copy selections, they are placed in the Office Clipboard. Regardless of which Office application you are using, you can view the Clipboard by clicking the Clipboard Dialog Box Launcher, as shown in Figure 1.43.

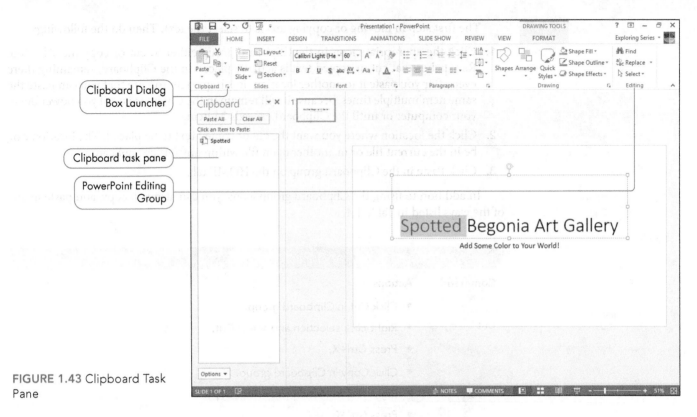

Clipboard Dialog Box Launcher

Clipboard task pane

PowerPoint Editing Group

Spotted Begonia Art Gallery

Add Some Color to Your World!

FIGURE 1.43 Clipboard Task Pane

Unless you specify otherwise when beginning a paste operation, the most recently added Clipboard item is pasted. You can, however, select an item from the Clipboard task pane to paste. Similarly, you can delete items from the Clipboard by making a selection in the Clipboard task pane. You can remove all items from the Clipboard by clicking Clear All. The Options button in the Clipboard task pane enables you to control when and where the Clipboard is displayed. Close the Clipboard task pane by clicking the Close (X) button in the top-right corner of the task pane or by clicking the arrow in the title bar of the Clipboard task pane and selecting Close.

Using the Editing Group Commands

The process of finding and replacing text is easily accomplished through options in the Editing group of the Home tab. The Editing group also enables you to select all contents of a project document, all text with similar formatting, or specific objects, such as pictures or charts. The Editing group is found at the far-right side of the Home tab in Excel, Word, and PowerPoint.

The Excel Editing group is unique in that it also includes options for sorting, filtering, and clearing cell contents; filling cells; and summarizing numeric data. Because those commands are relevant only to Excel, this chapter will not address them specifically.

Find and Replace Text

STEP 4 ›› Especially if you are working with a lengthy project, manually seeking a specific word or phrase can be time-consuming. Office enables you not only to *find* each occurrence of a series of characters, but also to *replace* what it finds with another series. You will at times find it necessary to locate each occurrence of a text item so that you can replace it with another or so that you can delete, move, or copy it. If you have consistently misspelled a person's name throughout a document, you can find the misspelling and replace it with the correct spelling in a matter of a few seconds, no matter how many times the misspelling occurs in the document. To begin the process of finding and replacing a specific item:

1. Click Replace in the Editing group on the HOME tab of Word or PowerPoint.
2. Or click Find & Select in the Editing group on the HOME tab of Excel. Then click Replace. The dialog box that displays enables you to indicate the word or phrase to find and replace.

The Advanced Find feature is one that you will use often as you work with documents in Word. It is beneficial to find each occurrence of a word you are searching for. But it is also very helpful to see all the occurrences of the word at once. Click Reading Highlight in the *Find and Replace* dialog box and select Highlight All to display each word highlighted, as shown in Figure 1.44. Click Reading Highlight again and select Clear Highlighting to remove the illumination.

FIGURE 1.44 Highlight All

TIP Using a Shortcut to Find Items

Ctrl+F is a shortcut used to find items in a Word, Excel, or PowerPoint file. When you press Ctrl+F, the *Find and Replace* dialog box displays in Excel and PowerPoint. Pressing Ctrl+F in Word displays a feature—the Navigation Pane—at the left side of a Word document. When you type a search term in the Search Document area, Word finds and highlights all occurrences of the search term. The Navigation Pane also makes it easy to move to sections of a document based on levels of headings.

To find and replace selected text, type the text to locate in the *Find what* box and the replacement text in the *Replace with* box. You can narrow the search to require matching case or find whole words only. If you want to replace all occurrences of the text, click Replace All. If you want to replace only some occurrences, click Find Next repeatedly until you reach the occurrence that you want to replace. At that point, click Replace. When you are finished, click the Close button (or click Cancel).

Use Advanced Find and Replace Features

The *Find and Replace* feature enables you not only to find and replace text, but also to restrict and alter the format of the text at the same time. To establish the format criteria associated with either the *Find or Replace* portion of the operation:

1. Click the More button to expand the dialog box options. Click Format in the bottom-left corner of the dialog box.
2. Add formatting characteristics from the Font dialog box or Paragraph dialog box (as well as many other formatting features).

In addition to applying special formatting parameters on a *Find and Replace* operation, you can specify that you want to find or replace special characters. Click Special at the bottom of the *Find and Replace* dialog box to view the punctuation characters from which you can choose. For example, you might want to look for all instances in a document where an exclamation point is being used and replace it with a period.

An Excel worksheet can include more than 1,000,000 rows of data. A Word document's length is unlimited. Moving to a specific point in large files created in either of those applications can be a challenge. That task is simplified by the Go To option, found in the Editing group as an option of the Find command in Word (or under Find & Select in Excel). Click Go To and enter the page number (or other item, such as section, comment, bookmark, or footnote) in Word or the specific Excel cell. Click Go To in Word (or OK in Excel).

Quick Concepts

1. After selecting text in a presentation or document, you see a small transparent bar with formatting options displayed just above the selection. What is the bar called and what is its purpose? *p. 46*

2. What is the difference between using a single-click on the Format Painter and using a double-click? *p. 50*

3. What is the first step in cutting or copying text? How are cutting and copying related to the concept of the Clipboard? *p. 51*

4. What feature can you use to very quickly locate and replace text in a document? Provide an example of when you might want to find text but not replace it. *p. 52*

Hands-On Exercises

5 Home Tab Tasks

You have created a list of potential contributors to the Spotted Begonia Art Gallery. You have used Excel to record that list in worksheet format. Now you will review the worksheet and format its appearance to make it more attractive. You will also modify a promotional flyer. In working with those projects, you will put into practice the formatting, copying, moving, and editing information from the preceding section.

Skills covered: Move, Copy, and Paste Text • Select Text, Apply Font Attributes, and Use the Mini Toolbar • Use Format Painter and Work with the Mini Toolbar • Use the Font Dialog Box and Find and Replace Text

STEP 1 ≫ MOVE, COPY, AND PASTE TEXT

Each contributor to the Spotted Begonia Art Gallery is assigned a contact person. You manage the worksheet that keeps track of those assignments, but the assignments sometimes change. You will copy and paste some worksheet selections to keep from having to retype data. You will also reposition an image to improve the worksheet's appearance. Refer to Figure 1.45 as you complete Step 1.

FIGURE 1.45 Contributor List
(Excel)

a. Navigate to the Start screen. Scroll across the tiles, if necessary, and click **Excel 2013**. Click **Open Other Workbooks**.

   You have opened Microsoft Excel because it is the program in which the contributors list is saved.

b. Open the student data file *f01h5Contributors*. Save the file as **f01h5Contributors_LastFirst** in the Office Records folder (a subfolder of Artists) you created.

   The potential contributors list shown in Figure 1.45 is displayed.

c. Click **cell C7** to select the cell that contains *Nester, Ali*, and click **Copy** in the Clipboard group on the HOME tab. Click **cell C15** to select the cell that contains *Sammons, Roger*, click **Paste** in the Clipboard group, and then press **Esc** to remove the selection from *Nester, Ali*.

Ali Nester has been assigned as the Spotted Begonia Art Gallery contact for Harris Foster, replacing Roger Sammons. You make that replacement on the worksheet by copying and pasting Ali Nester's name in the appropriate worksheet cell.

d. Click the picture of the begonia. A box displays around the image, indicating that it is selected. Click **Cut** in the Clipboard group, click **cell D2**, and then click **Paste**. Drag the picture to resize and position it as needed (see Figure 1.45) so that it does not block any information in the list. Click anywhere outside the begonia picture to deselect it.

You decide that the picture of the begonia will look better if it is placed on the right side of the worksheet instead of the left. You move the picture by cutting and pasting the object.

> **TROUBLESHOOTING:** A Paste Options icon might display in the worksheet after you have moved the begonia picture. It offers additional options related to the paste procedure. You do not need to change any options, so ignore the button.

e. Click **Save** on the Quick Access Toolbar. Click **Minimize** to minimize the worksheet without closing it.

STEP 2 ➤➤ SELECT TEXT, APPLY FONT ATTRIBUTES, AND USE THE MINI TOOLBAR

As the opening of a new showing at the Spotted Begonia Art Gallery draws near, you are active in preparing promotional materials. You are currently working on an informational flyer that is almost set to go. You will make a few improvements before approving the flyer for release. Refer to Figure 1.46 as you complete Step 2.

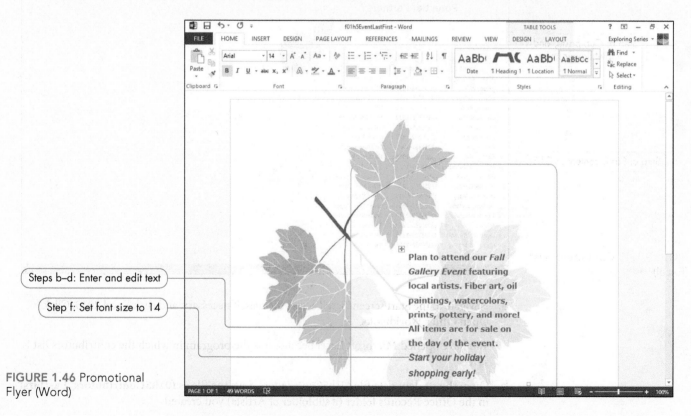

FIGURE 1.46 Promotional Flyer (Word)

Steps b–d: Enter and edit text

Step f: Set font size to 14

a. Navigate to the Start screen. Scroll across the tiles, if necessary, and click **Word 2013**. Click **Open Other Documents**. Open *f01h5Event* and save the document as **f01h5Event_LastFirst** in the Promotional Print folder (a subfolder of Artists) you created.

You plan to modify the promotional flyer slightly to include additional information about the Spotted Begonia Art Gallery.

> **TROUBLESHOOTING:** If you make any major mistakes in this exercise, you can close the file without saving it, open *f01h5Event* again, and then start this exercise over.

b. Click after the exclamation mark after the word *more* at the end of the first paragraph. Press **Enter** and type the following text. As you type, do not press Enter at the end of each line. Word will automatically wrap the lines of text.

All items are for sale on the day of the event. Start your holiday shopping early! You'll find gifts for everyone on your list.

> **TROUBLESHOOTING:** If you make any mistakes while typing, press Backspace and correct them.

c. Select the sentence beginning with *You'll find gifts*. Press **Delete**.

When you press Delete, selected text (or characters to the right of the insertion point) is removed. Deleted text is not placed in the Clipboard.

d. Select the words *Start your holiday shopping early!* Click **Italic** in the Font group on the HOME tab and click anywhere outside the selection to see the result.

e. Select both paragraphs but not the final italicized line. While still within the selection, move the mouse pointer slightly to display the Mini toolbar, click the **Font arrow** on the Mini toolbar, and then scroll to select **Verdana**.

> **TROUBLESHOOTING:** If you do not see the Mini toolbar, you might have moved too far away from the selection. In that case, click outside the selection and drag to select it once more. Without leaving the selection, move the mouse pointer slightly to display the Mini toolbar.

You have changed the font of the two paragraphs.

f. Click after the period following the word *event* before the last sentence in the second paragraph. Press **Enter** and press **Delete** to remove the extra space before the first letter, if necessary. Drag to select the new line, click **Font Size arrow** in the Font group, and then select **14**. Click anywhere outside the selected area. Your document should appear as shown in Figure 1.46.

You have increased font size to draw attention to the text.

g. Save the document and keep open for Step 3.

STEP 3 ≫ USE FORMAT PAINTER AND WORK WITH THE MINI TOOLBAR

You are on a short timeline for finalizing the promotional flyer, so you will use a few shortcuts to avoid retyping and reformatting more than is necessary. You know that you can easily copy formatting from one area to another using Format Painter. The Mini toolbar can also help you make changes quickly. Refer to Figure 1.47 as you complete Step 3.

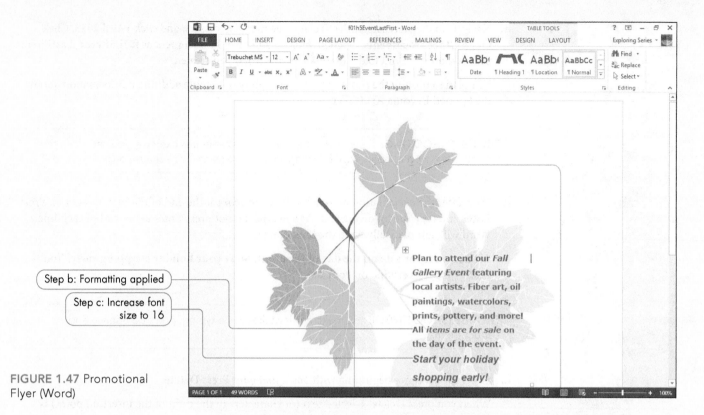

Step b: Formatting applied

Step c: Increase font size to 16

FIGURE 1.47 Promotional Flyer (Word)

a. Select the words *Fall Gallery Event* in the first paragraph and click **Format Painter** in the Clipboard group.

b. Select the words *items are for sale* in the sixth line. Click anywhere outside the selection to deselect the phrase.

The format of the area that you first selected (*Fall Gallery Event*) is applied to the line containing the phrase.

c. Select the text *Start your holiday shopping early!* in the Mini toolbar, click in the **Font Size box**, and then select **16** to increase the font size slightly. Click outside the selected area.

Figure 1.47 shows the final document as it should now appear.

d. Save the document as **f01h5Stp3Event_LastFirst** in the Promotional Print folder you created and close Word. Submit your file based on your instructor's directions.

The flyer will be saved with the same file name and in the same location as it was when you last saved the document in Step 2. As you close Word, the open document will also be closed.

STEP 4 ➤➤ USE THE FONT DIALOG BOX AND FIND AND REPLACE TEXT

The contributors worksheet is almost complete. However, you first want to make a few more formatting changes to improve the worksheet's appearance. You will also quickly change an incorrect area code by using Excel's *Find and Replace* feature. Refer to Figure 1.48 as you complete Step 4.

Step c: Open Fill Effects dialog box

Step c: Select a variant

FIGURE 1.48 Excel Format Cells Dialog Box

a. Click the **Excel icon** on the taskbar to redisplay the contributors worksheet that you minimized in Step 1.

The Excel potential contributors list displays.

> **TROUBLESHOOTING:** If you closed Excel, you can find the correct worksheet in your Recent Documents list.

b. Drag to select **cells A6** through **C6**.

> **TROUBLESHOOTING:** Make sure the mouse pointer looks like a large white plus sign before dragging. It is normal for the first cell in the selected area to be a different shade. If you click and drag when the mouse pointer does not resemble a white plus sign, text may be moved or duplicated. In that case, click Undo on the Quick Access Toolbar.

c. Click the **Dialog Box Launcher** in the Font group to display the Format Cells dialog box. Click the **Fill tab** and click **Fill Effects**, as shown in Figure 1.48. Click any style in the *Variants* section, click **OK**, and then click **OK** once more to close the Format Cells dialog box. Click outside the selected area to see the final result.

The headings of the worksheet are shaded more attractively.

d. Click **Find & Select** in the Editing group and click **Replace**. Type **410** in the **Find what box**. Type **411** in the **Replace with box**, click **Replace All**, and then click **OK** when notified that Excel has made seven replacements. Click **Close** in the *Find and Replace* dialog box.

You discovered that you consistently typed an incorrect area code. You used Find and Replace to make the corrections quickly.

e. Save the workbook as **f01h5Stp4Contributors_LastFirst** in the Office Records folder you created. Exit Excel, if necessary. Submit your files based on your instructor's directions.

Insert Tab Tasks

As its title implies, the Insert tab enables you to insert, or add, items into a file. Much of the Insert tab is specific to the particular application, with some commonalities to other Office applications. Word's Insert tab includes text-related commands, whereas Excel's is more focused on inserting such items as charts and tables. Word allows you to insert apps from the Microsoft app store, so you could add an application such as Merriam-Webster Dictionary. Both Word and Excel allow you to insert Apps for Office to build powerful Web-backed solutions. PowerPoint's Insert tab includes multimedia items and links. Despite their obvious differences in focus, all Office applications share a common group on the Insert tab—the Illustrations group. In addition, all Office applications enable you to insert headers, footers, text boxes, and symbols. Those options are also found on the Insert tab in various groups, depending on the particular application. In this section, you will work with common activities on the Insert tab, including inserting online pictures.

Inserting Objects

With few exceptions, all Office applications share common options in the Illustrations group of the Insert tab. PowerPoint places some of those common features in the Images group. You can insert pictures, shapes, and *SmartArt*. SmartArt is a diagram that presents information visually to effectively communicate a message. These items are considered objects, retaining their separate nature when they are inserted in files. That means that you can select them and manage them independently of the underlying document, worksheet, or presentation.

After an object has been inserted, you can click the object to select it or click anywhere outside the object to deselect it. When an object is selected, a border surrounds it with handles, or small dots, appearing at each corner and in the middle of each side. Figure 1.49 shows a selected object, surrounded by handles. Unless an object is selected, you cannot change or modify it. When an object is selected, the Ribbon expands to include one or more contextual tabs. Items on the contextual tabs relate to the selected object, enabling you to modify and manage it.

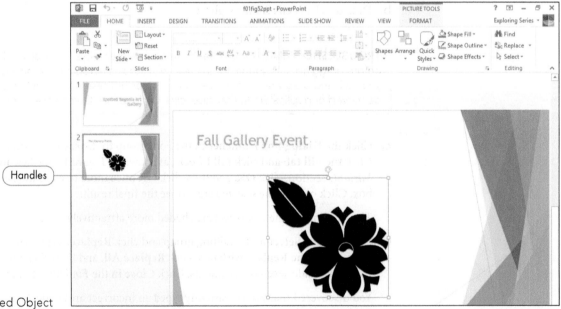

FIGURE 1.49 Selected Object

You can resize and move a selected object. Place the mouse pointer on any handle and drag (when the mouse pointer looks like a two-headed arrow) to resize the object. Be careful! If you drag a side handle, the object is likely to be skewed, possibly resulting in a poor image. Instead, drag a corner handle to proportionally resize the image. To move an object, drag the object when the mouse pointer looks like a four-headed arrow.

Insert Pictures

STEP 2 >> Documents, worksheets, and presentations can include much more than just words and numbers. You can easily add energy and additional description to the project by including pictures and other graphic elements. Although a *picture* is usually just that—a digital photo—it is actually defined as a graphic element retrieved from storage media such as a hard drive or a CD. A picture could actually be an image that you saved from the Internet onto your hard drive.

The process of inserting a picture is simple.

1. Click in the project where you want the picture to be placed. Make sure you know where the picture that you plan to use is stored.
2. Click the INSERT tab.
3. Click Pictures in the Illustrations group (or Images group in PowerPoint). The Insert Picture dialog box is shown in Figure 1.50. You can also use Online Pictures to search for and insert pictures.
4. Navigate to where your picture is saved and click Insert (or simply double-click the picture).

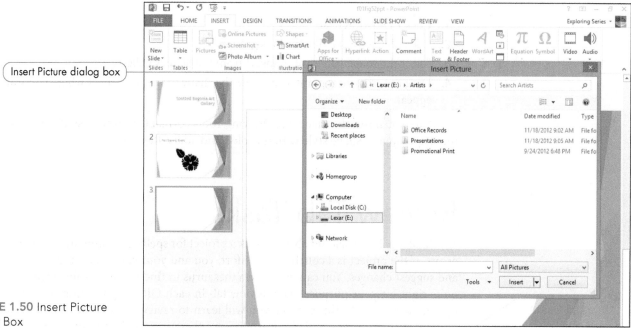

Insert Picture dialog box

FIGURE 1.50 Insert Picture Dialog Box

In addition, on some slide layouts, PowerPoint displays Pictures and Online Pictures buttons that you can click to search for and select a picture for the slide.

Insert and Modify SmartArt

The SmartArt feature enables you to create a diagram and to enter text to provide a visual representation of data. To create a SmartArt diagram, choose a diagram type that fits the purpose: List, Process, Cycle, Hierarchy, Relationships, Matrix, Pyramid, and Picture. You can get additional SmartArt diagrams at Office.com. To insert a SmartArt object, do the following:

1. Click the INSERT tab.
2. Click SmartArt in the Illustrations group to display the Choose a SmartArt Graphic dialog box.
3. Click the type of SmartArt diagram you want in the left pane of the dialog box.
4. Click the SmartArt subtype from the center pane.
5. Preview the selected SmartArt and subtype in the right pane and click OK.

Once you select the SmartArt diagram type and the subtype, a Text pane opens in which you can enter text. The text you enter displays within the selected object. If the SmartArt diagram contains more objects than you need, click the object and press Delete.

The SmartArt Tools Design tab enables you to customize the design of a SmartArt diagram. You can modify the diagram by changing its layout, colors, and style. The layout controls the construction of the diagram. The style controls the visual effects, such as embossing and rounded corners of the diagram. The SmartArt Tools Format tab controls the shape fill color, border, and size options.

Insert and Format Shapes

You can insert a shape to add a visual effect to a worksheet. You can insert various types of lines, rectangles, basic shapes (such as an oval, a pie shape, or a smiley face), block arrows, equation shapes, flowchart shapes, stars and banners, and callouts. You can insert shapes, such as a callout, to draw attention to particular worksheet data. To insert a shape, do the following:

1. Click the INSERT tab.
2. Click Shapes in the Illustrations group.
3. Select the shape you want to insert from the Shapes gallery.
4. Drag the cross-hair pointer to create the shape in the worksheet where you want it to appear.

After you insert the shape, the Drawing Tools Format tab displays so that you can change the shape, apply a shape style with fill color, and adjust the size.

Review Tab Tasks

As a final touch, you should always check a project for spelling, grammatical, and word usage errors. If the project is a collaborative effort, you and your colleagues might add comments and suggest changes. You can even use a thesaurus to find synonyms for words that are not quite right for your purpose. The Review tab in each Office application provides all these options and more. In this section, you will learn to review a file, checking for spelling and grammatical errors. You will also learn to use a thesaurus to identify synonyms.

Reviewing a File

As you create or edit a file, you will want to make sure no spelling or grammatical errors exist. You will also be concerned with wording, being sure to select words and phrases that best represent the purpose of the document, worksheet, or presentation. On occasion, you might even find yourself at a loss for an appropriate word. Not to worry. Word, Excel, and PowerPoint all provide standard tools for proofreading, including a spelling and grammar checker and a thesaurus.

Check Spelling and Grammar

STEP 1 > In general, all Office applications check your spelling and grammar as you type. If a word is unrecognized, it is flagged as misspelled or grammatically incorrect. Misspellings are identified with a red wavy underline, grammatical problems are underlined in green, and word usage errors (such as using *bear* instead of *bare*) have a blue underline. If the word or phrase is truly in error—that is, it is not a person's name or an unusual term that is not in the application's dictionary—you can correct it manually, or you can let the software correct it for you. If you right-click a word or phrase that is identified as a mistake, you will see a shortcut menu similar to that shown in Figure 1.51. If the application's dictionary can make a suggestion as to the correct spelling, you can click to accept the suggestion and make the change. If a grammatical rule is violated, you will have an opportunity to select a correction. However, if the text is actually correct, you can click Ignore or Ignore All (to bypass all occurrences of the flagged error in the current document). Click *Add to Dictionary* if you want the word to be considered correct whenever it appears in all documents. Similar selections on a shortcut menu enable you to ignore grammatical mistakes if they are not errors.

FIGURE 1.51 Correcting Misspelling

You might prefer the convenience of addressing possible misspellings and grammatical errors without having to examine each underlined word or phrase. To do so, click Spelling & Grammar in the Proofing group on the Review tab. Beginning at the top of the document, each identified error is highlighted in a pane similar to Figure 1.52. You can then choose how to address the problem by making a selection from the options in the pane.

Spelling pane

FIGURE 1.52 Checking for Spelling and Grammatical Errors

TIP Understanding Software Options

Many Office settings are considered *default* options. Thus, unless you specify otherwise, the default options are in effect. One such default option is the automatic spelling and grammar checker. If you prefer to enable and disable certain options or change default settings in an Office application, you can click the FILE tab and select Options. From that point, you can work through a series of categories, selecting or deselecting options at will. For example, if you want to change how the application corrects and formats text, you can select or deselect settings in the Proofing group.

Use the Thesaurus

As you write, there will be times when you are at a loss for an appropriate word. Perhaps you feel that you are overusing a word and want to find a suitable substitute. The Thesaurus is the Office tool to use in such a situation. Located in the Proofing group on the Review tab, Thesaurus enables you to search for synonyms, or words with similar meanings. Select a word and click Thesaurus in the Proofing group on the Review tab. A task pane displays on the right side of the screen, and synonyms are listed similar to those shown in Figure 1.53. You can also use the Thesaurus before typing a word to find substitutes. Simply click Thesaurus and type the word for which you are seeking a synonym in the Search box. Press Enter or click the magnifying glass to the right of the Search box for some suggestions. Finally, you can also identify synonyms when you right-click a word and point to Synonyms (if any are available). Click any word from the options offered to place it in the document.

Thesaurus pane

FIGURE 1.53 Thesaurus

Page Layout Tab Tasks

When you prepare a document or worksheet, you are concerned with the way the project appears onscreen and possibly in print. Unlike Word and Excel, a PowerPoint presentation is usually designed as a slide show, so it is not nearly as critical to concern yourself with page layout settings. The Page Layout tab in Word and Excel provides access to a full range of options such as margin settings and page orientation. In this section, you will identify page layout settings that are common to Office applications.

Because a document is most often designed to be printed, you will want to make sure it looks its best in printed form. That means that you will need to know how to adjust margins and how to change the page orientation. Perhaps the document or spreadsheet should be centered on the page vertically or the text should be aligned in columns. By adjusting page settings, you can do all these things and more. You will find the most common page settings, such as margins and page orientation, in the Page Setup group on the Page Layout tab. For less common settings, such as determining whether headers should print on odd or even pages, you can use the Page Setup dialog box.

Changing Margins

A *margin* is the area of blank space that displays to the left, right, top, and bottom of a document or worksheet. Margins are evident only if you are in Print Layout or Page Layout view or if you are in the Backstage view, previewing a document to print. To set or change margins, click the Page Layout tab. As shown in Figure 1.54, the Page Setup group enables you to change such items as margins and orientation. To change margins:

1. Click Margins in the Page Setup group on the PAGE LAYOUT tab.
2. If the margins that you intend to use are included in any of the preset margin options, click a selection. Otherwise, click Custom Margins to display the Page Setup dialog box in which you can create custom margin settings.
3. Click OK to accept the settings and close the dialog box.

You can also change margins when you click Print on the File tab.

FIGURE 1.54 Page Setup Group

Changing Page Orientation

STEP 3 » Documents and worksheets can be displayed in *portrait* orientation or in *landscape*. A page displayed or printed in portrait orientation is taller than it is wide. A page in landscape orientation is wider than it is tall. Word documents are usually more attractive displayed in portrait orientation, whereas Excel worksheets are often more suitable in landscape. To select page orientation, click Orientation in the Page Setup group on the Page Layout tab (see Figure 1.55). Orientation is also an option in the Print area of the Backstage view.

Using the Page Setup Dialog Box

The Page Setup group contains the most commonly used page options in the particular Office application. Some are unique to Excel, and others are more applicable to Word. Other less common settings are available in the Page Setup dialog box only, displayed when you click the Page Setup Dialog Box Launcher. The subsequent dialog box includes options for customizing margins, selecting page orientation, centering vertically, printing gridlines, and creating headers and footers, although some of those options are available only when working with Word; others are unique to Excel. Figure 1.55 shows both the Excel and Word Page Setup dialog boxes.

FIGURE 1.55 Page Setup Dialog Boxes

1. Give two ways to resize an object, such as a picture, that has been inserted in a document. *p. 61*

2. Often, an Office application will identify a word as misspelled that is not actually misspelled. How can that happen? If a word is flagged as misspelled, how can you correct it (or ignore it if it is not actually an error)? *p. 63*

3. Give two ways to change a document from a portrait orientation to landscape. Identify at least one document type that you think would be better suited for landscape orientation rather than portrait. *p. 66*

4. What dialog box includes options for selecting margins, centering vertically, and changing page orientation? *p. 66*

Watch the Video
for this Hands-
On Exercise!

MyITLab®
HOE6 Training

6 Insert Tab Tasks, Page Layout Tab Tasks, and Review Tab Tasks

A series of enrichment programs at the Spotted Begonia Art Gallery is nearing kickoff. You are helping plan a ceremony to commemorate the occasion. To encourage interest and participation, you will edit a PowerPoint presentation that is to be shown to civic groups, the local retiree association, and to city and county leaders to solicit additional funding. You know that pictures add energy to a presentation when used appropriately, so you will check for those elements, adding whatever is necessary. A major concern is making sure the presentation is error free and that it is available in print so that meeting participants can review it later. As a reminder, you also plan to have available a handout giving the time and date of the dedication ceremony. You will use the Insert tab to work with illustrations and the Review tab to check for errors, and you will use Word to generate an attractive handout as a reminder of the date.

Skills covered: Check Spelling and Use the Thesaurus • Insert Pictures • Change Margins and Page Orientation

STEP 1 ≫ CHECK SPELLING AND USE THE THESAURUS

As you check the PowerPoint presentation that will be shown to local groups, you make sure no misspellings or grammatical mistakes exist. You also use the Thesaurus to find a suitable substitution for a word you feel should be replaced. Refer to Figure 1.56 as you complete Step 1.

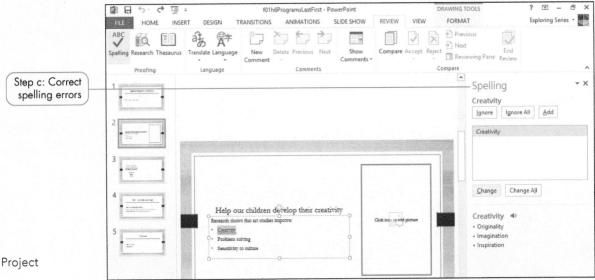

FIGURE 1.56 Project Presentation

a. Navigate to the Start screen. Scroll across the tiles, if necessary, and click **PowerPoint 2013**. Click **Open Other Presentations**. Open *f01h6Programs* and save the document as **f01h6Programs_LastFirst** in the Promotional Print folder (a subfolder of Artists) you created.

The PowerPoint presentation opens, with Slide 1 shown in Normal view.

b. Click the **SLIDE SHOW tab** and click **From Beginning** in the Start Slide Show group to view the presentation. Click to advance from one slide to another. After the last slide, click to return to Normal view.

c. Click the **REVIEW tab** and click **Spelling** in the Proofing group. Correct any words that are misspelled by clicking the correction and clicking Change or Ignore in the Spelling pane. Click **Change** to accept *Creativity* on Slide 2, click **workshops** and click **Change** on Slide 3, and click **Change** to accept *Thank* for Slide 5. Refer to Figure 1.56. Click **OK** when the spell check is complete and close the pane.

d. Click **Slide 2** in the Slides pane on the left. Double-click the bulleted word *Creativity*, click **Thesaurus** in the Proofing group, point to *Imagination* in the Thesaurus pane, click the arrow to the right of the word, and then select **Insert**.

The word *Creativity* is replaced with the word *Imagination*.

e. Click the **Close (X) button** in the top-right corner of the Thesaurus pane.

f. Save the presentation.

STEP 2 ≫ INSERT PICTURES

Although the presentation provides the necessary information and encourages viewers to become active participants in the enrichment programs, you believe that pictures might make it a little more exciting. Where appropriate, you will include a picture. Refer to Figure 1.57 as you complete Step 2.

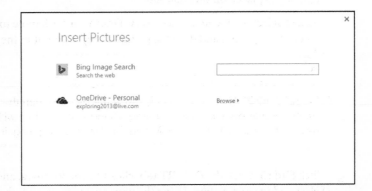

FIGURE 1.57 Inserting Pictures

a. Click **Slide 2** in the Slides pane on the left, if necessary. Click the **INSERT tab** and click **Online Pictures** in the Images group.

The Insert Pictures pane displays on the screen.

> **TROUBLESHOOTING:** You can add your own pictures to slides using the Pictures command. Or you can copy and paste images directly from a Web page.

b. Type **begonia** in the **Bing Image search box** and press **Enter**.

You will identify pictures that may be displayed on Slide 2.

c. Click to select a flower. Click **Insert**.

The picture may not be placed as you would like, but you will move and resize it in the next substep as necessary. Also, notice that the picture is selected, as indicated by the box and handles surrounding it.

> **TROUBLESHOOTING:** It is very easy to make the mistake of inserting duplicate pictures on a slide, perhaps because you clicked the image more than once in the task pane. If that should happen, you can remove any unwanted picture by clicking to select it and pressing Delete.

d. Click a corner handle—the small square on the border of the picture. Make sure the mouse pointer appears as a double-headed arrow. Drag to resize the image so that it fits well on the slide. Click in the center of the picture. The mouse pointer should appear as a four-headed arrow. Drag the picture slightly to the right corner of the slide. Make sure the picture is still selected (it should be surrounded by a box and handles). If it is not selected, click to select it.

> **TROUBLESHOOTING:** You may not need to perform this substep if the picture came in as desired. Proceed to the next substep if this occurs.

e. Click **Slide 5** in the Slides pane on the left. Click the **INSERT tab** and select **Online Pictures**. Type **happy art** in the **Bing Image search box** and press **Enter**. Click a picture of your choice and click **Insert**.

A picture is placed on the final slide.

f. Click to select the picture, if necessary. Drag a corner handle to resize the picture. Click the center of the picture and drag the picture to reposition it in the bottom-right corner of the slide.

> **TROUBLESHOOTING:** You can only move the picture when the mouse pointer looks like a four-headed arrow. If instead you drag a handle, the picture will be resized instead of moved. Click Undo on the Quick Access Toolbar and begin again.

g. Click **Slide 3**. Click the **INSERT tab**, click **Online Pictures**, and then search for **school art**. Select and insert a picture. Using the previously practiced technique, resize the image height and position as necessary to add the picture to the right side of the slide.

h. Save the presentation and exit PowerPoint. Submit your file based on your instructor's directions.

STEP 3 ›› CHANGE MARGINS AND PAGE ORIENTATION

You are ready to finalize the flyer promoting the workshops, but before printing it you want to see how it will look. You wonder if it would be better in landscape or portrait orientation, so you will try both. After adjusting the margins, you are ready to save the flyer for later printing and distribution. Refer to Figure 1.58 as you complete Step 3.

FIGURE 1.58 Page Setup Dialog Box

a. Navigate to the Start screen. Scroll across the tiles, if necessary, and click **Word 2013**. Click **Open Other Documents**. Open *f01h6Handout* and save the document as **f01h6Handout_ LastFirst** in the Promotional Print folder (a subfolder of Artists) you created.

b. Click the **PAGE LAYOUT tab**, click **Orientation** in the Page Setup group, and then select **Landscape** to view the flyer in landscape orientation.

You want to see how the handout will look in landscape orientation.

c. Click the **FILE tab**, click **Print**, and then click **Next Page** and click **Previous Page** (right- and left-pointing arrows at the bottom center of the preview page).

The second page of the handout shows only the last two bullets and the contact information. You can see that the two-page layout is not an attractive option.

d. Click the **Back arrow** in the top-left corner. Click **Undo** on the Quick Access Toolbar. Click the **FILE tab** and click **Print**.

The document fits on one page. Portrait orientation is a much better choice for the handout.

e. Click the **Back arrow** in the top-left corner. Click the **PAGE LAYOUT tab** if necessary, click **Margins** in the Page Setup group, and then select **Custom Margins**. Click the **spin arrow** beside the left margin box to increase the margin to **1.2**. Similarly, change the right margin to **1.2**. Refer to Figure 1.58. Click **OK**.

f. Save the document and exit Word. Submit your file based on your instructor's directions.

Chapter Objectives Review

After reading this chapter, you have accomplished the following objectives:

1. **Log in with your Microsoft account.**
   - Your Microsoft account connects you to all of Microsoft's Internet-based resources.

2. **Identify the Start screen components.**
   - The Start screen has a sleek, clean interface that is made up of tiles and Charms.

3. **Interact with the Start screen.**
   - Customize the Start screen to access programs and apps.

4. **Access the desktop.**
   - Simplified to accommodate mobile devices, laptops, and desktops.

5. **Use File Explorer.**
   - Understand and customize the interface: Change the view to provide as little or as much detail as you need.
   - Work with groups on the Navigation Pane: Provides access to all resources, folders, and files.

6. **Work with folders and files.**
   - Create a folder: A well-named folder structure can be created in File Explorer or within a program as you save a file.
   - Open, rename, and delete folders and files: File Explorer can be used to perform these tasks.
   - Save a file: When saving a file for the first time, you need to indicate the location and the name of the file.

7. **Select, copy, and move multiple files and folders.**
   - Select multiple files and folders: Folders and files can be selected as a group.
   - Copy and move files and folders: Folders and the files within them can be easily moved to the same or a different drive.

8. **Identify common interface components.**
   - Use the Backstage view and the Quick Access Toolbar: The Backstage view can perform several commands.
   - Familiarize yourself with the Ribbon: Provides access to common tasks.
   - Use the status bar: The status bar provides information relative to the open file and quick access to View and Zoom level options.

9. **Get Office Help.**
   - Use Office Help: The Help button links to online resources and technical support.
   - Use Enhanced ScreenTips: Provides the purpose of a command button as you point to it.
   - Get help with dialog boxes: Use the Help button in the top-right corner of a dialog box to get help relevant to the task.

10. **Open a file.**
    - Create a new file: A document can be created as a blank document or with a template.
    - Open a file using the Open dialog box: Previously saved files can be located and opened using a dialog box.

    - Open a file using the Recent Documents list: Documents that you have worked with recently display here.
    - Open a file from the Templates list: Templates are a convenient way to save time when designing a document.

11. **Print a file.**
    - Check and change orientation or perform other commands related to the look of your file before printing.

12. **Close a file and application.**
    - Close files you are not working on to avoid becoming overwhelmed.

13. **Select and edit text.**
    - Select text to edit: Commit to memory: "Select, then do."
    - Use the Mini toolbar: Provides instant access to common formatting commands after text is selected.
    - Apply font attributes: These can be applied to selected text with toggle commands.
    - Change the font: Choose from a set of fonts found within all Office applications.
    - Change the font size, color, and attributes: These commands are located in the Font group on the Ribbon.

14. **Use the Clipboard group commands.**
    - Copy formats with the Format Painter: Copy formatting features from one section of text to another.
    - Move and copy text: Text can be selected, copied, and moved between applications or within the same application.
    - Use the Office Clipboard: This pane stores up to 24 cut or copied selections for use later on in your computing session.

15. **Use the Editing group commands.**
    - Find and replace text: Finds each occurrence of a series of characters and replaces them with another series.
    - Use advanced find and replace feature: Change the format of every occurrence of a series of characters.

16. **Insert objects.**
    - Insert pictures: You can insert pictures from a CD or other media, or from an online resource such as Bing.com.
    - Insert and modify SmartArt: Create a diagram and to enter text to provide a visual of data.
    - Insert and format shapes: You can insert various types of lines and basic shapes.

17. **Review a file.**
    - Check spelling and grammar: All Office applications check and mark these error types as you type for later correction.
    - Use the Thesaurus: Enables you to search for synonyms.

18. **Use the Page Setup dialog box.**
    - Change margins: You can control the amount of blank space that surrounds the text in your document.
    - Change margins and page orientations, and create headers and footers.

Key Terms Matching

Match the key terms with their definitions. Write the key term letter by the appropriate numbered definition.

a. Backstage view
b. Charms
c. Cloud storage
d. Find
e. Font
f. Format Painter
g. Group
h. Mini toolbar
i. Navigation Pane
j. Operating system

k. Quick Access Toolbar
l. Ribbon
m. OneDrive
n. Snip
o. Snipping Tool
p. Start screen
q. Subfolder
r. Tile
s. Windows 8.1.1
t. Windows 8.1.1 app

1. _____ A tool that copies all formatting from one area to another. **p. 49**

2. _____ Software that directs computer activities such as checking all components, managing system resources, and communicating with application software. **p. 2**

3. _____ A task-oriented section of the Ribbon that contains related commands. **p. 25**

4. _____ An app used to store, access, and share files and folders. **p. 2**

5. _____ Any of the several colorful block images found on the Start screen that when clicked takes you to a program, file, folder, or other Windows 8.1.1 app. **p. 3**

6. _____ A component of Office 2013 that provides a concise collection of commands related to an open file. **p. 23**

7. _____ A tool that displays near selected text that contains formatting commands. **p. 46**

8. _____ A level of folder structure indicated as a folder within another folder. **p. 10**

9. _____ An application specifically designed to run in the Start screen interface of Windows 8.1.1. **p. 3**

10. _____ A command used to locate each occurrence of a series of characters. **p. 52**

11. _____ A Windows 8.1.1 accessory program that allows you to capture a screen display so that you can save, annotate, or share it. **p. 5**

12. _____ What you see after starting your Windows 8.1.1 computer and entering your username and password. **p. 2**

13. _____ Provides handy access to commonly executed tasks such as saving a file and undoing recent actions. **p. 23**

14. _____ A Microsoft operating system released in 2012 that is available on laptops, desktops, and tablet computers. **p. 2**

15. _____ A component made up of five icons that provide similar functionality to the Start button found in previous versions of Windows. **p. 3**

16. _____ The captured screen display created by the Snipping Tool. **p. 5**

17. _____ The long bar located just beneath the title bar containing tabs, groups, and commands. **p. 25**

18. _____ Provides access to computer resources, folders, files, and networked peripherals. **p. 11**

19. _____ A technology used to store files and to work with programs that are stored in a central location on the Internet. **p. 2**

20. _____ A character design or the way characters display onscreen. **p. 45**

Multiple Choice

1. The Recent Documents list shows documents that have been previously:
   (a) Printed.
   (b) Opened.
   (c) Saved in an earlier software version.
   (d) Deleted.

2. Which of the following File Explorer features collects related data from folders and gives them a single name?
   (a) Network
   (b) Favorites
   (c) Libraries
   (d) Computer

3. When you want to copy the format of a selection but not the content, you should:
   (a) Double-click Copy in the Clipboard group.
   (b) Right-click the selection and click Copy.
   (c) Click Copy Format in the Clipboard group.
   (d) Click Format Painter in the Clipboard group.

4. Which of the following is *not* a benefit of using OneDrive?
   (a) Save your folders and files in the cloud.
   (b) Share your files and folders with others.
   (c) Hold video conferences with others.
   (d) Simultaneously work on the same document with others.

5. What does a red wavy underline in a document, spreadsheet, or presentation mean?
   (a) A word is misspelled or not recognized by the Office dictionary
   (b) A grammatical mistake exists
   (c) An apparent word usage mistake exists
   (d) A word has been replaced with a synonym

6. When you close a file:
   (a) You are prompted to save the file (unless you have made no changes since last saving it).
   (b) The application (Word, Excel, or PowerPoint) is also closed.
   (c) You must first save the file.
   (d) You must change the file name.

7. Live Preview:
   (a) Opens a predesigned document or spreadsheet that is relevant to your task.
   (b) Provides a preview of the results of a choice you are considering before you make a final selection.
   (c) Provides a preview of an upcoming Office version.
   (d) Enlarges the font onscreen.

8. You can get help when working with an Office application in which one of the following areas?
   (a) Help button
   (b) Status bar
   (c) The Backstage view
   (d) Quick Access Toolbar

9. The *Find and Replace* feature enables you to do which of the following?
   (a) Find all instances of misspelling and automatically correct (or replace) them
   (b) Find any grammatical errors and automatically correct (or replace) them
   (c) Find any specified font settings and replace them with another selection
   (d) Find any character string and replace it with another

10. A document or worksheet printed in landscape orientation is:
    (a) Taller than it is wide.
    (b) Wider than it is tall.
    (c) A document with 2" left and right margins.
    (d) A document with 2" top and bottom margins.

Practice Exercises

1 Designing Web Pages

You have been asked to make a presentation to the local business association. With the mayor's renewed emphasis on growing the local economy, many businesses are interested in establishing a Web presence. The business owners would like to know a little bit more about how Web pages are designed. In preparation for the presentation, you need to proofread and edit your PowerPoint file. This exercise follows the same set of skills as used in Hands-On Exercises 1–6 in the chapter. Refer to Figure 1.59 as you complete this exercise.

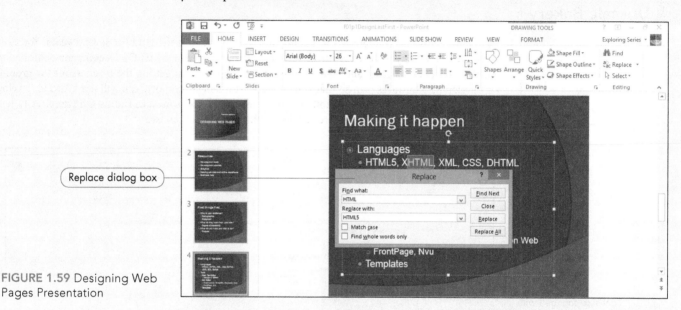

FIGURE 1.59 Designing Web Pages Presentation

a. Click **File Explorer** on the taskbar and select the location where you save your files. Click the **HOME tab** and click **New folder** in the New group. Type **Designing Web Pages** and press **Enter**.

   Take a snip, name it **f01p1DesignSnip_LastFirst**, and then save it in the Designing Web Pages folder. Close File Explorer.

b. Point to the bottom-right corner of your screen to display the Charms and click the **Start charm**. Scroll if necessary and click **PowerPoint 2013** to start PowerPoint. Open *f01p1Design* and save it as **f01p1Design_LastFirst** in the Designing Web Pages folder. In Slide 1, drag to select the text *Firstname Lastname* and type your own first and last names. Click an empty area of the slide to cancel the selection.

c. Click the **REVIEW tab** and click **Spelling** in the Proofing group. In the Spelling pane, click **Change** or **Ignore** to make or not make a change as needed. Most identified misspellings should be changed. The words *KompoZer* and *Nvu* are not misspelled, so you should ignore them when they are flagged. Click **OK** to end the spell check.

d. Click the **SLIDE SHOW tab**. Click **From Beginning** in the Start Slide Show group. Click each slide to view the show and press **Esc** on the last slide.

e. Click **Slide 2** in the Slides pane on the left. Drag to select the *Other tools* text and press **Backspace** on the keyboard to delete the text.

f. Click **Slide 4** in the Slides pane. Click the **HOME tab** and click **Replace** in the Editing group. Type **HTML** in the **Find what box** and **HTML5** in the **Replace with box**. Click **Find Next**. Read the slide and click **Replace** to change the first instance of *HTML*. Refer to Figure 1.59. Click **Close**.

g. Click **Replace** in the Editing group. Type **CSS** in the **Find what box** and **CSS5** in the **Replace with box**. Click **Replace All** and click **OK**. Click **Close**.

h. Drag to select the *FrontPage, Nvu* text and press **Backspace** on the keyboard to delete the text.

i. Press **Ctrl+End** to place the insertion point at the end of *Templates* and press **Enter**. Type **Database Connectivity** to create a new bulleted item.

j. Click the **FILE tab** and click **Print**. Click the **Full Page Slides arrow** and click **6 Slides Horizontal** to see a preview of all of the slides as a handout. Click the **Back arrow** and click the **HOME tab**.

k. Click **Slide 1** in the Slides pane to move to the beginning of the presentation.

l. Drag the **Zoom slider** on the status bar to the right to **130%** to magnify the text. Then use the **Zoom Slider** to return to **60%**.

m. Save and close the file. Submit your files based on your instructor's directions.

2 **Upscale Bakery**

You have always been interested in baking and have worked in the field for several years. You now have an opportunity to devote yourself full time to your career as the CEO of a company dedicated to baking cupcakes, pastries, and catering. One of the first steps in getting the business off the ground is developing a business plan so that you can request financial support. You will use Word to develop your business plan. This exercise follows the same set of skills as used in Hands-On Exercises 1, 3, 4, and 5 in the chapter. Refer to Figure 1.60 as you complete this exercise.

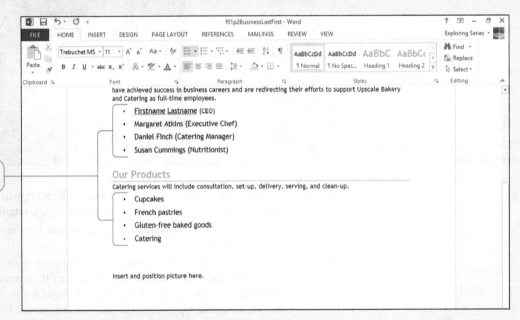

FIGURE 1.60 Business Plan Document

a. Click **File Explorer** on the taskbar and select the location where you save your files. Click the **HOME tab** and click **New folder** in the New group. Type **Business Plan** and press **Enter**.

Take a snip, name it **f01p2BusinessSnip_LastFirst**, and save it in the Business Plan folder. Close File Explorer.

b. Point to the bottom-right corner of your screen to display the Charms and click the **Start charm**. Scroll if necessary and click **Word 2013** to start Word. Open *f01p2Business* and save it as **f01p2Business_LastFirst** in the Business Plan folder.

c. Click the **REVIEW tab** and click **Spelling & Grammar** in the Proofing group. Click **Change** for all suggestions.

d. Drag the paragraphs beginning with *Our Staff* and ending with *(Nutritionist)*. Click the **HOME tab** and click **Cut** in the Clipboard group. Click to the left of *Our Products* and click **Paste**.

e. Select the text *Your name* in the first bullet and replace it with your first and last names. Select that entire bullet and use the Mini toolbar to use Live Preview to see some other Font sizes. Then click **11** to increase the size.

f. Double-click the **Format Painter** in the Clipboard group on the HOME tab. Drag the Format Painter to change the other *Our Staff* bullets to **11**. Drag all four *Our Products* bullets. Click the **Format Painter button** to toggle it off and click outside of the text to deselect it. Refer to Figure 1.60.

g. Select the last line in the document, which says *Insert and position picture here.*, and press **Delete**. Click the **INSERT tab** and click **Online Pictures** in the Illustrations group.

- Click in the **Bing Image search box**, type **Cupcakes**, and then press **Enter**.
- Select a Cupcake with a single birthday candle or select any image and click **Insert**. Do not deselect the image.
- Click the **PICTURE TOOLS FORMAT tab**, if necessary, click the **More button** in the Picture Styles group, and then click the **Soft Edge Rectangle** (sixth from the left on the top row).
- Click outside the picture.

h. Click the **FILE tab** and click **Print**. Change *Normal Margins* to **Moderate Margins**. Click the **Back arrow**.

i. Click the picture and click **Center** in the Paragraph group on the HOME tab.

j. Save and close the file. Submit your files based on your instructor's directions.

3 Best Friends Pet Care

You and a friend are starting a pet sitting service and have a few clients already. Billing will be a large part of your record keeping, so you are planning ahead by developing a series of folders to maintain those records. This exercise follows the same set of skills as used in Hands-On Exercises 1, 2, and 5 in the chapter. Refer to Figure 1.61 as you complete this exercise.

FIGURE 1.61 Best Friends Pet Care

a. Click **File Explorer** on the taskbar and select the location where you save your files. Click the **Home tab** and click **New folder** in the New group. Type **Best Friends** and press **Enter**.

b. Double-click **Best Friends** in the Content pane to open the folder. Create new subfolders as follows:

- Click the **Home tab** and click **New folder** in the New group. Type **Business Letters** and press **Enter**.
- Click the **Home tab** and click **New folder** in the New group. Type **Billing Records** and press **Enter**. Compare your results to Figure 1.61. Take a snip and name it **f01p3FriendsSnip_LastFirst**. Save it in the Billing Records subfolder of the Best Friends folder. Close File Explorer.

c. Navigate to the Start screen and click on **Word 2013**. Click **Open Other Documents** and open *f01p3Friends*. Save it as **f01p3Friends_LastFirst** in the Business Letters subfolder of the Best Friends folder.

d. Use *Find and Replace* to replace the text *Your Name* with your name by doing the following:

- Click **Replace** in the Editing group on the HOME tab.
- Type **Your name** in the **Find what box**. Type your first and last names in the **Replace with box**.
- Click **Replace** and click **OK**. Close the *Find and Replace* dialog box. Close, save changes to the document, and exit Word.

e. Click **File Explorer** on the taskbar so that you can rename one of your folders:
  - Click **Computer** in the Navigation Pane.
  - In the Content pane, navigate to the drive where you earlier created the Best Friends folder. Double-click the **Best Friends folder**.
  - Right-click **Billing Records**, click **Rename**, type **Accounting Records**, and then press **Enter**.

  f. Take a snip and name it **f01p3FolderSnip_LastFirst**. Save it in the Business Letters subfolder of the Best Friends folder. Submit your files based on your instructor's directions.

Mid-Level Exercises

1 Reference Letter

You are an instructor at a local community college. A student has asked you to provide her with a letter of reference for a job application. You have used Word to prepare the letter, but now you need to make a few changes before it is finalized.

a. Open File Explorer. Create a new folder named **References** in the location where you are saving your student files. Take a snip, name it **f01m1ReferencesSnip_LastFirst**, and save it in the References folder. Close File Explorer.

b. Start Word. Open *f01m1Letter* and save it in the References folder as **f01m1Letter_LastFirst**.

c. Select the date and point to several font sizes in the Mini toolbar. Use the Live Preview to compare them. Click **11**.

d. Double-click the date and use the **Format Painter** to change the rest of the letter to font size 11.

e. Apply bold to the student's name, *Stacy VanPatten*, in the first sentence.

f. Correct all errors using Spelling & Grammar. Her last name is spelled correctly. Use the Thesaurus to find a synonym for *intelligent* and replace wih **gifted**. Change the *an* to *a* just before the new word. Replace each occurrence of *Stacy* with **Stacey**.

g. Move the last paragraph—beginning with *In my opinion*—to position it before the second paragraph—beginning with *Stacey is a gifted*.

h. Move the insertion point to the beginning of the document.

i. Change the margins to **Narrow**.

j. Preview the document as it will appear when printed.

k. Save and close the file. Submit your files based on your instructor's directions.

2 Medical Monitoring

You are enrolled in a Health Informatics program of study in which you learn to manage databases related to health fields. For a class project, your instructor requires that you monitor your blood pressure, recording your findings in an Excel worksheet. You have recorded the week's data and will now make a few changes before printing the worksheet for submission.

a. Open File Explorer. Create a new folder named **Medical** in the location where you are saving your student files. Take a snip, name it **f01m2MedicalSnip_LastFirst**, and save it in the Medical folder. Close File Explorer.

b. Start Excel. Open *f01m2Tracker* and save it as **f01m2Tracker_LastFirst** in the Medical folder.

c. Preview the worksheet as it will appear when printed. Change the orientation of the worksheet to **Landscape**. Preview the worksheet again.

d. Click in the cell to the right of *Name* and type your first and last names. Press **Enter**.

e. Change the font of the text in **cell C1** to **Verdana**. Use Live Preview to try some font sizes. Change the font size to **20**.

f. Check the spelling for the worksheet.

g. Get help on showing decimal places. You want to increase the decimal places for the values in **cells E22, F22, and G22** so that each value shows two places to the right of the decimal. Use Excel Help to learn how to do that. You might use *Increase Decimals* as a Search term. When you find the answer, select the three cells and increase the decimal places to **2**.

h. Click **cell A1** and insert a picture of your choice related to blood pressure. Resize and position the picture so that it displays in an attractive manner. Format the picture with **Soft Edges** set to **4 pt**. Change the margins to **Wide**.

i. Open the Backstage view and adjust print settings to print two copies. You will not actually print two copies unless directed by your instructor.

j. Save and close the file. Submit your files based on your instructor's directions.

3 Today's Musical Artists

COLLABORATION CASE

CREATIVE CASE ★

With a few of your classmates, you will use PowerPoint to create a single presentation on your favorite musical artists. Each student must create at least one slide and then all of the slides will be added to the presentation. Because everyone's schedule is varied, you should use either your Outlook account or OneDrive to pass the presentation file among the group.

a. Open File Explorer. Create a new folder named **Musical** in the location where you are saving your student files. Take a snip, name it **f01m3MusicalSnip_LastFirst**, and then save it in the Musical folder. Close File Explorer.

b. Start PowerPoint. Create a new presentation and save it as **f01m3Music_GroupName** in the Musical folder.

c. Add one slide that contains the name of the artist, the genre, and two or three interesting facts about the artist.

d. Insert a picture of the artist or an image that represents the artist.

e. Put your name on the slide that you created. Save the presentation.

f. Pass the presentation to the next student so that he or she can perform the same tasks and save the presentation before passing it on to the next student. Continue until all group members have created a slide in the presentation.

g. Save and close the file. Submit your file based on your instructor's directions.

Beyond the Classroom

Fitness Planner

RESEARCH CASE

You will use Microsoft Excel to develop a fitness planner. Open *f01b2Exercise* and save it as **f01b2Exercise_LastFirst**. Because the fitness planner is a template, the exercise categories are listed, but without actual data. You will personalize the planner. Change the orientation to **Landscape**. Move the contents of **cell A2** (*Exercise Planner*) to **cell A1**. Click **cell A8** and use the Format Painter to copy the format of that selection to **cells A5** and **A6**. Increase the font size of **cell A1** to **26**. Use Excel Help to learn how to insert a header and put your name in the header. Begin the fitness planner, entering at least one activity in each category (warm-up, aerobics, strength, and cool-down). Submit as directed by your instructor.

Household Records

DISASTER RECOVERY

FROM SCRATCH

Use Microsoft Excel to create a detailed record of your household appliances and other items of value that are in your home. In case of burglary or disaster, an insurance claim is expedited if you are able to itemize what was lost along with identifying information such as serial numbers. You will then make a copy of the record on another storage device for safekeeping outside your home (in case your home is destroyed by a fire or weather-related catastrophe). Connect a flash drive to your computer and then use File Explorer to create a folder on the hard drive titled **Home Records**. Design a worksheet listing at least five fictional appliances and electronic equipment along with the serial number of each. Save the workbook as **f01b3Household_LastFirst** in the Home Records folder. Close the workbook and exit Excel. Use File Explorer to copy the Home Records folder from the hard drive to your flash drive. Use the Snipping Tool to create a full-screen snip of the screen display. Save it as **f01b3Disaster_LastFirst** in the Home Records folder. Close all open windows and submit as directed by your instructor.

Meetings

SOFT SKILLS CASE

FROM SCRATCH

After watching the Meetings video, you will use File Explorer to create a series of folders and subfolders to organize meetings by date. Each folder should be named by month, day, and year. Three subfolders should be created for each meeting. The subfolders should be named **Agenda**, **Handouts**, and **Meeting Notes**. Use the Snipping Tool to create a full-screen snip of the screen display. Save it as **f01b4Meetings_LastFirst**. Submit as directed by your instructor.

Capstone Exercise

You are a member of the Student Government Association (SGA) at your college. As a community project, the SGA is sponsoring a Stop Smoking drive designed to provide information on the health risks posed by smoking cigarettes and to offer solutions to those who want to quit. The SGA has partnered with the local branch of the American Cancer Society as well as the outreach program of the local hospital to sponsor free educational awareness seminars. As the secretary for the SGA, you will help prepare a PowerPoint presentation that will be displayed on plasma screens around campus and used in student seminars. You will use Microsoft Office to help with those tasks.

Manage Files and Folders

You will open, review, and save an Excel worksheet providing data on the personal monetary cost of smoking cigarettes over a period of years.

a. Create a folder called **SGA Drive**.

b. Start Excel. Open *f01c1Cost* from the student data files and save it in the SGA Drive folder as **f01c1Cost_LastFirst**.

c. Click **cell A10** and type your first and last names. Press **Enter**.

Modify the Font

To highlight some key figures on the worksheet, you will format those cells with additional font attributes.

a. Draw attention to the high cost of smoking for 10, 20, and 30 years by changing the font color in **cells G3 through I4** to **Red**.

b. Italicize the Annual Cost cells (**F3** and **F4**).

c. Click **Undo** on the Quick Access Toolbar to remove the italics. Click **Redo** to return the text to italics.

Insert a Picture

You will add a picture to the worksheet and then resize it and position it.

a. Click **cell G7** and insert an online picture appropriate for the topic of smoking.

b. Resize the picture and reposition it near cell B7.

c. Click outside the picture to deselect it.

Preview Print, Change Page Layout, and Print

To get an idea of how the worksheet will look when printed, you will preview the worksheet. Then you will change the orientation and margins before printing it.

a. Preview the document as it will appear when printed.

b. Change the page orientation to **Landscape**. Click the **PAGE LAYOUT tab** and change the margins to **Narrow**.

c. Preview the document as it will appear when printed.

d. Adjust the print settings to print two copies. You will not actually print two copies unless directed by your instructor.

e. Save and close the file.

Find and Replace

You have developed a PowerPoint presentation that you will use to present to student groups and for display on plasma screens across campus. The presentation is designed to increase awareness of the health problems associated with smoking. The PowerPoint presentation has come back from the reviewers with only one comment: A reviewer suggested that you spell out Centers for Disease Control and Prevention, instead of abbreviating it. You do not remember exactly which slide or slides the abbreviation might have been on, so you use *Find and Replace* to make the change quickly.

a. Start PowerPoint. Open *f01c1Quit* and save it in the SGA Drive folder as **f01c1Quit_LastFirst**.

b. Replace all occurrences of *CDC* with **Centers for Disease Control and Prevention**.

Cut and Paste and Insert a Text Box

The Mark Twain quote on Slide 1 might be more effective on the last slide in the presentation, so you will cut and paste it there in a text box.

a. On Slide 1, select the entire Mark Twain quote by clicking on the placeholder border. When the border is solid, the entire placeholder and its contents are selected.

b. On Slide 22, paste the quote, reposition it more attractively, and then format it in a larger font size.

Check Spelling and Change View

Before you call the presentation complete, you will spell check it and view it as a slide show.

a. Check spelling. The word *hairlike* is not misspelled, so it should not be corrected.

b. View the slide show and take the smoking quiz. Click after the last slide to return to the presentation.

c. Save and close the presentation. Exit PowerPoint. Submit both files included in this project as directed by your instructor.

Word

wavebreakmedia/Shutterstock

Introduction to Word

CHAPTER **1**

Organizing a Document

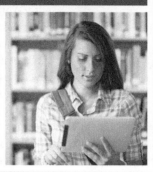

AFTER YOU READ THIS CHAPTER, YOU WILL BE ABLE TO:

1. Begin and edit a document p. 85
2. Customize Word p. 94
3. Use features that improve readability p. 103

4. View a document in different ways p. 108
5. Prepare a document for distribution p. 120
6. Modify document properties p. 124

CASE STUDY | Swan Creek National Wildlife Refuge

You have always been fascinated with wildlife in its natural habitat. For that reason, you are excited to be working with Swan Creek National Wildlife Refuge, assigned the task of promoting its educational programs to area schools and preparing documents to support the refuge's educational outreach. The wildlife refuge is situated near a large urban area that is dominated by a thriving industry of steel production. Emily Traynom, Swan Creek's site director, is concerned that children in the city have little opportunity to interact with nature. In fact, many spend their days indoors or on city streets, seldom having an opportunity to enjoy nature. She fears that a generation of children will mature into adults with little appreciation of the role of our country's natural resources in the overall balance of nature. Her passion is encouraging students to visit Swan Creek and become actively involved in environmental activities.

Ms. Traynom envisions summer day camps in which children will explore the wildlife refuge and participate in learning activities. She wants to provide internships for students, encouraging an ongoing relationship with nature. For those efforts and others, you will use your expertise in Microsoft Word to produce documents such as flyers, brochures, memos, contracts, and letters. As the school year draws to a close, Ms. Traynom has asked you to design and produce an article about a series of summer camps available to children from 5th through 8th grades. She has given you a rough draft of the article from which you will create an attractive document for distribution to schools and for posting on Swan Creek's Web site.

Introduction to Word Processing

Word processing software, often called a word processor, is one of the most commonly used types of software in homes, schools, and businesses. People around the world—students, office assistants, managers, and professionals in all areas—use word processing programs such as *Microsoft Word* for a variety of tasks. Microsoft Word 2013, included in the Microsoft Office suite of software, is the most current version of the popular word processor. You can create letters, reports, research papers, newsletters, brochures, and all sorts of documents with Word. You can even create and send e-mail, produce Web pages, post to social media sites, and update blogs with Word. Figure 1.1 shows examples of documents created in Word. If a project requires collaboration online or between offices, Word makes it easy to share documents, track changes, view comments, and efficiently produce a document to which several authors can contribute. By using Word to create a research paper, you can easily create citations, a bibliography, a table of contents, a cover page, an index, and other reference pages. To enhance a document, you can change colors, add interesting styles of text, insert graphics, and use tables to present data. With emphasis on saving documents to the cloud, Word enables you to share these documents with others or access them from any device. To say the least, Word is a very comprehensive word processing solution.

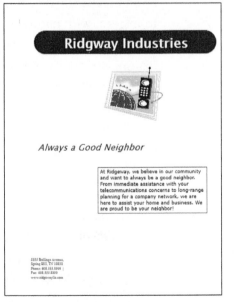

FIGURE 1.1 Word Documents

Communicating through the written word is an important task for any business or organization. In fact, it would be almost impossible to conduct business without written and oral communication. Word processing software, such as Word, simplifies the technical task of preparing documents, but a word processor does not replace the writer. Be careful when wording a document so you are sure it is appropriate for the intended audience. Always remember that once you distribute a document, either on paper or electronically, you cannot retract the words. Therefore, you should never send a document that you have not carefully checked several times to be sure it conveys your message in the best way possible. Also, you cannot depend completely on a word processor to identify all spelling and grammatical errors, so be sure to closely proofread every document you create. Although several word processors, including Word, provide predesigned documents (called *templates*) that include basic wording for various tasks, it is ultimately up to you to compose well-worded documents. The role of business communication, including the written word, in the success or failure of a business cannot be overemphasized.

In this section, you will explore Word's interface, learn how to create and save a document, explore the use of templates, and perform basic editing operations. You will learn how to move around in a document and to review spelling and word usage. Using Word options, you will explore ways to customize Word to suit your preferences, and you will learn to customize the Ribbon and the Quick Access Toolbar.

Beginning and Editing a Document

When you open Word 2013, your screen will be similar to Figure 1.2. You can create a blank document, or you can select from several categories of templates. Recently viewed files are shown on the left, for ease of access should you want to open any again.

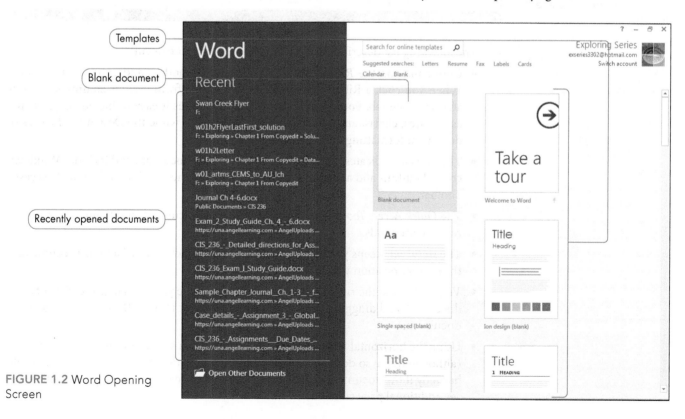

FIGURE 1.2 Word Opening Screen

To begin a blank document, click *Blank document* (or simply press Enter, if *Blank document* is selected). Word provides a clean, uncluttered area in which to type, with minimal distraction at the sides and across the top. Unlike earlier Word versions, Word 2013 provides a large, almost borderless area for your document, with an interface closely aligned with that of Windows 8.1.1. Using several basic features, including the Ribbon, Quick Access Toolbar, vertical and horizontal scroll bars, and the status bar, you can easily create an attractive document. Figure 1.3 shows a typical Word document.

FIGURE 1.3 Word Document Interface

The following list describes Word's basic features in more detail:

- Commands on the **Ribbon** enable you to create, modify, and enhance documents. When you click a Ribbon tab, you can then select from various commands associated with the tab. For example, the Insert tab makes it easy to include objects such as pictures, charts, and screenshots in a document, while the Design tab focuses on document formatting and color selections.

- The *title bar* indicates the file name of the current document and includes Windows control buttons and access to Word Help. It is also the location of the Quick Access Toolbar.

- The *Quick Access Toolbar* makes it easy to save a document, and to undo or redo recent commands.

- The *status bar* keeps you apprised of information such as word and page count, and the current position within the document.

- *View buttons* at the right side of the status bar enable you to change the view of a document, and dragging the *Zoom slider* enlarges or reduces the onscreen size of a document.

- Using the horizontal and vertical *scroll bars*, you can scroll through a document (although doing so does not actually move the insertion point). You will see a scroll bar only if the document is long enough and/or wide enough to require scrolling to see additional page content.

Many people enjoy having the Ribbon close at hand when developing or editing a document. Others might prefer an uncluttered workspace, free of distractions. Temporarily remove the Ribbon from view by clicking *Collapse the Ribbon* (see Figure 1.3). Tabs remain displayed, but all detail beneath them is hidden, resulting in a large amount of uncluttered typing space. To display the Ribbon again, click any tab and click *Pin the ribbon* (the toggle of *Collapse the Ribbon*) or simply double-click a tab on the Ribbon.

Ribbon Display Options (Figure 1.3) enables you to adjust the Ribbon view. You can choose to hide the Ribbon, providing a clear document space in which to edit or read a document. Click at the top of the Ribbon to show it again. You can also choose to show only the Ribbon tabs. Click a tab to display its options. Finally, you can choose to show all Ribbon tabs and commands, which is the default.

Use a Template

STEP 2 ▶ Wording a document can be difficult, especially if you are struck with writer's block! With that in mind, the developers of Word have included a library of **templates** from which you can select a predesigned document. You can then modify the document to suit your needs. Categories of templates are displayed when you first open Word, or when you click the File tab and click New. In addition to local templates—those that are available offline with a typical Word installation—Microsoft provides many more through Office.com. All of those templates are displayed or searchable within Word, as shown in Figure 1.4. Microsoft continually updates content in the template library, so you are assured of having access to all the latest templates each time you open Word.

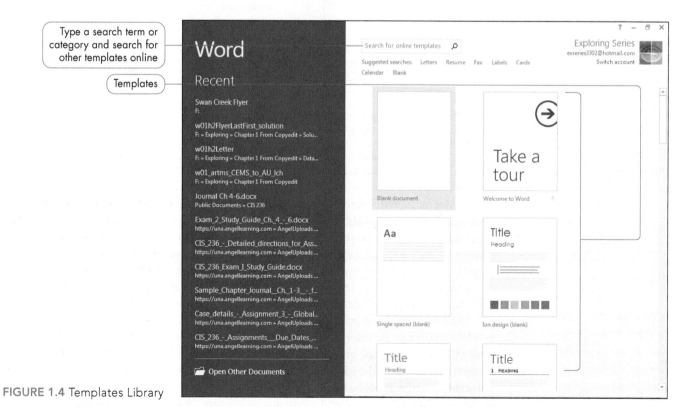

FIGURE 1.4 Templates Library

Some templates are likely to become your favorites. Because you will want quick access to those templates, you can pin them to the top of the templates menu so they will always be available. Simply right-click a favorite template and click *Pin to list*. To unpin a previously pinned template, repeat the process but select *Unpin from list*.

Create a Document

STEP 1 To create a blank document, click *Blank document* when Word opens (refer to Figure 1.2). As you type text, you will not need to think about how much text can fit on one line or how sentences progress from one line to the next. Word's ***word wrap*** feature automatically pushes words to the next line when you reach the right margin.

Word wrap is closely associated with another concept: the hard return and soft return. A *hard return* is created when you press Enter at the end of a line or paragraph. A *soft return* is created by Word as it wraps text from one line to the next. The locations of soft returns change automatically as text is inserted or deleted, or as page features or settings, such as objects or margins, are added or changed. Soft returns are not considered characters and cannot be deleted. However, a hard return is actually a nonprinting character, called a *paragraph mark*, that you can delete, if necessary. To display nonprinting characters, such as paragraph marks and tabs, click Show/Hide (¶) (see Figure 1.5). Just as you delete any other character by pressing Backspace or Delete (depending on whether the insertion point is positioned to the right or left of the item to remove), you can delete a paragraph mark. To remove the display of nonprinting characters, click Show/Hide (¶) again.

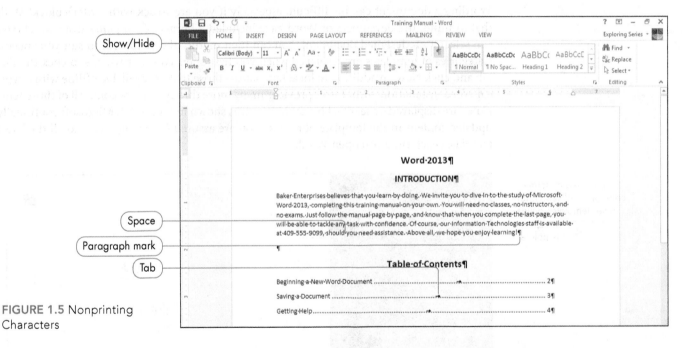

FIGURE 1.5 Nonprinting Characters

As you work with Word, you must understand that Word's definition of a paragraph and your definition are not likely to be the same. You would probably define a paragraph as a related set of sentences, which is correct in a literary sense. When the subject or direction of thought changes, a new paragraph begins. However, Word defines a paragraph as text that ends in a hard return. Even a blank line, created by pressing Enter, is considered a paragraph. Therefore, as a Word student, you will consider every line that ends in a hard return a paragraph. When you press Enter, a paragraph mark is displayed in the document (refer to Figure 1.5).

In addition to the nonprinting mark that Word inserts when you press Enter, other nonprinting characters are inserted when you press keys such as Tab or the Spacebar. Click Show/Hide (¶) in the Paragraph group on the Home tab to reveal all nonprinting characters in a document (refer to Figure 1.5). Nonprinting characters are generally not viewed when working in a document and will not be included when a document is printed, but they can assist you with troubleshooting a document and modifying its appearance before printing or distributing. For example, if lines in a document end awkwardly, some not even extending to the right margin, you can click Show/Hide (¶) to display nonprinting characters and check for the presence of poorly placed, or perhaps unnecessary, hard returns. Deleting the hard returns might realign the document so that lines end in better fashion.

Reuse Text

You might find occasion to reuse text from a previously created document because the wording fits well in a document on which you are working. For example, a memo to employees describing new insurance benefits might borrow wording from another document describing the same benefits to company retirees. In that case, you would simply insert text from a saved document into the currently open memo. With the insertion point positioned where the inserted text is to be placed, complete the following steps:

1. Click the INSERT tab.
2. Click the Object arrow (see Figure 1.6).
3. Click *Text from File.*
4. Navigate to the location of the saved document and double-click the file name.

FIGURE 1.6 Insert Text from Another Document

Save a Document

Saving a document makes it possible for you to access it later for editing, sharing, or printing. In fact, it is a good idea not to wait until a document is complete to save it, but to save a document periodically as you develop it. That way, you risk losing only what you created or edited since the last save operation if you experience a disruption of power. If you have ever worked with a word processor, you are probably familiar with the process of saving a document. Word 2013 recognizes not only the need to save files, but also the need to make them available on any device you might have access to and the need to share documents with others so you can collaborate on projects. To make that possible, Word encourages you to save documents to the cloud, or Internet, instead of a local drive, such as a hard drive or flash drive. It is always a good idea, however, to save a document in several places so that you always have a backup copy. You might save a document to a hard drive as well as OneDrive, which is free online storage space provided by Microsoft. If you plan to use the document on another computer, you could also save it to a flash drive for ease of transporting. To save a document, click the File tab and click Save (or Save As). You can also click Save on the Quick Access Toolbar.

If you are using Windows 8.1.1 as your operating system, you most likely provided a Windows Live ID, or e-mail address, when you installed the operating system. In that case, the address connects to your associated OneDrive storage and enables Word, and other Microsoft programs, to save files in that location by default. (A default setting is one that is automatically set unless you specify otherwise.) If you choose to share documents from your OneDrive storage, collaborators can easily access and edit them.

As you save a file, Word enables you to select a location to save to. Although OneDrive is the default, you can select another drive on your computer (see Figure 1.7).

Select to save to your OneDrive account (the default)

Select if you plan to save to local storage, such as a flash drive or hard drive

Click to navigate to a folder on the selected storage device or location

FIGURE 1.7 Saving a Document

TIP | **Saving Files**

Remember to save files often. If you open a document and plan to save it with the same file name and in the same location from which it was opened, click Save on the Quick Access Toolbar. You can also click the File tab and click Save. Otherwise, click the File tab and click Save As to change either the save location or the file name.

To save a document to local storage, such as a flash drive, hard drive, or local network location, click Computer (refer to Figure 1.7) and click Browse to navigate to the desired location. Provide a file name and either accept the default type (Word Document) or click the *Save as type* arrow (see Figure 1.8) and select another format. Users of Word 2007 and Word 2010 will be able to open a document saved in Word 2013 format, but some Word 2013 features might be disabled. However, if you plan to distribute a document to someone using a Word version earlier than Word 2007, change the type to Word 97-2003 Document. You will learn more about file compatibility later in this chapter.

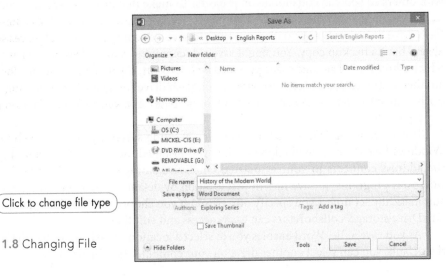

Click to change file type

FIGURE 1.8 Changing File Type

Open a Document

STEP 3 » Having saved a document, you can open it later when you start Word and then either select the document from the Recent list or click Open Other Documents and navigate to the saved file. Word remembers the position of the insertion point when you previously saved the file and suggests that you return to that same location (see Figure 1.9). Just click the link to return, or ignore it if you prefer the current display.

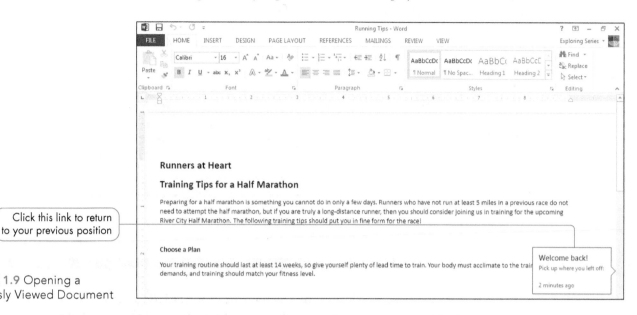

Click this link to return to your previous position

FIGURE 1.9 Opening a Previously Viewed Document

Move Around a Document and Edit a Document

The *insertion point* indicates where the text you type will be inserted. It is important to remain aware of the location of the insertion point and to know how to move it so that you can control where text is typed. Probably the easiest way to move the insertion point within a document is to simply click in the desired location. When you reposition the insertion point within existing text in a document and then type text, the text is inserted between pieces of existing text.

If a document contains more text than will display onscreen at one time, you can click the horizontal or vertical scroll arrows (or drag a scroll bar) to view different parts of the document. Then, when the desired text is shown onscreen, click to position the insertion point and continue editing the document. Be aware that using the scroll bar or scroll arrows to move the display does not reposition the insertion point. It merely lets you see different parts of the document, leaving the insertion point where it was last positioned. Only when you click in the document, or use a keyboard shortcut, is the insertion point moved.

Review Word Usage in a Document

It is important to create a document that is free of typographical and grammatical errors. One of the easiest ways to lose credibility with readers is to allow such errors to occur. You will also want to choose words that are appropriate and that best convey your intentions in writing or editing a document. Word provides tools on the Review tab that simplify the tasks of reviewing a document for errors, identifying proper wording, and defining words with which you are unfamiliar.

With the automated spelling and grammar tools in Word, it is relatively easy to produce an error-free document. A word that is considered by Word to be misspelled is underlined with a red wavy line. A possible grammatical mistake or word usage error is underlined in blue. Both types of errors are shown in Figure 1.10. Never depend completely on Word to catch all errors; always proofread a document yourself. For example, typing the word *fee* when you meant to type *free* is not an error that Word would typically catch, because the word is not actually misspelled and might not be flagged as a word usage error, depending upon the sentence context.

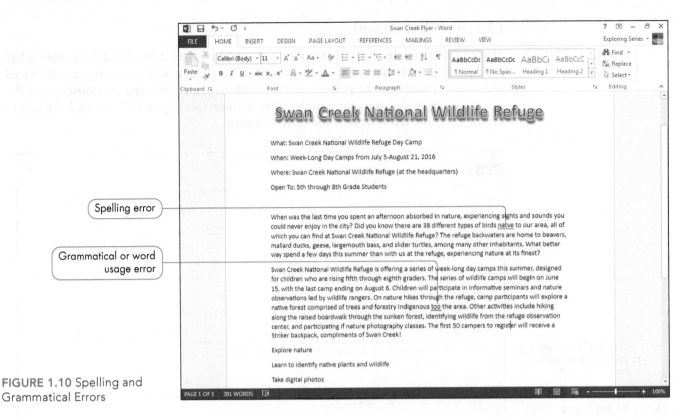

Spelling error

Grammatical or word usage error

FIGURE 1.10 Spelling and Grammatical Errors

To correct possible spelling, grammatical, or word usage errors in a document, you can right-click an underlined error and select an option from a shortcut menu. If possible, Word will attempt to provide a correction that you can select from the menu. If the word or text is not actually an error, you can choose to ignore it by making an appropriate selection from the shortcut menu.

STEP 4 >> Correcting each error by right-clicking can become time-consuming, especially if the mistakes are many. In that case, Word can check an entire document, pausing at each identified error so that you can determine whether to correct or ignore the problem. To check an entire document, click the Review tab and click Spelling & Grammar in the Proofing group (see Figure 1.11). For even quicker error identification, check the Proofing errors button on the status bar (see Figure 1.11). By default, Word will automatically check an entire open document for spelling, grammatical, and word usage errors, displaying an *X* on the Proofing errors button if errors are found. Click the button to either change or ignore all errors, one at a time. If, instead, you see a check mark on the Proofing errors button, the document appears to be error free. The document in Figure 1.11 contains errors, as indicated by the *X* on the Proofing errors button. Note that at a higher screen resolution than that shown in Figure 1.11, buttons in the Proofing group will be spelled out (Thesaurus, Define, and Word Count).

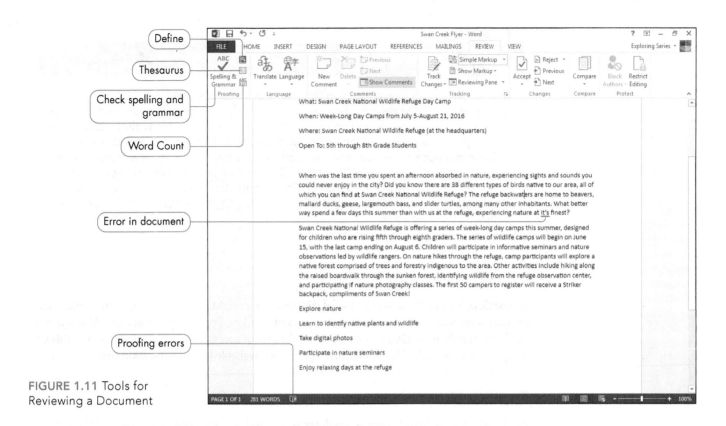

Labels pointing to the ribbon in the figure:
- Define
- Thesaurus
- Check spelling and grammar
- Word Count
- Error in document
- Proofing errors

FIGURE 1.11 Tools for Reviewing a Document

Words do not always come easily. Occasionally, you might need to find a synonym (a word with the same meaning as another) for a particular word but are unable to do so quickly. Word provides a handy *thesaurus* for just such an occasion. Select a word in a document and click the Review tab. Click Thesaurus (refer to Figure 1.11) and select from a group of synonyms. If you have installed a dictionary, you will see a definition of the selected word at the bottom of the Thesaurus pane. Otherwise, you can click a link to get a dictionary app.

> **TIP   Counting Words**
>
> Occasionally, you might need to know how many words are included in a document. For example, your English instructor might require a minimum word count for an essay. Click the Review tab and click Word Count (refer to Figure 1.11) to get a quick summary of words, characters, lines, pages, and paragraphs.

Especially when editing or collaborating on a document created by someone else, you might come across a word with which you are unfamiliar. After selecting a word, click the Review tab and click Define (refer to Figure 1.11). If a dictionary app is installed, the definition will display in the Dictionary pane.

New to Office 2013 is an online app store, providing replacements and additions to add-ins of previous Office versions. Several are especially useful for Word, such as Britannica Researcher, Merriam-Webster Dictionary, and Pingar Summaries (preparing a document summary). Locate those apps and more when you click the Insert tab and click *Apps for Office* in the Apps group. Click See All and click Featured Apps to view featured apps. You can find even more at the Office Store. Click an app link and follow prompts to download it. To insert the app, click *Apps for Office* on the Insert tab, click See All, Click *Find more apps at the Office Store*, and then click Refresh. Click the app and click Insert at the bottom of the dialog box.

Customizing Word

As installed, Word is immediately useful. However, you might find options that you would prefer to customize, add, or remove from the document window. For example, you can add frequently used commands to the Quick Access Toolbar for ease of access. You might prefer that the Ribbon is organized differently. These and other options are available for customization within Word.

Explore Word Options

By default, certain Word settings are determined and in place when you begin a Word document. For example, unless you specify otherwise, Word will automatically check spelling as you type. Similarly, the Mini toolbar will automatically display when text is selected. Although those and other settings are most likely what you will prefer, there may be occasions when you want to change them. When you change Word options, such as those just described, you change them for all documents—not just the currently open file. To modify Word options, click the File tab and click Options. As shown in Figure 1.12, you can select from several categories and then make appropriate adjustments. Word options that you change will remain in effect until you change them again, even after Word is closed and reopened. Keep in mind that if you are working in a school computer lab, you might not have permission to change options permanently.

STEP 5 »

FIGURE 1.12 Word Options

Customize the Ribbon

STEP 6>>

The Word 2013 Ribbon provides access to commands that make it easy to develop, edit, save, share, and print documents. If necessary, you can add and remove Ribbon tabs, as well as rename them. Simply click the File tab and click Options. Click Customize Ribbon. By deselecting a tab name (see Figure 1.13), you can remove a Ribbon tab. Later, you can select it again to redisplay it. Click a tab name and click Rename to change the name of the tab. Type a new name and press Enter. To return to showing all original tabs, click Reset and click *Reset all customizations.*

Review tab is deselected, so it will be removed from the Ribbon

Rename a tab

Add a new tab

Reset tabs to their original state

FIGURE 1.13 Customizing the Ribbon

Customize the Quick Access Toolbar

STEP 7>>

The *Quick Access Toolbar (QAT)* contains only a few commands, by default. With one click, you can save a document. Another QAT command enables you to undo a recent command, whereas another is the Redo command. Although it is helpful to have those options close at hand, you might want to include even more on the QAT. You can even remove commands that you do not use often. To customize the QAT, click Customize Quick Access Toolbar (see Figure 1.14) and select from a menu of options (or click More Commands for even more choices). You can also add a Ribbon command when you right-click it and select *Add to Quick Access Toolbar.* To remove a command from the QAT, right-click the command on the QAT and select *Remove from Quick Access Toolbar.*

Customize Quick
Access Toolbar

FIGURE 1.14 Customizing the
Quick Access Toolbar

Quick
Concepts ✓

1. When creating or editing a document, you can show nonprinting characters. In what ways might the display of nonprinting characters assist you with developing a document? *p. 88*

2. Word 2013 strongly encourages saving documents to a OneDrive account. In fact, OneDrive is the default save location. Provide at least two advantages of using OneDrive as a storage location for your documents. *p. 89*

3. It is very important to check a document for spelling, grammatical, and word usage errors—a task that Word 2013 can help you with. However, Word 2013 might not identify every error in a document. Why not? Provide an example of an error that Word might not identify. *p. 91*

4. In your position of employment, you must print documents often. Describe a way to customize Word to minimize the number of steps required to print a document. *p. 94*

1 Introduction to Word Processing

As an office assistant working with the wildlife refuge, you will prepare a document publicizing the summer day camps at Swan Creek. Your supervisor has worded a few paragraphs that you will modify and add to, creating an article for distribution to schools in the area. You will also open a document from a template, creating a calendar. Because you plan to use the office computer for future projects as well, you will explore ways to customize Word for ease of use.

Skills covered: Create and Save a Document • Use a Template • Move Around a Document and Edit a Document • Review Word Usage in a Document • Explore Word Options • Customize the Ribbon • Customize the Quick Access Toolbar

---

STEP 1 >> CREATE AND SAVE A DOCUMENT

As you create a new document, you will insert text provided by your supervisor at the wildlife refuge and then save the document for later editing. Refer to Figure 1.15 as you complete Step 1.

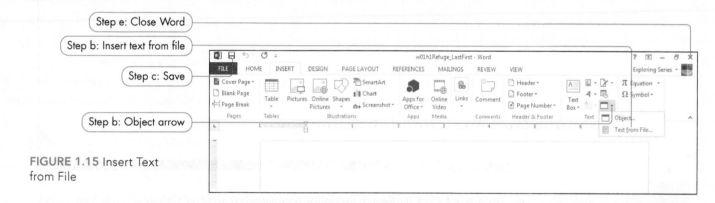

FIGURE 1.15 Insert Text from File

a. Open Word. Click **Blank document**. Click **Save** on the Quick Access Toolbar. In the right pane, click the location where you save your files and change the file name to **w01h1Refuge_LastFirst**. Click **Save**.

   When you save files, use your last and first names. For example, as the Word author, I would name my document *w01h1Refuge_HoganLynn*.

b. Click the **INSERT tab** and click the **Object arrow**. Click **Text from File**. Navigate to *w01h1Camps.docx* in the location of your student data files and double-click the file name. Press **Ctrl+Home** to move the insertion point to the beginning of the document.

c. Click **Save** on the Quick Access Toolbar.

   This saves the document with the same name and in the same location as the previous save.

d. Click the **FILE tab** and click **Close** to close the document.

   You will use this document again later in this Hands-On Exercise.

e. Click **Close** to exit Word.

STEP 2 ›› USE A TEMPLATE

As a multitasker, you are accustomed to working with several projects at once. Ms. Traynom, your supervisor, has asked that you print a calendar for the current year. She often must plan ahead and needs an at-a-glance calendar showing each month. You know that Word provides calendar templates, so you will locate one. Refer to Figure 1.16 as you complete Step 2.

Step c: Close

Step a: Select a year-at-a-glance calendar

FIGURE 1.16 Calendar Template

a. Open Word. Click the **Search for online templates box** and type **Calendar**. Press **Enter**. Click **Year-at-a-Glance** in the *Filter by* pane on the right. Scroll through the calendar templates presented and click to select one that presents the current year.

> **TROUBLESHOOTING:** The calendar template is only available if you are currently connected to the Internet.

b. Click **Create**. Save the calendar as **w01h1Calendar_LastFirst**.

    The location of your student files should display in the Recent Folders list on the right side of the Save As window. Click to select the location.

c. Click **Close** to exit Word.

STEP 3 ›› MOVE AROUND A DOCUMENT AND EDIT A DOCUMENT

Although Ms. Traynom provided you with a good start, you will add a bit more detail to the w01h1Refuge_LastFirst article. Refer to Figure 1.17 as you complete Step 3.

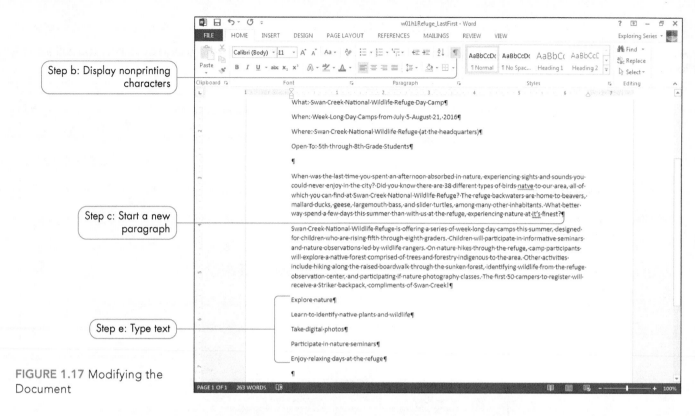

Step b: Display nonprinting characters

Step c: Start a new paragraph

Step e: Type text

FIGURE 1.17 Modifying the Document

a. Open Word. In the Recent list, click **w01h1Refuge_LastFirst**.

b. Click the **HOME tab**, if necessary, and click **Show/Hide (¶)** in the Paragraph group, if necessary, to display nonprinting formatting marks.

c. Click after the sentence ending in *finest?*—immediately after the question mark at the end of the fourth sentence in the body text—and press **Enter** to insert a hard return. Press **Delete** to remove the space before the word *Swan*.

> **TROUBLESHOOTING:** There will be no space before Swan if you clicked after the space instead of before it when you pressed Enter. In that case, there is no space to delete, so leave the text as is.

d. Scroll down and click after the word *Creek!*—immediately after the exclamation point after the second body paragraph—and press **Enter** to insert a hard return.

e. Type the following text, pressing **Enter** at the end of each line:

explore nature

learn to identify native plants and wildlife

take digital photos

participate in nature seminars

enjoy relaxing days at the refuge

As you type each line, the first letter is automatically capitalized. Unless you specify otherwise in Word Options, words that begin new paragraphs and sentences are capitalized. In this case, the capitalization is correct, so leave the words as they are capitalized by Word.

f. Press **Ctrl+End**. Press **Delete** to delete the final paragraph mark in the document.

STEP 4 » REVIEW WORD USAGE IN A DOCUMENT

As you continue to develop the article, you will check for spelling, grammar, and word usage mistakes. You will also identify a synonym and get a definition. Refer to Figure 1.18 as you complete Step 4.

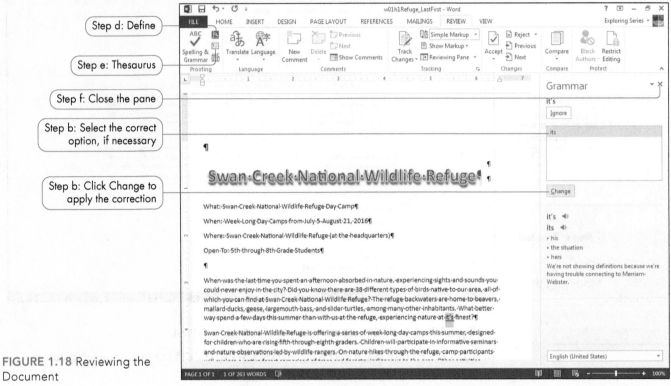

FIGURE 1.18 Reviewing the Document

a. Press **Ctrl+Home** to move to the beginning of the document. Right-click the red underlined word *natve* in the second line of the first body paragraph in the document. Click **native** on the shortcut menu to select the correct spelling.

b. Click the **REVIEW tab** and click **Spelling & Grammar** in the Proofing group. As each error is presented, click to select the correct option. The word *it's* should not include an apostrophe, so ensure the correct option is selected (see Figure 1.18) and click **Change**. The word *fo* should be *for*. Click **OK** when the check is complete.

c. At least one error in the document is not identified as a spelling or word usage error by Word. Read through the document to identify and correct the error.

d. Drag to select the word *immersed* in the first sentence of the first body paragraph (or double-click the word to select it). Click **Define** in the Proofing group. If a dictionary app is installed, you should see a definition of the word in the pane on the right. If a dictionary app is not installed, follow the prompts to install a dictionary app.

e. Close the pane on the right. With the word *immersed* still selected, click **Thesaurus** in the Proofing group. Point to the word *absorbed*, click the arrow at the right, and then select **Insert**.

f. Close the Thesaurus pane. Save the document.

STEP 5 » EXPLORE WORD OPTIONS

You will explore some Word options that will enable you to customize the computer assigned to you at the refuge. Such customization ensures that Word is configured to suit your preferences. Refer to Figure 1.19 as you complete Step 5.

FIGURE 1.19 Exploring Word Options

a. Click the **FILE tab** and click **Options**. Ensure that the General category in the left pane is selected.

   Note that you can change the User name and Initials that identify you as the author of documents you create. Because you might be working in a computer lab, you will not actually change anything at this time.

b. Click **Save** in the left pane of the Word Options dialog box.

   Note that you can adjust the AutoRecover time, a feature covered later in this chapter, by typing in the text box, replacing existing text, or by clicking the up or down arrow repeatedly.

c. Click **Cancel**, so you do not actually make changes.

STEP 6 ❯❯ CUSTOMIZE THE RIBBON

As you continue to explore ways to customize Word preferences, you will identify Ribbon tabs that you can add or remove. Refer to Figure 1.20 as you complete Step 6.

FIGURE 1.20 Customizing the Ribbon

a. Click the **FILE tab** and click **Options**. Click **Customize Ribbon** in the left pane. Under Main Tabs, click the **Mailings check box** to deselect the item.

> **TROUBLESHOOTING:** If *Mailings* is not deselected, you clicked the word *Mailings* instead of the check box next to it. Click the **Mailings check box**.

b. Click **Review** under Main Tabs (click the word *Review*, not the check mark beside the word). Click **Rename** (located beneath the list of Main Tabs) and type **Review Document**—but do not click OK.

c. Click **Cancel**, so that changes to the Ribbon are not saved to a lab computer. Click **Cancel** again.

STEP 7 ≫ CUSTOMIZE THE QUICK ACCESS TOOLBAR

You will customize the Quick Access Toolbar to include commands that you use often. Refer to Figure 1.21 as you complete Step 7.

FIGURE 1.21 Customizing the Quick Access Toolbar

a. Click **Customize Quick Access Toolbar**, located at the right side of the QAT, and select **Print Preview and Print** from the shortcut menu.

As shown in Figure 1.21, an additional button appears on the QAT, enabling you to preview and print a document when you click the button.

b. Click the **REVIEW tab**, if necessary, and right-click **Spelling & Grammar** in the Proofing group. Click **Add to Quick Access Toolbar**.

c. Right-click the **Print Preview and Print button** on the Quick Access Toolbar and select **Remove from Quick Access Toolbar**.

d. Repeat the process to remove Spelling & Grammar from the Quick Access Toolbar.

e. Save the document. Keep the document open if you plan to continue with the next Hands-On Exercise. If not, close the document and exit Word.

Document Organization

Most often, the reason for creating a document is for others to read; therefore, the document should be designed to meet the needs of the reading audience. It should not only be well worded and structured, but also might include features that better identify it, such as headers, footers, and *watermarks*. A watermark is text or graphics that displays behind text. In addition, adjusting margins and changing page orientation might better suit a document's purposes and improve its readability. Depending on its purpose, a document might need to fit on one page, or it could be very lengthy.

Before printing or saving a document, you will want to review it to ensure that it is attractive and appropriately organized. Word has various views, including Read Mode, Print Layout, Web Layout, Outline, and Draft, that you can use to get a good feel for the way the entire document looks in a variety of uses, regardless of its length. The view selected can also give a snapshot of overall document organization so you can be assured that the document is well structured and makes all points. In this section, you will explore features that improve readability, and you will learn to change the view of a document.

Using Features That Improve Readability

Choosing your words carefully will result in a well-worded document. However, no matter how well worded, a document that is not organized in an attractive manner so that it is easy to read and understand is not likely to impress the audience. Consider not only the content, but also how a document will look when printed or displayed. Special features that can improve readability, such as headers, footers, and symbols, are located on Word's Insert tab. Other settings, such as margins, page orientation, and paper size, are found on the Page Layout tab. The Design tab provides access to watermarks, which can help convey the purpose or originator of a document.

Insert Headers and Footers

Headers and *footers* can give a professional appearance to a document. A header consists of one or more lines at the top of each page. A footer displays at the bottom of each page. One advantage of using headers and footers is that you have to specify the content only once, after which it displays automatically on all pages. Although you can type the text yourself at the top or bottom of every page, it is time-consuming, and the possibility of making a mistake is great. Typically, the purpose of including a header or footer is to better identify the document. As a header, you might include an organization name or a class number so that each page identifies the document's origin or purpose. A page number is a typical footer, although it could just as easily be included as a header.

STEP 1 »   To insert a header or footer, click the Insert tab and click Header (or Footer) in the Header & Footer group. Select from a gallery of predefined header or footer styles or click Edit Header (or Edit Footer), as shown in Figure 1.22, to create an unformatted header or footer. After typing a header or footer, click *Close Header and Footer* to leave the header and footer area and return to the document (see Figure 1.23). In Print Layout view, you can also double-click in the document to close the header or footer. A header or footer can be formatted like any other text. It can be center, left, or right aligned, and formatted in any font or font size. When working with a header or footer, the main body text of the document is grayed out temporarily. When you return to the document, the body text is active, but the header or footer text is dim.

Choose from predesigned headers

Create an unformatted header

FIGURE 1.22 Inserting a Header

Click to close a header or footer

Header & Footer Tools contextual tab

FIGURE 1.23 Close a Header or Footer

Word provides fields, such as author, date, and file name, that you can choose to include in headers and footers. Some header and footer fields, such as page numbers, will actually change from one page to the next. Other fields, such as author name and date, will remain constant. Regardless, selecting fields (instead of typing the actual data) simplifies the task of creating headers and footers. Some of the most frequently accessed fields, such as Date & Time and Page Number, are available on the Header & Footer Tools Design contextual tab as separate commands (see Figure 1.24). Others, including Author, File Name, and Document Title, are available when you click Document Info in the Insert group. Depending on the field selected, you might have to indicate a specific format and/or placement. For example, you could display the date as *Monday, August 12, 2016*, or you might direct that a page number is centered.

Choose from a complete list of fields and settings related to headers and footers

Insert common headers and footers, such as author and file name

Insert date and time

Insert page number

FIGURE 1.24 Header and Footer Options

TIP Removing a Header from the First Page

Occasionally, you will want a header or footer on all pages except the first, such as when the first page is a report's cover page. In that case, select Different First Page in the Options group on the Header & Footer Tools Design tab (when a header or footer is selected).

You will find that you use some fields more often than others as headers and footers. Word 2013 provides one-click access to common fields such as Author, File Name, File Path, and Document Title when you click Document Info in the Insert group on the Header & Footer Tools Design tab. You can click Field for a complete list of fields to choose from (see Figure 1.25). The same fields are available when you click Quick Parts in the Insert group and click Field.

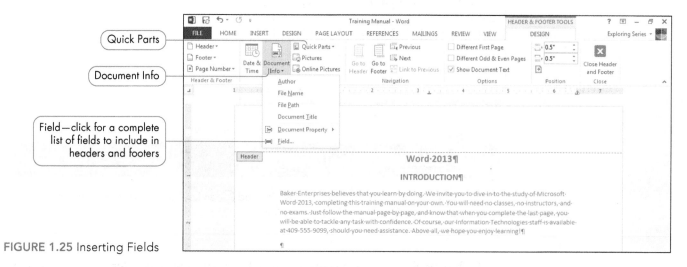

FIGURE 1.25 Inserting Fields

Insert a Symbol

A *symbol* is text, a graphic, or a foreign language character that can be inserted into a document. Most symbols are not located on the keyboard and are available only from Word's collection of symbols. Symbols such as © and ™ can be an integral part of a document; in fact, those particular symbols are necessary to properly acknowledge a source or product. Because they are typically not located on the keyboard, you need to find them in Word's library of symbols or use a shortcut key combination, if available.

Some symbols serve a very practical purpose. For example, it is unlikely you will want a hyphenated word to be divided between lines in a document. In that case, instead of typing a simple hyphen between words, you can insert a *nonbreaking hyphen*, which is available as a symbol. Similarly, you can insert a *nonbreaking space* when you do not want words divided between lines. For example, a person's first name on one line followed by the last name on the next line is not a very attractive placement. Instead, make the space between the words a nonbreaking space by inserting the symbol, so the names are never divided. Select a nonbreaking hyphen, nonbreaking space, and other special characters when you click the Insert tab, Symbol, More Symbols, and Special Characters. Click a special character and click Insert to place it in a document.

STEP 5 A typical Microsoft Office installation includes a wide variety of fonts. To view and select a symbol, click the Insert tab and click Symbol. A gallery of frequently accessed symbols displays, from which you can choose. If the symbol you seek is not in the list, click More Symbols. Figure 1.26 shows the dialog box from which you can search for a symbol. Depending upon the font selected (normal text is shown in Figure 1.26), your symbol choices will vary. Fonts such as Wingdings, Webdings, and Symbol contain a wealth of special symbols, many of which are actually pictures.

Select a font

Option to enter a character code

FIGURE 1.26 Inserting a Symbol

Each symbol is assigned a character code. If you know the character code, you can type the code (refer to Figure 1.26) instead of searching for the symbol itself or using a keyboard shortcut.

Adjust Margins

A *margin* is the area of blank space that displays to the left, right, top, and bottom of a document, between the text and the edge of the page. Although a 1" margin all around the document is the normal setting, you can easily adjust one or more margins for a particular document. You might adjust margins for several reasons. You can change a document's appearance and readability, perhaps even causing it to fit attractively on one page, by adjusting margins. Also, a style manual, such as you might use in an English class, will require certain margins for the preparation of papers and publications.

You can change margins in a couple of ways:

STEP 2 »

- Click the PAGE LAYOUT tab and click Margins in the Page Setup group. Select from one of the predefined margin settings (see Figure 1.27) or click Custom Margins to adjust each margin (left, right, top, and bottom) individually.

- Click the FILE tab and click Print. Click Normal Margins (or the previous margin setting) to change one or more margins.

Click to create custom margins

Predefined margin settings

FIGURE 1.27 Adjusting Margins

Change Page Orientation

You will find that some documents are more attractive in either **_portrait_** or **_landscape orientation_**. A document displayed in portrait orientation is taller than it is wide, whereas a document shown in landscape is wider than it is tall. Most certificates are designed in landscape orientation; letters and memos are typically presented in portrait orientation. You can change page orientation in several ways:

STEP 3 >>

- Click Orientation on the PAGE LAYOUT tab to select either Portrait or Landscape.
- Click Margins on the PAGE LAYOUT tab and click Custom Margins to display the Page Setup dialog box (see Figure 1.28). From there, select either Portrait or Landscape.
- Click the FILE tab, click Print, and then click Portrait Orientation (or Landscape Orientation if the document is in landscape orientation). Select either Portrait Orientation or Landscape Orientation.

Select Portrait or Landscape Orientation

FIGURE 1.28 Selecting Page Orientation

Insert a Watermark

A watermark, which is text or graphics that displays behind text on a page, is often used to display a very light, washed-out logo for a company or to indicate the status of a document. For example, a watermark displaying *Draft* indicates that the document is not in final form. The document shown in Figure 1.29 contains a watermark. Watermarks do not display on a document that is saved as a Web page, nor will they display in Word's Web Layout view (discussed later in this chapter). To insert a watermark, click the Design tab and click Watermark. Select from predesigned styles, or click Custom Watermark to create your own. To remove a previously created watermark (for example, when a draft becomes final), click the Design tab, click Watermark, and then select Remove Watermark.

STEP 4 >>

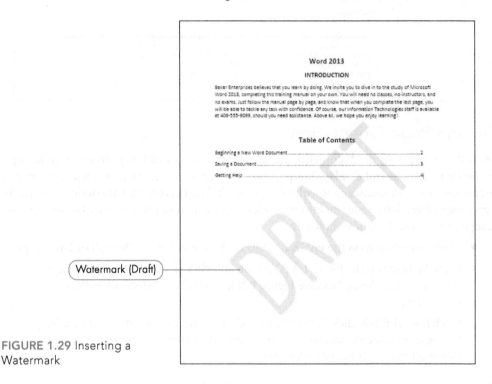

Watermark (Draft)

FIGURE 1.29 Inserting a Watermark

TIP | Formatting a Watermark

In selecting a custom watermark (click the Design tab, click Watermark, and then select Custom Watermark), you can select or change a watermark's color, size, font, and text. In addition, you can include a picture as a watermark.

Viewing a Document in Different Ways

Developing a document is a creative process. As you create, edit, or review a project, you will want to view the document in various ways. Word provides a view that enables you to see a document as it will print, as well as views that maximize typing space by removing page features. You might like to review a document in a magazine-type format for ease of reading, or perhaps a hierarchical view of headings and subheadings would help you better understand and proof the structure of a document. The ability to zoom in on text and objects can make a document easier to proofread, while viewing a document page by page helps you manage page flow—perhaps drawing attention to awkward page endings or beginnings. Taking advantage of the various views and view settings in Word, you will find it easy to create attractive, well-worded, and error-free documents.

Select a Document View

When you begin a new document, you will see the top, bottom, left, and right margins. The document view is called *Print Layout view*, and it is the default view. You can choose to view a document differently, which is something you might do if you are at a different step in its production. For example, as you type or edit a document, you might prefer *Draft view*, which provides the most typing space possible without regard to margins and special page features. Word's *Read Mode* facilitates proofreading and comprehension, whereas *Outline view* displays a document in hierarchical fashion, clearly delineating levels of heading detail. If a document is destined for the Web, you would want to view it in *Web Layout view*.

To change document view, click the View tab and select a view from the Views group (see Figure 1.30). Although slightly more limited in choice, the status bar also provides views to choose from (Read Mode, Print Layout, and Web Layout). Word views are summarized in Table 1.1.

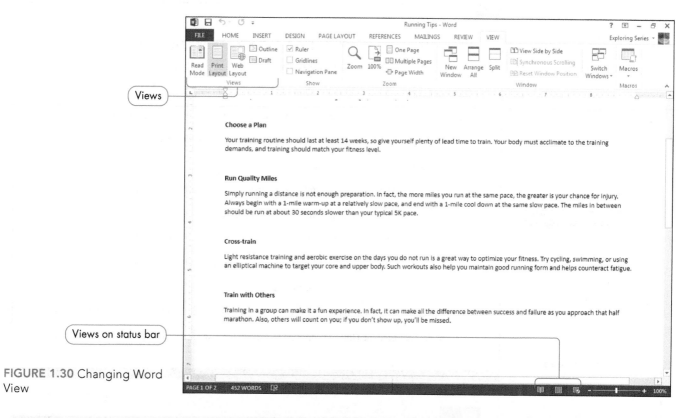

FIGURE 1.30 Changing Word View

TABLE 1.1 Word Views

View	Appearance
Read Mode	Primarily used for reading, with a document shown in pages, much like a magazine. The Ribbon is hidden, with only a limited number of menu selections shown.
Print Layout	Shows margins, headers, footers, graphics, and other page features—much like a document will look when printed.
Web Layout	Shows a document as it would appear on a Web page.
Outline	Shows level of organization and detail. You can collapse or expand detail to show only what is necessary. Often used as a springboard for a table of contents or a PowerPoint summary.
Draft	Provides the most space possible for typing. It does not show margins, headers, or other features, but it does include the Ribbon.

The Read Mode is new to Word 2013. Designed to make a document easy to read and to facilitate access across multiple devices, Read Mode presents a document in a left to right flow, automatically splitting text into columns, if necessary, for a magazine-like appearance. Text often displays in a two-page format. Text adjusts to fit any size screen, flowing easily from page to page with a simple flick of a finger (if using a tablet or touch-sensitive device) or click of the mouse. Users of touch-based devices can rotate the device between landscape and portrait modes, with the screen always divided into equally sized columns. When in Read Mode (see Figure 1.31), you will note that the Ribbon is removed from view. Instead, you have access to only three menu items: File, Tools, and View. One of the most exciting features of Read Mode is object zooming. Simply double-click an object, such as a table, chart, picture, or video, to zoom in. Press Esc to leave Read Mode. Although you can also leave Read Mode when you click the View tab and click Edit Document, doing so causes subsequently opened Word documents to automatically display in Read Mode when opened.

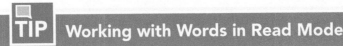

Read mode of document with object inserted

FIGURE 1.31 Using Read Mode

TIP   Working with Words in Read Mode

In Read Mode, right-click a word and choose Define from the shortcut menu for a quick definition and synonym. Select Translate, if the document is not in your native language.

Change the Zoom Setting

Regardless of the view selected, you can use Word's zoom feature to enlarge or reduce the view of text. Unlike zooming in on an object in Read Mode, the zoom feature available on the View tab enables you to enlarge text, not objects or videos. Enlarging text might make a document easier to read and proofread. However, changing the size of text onscreen does not actually change the font size of a document. Zooming in or out is simply a temporary change to the way a document appears onscreen. The View tab includes options that change the onscreen size of a document (see Figure 1.32). You can also enlarge or reduce the view of text by dragging the Zoom slider on the status bar. Click Zoom In and Zoom Out on the status bar to change the view incrementally by 10% for each click.

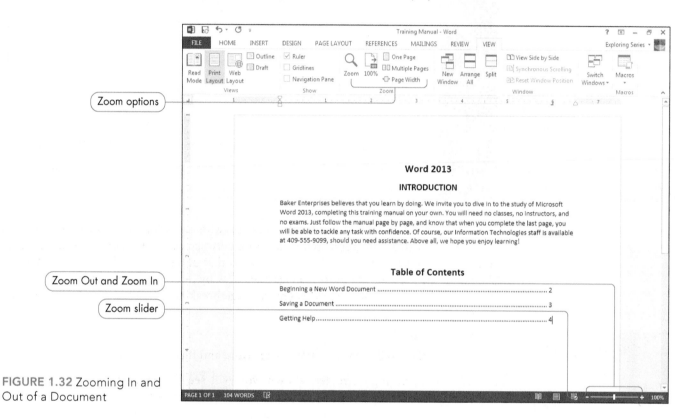

FIGURE 1.32 Zooming In and Out of a Document

Use the Zoom command on the View tab to select a percentage of zoom or to indicate a preset width (page width, text width, or whole page). Preset widths are also available as individual options in the Zoom group on the View tab (refer to Figure 1.32).

View a Document and Manage Page Flow

Document lengths can vary greatly. A research paper might span 20 pages, whereas a memo is seldom more than a few pages (most often, only one). Obviously, it is easier to view a memo onscreen than an entire research paper. Even so, Word enables you to get a good feel for the way a document will look when printed or distributed, regardless of document length.

STEP 6 >> Before printing, it is a good idea to view a document in its entirety. One way to do that is to click the File tab and click Print. A document is shown one page at a time in print preview (see Figure 1.33). Click the Next Page or Previous Page navigation arrow to proceed forward or backward in pages. You can also view a document by using options on the View tab (refer to Figure 1.32). Clicking One Page provides a snapshot of the current page, while Multiple Pages shows pages of a multiple-page document side by side (and on separate rows, in the case of more than two pages).

FIGURE 1.33 Previewing a Document

Occasionally, a page will end poorly—perhaps with a heading shown alone at the bottom of a page or with a paragraph split awkwardly between pages. Or perhaps it is necessary to begin a new page after a table of contents, so that other pages follow in the order they should. In those cases, you must manage page flow by forcing a page break where it would not normally occur. Simply click where the page break is to be placed and do one of the following:

- Press Ctrl+Enter.
- Click the PAGE LAYOUT tab, click Breaks, and then select Page.

With nonprinting characters shown, you will see the Page Break designation (see Figure 1.34). To remove the page break, click the Page Break indicator and press Delete.

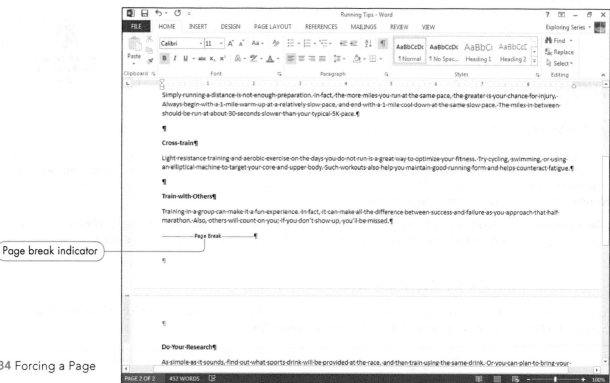

Page break indicator

FIGURE 1.34 Forcing a Page Break

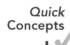

Quick
Concepts

1. Some header and footer items, such as author name and file name, serve to identify the document and its origin. Other header and footer fields portray data that changes. Provide at least two examples of fields that contain variable data. When would you want to exclude headers and footers from the first page of a document, and how would you do that? ***p. 103***

2. A watermark is often in the form of text, such as the word *Draft*, which indicates that a document is not in its final form. What other text and/or graphic watermarks might you include in a document? ***p. 108***

3. The status bar includes selections that change a document view. Compare and contrast the view selections on the status bar. ***p. 109***

4. You have just completed a multiple-page research paper, including a cover page. Before printing the paper, you will check it onscreen to determine how text flows from one page to the next, assuring attractive page endings (no heading shown alone at the end of a page, for example). Provide two ways to view the multiple-page document, so that at least one entire page is shown at a time. Also, assume that you find it necessary to break a page before a solo heading at the bottom of a page. How would you force a page break at that location? ***p. 111***

Hands-On Exercises

Watch the Video
for this Hands-
On Exercise!

MyITLab®
HOE2 Training

2 Document Organization

You are almost ready to submit a draft of the summer day camp article to your supervisor for approval. After inserting a footer to identify the document as originating with the U.S. Fish and Wildlife Service, you will adjust the margins and determine the best page orientation for the document. Next, you will insert a watermark to indicate it is a draft document. Finally, you will review the document for overall appearance and page flow.

Skills covered: Insert Headers and Footers • Adjust Margins • Change Page Orientation • Insert a Watermark • Insert a Symbol and Select a Document View • View a Document, Change the Zoom Setting, and Manage Page Flow

---

STEP 1 ≫ INSERT HEADERS AND FOOTERS

You will insert a footer to identify the article as a publication of the U.S. Fish and Wildlife Service. The footer will also include the file name. Refer to Figure 1.35 as you complete Step 1.

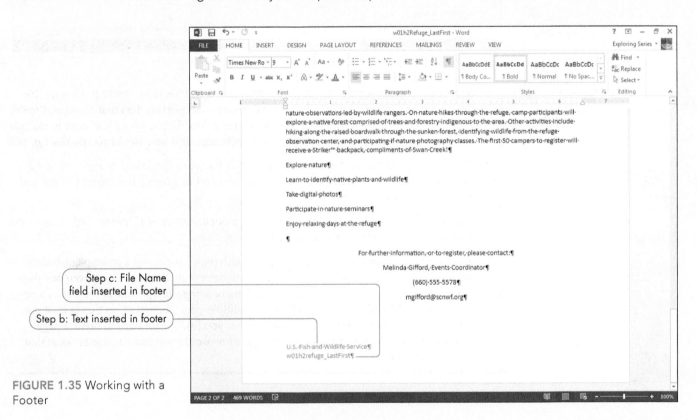

FIGURE 1.35 Working with a Footer

a. Open *w01h1Refuge_LastFirst* if you closed it at the end of Hands-On Exercise 1 and save it as **w01h2Refuge_LastFirst**, changing *h1* to *h2*.

> **TROUBLESHOOTING:** If you make any major mistakes in this exercise, you can close the file, open *w01h1Refuge_LastFirst* again, and then start this exercise over.

b. Click the **INSERT tab**, click **Footer** in the Header & Footer group, and then select **Edit Footer**. Type **U.S. Fish and Wildlife Service**. Press **Enter**.

> **TROUBLESHOOTING:** If you select a predefined footer instead of clicking *Edit Footer*, click **Undo** on the Quick Access Toolbar and repeat step b.

    c. Click **Document Info** in the Insert group and select **File Name**.

    d. Click **Close Header and Footer** in the Close group.

    e. Click after the first sentence of the second body paragraph, ending with *through eighth graders*. Be sure to click after the period ending the sentence. Press the **Spacebar** and type the following sentence: **The series of wildlife camps will begin on June 15, with the last camp ending on August 6.**

    f. Save the document.

STEP 2 ▶ ADJUST MARGINS

The article fits on one page, but you anticipate adding text. You suspect that with narrower margins, you might be able to add text while making sure the article requires only one page. You will experiment with a few margin settings. Refer to Figure 1.36 as you complete Step 2.

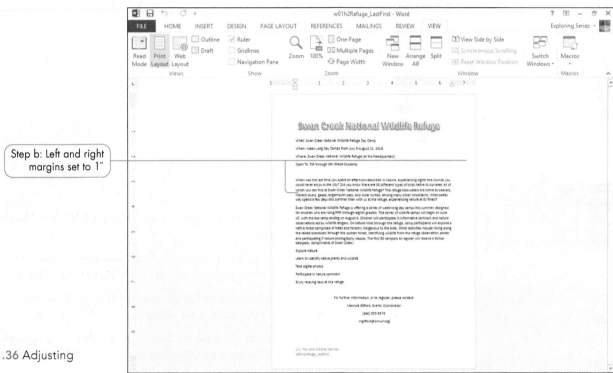

Step b: Left and right margins set to 1"

FIGURE 1.36 Adjusting Margins

    a. Click the **PAGE LAYOUT tab**, click **Margins** in the Page Setup group, and then select **Narrow**.

    At a glance, you determine the right and left margins are too narrow, so you will adjust them.

    b. Click **Margins** and select **Custom Margins**. Adjust the Left and Right margins to **1"** and click **OK**.

    c. Click the **VIEW tab** and click **One Page** in the Zoom group.

    The document appears to be well positioned on the page, with what appears to be room for a small amount of additional text, if necessary.

    d. Save the document.

STEP 3 >> CHANGE PAGE ORIENTATION

Ms. Traynom has asked that you prepare an abbreviated version of the article, retaining only the most pertinent information. You will prepare and save the shortened version, but you will also retain the lengthier version. The shortened article will provide a snapshot of the summer activity in an at-a-glance format. Refer to Figure 1.37 as you complete Step 3.

FIGURE 1.37 Viewing a Document

Step i: Save a file

Step h: Print Preview

a. Click **100%** in the Zoom group on the VIEW tab.

b. Make sure nonprinting characters display. If they do not, click **Show/Hide (¶)** in the Paragraph group on the Home tab.

c. Triple-click in the second body paragraph, beginning with *Swan Creek National Wildlife Refuge is offering*, to select the entire paragraph and press **Delete** to remove the paragraph.

d. Delete the single line paragraphs near the end of the document, beginning with *Explore nature* and ending with *Enjoy relaxing days at the refuge*.

e. Click the **FILE tab** and click **Save As**. Because the document is a shortened version of the original, you will save it with a different name. Save the file as **w01h2Flyer_LastFirst**.

Given the shortened nature of the document, you will see whether landscape orientation provides a more attractive view.

f. Click the **PAGE LAYOUT tab** and click **Orientation** in the Page Setup group. Click **Landscape**. Click the **VIEW tab,** and click **One Page**. The new orientation is not attractive, so click **Undo** on the Quick Access Toolbar.

The flyer is attractive, but you do not think it requires a footer. You will remove the footer.

g. Scroll down and double-click in the footer area. Select both footer lines and press **Delete** to remove the footer. Double-click in the document to close the footer.

h. Click the **FILE tab** and click **Print** to confirm the footer is removed.

i. Click **Save** in the left pane to save the document. Click the **FILE tab** and click **Close** to close the flyer without exiting Word.

STEP 4 ›› INSERT A WATERMARK

You will open the original article so that you can add the finishing touches, making sure to identify it as a draft and not the final copy. To do so, you will insert a DRAFT watermark, which can be removed after your supervisor has approved the document for distribution. Refer to Figure 1.38 as you complete Step 4.

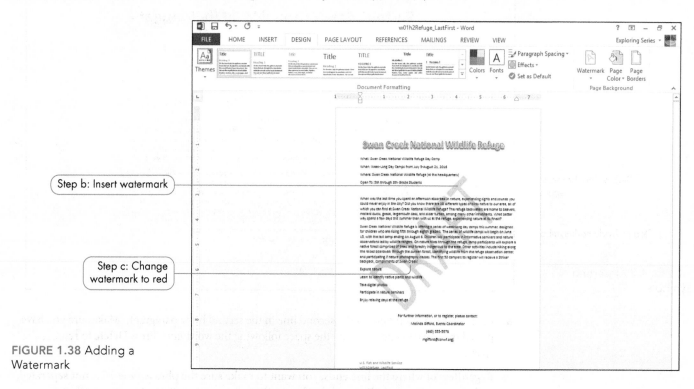

Step b: Insert watermark

Step c: Change watermark to red

FIGURE 1.38 Adding a Watermark

a. Click the **FILE tab** and click **w01h2Refuge_LastFirst** in the list of recent documents.

b. Click the **DESIGN tab** and click **Watermark** in the Page Background group. Scroll through the gallery of watermarks and click **DRAFT 1** (under *Disclaimers*).

The watermark is not as visible as you would like, so you will change the color.

c. Click **Watermark** again and select **Custom Watermark**. Click the **Color arrow** in the Printed Watermark dialog box and click **Red** (under *Standard Colors*). Click **OK**.

d. Save the document.

STEP 5 ›› INSERT A SYMBOL AND SELECT A DOCUMENT VIEW

The article you are preparing will be placed in numerous public venues, primarily schools. Given the widespread distribution of the document, you must consider any legality, such as appropriate recognition of name brands or proprietary mentions by inserting a trademark symbol. You will also ensure that words flow as they should, with no awkward or unintended breaks between words that should remain together. Refer to Figure 1.39 as you complete Step 5.

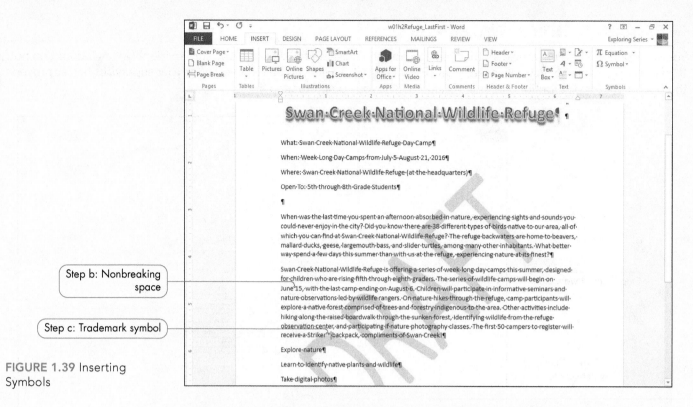

FIGURE 1.39 Inserting Symbols

Step b: Nonbreaking space

Step c: Trademark symbol

a. Click after the word *June* on the second line in the second body paragraph. Make sure you have placed the insertion point before the space following the word *June*. Press **Delete** to remove the space.

   Regardless of where the line ends, you want to make sure the phrase *June 15* is not separated, with the month on one line and the day on the following line. Therefore, you will insert a nonbreaking space.

b. Click the **INSERT tab** and click **Symbol** in the Symbols group. Click **More Symbols**. Click the **Special Characters tab**. Click **Nonbreaking Space**. Click **Insert** and click **Close**.

c. Click after the word *Striker* in the last sentence of the same paragraph. Click **Symbol** in the Symbols group and click **More Symbols**. Click **Special Characters**. Click **Trademark** to insert the Trademark symbol. Click **Insert** and click **Close**.

   You use the Trademark symbol to indicate that *Striker* is a brand name.

d. Click the **VIEW tab** and click **Draft** in the Views group. Click **Print Layout** in the Views group.

e. Save the document.

STEP 6 ⟩⟩ VIEW A DOCUMENT, CHANGE THE ZOOM SETTING, AND MANAGE PAGE FLOW

Ms. Traynom has provided you with a cover letter to include with the article. You will incorporate the letter text into the article as the first page, remove the footer from the first page, proofread the document, and ensure that both pages are attractively designed. Refer to Figure 1.40 as you complete Step 6.

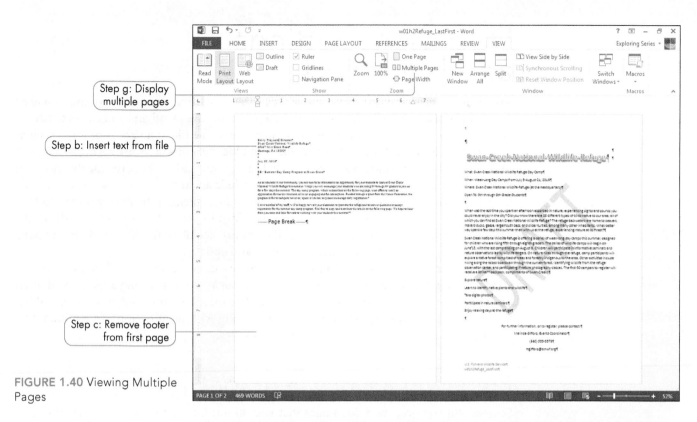

Step g: Display multiple pages

Step b: Insert text from file

Step c: Remove footer from first page

FIGURE 1.40 Viewing Multiple Pages

a. Press **Ctrl+Home** to position the insertion point at the top of the article. Press **Ctrl+Enter** to insert a blank page at the top. Press **Ctrl+Home** to move to the top of the new page.

Note that both the watermark and the footer display on the new page. That is because those features are designed to appear by default on all pages of a document.

b. Click the **INSERT tab**, if necessary, and click the **Object arrow** in the Text group. Click **Text from File**. Navigate to *w01h2Letter* in your student data files and double-click the file name.

c. Double-click in the footer area of the first page. Click **Different First Page** in the Options group of the HEADER & FOOTER TOOLS DESIGN tab.

You have indicated that the watermark and footer are not to appear on the first page, but will remain on all others.

d. Click **Close Header and Footer** in the Close group.

e. Press **Ctrl+Home**. Click the **VIEW tab** and click **Zoom** in the Zoom group. Click in the **Percent box** and change the Zoom to **125%**. Click **OK**.

f. Scroll through the document, proofreading for spelling and grammatical errors. Right-click any underlined error and either correct or ignore it. Manually correct any errors that Word has not flagged.

g. Click **Multiple Pages** in the Zoom group.

h. Click the **FILE tab** and click **Print**. Click **Next Page** (the arrow that follows *1 of 2* at the bottom of the screen) to view the article. Click **Previous Page** to return to the letter.

The letter appears to be too high on the page, so you will move the text down a bit.

i. Click **Back** (the arrow at the top left) to return to the document. Click **100%** in the Zoom group. Press **Ctrl+Home** to move to the top of the document. Press **Enter** three times to move the text down the page.

j. Click the **FILE tab** and click **Print**. The first page should be better situated on the page, with additional space at the top.

k. Save the document. Keep the document open if you plan to continue with the next Hands-On Exercise. If not, close the document and exit Word.

Document Settings and Properties

After you organize your document and make all the formatting changes you desire, you need to save the document in its final form and prepare it for use by others. You can take advantage of features in Word that enable you to manipulate the file in a variety of ways, such as identifying features that are not compatible with older versions of Word, saving in a format that is compatible with older versions, and including information about the file that does not display in the document. For example, you can include an author name, a subject, and even keywords—all information that does not display in the content of the document but further identifies the file, and can be used as a basis on which to search for or categorize the document later. Because you are well aware of the importance of saving files, and even making backup copies of those files, you will explore backup options.

In this section, you will explore ways to prepare a document for distribution, including saving in a format compatible with earlier versions of Word, converting a file created in an earlier version to Office 2013, checking for sensitive information included in a file, making backup copies of important documents, and working with print options. In addition, you will learn to customize and print document properties.

Preparing a Document for Distribution

Seldom will you prepare a document that you do not intend to distribute. Whether it is a report to submit to your instructor or a memo on which you collaborated, most likely the document is something that will be shared with others. Regardless of how you plan to develop, save, and distribute a document, you will not want to chance losing your work because you did not save it properly or failed to make a backup copy. Inevitably, files are lost, systems crash, and viruses infect a system. That said, the importance of saving work frequently and ensuring that backup copies exist cannot be overemphasized.

With the frequency of new Word versions, there is always a chance that someone who needs to read your document is working with a version that is not compatible with yours, or perhaps the person is not working with Word at all. You can eliminate that source of frustration by saving a document in a compatible format before distributing it. Another source of concern when distributing a document is the hidden or personal data that might be stored in document properties, such as the author's or organization's name. Backing up documents, ensuring their compatibility with other software versions, and removing document information that is either unnecessary or has the potential for too much disclosure should definitely be considered before finalizing a project or allowing others to see it.

Ensure Document Compatibility

Earlier in this chapter, in the section on saving files, you learned how to save a document in an earlier Word version so that someone without access to Word 2013 might still open the file. You might also consider saving a file in Rich Text Format, which adds even more flexibility, as such a file can be opened by other word processing software in addition to Word. Be aware, however, that doing so might compromise the document somewhat because Rich Text Format, and even earlier Word versions, cannot accommodate all of the current Word version's special features. (See the section in this chapter on saving a file for information on how to change the file type.)

When you open a file created in an earlier Word version, the words *Compatibility Mode* are included in the title bar, advising you that some of Word 2013's features will not be available or viewable in the document. While in Compatibility Mode, you might not be able to use new and enhanced features of the most current Word version; by keeping the file in Compatibility Mode, you ensure that people with earlier Word versions will still have full editing capability when they receive the document. However, if you want to convert the file to Office 2013, complete the following steps:

1. Click the FILE tab. Info should be selected; if not, click to select it.
2. Click Convert (beside Compatibility Mode). The Convert option will not be displayed if the file is currently in Office 2013 format.
3. Click OK.

When you convert a file, you change the original file to a newer version of Word. When you subsequently save the file, it is saved in the newest Word version.

Documents saved in Word 2013 can be opened by users of Word 2010 and Word 2007. Even so, documents developed in Word 2013 might contain features that are not recognizable by those or earlier versions. In some cases, it might be necessary for a user of Word 2007 or Word 2010 to install a service pack or otherwise download a software solution in order to view a Word 2013 file in its entirety.

Before distributing a document, you can check it for compatibility, ensuring that it can be read in its entirety by users of earlier Word versions. To check a document for compatibility, do the following:

STEP 1 »

1. Click the FILE tab.
2. Click Check for Issues (beside Inspect Document).
3. Click Check Compatibility.
4. Click *Select versions to show* and then select one or more versions of Word to check (or simply leave them all selected).
5. After reading a summary of any features that are incompatible, click OK.

Understand Backup Options

Word enables you to back up files in different ways. One option is to use a feature called **AutoRecover**. If Word crashes when AutoRecover is enabled, the program will be able to recover a previous version of your document when you restart the program. The only work you will lose is anything you did between the time of the last AutoRecover operation and the time of the crash, unless you happen to save the document in the meantime. By default, file information is saved every 10 minutes (see Figure 1.41), but you can adjust the setting so that the AutoRecover process occurs more or less frequently.

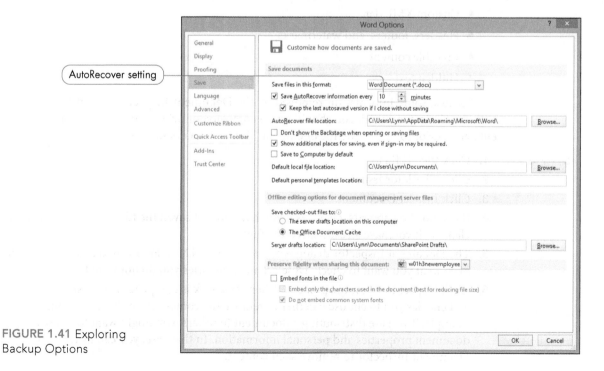

FIGURE 1.41 Exploring Backup Options

You can also configure Word to create a backup copy each time a document is saved. Although the setting to always create a backup copy is not enabled by default, you can enable it from Word Options in the Advanced category. Scroll through categories under Advanced options to locate the Save group, in which you can choose to always create a backup copy. Word will create a backup copy in this way. Assume that you have created the simple document with the phrase *The fox jumped over the fence*, and have saved it under the name *Fox*. Assume further that you edit the document to read *The quick brown fox jumped over the fence*, and that you save it a second time. The second Save command changes the name of the original document (containing the text *The fox jumped over the fence*) from *Fox* to *Backup of Fox*, then saves the current contents (*The quick brown fox jumped over the fence*) as *Fox*. In other words, the disk now contains two instances of the document: the current *Fox* document and the document containing the original text—*Backup of Fox*.

The cycle goes on indefinitely, with *Fox* always containing the current document and *Backup of Fox* the most recent instance. So, if you revise and save the document a third time, the original wording of the document is no longer available, because only two instances of the document are kept. The contents of *Fox* and *Backup of Fox* are different, but the existence of the latter enables you to retrieve the previous iteration if you inadvertently edit beyond repair or accidentally erase the current *Fox* document. To enable an automatic backup:

STEP 2 ▶
1. Click the FILE tab.
2. Click Options.
3. Click Advanced.
4. Scroll to the Save group and click *Always create backup copy*. Click OK.

Run the Document Inspector

Before you send or give a document to another person, you should run the **Document Inspector** to reveal any hidden or personal data in the file. For privacy or security reasons, you might want to remove certain items contained in the document such as author name, comments made by one or more persons who have access to the document, or document server locations. Word's Document Inspector will check for and enable you to remove various types of identifying information, including:

- Comments, revisions, versions, and annotations
- Document properties and personal information
- Custom XML data
- Headers, footers, and watermarks
- Invisible content
- Hidden text

Because some information removed by the Document Inspector cannot be recovered with the Undo command, you should save a copy of your original document, using a different name, prior to inspecting the document. To inspect a document:

STEP 3 ▶
1. Click the FILE tab.
2. Click Check for Issues.
3. Click Inspect Document.
4. If a dialog box appears, click Yes if you have not yet saved the file and want to do so (or click No if you have already saved the file).
5. The Document Inspector dialog box (see Figure 1.42) enables you to confirm the types of content you want to check. Deselect any categories you do not want to check.
6. Click Inspect to begin the process. When the check is complete, Word lists the results and enables you to choose whether to remove the content from the document. For example, if you are distributing a document to others, you might want to remove all document properties and personal information. In that case, you can instruct the Document Inspector to remove such content.

FIGURE 1.42 Document Inspector

Select Print Options

It is far too easy to print an entire document when you intend to print only a few pages. That is because you might not pay enough attention to print options, one of which enables you to print the entire document unless you specify otherwise. You will find that print setting, and others, when you click the File tab and click Print. The current printer is shown, although you can change to another installed printer, if you like (see Figure 1.43). The Print settings shown in Figure 1.43 enable you to select the number of copies, the pages or range of pages to print, the printer to use, whether to collate pages, whether to print on only one side of the paper, and how many pages to print per sheet. In addition, you can adjust page orientation, paper size, and even customize a document's margins—all by paying attention to print options. Please note that the wording of some Print options will vary, depending on whether you have previously selected the option and indicated a custom setting. For example, if you recently selected Print All Pages and indicated a specific range to print, then the Print All Pages option will display the most recent range of pages printed or selected.

FIGURE 1.43 Exploring Print Settings

Print options display to the left of the document preview (refer to Figure 1.43). You can click the Next Page or Previous Page navigation arrow to move among pages in the document preview. You can also drag the Zoom slider to enlarge or reduce the size of the document preview.

Modifying Document Properties

Occasionally, you might want to include information to identify a document, such as author, document purpose, intended audience, or general comments. Those data elements, or *metadata*, are saved with the document, but do not appear in the document as it displays onscreen or is printed. Instead, you can use the *Document Panel* to display descriptive information. You can even search for a file based on identifying information you assign a document. For example, suppose you apply a keyword of *CIS 225* to all documents you create that are associated with that particular college class. Later, you can use that keyword as a search term, locating all associated documents.

For statistical information related to the current document, click the File tab and make sure that Info is selected. Data such as file size, number of pages, and total words are presented (see Figure 1.44). You can modify some document information in this view, such as adding a title or comments, but for more possibilities, display the full Document Panel (see Figure 1.45). To display the Document Panel:

1. Click the FILE tab.
2. Click the Properties arrow.
3. Click Show Document Panel.

FIGURE 1.44 Opening the Document Panel

FIGURE 1.45 Viewing the Document Panel

When you save the document, Word saves this information with the document. You can update the descriptive information at any time by opening the Document Panel for the respective document.

Customize Document Properties

In addition to creating, modifying, and viewing a document summary, you may want to customize document properties in the Document Panel. For example, you might want to add a *Date completed* property and specify an exact date for reference. This date would reflect the completion date, not the date the file was last saved. You also might create a field to track company information such as warehouse location or product numbers.

To customize document properties:

1. Click the FILE tab and click Info, if necessary. Click Properties and click Advanced Properties. The Properties dialog box displays, showing commonly used properties on the General tab.
2. Click the Custom tab of the Properties dialog box to add custom property categories and assign values to them.
3. Click Add, after assigning a value to a custom category, and click OK.

> **TIP** | **Checking Statistics**
>
> When working with Advanced Properties, you might want to check document statistics, such as the date the document was created, the total editing time, or the word count. Click the File tab, select Info, and then click Properties. Click Advanced Properties and click the Statistics tab to view statistics related to the current document.

Print Document Properties

You can print document properties to store hard copies for easy reference. To do this:

1. Click the FILE tab.
2. Click Print.
3. Click Print All Pages.
4. Click Document Info.
5. Click Print.

Quick
Concepts

1. A coworker who uses Office 2007 has sent you a document for review. When you open the document, the words *[Compatibility Mode]* display in the title bar after the file name. Is there any reason you might want to remove the document from Compatibility Mode? And if so, how would you convert the document to Word 2013 format? **p. 120**

2. You are aware that it is very important to create backup copies of important documents. Describe the process of using Word 2013 options to ensure that backup copies are automatically created. **p. 121**

3. Before distributing a document, you want to make sure any personally identifying information, such as author and comments, are removed. How would you accomplish that? **p. 122**

4. Before printing pages 3 through 5 of the current document, you want to preview the document and then print only those pages. In a separate print procedure, you also want to print document properties that are associated with the current document. What steps would you follow to preview and print those pages? **p. 123**

Watch the Video
for this Hands-
On Exercise!

MyITLab®
HOE3 Training

3 Document Settings and Properties

As the office assistant for Swan Creek National Wildlife Refuge, you are responsible for the security, management, and backup of the organization's documents. The article promoting the summer day camps is ready for final approval. Before that happens, however, you want to check it one last time yourself, making sure it is saved in a format that others can read and that you have sufficient backup copies. You will also include appropriate document properties for additional identification, and you will consider print options. Privacy and security are to be considered as well, so you will check for identifiers that should be removed before distributing the document.

Skills covered: Ensure Document Compatibility • Understand Backup Options • Run the Document Inspector and Select Print Options • Customize and Print Document Properties

STEP 1 ➤➤ ENSURE DOCUMENT COMPATIBILITY

You know Ms. Traynom is anxious to review a copy of this document; however, she has not yet upgraded to Office 2013. Instead, her office computer has Office 2007 installed. To make sure she can open and read the document, you will check the document for compatibility with earlier Word versions. Refer to Figure 1.46 as you complete Step 1.

Memo

To: Swan Creek Staff

From: Joseph Blackstone, Personnel Director

Date: July 28, 2016

Re: Adrian Sammons (new employee)

Please give a warm welcome to our newest employee, Adrian Sammons, who will be leading our Nature Conservancy office. Adrian comes to us with a wealth of experience in managing wildlife programs. His most recent assignment was with the South Florida Sea Lab, where he directed several successful grant programs and helped develop the first student-led symposium in Florida. Until his new office is renovated, Adrian will share quarters with Ms. Emily Traynom. Please join me in welcoming Adrian to Swan Creek!

FIGURE 1.46 Converted Document

a. Open *w01h2Refuge_LastFirst* if you closed it at the end of Hands-On Exercise 2 and save it as **w01h3Refuge_LastFirst**, changing *h2* to *h3*.

b. Click the **FILE tab**, make sure that *Info* is selected, and then click **Check for Issues** (beside *Inspect Document*).

c. Click **Check Compatibility**. Click **Select versions to show** and deselect **Word 97-2003** to make sure only *Word 2007* and *Word 2010* are selected.

   Note that some formatting features are not supported and will not be available in the version you are preparing for Ms. Traynom.

d. Click **OK**. Save the document.

   Because the compatibility issues are few and are restricted to what appear to be minor text effects, you feel confident that Ms. Traynom will be able to open the document in Word 2007. You will also provide her with a printed copy, just in case.

e. Click the **FILE tab** and close the document.

   The personnel director has prepared a draft of a memo introducing a new employee. He has asked that you proof the document and prepare it for printing. However, he created and saved the memo using Word 2007. You will open the file and convert it to Word 2013 format.

f. Open *w01h3NewEmployee* from your data files.

   The title bar displays *[Compatibility Mode]* following the file name *w01h3NewEmployee*, indicating that it is not a file saved with Word 2013.

g. Click the **FILE tab** and click **Convert** (beside *Compatibility Mode*). A message box displays explaining the consequences of upgrading the document. Click **OK**.

   The Compatibility Mode designation is removed from the title bar.

h. Save the document as **w01h3NewEmployee_LastFirst**.

STEP 2 » UNDERSTAND BACKUP OPTIONS

The timeline for preparing for the summer day camps is short. Given the time spent in developing the article, you know that if it were lost, recreating it in a timely fashion would be difficult. In fact, it is critical to ensure appropriate backups for *all* files for which you are responsible at Swan Creek. You will explore backup options on your computer to verify that files are saved periodically and that backups are automatically created. Refer to Figure 1.47 as you complete Step 2.

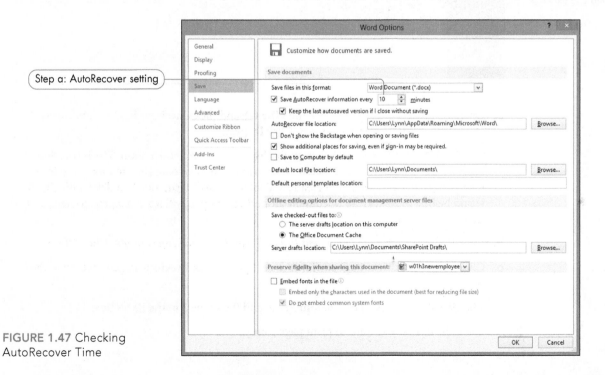

FIGURE 1.47 Checking AutoRecover Time

a. Click the **FILE tab** and click **Options**. Click **Save** in the left pane of the Word Options dialog box. If *Save AutoRecover information every* is checked, note the number of minutes between saves.

b. Click **Advanced**. Scroll to the Save area and note whether *Always create backup copy* is selected.

You will not select the setting at this time, although you should consider doing so on your own computer or a computer at a workplace.

c. Click **Cancel**. Close the document.

STEP 3 ≫ RUN THE DOCUMENT INSPECTOR AND SELECT PRINT OPTIONS

Before distributing the article, you will run the Document Inspector to identify any information that should first be removed. You will also prepare to print the document. Refer to Figure 1.48 as you complete Step 3.

Step e: Indicate number of copies

Step d: Select pages to print

Step c: Next Page

Step c: Previous Page

FIGURE 1.48 Selecting Print Settings

a. Open *w01h3Refuge_LastFirst*. Click the **FILE tab** and click **Check for Issues** (beside *Inspect Document*). Click **Inspect Document**. Click **Inspect**.

You check for document areas that might display sensitive information. The inspection suggests that the category of Document Properties and Personal Information contains identifying data, as does that of Headers, Footers, and Watermarks. You determine that it would be best to remove all document properties, but you will leave headers, footers, and watermarks.

b. Click **Remove All** beside *Document Properties and Personal Information*. Click **Close**.

c. Click **Print**. Click **Next Page** to view the next page. Click **Previous Page** to return to the first page.

d. Click **Print All Pages**, click **Custom Print**, and then type **2** in the Pages box.

You indicate that you want to print page 2 only.

e. Click the **Copies up arrow** repeatedly to print five copies.

You have indicated that you want to print five copies of page 2.

f. Press **Esc** to return to the document without printing.

STEP 4 ≫ CUSTOMIZE AND PRINT DOCUMENT PROPERTIES

You will assign document properties to the document to identify its author and purpose. You will also create an additional property to record a project identifier. Finally, you will prepare to print document properties. Refer to Figure 1.49 as you complete Step 4.

FIGURE 1.49 Advanced Document Properties

a. Save the document as **w01h4Refuge_LastFirst**, changing *h3* to *h4*. Click the **FILE tab**, click **Properties** in the right pane, and then click **Show Document Panel**.

The Document Panel displays above your document.

b. Ensure that the Author box contains your name. Type your name, if necessary. Click one time in the **Comments box** and type **Summer Camp Information**.

c. Click the **Document Properties arrow** in the top-left of the Document Properties panel and click **Advanced Properties** to display the w01h4Refuge_LastFirst Properties dialog box.

d. Create a custom property by completing the following steps:

- Click the **Custom tab** and select **Project** in the **Name list**.
- Type **School Information** in the **Value box**, as shown in Figure 1.56, and click **Add**.
- Click **OK** to close the dialog box.

You want to catalog the documents you create for Swan Creek National Wildlife Refuge, and one way to do that is to assign a project scope using the custom properties that are stored with each document. Because you set up a custom field in the Document Properties, you can later perform searches and find all documents in that Project category.

e. Click **Close the Document Information Panel** in the top-right corner of Document Properties. Save the document.

f. Click the **FILE tab**, click **Print**, click **Custom Print**, and then click **Document Info**. If your computer is in communication with, or connected to, a printer, click **Print**. Otherwise, continue to step g.

g. Save and close *w01h4Refuge_LastFirst*, and submit based on your instructor's directions.

Chapter Objectives Review

After reading this chapter, you have accomplished the following objectives:

1. **Begin and edit a document.**
   - Use a template: Predesigned documents save time by providing a starting point.
   - Create a document: Create a blank document by clicking *Blank document* when Word opens.
   - Save a document: Saving a document makes it possible to access it later for editing, sharing, or printing.
   - Open a document: Open a saved document by selecting the document from the Recent Documents List or browsing for other documents.
   - Move around a document and edit a document: Use scroll bars or keyboard shortcuts to move around in a document.
   - Review Word usage in a document: Use the Review tab to make sure all documents are free of typographical and grammatical errors.

2. **Customize Word.**
   - Explore Word options: Word options are global settings you can select, such as whether to check spelling automatically, or where to save a file by default.
   - Customize the Ribbon: Customize the Ribbon, using Word Options, to add, remove, or rename Ribbon tabs.
   - Customize the Quick Access Toolbar: The Quick Access Toolbar contains a few commands by default, but you can add more when you click *Customize the Quick Access Toolbar* and select from a menu.

3. **Use features that improve readability.**
   - Insert headers and footers: Headers and footers provide information, such as page number and organization name, in the top and bottom margins of a document.
   - Insert a symbol: A symbol is typically a character or graphic that is not found on the keyboard, such as ©.
   - Adjust margins: You can change margins, selecting predefined settings or creating your own.
   - Change page orientation: Select Landscape (located on the Page Layout tab) to show a document that is wider than it is tall, or Portrait to show a document taller than it is wide.

   - Insert a watermark: A watermark is text or a graphic that displays behind text to identify such items as a document's purpose, owner, or status.

4. **View a document in different ways.**
   - Select a document view: A view is the way a document displays onscreen; available Word views include Print Layout, Read Mode, Outline, Web Layout, and Draft.
   - Change the zoom setting: By changing the zoom setting (available on the View tab as well as the status bar), you can enlarge or reduce text size onscreen.
   - View a document and manage page flow: Forcing a page break is useful to divide document sections (for example, to separate a cover page from other report pages), or to better manage page flow so that pages do not end awkwardly.

5. **Prepare a document for distribution.**
   - Ensure document compatibility: Using Word 2013, you can convert documents to the most recent version and you can also ensure a document's compatibility with earlier versions.
   - Understand backup options: Backup options include AutoRecover and the ability to always create a backup copy of a saved document.
   - Run the Document Inspector: Word's Document Inspector reveals any hidden or personal data in a file and enables you to remove sensitive information.
   - Select print options: Using Word's print options (available when you click the File tab and click Print), you can specify the pages to print, the number of copies, and various other print selections.

6. **Modify document properties.**
   - Customize document properties: Document properties are items you can add to a document to further describe it, such as author, keywords, and comments.
   - Print document properties: For documentation purposes, you might want to print Document Properties.

Key Terms Matching

Match the key terms with their definitions. Write the key term letter by the appropriate numbered definition.

a. AutoRecover
b. Document Inspector
c. Document Panel
d. Draft view
e. Header and Footer
f. Insertion point
g. Landscape orientation
h. Microsoft Word
i. Outline view
j. Portrait orientation

k. Print Layout view
l. Quick Access Toolbar
m. Read Mode
n. Ribbon
o. Symbol
p. Template
q. Watermark
r. Word processing software
s. Word wrap

1. _____ The long bar of tabs, groups, and commands located just beneath the Title bar. **p. 86**

2. _____ Text or graphic that displays behind text. **p. 103**

3. _____ A structural view of a document or presentation that can be collapsed or expanded as necessary. **p. 109**

4. _____ Area that provides one-click access to commonly used commands. **p. 95**

5. _____ Document that is displayed taller than it is wide. **p. 107**

6. _____ The feature that automatically moves words to the next line if they do not fit on the current line. **p. 88**

7. _____ Enables Word to recover a previous version of a document. **p. 121**

8. _____ A computer application, such as Microsoft Word, used primarily with text to create, edit, and format documents. **p. 84**

9. _____ View in which text reflows to screen-sized pages to make it easier to read. **p. 109**

10. _____ Word processing application included in the Microsoft Office software suite. **p. 84**

11. _____ A predesigned document that may include format and wording that can be modified. **p. 87**

12. _____ Document that is displayed wider than it is tall. **p. 107**

13. _____ View that closely resembles the way a document will look when printed. **p. 109**

14. _____ A character or graphic not normally included on a keyboard. **p. 105**

15. _____ Checks for and removes certain hidden and personal information from a document. **p. 122**

16. _____ Information that displays at the top or bottom of each document page. **p. 103**

17. _____ View that shows a great deal of document space, but no margins, headers, footers, or other special features. **p. 109**

18. _____ Blinking bar that indicates where text that you next type will appear. **p. 91**

19. _____ Provides descriptive information about a document, such as a title, subject, author, keywords, and comments. **p. 124**

Multiple Choice

1. The view that presents a document in screen-sized pages with two shown at a time, for ease of comprehension and sharing, is the:

   (a) Read Mode.
   (b) Print Layout view.
   (c) Draft view.
   (d) Full Screen Mode.

2. One reason to display nonprinting characters is to:

   (a) Simplify the process of converting a document to an earlier Word version.
   (b) Enable spell checking on the document.
   (c) Enable document properties to be added to a document.
   (d) Assist with troubleshooting a document and modifying its appearance.

3. You are the only person in your office to upgrade to Word 2013. Before you share documents with coworkers, you should do which of the following?

   (a) Print out a backup copy.
   (b) Run the Compatibility Checker.
   (c) Burn all documents to CD.
   (d) Have no concerns that coworkers can open your documents.

4. Word 2013 encourages saving files so they can be accessed from multiple devices. One way that is accomplished is by:

   (a) Creating an automatic backup copy of every file, regardless of where it is saved.
   (b) Saving to your OneDrive account.
   (c) Shortening the AutoRecover interval so save operations occur more frequently and in various locations.
   (d) Saving all files to flash storage by default, so files can then be transferred to other devices.

5. Which of the following is detected by the contextual spelling check feature?

   (a) Incorrectly divided words that flow from one line to the next
   (b) Use of the word *their* when you should use *there*
   (c) Irregular capitalization
   (d) Improper use of commas

6. Suppose you are preparing a report that requires a cover page followed by text on the next page. To keep the cover page on its own page, you would position the insertion point at the end of the cover page and do which of the following?

   (a) Press Enter.
   (b) Click the PAGE LAYOUT tab, click Breaks, and then select Line Numbers.

   (c) Press Ctrl+Enter.
   (d) Press Ctrl+Page Down.

7. You need to prepare a resume to assist in your job search but are challenged with the design of the document. You have a classic case of writer's block! Word provides assistance in the form of a predesigned document called a:

   (a) Template.
   (b) Pattern.
   (c) Document Inspector.
   (d) Shell.

8. You have just opened a document provided by a coworker, and the title bar includes not only the file name but also the words *Compatibility Mode*. What does that mean?

   (a) The file was created in an earlier version of Word but saved as a Word 2013 file.
   (b) The file was created using another operating system, but opened under a version of Windows.
   (c) Word 2013 has placed the document in read-only mode, which means you will not be able to edit it.
   (d) The file was created in an earlier version of Word and might not be able to accommodate newer Word 2013 features unless you convert it.

9. To identify a document as a draft, and not in final form, which of the following could you add to the document?

   (a) Symbol
   (b) Watermark
   (c) Template
   (d) Document property

10. You plan to print only the current page of a Word document. Instead, the entire document prints. What should you have done to print only one page?

    (a) Click Print on the PRINT LAYOUT tab and click Current Page.
    (b) Click Print on the Quick Access Toolbar.
    (c) Click Print on the FILE tab and change the print setting to print only the current page.
    (d) Click Info on the FILE tab and change the print document property to only the current page.

1 | Interview Tips

You are a student assistant in your college's Career Placement Center (CPC). The CPC provides assistance with job searches, hosts job fairs on campus, collects student resumes for inclusion in departmental "resume yearbooks," and encourages many other forms of college-to-career activities. The newest project is the preparation of a guidebook for students who are nearing graduation or are otherwise seeking a career track. You are charged with the task of modifying a description of interview skills that was actually included in an earlier guidebook. The only problem is that the document was saved in Word 2007 format, so you must make sure it is converted to the most current Word version before beginning to modify it (in case you want to include any special features of the newest version). This exercise follows the same set of skills as used in Hands-On Exercises 1–3 in the chapter. Refer to Figure 1.50 as you complete this exercise.

FIGURE 1.50 Modifying Interview Skills

a. Open the *w01p1Interview* document.

The words *[Compatibility Mode]* inform you the document was created in an earlier version of Word.

b. Click the **FILE tab**, and then click **Save As**. Save the document as **w01p1Interview_LastFirst**. Click **Save**. You will be presented with a dialog box letting you know the document will be upgraded to the newest file format. Click **OK**.

c. Press **Ctrl+Home** to make sure the insertion point is at the beginning of the document and check the document for errors:

- Click the **REVIEW tab** and click **Spelling & Grammar** in the Proofing group. The university's name is Montclare, so it is not misspelled. Click **Ignore All**.
- Correct any other identified errors, if they are actually incorrect.
- Read over the document again, checking for errors the spell check might have missed.

d. Double-click to select the word *ongoing* in the paragraph that begins with *We know you are serious* and click **Define** in the Proofing group to get a definition. If a definition does not display, you might not have a dictionary app installed. Follow the prompts to install a dictionary. Close the Define pane on the right. Click **Thesaurus** in the Proofing group to get an alternative word for *ongoing*. Locate the word *current* in the Thesaurus pane, click its arrow, and then click **Insert**. Close the Thesaurus pane.

e. Make the following edits in the document:

- Remove the words *if possible* (including the following comma and space) from the paragraph following the *Do your homework* heading by selecting the text and pressing **Delete**.
- Begin the same sentence with the capitalized word *Visit*.
- Rearrange the words *first practicing* in the *Practice* paragraph, so they read **practicing first**.

f. Select the hyphen between the words *midriff* and *showing* in the *Dress for success* paragraph. Click the **INSERT tab** and click **Symbol** in the Symbols group. Click **More Symbols**. Click the **Special Characters tab**. Click **Nonbreaking Hyphen**. Click **Insert** and click **Close**. You have made sure the words will not be divided between lines. Select the double "hyphen" between the words *confident* and *which* in the *Practice* paragraph. Following the same steps, insert an em dash. Close the Symbols dialog box.

g. Click the **DESIGN tab** and click **Watermark** in the Page Background group. Scroll through the watermarks and click **Draft 2**. Click **Watermark**, click **Custom Watermark**, and then deselect **Semitransparent**. Click **Color**, select **Red, Accent 2**, and then click **OK**. You have inserted a watermark that indicates the document is not yet final.

h. Set up a footer:

- Click the **INSERT tab** and click **Footer** in the Header & Footer group.
- Click **Edit Footer**. Type **Career Placement Center** and press Enter.
- Click **Document Info** on the Header & Footer Tools Design tab and select **File Name**.
- Click **Close Header and Footer** (or double-click in the body of the document).

i. Because the document will be bound in a notebook, you will make the left margin larger:

- Click the **PAGE LAYOUT tab** and click **Margins** in the Page Setup Group.
- Click **Custom Margins**.
- Change the left margin to **2"** and click **OK**.
- Click the **VIEW tab** and click **Multiple Pages** in the Zoom group to see how the text is lining up on the pages.

j. Because the *Practice* paragraph is split between two pages, you will insert a page break before the paragraph heading:

- Click before the *Practice* heading. If nonprinting characters are not displayed, click the **HOME tab** and click **Show/Hide (¶)**.
- Press **Ctrl+Enter** to insert a page break.

k. Press **Ctrl+Home**. Click the **VIEW tab** and click **Read Mode** in the Views group. Click the arrow on the right to move from one page to the next. Press **Esc** to return to the previous document view.

l. Save the document. Before distributing the document, you will check it for sensitive information:

- Click the **FILE tab** and click **Check for Issues**.
- Click **Inspect Document** and click **Inspect**.
- Click **Remove All** beside *Document Properties and Personal Information*. Click **Close**.

m. Finally, you will check the document for compatibility with earlier Word versions:

- Click **Check for Issues** and click **Check Compatibility**.
- Click **Select versions to show** and make sure that all earlier Word versions are selected. Click **Select versions to show again** to close the list. One compatibility issue is found.
- Click **OK**.

n. Click **Save** on the Quick Access Toolbar to save the document. It is saved as a Word 2013 file. One of your coworkers is still using Word 2003, so you will also save the document in that format:

- Click the **FILE tab** and click **Save As**.

- Click the location where you save your files in the Recent Folders list (or click **Computer** and navigate to the location).
- Click the **Save as type box** and click **Word 97-2003 Document**. Click **Continue**.
- Click **Save**. Although the file name remains the same, you have actually saved two files in this step. One is named *w01p1Interview_LastFirst.docx* (the Word 2013 version), and the other is called *w01p1Interview_LastFirst.doc* (the Word 97-2003 version).

o. Close the file and submit based on your instructor's directions.

2 Aztec Computers

As the co-owner of Aztec Computers, you are frequently asked to provide information about computer viruses and backup procedures. You are quick to tell anyone who asks about data loss that it is not a question of if it will happen, but when—hard drives fail, removable disks are lost, and viruses may infect systems. You advise customers and friends alike that they can prepare for the inevitable by creating an adequate backup before the problem occurs. Because people appreciate a document to refer to about this information, you have started one that contains information that should be taken seriously. After a few finishing touches, you will feel comfortable about passing it out to people who have questions about this topic. This exercise follows the same set of skills as used in Hands-On Exercises 1–3 in the chapter. Refer to Figure 1.51 as you complete this exercise.

FIGURE 1.51 Multiple Pages View

a. Open *w01p2Virus* and save it as **w01p2Virus_LastFirst**.

b. Press **Ctrl+Enter** to insert a page break, creating a blank page at the beginning. Press **Ctrl+Home** to move the insertion point to the beginning of the first page.

c. You will insert a short paragraph prepared by your partner, promoting the company and encouraging the use of computer security tools. The paragraph will be shown on a page by itself, as a lead-in to the article. To insert the paragraph:

- Click the **INSERT tab** and click the **Object arrow** in the Text group.
- Click **Text from File**.
- Locate and click **w01p2Summary** and click **Insert**.

d. Press **Ctrl+Home**. You want to add a heading above the paragraph, so type **Aztec Computers**. Press **Enter**. Type **Your Total Computer Solution**. Press **Enter** twice.

e. Scroll to the bottom of the second page and click before the title *The Essence of Backup*. Click the **PAGE LAYOUT tab**, click **Breaks** in the Page Setup group, and then click **Page**. Click the **VIEW tab** and click **Multiple Pages** in the Zoom group. Scroll to view all pages. Click **100%** in the Zoom group.

f. You will add a footer to better identify the document:

- Click the **INSERT tab** and click **Footer** in the Header & Footer group.
- Click **Edit Footer**.
- Click **Page Number** in the Header & Footer group, point to **Current Position**, and then click **Plain Number**. You have created a page number footer.

g. Scroll to the top of the current page and click in the Header area. Type your first name and last name. Double-click in the document to close the header.

h. Click the **FILE tab** and click **Print**. Click **Previous Page** to view the previous page. Click **Back** (the arrow at the top left) to return to the document.

i. If nonprinting characters are not displayed, click the **HOME tab** and click **Show/Hide (¶)**. You will make edits to the text:

- The second to last sentence in the first body paragraph on page 2 should begin with the word *Unusual* instead of *Usual*. Make that change.
- Click before the paragraph mark after the word *worm* in the second body paragraph. Delete the paragraph mark so the two paragraphs become one.
- Locate the words *will it* in the last paragraph on the second page (in the sentence beginning with *If you are prone to think this way*). Reverse those words so the sentence reads *it will* instead of *will it*.

j. Press **Ctrl+Home**. Click the **REVIEW tab** and click **Spelling & Grammar** in the Proofing group. Correct any identified errors, if they are actual errors. The word *Trojan* should be capitalized and *backup* should be two words, in the context in which it is presented. Click **OK** when the spelling check is complete.

k. Press **Ctrl+Home**. Click the **VIEW tab** and click **Read Mode** in the Views group. Move to the second page and double-click the graphic. Click the arrow at the top-right corner of the graphic to enlarge it. Press **Esc**. Press **Esc** again to return to Print Layout view.

l. Click the **PAGE LAYOUT tab**, click **Margins** in the Page Setup group, and then select **Custom Margins**. Change the left and right margins to **0.75"**. Click **Landscape** and click **OK**. Because the document is adjusted to landscape orientation, the newly created left and right margins (0.75") are now considered the top and bottom margins.

m. Click the **FILE tab** and click **Print**. Click **Next Page** and/or **Previous Page** repeatedly to view all pages. You decide portrait orientation is a better choice for this document. Click **Landscape Orientation** and click **Portrait Orientation**.

n. Click **Info**, click **Properties**, and then click **Show Document Panel**. Click in the **Comments box** and type **General information for understanding computer viruses**. Click **Close the Document Information Panel** (on the top-right side of the Document Panel).

o. Save the document. Click the **FILE tab**, click **Check for Issues**, and then click **Check Compatibility**. There are no compatibility issues with earlier Word versions, so click **OK**.

p. Click the **FILE tab**, click **Check for Issues**, click **Inspect Document**, click **No**, and then click **Inspect**. Click **Close** after you review the results.

q. Click **Print**. Click **Print All Pages**, click **Custom Print**, and then type **2-3** to indicate that you want to print only the second and third pages. Because you are likely in a lab setting, you will not print the pages.

r. Press **Esc** twice to return to the document. Save and close the file, and submit based on your instructor's directions.

Mid-Level Exercises

1 Runners at Heart

CREATIVE CASE

A local cross-country team, Runners at Heart, is comprised of people who are recovering from a heart ailment or who support the cause of fitness for former heart patients. A half marathon is coming up in five months, and the Runners at Heart cross-country team wants to be prepared. A half marathon is a run/walk of 13 miles. You and others have researched tips on preparing for a half marathon. You have begun a document containing a few of those tips, and will collect ideas from other club members as well. You will finalize the tips document and make it available in plenty of time for the runners to prepare.

a. Open *w01m1Running* and save it as **w01m1Running_LastFirst**.

b. Move to the end of the document and press **Enter**. Insert the text from *w01m1Tips*, a list of running tips provided by another club member.

c. Make sure nonprinting characters display. View each page of the document and note that the first page ends awkwardly, with a single heading at the bottom. Insert a page break before the *Prepare mentally* heading.

d. The headings from the *w01m1Tips* file should be capitalized to be consistent with those you typed earlier. Make that correction. They should read: *Train with Others, Do Your Research, Rest, What to Wear,* and *Prepare Mentally*.

e. Insert a hard return before each heading except *Prepare Mentally* (beginning with *Choose a Plan* and ending with *What to Wear*) to increase the space between them. Make sure you are in Print Layout view. Because the page break is no longer necessary in its current position, click on the **Page Break line** and press **Delete**. Insert a hard return before the *Prepare Mentally* heading.

f. View the document and insert a page break, if necessary, wherever a heading stands alone.

g. Identify synonyms for the word *regimen* in the *Choose a Plan* section. Insert the word *routine*. Check for spelling and word usage errors, correcting any that are identified. The brand of clothing is correctly spelled *Dri-Fit*. Proofread the document carefully to identify any errors that Word might have missed.

h. Insert a page number footer as a **Plain Number** in the current position (on the left side of the footer). As a header, include the file name as a field.

i. Select the hyphen between the words *long* and *distance* in the paragraph following *Training Tips for a Half Marathon*. Insert a nonbreaking hyphen. Insert a trademark symbol immediately after the words *Nike Dri-Fit* in the *What to Wear* paragraph.

j. Add a custom watermark, with a text or graphic of your choice. The watermark should be clearly visible, and colored, if you like.

k. Change the page orientation to landscape. Preview the document to determine if the orientation is appropriate. Return to the document and delete the page break before the *Rest* heading. Remove one of the blank paragraphs before the *Rest* heading.

l. Save the document. Because one of your club members, who will contribute to the document later, uses Word 2003, save the document in that format, with the same file name. Click **Continue** if warned of unsupported features. Save it again as a Word 2013 file by changing the file type (during the save operation) to **Word Document**. Agree to replace the existing file and click **OK**. Click **OK** when advised that the file will be upgraded to the newest format.

m. Open the **Document Panel** and replace the current author with your first and last names. In the *Comments* section, type **Tips for a Half Marathon**. Close the Document Panel.

n. Preview the document and then remove the watermark. Print the document properties if approved by your instructor.

o. Save and close the file, and submit based on your instructor's directions.

2 Health Fair

You are a pediatric health assistant in a pediatrician's office. The local community college is hosting a health fair and has asked that your office staff a table promoting childhood vaccinations. Having worked in the office for several years, you are well aware of the benefits of immunization against a host of serious illnesses, so you are happy to help. You want to prepare a document summarizing in an at-a-glance fashion the advantages of immunization and the problems with avoiding it. However, because you are not a physician, you will depend on the doctor you work with to provide a bit of research and statistics that you will then compile into a more complete document for distribution.

a. Open *w01m2Vaccines* and save it as **w01m2Vaccines_LastFirst**.

b. Preview the document to get a feel for the text flow.

c. Check for spelling and word usage errors. Proofread the document to identify and correct errors that Word might have missed. (Hint: Most, but not all, vaccines have a low risk of side effects.)

d. Remove the words *as well* from the last sentence in the second body paragraph. The sentence should end with *child*, so you should also remove the comma and space before the words *as well*. Remove the word *actually* from the last sentence of the third body paragraph. In the same paragraph, click before the word *Vaccines* in the sentence beginning *Vaccines contain a weak form*. Insert a hard return.

e. Identify a synonym for the word *counteracted* in the third sentence of the third body paragraph. Replace the word with **thwarted**. Your document is limited to 500 words. Check the status bar for a word count (or click **Word Count** in the Proofing group) to see if you are above or below the limit.

f. Select the hyphen between the words *day* and *a* in the third body paragraph. Replace the selection with an **em dash symbol**.

DISCOVER

g. Select the word *Vaccines* anywhere in the document and use Word's Translate Language tool to identify the equivalent word in Spanish. You do not need to make the change in the document.

h. Change all margins to **0.75"**. Preview the document.

i. Include the file name in the footer area. On a separate line in the footer, type your first name and last name.

j. View each page of the document and make any adjustments necessary to ensure that only two pages are included, with the required vaccinations shown on the second page.

k. Add a watermark with the text **Health Fair** shown in red. The watermark should be horizontal. Save the document.

l. List yourself as the author in Document Properties. The subject is **Childhood Vaccinations**.

m. Run the Compatibility Checker to make sure the file is compatible with earlier Word versions.

n. Save and close the file, and submit based on your instructor's directions.

3 College Events

COLLABORATION CASE

FROM SCRATCH

You and a group of your fellow students are assigned the project of preparing a document describing several upcoming events at your college or university. Identify a few events to highlight, and assign each event to a student. Although each student will conduct independent research on an event, all event descriptions will be collected and combined into one document for submission to your instructor. To complete the project:

a. Identify a unique name for the group (perhaps assigned by your instructor).

b. Identify events (perhaps conduct research online) and assign one event to each student.

c. Each student will collect information on the event (general description, location, cost, etc.).

d. Compose a cover letter to the instructor, identifying group members and noting events to be included in the document. The cover letter should be attractive and error-free.

e. Insert a hard return at the end of the cover letter so that the first event description begins on a new page.

f. Save the document to OneDrive as **w01m3Events_GroupName** (replacing *GroupName* with the actual group name). Go to http://onedrive.live.com, sign in, and then open *w01b3EventsGroup-Name*. Click **Share** and click **Get link**. Click **Shorten** to get a shorter version of the URL. Provide the URL to group members so each member can access and edit the file.

g. Each group member will access the file from the URL. When the document opens, click **Edit Document**, and then click **Edit in Word**. Enter any login information (Windows Live ID) and edit the document to add event information. When a description is complete, insert a hard return so that the next description begins on a new page. Click **Save** on the Quick Access Toolbar to save the document back to OneDrive.

h. Submit the completed document based on instructor's directions.

Dream Destination

You work with a local radio station that will award a dream vacation of one week in a resort area to a lucky listener. Select a destination and conduct some research to determine approximately how much it will cost your employer to make the vacation available. What travel arrangements are possible? What type of accommodations do you recommend? What activities are there to enjoy in the area, and what are some outstanding restaurants? Prepare a one- to two-page document, outlining what you think are the best selling points for the area and approximately how much the travel and hotel accommodations will cost the radio station. Because the document is for internal distribution in draft format, you do not need to be overly concerned with format. However, you should use skills from this chapter to properly identify the document (headers, footers, and watermarks) and to position it on the page. The document should be error-free. Modify document properties to include yourself as the author. Save the file as **w01b2Vacation_LastFirst** and submit based on your instructor's directions.

Logo Policy

Open *w01b3Policy* and save it as a Word 2013 file with the file name **w01b3Policy_LastFirst**. The document was started by an office assistant, but was not finished. You must complete the document, ensuring that it is error-free and attractive. The current header includes a page number at the top right. Remove the page number from the header and create a footer with a centered page number instead. Remove the word *copyright* where it appears in the document and replace it with the copyright symbol. Show nonprinting characters and remove any unnecessary or improperly placed paragraph marks. Insert hard returns where necessary to better space paragraphs. The hyphenated word *non-Association* should not be divided between lines, so use a nonbreaking hyphen, if necessary. Modify document properties to include yourself as the author and assign relevant keywords. Finally, use a watermark to indicate that the document is not in final form. Save the document as a Word 2013 file and as a separate Word 97-2003 document with the same file name. Submit both files based on your instructor's directions.

Time Management

After watching the video on time management and organization skills, think about how you could put into practice some of the tips suggested in the video. Specifically, consider how you might better manage your time with respect to completing class assignments, studying for quizzes and exams, and preparing for class. Then write an informal one-to-two page paper, saving it as **w01b4Time_LastFirst**, outlining changes you plan to make. You will use Word's default line and paragraph spacing settings, but you should make sure the document also includes the following items:

- A left-aligned header with your name, and a centered footer including the page number.
- Top and bottom margins of 1" and left and right margins of 1.5".
- A *Draft* watermark of your choice.
- A smiley face symbol in an appropriate place within the document.
- Your name in the Document Properties Author area.
- No spelling or grammatical errors.

Capstone Exercise

Ethical conflicts occur all the time and result when one person or group benefits at the expense of another. Your Philosophy 101 instructor assigned a class project whereby students must consider the question of ethics and society. The result of your research includes a collection of questions every person should ask him- or herself. Your paper is nearly complete but needs a few modifications before you submit it.

Spelling, Margins, Watermarks, and Editing

You notice Word displays spelling and grammatical errors with colored underlines, so you must correct those as soon as possible. Additionally, you want to adjust the margins and then insert a watermark that displays when you print so that you will remember that this is not the final version.

a. Open *w01c1Ethics* and save it as **w01c1Ethics_LastFirst**.

b. Run the Spelling & Grammar tool to correct all misspelled words and contextual errors. Identify and insert a synonym for the word *whereas* in the *$50 Bill* paragraph.

c. Change the margins to **0.75"** on all sides.

d. Insert a diagonal watermark that displays **Version 1**. (Hint: Insert a Custom watermark, select Text watermark, and then type **Version 1** in the text box.) Color the watermark blue.

e. Remove the word *new* from the first body paragraph, beginning with *Ethics refers to the principals or standards*. You realize that the word *principals* is incorrectly used in the first sentence of the same paragraph. Change the word to **principles**. Proofread the document to find any spelling or word usage errors that Word missed.

Headers, Footers, and Features That Improve Readability

You will set up page numbering and will include a descriptive header. Because you are going to customize headers and footers precisely, you must use several of the custom settings available for headers and footers.

a. Insert a centered page number at the bottom of the report. Type your first name and last name in the header area. The header and footer should not display on the first page.

b. Insert a space and then a frownie face symbol after the word *exam* in the first sentence of the *Honor Code* section. You can find a frownie face symbol in the Wingdings font.

c. Insert a ™ symbol after *Office 2013*, in the *Office CD* paragraph.

Set Properties and Finalize Document

After improving the readability of the document, you remember that you have not yet saved it. Your professor still uses an older version of Word, so you save the document in a compatible format that will display easily.

a. Save the document.

b. Run the Compatibility Checker and Document Inspector, but do not take any suggested actions at this time.

c. Add **Ethics**, **Responsibility**, and **Morals** to the Keywords field in the document properties. Change the author to your first name and last name. Close the Document Panel.

d. Preview the document.

e. Save and close the file, and submit based on your instructor's directions.

Document Presentation

Editing and Formatting

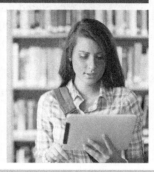

OBJECTIVES AFTER READING THIS CHAPTER, YOU WILL BE ABLE TO:

1. Apply font attributes p. 144
2. Format a paragraph p. 149
3. Format a document p. 163
4. Apply styles p. 166
5. Insert and format objects p. 177

CASE STUDY | Phillips Studio L Photography

Having recently opened your own photography studio, you are involved in marketing the business. Not only do you hope to attract customers from the local community who want photos of special events, but also you will offer classes in basic photography for interested amateur photographers. You have even designed a Web site to promote the business and provide details on upcoming events and classes. You are not yet a large enough business to employ an office staff, so much of the work of developing promotional material falls to you.

Among other projects, you are currently developing material to include in a quarterly mailing to people who have expressed an interest in upcoming studio events. You have prepared a rough draft of a newsletter describing photography basics—a document that must be formatted and properly organized before it is distributed to people on your mailing list. You will modify the document to ensure attractive line and paragraph spacing, and you will format text to draw attention to pertinent points. Formatted in columns, the document will be easy to read. The newsletter is somewhat informal, and you will make appropriate use of color, borders, and pictures so that it is well received by your audience.

Text and Paragraph Formatting

When you format text, you change the way it looks. Your goal in designing a document is to ensure that it is well received and understood by an audience of readers. Seldom will your first attempt at designing a document be the only time you work with it. Inevitably, you will identify text that should be reworded or emphasized differently, paragraphs that might be more attractive in another alignment, or the need to bold, underline, or use italics to call attention to selected text. As you develop a document, or after reopening a previously completed document, you can make all these modifications and more. That process is called *formatting*.

In this section, you will learn to change font and font size, and format text with character attributes, such as bold, underline, and italics. At the paragraph level, you will adjust paragraph and line spacing, set tabs, change alignment, and apply bullets and numbering.

Applying Font Attributes

A *font* is a combination of typeface and type style. The font you select should reinforce the message of the text without calling attention to itself, and it should be consistent with the information you want to convey. For example, a paper prepared for a professional purpose, such as a resume, should have a standard font, such as Times New Roman, instead of one that looks funny or frilly, such as Comic Sans. Additionally, you will want to minimize the variety of fonts in a document to maintain a professional look. Typically, you should use three or fewer fonts within a document. A header might be formatted in one font, while body text is shown in another. Word enables you to format text in a variety of ways. Not only can you change a font, but you can apply text attributes, such as bold, italic, or underline, to selected text, or to text that you are about to type. Several of the most commonly used text formatting commands are located in the Font group on the Home tab.

Select Font Options

When you begin a new, blank document, a default font is applied, which you can change for the current document if you like. The default font is Calibri 11 pt. To change the font for selected text, or for a document you are beginning, click the Font arrow and select a font from those displayed (see Figure 2.1). Each font shown is a sample of the actual font. With text selected, you can point to any font in the list, without clicking, to see a preview of the way selected text will look in that particular font. The feature whereby you can preview the effect of a formatting selection is called *Live Preview*.

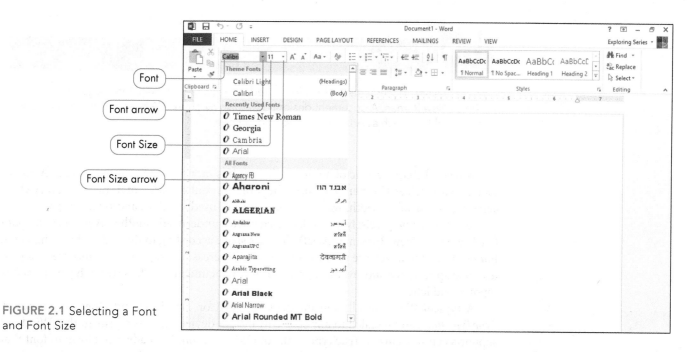

FIGURE 2.1 Selecting a Font and Font Size

You can also change font size when you click the Font Size arrow (refer to Figure 2.1) and select a point size. Each point size is equivalent to 1/72 of an inch; therefore, the larger the point size, the larger the font. A document often contains various sizes of the same font. For example, a document that includes levels of headings and subheadings might have major headings formatted in a larger point size than lesser headings.

A definitive characteristic of any font is the presence or absence of thin lines that end the main strokes of each letter. A *serif font* contains a thin line or extension at the top and bottom of the primary strokes on characters. Times New Roman is an example of a serif font. A *sans serif font* (*sans* from the French word meaning *without*) does not contain the thin lines on characters. Arial is a sans serif font.

Serifs (the thin lines that begin and end each character formatted in a serif font) help the eye connect one letter with the next and generally are used with large amounts of text. The paragraphs in this book, for example, are set in a serif font. Body text of newspapers and magazines is usually formatted in a serif font, as well. A sans serif font, such as Arial or Verdana, is more effective with smaller amounts of text such as titles, headlines, corporate logos, and Web pages. For example, the heading *Select Font Options*, at the beginning of this section, is set in a sans serif font. Web developers often prefer a sans serif font because the extra strokes that begin and end letters in a serif font can blur or fade into a Web page, making it difficult to read. Examples of serif and sans serif fonts are shown in Figure 2.2.

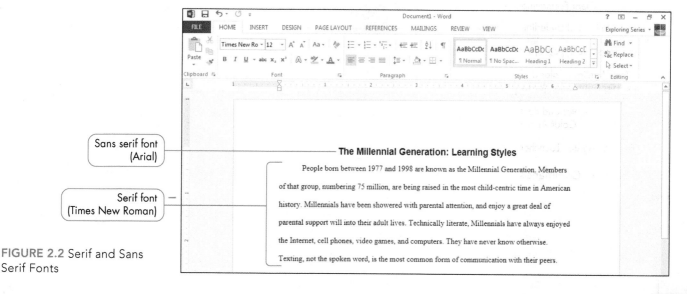

FIGURE 2.2 Serif and Sans Serif Fonts

A second characteristic of a font is whether it is monospaced or proportional. A *monospaced font* (such as Courier New) uses the same amount of horizontal space for every character regardless of its width. Monospaced fonts are used in tables and financial projections where text must be precisely aligned, one character underneath another. A *proportional font* (such as Times New Roman or Arial) allocates space according to the width of the character. For example, the lowercase *m* is wider than the lowercase *i*. Proportional fonts create a professional appearance and are appropriate for most documents, such as research papers, status reports, and letters.

A typical Word installation includes support for TrueType and OpenType fonts. A *TrueType font* can be scaled to any size. Any output device, such as a printer, that Windows supports can recognize a TrueType font. An *OpenType font* is an advanced form of font that is designed for all platforms, including Windows and Macintosh. OpenType fonts incorporate a greater extension of the basic character set. Most fonts included in a typical Word installation are OpenType.

Change Text Appearance

Commonly accessed commands related to font settings are located in the Font group on the Home tab (see Figure 2.3). Word 2013 enables you to bold, underline, and italicize text, apply text highlighting, change font color, and work with various text effects and other formatting options from commands in the Font group. For even more choices, click the Font Dialog Box Launcher in the Font group and select from additional formatting commands available in the Font dialog box (see Figure 2.4). With text selected, you will see the Mini Toolbar when you move the pointer near the selection. The *Mini Toolbar* (see Figure 2.5), which contains several of the most commonly accessed formatting and alignment commands, makes it convenient to quickly select a format (instead of locating it on the Ribbon or using a keyboard shortcut).

FIGURE 2.3 Font Commands

FIGURE 2.4 Font Dialog Box

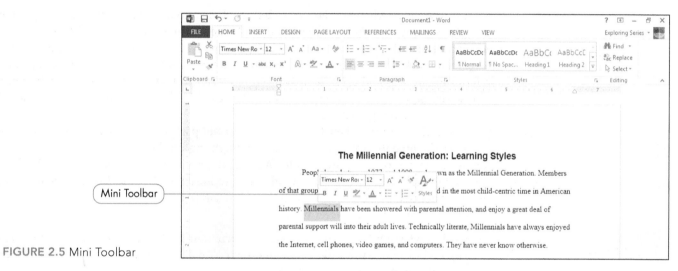

FIGURE 2.5 Mini Toolbar

STEP 1

To bold, underline, or italicize text, do either of the following:

• Select text to be formatted. Click Bold, Italic, or Underline in the Font group on the HOME tab.

• Click Bold, Italic, or Underline in the Font group on the HOME tab and type text to be formatted. Click the same command to turn off the formatting effect.

Word 2013 includes a variety of text effects that enable you to add a shadow, outline, reflection, or glow to text. The *Text Effects and Typography* gallery (see Figure 2.6) provides access to those effects as well as to WordArt styles, number styles, ligatures, and stylistic sets that you can apply to text.

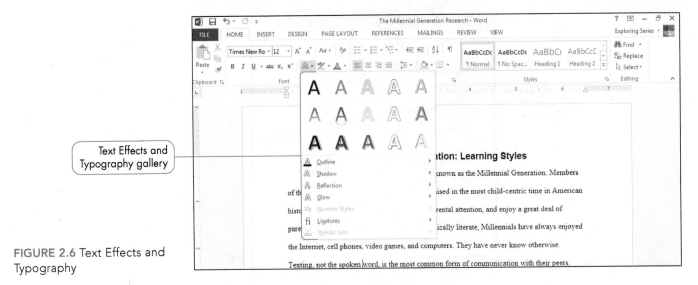

Text Effects and Typography gallery

FIGURE 2.6 Text Effects and Typography

A *ligature* is two letters that are crafted together into a single character, or *glyph*. For example, you often see the letters *f* and *i* bound together in a ligature. A *stylistic set* is a collection of letter styles that you can apply to OpenType fonts. Some fonts include more stylistic sets than others. To explore advanced font settings, click the Font Dialog Box Launcher (refer to Figure 2.3) and click the Advanced tab (refer to Figure 2.4). Select a ligature and stylistic set. Stylistic sets and ligatures are often used in the preparation of formal documents such as wedding invitations.

As a student, you are likely to highlight important parts of textbooks, magazine articles, and other documents. You probably use a highlighting marker to shade parts of text you want to remember or draw attention to. Word 2013 provides an equivalent tool with which you can highlight text you want to stand out or to locate easily—the Text Highlight Color command, located in the Font group on the Home tab (refer to Figure 2.3).

To highlight text *before* selecting it:

1. Click Text Highlight Color to select the current highlight color or click the Text Highlight Color arrow and choose another color. The mouse pointer resembles a pen when you move it over the document.
2. Drag across text to highlight it.
3. Click Text Highlight Color or press Esc to stop highlighting.

To highlight text *after* selecting it, click Text Highlight Color or click the Text Highlight Color arrow and choose another color. To remove highlights, select the highlighted text, click the Text Highlight Color arrow, and then select No Color.

When creating a document, you must consider when and how to capitalize text. Titles are occasionally in all caps, sentences begin with a capital letter, and each key word of a heading is typically capitalized. Use the Change Case option in the Font group on the Home tab to quickly change the capitalization of document text (refer to Figure 2.3).

By default, text is shown in black as you type a document. For a bit of interest, or to draw attention to text within a document, you can change the font color of previously typed text or of text that you are about to type. Click the Font Color arrow (refer to Figure 2.3) and select from a gallery of colors. For even more choices, click More Colors and select from a variety of hues or shades. As shown in Figure 2.7, you can click the Custom tab in the Colors dialog box and click to select a color hue, while honing in on a variation of that hue by dragging along a continuum.

Drag to select a variation of the color hue

Click to select a color hue or shade

FIGURE 2.7 Applying a Custom Color

TIP Matching Font Color

If you have created a custom font color, matching text that you type later to that particular shade can be a challenge. It is easy to match color, however, when you click the Font Color arrow and select the shade from the Recent Colors area.

Formatting a Paragraph

Formatting selected text is only one way to alter the appearance of a document. You can also change the alignment, indentation, tab stops, or line spacing for any paragraph within the document. Recall that Word defines a paragraph as text followed by a hard return, or even a hard return on a line by itself (indicating a blank paragraph). You can include borders or shading for added emphasis around selected paragraphs, and you can number paragraphs or enhance them with bullets. The Paragraph group on the Home tab contains several paragraph formatting commands (see Figure 2.8). If you are formatting only one paragraph, you do not have to select the entire paragraph. Simply click to place the insertion point within the paragraph and apply a paragraph format. However, if you are formatting several paragraphs, you must select them before formatting.

Align Left

Center

Align Right

Justify

Line and Paragraph Spacing

Paragraph Dialog Box Launcher

FIGURE 2.8 Paragraph Commands

Select Paragraph Alignment

Left alignment is the most common alignment, often seen in letters, reports, and memos. When you begin a new blank Word document, paragraphs are left aligned by default. Text begins evenly at the left margin and ends in an uneven right edge. The reverse of left alignment is *right alignment*, a setting in which text is aligned at the right margin with a ragged left edge. Short lines including dates, figure captions, and headers are often right aligned. A *centered* paragraph is horizontally located in the center, an equal distance from the left and right edges. Report titles and major headings are typically centered. Finally, *justified alignment* spreads text evenly between the left and right margins so that text begins at the left margin and ends uniformly at the right margin. Newspaper and magazine articles are often justified. Such text alignment often causes awkward spacing as text is stretched to fit evenly between margins. Figure 2.9 shows examples of paragraph alignments.

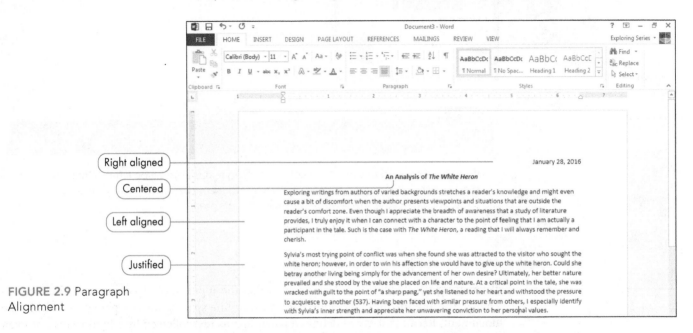

FIGURE 2.9 Paragraph Alignment

STEP 2 To change paragraph alignment, select text (or click to position the insertion point in a paragraph, if only one paragraph is to be affected) and select an alignment from the Paragraph group on the Home tab (refer to Figure 2.8). You can also change alignment by making a selection from the Paragraph dialog box (see Figure 2.10), which opens when you click the Paragraph Dialog Box Launcher (refer to Figure 2.8).

FIGURE 2.10 Paragraph Dialog Box

Select Line and Paragraph Spacing

Paragraph spacing is the amount of space between paragraphs, measured in points. (Recall that one point is 1/72 of an inch.) Paragraph spacing is a good way to differentiate between paragraphs, especially if the beginning of each paragraph is not clearly identified by an indented line. In such a case, paragraph spacing makes it clear where one paragraph ends and another begins. Spacing used to separate paragraphs usually comes *after* each affected paragraph, although you can specify that it is placed *before*. Use the Paragraph dialog box to select paragraph spacing (refer to Figure 2.10).

Word provides several ways to select paragraph spacing, as described in the following steps:

- Click the HOME tab. Click *Line and Paragraph Spacing* in the Paragraph group on the HOME tab (see Figure 2.11). Click to Add Space Before Paragraph (or to Remove Space After Paragraph).
- Click the Paragraph Dialog Box Launcher in the Paragraph group on the HOME tab. Type spacing Before or After in the respective areas (refer to Figure 2.10) or click the spin arrows to adjust spacing. Click OK.
- Click the PAGE LAYOUT tab. Change the Before or After spacing in the Paragraph group (see Figure 2.12).

FIGURE 2.11 Spacing Options

FIGURE 2.12 Paragraph Spacing and Indents

Just as paragraph spacing is the amount of space between paragraphs, **line spacing** is the amount of space between lines. Typically, line spacing is determined before beginning a document, such as when you know that a research paper should be double-spaced, so you identify that setting before typing. Of course, you can change line spacing of a current paragraph or selected text at any point as well. Change line spacing in one of the following ways:

- Click the HOME tab. Click *Line and Paragraph Spacing* (refer to Figure 2.11). Select line spacing or click Line Spacing Options for more choices.
- Click the Paragraph Dialog Box Launcher on the HOME tab. Click the *Line spacing* arrow and select spacing (refer to Figure 2.10). Click OK.

The most common line spacing options are single, double, or 1.5. Word provides those options and more. From the Paragraph dialog box (refer to Figure 2.10), you can select Exactly, At Least, or Multiple. To specify an exact point size for spacing, select Exactly. If you select At Least, you will indicate a minimum line spacing size while allowing Word to adjust the height, if necessary, to accommodate such features as drop caps (oversized letters that sometimes begin paragraphs). The Multiple setting enables you to select a line spacing interval other than single, double, or 1.5.

Select Indents

An *indent* is a setting associated with how part of a paragraph is distanced from one or more margins. One of the most common indents is a *first line indent*, in which the first line of each paragraph is set off from the left margin. For instance, your English instructor might require that the first line of each paragraph in a writing assignment is indented 0.5" from the left margin, a typical first line indent. If you have ever prepared a bibliography for a research paper, you have most likely specified a *hanging indent*, where the first line of a source begins at the left margin, but all other lines in the source are indented. Indenting an entire paragraph from the left margin is a *left indent*, while indenting an entire paragraph from the right margin is a *right indent*. A lengthy quote is often set apart by indenting from both the left and right margins.

Using the Paragraph dialog box (refer to Figure 2.10), you can select an indent setting for one or more paragraphs. First line and hanging indents are considered special indents. You can select left and right indents from either the Paragraph dialog box or from the Paragraph group on the Page Layout tab (refer to Figure 2.12).

STEP 2 >> You can use the Word ruler to set indents. If the ruler does not display above the document space, click the View tab and click Ruler (see Figure 2.13). The three-part indicator at the left side of the ruler enables you to set a left indent, a hanging indent, or a first line indent. Drag the desired indent along the ruler to apply the indent to the current paragraph (or selected paragraphs). Figure 2.13 shows the first line indent moved to the 0.5" mark, resulting in the first line of a paragraph being indented by 0.5".

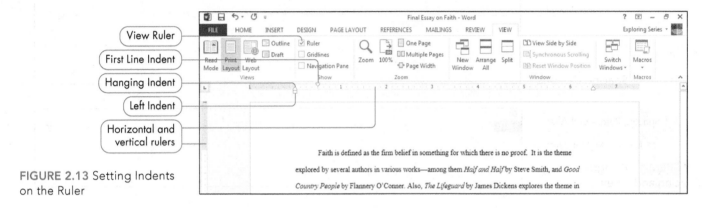

FIGURE 2.13 Setting Indents on the Ruler

Set Tabs

A tab is a marker that specifies a position for aligning text. By using *tabs*, you can easily arrange text in columns or position text a certain distance from the left or right margins. Tabs enable you to add organization to a document, arranging text in easy-to-read columns. A table of contents is an example of tabbed text, as is a restaurant menu. You can select from various types of tabs, with the most common being *left*, *right*, *center*, and *decimal*. By default, a left tab is set every 0.5" when you start a new document. Each time you press Tab on the keyboard, the insertion point will move to the left by 0.5". Typically, you would set a first line indent or simply press Tab to indent the first line of each new paragraph within a document. Table 2.1 describes various types of tabs.

TABLE 2.1	Tab Markers	
Tab Icon on Ruler	**Type of Tab**	**Function**
[L]	Left tab	Sets the start position on the left so as you type; text moves to the right of the tab setting.
[⊥]	Center tab	Sets the middle point of the text you type; whatever you type will be centered on that tab setting.
[⌐]	Right tab	Sets the start position on the right so as you type; text moves to the left of that tab setting and aligns on the right.
[⊥·]	Decimal tab	Aligns numbers on a decimal point. Regardless of how long the number, each number lines up with the decimal point in the same position.
[|]	Bar tab	This tab does not position text or decimals; but inserts a vertical bar at the tab setting. This bar is useful as a separator for text printed on the same line.

STEP 3 » Tabs that you set override default tabs. For example, suppose you set a left tab at 1". That means the default tab of 0.5" is no longer in effect, nor is any other 0.5" default tab still in place. Perhaps the easiest way to set tabs, if not the most precise, is to use the ruler. Click the tab selector (see Figure 2.14) repeatedly to cycle through tabs, including left, center, right, decimal, bar, first line indent, and hanging indent. Then simply click a position on the ruler to set a tab. You can drag a tab along the ruler to reposition it, or you can drag a tab off the ruler to remove it. Figure 2.14 shows a left tab at 1" and a right tab at 5.5". To apply one or more tabs, you can select text and set tabs (applying tabs to the selected text), or you can set a tab and type text (applying tabs to text typed after setting tabs).

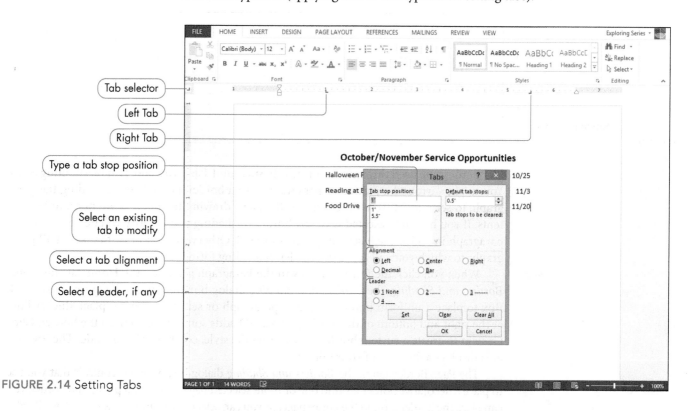

FIGURE 2.14 Setting Tabs

To include *leaders* (the series of dots or hyphens that leads the reader's eye across the page to connect two columns of information), use the Tabs dialog box, shown in Figure 2.14.

The row of dots that typically connects a food item with its price on a restaurant menu is an example of a leader. To set a tab with a leader:

1. Click the Paragraph Dialog Box Launcher in the Paragraph group on the HOME tab and click Tabs from the *Indents and Spacing* tab. Alternatively, double-click a tab on the ruler.
2. Type the location where you want to set the tab. The number you type is assumed to be in inches, so typing *2* would place a tab at 2".
3. Select a tab alignment (Left, Right, etc.).
4. Specify a leader, if desired.
5. Click OK (or click Set and continue specifying tabs).

TIP | Deleting Tabs

To manually delete a tab you have set, simply drag it off the ruler. An alternative is to click the Paragraph Dialog Box Launcher, click Tabs, select the tab (in the Tab stop position box), and then click Clear. Click OK.

Apply Borders and Shading

You can draw attention to a document or an area of a document by using the *Borders and Shading* command. A ***border*** is a line that surrounds a paragraph, a page, a table, or an image, similar to how a picture frame surrounds a photograph or piece of art. A border can also display at the top, bottom, left, or right of a selection. ***Shading*** is a background color that appears behind text in a paragraph, a page, or a table. Figure 2.15 illustrates the use of borders and shading.

October/November Service Opportunities	
Halloween Fun Run	10/25
Salvation Army Fundraiser	11/3
Reading at Brandon Elementary	11/18
Food Drive	11/20

FIGURE 2.15 Borders and Shading

Borders are used throughout this text to surround Tip boxes and Troubleshooting areas. You might surround a particular paragraph with a border, possibly even shading the paragraph, to set it apart from other text on the page, drawing the reader's attention to its contents. If you have not selected text, any border or shading you identify will be applied to the paragraph in which the insertion point is located. Otherwise, you must first select all paragraphs to which you will apply the border or shading formats.

STEP 4》 When you click the Borders arrow in the Paragraph group on the Home tab and select *Borders and Shading*, the *Borders and Shading* dialog box displays (see Figure 2.16). Click Box to place a uniform border around a paragraph or select Shadow to place thicker lines at the right and bottom of the bordered area. 3D adds some dimension to the border. Click Custom to create a custom border by selecting the style, color, width, and side. The Preview area displays a diagram of your border.

The Page Border tab in the *Borders and Shading* dialog box provides controls that you use to place a decorative border around one or more selected pages. As with a paragraph border, you can place the border around the entire page, or you can select one or more sides. The Page Border tab also provides an additional option to use preselected image as a border instead of ordinary lines. Note that it is appropriate to use page borders on documents such as flyers, newsletters, and invitations, but not on formal documents such as research papers and professional reports.

To apply shading to one or more selected paragraphs, click the Shading arrow in the Paragraph group on the Home tab. You can select a solid color, or a lighter or darker variation of the color, for the shaded background. Click More Colors for even more selection. You can also select shading from the Shading tab of the *Borders and Shading* dialog box (see Figure 2.16).

FIGURE 2.16 Selecting a Border

Create Bulleted and Numbered Lists

A list organizes information by topic or in a sequence. Use a ***numbered list*** if the list is a sequence of steps. If the list is not of a sequential nature, but is a simple itemization of points, use a ***bulleted list*** (see Figure 2.17). The numerical sequence in a numbered list is automatically updated to accommodate additions or deletions, which means that if you add or remove items, the list items are renumbered. A *multilevel list* extends a numbered or bulleted list to several levels, and it, too, is updated automatically when topics are added or deleted. You create each of these lists from the Paragraph group on the Home tab.

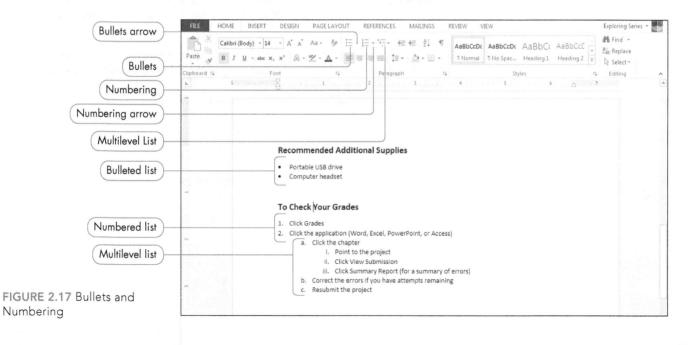

FIGURE 2.17 Bullets and Numbering

To define a new bullet or customize the formatting (such as color or special effect) of a selected bullet, click the Bullets arrow in the Paragraph group on the Home tab and click Define New Bullet. Make selections from the Define New Bullet dialog box and click OK.

STEP 5 To apply bullets, numbering, or multiple levels to a list:

1. Select the items to be bulleted or numbered, or click where you will begin typing the items. Click Bullets (or Numbering) to apply the default bullet or numbering style. To select another style, click the Bullets (or Numbering) arrow in the Paragraph group on the HOME tab and point to one of the predefined symbols or numbering styles in the library. A preview of the style will display in your document. Click the style you want to use. If creating a multilevel list, click Multilevel List (instead of the Bullets arrow or Numbering arrow) and select a style.

2. If you previously selected items to bullet or number, the style will be applied to the selection. Otherwise, type items, pressing Enter after each; when the list is complete, click Bullets (or Numbering) again to turn off the toggle.

TIP Renumbering a List

Especially when creating several numbered lists in a document, you might find that Word continues the numbering sequence from one list to the next, when your intention was to begin numbering each list at 1. To restart numbering at a new value, right-click the item that is not numbered correctly, and click *Restart at 1*. Alternatively, you can click the Numbering arrow and select Set Numbering Value. Indicate a starting value in the subsequent dialog box.

Quick Concepts

1. Describe the difference between a serif and sans serif font. Give examples of when you might use each. *p. 145*

2. Suppose a document is single spaced. However, when you type a series of bulleted lines, the lines are not single spaced; instead there is a much larger distance between each. What could cause the larger space, and how would you correct it so that the bulleted items are also single spaced? *p. 151*

3. You are working with a campus organization, helping plan a charity dinner. You will use Word to create the menu. What type of tabs would you use, and approximately how would you space them? *p. 153*

4. You are preparing a document of tips for an upcoming camping trip. You will include a list of items to bring along for the overnight adventure. What Word feature could you use to draw attention to the list? *p. 155*

Hands-On Exercises

Watch the Video
for this Hands-
On Exercise!

MyITLab®
HOE1 Training

1 Text and Paragraph Formatting

The newsletter you are developing needs a lot of work. The first thing to do is to make sure it is error free, and to format it so it is much easier to read. After selecting an appropriate font and font size, you will emphasize selected text with bold and italic text formatting. Paragraphs must be spaced so they are easy to read. You know that to be effective, a document must capture the reader's attention while conveying a message. You will begin the process of formatting and preparing the newsletter in this exercise.

Skills covered: Select Font Options and Change Text Appearance • Select Paragraph Alignment, Spacing, and Indenting • Set Tabs • Apply Borders and Shading • Create Bulleted and Numbered Lists

STEP 1 ≫ SELECT FONT OPTIONS AND CHANGE TEXT APPEARANCE

The newsletter will be printed and distributed by mail. As a printed document, you know that certain font options are better suited for reading. Specifically, you want to use a serif font in an easy-to-read size. Refer to Figure 2.18 as you complete Step 1.

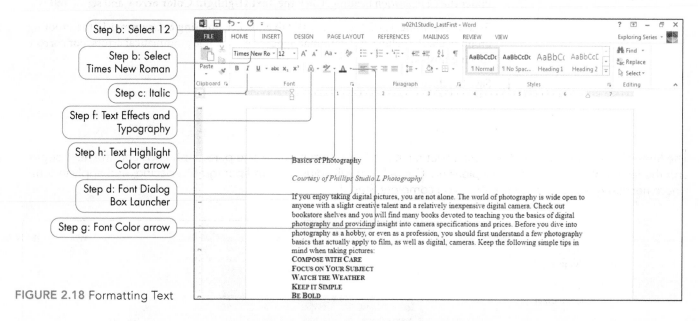

FIGURE 2.18 Formatting Text

a. Open *w02h1Studio* and save it as **w02h1Studio_LastFirst**.

   When you save files, use your last and first names. For example, as the Word author, I would name my document *w02h1Studio_HoganLynn*.

TROUBLESHOOTING: If you make any major mistakes in this exercise, you can close the file, open *w02h1Studio* again, and then start this exercise over.

---

b. Press **Ctrl+A** to select all of the text in the document. Click the **Font arrow** in the Font group on the HOME tab and scroll, if necessary, to select **Times New Roman**. Click the **Font Size arrow** in the Font group and select **12**.

   You use a 12-pt serif font on the whole document because it is easier to read in print.

c. Select the second line of text in the document, *Courtesy of Phillips Studio L Photography*. Click **Italic** on the Mini Toolbar. Scroll down, if necessary, and double-click *boxy* in the paragraph below *Camera Body*. Click **Italic** in the Font group.

> **TROUBLESHOOTING:** If the Mini Toolbar does not display or disappears, click Italic in the Font group on the HOME tab.

d. Select the five paragraphs beginning with *Compose with Care* and ending with *Be Bold*. Click the **Font Dialog Box Launcher** in the Font group.

The Font dialog box displays with font options.

e. Click the **Font tab**, if necessary, and click **Bold** in the Font style box. Click to select the **Small caps check box** under *Effects*. Click **OK**.

f. Press **Ctrl+End** to move the insertion point to the end of the document. Select the last line in the document, *Let Phillips Studio L Photography Preserve Your Memories!* Click **Text Effects and Typography** in the Font group. Select **Fill – Blue, Accent 1, Outline – Background 1, Hard Shadow – Accent 1** (third row, third column). Change the font size of the selected text to **16**. Click anywhere to deselect the text.

g. Press **Ctrl+Home** to position the insertion point at the beginning of the document. Select the second line in the document, *Courtesy of Phillips Studio L Photography*. Click the **Font Color arrow** and select **Blue, Accent 5, Darker 25%** (fifth row, ninth column).

h. Select the words *you should consider how to become a better photographer* in the paragraph under the *Composition* heading. Click the **Text Highlight Color arrow** and select **Yellow**.

i. Press **Ctrl+Home**. Click the **REVIEW tab** and click **Spelling & Grammar** in the Proofing group to check spelling and grammar. Ignore any possible grammatical errors, but correct spelling mistakes.

j. Save the document.

STEP 2 ≫ SELECT PARAGRAPH ALIGNMENT, SPACING, AND INDENTING

The lines of the newsletter are too close together. It is difficult to tell where one paragraph ends and the next begins, and the layout of the text is not very pleasing. Overall, you will adjust line and paragraph spacing, and apply indents where necessary. Refer to Figure 2.19 as you complete Step 2.

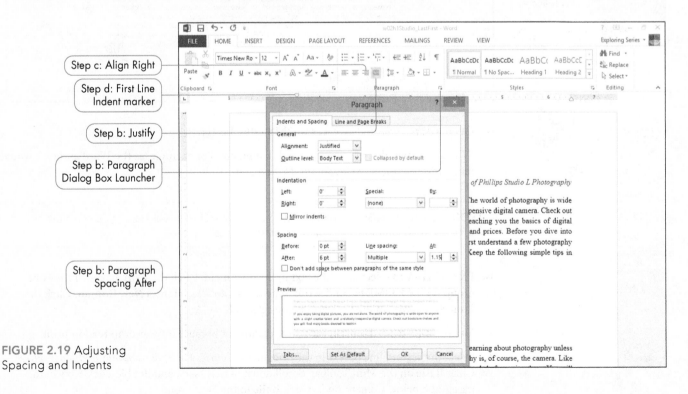

FIGURE 2.19 Adjusting Spacing and Indents

a. Select most of the document beginning with the sentence *If you enjoy taking digital pictures* and ending with *emotion expressed before even greeting Santa*. Click the **HOME tab**. Click **Line and Paragraph Spacing** in the Paragraph group. Select **1.15**. Do not deselect the text.

All lines within the selected text are spaced by 1.15.

b. Click **Justify** in the Paragraph group. Click the **Paragraph Dialog Box Launcher**. With the Indents and Spacing tab selected, click the **After spin arrow** in the *Spacing* section once to increase spacing after to **6 pt**. Click **OK**. Click anywhere to deselect the text.

You have placed 6 pt spacing after each paragraph in the selected area. Selected paragraphs are also aligned with justify, which means text is evenly distributed between the left and right margins.

c. Press **Ctrl+End**. Click anywhere on the last line in the document, *Let Phillips Studio L Photography Preserve Your Memories!* Click **Center** in the Paragraph group. Press **Ctrl+Home**. Click anywhere on the second line of text in the document, *Courtesy of Phillips Studio L Photography*. Click **Align Right** in the Paragraph group.

d. Click the **VIEW tab** and click **Ruler** in the Show group to display the ruler, if necessary. Click anywhere in the first body paragraph, beginning with *If you enjoy taking digital pictures*. Click the **HOME tab**, if necessary, and click the **Paragraph Dialog Box Launcher**. Click the **Special arrow** in the Indentation group and select **First line**. Click **OK**. Click anywhere in the second multiline paragraph—the paragraph beginning with *First things first*. Position the mouse pointer on the First Line Indent marker and drag the marker to the **0.5"** mark on the horizontal ruler.

The first line of both multiline paragraphs that begin the document are indented by 0.5 inches.

e. Save the document.

STEP 3 ≫ SET TABS

You realize that you left off the studio hours and want to include them at the end of the document. Refer to Figure 2.20 as you complete Step 3.

FIGURE 2.20 Setting Tabs

a. Press **Ctrl+End**. If necessary, click **Show/Hide** in the Paragraph group to display nonprinting characters. Press **Enter** twice. Click **Clear All Formatting** in the Font group on the HOME tab. Select **Times New Roman font** and **16 pt size**.

You clicked Clear All Formatting so that the text effect formatting from the line above the insertion point is not carried forward to text that you will type next.

b. Make sure the tab selector (shown at the top of the vertical ruler) specifies a Left Tab and click at **1"** on the ruler to set a left tab. Click the tab selector twice to select a right tab and click at **5.5"** on the ruler to set a right tab.

You set a left tab at 1" and a right tab at 5.5".

> **TROUBLESHOOTING:** If the tabs you set are incorrectly placed on the ruler, click Undo in the Quick Access Toolbar and repeat step b. You can also simply drag a tab off the ruler to remove it, or drag it along the ruler to reposition it.

c. Click the **Paragraph Dialog Box Launcher** and click **Tabs** at the bottom-left corner. Click **5.5"** in the Tab stop position box. Click **2** in the *Leader* section and click **OK**.

You modified the right tab to include dot leaders, which means dots will display before text at the right tab.

d. Press **Tab**. Type **Monday – Friday** and press **Tab**. Type **9:00 – 4:00**. Press **Enter**. Press **Tab**. Type **Saturday** and press **Tab**. Type **9:00 – 2:00**. Press **Enter**. Press **Tab**. Type **Closed Sunday**.

e. Save the document.

STEP 4 ›› APPLY BORDERS AND SHADING

To draw attention to the business hours, you will shade and border the information you typed. Refer to Figure 2.21 as you complete Step 4.

FIGURE 2.21 Bordering and Shading Text

a. Select the three lines at the end of the document, beginning with *Monday – Friday* and ending with *Closed Sunday*. Click the **Borders arrow** in the Paragraph group on the HOME tab and select **Borders and Shading**.

> **TROUBLESHOOTING:** If you click Borders instead of the Borders arrow, you will not see the *Borders and Shading* dialog box and the most recent border will be applied to selected text. Click Undo on the Quick Access Toolbar and click the Borders arrow. Then click *Borders and Shading*.

b. Click **Shadow** in the *Setting* section. Scroll through the **Style box** and select the seventh style—double line. Click **OK**. Do not deselect text. Click the **Shading arrow** and select **Blue, Accent 1, Lighter 60%** (third row, fifth column). Click anywhere to deselect the text.

Studio hours are bordered and shaded.

c. Save the document.

STEP 5 ❯❯ CREATE BULLETED AND NUMBERED LISTS

At several points in the newsletter, you include either a list of items or a sequence of steps. You will add bullets to the lists and number the steps. Refer to Figure 2.22 as you complete Step 5.

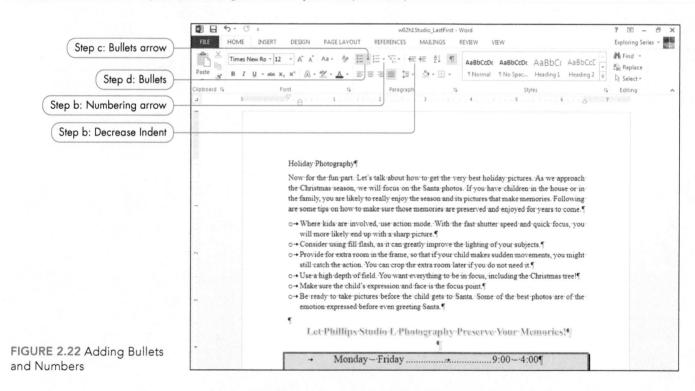

FIGURE 2.22 Adding Bullets and Numbers

a. Press **Ctrl+Home**. Select the five boldfaced paragraphs, beginning with *Compose with Care* and ending with *Be Bold*.

b. Click the **Numbering arrow** and select **Number alignment: Left** (third option on the first row in the Numbering Library, showing each number followed by a right parenthesis). Click **Decrease Indent** in the Paragraph group to move the numbered items to the left margin. Click anywhere to deselect the text.

c. Scroll to the second page and select four paragraphs following the sentence *Depth of field is determined by several factors:*, beginning with *Aperture/F-Stop* and ending with *Point of View*. Click the **Bullets arrow** and select the hollow round bullet. Decrease the indent to move the selected text to the left margin. Deselect the text.

d. Press **Ctrl+End** and select the six paragraphs beginning with *Where kids are involved*, and ending *even greeting Santa*. Click **Bullets** to apply a hollow round bullet to the selected paragraphs. Decrease the indent so the bullets begin at the left margin.

Clicking Bullets applied the most recently selected bullet style to selected text. You did not have to click the Bullets arrow and select from the Bullet Library.

e. Save the document. Keep the document open if you plan to continue with the next Hands-On Exercise. If not, close the document and exit Word.

Document Appearance

The overall appearance and organization of a document is the first opportunity to effectively convey your message to readers. You should ensure that a document is formatted attractively with coordinated and consistent style elements. Not only should a document be organized by topic, but also it should be organized by design, so that it is easy to read and so that topics of the same level of emphasis are similar in appearance. For example, major headings are typically formatted identically, with subheadings formatted to indicate a subordinate relationship—in a smaller font, for example. Word 2013 includes tools on the Design tab that help you create a polished and professional-looking document. You will find options for creating a themed document, with color-coordinated design elements, as well as *style sets*, which are predefined combinations of font, style, color, and font size that can be applied to selected text. Organizing a document into sections enables you to combine diverse units into a whole, formatting sections independently of one another.

In this section, you will explore document formatting options, including themes and style sets. In addition, you will learn to create and apply styles. You will work with sections and columns, learning to organize and format sections independently of one another, to create an attractive document that conveys your message.

Formatting a Document

A *document theme* is a set of coordinating fonts, colors, and special effects, such as shadowing or glows that are combined into a package to provide a stylish appearance. Applying a theme enables you to visually coordinate various page elements. In some cases, adding a page border or page background can also yield a more attractive and effective document. All these design options are available on the Design tab, which is new to Word 2013. As you consider ways to organize a document, you might find it necessary to divide it into sections, with each section arranged or formatted independently of others. For example, a cover page (or section) might be centered vertically, while all other pages are aligned at the top. By arranging text in columns, you can easily create an attractive newsletter or brochure. The Page Layout tab facilitates the use of sections and formatting in columns. When formatting a document, you should always keep in mind the document's purpose and its intended audience. Whereas a newsletter might use more color and playful text and design effects, a legal document should be more conservative. With the broad range of document formatting options available in Word, you can be as playful or conservative as necessary.

Select a Document Theme

A document theme combines color, font, and graphics, simplifying the task of creating a professional, color-coordinated document. When you select a theme for a document, a unified set of design elements, including font style, color, and special effects, is applied to the entire document. The Design tab includes selections related to themes (see Figure 2.23). Themes are not limited to Word, but are also available in other Office 2013 applications. A Word document, color-coordinated to match a supporting PowerPoint presentation, adds professionalism and encourages continuity of purpose between the two projects. Even a new blank Word document is based on a theme by default—the Office theme. Click the Font arrow in the Font group on the Home tab to see the theme fonts (both Heading and Body) for the Office theme. Of course, you can select from other fonts in the list if you prefer. Similarly, you will see Office theme font colors when you click the Font Color arrow.

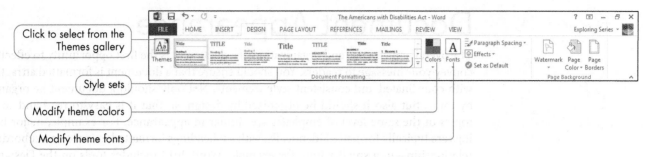

Click to select from the
Themes gallery

Style sets

Modify theme colors

Modify theme fonts

FIGURE 2.23 Design Tab

STEP 1 » Themes are located in the Document Formatting group on the Design tab (refer to Figure 2.23). Click Themes to select from the Themes gallery. As you point to a theme, you will see a preview of the effect on document text. Depending on document features and color selections already in place, you might not see an immediate change when previewing or selecting a document theme. Click a theme to select it. Perhaps you are pleased with most of the theme effects, but want to modify the color or font selection. Click Colors or Fonts in the Document Formatting group on the Design tab to adjust the theme slightly. Each group of coordinated colors or font selections is summarized and identified by a unique name. Click to select a color or font group to adjust the selected theme in the document. To apply themed effects to objects in a document, click Effects in the Document Formatting group on the Design tab and select from a gallery of effects.

Work with Sections

It sometimes becomes necessary to vary the layout of a document within a page or between pages, and incorporate sections into a document. A headline of an article might center horizontally across the width of a page, while remaining article text is divided into columns. The headline could be situated in one section, while article text resides in another. So that sections can be managed separately, you must indicate with section breaks where one section ends and another begins. A *section break* is a marker that divides a document into sections. Word stores the formatting characteristics of each section within the section break at the end of a section. Therefore, if you delete a section break, you also delete the formatting for that section, causing the text above the break to assume the formatting characteristics of the previous section. To delete a section break, click the section break indicator (see Figure 2.24) and press Delete.

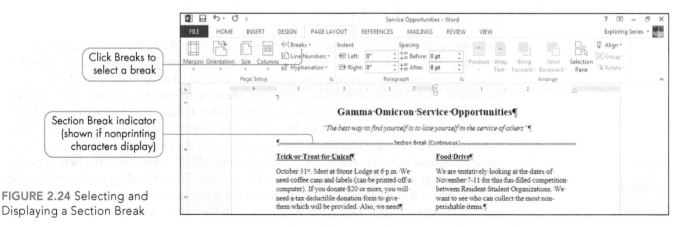

Click Breaks to
select a break

Section Break indicator
(shown if nonprinting
characters display)

FIGURE 2.24 Selecting and
Displaying a Section Break

You can choose from four types of section breaks, as shown in Table 2.2. You can select a section break type when you click the Page Layout tab and click Breaks in the Page Setup group. Before inserting a break, the insertion point should be at the point where the break is to occur.

TABLE 2.2 Section Breaks

Type	Description	Example
Next Page	Text that follows must begin at the top of the next page.	Use to force a chapter to start at the top of a page.
Continuous	Text that follows can continue on the same page.	Use to format text in the middle of the page into columns.
Even Page	Text that follows must begin at the top of the next even-numbered page.	Use to force a chapter to begin at the top of an even-numbered page.
Odd Page	Text that follows must begin at the top of the next odd-numbered page.	Use to force a chapter to begin at the top of an odd-numbered page.

To place a section break in a document:

1. Click at the location where the section break should occur.
2. Click the PAGE LAYOUT tab. Click Breaks in the Page Setup group.
3. Select a section break type (see Table 2.2). If nonprinting characters display, you will see a section break (refer to Figure 2.24).

Format Text into Columns

STEP 2>> *Columns* format a document or section of a document into side-by-side vertical blocks in which the text flows down the first column and continues at the top of the next column. To format text into columns, click the Page Layout tab and click Columns in the Page Setup group. Specify the number of columns or select More Columns to display the Columns dialog box. The Columns dialog box (see Figure 2.25) provides options for setting the number of columns and spacing between columns.

FIGURE 2.25 Columns Dialog Box

Having created a two-column document, you should preview the document to ensure an attractive arrangement of columns. Try to avoid columns that end awkwardly, perhaps with a column heading at the bottom of one column, while remaining text continues at the top of the next column. In addition, columns should be somewhat balanced, if possible, so that one column is not lengthy, while the next is very short. To force a column break, click in the document where the break is to occur, click the Page Layout tab, click Breaks, and then click Column in the *Page Breaks* section. With nonprinting characters displayed, you will see the Column break indicator at the location where one column ends and the next begins.

Applying Styles

As you complete reports, assignments, and other projects, you probably apply the same text, paragraph, table, and list formatting for similar documents. Instead of formatting each element of each document individually, you can create your own custom format for each element—called a style—to save time in designing titles, headings, and paragraphs. A characteristic of a professional document is uniform formatting. All major headings look the same, with uniform subheadings. Even paragraphs can be styled to lend consistency to a document. If styles are appropriately assigned, Word can automatically generate reference pages such as a table of contents and indexes.

A *style* is a named collection of formatting characteristics. Styles automate the formatting process and provide a consistent appearance to a document. It is possible to store any type of character or paragraph formatting within a style, and once a style is defined, you can apply it to any element within a document to produce identical formatting. Word provides a gallery of styles from which you can choose, or you can create your own style. For example, having formatted a major report heading with various settings, such as font type, color, and size, you can create a style from the heading, calling it *Major_Heading*. The next time you type a major heading, simply apply the *Major_Heading* style so that the two headings are identical in format. Subsequent major headings can be formatted in exactly the same way. If you later decide to modify the *Major_Heading* style, all text based on that style will automatically adjust as well.

Select and Modify Styles

Some styles are considered either character or paragraph styles. A *character* style formats one or more selected characters within a paragraph, often applying font formats found in the Font group on the Home tab. A *paragraph* style changes the entire paragraph in which the insertion point is located, or changes multiple selected paragraphs. A paragraph style typically includes paragraph formats found in the Paragraph group on the Home tab, such as alignment, line spacing, indents, tabs, and borders. Other styles are neither character nor paragraph, but are instead *linked* styles in which both character and paragraph formatting are included. A linked style applies formatting dependent upon the text selected. For example, when the insertion point is located within a paragraph, but no text is selected, a linked style applies both font characteristics (such as bold or italic) and paragraph formats (such as paragraph and line spacing) to the entire paragraph. However, if text is selected within a paragraph when a linked style is applied, the style will apply font formatting only.

By default, the Normal style is applied to new Word documents. Normal style is a paragraph style with specific font and paragraph formatting. If that style is not appropriate for a document you are developing, you can select another style from Word's style gallery. The most frequently accessed styles are shown in the Styles group on the Home tab (see Figure 2.26). To apply a style to selected text or to an existing paragraph, select the text (or place the insertion point within the paragraph) and click a style in the Styles group on the Home tab. For even more style choice, click the Styles Dialog Box Launcher (see Figure 2.26) to display the Styles pane (see Figure 2.26) and click to select a style.

Styles group
Styles Dialog Box Launcher
Styles pane
Options
Show Preview
New Style

James Canyon Hot Air Balloon Festival

See the Canyon From On High!

May 25-26, 2016

The James Canyon Hot Air Balloon Festival, presented by New Mexico Explore Outdoors, welcomes more than 65 hot air balloonists from across the country. One of the largest free hot-air balloon festivals in the Southwest, the event features hot air balloon races, a key grab, tether rides, and our always well-attended Ballumination! Tour Point Shepherd Park, enjoy a free arts and crafts show, visit the multiple food vendors, and get up close with antique cars and tractors. As the sun

As for entertainment, you're in luck! Spread out your blanket, grab a cold drink, and enjoy a variety of live music daily, from country to rock and roll. With activities for the kids, shopping and entertainment for adults, and plenty of photo ops, this is a festival you won't want to miss!

This year's music acts include EZ Star, Black Dog, Rachel Mac, and the LLC Five Star Jazz Orchestra. Plenty of others will be on hand, as well. Stroll the park, visiting each live music stage, to enjoy just about any type of musical

FIGURE 2.26 Styles

STEP 3 ≫

To modify a style:

1. Click the Styles Dialog Box Launcher.
2. Point to a style in the Styles pane and click the arrow on the right.
3. Click Modify. The Modify Style dialog box displays (see Figure 2.27).
4. Change any font and paragraph formatting or click Format for even more choices.
5. Click *Add to the Styles gallery* if the style is one you are likely to use often.
6. Indicate whether the style should be available only in the current document, or in new documents based on the current template.
7. Click OK.

Modifying a style, or even creating a new style, affects only the current document, by default. However, you can cause the style to be available to all documents that are based on the current template when you select *New documents based on this template* in the Modify Style dialog box (see Figure 2.27). Unless you make that selection, however, the changes are not carried over to new documents you create or to others that you open. As an example, the specifications for the Title style are shown in Figure 2.27.

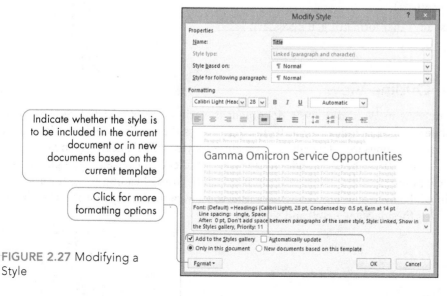

Indicate whether the style is to be included in the current document or in new documents based on the current template

Click for more formatting options

FIGURE 2.27 Modifying a Style

Use a Style Set

A style set is a combination of title, heading, and paragraph styles. Using a style set, you can format all of those elements in a document at one time. Style sets are included on the Design tab in the Document Formatting group (refer to Figure 2.23). Simply click a style set to apply the format combination to the document.

 TIP **Styles Versus Format Painter**

To copy formatting from one selection to another, you can certainly use Format Painter. Another alternative is to create a new style from the selection and apply it to additional text. Both processes seem to produce the same results. However, unlike changes made using Format Painter, a style remains available in both the current document and in other documents based on the same template, if you indicate that preference when you create the style. That way, the same formatting changes can be applied repeatedly in various documents or positions within the same document, even after a document is closed and reopened. Formatting changes made as a result of using Format Painter are not available later. Also, styles that indicate a hierarchy (such as Heading 1, Heading 2) can be used to prepare a table of contents or outline.

Create a New Style from Text

Having applied several formatting characteristics to text, you might want to repeat that formatting on other selections that are similar in purpose. For example, suppose you format a page title with a specific font size, font color, and bordering. Subsequent page titles should be formatted identically. You can select the formatted page title and create a new style based on the formatting of the selected text. Then simply select the next title to which the formatting should be applied and choose the newly created style name from the Styles group or from the Styles pane.

STEP 4>> To create a new style from existing text:

1. Select the text from which the new style should be created or click in a paragraph containing paragraph characteristics you want to include in the new style.
2. Click the Styles Dialog Box Launcher (refer to Figure 2.26) to open the Styles pane.
3. Click New Style, located in the bottom-left corner of the Styles pane (refer to Figure 2.26).
4. Enter a name for the new style. Do not use the name of an existing style.
5. Click the *Style type* arrow and select a style type (paragraph, character, or linked, among others).
6. Adjust any other formatting, if necessary.
7. Click OK.

Use the Outline View

The Outline view in Word displays a document in various levels of detail, according to heading styles applied in a document. Figure 2.28 shows the Outline view of a document in which major headings were formatted in Heading 1 style, with subheadings in Heading 2 style. You can modify the heading styles to suit your preference; however, if you plan to use Outline view to summarize a document, you must apply Word's heading styles (even if you have modified them) to your text. To select a level to view, perhaps only first-level headings, click All Levels (beside *Show Level*) and select a level.

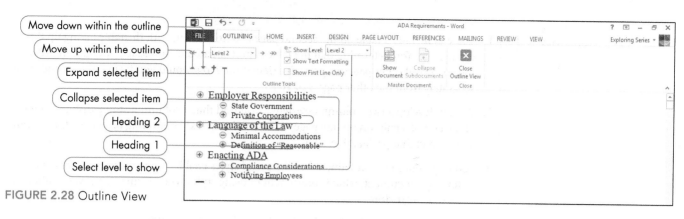

Move down within the outline
Move up within the outline
Expand selected item
Collapse selected item
Heading 2
Heading 1
Select level to show

FIGURE 2.28 Outline View

STEP 5 »

To collapse or expand a single heading, click the heading in Outline view and click + (to expand) or – (to collapse) on the Ribbon. For example, having clicked text formatted as Heading 1, click + to show any lower-level headings associated with the particular heading (refer to Figure 2.28). Text other than that associated with the selected heading will remain unaffected. As shown in Figure 2.28, you can move a heading (along with all associated sub-headings) up or down in the document. In Outline view, you can also drag the + or – beside a heading to move the entire group, including all sublevels, to another location.

In Print Layout view, you can quickly collapse everything except the section you want to work with. Point to a heading and click the small triangle that displays beside the heading (see Figure 2.29) to collapse or expand the following body text and sublevels. Collapsing text in that manner is a handy way to provide your readers with a summary.

Click to collapse view (or expand if already collapsed)

FIGURE 2.29 Expanding and Collapsing Detail

Use Outline view to glimpse or confirm a document's structure. Especially when developing lengthy reports, you will want to make sure headings are shown at the correct level of detail. A document shown in Outline view can also be easily converted to a PowerPoint presentation, with each level shown as a point on a slide. Also, a table of contents is automatically generated when you click *Table of Contents* on the References tab.

You can also quickly move through a document in Outline view, and you can restructure a document:

- With levels collapsed so that body text does not display, just click a heading to move to and change the view to Print Layout or another view. The document will expand, and the insertion point will be in the section identified by the heading you clicked. Using Outline view to move through a lengthy document can save a great deal of time because it is not necessary to page through a document looking for a particular section heading.

- Use Outline view to restructure a document. Simply drag and drop a heading to reposition it within a document, or use the Move Up or Move Down buttons. If subheadings are associated, they will move with the heading as well.

**Quick
Concepts** ✓

1. You will include a table on the second page of a document, with the table taking up the entire page. You determine that the table is best situated in landscape orientation, with the text on all other pages in portrait orientation. How would you format the second page separately from the other pages? *p. 164*

2. As you develop a two-column newsletter, you find that a column heading displays alone at the end of a column on one page, with remaining text continuing on the next. How can you correct that problem? *p. 165*

3. Although both Format Painter and the use of styles enable you to change the appearance of text in a document, what is the benefit of using styles when formatting several different areas of text? *p. 166*

4. How is the concept of styles related to the Outline view? *p. 168*

Hands-On Exercises

Watch the Video
for this Hands-
On Exercise!

MyITLab®
HOE2 Training

2 Document Formatting

The next step in preparing the photography newsletter for distribution is to apply document formatting to several areas of the document that will make it easier to read. By applying a theme and formatting the document in columns, you will add to the visual appeal. Using styles, you can ensure consistent formatting of document text. Finally, you will check the document's organization by viewing it in Outline view.

Skills covered: Select a Document Theme • Work with Sections and Format Text into Columns • Select and Modify Styles • Use a Style Set and Create a New Style • Use the Outline View

STEP 1 ≫ SELECT A DOCUMENT THEME

A document theme provides color and font coordination, simplifying your design task. You will apply a document theme to the newsletter as a simple way to ensure that yours is an attractive document with well-coordinated features. Refer to Figure 2.30 as you complete Step 1.

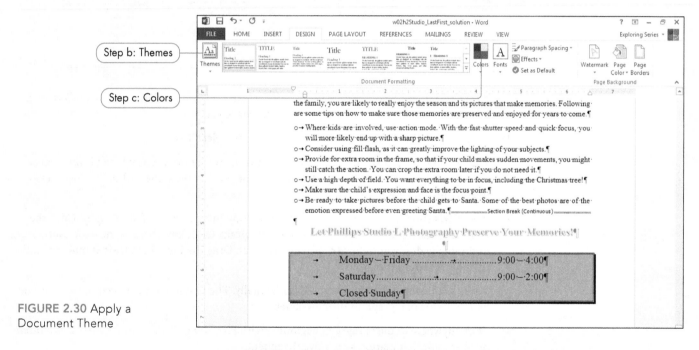

FIGURE 2.30 Apply a
Document Theme

a. Open *w02h1Studio_LastFirst* if you closed it at the end of Hands-On Exercise 1 and save it as **w02h2Studio_LastFirst**, changing *h1* to *h2*.

b. Press **Ctrl+Home**. Click the **DESIGN tab** and click **Themes** in the Document Formatting group. Select **Organic**.

   Note the color change applied to the second line of the document, *Courtesy of Phillips Studio L Photography*.

c. Click **Colors** in the Document Formatting group and select **Violet II**.

   The second line of the document, *Courtesy of Phillips Studio L Photography*, has changed colors because you selected a new color scheme within the theme. The table of studio hours on the last page of the document also changed colors.

d. Save the document.

STEP 2 » WORK WITH SECTIONS AND FORMAT TEXT INTO COLUMNS

The document should be formatted as a newsletter. Most often, newsletters display in columns, so you will apply columns to the newsletter. A few items, such as the newsletter heading and the store hours at the end of the document, should be centered horizontally across the page instead of within a column. Using sections, you will format those items differently from column text. Refer to Figure 2.31 as you complete Step 2.

FIGURE 2.31 Formatting in Columns

a. Press **Ctrl+Home**. Select most of the document text, beginning with *Courtesy of Phillips Studio L Photography* and ending with *before even greeting Santa.*

b. Click the **PAGE LAYOUT tab** and click **Columns**. Select **Two**.

   The selected text is formatted into two columns. A continuous section break is inserted at the beginning of the document, after the document title, and at the end of the document (before the final line).

c. Press **Ctrl+Home**. Click anywhere on the line containing *Basics of Photography*. Click the **HOME tab** and click **Center** in the Paragraph group. Click anywhere in the paragraph beginning with *If you enjoy taking digital pictures*. Drag the **First Line Indent marker** on the ruler back to the left margin.

   The title of the newsletter is centered horizontally. The first line indent is removed from the first multiline paragraph in the newsletter.

d. Click anywhere in the paragraph beginning with *First things first*. Drag the **First Line Indent marker** to the left margin to remove the indent.

e. Click the **VIEW tab** and click **Multiple Pages** in the Zoom group. Scroll down to view all pages, getting an idea of how text is positioned on all pages. Click **100%** in the Zoom group.

f. Save the document.

STEP 3 » SELECT AND MODIFY STYLES

The newsletter is improving in appearance, but you note that the headings (Camera, Composition, etc.) are not as evident as they should be. Also, some headings are subordinate to others, and should be identified accordingly. You will apply heading styles to headings in the newsletter. Refer to Figure 2.32 as you complete Step 3.

Step d: Format Painter

Troubleshooting: Spin down arrow

Step e: Styles Dialog Box Launcher

Step e: Underline style

Step e: Heading 1 arrow

Step e: Format

FIGURE 2.32 Working with Styles

a. Select the text *Camera Body* on the first page of the newsletter. Click the **HOME tab** and select **Heading 1** in the Styles group. On the same page, in the column on the right, select *Lens* and apply **Heading 1**. Select *Composition* and apply **Heading 1**.

b. Apply **Heading 1** to *Juxtaposition*, *Common Photography Mistakes*, and *Holiday Photography* on the second and third pages of the newsletter.

c. Select *Rule of Thirds* on the first page and press and hold **Ctrl** on the keyboard as you also select *Depth of Field*, *Becoming the Subject*, *Shooting from Below*, and *Shooting from Above* on the second page. Release Ctrl. Click **Heading 2** in the Styles group on the HOME tab. Do not deselect text.

d. Double-click **Format Painter** in the Clipboard group. Select *Dark Photos* on the third page. Select *Blurry Images*. Press **Esc**. Select *Blurry Images Due to Focus* on the third page. Click **Heading 3** in the Styles group. Select *Blurry Images Due to Camera Shake* on the third page and apply **Heading 3** style.

> **TROUBLESHOOTING:** If you do not see Heading 3 in the Styles group, click the More arrow beside the styles in the Styles group and select Heading 3.

Using Format Painter, you copied the format of the Heading 2 style to a few headings. Headings throughout the newsletter are formatted according to their hierarchy, with major headings in Heading 1 style and others in correct order beneath the first level.

e. Click the **Styles Dialog Box Launcher** to display the Styles pane. Point to *Heading 1* and click the **Heading 1 arrow**. Click **Modify**. Click **Format** in the Modify Style dialog box and click **Font**. Click the **Underline style arrow** and click the second underline style (double underline). Click **OK**. Click **OK** again.

You modified Heading 1 style to include a double underline. Every heading formatted in Heading 1 style is automatically updated to include an underline.

f. Save the document.

STEP 4 ›› USE A STYLE SET AND CREATE A NEW STYLE

Although you are pleased with the heading styles you selected in the previous step, you want to explore Word's built-in style sets to determine if another style might be more attractive. You will also create a style for all bulleted paragraphs in the newsletter. Refer to Figure 2.33 as you complete Step 4.

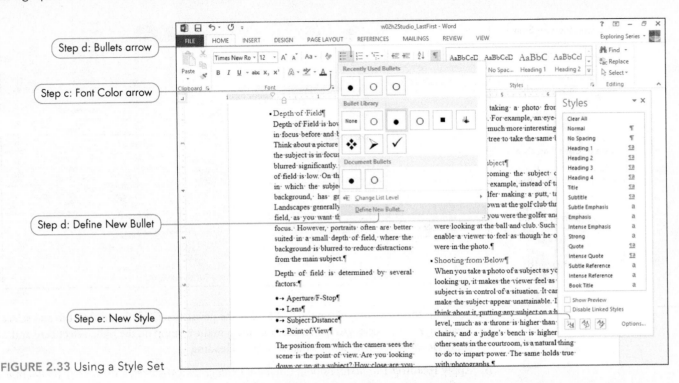

FIGURE 2.33 Using a Style Set

Callouts in figure:
- Step d: Bullets arrow
- Step c: Font Color arrow
- Step d: Define New Bullet
- Step e: New Style

a. Press **Ctrl+Home**. Click the **DESIGN tab**. Point to any style set in the Document Formatting group, without clicking, to view the effect on the document. Specifically, see how the previewed style affects the *Lens* heading shown in the right column. Click the **More arrow** beside the style sets and select **Lines (Simple)** (second row, third column under *Built-In*).

   When you apply a style set, headings are formatted according to the style settings, overriding any formatting characteristics you might have set earlier.

b. Click the **VIEW tab** and click **One Page** in the Zoom group to view the first page.

   Note the format of the major headings—*Camera Body*, *Lens*, and *Composition*—has been modified, removing the underline you set earlier, and now displays the format of the Lines (Simple) style set.

c. Click **100%** in the Zoom group. Select the second line in the document, *Courtesy of Phillips Studio L Photography*. Click the **HOME tab**. Click the **Font Color arrow** and select **Plum, Accent 1, Darker 25%** (fifth row, fifth column).

   You select a coordinating text color for the second line in the document.

d. Scroll to the second page and click anywhere in the bulleted paragraph containing the text *Aperture/F-Stop*. Click the **Bullets arrow** and select a solid round black bullet. Click the **Bullets arrow** and click **Define New Bullet**. Click **Font**. Click the **Font color arrow** and select **Plum, Accent 1, Darker 25%**. Click **OK**. Click **OK** again.

   Having modified the format of one bulleted item, you will create a style from that format to apply to all other bulleted items in the document.

e. Click **New Style** in the Styles pane. Type **Bullet Paragraph** in the **Name box** and click **OK**.

   You should see a new style in the Styles pane titled *Bullet Paragraph*.

f. Select the three bulleted paragraphs below *Aperture/F-Stop* and click **Bullet Paragraph** in the Styles pane. Scroll to the third page, select the three bulleted paragraphs at the bottom of the right column, and then click **Bullet Paragraph** in the Styles pane. Scroll to the fourth page, select the three bulleted paragraphs at the top of the page (in both columns), and then apply the **Bullet Paragraph style**. Close the Styles pane.

g. Save the document.

STEP 5 ≫ USE THE OUTLINE VIEW

The newsletter spans four pages, with headings identifying various levels of detail. You will check to make sure you have formatted headings according to the correct hierarchy. To do so, you will view the newsletter in Outline view. Refer to Figure 2.34 as you complete Step 5.

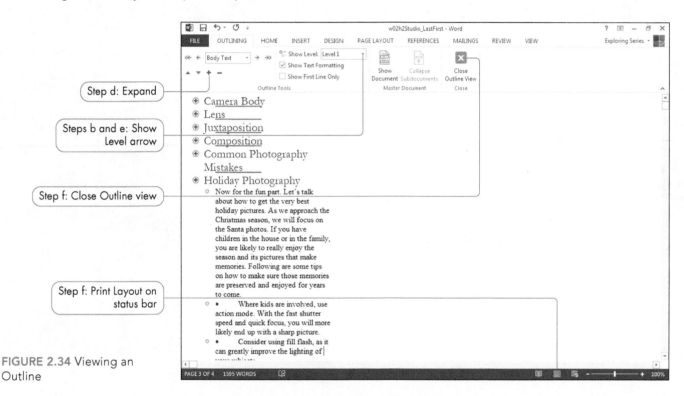

FIGURE 2.34 Viewing an Outline

a. Press **Ctrl+Home**. Click the **VIEW tab** and click **Outline** in the Views group. Scroll down slightly to see the first major heading (with a + on the left)—*Camera Body*.

b. Click the **Show Level arrow** and click **Level 3**.

You formatted headings in the newsletter as headings, in three levels of detail. Because you did so, you are able to view the document structure according to the hierarchy of headings.

c. Position the pointer on the + that precedes *Blurry Images Due to Camera Shake* (so the pointer becomes a four-headed arrow). Drag the heading above the preceding level (*Blurry Images Due to Focus*). When you see a small black triangle above the preceding level, release the mouse button to reposition the section.

d. Using the same procedure as in step c, move the *Juxtaposition* section above *Composition*. Click **Expand** in the Outline Tools group to view the content of the *Juxtaposition* section.

e. Click the **Show Level arrow** and select **Level 1** to display Level 1 headings only. Select *Holiday Photography* and click **Expand** in the Outline Tools group.

The *Holiday Photography* section is expanded. Other Level 1 headings remain collapsed.

f. Click **Close Outline View** in the Close group on the Outlining tab. If both columns do not display, click **Print Layout** on the status bar.

g. Save the document. Keep the document open if you plan to continue with the next Hands-On Exercise. If not, close the document and exit Word.

Objects

An **object** is an item that can be individually selected and manipulated within a document. Objects, such as pictures, text boxes, tables, and other graphic types are often included in documents to add interest or convey a point (see Figure 2.35). Newsletters typically include pictures and other decorative elements to liven up what might otherwise be a somewhat mundane document. As you work with a document, you can conduct a quick search for appropriate pictures and graphics online—all without ever leaving your document workspace.

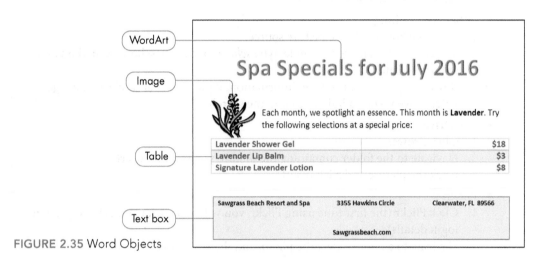

FIGURE 2.35 Word Objects

One thing all objects have in common is that they can be selected and worked with independently of surrounding text. You can resize them, add special effects, and even move them to other locations within the document. Word 2013 includes convenient text wrapping controls so that you can quickly adjust the way text wraps around an object. With Live Layout and alignment guides, you can easily line up pictures and other diagrams with existing text.

In this section, you will explore the use of objects in a Word document. Specifically, you will learn to include pictures, searching for them online as well as obtaining them from your own storage device. You will learn to create impressive text displays with WordArt. A text box is a bordered area you can use to draw attention to specific text. You will create text boxes, as well.

Inserting and Formatting Objects

Objects can be collected from the Web or from a storage device, as with pictures and illustrations. You can create other objects, such as WordArt, text boxes, charts, and tables. When you insert an object, it is automatically selected so that you can manipulate it independently of surrounding text. A contextual tab displays on the Ribbon with options related to the selected object, making it easy to quickly modify and enhance an object.

Insert a Picture

A **picture** is a graphic image, such as a drawing or photograph. You can insert pictures in a document from your own library of digital pictures you have saved, or you can access Microsoft's abundant picture through Bing Image Search. From within a document, you can conduct a Web search to locate even more picture possibilities. Inserting a picture is only the first step in the process. Once incorporated into your document, a picture can be resized and modified with special bordering and artistic effects. Other options enable you to easily align a picture with surrounding text, rotate or crop it, if necessary, and even recolor it so it blends in with an existing color scheme.

You might find it necessary to include a picture within an open document. If you do not have a picture already saved on your computer, you can go online to locate a suitable image. Without closing or minimizing the document, and without opening a browser to search the Web, you can immediately peruse Office.com, Bing Image Search, OneDrive, and even your Flickr account for a picture. It is not necessary to obtain an image from the Web and save it to a storage device before inserting it in the document. The picture is inserted directly from the Web, after which you can resize and reposition it.

To insert an online picture, click to place the insertion point in the document in the location where the picture is to be inserted. Click the Insert tab and click Online Pictures (see Figure 2.36) to insert a picture from:

- Office.com or Bing:
    1. Click the box beside the picture source.
    2. Type a search term (for example, type *school* to identify school-related images) and press Enter.
    3. Review any relevant licensing information, if presented, and select an image. Alternatively, click a link to expand the search.

- OneDrive:
    1. Click Browse.
    2. Navigate to the folder containing the picture you want to insert.
    3. Click the picture and click Insert.

- Flickr:
    1. Click Flickr (the first time using Flickr, you will first click Connect and provide login details).
    2. Navigate to a photo, select the photo, and then click Insert.

FIGURE 2.36 Inserting an Online Picture

 Insert a Screenshot

When describing a process, you might find occasion to include a screenshot of a computer display in a document. You can capture a screenshot and insert it in a document as an object. With the item to capture displayed on the computer screen, open the document in which you plan to place the screenshot. Click the Insert tab and click Screenshot in the Illustrations group. Click Screen Clipping. The document is removed from view, leaving the original screen display. Drag to select any part of the screen display. The document displays again, with the selection included as an object.

STEP 1 >> If you enjoy taking digital pictures, you most likely have a great many of your pictures saved to a storage device you can access with a computer. Suppose you are using Word to prepare a flyer or newsletter. In that case, you might want to insert one or more of your pictures into the document. Inserting pictures from a storage device is a simple process. To do so:

1. Position the insertion point in the document where the picture is to be inserted.
2. Click the INSERT tab.
3. Click Pictures in the Illustrations group (refer to Figure 2.36).
4. Navigate to the folder in which your photos are stored.
5. Select a photo to insert.
6. Click Insert.

Resize, Move, and Align a Picture

A new Ribbon tab, with one or more associated tabs beneath it, is added to the Ribbon when you insert and select an object. The new Ribbon tab, called a *contextual tab*, includes commands relevant to the type of object selected. As shown in Figure 2.37, the Picture Tools Format tab includes settings and selections related to the inserted picture.

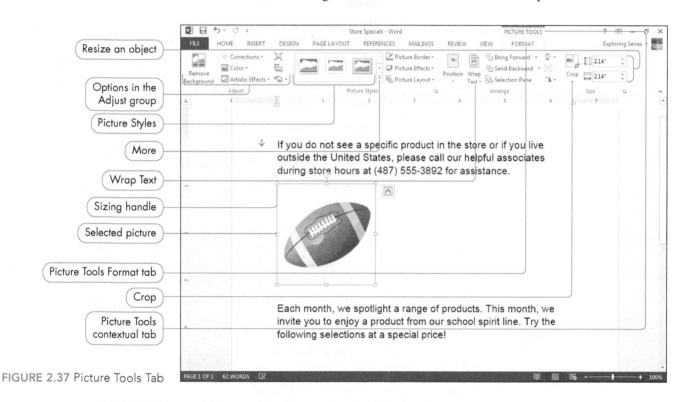

FIGURE 2.37 Picture Tools Tab

STEP 2 >> Although an inserted picture is considered a separate object, you will want to position it so that it flows well with document text and does not appear to be a separate unit. One way to make that happen is to wrap text around the picture. The Format tab includes an option to wrap text around a selected picture (refer to Figure 2.37). You can select from the text wrapping styles shown in Table 2.3 when you click Wrap Text. You can also choose to allow the object to move with text as text is added or deleted, or you can keep the object in the same place on the page, regardless of text changes.

Word 2013 includes a new feature that simplifies text wrapping around an object—Layout Options. Located next to a selected object, the Layout Options control (see Figure 2.38) includes the same selections shown in Table 2.3. The close proximity of the control to the selected object makes it easy to quickly adjust text wrapping.

FIGURE 2.38 Layout Options

TABLE 2.3	Text Wrap Options
Type	**Effect**
In Line with Text	The image is part of the line of text in which it is inserted. Typically, text wraps above and below the object.
Square	Text wraps on all sides of an object, following an invisible square.
Tight	Text follows the shape of the object, but does not overlap the object.
Through	Text follows the shape, filling any open spaces in the shape.
Top and Bottom	Text flows above and below the borders of the object
Behind Text	The object is positioned behind text. Both the object and text are visible (unless the fill color exactly matches the text color).
In Front of Text	The object is positioned in front of text, often obscuring the text.

New to Word 2013 are *Live Layout* and *alignment guides*. **Live Layout** enables you to watch text flow around an object as you move it, so you can position the object exactly as you want it. **Alignment guides** are horizontal or vertical green bars that appear as you drag an object, so you can line up an object with text or with another object. The green alignment guide shown in Figure 2.39 helps align the football object with paragraph text.

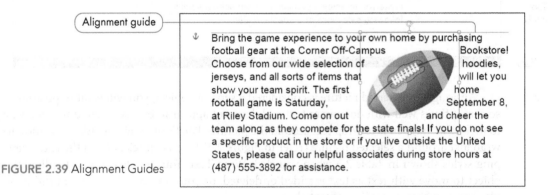

FIGURE 2.39 Alignment Guides

Often, a picture is inserted in a size that is too large or too small for your purposes. To resize a picture, you can drag a corner *sizing handle*. You should never resize a picture by dragging a center sizing handle, as doing so would skew the picture. You can also resize a picture by adjusting settings in the Size group of the Picture Tools Format tab (refer to Figure 2.37).

Modify a Picture

The Picture Tools Format tab (refer to Figure 2.37) includes options for modifying a picture. You can apply a picture style or effect, as well as add a picture border, from selections in the Picture Styles group. Click More (refer to Figure 2.37) to view a gallery of picture styles. As you point to a style, the style is shown in Live Preview, but the style is not applied until you click it. Options in the Adjust group (refer to Figure 2.37) simplify changing a color scheme, applying creative artistic effects, and even adjusting the brightness, contrast, and sharpness of an image.

STEP 3 >> If a picture contains more detail than is necessary, you can *crop* it, which is the process of trimming edges that you do not want to display. The Crop tool is located on the Picture Tools Format tab (refer to Figure 2.37). Even though cropping enables you to adjust the amount of a picture that displays, it does not actually delete the portions that are cropped out. Therefore, you can later recover parts of the picture, if necessary. Cropping a picture does not reduce the file size of the picture and the Word document in which it displays.

Other common adjustments to a picture include contrast and/or brightness. Adjusting *contrast* increases or decreases the difference in dark and light areas of the image. Adjusting *brightness* lightens or darkens the overall image. These adjustments often are made on a picture taken with a digital camera in poor lighting or if a picture is too bright or dull to match other objects in your document. The Brightness/Contrast adjustment is available when you click Corrections in the Adjust group on the Format tab (refer to Figure 2.37).

Insert a Text Box

Text in a *text box* is bordered, sometimes shaded, and set apart from other text in a document. Depending on the outline selected, a border might not even be visible, so it is not always possible to identify a text box in a document. In most cases, however, you will find a text box as a boxed area of text—usually providing additional details or drawing attention to an important point. A text box could contain a *pull quote*, which is a short text excerpt that is reinforced from a report, or a text box could be used as a banner for a newsletter. Place any text you want to draw attention to or set apart from the body of a document in a text box. Figure 2.40 shows a simple text box that provides business information. Remember that a text box is an object. As such, you can select, move, resize, and modify it, much as you learned you could do with pictures in the preceding sections of this chapter. Layout Options enable you to wrap text around a text box, and alignment guides assist with positioning a text box within existing text.

TIP Removing Background

Word 2013 makes it easy to remove the background or portions of a picture you do not want to keep. When you select a picture and click the Remove Background tool in the Adjust group on the Format tab, Word creates a marquee selection area in the picture that determines the *background*, or area to be removed, and the *foreground*, or area to be kept. Word identifies the background selection with magenta coloring. Using tools on the Background Removal tab, you can mark areas to keep or mark additional areas to remove. Click Keep Changes to remove the background.

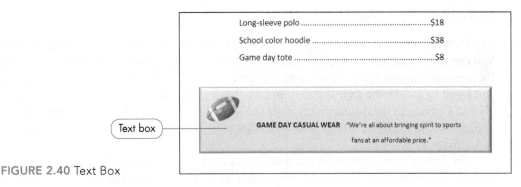

Long-sleeve polo $18

School color hoodie $38

Game day tote $8

GAME DAY CASUAL WEAR "We're all about bringing spirit to sports fans at an affordable price."

Text box →

FIGURE 2.40 Text Box

STEP 4 ›› To insert a text box:

1. Click the INSERT tab.
2. Click Text Box in the Text group.
3. Click Draw Text Box or select a predefined text box style (see Figure 2.41).
4. Drag to draw a box (unless you selected a predefined text box style, in which case, the text box will be automatically drawn). The dimensions of the text box are not that critical, as you can adjust the size using the Ribbon.
5. Type text in the text box.

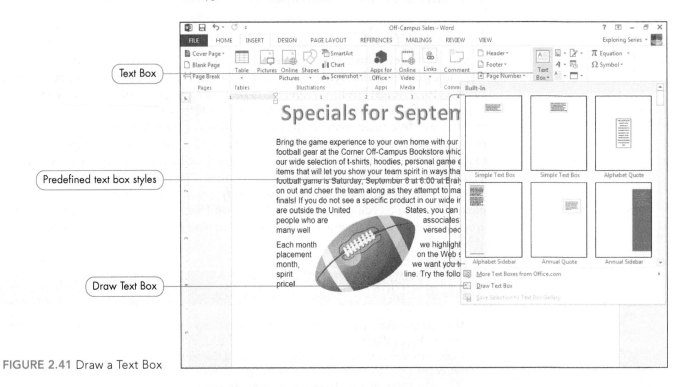

Text Box →

Predefined text box styles →

Draw Text Box →

FIGURE 2.41 Draw a Text Box

TIP **Formatting Text in a Text Box**

Before formatting text in a text box, you should select the text to be affected. To do so, drag to select the text to be formatted. Or, if you want to select *all* text, you might appreciate learning a shortcut. You can select all of the text when you click the dashed border surrounding the text box (when the pointer is a small four-headed shape). The dashed line should become solid, indicating that all text is selected. At that point, any formatting selections you make related to text are applied to all text in the text box.

Resize, Move, and Modify a Text Box

The Drawing Tools Format tab includes a multitude of options for adding color, background, and style to a text box. In addition, you can select from predefined text styles or design your own text fill, outline, and text effects. Positioning a text box is a simple task, with text wrap options available to arrange text evenly around the text box. You can even indicate the exact height and width of a text box using the Format tab (see Figure 2.42).

Change text box size

Shape styles, fills, outlines, and effects

FIGURE 2.42 Modify a Text Box

One way to resize a text box is to drag a sizing handle. Although not as precise as using the Size group on the Format tab to indicate an exact measurement, dragging to resize a text box is done quickly. Depending on how you want to resize the object, you can either drag a corner handle (to resize two sides at once) or a center handle (to adjust the size in only one direction). Although you should not drag a center handle when resizing a *picture* (because doing so will skew the picture), dragging a center handle in a *text box* is an appropriate way to resize a text box.

You can be as creative as you like when designing a text box. Options on the Format tab enable you to add color and definition to a text box with shape fill and outline selections, or select from a gallery of shape styles. Select text within a text box and select an alignment option on the Home tab to left align, right align, center, or justify text.

You can move a text box by dragging it from one area to another. You should first select or confirm a text wrapping option. Text will then wrap automatically around the text box as you move it. Position the pointer on a border of the text box so it appears as a black, four-headed arrow. Drag to reposition the text box. As you drag the box, green alignment guides assist in positioning it neatly. The Format tab includes a Position option in the Arrange group that enables you to align the text box in various ways within existing text.

Insert WordArt

WordArt is a feature that modifies text to include special effects, including colors, shadows, gradients, and 3-D effects (see Figure 2.43). It is a quick way to format text so that it is vibrant and eye-catching. Of course, WordArt is not appropriate for all documents, especially more conservative business correspondence, but it can give life to newsletters, flyers, and other more informal projects, especially when applied to headings and titles. WordArt is well suited for single lines, such as document headings, where the larger print and text design draws attention and adds style to a document title. However, it is not appropriate for body text, because a WordArt object is managed independently of surrounding text and cannot be formatted as a document (with specific margins, headers, footers, etc.). In addition, if WordArt were incorporated into body text, the more ornate text design would adversely affect the readability of the document.

Off-Campus School Spirit Sale

WordArt

We welcome the opportunity to serve you, especially during the football season at the university. Our store is filled with special sales this time of year.

FIGURE 2.43 WordArt

You can format existing text as WordArt, or you can insert new WordArt text into a document. WordArt is considered an object; as such, the preceding discussion related to positioning pictures and text boxes applies to WordArt as well. Also, Live Layout and alignment guides are available to facilitate ease of positioning, and you can select a text wrapping style with layout options.

STEP 5 >>

To format existing text as WordArt:

1. Select text to be formatted.
2. Click the INSERT tab.
3. Click WordArt in the Text group.
4. Select a WordArt style.

To insert new text as WordArt:

1. Place the insertion point at the point where WordArt should appear.
2. Click the INSERT tab.
3. Click WordArt in the Text group.
4. Select a WordArt style.
5. Type text.

Depending upon the purpose of a document and its intended audience, objects such as pictures, text boxes, and WordArt can help convey a message and add interest. As you learn to incorporate objects visually within a document so that they appear to flow seamlessly within existing text, you will find it easy to create attractive, informative documents that contain an element of design apart from simple text.

Quick
Concepts

1. How would you determine what type of text wrapping to use when positioning a picture in a document? *p. 177*

2. Describe two methods to modify the height and width of a picture. *p. 181*

3. Although a text box can appear similar to text in a document that has simply been bordered and shaded, a text box is actually an object. What does that fact tell you about a text box that makes it very different from simple shaded text? *p. 181*

4. Why is WordArt most often used to format headings or titles, and not text in the body of a document? *p. 183*

Hands-On Exercises

3 Objects

You will add interest to the newsletter by including pictures that illustrate points, a text box with business information, and WordArt that livens up the newsletter heading.

Skills covered: Insert a Picture • Resize, Move, and Align a Picture • Modify a Picture • Insert and Modify a Text Box • Insert WordArt

---

STEP 1 》 INSERT A PICTURE

You will include pictures in the newsletter to represent photographs shot from various angles, as well as holiday graphics. Pictures will be formatted with appropriate picture styles and effects and positioned within existing text. Refer to Figure 2.44 as you complete Step 1.

FIGURE 2.44 Inserting and Rotating Pictures

a. Open *w02h2Studio_LastFirst* if you closed it at the end of Hands-On Exercise 2 and save it as **w02h3Studio_LastFirst**, changing *h2* to *h3*.

b. Scroll to the second page of the document and click to place the insertion point before the words *Depth of Field is how much of the image*. Click the **INSERT tab** and click **Pictures** in the Illustrations group. Navigate to the location of your student data files and double-click *w02h3Kayak*.

 The picture is inserted, but must be rotated.

c. With the picture selected (surrounded by a border and sizing handles), click **Rotate Objects** in the Arrange group on the PICTURE TOOLS FORMAT tab and click **Rotate Right 90°**. Click outside the picture to deselect it.

> **TROUBLESHOOTING:** If you do not see Rotate Objects or the Format tab, click the picture to select it. Then click the Format tab, if necessary.

d. Scroll to the third page and click to place the insertion point before *The most common reason for a blurred image* under the *Blurry Images Due to Focus* heading. Click the **INSERT tab**, click **Pictures** in the Illustrations group, and then double-click *w02h3Float* in your student data files. If necessary, rotate the picture to the right. Click outside the picture to deselect it.

> **TROUBLESHOOTING:** The placement of the picture will vary, so it is OK if it is not positioned directly below the *Blurry Images Due to Focus* heading. You will move it later.

e. Scroll to the *Holiday Photography* section and click to place the insertion point before *Now for the fun part*. Click the **INSERT tab**. Click **Online Pictures** in the Illustrations group. In the box beside Bing Image Search, type **Ski** and press **Enter**. Select the picture shown in Figure 2.45b (or one that is very similar). Click **Insert**.

The picture is placed within or very near the *Holiday Photography* section. You will reposition it and resize it later.

f. Save the document.

STEP 2 ≫ RESIZE, MOVE, AND ALIGN A PICTURE

The pictures you inserted are a bit large, so you will resize them. You will also position them within the column and select an appropriate text wrapping style. Refer to Figure 2.45 as you complete Step 2.

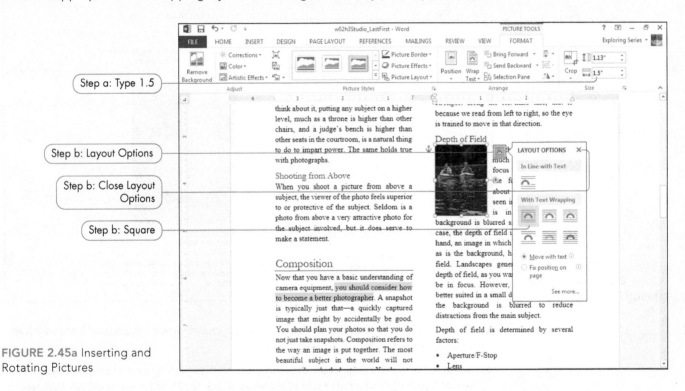

FIGURE 2.45a Inserting and Rotating Pictures

FIGURE 2.45b Inserting and Rotating Pictures

a. Scroll up and click to select the picture near the *Depth of Field* section. Click in the **Width box** in the Size group on the FORMAT tab and type **1.5**. Press **Enter**.

By default, the *Lock aspect ratio* setting is on, which means that when you change a dimension—either width or height—of a picture, the other dimension is automatically adjusted as well. To confirm, or deselect the Lock aspect ratio, click the **Size Dialog Box Launcher** and adjust the setting in the Layout dialog box. Unless you deselect the setting, you cannot change both width and height manually, as that would skew the picture.

b. Click **Layout Options** (beside the selected picture) and select **Square** (first selection under *With Text Wrapping*). Close Layout Options. Check the placement of the image with that shown in Figure 2.45a, and adjust if necessary.

c. Scroll down and select the second picture near the *Blurry Images Due to Focus* heading. Change the text wrapping to **Square** and change the width to **1.5**. Close Layout Options. If necessary, drag the picture (when the pointer is a four-headed arrow) so it displays immediately beneath the section heading.

d. Scroll down and select the ski picture in, or near, the *Holiday Photography* section. Change text wrapping to **Tight**, change the width to **1.5**, close Layout Options, and then drag to position the picture as shown in Figure 2.45b. Words may not wrap exactly as shown in Figure 2.45b, but they should be approximately as shown.

e. Save the document.

STEP 3 ›› MODIFY A PICTURE

You will apply a picture style and picture effects to the pictures included in the newsletter. You will also crop a picture to remove unnecessary detail. Refer to Figure 2.46 as you complete Step 3.

FIGURE 2.46a Modifying a Picture

FIGURE 2.46b Modifying a Picture

a. Select the picture in the *Depth of Field* section. Click the **FORMAT tab**, if necessary. Click **Crop** in the Size group on the FORMAT tab. Be sure to click *Crop*, not the *Crop arrow*. Drag the crop indicator in the bottom center of the photograph up slightly to remove some of the water, as shown in Figure 2.46a. Click **Crop** to toggle the selection off. If necessary, drag to position the picture as shown in Figure 2.46b.

> **TROUBLESHOOTING:** If the picture becomes skewed as you drag, instead of simply shading the water to remove, you are dragging a sizing handle instead of the crop indicator. Only drag when the pointer is a thick black T, not a two-headed arrow. Click Undo and repeat the crop.

b. If necessary, click to select the picture in the *Depth of Field* section. Click **More** beside the Picture Styles gallery in the Picture Styles group. Select **Soft Edge Rectangle**.

> **TROUBLESHOOTING:** If you do not see options related to the picture, make sure the picture is selected and click the Format tab, if necessary.

c. Select the picture in the *Blurry Images Due to Focus* section. Click **Corrections** in the Adjust group on the FORMAT tab. Select **Brightness: 0% (Normal), Contrast: +20%** (fourth row, third column under *Brightness/Contrast*).

You used Word's image editing feature to change brightness and contrast.

d. Select the ski picture. Click **Remove Background** in the Adjust group on the FORMAT tab. Wait a few seconds until the background is shaded in magenta. Click **Keep Changes**. Deselect the picture.

e. Save the document.

STEP 4 ≫ INSERT AND MODIFY A TEXT BOX

By placing text in a text box, you can draw attention to information you want your readers to notice. You will insert a text box, including the studio's contact information, near the beginning of the document. You will then modify the text to coordinate with other page elements. Refer to Figure 2.47 as you complete Step 4.

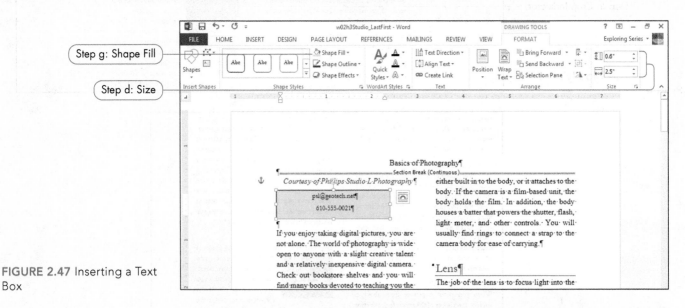

FIGURE 2.47 Inserting a Text Box

a. Press **Ctrl+Home**. If nonprinting characters do not display, click **Show/Hide** in the Paragraph group on the HOME tab.

b. Click the **INSERT tab** and click **Text Box** in the Text group. Click **Draw Text Box**. Point to the blank paragraph mark below *Courtesy of Phillips Studio L Photography* and drag to draw a small box. The dimensions are not important, as you will resize the text box later.

A small text box is drawn in the document.

c. Click **Layout Options** (beside the text box) and select **Top and Bottom** (second row, first column under *Text Wrapping*). Close Layout Options.

Text wraps above and below the text box.

d. Click the **Height box** in the Size group on the FORMAT tab and type **0.6**. Click the Width box and type **2.5**. Press **Enter**.

e. Click in the text box, if necessary, to position the insertion point. Type **psl@geotech.net** and press **Enter**. Type **610-555-0021**. Right-click the underlined e-mail link in the text box and select **Remove Hyperlink**.

f. Click the dashed line surrounding the text box to make it solid, so that all text in the text box is selected (although it is not shaded). Click the **HOME tab** and click **Center** in the Paragraph group.

All text is centered in the text box.

g. Click the **FORMAT tab**. Click **Shape Fill** in the Shape Styles group. Select **Plum, Accent 1, Lighter 80%** (second row, fifth column).

The text box background is shaded to match the document theme.

h. Position the pointer near a border of the text box so that the pointer appears as a four-headed arrow. Drag to the left edge of the column, until the green alignment guide indicates the text box is aligned at the left edge of the column. Release the mouse button. The text box should appear as shown in Figure 2.47.

i. Save the document.

STEP 5 ›› INSERT WORDART

The newsletter is near completion, but you need to work with the heading—*Basics of Photography*. You will format the heading with WordArt to add some visual appeal. Refer to Figure 2.48 as you complete Step 5.

FIGURE 2.48 Inserting and Rotating Pictures

a. Select *Basics of Photography* on the first line of the newsletter, including the following paragraph mark. Be careful not to select the Section Break indicator following the paragraph mark. Click the **INSERT tab** and click **WordArt** in the Text group. Select **Fill – Plum, Accent 1, Shadow** (first row, second column).

TROUBLESHOOTING: If you do not see a Section Break indicator, click Show/Hide in the Paragraph group on the Home tab.

The heading is formatted in WordArt, in a shade that coordinates with other text formatting in the newsletter.

b. Click **Layout Options** and click **Top and Bottom**. Close Layout Options.

c. Click outside the WordArt object to deselect it. Click the **FILE tab** and click **Print**. The first page shows in preview in the right pane (refer to Figure 2.48). Click **Next Page** (at the bottom of the preview page) to move to the next page.

d. Save and close the file, and submit the file based on your instructor's directions.

Chapter Objectives Review

After reading this chapter, you have accomplished the following objectives:

1. **Apply font attributes.**
   - Select font options: Font options include serif or sans serif font, as well as monospaced or proportional font. The Font group on the Home tab includes font selections.
   - Change text appearance: Format characters by applying bold, italics, underline, font color, text highlighting, and text effects.

2. **Format a paragraph.**
   - Select paragraph alignment: Align paragraphs to be left or right aligned, centered, or justified.
   - Select line and paragraph spacing: Line spacing refers to the amount of space between lines within a paragraph, whereas paragraph spacing is concerned with the amount of space between paragraphs.
   - Select indents: Options for indenting paragraphs include left indent, right indent, hanging indent, and first line indent.
   - Set tabs: Use tabs to arrange text in columns, including leaders if desired.
   - Apply borders and shading: Draw attention to selected paragraphs when you add borders and shading.
   - Create bulleted and numbered lists: Itemized lists can be set apart from other text with bullets, while sequential lists are often formatted with numbers.

3. **Format a document.**
   - Select a document theme: Use a theme to create a color-coordinated document, with page elements based on themed settings.
   - Work with sections: Divide a document into sections, so that each area can be formatted independently of others.
   - Format text into columns: Some documents, such as newsletters, are formatted in columns.

4. **Apply styles.**
   - Select and modify styles: Styles enable you to apply identical formatting to page features, such as headings. When a style is modified, changes apply to all text formatted in that style.
   - Use a style set: Select a style set to quickly format page elements, such as headers and paragraph text.
   - Create a new style from text: Format text and create a style from the text so that formatting characteristics can be easily applied to other text in the document.
   - Use the Outline view: Expand and collapse sections, view document structure, and easily rearrange document sections in Outline view.

5. **Insert and format objects.**
   - Insert a picture: Insert pictures from online sources or from a storage device connected to your computer.
   - Resize, move, and align a picture: Reposition objects easily using Live Layout and alignment guides. You can also resize objects and wrap text around objects.
   - Modify a picture: Apply a picture style or effect, adjust the color, contrast, and brightness of a picture, and crop a picture to modify a picture's appearance.
   - Insert a text box: Include text in a bordered area when you insert a text box. You can format a text box with shape styles and effects, and you can align text within a text box.
   - Resize, move, and modify a text box: As an object, a text box can be moved, resized, and modified with options on the Format tab.
   - Insert WordArt: A WordArt object displays text with special effects, such as color, size, gradient, and 3-D appearance.

Key Terms Matching

Match the key terms with their definitions. Write the key term letter by the appropriate numbered definition.

a. Alignment guide
b. Border
c. Bulleted list
d. Column
e. Document theme
f. First line indent
g. Font
h. Indent
i. Line spacing
j. Live Layout

k. Object
l. Paragraph spacing
m. Picture
n. Section break
o. Sizing handles
p. Style
q. Style set
r. Tab
s. Text box
t. WordArt

1. _____ An item, such as a picture or text box, that can be individually selected and manipulated. **p. 177**

2. _____ The small circles and squares that appear around a selected object and enable you to adjust its size. **p. 180**

3. _____ A list of points that is not sequential. **p. 155**

4. _____ A feature that modifies text to include special effects, such as color, shadow, gradient, and 3-D appearance. **p. 183**

5. _____ The vertical space between the lines in a paragraph. **p. 151**

6. _____ A typeface or complete set of characters. **p. 144**

7. _____ The horizontal or vertical green bar that appears as you move an object, assisting with lining up an object. **p. 180**

8. _____ Marks the location to indent only the first line in a paragraph. **p. 151**

9. _____ A named collection of formatting characteristics that can be applied to characters or paragraphs. **p. 166**

10. _____ A combination of title, heading, and paragraph styles that can be used to format all of those elements at one time. **p. 168**

11. _____ A format that separates document text into side-by-side vertical blocks, often used in newsletters. **p. 165**

12. _____ A marker that specifies the position for aligning text, sometimes including a leader. **p. 153**

13. _____ The amount of space before or after a paragraph. **p. 158**

14. _____ A feature that enables you to watch text flow around an object as you move the object. **p. 180**

15. _____ A setting associated with the way a paragraph is distanced from one or more margins. **p. 149**

16. _____ An indicator that divides a document into parts, enabling different formatting in each section. **p. 163**

17. _____ A boxed object that can be bordered and shaded, providing space for text. **p. 181**

18. _____ A line that surrounds a paragraph or a page. **p. 154**

19. _____ A graphic file that is obtained from the Internet or a storage device. **p. 177**

20. _____ A unified set of design elements, including font style, color, and special effects, that is applied to an entire document. **p. 163**

Multiple Choice

1. How does a document theme differ from a style?

   (a) A theme applies an overall design to a document, with no requirement that any text is selected. A style applies formatting characteristics to selected text or to a current paragraph.

   (b) A theme applies color-coordinated design to selected page elements. A style applies formatting to an entire document.

   (c) A theme and a style are actually the same feature.

   (d) A theme applies font characteristics, whereas a style applies paragraph formatting.

2. To identify a series of sequential steps, you could use:

   (a) Outlining.

   (b) Bullets.

   (c) Tabs.

   (d) Numbering.

3. The feature that modifies text to include special effects, such as color, shadow, and gradients, is:

   (a) WordArt.

   (b) Themes.

   (c) Live Layout.

   (d) Text box.

4. If you have not selected text when you identify a shading color, what part of a document is shaded?

   (a) The paragraph in which the insertion point is located.

   (b) The entire document.

   (c) The currently displayed page.

   (d) The most recent selection of text.

5. Having applied a particular heading style to several headings within a document, you modify the style to include bold and italic font formatting. What happens to the headings that were previously formatted in that style, and why?

   (a) They remain as they are. Changes in style affect only text typed from that point forward.

   (b) They remain as they are. You cannot modify a style that has already been applied to text in the current document.

   (c) They are updated to reflect the modified heading style settings. When a heading style is modified, all text formatted in that style is updated.

   (d) Each heading reverts to its original setting. When you modify styles, you make them unavailable to previously formatted styles.

6. To divide a document so that one area can be formatted independently of the next, you can use a(n):

   (a) Column.

   (b) Indent.

   (c) Section break.

   (d) Page break.

7. If you select text and apply a linked style, what happens?

   (a) Paragraph formats are applied, but not character formats.

   (b) Both paragraph and character formats are applied.

   (c) Linked formats are applied.

   (d) Character formats are applied, but not paragraph formats.

8. To draw attention to such items as contact information or store hours, you could place text in a bordered area called a:

   (a) Text box.

   (b) Dot leader.

   (c) Section.

   (d) Tabbed indent.

9. Viewing a document in Outline view can be helpful in which one of the following ways?

   (a) It simplifies the application of formatting to entire sections.

   (b) It streamlines the process of applying heading styles to selected text.

   (c) It color coordinates various heading levels.

   (d) It enables you to expand and collapse levels, dragging to reposition them within the document.

10. The feature that enables you to watch text flow around an object as you move the object is called:

    (a) Alignment guide.

    (b) Live Layout.

    (c) Text wrap.

    (d) Layout Options.

Practice Exercises

1 Campus Safety

You are the office assistant for the police department at a local university. As a service to students, staff, and the community, the police department publishes a campus safety guide, available both in print and online. With national emphasis on homeland security, and local incidents of theft and robbery, it is obvious that the safety guide should be updated and distributed. You will work with a draft document, formatting it to make it more attractive and ready for print. This exercise follows the same set of skills used in Hands-On Exercises 1–3 in the chapter. Refer to Figure 2.49 as you complete this exercise.

FIGURE 2.49 Format a Document

a. Open *w02p1Safety* and save the document as **w02p1Safety_LastFirst**. Click **Show/Hide** in the Paragraph group to show nonprinting characters, if necessary.

b. Click the **DESIGN tab**. Click **Themes** in the Document Formatting group and select **Retrospect**. Click **Colors** in the Document Formatting group and select **Blue**. Click **Fonts** in the Document Formatting group and select **Century Schoolbook**.

c. Click the **HOME tab**. Select the first line in the document and click **Center** in the Paragraph group. Click the **Font Color arrow** in the Font group and select **Blue, Accent 1**. Click the **Font Size arrow** and select **26**. Click **Change Case** in the Font group and select **UPPERCASE**. Double-click *of* in the first line in the document, click **Change Case**, and then select **lowercase**. Select the second line in the document. Center the line, change the font color to **Blue, Accent 1**, change the font size to **16**, and then change the case to **Capitalize Each Word**. Do not deselect the text.

d. Click the **Borders arrow** in the Paragraph group and click **Borders and Shading**. Click **Custom** in the *Setting* section of the Borders and Shading dialog box. Click the **Color arrow** and select **Blue, Accent 1**. Scroll through styles in the Style box and select the seventh style (double line). Click the **Width arrow** and select **1 1/2 pt**. Click **Bottom** in the Preview group and click **OK**.

e. Select the line containing the text *Your reference to campus safety*. Click **Font Color** on the Mini toolbar to apply the most recent font color selection. Use either the Mini toolbar or selections on the HOME tab to change the font to **Lucida Calligraphy** and center the selection.

f. Click at the end of the currently selected line to position the insertion point immediately after *Your reference to campus safety*. Click the **INSERT tab** and click **Pictures** in the Illustrations group. Navigate to the location of your student data files and double-click *w02p1Campus*.

g. Click **Height** in the Size group on the FORMAT tab and type **5**. Press **Enter**. Click **Corrections** in the Adjust group and select **Brightness: 0% (Normal), Contrast: +20%** under *Brightness/Contrast*.

h. Click before the words *University of East Maine* immediately below the picture and press **Ctrl+Enter** to insert a manual page break. Scroll up and select the first line on page 1 of the document. Click the **HOME tab**, if necessary, and click **Format Painter** in the Clipboard group. Scroll to the second page and select the first line (*University of East Maine*) to copy the formatting. Change the font color of the selected line to **Black, Text 1**.

i. Select the second line on page 2, containing the text *Police Department*. Apply **Center**, **Bold**, and **Italic** to the selection. Change the font size to **16 pt**. Select text in the document beginning with *Mission Statement* and ending with *prevention, partnerships, and problem solving* (on the same page). Click **Line and Paragraph Spacing** in the Paragraph group and select **1.5**. Click the **Paragraph Dialog Box Launcher** and change **Spacing After** to **6 pt**. Click **OK**. Click to position the insertion point after the words *Police Department* and press **Enter** twice.

j. Select the *Mission Statement* heading near the top of page 2 and change the font color to **Blue, Accent 1**. Center the selection and change the font size to **16** and the font to **Lucida Calligraphy**. Copy the format of the selection to the *Vision* heading on the same page. Insert a page break after the sentence ending with the words *problem solving* on page 2.

k. Select the paragraphs on page 2 beginning with *University police officers are committed to* and ending with *prevention, partnerships, and problem solving*. Click the **Bullets arrow** in the Paragraph group and select the square filled bullet. Click **Decrease Indent** in the Paragraph group to move bullets to the left margin.

l. Scroll to page 3. Click the **Styles Dialog Box Launcher**. Complete the following steps to apply styles to selected text.

- Click in the line containing *Emergency Notifications*. Click **Heading 1** in the Styles pane. Scroll down and apply Heading 1 style to the headings *Personal Safety*, *Medical Emergencies*, *Fire Emergencies*, *Homeland Security*, and *Personal Safety on Campus*.
- Click in the line on page 4 containing the text *Summary*. Click **Heading 2** in the Styles pane. Scroll down and apply Heading 2 style to the headings *Security and Access to Campus Facilities* and *Emergency Phones*.

m. Point to *Heading 2* in the Styles pane, and click the **Heading 2 arrow**. Click **Modify**. Click **Underline** and click **OK**.

Heading 2 is modified to include an underline. All text previously formatted in Heading 2 style now includes an underline.

n. Scroll to page 3 and select the five paragraphs in the *Emergency Notifications* section, beginning with *Phone* and ending with *provide additional information*. Apply square filled bullets to the selection. Decrease indent to the left margin. Click **New Style** in the Styles pane, type **Bulleted Text** in the **Name box**, and then click **OK**.

o. Select the seven paragraphs in the *Personal Safety* section, beginning with *Seek a safe location* and ending with *follow all directions immediately*. Click **Bulleted Text** in the Styles pane to apply the style to the selection. Apply the same style to the seven paragraphs in the *Medical Emergencies* section, beginning with *The victim should not be moved* and ending with *information is needed*. Close the Styles pane.

p. Press **Ctrl+Home** to move to the beginning of the document. Spell check the document. The word *of* in the university name is correct in lowercase, so do not correct it.

q. Scroll to page 3 and select all text beginning with *The University of East Maine* and ending at the end of the document. Click the **PAGE LAYOUT tab**, click **Columns**, and then select **Two**. Click the **VIEW tab** and click **Multiple Pages** in the Zoom group to view pages of the document. Scroll up or down to check the document for text positioning and any awkward column endings. Click **100%** in the Zoom group.

r. Click **Outline** in the Views group. Click the **Show Level arrow** in the Outline Tools group and click **Level 1**. Click + beside *Personal Safety on Campus* and click **Expand** in the Outline Tools group. Point to + beside *Emergency Phones* and drag to position the *Emergency Phones* section above *Security and Access to Campus Facilities.* Click **Print Layout** on the status bar.

s. Press **Ctrl+Home** to move to the beginning of the document. Click the **FILE tab** and click **Print** to preview the document. Click **Next Page** to move through the pages of the document. Click **Back** at the top-left corner of the screen to leave print preview.

t. Compare your work to Figure 2.49. Save and close the file, and submit based on your instructor's directions.

2 Alcohol Awareness

You have been employed to oversee a grant program that your city has been awarded to develop material on alcohol awareness. The purpose of the grant is to increase awareness among youth of the dangers of abusing alcohol and the long-term repercussions of alcohol dependency. You will make presentations to various groups around the city, including civic clubs and student organizations. Along with using a PowerPoint presentation to support your discussions, you also have on hand articles, flyers, and brochures that help convey the message. One such document, a summary of medical facts regarding alcohol abuse, is near completion. However, your assistant was called away and you must finish it. It is in need of proofreading, formatting, and a few other features that will result in a polished handout for your next presentation. This exercise follows the same set of skills as used in Hands-On Exercises 1–3 in the chapter. Refer to Figure 2.50 as you complete this exercise.

FIGURE 2.50 Finish a Handout

a. Open *w02p2Alcohol* and save it as **w02p2Alcohol_LastFirst**.

b. Click the **HOME tab** and click **Show/Hide** if nonprinting characters are not displayed. Press **Ctrl+A** to select all document text. Click the **Font arrow** and select **Times New Roman**. Click anywhere to deselect the text. Check the document for spelling and grammatical errors. Ignore the identified grammatical mistake.

c. Press **Ctrl+Home** to move to the beginning of the document. Select the first line in the document, *Center Hill Community Affairs Division.* Click the **INSERT tab** and select **WordArt** in the Text group. Click **Fill – Black, Text 1 – Outline – Background 1, Hard Shadow – Background 1** (third row, first column). Click the **Shape Fill arrow** in the Shape Styles group on the DRAWING TOOLS FORMAT tab. Select **White, Background 1, Darker 25%** (fourth row, first column). Click the **HOME tab** and change the font size to **24**.

d. Click **Layout Options** and click **Top and Bottom**. Close Layout Options. Point to the WordArt object and drag to visually center it. You should drag when the mouse pointer resembles a four-headed arrow.

e. Select the second line in the document, *Alcohol Awareness Month*. When you select the text, the WordArt is also selected because it is anchored to the selected paragraph. Center and bold the selected text and change the font size to **14**.

f. Click anywhere in the paragraph that begins *Alcohol abuse is a serious concern*. Center the paragraph. Click **Line and Paragraph Spacing** in the Paragraph group and select **2.0**. Click before the paragraph mark ending the paragraph that begins *Alcohol abuse is a serious concern*. Click the **PAGE LAYOUT tab** and click **Breaks**. Click **Next Page** in the Section Breaks group. Press **Delete** to remove the paragraph mark at the top of page 2.

g. Click the **HOME tab**. Select the first line on page 2, *Dealing with Alcohol*. Click **Heading 1** in the Styles group. Select *What You Should Know* and select **Heading 2**.

h. Select *What Happens When You Get Alcohol Poisoning?* Change the font to **Arial**, click **Underline** in the Font group, click the **Font Color arrow**, and change the font color to **Blue, Accent 1**. Click the **Styles Dialog Box Launcher**. Click **New Style**. Type **Lower Item** in the **Name box** and click **OK**. Select the heading *What about Blood Alcohol Concentration (BAC)?* Click **Lower Item** in the Styles pane to apply the newly created style to the selected text.

i. Point to *Heading 1* in the Styles pane and click the **Heading 1 arrow**. Click **Modify**. Click **Bold** and click **OK**. Scroll up, if necessary, to see that the heading *Dealing with Alcohol* is bold. Close the Styles pane.

j. Select three paragraphs in the *Dealing with Alcohol* section, beginning with *Do you know about the dangers* and ending with *excessive drinking when you are young?* Click the **Bullets arrow** and select the hollow round bullet.

k. Select seven paragraphs in the *What about Blood Alcohol Concentration (BAC)?* section, beginning with *How much alcohol you drink* and ending with *because they have less water in their bodies*. Apply a check mark bullet to the selected paragraphs. Click **Decrease Indent** to move bulleted items to the left margin.

l. Scroll to page 3 and select the last six paragraphs, beginning with *Commit to stop drinking* and ending with *Get support*. Click **Numbering** in the Paragraph group to apply default numbers to the selection.

m. Click after the sentence ending with *unacceptable levels* on the same page. Press **Enter**. If the ruler is not displayed above the document area, click the **VIEW tab** and click **Ruler** in the Show group. Ensure that the tab selector, shown just above the vertical ruler, shows a left tab. Click **1"** to set a left tab. Click **3"** to set another left tab. Press **Tab**. Type **Weight**. Press **Tab**. Type **Number of Drinks Consumed**. Press **Enter**.

n. Drag the 3" left tab off the ruler to remove it. Click the tab selector twice to select a right tab. Click **2"** to set a right tab. Click **3"**, **4"**, **5"**, and **6"** to set four more right tabs.

o. Press **Tab**. Press **Tab** again. Type **1**. Press **Tab**. Type **2**. Press **Tab**. Type **3**. Press **Tab**. Type **4**. Press **Tab**. Type **5**. Press **Enter**. Press **Tab**. Type the following data, pressing **Tab** between each entry and pressing **Enter** at the end of each line except the last line:

100 lbs.	.043	.097	.130	.174	.217
125 lbs.	.034	.089	.103	.139	.173
150 lbs.	.029	.078	.087	.116	.145
175 lbs.	.025	.070	.075	.100	.125
200 lbs.	.022	.063	.065	.087	.108

p. Scroll to page 2 and click before the first sentence in the *What You Should Know* section. Click the **INSERT tab** and click **Online Pictures** in the Illustrations group. Type **alcohol** in the **Bing Image Search box**. Press **Enter**. Double-click the image shown in Figure 2.50 (or select one very similar if it is unavailable). Change the height of the picture to **1.5** in the Size group on the PICTURE TOOLS FORMAT tab. Click **Layout Options** and select **Square**. Close Layout Options. Drag to position the image as shown in Figure 2.50.

q. Press **Ctrl+End** to move to the end of the document. Select the six numbered paragraphs. Click the **HOME tab** and click the **Borders arrow** in the Paragraph group. Click **Borders and Shading**. Click **Shadow** in the *Setting* section. Click the **Shading tab**. Click the **Color arrow** in the *Fill* section and select **White, Background 1, Darker 15%**. Click **OK**.

r. Click after the last sentence in the *What You Should Know* section. Click the **INSERT tab** and click **Text Box** in the Text group. Click **Draw Text Box**. Drag to draw a box approximately 1" high and 6" wide below the *What You Should Know* section. If necessary, change the height to **1"** and the width to **6"** in the Size group on the DRAWING TOOLS FORMAT tab. Click **Layout Options**. Click **Top and Bottom**. Click to place the insertion point in the text box, if necessary.

s. Click the **HOME tab** and click **Bold** in the Font group. Change the font size to **16**. Type **REALITY CHECK** and press **Enter**. Click **Line and Paragraph Spacing** in the Paragraph group and click **1.0**. Click the **Paragraph Dialog Box Launcher**. Change **Paragraph Spacing After** to **0 pt**. Click **OK**. Change the font size to **10**. Type the following, pressing **Enter** after each line:

It takes a long time to sober up.

A person with a blood alcohol concentration of .08% takes more than 5 hours to become completely sober.

t. Apply check mark bullets to the two sentences you just typed. Click the **FORMAT tab**. Click **More** beside Shape Styles. Select **Subtle Effect – Blue, Accent 5** (fourth row, sixth column). Point in the text box so that the pointer displays as a four-headed arrow. Drag to position the text box as shown in Figure 2.50.

u. Compare your work to Figure 2.50. Save and close the file, and submit based on your instructor's directions.

1 Balloon Festival

As chair of the James Canyon Balloon Festival, you are responsible for promoting the upcoming event. You have begun a document providing details on the festival. You plan to distribute the document both in print and online. First, you must format the document to make it more attractive and well designed. You will use styles, bullets, and line and paragraph spacing to coordinate various parts of the document. In addition, you will add interest by including objects, such as pictures, text boxes, and WordArt.

a. Open *w02m1Balloons* and save it as **w02m1Balloons_LastFirst**.

b. Change the document theme to **Slice**. Select the first line in the document, *James Canyon Balloon Festival*. Insert WordArt, selecting **Fill – Dark Purple, Accent 2, Outline – Accent 2** (first row, third column). Change the font size of the WordArt object to **20**.

c. Wrap text around the WordArt object as **Top and Bottom**. Format the WordArt object with Shape Style **Subtle Effect – Dark Purple, Accent 2** (fourth row, third column). Visually center the WordArt object on the first line of the document.

d. Select the second line in the document, *See the Canyon From on High!* Center and bold the text and apply a font color of **Dark Purple, Accent 2**.

e. Select the remaining text on page 1, beginning with *May 25-26, 2016* and ending with *on the festival grounds*. Format the selected text into two columns. Insert a page break (not a section break) after the sentence ending with *on the festival grounds*. Change the font of the columned text on page 1 to **Century Schoolbook**.

f. Check spelling and grammar—the word *Ballumination* is not misspelled (for the purposes of this document).

g. Click in the third line on page 1—*May 25-26, 2016*—and right align it. Select all columned text, including the line containing festival dates, and select a line spacing of **1.5** and paragraph spacing after of **6 pt**. Insert a column break before the paragraph beginning with *And don't forget the dogs!*

h. Click to place the insertion point before the paragraph beginning *As for the kids*. Insert an online picture from Bing.com relating to hot air balloons. Size the picture with a height of **1.5"**. Select **Square text wrapping** and a picture style of **Rotated, White**. Position the picture so that it is on the left side of the paragraph beginning with *As for the kids*, but still in the right column.

DISCOVER

i. Select the picture and recolor it to coordinate with the purple theme of the document. Choose an artistic effect of **Photocopy**.

j. Scroll to page 3 and select the heading, *When is the best time to see balloons?* Bold the selection and change the font color to **Dark Purple, Accent 2**. Do not deselect the heading. Open the Styles pane and create a new style named **Questions**. Apply the **Questions style** to other questions (headings) on page 3.

k. Scroll to page 4 and apply solid round bullets to the first nine paragraphs on the page. Decrease the indent so the bullets begin at the left margin. With the bulleted items selected, click the **Bullets arrow** and click **Define New Bullet**. Click **Font** and change the font color to **Dark Purple, Accent 2**. Click **OK**. Click **OK** again.

l. Insert a page break (not a section break) before the heading *How can I plan for the best experience?* on page 3.

m. Select the schedule of items under the heading *Saturday (5/25/16)*, beginning with *6:00 AM* and ending with *Balloon Glow*. Set a left tab at **1"**. Press **Tab** to move selected paragraphs to the left tab. Select the schedule of items under *Sunday (5/26/16)*, set a left tab at **1"**, and then tab selected paragraphs.

n. Save and close the file, and submit based on your instructor's directions.

CREATIVE CASE

You are the office manager for a pediatric dentist who periodically conducts informational sessions for young children. You have written a letter to children in the neighborhood reminding them about the upcoming monthly session, but you want to make the letter more professional looking. You decide to use paragraph formatting such as alignment, paragraph spacing, borders and shading, and bullets that describe some of the fun activities of the day. You will also want to add the dentist's e-mail address and appropriate images to the letter.

a. Open the document *w02m2Dentist* and save it as **w02m2Dentist_LastFirst**.

b. Change the capitalization of the recipient *Ms. Catherine Ellis* and her address so that each word is capitalized and the state abbreviation displays in uppercase. Change Dr. Block's name to your full name in the signature block. Type your e-mail address (or a fictitious e-mail address) on the next line below your name.

c. Show nonprinting characters, if they are not already displayed. Apply **Justify alignment** to body paragraphs beginning with *On behalf* and ending with *July 14*. At the paragraph mark under the first body paragraph, create a bulleted list, selecting a bullet of your choice. Type the following items in the bulleted list. Do not press Enter after the last item in the list.

Participating in the dental crossword puzzle challenge
Writing a convincing letter to the tooth fairy
Digging through the dental treasure chest
Finding hidden toothbrushes in the dental office

d. Select text from the salutation *Dear Catherine*: through the last paragraph that ends with *seeing you on July 14*. Set **12 pt Spacing After paragraph**.

e. Use small caps on *Dr. Block Pediatric Dental Center* in the first paragraph.

f. Select the italicized lines of text that give date, time, and location of the meeting. Remove the italics, do not deselect the text, and then complete the following:

   • Increase left and right indents to **1.25** and set **0 pt Spacing After paragraph**.
   • Apply a **double-line box border** with the color **Red, Accent 2, Darker 50%** and a line width of **3/4 pt**. Shade selected text with the **Red, Accent 2, Lighter 40% shading color**.
   • Delete the extra tab formatting marks to the left of the lines containing *July 14, 2012; 4:00 p.m.*; and *Dr. Block Pediatric Dental Center* to align them with other text in the bordered area.
   • Remove the paragraph mark before the paragraph that begins with *Please call our office*.

g. Click the line containing the text *Glen Allen, VA 23060*, and set **12 pt Spacing After** the paragraph. Click the line containing *Sincerely* and set **6 pt Spacing Before** the paragraph. Add **6 pt Spacing Before** the paragraph beginning with the text *Dr. Block is pleased to let you know*.

h. Select the entire document and change the font to **12-pt Bookman Old Style**.

★ i. Move to the beginning of the document. Search online for a picture related to *tooth*. Insert an appropriate image from the results and apply a square text wrap. Position the picture in the top-right corner of the document, just below the header area. Resize the graphic to **1.1"** high. Apply the **Bevel Perspective Left, White picture style** (fourth row, third column).

j. Move to the end of the document. Insert a Next Page section break. Change the orientation to **Landscape**. Change **Paragraph Spacing After** to **6 pt**. Change the font size to **14**. Center the first line. Type **Ariat Lake Water Park Fun Day!** Press **Enter** and type **July 5, 2016**. Press **Enter** and change the alignment to **Left**. Change the font size to **12**. Set a left tab at **2"** and a right tab at **7"**. Type the following text, with the first column at the 2" tab and the next column at the 7" tab. Do not press Enter after typing the last line.

Check-in	9:00
Water slide	9:30-11:00
Lunch at the pavilion	11:00-12:00
Wave pool	12:00-2:00
Bungee	2:00-3:00
Parent pickup at the gate	3:00-3:30

k. Select **Ariat Lake Water Park Fun Day!** on page 2 and insert WordArt with the style **Fill – Aqua, Accent 1, Outline – Background 1, Hard Shadow – Accent 1** (third row, third column). Wrap text around the WordArt object at **Top and Bottom**, change the font size of the WordArt object to **24**, and drag to center the object horizontally on the first line.

l. Select the tabbed text, beginning with *Check-in* and ending with *3:00-3:30*. Modify the 7" right tab to include a dot leader.

m. Change the theme to **Integral**. Check spelling and grammar, correcting any errors and ignoring those that are not errors.

n. Save and close the file, and submit based on your instructor's directions.

3 A Music CD Cover

COLLABORATION
CASE

FROM
SCRATCH

You play bass guitar with a local band, Twilight Hour. You love playing with the band, but you also enjoy the business side of music, and plan to pursue a career in music production. To that end, you are completing requirements for a B.S. degree. This semester, you are participating in a seminar on music marketing and production. You are in a group that is required to design the front and back of a CD cover for a band, real or fictitious, and your group decides to create a cover for your band, Twilight Hour. You will begin a document and share it with members of the group, who will each contribute to the CD cover. Your group will first locate a music CD case to use as a model. The front of the CD typically displays the band or artist name, along with a graphic or background design.

Before continuing with this case, all group members must have a Microsoft account. An account can be obtained at www.outlook.com.

a. One person in your group should complete the following two steps:
- Open a new Word document. Include the group name in the header. Click the **FILE tab** and click **Share**. Click **Save to Cloud** and click the **OneDrive link**. Select a recently accessed folder, or click **Browse**, and navigate to, or create, another folder.
- Change the file name to **w02m3Cover_GroupName** and click **Save**. Click **Get a Link**. Click **Create Link** beside the *Edit Link* section. Share the link with group members so that they can access the document online.

b. Each group member should enter the link in a browser to access the shared document. When the document opens in Word Online, click **Edit Document** and click **Edit in Word**.
- One or more group members will focus on developing the front cover, including WordArt, pictures, and/or text boxes where appropriate. Use font and paragraph formatting, as needed, to produce an attractive front cover. The front cover should occupy the first page, or first section, of the shared document. Save the document often, ensuring the save location is OneDrive.
- One or more group members will focus on the back cover, including a list of songs, numbered and in two columns. In addition, give attention to the design of text and headings, formatting all items to produce an attractive back cover. The back cover will occupy the second page, or second section, of the shared document. Save the document often, ensuring the save location is OneDrive.
- The dimensions of the final document will not necessarily be that of an actual CD. You are concerned with the design only.

c. The final version of the CD cover should be saved to OneDrive and printed and submitted according to your instructor's directions.

Invitation

RESEARCH CASE

FROM SCRATCH

Search the Internet for an upcoming local event at your school or in your community and produce the perfect invitation. You can invite people to a charity ball, a fun run, or to a fraternity party. Your color printer and abundance of fancy fonts, as well as your ability to insert page borders, enable you to do anything a professional printer can do. Save your work as **w02b2Invitation_LastFirst** and submit based on your instructor's directions.

Fundraising Letter

DISASTER RECOVERY

Each year, you update a letter to several community partners soliciting support for an auction. The auction raises funds for your organization, and your letter should impress your supporters. Open *w02b3Auction* and notice how unprofessional and unorganized the document looks so far. You must make changes immediately to improve the appearance. Consider replacing much of the formatting that is in place now and instead using columns for auction items, bullets to draw attention to the list of forms, page borders, and pictures—and that is just for starters! Save your work as **w02b3Auction_LastFirst** and submit based on your instructor's directions.

Job Search Strategies

SOFT SKILLS CASE

FROM SCRATCH

After watching the video on Job Search Strategies, develop a two-page document providing suggestions on searching for a job and listing numbered and/or bulleted strategies that you would suggest. The document should be error-free and must include at least one graphic (picture, text box, or WordArt). Use appropriate paragraph and line spacing, and include appropriate heading styles for sections within the paper. Save your work as **w02b4Strategy_LastFirst** and submit based on your instructor's directions.

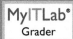
In this project, you work with a document prepared for managers involved in the hiring process. This report analyzes the validity of the interview process and suggests that selection does not depend only on quality information, but on the quality of the interpretation of information. The document requires formatting to enhance readability and important information; you will use skills from this chapter to format multiple levels of headings, arrange and space text, and insert graphics.

Applying Styles

This document is ready for enhancements, and the styles feature is a good tool that enables you to add them quickly and easily.

a. Open *w02c1Interview* and save it as **w02c1Interview_ LastFirst**.

b. Press **Ctrl+Home**. Create a paragraph style named **Title_Page_1** with these formats: **22-pt font size** and **Dark Blue, Text 2, Darker 50% font color**. Ensure that this style is applied to the first line of the document, *Understanding the Personal Interview*.

c. Select the second line, *A Study for Managers Involved in the Hiring Process*. Change the font size to **16** and apply a font color of **Dark Blue, Text 2, Darker 50%**.

d. Click the line following *Updated by:* and type your first and last names. Change the capitalization for your name to uppercase.

e. Select the remainder of the text in the document that follows your name, starting with *The Personal Interview*. Justify the alignment of all paragraphs and change line spacing to **1.15**. Place the insertion point on the left side of the title *The Personal Interview* and insert a page break (not a section break).

f. Apply **Heading 1 style** to *The Personal Interview*. Apply **Heading 2 style** to paragraph headings, including *Introduction, Pre-interview Impression Effects, The Bias of Information Processing, Interviewer Decision Styles, Nonverbal Communications, Physical Characteristics*, and *Stereotypes*.

g. Modify the Heading 2 style to use **Dark Red font color**.

Formatting the Paragraphs

Next, you will apply paragraph formatting to the document. These format options will further increase the readability and attractiveness of your document.

a. Apply a bulleted list format for the five-item list in the *Introduction*. Use the symbol of a four-sided star.

b. Select the second paragraph in the *Introduction* section, which begins with *Personal interviewing continues*, and apply these formats: **0.6" left and right indents**, **6 pt spacing after the paragraph**, **boxed 1 1/2 pt border** using the color **Dark Blue, Text 2, Darker 25%**, and the shading color **Dark Blue, Text 2, Lighter 80%**.

c. Apply the first numbered-list format (1., 2., 3.) to the three phases in the *Pre-interview Impression Effects* section.

d. Select the last two multiline paragraphs in the *Pre-Interview Impression Effects* section and display them in two columns with a line between the columns. To do so, click the **PAGE LAYOUT tab**, click **Columns**, and then select **More Columns**. Click **Two** and select **Line between**. Click **OK**.

Inserting Graphics

To put the finishing touches on your document, you will add graphics that enhance the explanations given in some paragraphs.

a. Insert the picture file *w02c1Perceptions.jpg* at the beginning of the line that contains *First, we discuss some of the psychological pitfalls*, near the bottom of page 2. Change the height of the picture to **3"**. Change text wrapping to **Top and Bottom**. Position the picture so that it appears at the top of page 3. Click **Align Objects** in the Arrange group and click **Align Center** to center the graphic horizontally. Apply the **Rounded Diagonal Corner, White picture style**.

b. Insert the picture file *w02c1_Phases.jpg* at the beginning of the line on page 3 that begins with *Hakel, in 2002*. Ensure that text wrapping is **Top and Bottom**, position the picture so it appears immediately above the line beginning *Hakel, in 2002*. Apply **Offset Center Shadow Picture Effect** (second row, second column under *Outer*) to the graphic.

c. Spell check and review the entire document—no author names are misspelled.

d. Display the document in Outline view. Collapse all paragraphs so only lines formatted as Heading 1 or Heading 2 display. Move the *Stereotypes* section above *Physical Characteristics*. Close Outline view.

e. Save and close the file, and submit based on your instructor's directions.

Document Productivity

Working with Tables and Mail Merge

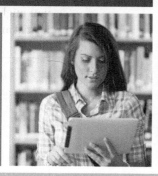

OBJECTIVES | AFTER YOU READ THIS CHAPTER, YOU WILL BE ABLE TO:

1. Insert a table p. 206
2. Format a table p. 211
3. Manage table data p. 220

4. Enhance table data p. 225
5. Create a Mail Merge document p. 235
6. Complete a Mail Merge p. 239

CASE STUDY | Traylor University Economic Impact Study

As director of marketing and research for Traylor University, a mid-sized university in northwest Nebraska, you have been involved with an economic impact study during the past year. The study is designed to measure as closely as possible the contribution of the university to the local and state economy. The scale of the study is large, measuring direct, indirect, and induced effects on employment, employee compensation, and spending. An evaluation of data led university researchers to conclude that Traylor University serves as a critical economic driver in the local community and, to a lesser extent, the state of Nebraska. It is your job to summarize those findings and see that they are accurately reflected in the final report.

Your assistant has prepared a draft of an executive summary that you will present to the board of trustees, outlining the major findings and conclusions. The summary is designed to provide a snapshot of the study process and findings. The best way to present some of the data analysis will be through tables, which your assistant is not very familiar with, so you will take responsibility for that phase of the summary preparation. The economic impact study is of interest to community leaders and groups throughout the university's service area, so you will send the executive summary, along with a cover letter, to those individuals. You will use Word's mail merge feature to prepare personalized letters and mailing labels.

Tables

A *table* is a grid of columns and rows that organizes data. As shown in Figure 3.1, a table is typically configured with headings in the first row and related data in following rows. The intersection of each column and row is a *cell*, in which you can type data. A table is an excellent format in which to summarize numeric data because you can easily align numbers and even include formulas to sum or average numbers in a column or row. Text can be included in a table as well. Although you can use tabs to align text in columns in a Word document, you might find it quicker to create a table than to set tabs, and you have more control over format and design when using a table.

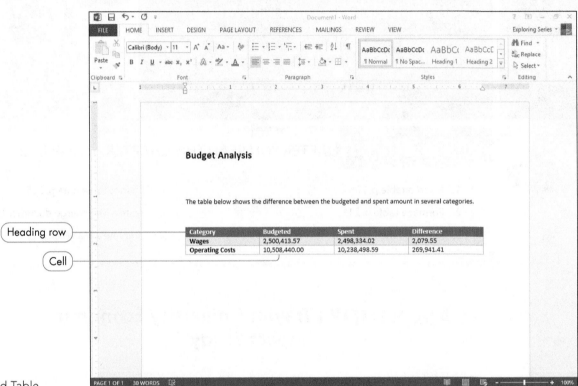

FIGURE 3.1 Word Table

Word's Table feature is a comprehensive but easy-to-use tool, enabling you to create a table, add and remove rows and columns, format table elements, include formulas to summarize numbers in a table, and customize borders and shading. When you create a table, you specify the number of columns and rows that should be included. For example, the table shown in Figure 3.1 is a 4x3 table, which means it contains 4 columns and 3 rows. Often, the number that you indicate turns out to be more or less than is actually necessary. Adding and deleting columns and rows is a simple task. In addition, you can merge cells, adjust row height and column width, and change alignment within cells.

In this section, you will learn to create a table. After positioning the table within a document, you will explore inserting and deleting columns and rows, merging and splitting cells, and adjusting row height and column width. Using Table styles, you will modify the appearance of a table, and you will adjust table position and alignment.

Inserting a Table

Inserting a table in a document is an easy task. You can either create a table with uniformly spaced rows and columns, or you can draw a table with the mouse pointer, creating rows and columns of varying heights and widths. Regardless of how a table is created, you can always change table settings so that rows and columns fit the data included in the table.

A table is an object; as such, it can be selected and manipulated independently of surrounding text. Although you can indicate precise table settings, such as column width and row height, you can also simply drag to increase or reduce the size of table elements, or adjust table settings by making selections from a dialog box. After selecting a column or row, you can delete or resize the item. You can even drag the entire table to reposition it, if necessary.

> **TIP Insert an Excel Spreadsheet**
>
> If you are familiar with Microsoft Excel, you can insert an Excel spreadsheet into a document and format it as a Word table. The advantage is that when you double-click a cell in the table, it reverts to an Excel spreadsheet, so you can use Excel commands and functionality with which you are familiar to modify the table and create formulas. To insert an Excel spreadsheet, click the Insert tab, click Table, and then click Excel Spreadsheet. Enter data in the Excel spreadsheet and click outside the spreadsheet to view it as a Word table. Double-click any cell to return to Excel.

Create or Draw a Table

STEP 1 To insert a table with identically sized rows and columns, click Table in the Tables group on the Insert tab. Drag to select the number of columns and rows to include in the table, as shown in Figure 3.2, or click Insert Table to display the Insert Table dialog box, where you can indicate the number of rows and columns you want to include.

Point to number of columns and rows to include
Insert a table
Draw a table
Select from Quick Tables

FIGURE 3.2 Inserting a Table

Instead of inserting a table, you can draw a table. You might choose to draw a table if you know that rows and/or columns should have varying heights or widths. It is sometimes easier to draw rows and columns of varying dimensions when a table is created rather than to modify the dimensions later, as would be necessary if you inserted a table instead of drawing it. To draw a table, click the Insert tab, click Table in the Tables group, and then select Draw Table. As you move the mouse pointer over the document, it resembles a pencil. Drag a rectangle and then draw horizontal and vertical lines to create rows and columns within the rectangular table space. Press Esc when the table is complete. To erase a grid line, click the Table Tools Layout contextual tab and click Eraser in the Draw group (see Figure 3.3). Click a grid line to erase. When the line is erased, press Esc.

After the table structure is created, you can enter characters, numbers, or graphics in cells, moving from one cell to another when you press Tab or a directional arrow key. You can also simply click a cell to move to. As you type text in a cell, Word will wrap text to the next line when it reaches the right edge of the cell, adjusting row height if necessary to accommodate cell contents. To force text to a new line in a cell (before reaching the right cell border), press Enter.

Seldom will you create a table that is in final form as soon as data is entered. Instead, you are likely to find that additional rows or columns are necessary or that you have too many rows or columns. You might want to apply a table design to enhance the appearance or modify borders or text alignment. All of those activities are possible if you know how to select a table or individual table components.

Insert and Delete Rows and Columns

Having inserted a table, you might find the need for additional rows or columns. Or perhaps you overestimated the number of rows or columns needed and want to remove some. Word makes it easy to insert and delete rows and columns.

In a typical scenario, you have inserted a table and entered text in cells. As you complete the last row in the table, you find that an additional row is required. Simply press Tab to begin a new row. Continue entering data and pressing Tab to create new rows until the table is complete. Occasionally, you will want to insert a row above or below an existing row, when the row is not the last row in the table. You might even want to insert a column to the left or right of a column in a table. Word 2013 includes a new feature whereby you can insert rows or columns by clicking an *insert control* that displays when you point to the edge of a row or column gridline, as shown in Figure 3.3. To insert several rows or columns, drag to select the number of rows or columns to insert and click the insert control.

FIGURE 3.3 Inserting Rows and Columns

TIP **Delete a Table**

If you find you no longer need a particular table in a document, you can delete the table. Click the Table Select indicator (visible at the top-left corner of the table when you move the mouse pointer over any cell in the table or click a cell in the table), shown in Figure 3.3. Click the Table Tools Layout tab, if necessary, and click Delete in the Rows & Columns group. Click Delete Table.

You can also use commands on the Table Tools Layout tab to insert rows or columns, as described in the following steps:

1. Click in the row that is to appear *above* the new row or the row that is to appear *below* the new row. If inserting a column, click in the column that is to appear to the *left* of the new column or click in the column that is to appear to the *right* of the new column.

2. To insert a new row, click Insert Above or Insert Below in the Rows & Columns group. To insert a new column, click Insert Left or Insert Right in the Rows & Columns group.

As you develop a table, you might determine that one or more rows or columns are unnecessary. If you want to delete an entire row or column (not merely the cell contents of a row or column), complete the following steps:

1. Select the row or column to delete (or drag to select multiple rows or columns). Position the pointer just outside the left edge of a row or just above the top edge of a column and click to select the row or column.

2. Click Delete in the Rows & Columns group (see Figure 3.3).

3. Click Delete Columns or Delete Rows. Additional selections on the Delete menu enable you to delete individual cells or an entire table.

OR

1. Select the row or column to delete (or drag to select multiple rows or columns).

2. Right-click the selected row(s) or column(s) and click Delete Rows or Delete Columns.

TIP **Delete Cell Contents**

To delete cell contents without removing a row or column, position the pointer just inside the left edge of the cell so that the pointer appears as a small right-directed black arrow. Click to select all cell contents (or drag to saelect contents of multiple adjacent cells). Press Delete.

Merge and Split Cells

The first row of the table shown in Figure 3.3 is actually a merged cell. If you want to place a title across the top of a table or center a label over columns or rows of data, you can merge cells. Align data in a merged cell, perhaps by centering it, and change the font size to create a table title. Merging cells is a simple process, as described in the following steps:

1. Select the row or column in which to merge cells (or drag to select multiple rows or columns).

2. Click the TABLE TOOLS LAYOUT tab and click Merge Cells in the Merge group (see Figure 3.3).

Conversely, you might find occasion to split a single cell into multiple cells. You might find it necessary to split a row or column to provide additional detail in separate cells. Splitting cells is an option on the Table Tools Layout tab. Select a row or column to split and click Split Cells in the Merge group. Respond to selections in the Split Cells dialog box and click OK. Especially when splitting a previously merged cell, it is likely that you will have to reposition text in cells (by retyping, or cutting and pasting).

Change Row Height and Column Width

When you create a table by inserting it, Word builds a grid with evenly spaced columns and rows. If text that you type requires more than one row within a cell, Word automatically wraps the text and adjusts row height to accommodate the entry. Row height is the vertical distance from the top to the bottom of a row, whereas column width is the horizontal space from the left to the right edge of a column. On occasion, you might want to manually adjust row height or column width to modify the appearance of a table, perhaps making it more readable or more attractive. Increasing row height can better fit a header that has been enlarged for emphasis. You might increase column width to display a wide area of text, such as a first and last name, to prevent wrapping of text in a cell.

You can distribute selected columns and rows to ensure that they are the same size and width. Simply select the columns and rows to affect and click Distribute Rows (or Distribute Columns) in the Cell Size group on the Table Tools Layout tab. Distributing rows and columns is an easy way to ensure uniformity within a table.

A simple, but not very precise way to change row height or column width is to position the pointer on a border so that it displays as a double-headed arrow and drag to increase or reduce height or width. For more precision, select a row or column to be adjusted (or select multiple rows or columns). Then change the row height or column width in the Cell Size group on the Table Tools Layout tab. You can also simply right-click the selected row or column and select Table Properties on the shortcut menu. Click the Column tab or Row tab and indicate a measurement in inches, as shown in Figure 3.4.

FIGURE 3.4 Changing Row Height and Column Width

Formatting a Table

After a table is inserted in a document, you can enhance its appearance by applying a predesigned *table style*, in which colors, borders, shading, and other design elements are coordinated. Edit text within a table by underlining, boldfacing, or italicizing it. You can also align text within cells by selecting an alignment from the Alignment group on the Table Tools Layout tab. Lists or series within cells can be bulleted or numbered, and you can indent table text. Use the Properties control on the Table Tools Layout tab, or right-click a table and select Table Properties, to reposition a table by centering it horizontally or vertically, or simply drag a table to change its position on the page.

Apply Table Styles

Word provides several predesigned table styles that contain borders, shading, font sizes, and other attributes that enhance the readability of a document. Use a table style when:

- You want to create a color-coordinated, professional document.
- You are coordinating a table with elements of Word, Excel, or PowerPoint files, so that the table can be shared among the Office applications.
- You do not have time to design your own custom borders and shading.

As shown in Figure 3.5, the Table Styles gallery provides styles that work well for presenting lists and others that are suited for displaying data in a grid (which typically includes a shaded first row and/or column with headings). Word 2013 has added black-and-white styles to the gallery as well.

FIGURE 3.5 Working with Table Styles

STEP 3 » To apply a table style, click anywhere in a table and click the Table Tools Layout tab, if necessary. Select a style from the Table Styles group (see Figure 3.5) or click More for even more choices. When you point to a style in the gallery, Live Preview shows the result of the style selection in the table.

TIP | Modify a Table Style

Having selected a table style, you can modify it when you click Modify Table Style (see Figure 3.5) and adjust the format in the Modify Table Style dialog box. As you modify a table style, you can apply changes to the entire table or to elements such as the header row. In that way, you can adjust a style so that it better suits your purposes for the current table as well as for others that are based on the style. Save the changes for use in the current document only, or in new documents based on the current template.

Adjust Table Position and Alignment

Table alignment refers to the position of a table between the left and right document margins. When you insert a table, Word automatically aligns it at the left margin. To change table alignment, as well as to adjust text wrapping around a table, right-click an empty area of a table cell and select Table Properties. You can also select Properties from the Table Tools Layout tab. The Table tab of the Table Properties dialog box shown in Figure 3.6 includes options to align a table horizontally on the left, center, or right side of a document. If you select left alignment but want the table positioned slightly away from the left margin, you can indicate the number of inches to indent the table from the left.

FIGURE 3.6 Table and Text Alignment

Move a table to any location within the document when you drag the Table Select indicator. As you move the table, a dashed border displays, indicating the position of the table. Release the mouse button to position the table.

Especially when working with a small table that does not require much document space, you might find it useful to wrap text around the table so that the table is better incorporated visually into the document. Select Around in the *Text wrapping* section of the Table tab of the Table Properties dialog box (refer to Figure 3.6) to wrap text around a table. Text will wrap on the right side of a left-aligned table, on both sides of a centered table, and on the left side of a right-aligned table. If you select None in the *Text wrapping* section, text is prevented from wrapping, ensuring that text displays only at the top and bottom of a table.

Text within cells can be aligned as well. To align text in a cell, click the cell and select an alignment option in the Alignment group on the Table Tools Layout tab. You can align cell contents both vertically and horizontally within the current cell, as indicated in Figure 3.6.

Format Table Text

Text within a cell can be formatted just as any other text in a document. Select text to format and apply one or more font attributes such as font type, font size, underline, boldface, or italics. Although you can drag text to select it, you can also quickly select all cell contents when you click just inside the left edge of a cell. Select a font attribute to apply to the selected cell text.

By default, text within a cell is oriented horizontally so that it reads from left to right. On occasion, you might want to change that direction. Lengthy column headings can be oriented vertically, so that they require less space. Or perhaps a table includes a row of cells repeating a business telephone number, with each cell designed to be ripped off. Such cells are often in a vertical format for ease of removal. To change cell orientation, click Text Direction in the Alignment group on the Table Tools Layout tab (see Figure 3.6). Each time you click the Text Direction option, text in the current cell or selection rotates.

The Cell Margins command in the Alignment group enables you to adjust the amount of white space inside a cell as well as spacing between cells. With additional empty space shown between typed entries, a table can appear more open and readable.

Quick
Concepts

1. Assume you are describing a table to someone who has never worked with one. Using correct terminology, explain the basics of how a table is organized. **p. 206**

2. You can create a table by inserting it or by drawing it. When might you prefer one method over the other? **p. 207**

3. You can align a table and the text within each cell in various ways. Discuss the ways you can apply alignment to a table and its content. **p. 212**

Hands-On Exercises

Watch the Video for this Hands-On Exercise!

MyITLab®
HOE1 Training

1 Tables

The executive summary is the first section of the complete economic impact report for Traylor University. You will present the executive summary at the upcoming board of trustees meeting. Although the summary is already well organized, the data analysis part of the summary needs some attention. Specifically, you will develop tables to organize major findings so the trustees will understand the general outcome of the study.

Skills covered: Create a Table and Insert and Delete Rows and Columns • Merge and Split Cells and Change Row Height and Column Width • Apply Table Styles, Adjust Table Position and Alignment, and Format Table Data

STEP 1 ≫ CREATE A TABLE AND INSERT AND DELETE ROWS AND COLUMNS

You will create a couple of tables to summarize study findings, including those tables in the executive summary. As you develop the tables, you will find it necessary to insert rows to accommodate additional data and to delete columns that are not actually required. Refer to Figure 3.7 as you complete Step 1.

Key Findings

Table 1 shows the top industry sectors in which Traylor University makes a difference in terms of economic impact.

Table 1 – Top Industry Sectors

Sector	Description	Economic Impact
487	Colleges and universities	1,770,281,355
354	Private hospitals	544,871,166
215	Retail interests	1,256,390,688
589	Food services and drinking establishments	321,381,992
501	Real estate companies	348,950,342

Step c: Insert Table 1

Table 2 presents impact sources, with a description of each.

Table 2 – Impact Sources

Step g: Draw Table 2

Employee Compensation	Salary and wages to faculty and staff circulate in the local and regional economy
Other Expenditures	Non-salary expenditures for goods and services needed to support ongoing operations
Capital Investment	New construction expenditures, creating additional "indirect" and "induced" jobs

FIGURE 3.7 Report Tables

a. Open *w03h1Traylor* and save it as **w03h1Traylor_LastFirst**.

> **TROUBLESHOOTING:** If you make any major mistakes in this exercise, you can close the file, open *w03h1Traylor* again, and then start this exercise over.

b. Click the **VIEW tab** and click **Ruler** in the Show group, if necessary. Scroll through the document to view its contents. Press **Ctrl+End** to move to the end of the document. Type **Table 1 shows the top industry sectors in which Traylor University makes a difference in terms of economic impact.** Press Enter.

c. Click the **INSERT tab** and click **Table** in the Tables group. Drag to select a four column by five row table and click.

A four column by five row table is inserted. The insertion point is located in the top-left cell.

d. Type **Sector** and press **Tab**. Type **Description** and press **Tab**. Type **Category**, press **Tab**, and then type **Economic Impact**.

e. Press **Tab** and type the following entries, tabbing between each item, but not tabbing after the last cell on the last row. Text will wrap, where necessary, in each cell.

487	Colleges and universities	Education	1,770,281,355
354	Private hospitals	Health	544,871,166
589	Food services and drinking establishments	Retail	321,381,992
501	Real estate companies	Land	348,999,342

You entered data in the table to indicate community and state interests positively impacted by the presence of Traylor University.

TROUBLESHOOTING: If you press Tab after the last entry, a new row is created. Click Undo.

TROUBLESHOOTING: If the insertion point returns to a new line within a cell instead of advancing to another cell or row, you pressed Enter instead of Tab between entries. Press Backspace and press Tab.

---

f. Press **Ctrl+End** and press **Enter**. Type **Table 2 presents impact sources, with a description of each.** Press **Enter**.

g. Click the **INSERT tab**, click **Table** in the Tables group, and then click **Draw Table**. The mouse pointer appears as a pencil. Drag a box approximately 6 inches wide and 4 inches tall, using the vertical and horizontal rulers as guides. Draw grid lines to create three approximately evenly spaced columns of about 2 inches each. Draw horizontal grid lines to divide the table into four approximately evenly spaced rows of about 1 inch each. Press **Esc**.

TROUBLESHOOTING: It is possible that the lines you draw to form the table are in a color or style other than black. That occurs if someone using the same computer previously selected a different pen color. For this exercise, it will not matter what color the table borders are.

It is OK if the height and width of rows and columns is not identical. Simply approximate the required height and width for each.

h. Click **Eraser** in the Draw group and click to erase the third vertical gridline from the left in each cell. The table design should result in a two-column, four-row table, although the columns will not be evenly spaced. With the Eraser tool still selected, erase the vertical gridline in the first row, so that the row includes only one column. Click **Eraser** to toggle off the eraser or press **Esc**.

TROUBLESHOOTING: If you make any mistakes while erasing gridlines, press Esc. Then click Undo (repeatedly, if necessary) to undo your actions.

---

i. With the insertion point in the first row, type **Table 2 - Impact Sources**. (Do not type the period.) Press **Tab** and complete the table as follows:

Employee Compensation	Salary and wages to faculty and staff circulate in the local and regional economy
Other Expenditures	Non-salary expenditures for goods and services needed to support ongoing operations
Capital Investment	New construction expenditures, creating additional "indirect" and "induced" jobs

Text you type may wrap within a cell. You will resize the columns later, so leave the text as it appears.

j. Position the pointer just above the Category column in Table 1, so that the pointer resembles a downward-directed black arrow. Click to select the column. Click **Delete** in the Rows & Columns group on the TABLE TOOLS LAYOUT tab and select **Delete Columns**.

k. Click anywhere in row 1 of Table 1. Click **Insert Above** in the Rows & Columns group. Click in the first cell in the new row and type **Table 1 - Top Industry Sectors**.

l. Point to the left edge of the horizontal gridline dividing Sector 354 from 589 to display an insert control. Click the + indicator on the end of the insert control to insert a new row. Click the first cell in the new row and type the following. Press **Tab** between cells. Do not press Tab after the last entry.

    215   **Retail interests**   **1,256,390,688**

m. Click anywhere in Table 2 to select the table. Use the **insert control** to insert a row above row 2 (*Employee Compensation*). Leave the row blank, for now.

n. Save the document.

STEP 2 ➤ MERGE AND SPLIT CELLS AND CHANGE ROW HEIGHT AND COLUMN WIDTH

As you work with the tables in the executive summary, you notice that the first row of Table 1 is not very attractive. The title in that row should not be limited to one small cell. Instead, you will merge cells in the row to provide more space for the entry. More uniformity of row height and column width might also improve the appearance of Table 2, and you need to add data to the second row. You will explore ways to modify both tables by merging and splitting cells and changing row height and column width. Refer to Figure 3.8 as you complete Step 2.

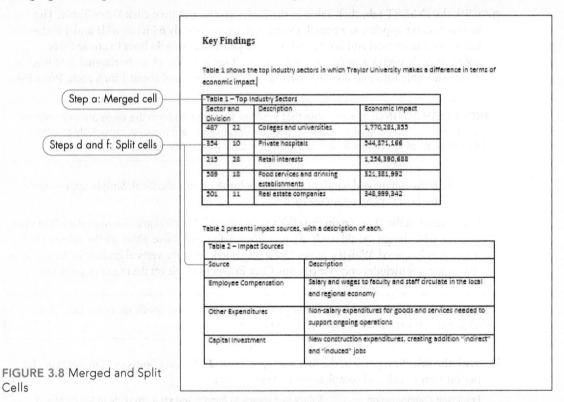

Step a: Merged cell

Steps d and f: Split cells

FIGURE 3.8 Merged and Split Cells

a. Position the mouse pointer just outside the left edge of the first row of Table 1, so that it resembles a right-directed diagonal arrow. Click to select row 1. Click the **TABLE TOOLS LAYOUT tab**, if necessary. Click **Merge Cells** in the Merge group.

You merge the cells in row 1 to create one cell in which text can be better positioned across the table.

b. Position the mouse pointer in row 2 on the border between the first and second column of Table 1. The pointer appears as a double-headed arrow. Click and drag to the left to reduce the column width to approximately 1 inch to better accommodate the contents of the column.

c. Position the mouse pointer just outside the left edge of row 2 in Table 1 and drag down to select row 2 as well as all remaining rows. With the TABLE TOOLS LAYOUT tab selected, click the **top spin arrow** beside Height in the Cell Size group to change the height to **0.3"**.

Row height of rows 2, 3, 4, 5, and 7 is adjusted to 0.3". However, because text wraps in row 6, the height of that row is not adjusted to 0.3".

> **TROUBLESHOOTING:** If items in the first column are selected instead of every cell in every row, you selected cells instead of rows. Repeat step c, making sure to position the mouse pointer *outside* the table and very near the left edge.

The first column of Table 1 lists a sector in which an area of economic impact is identified. Each sector should be further identified by a division, which you now need to add. You will split column 1 into two columns so that the first column includes the sector, and the second contains the associated division.

d. Position the mouse pointer just *inside* the left edge of the third row of Table 1 (containing *487*). The pointer should resemble a right-directed black arrow. Drag down to select the contents of the first column in row 3 as well as all remaining rows. Click **Split Cells** in the Merge group. Check to ensure that *2* displays as the number of columns and *5* displays as the number of rows. Make adjustments, if necessary. Deselect **Merge cells before split**. Click **OK**.

> **TROUBLESHOOTING:** If all sector numbers appear in the first cell, instead of remaining in separate cells, you did not deselect *Merge cells before split*. Click Undo and repeat step d.

e. Click in the first cell on the second row in Table 1 (containing *Sector*). Type **and Division** after *Sector*. Complete the data underneath the heading as follows, using Figure 3.8 as a guide:

487	**22**
354	**10**
215	**28**
589	**18**
501	**11**

f. Click in the second row of Table 2. Click **Split Cells** in the Merge group. Check to ensure that *2* displays as the number of columns and *1* displays as the number of rows. Adjust, if necessary. Click **OK**. Place the mouse pointer on the vertical gridline dividing the two columns in row 2. The pointer displays as a double-headed arrow. Click and drag to the left to align the gridline with the vertical gridline in row 3.

g. Click in the first cell of row 2 in Table 2 and type **Source**. Press **Tab**. Type **Description**.

h. Click the **Table Select indicator** (at the top-left corner of Table 2) to select the entire table. Click the **bottom spin arrow** beside *Height* in the Cell Size group to reduce the height to **0.01"**.

Row height of all rows in Table 2 is reduced, resulting in a more attractive table.

i. Save the document.

The tables included in the *Key Findings* section are complete with respect to content, but you realize that they could be far more attractive with a bit of color and appropriate shading. You will explore Word's gallery of table styles. You will bold and center column headings and explore aligning the tables horizontally on the page. Refer to Figure 3.9 as you complete Step 3.

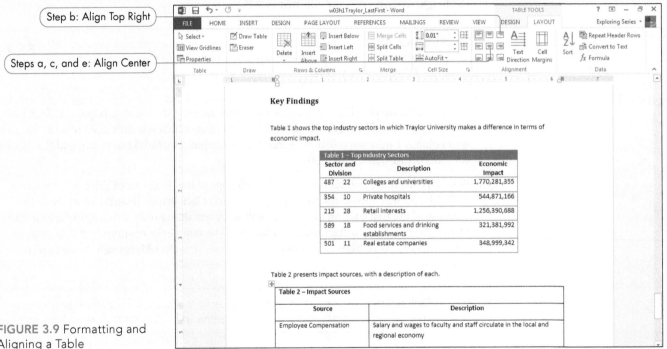

FIGURE 3.9 Formatting and Aligning a Table

a. Select the second row in Table 1. Click the **TABLE TOOLS LAYOUT tab,** if necessary. Click **Align Center** in the Alignment group to center text in row 2 both vertically and horizontally within each cell.

b. Select the cells containing numbers in the rightmost column of Table 1 (beginning with *1,770,281,355* and ending with *348,999,342*). Click **Align Top Right** in the Alignment group. Click anywhere to deselect the cells. Position the mouse pointer on the right border of the rightmost column so that it resembles a double-headed arrow. Drag to the left to reduce the column so that the width is approximately 1", better accommodating the contents of the column.

    Numbers are usually right aligned, so you right align numbers in Table 1.

c. Select the second row in Table 2, containing column headings. Click **Align Center** in the Alignment group. With the column headings selected, click the **HOME tab** and click **Bold** in the Font group. Bold the contents of row 1 in Table 2. Bold the contents of the first two rows in Table 1.

d. Click anywhere in Table 1. Click the **TABLE TOOLS DESIGN tab** and click **More** in the Table Styles group. Scroll through the gallery and select **List Table 3 - Accent 1** (third row, second column under *List Tables*).

    The table style removed some of the formatting from step c, applying color-coordinated font color, shading, and a colored border. The style also removed the inside vertical borders.

e. Remove bold formatting from all numeric entries in column 1 of Table 1 (*Sector and Division*). Click the **TABLE TOOLS LAYOUT tab**. Select row 2 in Table 1 (containing column headings) and click **Align Center** in the Alignment group. Ensure that all entries in row 2 of Table 1 are bold.

f. Click the **VIEW tab** and click **One Page** in the Zoom group to view the current page. Note that the tables are not centered on the page horizontally. Click **100%** in the Zoom group.

g. Right-click anywhere in Table 1 and select **Table Properties**. Click **Center** in the Alignment group of the Table tab in the Table Properties dialog box to center the table horizontally. Click **OK**. Repeat this technique to center Table 2 horizontally. Click **One Page** in the Zoom group to view the effects of the realignment. Click **100%**.

h. Save the document and keep it onscreen if you plan to continue with the next Hands-On Exercise. If not, close the document and exit Word.

Advanced Table Features

Developing a basic Word table to organize data in columns is a fairly simple task. With a bit more effort, you can enhance a table using features that improve its readability and summarize table data. Many of the tasks typically associated with an Excel spreadsheet can be accomplished in a Word table, such as summing or averaging a numeric column or row. By using advanced table features in Word, you can create tables that not only organize data, but also present table contents in an attractive, easy-to-read format.

In this section, you will use Word to enhance tables with borders and shading of your choice. In addition, you will sort table data and learn to total and average numbers in a table. You will learn to include captions with tables, so that tables are correctly identified. By indicating that a heading row should recur on each printed page in which a table displays, you will ensure that table contents are easily identified, even if table rows are carried over to another page. Finally, you will simplify the task of creating a table by converting plain text into a table, and you will learn to convert a table to plain text.

Managing Table Data

A table is often used to summarize numeric data. For example, the table shown in Figure 3.10 organizes a list of students receiving a particular college scholarship. Scholarship amounts vary, so there is no standard amount awarded. The last row of the table shows a total scholarship amount, although for illustration, the formula that produces the total is shown in Figure 3.10. The table is sorted by student last name. Because the company awards many individual scholarships, there is a likelihood that the table could extend beyond one page. In that case, the first row (containing table headings) should be set to recur across all pages so that table data is identified by column headings, regardless of the page on which the table is continued. Using Word, you can manage table data to include calculations, sort table contents, and cause heading rows to recur across pages. Planning a table ahead of time is always preferable to recognizing the need for a table after text has already been typed. However, in some cases, you can convert plain text into a table. Conversely, after a table has been created, you can convert table text back to plain text.

Calculate Using Table Formulas and Functions

Organizing numbers in columns and rows within a Word table not only creates an attractive and easy-to-read display, but also simplifies the task of totaling, averaging, or otherwise summarizing those numbers. A *formula* is a calculation that can add, subtract, divide, or multiply cell contents. Although Word is not designed to perform heavy-duty statistical calculations, it is possible to determine basic items, such as a sum, an average, or a count, of items in cells. Word provides *functions*, which are built-in formulas, to simplify the task of performing basic calculations. A function uses values in a table to produce a result. For example, the SUM function totals values in a series of cells, whereas the COUNT function identifies the number of entries in a series of cells. The total scholarship amount shown in Figure 3.10 was calculated with a SUM function. In most cases, a function provides an alternative to what would otherwise be a much lengthier calculation.

Recipient Name	Major	Date Awarded	Amount Awarded	Amount Spent	Amount Left
Alim, Nisheeth	Accounting	5/15/2016	1,850	650	
Blair, Walter	Finance	4/23/2016	1,200	1,200	
Diminsha, Ahmed	Management	2/1/2016	1,350	728	
Don, Clarice	Finance	6/4/2016	2,550	1,014	
Edge, Latisha	Accounting	2/16/2016	1,500	0	
Gonzalez, Patricia	Entrepreneurship	3/12/2016	1,225	1,225	
Green, Amber	CIS	5/10/2016	2,890	856	
James, Greg	Marketing	4/23/2016	2,335	2,010	
McDonald, Barbara	Accounting	5/15/2016	1,675	981	
Marish, Tia	CIS	2/10/2016	1,895	1,400	
Pintlala, Sarah	Management	6/2/2016	2,350	2,482	
Tellez, Anthony	Finance	8/1/2016	3,950	2,100	
Wallace, April	Marketing	2/28/2016	1,100	250	
		TOTAL	=SUM(ABOVE)		

Function to show total scholarship amount

FIGURE 3.10 Managing Table Data

Use a Formula

To use formulas, you must understand the concept of cell addresses. A Word table is very similar to an Excel worksheet, so if you are familiar with Excel, you will understand how Word addresses cells and develops formulas. Each cell in a Word table has a unique address. Columns are labeled with letters (although such labeling is understood—letters do not actually display above each column) and rows with numbers. For example, Nisheeth Alim's award amount, shown in Figure 3.10, is in cell D2 (second row fourth column). The amount he has spent is in cell E2, and the amount left is to be calculated in cell F2. The formula to calculate the amount left is =D2-E2, which subtracts the amount spent from the award amount. When indicating a cell reference, you do not have to capitalize the address. For example, =A10+A11 is evaluated identically to =a10+a11.

Unlike the way you would manage formulas in an Excel worksheet, you do not actually type a formula or function in a cell. Instead, you use a Formula dialog box to build a formula or use a function. To create a formula in a Word table:

STEP 1 ▶

1. Click in the cell that is to contain the result of the calculation. For example, click in cell F2 to begin the formula to determine the amount of scholarship award left.
2. Click the TABLE TOOLS LAYOUT tab, if necessary.
3. Click Formula in the Data group.
4. The Formula dialog box (see Figure 3.11) displays with a suggested function in the Formula box. The suggested =SUM formula is not appropriate because you are not summing the two values in row 2; instead, you are subtracting one from the other. Backspace to remove the function from the box, but leave the = (because all formulas must begin with =).
5. In calculating Nisheeth's remaining amount, you would subtract his amount spent from his amount awarded. Type D2-E2, subtracting the contents of cell E2 from those of cell D2. The resulting formula should read *=D2-E2*. Because you began the formula in cell F2, the resulting amount left will be shown there when the formula is complete.
6. Click the *Number format* arrow and select a format. Click OK.

FIGURE 3.11 Formula Dialog Box

A formula can contain more than one mathematical operator. The minus sign in the formula described in the preceding steps is considered an *operator*. Mathematical operators that you can use in creating formulas are described below.

- Exponentiation: ^
- Multiplication: *
- Division: /
- Addition: +
- Subtraction: -

When more than one operator is included in a formula, evaluation of the formula follows a set procedure, called the ***order of operations***, or ***order of precedence***. The order of operations requires that the following operations be evaluated in order from highest to lowest.

1. Parenthetical information (anything in parentheses)
2. Exponentiation
3. Multiplication and Division—evaluated from left to right if both operators are present in a formula
4. Addition and Subtraction—evaluated from left to right if both operators are present in a formula

As an example, the expression =C12+C15*1.8 is evaluated as follows: Multiply cell C15 by 1.8 and add the result to cell C12.

On occasion, you might develop a formula with multiple operators, but want to force one operation to be evaluated before another, even if it violates the order of operations. For example, the formula =B3+B4/2 calculates the average of the numbers in cells B3 and B4, except that the order of operations indicates that the division will occur first. That would divide B4 by 2 before adding it to B3, obviously resulting in an incorrect average. To force the addition to occur first, use parentheses around the terms that should be calculated first, for example, =(B3+B4)/2. By enclosing the addition operation in parentheses, it is evaluated first, with the division occurring second.

TIP Inserting Equations in a Document

Occasionally, you might find it necessary to include a formula, or complicated equation, in a document, even outside a table. Most math symbols and operators are not located on the keyboard; however, you can create a formula so that it seamlessly integrates with surrounding text when you make selections from the Symbols group on the Insert tab. Word even makes common equations, such as the area of a circle, available with a single click.

To use Word's equation tools to assist in developing a formula in a document (or to insert a common equation), click the Insert tab and click Equation in the Symbols group. Select from options on the Equation Tools Design tab to create a formula, no matter how complex. A formula is created in a placeholder, so you can manage it independently of surrounding text. To insert a common equation, such as the Quadratic Formula, click Equation on the Equation Tools Design tab.

Use a Function

To determine a final scholarship amount in the Total row of the table shown in Figure 3.10, you could click in the cell underneath the last scholarship award amount and add all cells in the fourth column, as in =D2+D3+D4+D5+D6…, continuing to list cells in the range through D14. A *range* is a series of adjacent cells. Although the formula would produce a final total, the formula would be extremely lengthy. Imagine the formula length in a more realistic situation in which hundreds of students received a scholarship! A much more efficient approach would be to include a SUM function, in which you indicate, by position, the series of cells to total. For example, the function to produce a total scholarship amount is =SUM(ABOVE). Similarly, a function to produce an average scholarship amount is =AVERAGE(ABOVE). In fact, you can select from various table functions, as shown in Table 3.1. The positional information within parentheses is referred to as an *argument*. Positional information refers to the position of the data being calculated. You can use positional notation of ABOVE, BELOW, LEFT, or RIGHT as arguments. An argument of ABOVE indicates that data to be summarized is located above the cell containing the function. A similar function to determine an average scholarship amount is =AVERAGE(ABOVE). Although not a comprehensive list, the functions shown in Table 3.1 are commonly used. Note that an argument will be included within parentheses in each function.

TABLE 3.1 Table Functions

Function	Action
=SUM(argument)	Totals a series of cells
=AVERAGE(argument)	Averages a series of cells
=COUNT(argument)	Counts the number of entries in a series of cells
=MAX(argument)	Displays the largest number in a series of cells
=MIN(argument)	Displays the smallest number in a series of cells

To place a function in a table cell:

1. Click in the cell that is to contain the result of the calculation. For example, click in cell D15 of the table shown in Figure 3.10 to include a function totaling all scholarship amounts.
2. Click the TABLE TOOLS LAYOUT tab, if necessary.
3. Click Formula in the Data group.
4. The Formula dialog box (see Figure 3.11) displays with a suggested =SUM function in the Formula box. To select a different function, press Backspace or delete the existing function and click *Paste function*. Select a function and type an argument. Click OK.

TIP Combining Arguments

Combine arguments in a function to indicate cells to include. For example, =SUM(ABOVE,BELOW) totals numeric cells above and below the current cell. =SUM(LEFT,ABOVE) totals numeric cells to the left and above the current cell, whereas =SUM(RIGHT,BELOW) totals numeric cells to the right and below the current cell. Combine any two arguments, separated by a comma, to indicate cells to include.

Sort Data in a Table

Columns of text, dates, or numbers in a Word table can be sorted alphabetically, chronologically, or numerically. The table shown in Figure 3.10 is sorted alphabetically in ascending order by student name. It might be beneficial to sort the data in Figure 3.10 by date, so that scholarship awards are shown in chronological order. Or you could sort table rows numerically by award amount, with highest awards shown first, followed in descending order by lesser award amounts. You might even want to sort awards alphabetically by major, with scholarship award amounts within programs of study shown in order from low to high. Such a sort uses a primary category (major, in this case) and a secondary category (award amount). You can sort a Word table by up to three categories.

To sort table rows:

STEP 2 »
1. Click anywhere in the table (or select the column to sort by) and click the TABLE TOOLS LAYOUT tab.
2. Click Sort in the Data group.
3. Indicate or confirm the primary category, or column, to sort by (along with the sort order, either ascending or descending), as shown in Figure 3.12.
4. Select any other sort columns and indicate or confirm the sort order.
5. Specify whether the table includes a header row and click OK.

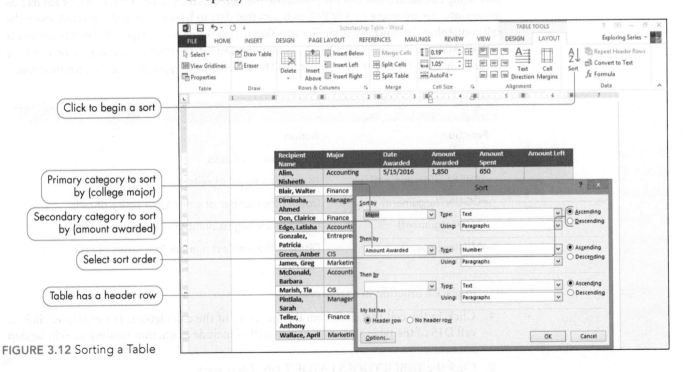

- Click to begin a sort
- Primary category to sort by (college major)
- Secondary category to sort by (amount awarded)
- Select sort order
- Table has a header row

FIGURE 3.12 Sorting a Table

Include a Recurring Table Header

A table is typically comprised of a heading row followed by several rows of data. The heading row in Figure 3.10 includes text identifying the first column as *Recipient Name*, the second as *Major*, and so forth. With a large number of students receiving scholarships, the table could easily extend beyond one page. In that case, table rows on the additional pages would have no identifying heading row. To remedy that situation, you can cause one or more rows of headings to repeat at the top of every page on which a table extends. Repeated table heading rows are visible only in Print Layout view. To cause one or more header rows to recur:

1. Select the heading row(s).
2. Click the TABLE TOOLS LAYOUT tab, if necessary, and click Repeat Header Rows in the Data group.

Converting Text to a Table (and Converting a Table to Text)

Suppose you are working with a list of items organized into two columns, separated by a tab. You know that if the columns were organized as a table, you could easily apply a table style, sort rows, and even use formulas to summarize numeric information. Conversely, you might identify a need to convert table text to plain text, removing special table features and organizing columns into simple tabbed columns.

To convert text into a table:

STEP 4

1. Select text to be converted.
2. Click the INSERT tab and click Table in the Tables group.
3. Click *Convert Text to Table*.
4. Select options from the Convert Text to Table dialog box (see Figure 3.13), including the number of columns and rows to include.
5. Click OK.

FIGURE 3.13 Converting Text to a Table

To convert a table into text:

1. Click anywhere in the table.
2. Click the TABLE TOOLS LAYOUT tab, if necessary.
3. Click *Convert to Text* in the Data group.
4. In the *Convert Table to Text* dialog box, indicate how table text is to be divided (see Figure 3.14).
5. Click OK.

FIGURE 3.14 Converting a Table to Text

Enhancing Table Data

You include data in a table to organize it in a way that makes it easy for a reader to comprehend. Using table styles and table formulas, you have learned to configure a table so it is attractive and so that it provides any necessary summary information. To further enhance table data, you can select custom shading and borders, and you can include images in cells. Certain writing styles require the use of captions to identify tables included in reports; you will learn to work with captions in this section.

Include Borders and Shading

Enhancing a table with custom borders and shading is a simple task when you use Word 2013's Border tools. A **border** is a line style you can apply to individual cells, an entire table, or to individual areas within a table. You can design your own border, selecting a pen color, line style, and line weight, or you can select from a gallery of predesigned borders that coordinate with existing table styles. New to Word 2013 is **Border Painter**, a tool that enables you to easily apply border settings you have identified (or a border style selected from the Borders gallery) to one or more table borders. Using Border Painter, you can apply preselected borders by simply "brushing" them on a table border with the mouse. Figure 3.15 shows various border selections that are available on the Table Tools Design tab when a table is selected.

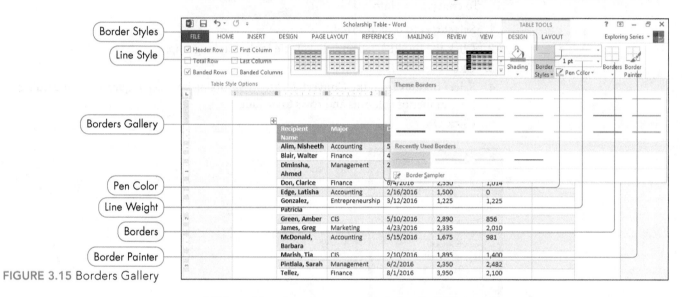

FIGURE 3.15 Borders Gallery

With a table selected, you can apply borders in several ways:

- To create a *custom* border:

    1. Choose a pen color, line style, and line weight (refer to Figure 3.15).
    2. The pointer displays as an ink pen, with Border Painter active. Click a table border to apply the border selection (or click and drag to brush the selection on several borders).
    3. Click Border Painter to toggle off the feature, or press Esc.

- To apply a border *style*:

    STEP 3

    1. Click Border Styles (refer to Figure 3.15) and select a border style. Each border style combines border width, color, and size. If you change the document theme later, the border style will change to match the theme.
    2. The pointer displays as an ink pen, with Border Painter active. Click a table border to apply the border style (or drag to brush the style on several borders).
    3. Click Border Painter to toggle off the feature, or press Esc.

Regardless of whether you are applying a custom border or a predesigned style, you can select the borders to which to apply the selection when you click Borders (see Figure 3.15) and select a type (Outside Borders, Right Border, Left Border, etc.).

As shown in Figure 3.16, the Design tab also includes options for selecting shading. **Shading** applies color or a pattern to the background of a cell or group of cells. You might want to apply shading to a heading row to emphasize it, setting it apart from the rows beneath. Click the Borders arrow in the Table Styles group and select a border position, or click *Borders and Shading* to display the *Borders and Shading* dialog box, which includes additional options related to border and shading design.

TIP Border Sampler

Having applied a custom border or border style to one or more borders in a table, you might want to copy the selection to other table borders. Using Border Sampler, you can easily accomplish that task. Click the Border Styles arrow and click Border Sampler. The mouse pointer becomes an eyedropper tool; click a table border that you want to copy. Automatically, the pointer switches to the Border Painter tool, as indicated by the ink pen designation, so you can brush another border to apply the border selection.

Shading arrow

Borders arrow

Borders and Shading dialog box

FIGURE 3.16 Using Borders and Shading

When a table is created, it is automatically formatted in Table Grid style, with all cells bordered with a 1/2 pt single line border. To use the *Borders and Shading* dialog box to change borders in a table:

1. Select the cells to modify (or click the Table Select indicator to select the entire table).
2. Click the Borders arrow in the Table Styles group on the TABLE TOOLS DESIGN tab. Click *Borders and Shading* to display the *Borders and Shading* dialog box (see Figure 3.16).
3. Select from options in the dialog box to add, remove, or modify table and cell borders. In addition, you can select shading when you click the Shading tab in the dialog box.

Include a Table Caption

A *caption*, such as *Table 1*, is a numbered item of text that identifies a table, figure, or other object in a Word document. A caption typically includes a *label*, such as the word *Figure* or *Table*, followed by a sequential number that can be automatically updated with the addition of new tables or captioned objects.

To include a table caption:

1. Click a cell in the table.
2. Click the REFERENCES tab and click Insert Caption in the Captions group. The Caption dialog box displays, as shown in Figure 3.17.

3. Click the Label arrow and select a type (Table, Figure, or Equation), or click New Label and type a new label.
4. Click the Position arrow and indicate a caption position—above or below the table.
5. If you prefer that the label is excluded from display, select *Exclude label from caption*.
6. Click Numbering to select a numbering style (*1, 2, 3,* or *A, B, C,* for example).
7. Click OK (repeatedly, if necessary).

FIGURE 3.17 Inserting a Caption

When a caption is created, it is formatted in Caption style. You can use the Styles pane to modify the Caption style applied to all captions in the document. Click the Styles Dialog Box Launcher in the Styles group on the Home tab. Point to the Caption style in the Styles pane and click the Caption arrow. Click Modify. Adjust the style format by making selections in the Modify Style dialog box and click OK (repeatedly, if necessary).

As you continue to add captions to tables in a document, each caption is shown in sequence. For example, if the first caption is *Table 1,* then the second caption you add will automatically be labeled *Table 2.* If you should insert a table between existing tables, the caption you add to the table will automatically be shown in sequence, with captions on following tables updated accordingly. However, if you delete a table from a document, remaining captions are not automatically renumbered. To update all captions in a document, press Ctrl+A to select all document text, right-click anywhere in the selection, and then select Update Field. To update only one caption, right-click the caption number and click Update Field.

Quick Concepts

1. When summing a long column of values in a Word table, would you use a function or a formula? In general terms, how would the function or formula be developed? **p. 220**

2. A table contains several columns; among them is one containing employee last name and another containing department. You want to sort the table so that departments are shown in alphabetical order, with employee last names sorted alphabetically within departments. What steps would you follow to complete that sort operation? **p. 224**

3. A table is split between two pages, with a heading row identifying columns on the first page. However, the heading row does not display above the table rows that continue on the second page, so it is difficult to determine what each column represents. How would you remedy that situation? **p. 224**

4. What steps would you take to convert a list of names and addresses into a table? **p. 225**

2 Advanced Table Features

As you continue to work with the *Key Findings* section of the executive summary, you will modify the two tables you previously created. The first table, showing major areas in which the university contributed to the economy, will be modified to include a total row and to indicate the percentage represented by each category. You will explore Word's Borders Gallery as you customize the tables to reflect the color scheme of the university. Adding a caption to each table will serve to identify the table and will be useful for your assistant when she prepares a Table of Figures later. You will also apply a sort order to each table to organize each in a more understandable manner.

Skills covered: Calculate Using Table Formulas • Sort Data in a Table and Include Recurring Rows • Include Borders and Shading and a Table Caption • Convert Text to a Table

STEP 1 ≫ CALCULATE USING TABLE FORMULAS

Table 1 includes a numeric column showing Traylor University's economic impact in several sectors. You will add a row showing the total for all of the sectors. You will also insert a column showing the percentage of the total represented by each sector's value. Refer to Figure 3.18 as you complete Step 1.

Key Findings

Table 1 shows the top industry sectors in which Traylor University makes a difference in terms of economic impact.

Table 1 – Top Industry Sectors				
Sector and Division		**Description**	**Economic Impact**	**Percentage of Total**
487	22	Colleges and universities	1,770,281,355	41.83%
354	10	Private hospitals	544,871,166	12.88%
215	28	Retail interests	1,256,390,688	29.69%
589	18	Food services and drinking establishments	321,381,992	7.59%
501	11	Real estate companies	338,999,342	8.01%
		Total	4,231,924,543	

Step h: Updated total and percentages

FIGURE 3.18 Working with Table Formulas

a. Open the *w03h1Traylor_LastFirst* document if you closed it after the last Hands-On Exercise and save it as **w03h2Traylor_LastFirst**, changing *h1* to *h2*.

b. Scroll to page 5, if necessary, to display Table 1 and Table 2. Click in the last row of Table 1 and click the **TABLE TOOLS LAYOUT tab**, if necessary. Click **Insert Below** in the Rows & Columns group on the TABLE TOOLS LAYOUT tab. Click in the third column of the new row (the Description column) and type **Total**. Bold the word *Total*. With Total still selected, click the **TABLE TOOLS LAYOUT tab**, if necessary, and click **Align Top Right** in the Alignment group.

You have added a row in which to place a total economic impact figure.

c. Click in the cell immediately below the last economic impact number. Click **Formula** in the Data group. The suggested function, *=SUM(ABOVE)*, will total all values in the row. Click the **Number format arrow** and select (#,##0). Click **OK**.

The total economic impact is 4,241,924,543.

> **TROUBLESHOOTING:** If the total is incorrect, you most likely typed a number incorrectly in the column above. Refer to Figure 3.9 in the previous Hands-On Exercise for the correct numbers. Make any necessary corrections in Table 1. The total will not show the correct number until you complete step h to update the field.

d. Click **Insert Right** in the Rows & Columns group. Click the last cell in the second row of the new column and type **Percentage of Total**. If necessary, center align the new entry.

Text will wrap in the cell. You have added a new column that will show the percentage each sector's value represents of the total economic impact. You will create a formula to obtain that result.

e. Click in the third row of the last column (in the *Colleges and universities* row). Click **Formula** in the Data group. Press **Backspace** repeatedly to remove the suggested function from the Formula box. Type **=D3/D8*100**. Click the **Number format arrow**, scroll through the options, and then select **0.00%**. Click **OK**.

The formula divides the value in the cell to the left (cell D3) by the total value of economic impact in the last row of the table (cell D8). The result is multiplied by 100 to convert it to a percentage. The format you chose displays the result with a percent sign and two places to the right of the decimal. The percentage represented by *Colleges and universities* is 41.73%.

> **TROUBLESHOOTING:** If an error message displays in the cell instead of a percentage, or if the percentage is incorrect, click Undo and repeat step e.

f. Click in the last column of the *Private hospitals* row. Click **Formula** in the Data group. Press **Backspace** to remove the suggested function from the Formula box. Type **=D4/D8*100**. Click **OK**.

The number format remains at 0.00%, so there is no need to change it.

g. Click in the last column of the *Retail interests* row and repeat step f, changing *D4* in the formula to **D5** (because you are working with a value on the fifth row). Create a formula for *Food services and drinking establishments* and *Real estate companies,* adjusting the row reference in each formula.

h. Change the number in Economic Impact for *Real estate companies* in the second to last row in the table from *348,999,342* to **338,999,342**. Right-click the total in the next row, *4,241,924,543,* and click **Update Field** to update the total. Right-click the percentage of total for *Real estate companies* in the last column of the second to last row. Click **Update Field**. Right-click each remaining percentage figure in the last column, updating each field.

i. Save the document.

STEP 2 ›› SORT DATA IN A TABLE AND INCLUDE RECURRING ROWS

You will sort Table 1 so that the dollar amounts in Table 1 are arranged in descending order. That way, it is very clear in which sectors the university had the most impact. You will sort Table 2 in alphabetical order by Source. The resulting table will appear well organized. After inserting text from another file, Table 2 will be split between two pages. You will repeat Table 2 heading rows to better identify table rows that are carried over to another page. Refer to Figure 3.19 as you complete Step 2.

FIGURE 3.19 Sorted Tables

a. Show nonprinting characters if they are not already displayed. Position the mouse pointer just outside the left edge of the third row of Table 1 (beginning with *487*). The pointer should be a right-oriented white arrow. Drag down to select the five rows containing a description. Do not include the final total row.

You have selected the table rows that are to be sorted. You do not want to include the first two rows or the final total row in the sort because they do not contain individual values to sort.

b. Click the **TABLE TOOLS LAYOUT tab**, if necessary. Click **Sort** in the Data group. Click the **Sort by arrow** and select **Column 4**. Click **Descending** (in the *Column 4* section). Click **OK**.

You have sorted the five rows containing a sector name (*Colleges and universities, Retail interests,* etc.) in descending order by the value in the fourth column (Economic Impact). It is clear that the sector most affected is *Colleges and universities.*

c. Position the mouse pointer just outside the left edge of the third row of Table 2. Drag to select the remaining rows. Click **Sort** in the Data group. Make sure *Column 1* displays in the **Sort by box**. Click **Ascending** and click **OK**.

You have sorted the three rows containing a source (Capital Investment, etc.) in ascending order alphabetically.

d. Click before the words *Table 1* in the first multi-line paragraph on page 5. Press **Enter**. Click before the second blank paragraph under *Key Findings*. Click the **INSERT tab**, click the **Object arrow** in the Text group, and then select **Text from File**. Navigate to your student data files and double-click **w03h2KeyFindings**.

> **TROUBLESHOOTING:** If you see an Object dialog box instead of text from the inserted file, you clicked *Object* instead of the *Object arrow*. Close the dialog box and repeat step d.

e. Scroll to the bottom of page 5 and note that Table 2 is now split between pages, with several rows on page 6. Those rows are not identified by column headings (Source and Description). Select the first two rows of Table 2 (on page 5). Click the **TABLE TOOLS LAYOUT tab**, if necessary. Click **Repeat Header Rows** in the Data group.

The first two rows of Table 2 repeat above the remaining rows of Table 2 shown on page 6.

f. Click **Undo**. Click before the words *Table 2 presents impact sources* on page 5. Press **Ctrl+Enter** to insert a manual page break.

You determine that the way Table 2 is divided between pages 5 and 6 is very unattractive, even with repeating heading rows, so you remove the repeating rows and insert a manual page break to force the entire table onto another page.

g. Save the document.

STEP 3 ≫ INCLUDE BORDERS AND SHADING AND A TABLE CAPTION

You expect to add more tables later, but will go ahead and format Tables 1 and 2 so they are more attractive and color-coordinated. You will explore border and shading options, learning to "paint" borders and considering border selections from the Borders Gallery. Because you expect to include numerous figures throughout the report, you will insert captions to identify those tables. Refer to Figure 3.20 as you complete Step 3.

FIGURE 3.20 Including Borders, Shading, and Captions

a. Scroll to page 6. Click the **Table Select indicator** to select Table 2. Click the **TABLE TOOLS DESIGN tab** and click **Border Styles** in the Borders group. Click **Double solid lines, 1/2 pt, Accent 4** (third row, fifth column under *Theme Borders*). Click the **Borders arrow** in the Borders group and click **All Borders**.

> **TROUBLESHOOTING:** If you do not see the Table Select indicator, click any cell in the table and move to the top-left corner of the table to click the Table Select indicator.

Traylor University's school colors are purple and gold, so you will design tables with that color combination. Here, you apply a border style (double solid line) to all cells in Table 2.

b. Select row 1 in Table 2. Click the **Shading arrow** in the Table Styles group and select **More Colors**. Click the **Custom tab** and adjust Red to **240**, Green to **239**, and Blue to **29**. Click **OK**.

c. Select rows 2, 3, 4, and 5 in Table 2. Click the **Shading arrow** and click **Purple, Accent 4, Lighter 40%** (fourth row, eighth column).

d. Click **Pen Color** in the Borders group. Click the **Yellow color** shown under *Recent Colors*. The mouse pointer displays as an ink pen, indicating that Border Painter is active. Drag the pen along the horizontal border dividing row 1 from row 2. Next, drag the pen along the horizontal border dividing row 2 from row 3. Do the same for the next two horizontal borders dividing row 3 from row 4, and row 4 from row 5. Drag the pen along the vertical border dividing the first column from the second (in the purple shaded area). Press **Esc** to turn off the Border Painter.

> **TROUBLESHOOTING:** If you make a mistake as you color borders, press Esc to turn off the pen and click Undo (repeatedly, if necessary) to undo your action(s). Repeat step d.

e. Select the first two rows in Table 2. Right-click the selection and click **Table Properties**. Click the **Row tab**. Make sure *Specify height* is checked and change the height to **0.4"**. Click **OK**.

The first two rows in Table 2 are resized slightly.

f. Click **Border Painter** in the Borders group. Scroll to page 5 and drag the pen along the horizontal border dividing row 2 from 3 in Table 1. Do the same for the horizontal borders dividing all other rows, but do not drag the bottom border of the table or the horizontal border dividing row 1 from row 2. Drag the pen along the vertical gridlines dividing all columns, but do not drag the outside borders of the table. Press **Esc**.

> **TROUBLESHOOTING:** If you make a mistake as you color borders, press Esc to turn off the pen and click Undo (repeatedly, if necessary) to undo your action(s). Repeat step f.

You used Border Painter to "paint" the currently selected yellow border on the gridlines dividing rows and columns in Table 1.

g. Click anywhere in Table 1 and click the **Table Select indicator** to select Table 1. Click the **Border Styles arrow**. Select **Double solid lines, 1/2 pt, Accent 4** (third row, fifth column). Click the **Borders arrow** and click **Outside Borders**.

You selected a border style and applied it to the outside borders of the selected table.

h. Select **row 1** in Table 1. Click the **Shading arrow** in the Table Styles group and click **Purple Accent 4** (first row, eighth column). Select **rows 2 through 8** in Table 1. Click the **Shading arrow** and click **Purple, Accent 4, Lighter 40%** (fourth row, eighth column under *Theme Colors*).

i. Click the **Table Select indicator** to select Table 1. Click the **Borders arrow** and click **Borders and Shading**. Click **All** in the Setting area and scroll up and click the first selection in the Style box (single purple line). Click **Width** and select **1 pt**. Click **OK**.

You decide a more conservative format would be attractive, so you use the *Borders and Shading* dialog box to apply a purple border between all cells.

j. Click anywhere in Table 1. Click the **References tab**. Click **Insert Caption** in the Captions group. With the insertion point immediately after Table 1 in the Caption box, type : and press the **Spacebar**. Type **Economic Impact by Industry**. Click the **Position arrow** and select **Below selected item**. Click **OK**. Click the **HOME tab** and click **Increase Indent** in the Paragraph group. Click anywhere in Table 2 and insert a caption below the selected item. The caption should read **Table 2: Sources of Economic Impact**.

k. Click the **HOME tab**. Click the **Styles Dialog Box Launcher**. Scroll down and point to *Caption* in the Styles pane. Click the **Caption arrow** and click **Modify**. Change the font size to **11** and the font color to **Purple, Accent 4**. Click **OK**. Close the Styles pane.

You modified the Caption style to include purple font so the caption text coordinates with the table color scheme.

l. Save the document.

STEP 4 ≫ CONVERT TEXT TO A TABLE

One additional table is necessary to complete the executive summary, but the necessary data are arranged in a tabbed format instead of a table. You will convert the columns of data into a table. Refer to Figure 3.21 as you complete Step 4.

Table 2 presents impact sources, with a description of each.

Table 2 – Impact Sources	
Source	**Description**
Capital Investment	New construction expenditures, creating addition "indirect" and "induced" jobs
Employee Compensation	Salary and wages to faculty and staff circulate in the local and regional economy
Other Expenditures	Non-salary expenditures for goods and services needed to support ongoing operations

Table 2: Sources of Economic Impact

Table 3 summarizes the total employment impact of Traylor University.

Description	Total Employment
Colleges and universities	902 jobs
Nursing and residential care facilities	420 jobs
Offices of physicians and health practitioners	319 jobs
Retail stores – general merchandise	311 jobs
Retail stores – food and beverage	281 jobs
Private hospitals	178 jobs

Table 3: Economic Impact by Employment

FIGURE 3.21 Caption Dialog Box

a. Press **Ctrl+End** to move to the end of the document. Press **Enter** twice. Click the **INSERT tab**, click the **Object arrow**, and then select **Text from File**. Navigate to the location of your student data files and double-click **w03h2Text**.

Columned text is inserted in the document, with each column separated by a tab.

b. Select the newly inserted text, beginning with *Description* and ending with *178 jobs*. Click **Table** in the Tables group and click **Convert Text to Table**. Click **OK** to accept the default settings of 2 columns and 7 rows.

c. Click **More** in the Table Styles group. Click **Grid Table 2 - Accent 4** (second row, fifth column in the *Grid Tables* section).

d. Click in the newly created table, click the **REFERENCES tab**, and then click **Insert Caption** in the Captions group. The caption should read **Table 3: Economic Impact by Employment**. Ensure that the position is *Below selected item*. Click **OK**.

Note that the caption is formatted with the purple font that you indicated earlier.

e. Click before the blank paragraph preceding Table 3 and type **Table 3 summarizes the total employment impact of Traylor University.**

f. Save the document and exit Word. Submit the file based on your instructor's directions.

Mail Merge

At some point in your personal or professional life, you will need to send the same document to a number of different people. The document might be an invitation, a letter, or a memo. For the most part, document text will be the same, regardless of how many people receive it. However, certain parts of the document are likely to be unique to the recipient, such as the inside address included in a letter. Consider the task of conducting a job search. Having prepared a cover letter to accompany your résumé for a job search, you will want to include the recipient's name and address in the letter so that the document appears to have been prepared especially for the company to which you are applying. Word's **Mail Merge** feature enables you to easily generate those types of documents. Mail Merge is a process that combines content from a **main document** and a **data source**, with the option of creating a new document.

Mail merge is often used to send personalized e-mail messages to multiple recipients. Unlike sending e-mail to a group of recipients or listing recipients as blind carbon copies, creating a mail-merged e-mail makes it appear as if each recipient is the sole addressee. You can also use mail merge to send an e-mail in which the message is personalized for each recipient, perhaps referring to the recipient by name within the body of the message.

You might use Mail Merge to create a set of form letters, personalizing or modifying each one for the recipient. A **form letter** is a document that is often mass produced and sent to multiple recipients. The small amount of personal information included in the form letter—perhaps the salutation or the recipient's address—can be inserted during the mail merge procedure. In this section, you will learn to use Mail Merge to create a main document and select a recipient list. You will then combine, or merge, the main document and data source to produce a document that is personalized for each recipient.

Creating a Mail Merge Document

The mail merge process begins with a document that contains wording that remains the same for all recipients. In the case of the cover letter used in your job search, the main document would include paragraphs that are intended for all recipients to read—perhaps those that describe your qualifications and professional goals. **Merge fields** are also included in the main document. A merge field is a placeholder for variable data, which might include a recipient's address or a salutation directed to a particular person. During the mail merge process, a **data source** that contains variable data is combined with the main document to produce personalized documents. You might merge a data source of employer addresses with a main document to produce a personalized letter for each potential employer. Mail merge also enables you to print labels or envelopes, obtaining addresses from a data source.

To begin a mail merge, open a main document, which you might have prepared earlier. The main document is likely to contain merge fields for combining with a data source. You will learn to create merge fields later in this chapter. The main document can also be blank, as would be the case when preparing mailing labels that you intend to merge with an address data source. Click the Mailings tab and click Start Mail Merge in the Start Mail Merge group. Although you can select from several document types, including Letters, E-mail Messages, Envelopes, Labels, or a Directory, you can simply click Start Mail Merge Wizard for a step-by-step approach to developing a merged document. A **wizard** guides you through a process one step at a time, asking questions and using the responses to direct the end result. In the case of the Mail Merge wizard, step-by-step directions display in the Mail Merge pane on the right side of the main document. The self-explanatory options for the current step appear in the top portion of the pane, with a link to the next step shown at the bottom of the same pane. Figure 3.22 shows the first step in the Mail Merge process.

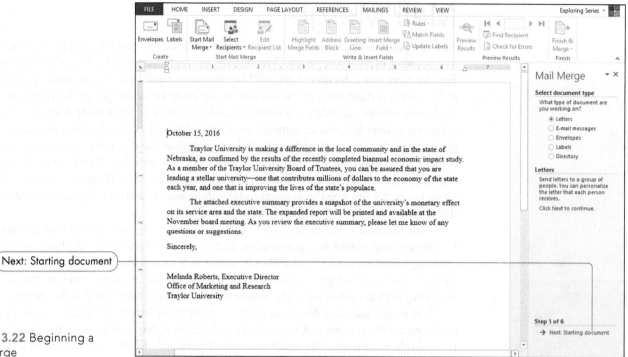

FIGURE 3.22 Beginning a Mail Merge

Click the link to the next step at the bottom of the pane to move forward in the mail merge process. In subsequent steps, you can click a link to the previous step to correct any mistakes you might have made. As is typical of wizards, the Mail Merge wizard simplifies a task so you can follow obvious links to complete the process.

Select or Create a Recipient List

STEP 1» The first step in the mail merge process, shown in Figure 3.22, is to identify the type of document you are producing—letters, e-mail messages, envelopes, labels, or directory. If creating a form letter in which certain variable data will be inserted, you can begin with the main document, or letter, open (if you have already included merge fields in the document). If you have not yet created the form letter, you will begin with a blank document. Similarly, you would begin with a blank document when creating envelopes or labels. After indicating the document type, click *Next: Starting document* at the bottom of the Mail Merge task pane (refer to Figure 3.22). To use the current document, which is the default selection, click *Next: Select recipients*. Otherwise, you can select *Start from existing document* to begin the mail merge with an existing mail merge document, making changes to the content or recipients. If a template is available, you can also begin with a template.

The data source provides variable data to include in the document, such as recipient name, address, phone number, and company information. Each item of information is referred to as a *field*. For example, the data source might include a last name field, a first name field, a street address field, etc. A group of fields for a particular person or thing, presented as a row in the data source, is called a *record*. Figure 3.23 illustrates a sample data source. Note that each record in the data source represents a person, with each record subdivided into fields. The data source shown in Figure 3.23 is an Access database table.

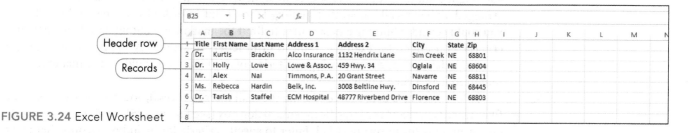

FIGURE 3.23 Mail Merge Data Source

FirstName	LastName	Address	City	State	Zip Code
Catherine	McQuaide	31 Oakmont Circle	Beebe	AR	72012
Danica	Boothe	3646 Seton Hall Way	Beebe	AR	72012
Shelly	Martin	123 North Street	Conway	AR	72032
Jerry	Kripton	456 North Street	Conway	AR	72032
Huong	Pham	P.O. Box ABC	Conway	AR	72032
Marion	McMahon	2216 Catharine Street	Conway	AR	72032
Christopher	Martinez	15709 Holly Grove Rd.	Conway	AR	72032
Georgianna	McFall	123 North Street	Conway	AR	72032
Dan	Reed	901 North Street	Conway	AR	72032
Robert	McMahon	2216 Catharine Street	Conway	AR	72032
Dewey	Francani	800 North Street	Conway	AR	72032
Benita	Brown	143 Sunset Avenue	Conway	AR	72032
Catherine	McCue	31 Oakmont Circle	Conway	AR	72032
Natalie	Barguno	1661 Cardinal Drive	Conway	AR	72032
Gigi	Mican	3509 Carla Drive	Greenbriar	AR	72058
Huong	Ngyun	P.O. Box ABC	Greenbriar	AR	72058
Kim	Jansen	678 North Street	Mayflower	AR	72106
Donna	Reed	901 North Street	Mayflower	AR	72106
Kim	Jones	678 North Street	Morrilton	AR	72110
Michael	Anderson	1 Clark Smith Drive	Morrilton	AR	72110
Roanne	Hall	P. O. Box 121802	Plumerville	AR	72127

A data source can be obtained from:

- A Word document that contains records stored in a table, where each row after the first is a record and the top row contains headings (field names)
- An Access database table
- An Excel worksheet, where each row after the first contains records and the top row shows headings (field names)
- A group of Outlook Contacts

The first row in the data source is called the **header row** and identifies the fields in the remaining rows. Each row beneath the header row contains a record, and every record contains the same fields in the same order—for example, Title, FirstName, LastName, etc.

If you do not have a preexisting list to use as a data source, you can create one. Select *Type a New List* in the Mail Merge pane to create a data source. Click Create in the *Type a new list* area. A New Address List dialog box displays with the most commonly used fields for a mail merge. You can enter data immediately or click Customize Columns to add, delete, or rename the fields to meet your particular needs. The data source is saved as an Access database file.

Use an Excel Worksheet as a Data Source

Because an Excel worksheet organizes data in columns and rows, it can be used to develop a data source that can be merged with a main document during a mail merge. With only a bit of introduction, you can learn to enter data in an Excel worksheet, designing columns and rows of data so that a lengthy address list can be easily maintained. With millions of columns and rows available in a single worksheet, Excel can store a huge number of records, making them available as you create a mail merge document. Figure 3.24 shows an Excel worksheet that can be used as a data source. Note the header row, with records beneath.

FIGURE 3.24 Excel Worksheet

To merge a Word document with an Excel data source, select *Use an existing list* in Step 3 of the mail merge process (see Figure 3.25). Click Browse. Navigate to the Excel workbook and double-click the file.

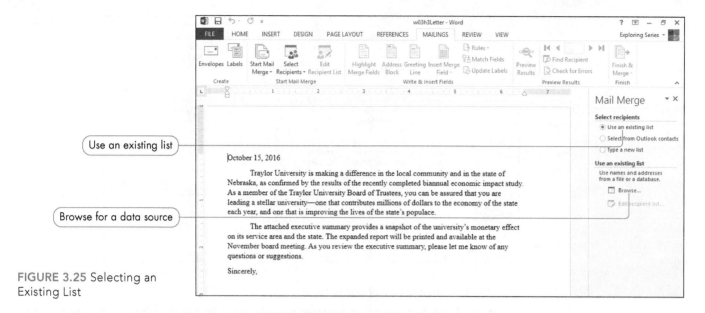

Use an existing list

Browse for a data source

FIGURE 3.25 Selecting an Existing List

Use an Access Database as a Data Source

As a database program, Microsoft Access is designed to manage large amounts of data. An Access database typically contains one or more tables; each table is a collection of related records that contain fields of information. Access enables you to *query* a table, which is the process of filtering records to show only those that meet certain search criteria. For example, you might want to view only the records of employees who work in the Accounting department. If you want to send a personalized communication, such as a letter or e-mail, to all employees in the Accounting department, you could use the query as a basis for a mail merge. An Access table is well suited for use as a mail merge data source, due to its datasheet design (approximating an Excel worksheet) and its propensity for filtering records. Figure 3.23 shows a sample Access table that could be used as a data source.

Use a Word Table or an Outlook List as a Data Source

A Word table is organized in rows and columns, which is ideal for use as a data source in a mail merge. The first row in the Word table should include descriptive headers, with each subsequent row including a record from which data can be extracted during a mail merge process. The document used in a mail merge must contain a single table. You can also use a list of Outlook contacts as a data source. Select the list during the mail merge process.

Sort and Filter Records in a Data Source

Before merging a data source with the main document, you might want to rearrange records in the data source so that output from a mail merge is arranged accordingly. For example, you might want to sort the data source in alphabetical order by last name so that letters are arranged alphabetically or so that mailing labels print in order by last name. In addition, you could consider filtering a data source to limit the mail merge output based on particular criteria. You might, for example, want to print letters to send to Alabama clients only. By filtering a data source by state, using a criterion of *Alabama*, you could ensure that letters are sent to Alabama clients only.

STEP 2 ⟫ After selecting a data source (during the mail merge process), you can choose to sort or filter records in the Mail Merge Recipients dialog box (see Figure 3.26). Click Sort to indicate one or more fields to sort by. Click Filter to specify criteria for including records that meet certain conditions during the merge process.

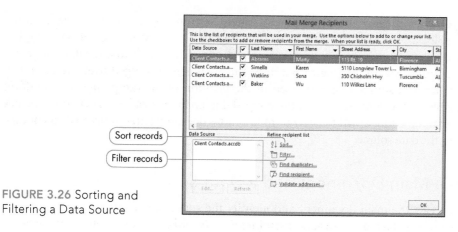

FIGURE 3.26 Sorting and Filtering a Data Source

Completing a Mail Merge

The goal of a mail merge is often to produce a personalized document or e-mail that can be sent to multiple recipients. As the document is prepared, you will indicate locations of variable data, such as a mailing address or a personalized greeting. Such areas of information are called merge fields. After inserting merge fields, you will combine the main document with a data source, a process that results in a single document that includes items (often letters or labels) that are personalized for each recipient. For example, if a data source contains 60 recipient addresses that are then merged with a main document (a letter with placeholders for variable data such as recipient name and address), the resulting merged document will contain 60 letters.

Insert Merge Fields

STEP 3 When you write a letter or create an e-mail in preparation for a mail merge, you will insert one or more merge fields in the main document in the location(s) of variable data. As shown in Figure 3.27, the Mail Merge wizard enables you to select an Address block, Greeting line, or other item that can be included as a placeholder in the main document. The data source must contain fields that are recognizably named. For example, a field containing last names should be given a field name that is likely to be recognized as containing a person's last name, such as Last Name. Because a merge field corresponds with a field in the data source, matching the two fields guarantees that the right data will be inserted into the main document when you complete the merge.

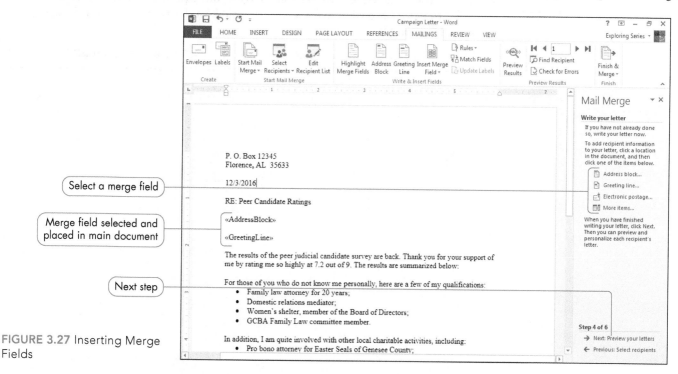

FIGURE 3.27 Inserting Merge Fields

Merge fields display in the main document within angle brackets, for example <<AddressBlock>>, <<FirstName>>, or <<Donation>>. Those entries are not typed explicitly but are entered automatically when you select one of the fields that displays in Step 4 of the Mail Merge wizard (see Figure 3.27). As the document is merged with a data source, data from the data source will be placed in the position of the merge fields. Therefore, <<AddressBlock>> will not display in the merged document; instead a particular recipient's multiline mailing address will be shown, followed by the same letter addressed to another recipient in the data source.

Merge a Main Document and a Data Source

After you create the main document and identify the source data, you are ready to begin the merge process. The merge process examines each record in the data source, and when a match is found, it replaces the merge field in the main document with the information from the data source. A copy of the main document is created for each record in the data source, creating individualized documents.

STEP 4 To complete the merge, click *Next: Preview your letters* (see Figure 3.27). You can view each merged document, making changes to the recipient list, if necessary. Click *Next: Complete the merge*. Two options display: *Edit individual letters* (or other document) and Print. To create a merged document, select *Edit individual letters*. This enables you to preview each page of the merged document prior to saving or printing. If you select Print, you will have the opportunity to specify which pages to print; however, you cannot preview the document prior to printing. To conserve paper, you should choose *Edit individual letters* and use Print only when you are ready to print.

The same data source can be used to create multiple sets of form documents. You could, for example, create a marketing campaign in which you send an initial letter to the entire list, and then send follow-up letters at periodic intervals to the same mailing list. Alternatively, you could filter the original mailing list to include only a subset of names, such as the individuals who responded to the initial letter. You could also create a different set of documents, such as envelopes, labels, or e-mail messages.

Quick
Concepts

1. What forms of output can you create as an end result of a mail merge? *p. 235*

2. Assume you are describing Word's Mail Merge feature to a person who is unfamiliar with Word. How would you describe it, and what would you say is a major reason for using Mail Merge? *p. 235*

3. List three types of data sources that can be used in a mail merge process. *p. 237*

Hands-On Exercises

3 Mail Merge

This executive summary is ready to send to members of the board of trustees. You will merge a form letter with a data source of addresses, merging fields in the process to personalize each letter.

Skills covered: Create a Recipient List • Sort and Filter Records in a Data Source • Insert Merge Fields • Merge a Main Document and a Data Source

STEP 1 ≫ CREATE A RECIPIENT LIST

You will use Word to create a recipient list, including the names and addresses of members of the board of trustees. Refer to Figure 3.28 as you complete Step 1.

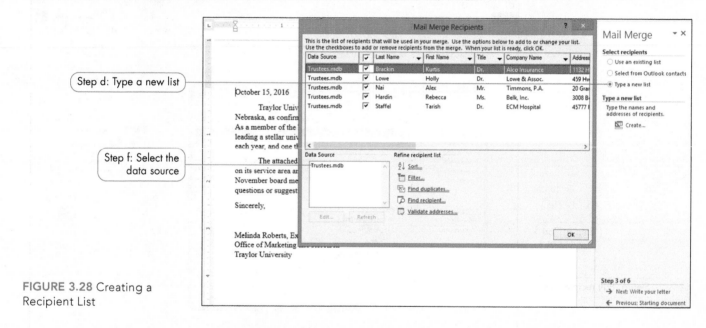

FIGURE 3.28 Creating a Recipient List

a. Open *w03h3Letter*.

b. Click the **MAILINGS tab** and click **Start Mail Merge** in the Start Mail Merge group. Click **Step-by-Step Mail Merge Wizard**. Ensure that *Letters* is selected in the *Select document type* area of the Mail Merge pane and click **Next: Starting document** at the bottom of the Mail Merge pane.

c. Ensure that *Use the current document* is selected in the *Select starting document* area. Click **Next: Select recipients**.

d. Select **Type a new list** in the *Select recipients* area and click **Create**. Type the information in the table below, pressing **Tab** to move from one field (column) to another. You will not include data in the country, phone, or e-mail fields. Tab through all fields and continue entering data on a new row for a new record. After typing the last record, click **OK**.

Title	First Name	Last Name	Company	Address 1	Address 2	City	State	ZIP
Dr.	Kurtis	Brackin	Alco Insurance	1132 Hendrix Lane		Sim Creek	NE	68801
Dr.	Holly	Lowe	Lowe & Assoc.	459 Hwy. 34		Oglala	NE	68604
Mr.	Alex	Nai	Timmons, P.A.	20 Grant Street		Navarre	NE	68811
Ms.	Rebecca	Hardin	Belk, Inc.	3008 Beltline Hwy.	Suite 10	Dinsford	NE	68445
Dr.	Tarish	Staffel	ECM Hospital	45777 Riverbend Drive		Florence	NE	68803

e. Type **Trustees** in the **File name box** and click **Save** to save the data source with your student files.

The address list displays as shown in Figure 3.28, with all recipients checked. It is an Access database. Note that you can deselect any recipients to which you do not want to send the letter. In this case, you will send the letter to all.

f. Click **Trustees.mdb** in the Data Source box. Click **Edit**. Click **New Entry** and add the following record. After typing the record, click **OK**. Click **Yes**. Click **OK**.

Mr. Robert Cobb Tremont Insurance Rt. 19 Navarre NE 68811

You inadvertently left off one of the trustees, so you add him to the data source.

STEP 2 ➤➤ SORT AND FILTER RECORDS IN A DATA SOURCE

You will sort the records alphabetically by city and then by recipient last name. Refer to Figure 3.29 as you complete Step 2.

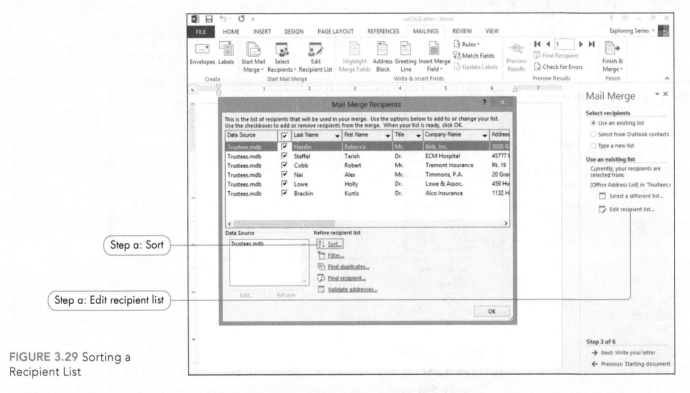

FIGURE 3.29 Sorting a Recipient List

a. Click **Edit recipient list** in the *Use an existing list* area on the Mail Merge pane. Click **Sort** in the *Refine recipient list* area of the Mail Merge Recipients dialog box.

You open the data source in order to sort it.

b. Click the **Sort by arrow**, scroll down, and then click **City**. Sort order is *Ascending*. Click the **Then by arrow** and click **Last Name**. Sort order should be *Ascending*. Click **OK**.

c. Scroll to the right to confirm that records are sorted by City. Scroll back to the left and confirm that the two records with a city of *Navarre* (records 3 and 4) are also sorted by Last Name. Click **OK**.

STEP 3 >> INSERT MERGE FIELDS

Although the body of the letter will be the same for all recipients, you will create merge fields to accommodate variable data, including each recipient's name and address. Refer to Figure 3.30 as you complete Step 3.

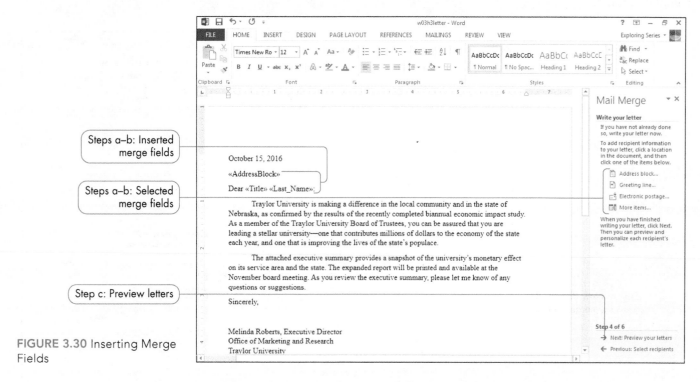

Steps a–b: Inserted merge fields

Steps a–b: Selected merge fields

Step c: Preview letters

FIGURE 3.30 Inserting Merge Fields

a. Click after *2016* in the first line of the document. Press **Enter**. Click **Next: Write your letter** at the bottom of the Mail Merge pane. Click **Address block** in the Mail Merge pane. Note the address in the Preview area. Ensure that *Insert recipient's name in this format, Insert company name,* and *Insert postal address* are selected. Click **OK**.

The AddressBlock merge field is inserted, with double chevrons on each side, indicating its status.

b. Press **Enter**. Type **Dear** and press **Space**. Click **More items** in the Mail Merge pane. With *Title* selected, click **Insert**. Click **Close**. Press **Space**. Click **More items**, click **Last Name**, click **Insert**, and then click **Close**. Type **:**.

You add a salutation, including the title and last name, followed by a colon (:).

> **TROUBLESHOOTING:** If you make a mistake when entering merge fields, you can backspace or otherwise delete a field.

c. Click **Next: Preview your letters** in the Mail Merge pane. Select the address block, from the recipient name through the line preceding the city and state. Do not select the line containing the city, state, and ZIP code. Click the **HOME tab**, click the **Paragraph Dialog Box Launcher**, and then change the paragraph spacing after to **0 pt**. Click **OK**.

One letter is shown. Note the personalized inside address and salutation.

Having inserted merge fields into the form letter, the letter is complete. You will now merge the main document with the data source so that each letter is personally addressed and ready to be printed. Refer to Figure 3.31 as you complete Step 4.

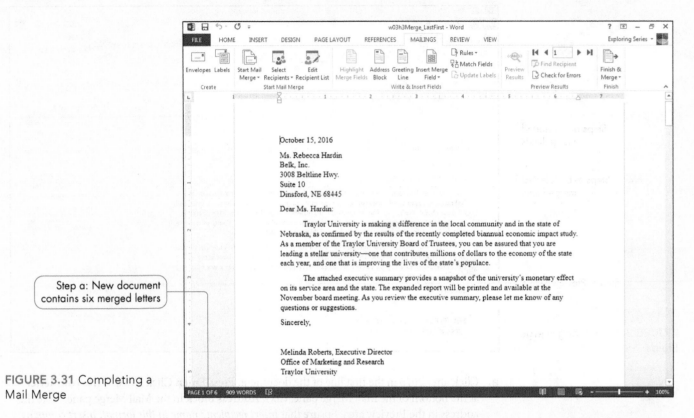

Step a: New document contains six merged letters

FIGURE 3.31 Completing a Mail Merge

a. Click **Next: Complete the merge** at the bottom of the Mail Merge pane. Click **Edit individual letters**. Ensure that *All* is selected in the *Merge to New Document* dialog box and click **OK**.

   Scroll through the letters, noting that each address and salutation is unique to the recipient. The main document and data source were merged to create a new document titled *Letters1*. You will save the document.

b. Click the **FILE tab** and click **Save As**. Navigate to the location where you save your files and change the file name to *w03h3Merge_LastFirst*. Click **Save**. Close the document. Close *w03h3Letter* without saving it.

c. Exit Word and submit the merged document as directed by your instructor.

Chapter Objectives Review

1. **Insert a table.**
   - Create or draw a table: You can include a table in a document by indicating the number of rows and columns, allowing Word to create the table, or you can draw the table, designing rows and columns of varying height and width.
   - Insert and delete rows and columns: You will often find it necessary to insert or delete rows and columns in a table to accommodate additional data or to otherwise update a table.
   - Merge and split cells: As you update a table, you can merge cells in a row, accommodating text that is to be aligned within the row, and you can split cells within an existing column as well.
   - Change row height and column width: You can increase or decrease row height and column width in several ways—using selections on the Table Tools Layout tab as well as manually dragging column or row borders.

2. **Format a table.**
   - Apply table styles: Apply predesigned color, borders, and shading to a table by selecting a table style.
   - Adjust table position and alignment: A table can be aligned horizontally on a page; in addition, you can align cell contents within each cell horizontally and vertically.
   - Format table text: Format text included in a cell just as you would format text outside a table, with bold, italics, underlining, etc. You can also apply paragraph formatting, such as alignment, bullets, and numbering.

3. **Manage table data.**
   - Use a formula: A formula includes table cells and mathematical operators to calculate data in a table.
   - Use a function: A function is a simplified formula, such as SUM or AVERAGE, that can be included in a table cell.
   - Sort data in a table: You can sort table columns in ascending or descending order, including up to three sort categories. For example, you can sort a table by department name, and then by employee name within department.
   - Include a recurring table header: When table rows are divided between pages, you can repeat heading rows so that they display at the top of table rows on a new page.
   - Convert text to a table (and convert a table to text): Text that is arranged in columns, with tabs separating columns, can be converted to a table. Conversely, text arranged in a table can be converted to text that is tabbed or otherwise divided into columns.

4. **Enhance table data.**
   - Include borders and shading: Use borders and shading to customize a table's design. You can use Word's Borders Styles Gallery, Border Painter, or the *Borders and Shading* dialog box to enhance a table with borders and shading.
   - Include a table caption: A table caption identifies a table, numbering each table in a document sequentially. You can modify the caption style and update caption numbering when tables are deleted.

5. **Create a Mail Merge document.**
   - Select or create a recipient list: To prepare a form letter or other document type so that it is personalized with variable data, such as recipient name and address, you will select or create a recipient list that will be merged with the main document.
   - Use an Excel worksheet as a data source: A worksheet, comprised of columns and rows, can be used as a data source containing records used in a mail merge.
   - Use an Access database as a data source: An Access table or query, containing records with data that can be merged with a main document, is often used as a data source for a mail merge.
   - Use a Word table or an Outlook list as a data source: A Word table is often used as a data source, with data merged into a main document. Similarly, Outlook contacts can be incorporated into a main document during a mail merge.
   - Sort and filter records in a data source: Records in a data source can be sorted or filtered before they are merged with the main document.

6. **Complete a Mail Merge.**
   - Insert merge fields: Merge fields are placeholders in a main document to accommodate variable data obtained from a data source.
   - Merge a main document and a data source: As you complete a mail merge procedure, you will update a main document with variable data from a data source, resulting in a new document that is a combination of the two.

Key Terms Matching

Match the key terms with their definitions. Write the key term letter by the appropriate numbered definition.

a. Argument
b. Border
c. Border Painter
d. Caption
e. Cell
f. Data source
g. Form letter
h. Formula
i. Function
j. Insert control

k. Mail Merge
l. Main document
m. Merge field
n. Order of operations
o. Record
p. Shading
q. Table
r. Table alignment
s. Table style
t. Wizard

1. _____ The position of a table between the left and right document margins. **p. 212**

2. _____ A descriptive title for a table. **p. 227**

3. _____ A document with standard information that you personalize with recipient information, which you might print or e-mail to many people. **p. 235**

4. _____ A line that surrounds a Word table, cell, row, or column. **p. 226**

5. _____ A named collection of color, font, and border design that can be applied to a table. **p. 211**

6. _____ A background color that displays behind text in a table, cell, row, or column. **p. 226**

7. _____ A combination of cell references, operators, and values used to perform a calculation. **p. 220**

8. _____ The intersection of a column and row in a table. **p. 206**

9. _____ A process that combines content from a main document and a data source. **p. 235**

10. _____ Contains the information that stays the same for all recipients in a mail merge. **p. 235**

11. _____ An indicator that displays between rows or columns in a table; click the indicator to insert one or more rows or columns. **p. 208**

12. _____ Organizes information in a series of rows and columns. **p. 206**

13. _____ A list of information that is merged with a main document during a mail merge procedure. **p. 235**

14. _____ A tool that makes a process easier by asking a series of questions, then creates a structure based on your answers. **p. 235**

15. _____ Determines the sequence by which operations are calculated in an expression. **p. 222**

16. _____ Serves as a placeholder for the variable data that will be inserted into the main document during a mail merge procedure. **p. 235**

17. _____ A pre-built formula that simplifies creating a complex calculation. **p. 220**

18. _____ Feature that enables you to choose border formatting and click on any table border to apply the formatting. **p. 226**

19. _____ A positional reference contained in parentheses within a function. **p. 223**

20. _____ A group of related fields representing one entity, such as a person, place, or event. **p. 236**

Multiple Choice

1. Having applied custom borders to a table, you can use this feature to copy the border style to another table:

   (a) Borders Gallery
   (b) Format Painter
   (c) Border Painter
   (d) Border Style

2. When used in a table, an insert control enables you to insert a(n):

   (a) Blank row or column.
   (b) Table in a document.
   (c) Caption above or below a table.
   (d) Image in a cell.

3. A mail merge procedure combines two items—a main document and a(n):

   (a) Merge field.
   (b) Data table.
   (c) Data source.
   (d) Address list.

4. To center a table heading in row 1 across several columns of data (when row 1 is *not* already merged):

   (a) Select row 1 and click Align Center on the Table Tools Layout tab.
   (b) Click the Home tab and click Center in the Font group.
   (c) Merge the cells in row 1 and center the contents of the merged cell.
   (d) Split the cells in row 1 and center the contents of the split cells.

5. Which of the following documents is not included as an option in the mail merge procedure?

   (a) Directory
   (b) Labels
   (c) Envelopes
   (d) Report

6. You plan to place a function or formula in cell C4 of a Word table to total the cells in the column above. How would that function or formula appear?

   (a) =SUM(ABOVE)
   (b) -C1+C2+C3+C4
   (c) =TOTAL(ABOVE)
   (d) =SUM(C1-C3)

7. If a table with a heading row extends from one page to another, rows on the second page will not be identified by a heading row. How would you correct that situation?

   (a) Drag the heading row(s) to the top of the second page.
   (b) Insert a manual page break at the top of the second page.
   (c) Select the heading row(s) and cut and paste them to the top of the rows on the second page.
   (d) Select the heading row(s) and click Repeat Header Rows on the Table Tools Layout tab.

8. You have created a table containing numerical values and have entered the =SUM(ABOVE) function at the bottom of a column. You then delete one of the rows included in the sum. Which of the following is *true*?

   (a) The row cannot be deleted because it contains a cell that is referred to in the =SUM function.
   (b) The sum is updated automatically.
   (c) The sum cannot be updated.
   (d) The sum will be updated after you right-click the cell and click the Update Field command.

9. During a mail merge process, what operation can you perform on a data source so only data that meet specific criteria, such as a particular city, are included in the merge?

   (a) Sort
   (b) Propagate
   (c) Delete
   (d) Filter

10. What happens when you press Tab from within the last cell of a table?

   (a) A Tab character is inserted just as it would be for ordinary text.
   (b) Word inserts a new row below the current row.
   (c) Word inserts a new column to the right of the current column.
   (d) The insertion point displays in the paragraph below the table.

1 Rental Car Business

As an executive assistant working for the state of Arkansas, you are involved with a project in which the state has selected a rental car company to supply rental cars for state employees. An employee conducting state business will be assigned a rental car if a state car is not available. Roadway Rentals was awarded the contract and has provided a price list for daily and weekly rentals. You will prepare Word tables to summarize the bid process and the subsequent contract award. This exercise follows the same set of skills as used in Hands-On Exercises 1 and 2 in the chapter. Refer to Figure 3.32 as you complete this exercise.

FIGURE 3.32 Rental Car Contract

a. Open *w03p1Rental* and save the document as **w03p1Rental_LastFirst**. Click **Show/Hide** in the Paragraph group to show nonprinting characters, if necessary.

b. Click before the blank paragraph mark after the Terms heading and press **Enter**. Click the **INSERT tab** and click **Table** in the Tables group. Drag to insert a 2x11 table. Beginning in the top-left cell, enter the following text, pressing **Tab** after each entry. However, do not press Tab after the last entry on the last row. The e-mail address will be formatted as a hyperlink.

Contract No. 975A	
State of Arkansas, Department of Administration	
Division of Purchase and Contract	
198 West James Street, Little Rock AR 27655	
Term Contract	975A
Bid Number	3897701
Administrator	Corey Smithers
Phone	(355) 555-0476
Fax	(355) 555-0487
E-Mail	Corey.Smithers@doad.ar.us
Last Updated	September 25, 2016

c. Point to the border dividing the Term Contract row from the Bid Number row, slightly outside the left edge of the table. Click the **Insert control**. Click in the left cell of the new row. Type the following text, tabbing to position each entry in a separate cell on the new row:

Effective Dates   **February 1, 2016 through January 31, 2017**

d. Select the first four rows. Click the **TABLE TOOLS LAYOUT tab** and click **Merge Cells** in the Merge group. Click **Align Center** in the Alignment group. Click the **HOME tab** and click **Bold**. Do not deselect the first row.

e. Click the **TABLE TOOLS DESIGN tab**, click the **Shading arrow**, and then click **White Background 1, Darker 15%** (third row, first column). Select all text in the first column under the merged row, beginning with *Term Contract* and ending with *Last Updated*. Bold the selection.

f. Right-click the e-mail hyperlink, *Corey.Smithers@doad.au.us*, and select **Remove Hyperlink**. Select the second row, beginning with *Term Contract*. Click the **TABLE TOOLS LAYOUT tab** and click **Split Cells** in the Merge group. Change the number of columns to **3** and ensure that the number of rows is 1. Make sure *Merge cells before split* is checked. Click **OK**.

g. Click in the third cell in the newly split row and type **Rental**. Select the newly split row and click **Align Center** in the Alignment group. Remove the bold formatting from *Term Contract*.

h. Scroll down to the *Rates* section and select all text from *Roadway Rentals* through *$275.00*. Do not select the paragraph mark following *$275.00*. Click the **Insert tab** and click **Table** in the Tables group. Click **Convert Text to Table**. Accept the default settings of 3 columns and 15 rows in the *Convert Text to Table* dialog box and click **OK**.

i. Deselect the table. Place the pointer above the first column so that it appears as a downward-pointing black arrow. Click to select the first column. Right-click in the selected column and select **Table Properties**. Click the **Column tab** in the Table Properties dialog box. Change the width to **2.5"**. Click **OK**.

j. Select the first row. Click the **TABLE TOOLS LAYOUT tab**. Click **Align Center** in the Alignment group. Click the **TABLE TOOLS DESIGN tab** and click **More** beside *Table Styles* to display the Table Styles gallery. Select **Grid Table 4 - Accent 3** (fourth row, fourth column under *Grid Tables*).

k. Click the **TABLE TOOLS LAYOUT tab** and click **Repeat Header Rows** in the Data group.

l. Display the ruler, if it is not already shown. (Click the **VIEW tab** and click **Ruler**.) Click before the second blank paragraph under *4. Contractor Contact*. Click the **INSERT tab**, click **Table** in the Tables group, and then select **Draw Table**. Use the mouse to draw a box, beginning at the second blank paragraph mark, extending to approximately 6" on the ruler, and down approximately 2".

TROUBLESHOOTING: If the pen color that displays when you draw the table is not black, click the Table Tools Design tab and click Pen Color. Click Black, Text 1 (first row, second column under *Theme Colors*). Click Border Painter. Click the Borders arrow and select Outside Borders. Click the Insert tab, click Table, and then select Draw Table. Continue to step m.

---

m. Draw three vertical borders in the box, each beginning approximately 1.5" from the previous border. Draw three horizontal borders in the table area, each beginning approximately 0.5" from the previous. The borders do not have to be precise, as they will be adjusted later. Press **Esc**.

n. Click **Eraser** in the Draw group on the TABLE TOOLS LAYOUT tab. Click the left border of the last cell on the first row. The left border of that cell is removed. Click the left border of the last cell on the second row to remove it. Similarly, remove the left border of the last cell in the third and fourth rows. Press **Esc**.

o. Point to the vertical grid line dividing the second column from the third so that the pointer displays as a double-headed arrow. Drag to the right to resize the last column to approximately 2". Resize the remaining columns to approximately 2".

p. Type the following text in the table. Press **Enter** to place the address on two rows within each cell in the second column, and after typing the table, adjust the width of the first column to display all text on a single line. The table appearance should be similar to that shown below.

Contractor Name	Address	Customer Service
Roadway Rentals (Clairview)	55 Court Street Clairview, AR 27400	(800) 555-6888
Roadway Rentals (Downtown)	38099 Bounds Drive Little Rock, AR 27655	(800) 555-7112
Roadway Rentals (Northrup)	790 Overlook Circle Northrup, AR 27422	(800) 555-0002

q. Select the first row. Click the **TABLE TOOLS LAYOUT tab**, if necessary, and click **Align Center** in the Alignment group. Click the **TABLE TOOLS DESIGN tab** and click the **Shading arrow**. Select **Gray - 25%, Background 2, Darker 25%** (third row, third column). Click the **HOME tab** and bold the text in row 1.

r. Save the document and exit Word. Submit *w03p1Rental_LastFirst* according to your instructor's directions.

2 Restaurant Letter

You are the manager of a local steak and seafood restaurant. At the end of each month, you balance the books and process the accounts payable. You then write a letter to all your suppliers, thank them for the prompt delivery services, and enclose a check for the monthly balance. Because you already have the suppliers' information stored in a spreadsheet, you decide to create a mail merge document that you can use to quickly create letters to send to each supplier. There is no need to send payments to suppliers with a zero balance, so you use a filter to remove their names from the merge process. This exercise follows the same set of skills as used in Hands-On Exercise 3 in the chapter. Refer to Figure 3.33 as you complete this exercise.

FIGURE 3.33 Completed Letter

a. Open *w03p2Letter*. Show nonprinting characters if they are not already displayed.

b. Click the **MAILINGS tab** and click **Start Mail Merge** in the Start Mail Merge group. Click **Step-by-Step Mail Merge Wizard**. Make sure *Letters* is selected in the *Select document type* area of the Mail Merge pane and click **Next: Starting document**. Make sure *Use the current document* is selected in the *Select starting document* area and click **Next: Select recipients**.

c. Make sure *Use an existing list* is selected and click **Browse**. Navigate to the location where data files are stored and double-click **w03p2Suppliers.xlsx**. Make sure *Sheet1$* is selected in the Select Table dialog box and click **OK**. Click **OK** again. Click **Next: Write your letter**.

d. Insert merge fields by completing the following steps:

- Click before the blank paragraph mark below the date. Click **Address block** in the Mail Merge pane and click **OK** to insert the default format of the supplier's address at the top of the letter.
- Place the insertion point at the left of the comma in the salutation line beginning with *Dear*. Click **More items** in the Mail Merge pane. Click **FirstName**, click **Insert**, and then click **Close**. With the insertion point at the right of *FirstName*, press **Space** and click **More items**. With *LastName* selected, click **Insert** and click **Close**.
- Place the insertion point at the right side of the dollar sign in the first sentence of the second body paragraph. Click **More items** and click **Balance**. Click **Insert** and click **Close**.

e. Click **Next: Preview your letters**. To correct the extra lines around the address block, complete these steps:

- Select the four lines that comprise the address block (the address block is located beneath *October 12, 2016*).
- Click the **PAGE LAYOUT tab**.
- Change the paragraph spacing Before and After to **0 pt**.

f. Click **Next: Complete the merge**. Click **Edit individual letters**. Click **All**, if necessary, and click **OK**. The letters are shown in a new document, titled *Letters1*, with one letter shown for each recipient (10 letters in all). Save the new document as **w03p2SupplierLetters1_LastFirst**. Close the document.

g. You are returned to the original document, *w03p2Letter*. Close the Mail Merge pane. Filter the recipient list in preparation for limiting letters to include only suppliers with a positive balance by completing the following steps:

- Click the **MAILINGS tab** and click **Edit Recipient List** in the Start Mail Merge group.
- Click **Filter** to display the *Filter and Sort* dialog box. Click the **Filter Records tab**, if necessary.
- Click the **Field arrow** and click **Balance**.
- Click the **Comparison arrow** and click **Greater than**.
- Type **0** in the **Compare to box** and click **OK**.
- Click **OK** again to close the Mail Merge Recipients dialog box.

h. Click **Finish & Merge** in the Finish group on the right side of the Ribbon, click **Edit Individual Documents**, click **All**, if necessary, and then click **OK**.

i. The new document, titled *Letters2*, contains eight letters—each recipient's balance is greater than 0. Save the new document as **w03p2SupplierLetters2_LastFirst**. Close the document.

j. Close *w03p2Letter* without saving it and exit Word. Submit *w03p2SupplierLetters1_LastFirst* and *w03p2SupplierLetters2_LastFirst* based on your instructor's directions.

1 Football Statistics

CREATIVE CASE

As an intern for the Southern Athletic Conference, you are preparing a summary of football statistics for inclusion in material published and placed online by the conference. Specifically, you will highlight stats from the offensive units of leading teams in the conference. A Word table is an ideal way to summarize those statistics, so you will prepare and populate several tables. Where appropriate, you will include formulas to summarize table data. The tables must be attractively formatted, so you will use Word's design and bordering tools as well.

DISCOVER

a. Open *w03m1Football* and save it as **w03m1Football_LastFirst**.

b. Select text in the document from # (in the top-left corner) to *13.4* (in the bottom-right corner) and convert the text to a table. The number of columns is 15, and the number of rows is 18. Table data are separated by tabs. After creating the table, change page orientation to **Landscape**.

c. Delete column 1. Change the font of all table data to **Cambria**. Change the font size of all table text to **10**. AutoFit the contents of the table.

d. Change the font of the first two lines (*Southern Athletic Conference* and *Season Statistics*) to **Cambria 16 pt**.

e. Insert a row above row 1 in the table. Complete the following activities to populate and format the new row:
   • Type **Offensive Statistics** in the first cell on the new row.
   • Type **Rushing Statistics** in the next cell on the first row.
   • Select the second, third, fourth, fifth, and sixth cells on the first row. Merge the selected cells.
   • Align *Rushing Statistics* in the center of the merged cell.
   • Type **Passing Statistics** in the next cell on the first row.
   • Select the cell containing *Passing Statistics* and the next three cells on the first row. Merge the cells.
   • Align *Passing Statistics* in the center of the merged cell.
   • Merge the remaining cells on row 1, type **Total** in the merged cell, and then center *Total*.

f. Insert a row between *HARKINSVILLE* and *DAKOTA STATE* and type the following data in the new row.

   JAMES COLLEGE 38.2 41.0 220.5 4.2 19.7 32.7 0.601 199.2 7.6 57.9 449.3 5.9 12.7

g. Select a table style of **Grid Table 5 Dark - Accent 2** (fifth row, third column under *Grid Tables*). Click the **Table Select indicator** to select all table text. Change the Pen Color to **Orange, Accent 2, Darker 50%** (sixth row, sixth column under *Theme Colors*). Click **Borders** and apply the color to Outside Borders.

h. Select a border style of your choice and apply it to the border along the horizontal line separating row 1 from row 2, and also along the vertical line separating the first column from the second.

i. Move to the end of the document. Press **Enter** twice and insert a 3x5 table. Enter the following data in the table.

Calvin Spraggins	SPR	1428
Demaryius Schuster	DEN	1197
Brandon Marchant	CHI	1182
Wayne McAnalley	IND	1156
Sparky Hall	HOU	1114

j. Insert a new blank row at the top of the table and complete the following steps:
   • Type **Receiving Yards** in the first cell on row 1.
   • Change the font size of the entry on row 1 to **14 pt**.
   • Merge all cells on row 1.
   • Align Center *Receiving Yards*.

k. Manually adjust each column of data to approximately 1.5" wide. Center all entries in the last two columns.

l. Select the first row and apply a shading of **Orange, Accent 2, Lighter 60%** (third row, sixth column under *Theme Colors*).

m. Add a new blank row at the end of the table and type **Total** in the first cell of the new row. Enter a formula in the last cell of the new row to sum all entries in the column above. You do not need to select a number format.

n. Align both tables horizontally in the center of the page.

o. Change the receiving yards for *Calvin Spraggins* to **1451**. Update the formula to reflect the change.

p. Add a caption below the bottom of the first table. The caption should read **Table 1: Southern Athletic Conference Offensive Statistics**. Add a caption below the bottom of the second table that reads **Table 2: Total Receiving Yards**. Modify the Caption style to include a font color of **Orange, Accent 2, Darker 50%** (sixth row, sixth column under *Theme Colors*). Change the Caption style font to **Bold** (not italicized) and **Centered**.

q. Save and submit *w03m1Football_LastFirst* based on your instructor's directions.

2 Pool Places

 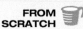

You own a swimming pool company, installing in-ground pools, providing pool services (such as replacing liners and repairing pumps), and selling pool supplies and covers. Each month, you bill for sales and services. Traditionally, you type the total amount of your services in the document, but after a discussion with another business owner you discover how to use table formulas and begin to use them to calculate total fees on the invoice. In this exercise, you develop a professional-looking invoice and use formulas to calculate totals within the table. You will also create a mail merge document.

a. Begin a blank document and save it as **w03m2Pool_LastFirst**.

b. Insert a 1x3 table. Type **Party Pools, LLC** in the first cell of the first row. Change the font size of the text in row 1 to **28** and center the text.

c. Select the second and third rows. Split cells, resulting in 2 columns by 2 rows.

d. Complete the table as shown below, adding rows where necessary:

Invoice Number: 300	Invoice Date: 8/20/2016
Bill to:	Submit Payment to:
Ladean Murphy	Party Pools, LLC
33252 S. Campbell Ave.	2048 S. Glenn Ave.
Springfield, MO 65807	Springfield, MO 65807

e. Change the font size of the text you just typed to **14**.

f. Select the second row of the table, click the **PAGE LAYOUT tab**, and increase both **Spacing before** and **Spacing after** to **6 pt**. Bold entries in the second row.

g. Format the table as follows:
   - Select the table. Open the *Borders and Shading* dialog box and select the **Box setting**. Accept default line selections and click **OK**.
   - Select the second row of the table. Change the pen color to **Blue, Accent 1, Darker 25%** (fifth row, fifth column under *Theme Colors*). Apply the color to outside borders of the selection. Press **Esc**.
   - Shade the first row with **Blue, Accent 1, Lighter 40%**.

h. Move to the end of the document and press **Enter** twice. Insert a 4x5 table. Type the following column headings in the first row.

File #	Service Date	Property Address	Service Charge

i. Change the column width of all columns to **1"**. Center align all entries on row 1 so that entries are centered both horizontally and vertically. Adjust the column width of only the third column (Property Address) to **2"**.

j. Type the following information in rows 2 through 4.

65	8/4/2016	2402 E. Lee St., Republic	300.00
70	8/2/2016	105 Amanda Ln., Nixa	300.00
75	8/1/2016	335 Valley Vista Dr., Springfield	800.00

k. Adjust the width of the third column to accommodate the longest entry, if necessary. Create a total row in row 5 by completing the following steps:

- Merge the first three cells in row 5.
- Type **Total** in the first cell in row 5 and right align the entry.
- Insert a formula or function in the last cell on row 5 to total the service charges in the column above. The number format should show a dollar sign and two decimal places. Right align all numbers in the last column of the table. However, the words *Service Charge* should remain centered in the top cell of the last column.

l. Add another row to the end of the table. Merge all cells in the final row and type **Thank you for your business.** (Include the period.) Center the entry in the last row.

m. Insert a row after the row containing File # 75. Add the following text to the new row:

| 77 | 8/4/2016 | 3324 N. Hickory Hills Ct., Nixa | 100.00 |

n. Update the total on the last row to include the new row information. Sort the rows containing service charges by Service Date and then by Service Charge, both in ascending order. *Do not include the header row, total row, or last row in the table in the sort selection.*

o. Center both tables horizontally on the page. Save and close the document.

p. Open *w03m2BillLetter*. Begin a mail merge, using the Step-by-Step Mail Merge Wizard. Complete the following steps:

- Ensure that *Letters* is selected and click **Next: Starting document**.
- Ensure that *Use the current document* is selected and click **Next: Select recipients**.
- Browse and select **w03m2Clients.xlsx** from your data files as the data source. Select **Sheet1** and click **OK**. Sort the data source by **Last Name** in ascending order.
- Click **Next: Write your letter**. Click before the second blank paragraph after the inside address. Insert an Address Block, using default settings.
- Click after the space following the word *Dear* (and before the colon). Click **More items**. Click **First Name**, click **Insert**, and then click **Close**. Press **Space**. Click **More items** and insert the **Last Name**.
- Click **Next: Preview your letters**. Adjust the paragraph spacing of the address block (beginning with *Ashley Dugan* and ending with *Midlothian, VA 23113*) to **0 pt** paragraph spacing before and after. Click **Next: Complete the merge**. Click **Edit individual letters** and ensure that all letters will be merged to a new document. Click **OK**.

q. Save the merged document, containing four pages, as **w03m2Merge_LastFirst** and close it. Close *w03m2BillLetter* without saving it.

r. Submit *w03m2Pool_LastFirst* and *w03m2Merge_LastFirst* based on your instructor's directions.

3 Remodeling

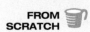

As a general contractor, you are often called upon to help plan remodeling projects. A local shelter for women and children is considering updating a bathroom and has asked for your help in identifying necessary construction materials and an estimated cost for the equipment. The shelter is run by a board of directors to whom you will send a letter of introduction that includes a table of materials. This project is designed to be completed by a group of three students. The project is completed as follows:

a. The team will decide on a shared location in which to place files, such as OneDrive, Dropbox, or server space allotted by the college or university. All team members should become familiar with the shared space and any login requirements.

b. Determine a group name to be used throughout this project, or use one assigned by your instructor. Allocate one of three major tasks to each team member. One student will develop a main document to be used in a mail merge, one student will develop a data source to merge with the main document, and one student will develop a table of building materials to include in the main document before it is merged.

Student 1:

c. Develop an introduction letter to each member of the board of trustees. The letter will be designed as the main document in a mail merge; as such it will include fields for variable data such as each board member's name and mailing address. Indicate in the letter that the included table of materials outlines an estimated cost for each item as well as a total estimate for the remodeling project. The letter should be worded so that another student can easily insert the table of materials.

d. Format the letter attractively, using appropriate alignment, line spacing, and paragraph spacing. The letter should be error-free and grammatically correct. When complete, although without the table that will be inserted later, save the letter as **w03m3Introduction_GroupName**. Upload the letter to the shared location and contact the next student.

Student 2:

e. Develop a data source containing the names and addresses of all six board members. The data source can be a Word table, an Access database table or query, or an Excel worksheet.

f. Use descriptive field names and design the data source so it can be merged with a Word document. Include at least six records. Save the data source as **w03m3Trustees_GroupName** and upload the document to the shared location. Contact Student 3.

Student 3:

g. Convert the text found in *w03m3Construction* into a Word table and format the table so it is attractive, well structured, and descriptive. The table initially contains three columns, including description, quantity, and unit cost. A fourth column should be added to include a formula for each item (multiplying the quantity by the unit cost). Save the table as **w03m3Construction_GroupName** and upload the document to the shared location. Contact Student 2.

Student 2:

h. From the shared location, access or download *w03m3Introduction_GroupName* and *w03m3Construction_GroupName*. Insert text from (or copy and paste) the table into *w03m3Introduction_GroupName*, adjusting wording within the letter, if necessary, to assimilate the table. Save the revised letter as **w03m3Introduction_GroupName** and upload the file to the shared location, replacing the previous version with the new. Contact Student 1.

Student 1:

i. Download *w03m3Introduction_GroupName* and *w03m3Construction_GroupName*. Merge the two documents through Word's mail merge process, incorporating variable data where indicated in the letter. Save the merged document as **w03m3ConstructionLetter_GroupName**.

j. Submit the document based on your instructor's directions.

Beyond the Classroom

Personal Budget Report

RESEARCH CASE

FROM SCRATCH

You are taking a personal finance class this semester and one of the assignments is to provide a report about your income, expenses, and spending habits for a 12-month period. Begin a new document and type two paragraphs that describe your spending habits. Be as general as you like, and feel free to create a fictional account of your spending, if you prefer. In the first paragraph, include your primary sources of income and how you allocate your income to different sources such as savings accounts and expenses. In the second paragraph, describe your major expenses. Create a Word table that details your budget under various major categories such as **Income**, **Expenses**, and **Savings**. Include subcategories such as **Fixed Expenses** and **Variable Expenses**. Examples of fixed expenses include tuition, rent, auto insurance, cable, and cell phone subscriptions. Variable expenses include food, books, school supplies, and utilities. Create multiple columns that enable you to break down your income and costs by category and by month, and then add formulas to show subtotals for each month and the grand total for the 12-month period. Save your report as **w03b2Budget_LastFirst**. Close the document and submit based on your instructor's directions.

Assignment Planner

DISASTER RECOVERY ✚

Your computer applications instructor has assigned the task of using your Word skills to design an assignment planner. She has challenged you to use what you have learned about Word tables to design an attractive document, with a table grid set up so you can enter class assignments for each week. The assignment is a group project, so you and your classmates decide to pattern the assignment planner table after a notebook you already use to record assignments. The first attempt at table design did not go so well, and the classmate who began the project needs help. Open *w03b3Planner* and redesign the document to produce an attractive planner that you could actually use. Do not settle for a mundane table. Use what you have learned about table styles, creating borders, adjusting row height and column width, and alignment to create a stunning table. Make sure your table has enough space for a five-day week and six subjects. Complete the table with a sample week of assignments in classes in which you are enrolled. Save the completed document as **w03b3Planner_LastFirst** and submit based on your instructor's directions.

Pre-Interview Activities

SOFT SKILLS CASE S

FROM SCRATCH

As an assistant in the Office of Student Development, you will create a short document for mailing to all graduating seniors. The document is in the form of a memo, with a placeholder for each student recipient's first and last names, as indicated by the starred placeholders in the sample below:

M E M O
TO: *First Name* *Last Name*
FROM: Office of Student Development
DATE: Current Date
Memo Text

Develop the memo as a main document for inclusion in a mail merge, containing a table you will create after watching the video on pre-interview skills. In the memo, you will let students know how important it is to prepare for an interview, and you will develop a table within the memo with at least three columns and several rows. Column headings might include such categories as Activities, Timeline, and Expected Outcome. The table should be attractively formatted, using appropriate column width, headings, and style. Be creative, designing your own style with shading and border tools. When the memo is complete, develop a data source with the first and last names as well as major program of study for at least eight fictional graduating seniors. Finally, merge the main document with the data source. Save the final merged document as **w03b4PreInterview_LastFirst**. Submit the file based on your instructor's directions.

Capstone Exercise

You work as the business manager for the local Sports Medicine Clinic and are responsible for many forms of correspondence. This week, you want to send a letter of welcome to three physical therapists recently hired at the clinic. Additionally, you need to send your weekly reminders to patients who are scheduled for upcoming treatment or consultations. In the past, the letters were generated manually and names were typed in each letter separately. However, because you now use Word 2013, you decide to create and use source data documents and implement a mail merge so you can produce the letters quickly and accurately.

Create a Table Containing Therapist Information

You will create a new document that includes a table of information about the new physical therapists. Then you will personalize the welcome letter created for the therapists and use information from the table to create a personal letter for each person.

a. Open a new blank document and save it as **w03c1Therapists_LastFirst**.

b. Create a table with the following information:

Name	Credentials	Street Address	Days Working	Salary
Mike Salat	M.S., ATC	2342 W. Cardinal Street	Monday-Thursday	$65,000
Justin Ebert	M.S., ATC	34234 S. Callie Place	Monday-Friday	$68,000
Karen Rakowski	ATC, PT	98234 E. Shepherd Lane	Monday-Friday	$65,000

c. Separate each name, including the column heading, into two columns, because it will be easier to use in form letters using mail merge features. (Hint: Uncheck the option *Merge cells before split* in the Split Cells dialog box.) Make necessary changes to the table to display the therapists' first and last names in two separate columns. The first column should include first names, while the second column contains last names. The first cell in the first row should include **First Name**, and the second cell in the first row should include **Last Name**.

d. Insert three new columns after the Street column for the City, State, and Zip information. Add a column heading to each new column, with **City**, **State**, and **Zip**, from left to right. Center entries in row 1 both horizontally and vertically. Populate each cell in the City column with **Conway**. Each cell in the State column should contain **AR**, and each cell in the Zip column should contain **72032**. Center all entries in rows 2, 3, and 4 both horizontally and vertically.

e. Create a new row at the end of the table. Type the word **Average** in the eighth cell on the last row and right align it. Use a formula to average the Salary column in the next

cell on the last row. (Hint: In the Formula dialog box, remove the suggested function, but leave the = and paste an Average function, indicating that the average should include the numbers *Above*.) Select a currency number format, displaying a dollar sign and two places to the right of the decimal.

f. Select a table style of **Grid Table 6 Colorful - Accent 6** (sixth row, seventh column, under *Grid Tables*). Select a pen color of **Green, Accent 6** and a double underline line style (seventh selection under *Line Style*). Brush the border dividing the first row from the second. Press **Esc**. Remove bold formatting from the first names in column 1.

g. Click the **Border Styles arrow** and select **Border Sampler**. Click to sample the new border dividing the first and second rows and brush it along the bottom border of the table. Press **Esc**.

h. Sort the data in the table (but do not include the header or total rows) by Last Name in ascending order. Save and close the document.

Merge Therapist Information into a Welcome Letter

You have documented information about the new physical therapists; you can use it as a source for the welcome letter.

a. Open *w03c1Welcome*. Start a mail merge using the welcome letter as the source document. The recipient information will come from *w03c1Therapists_LastFirst*. Be sure to deselect the last record in the data source so the Average row is not included in the merge.

b. Replace the bracketed *Current Date* with today's date. Replace the starred placeholders in the letter with fields from the recipient table. Insert an Address Block using the default settings. Include a first name in the salutation and replace *days of week* in the body of the letter with data from the Days_Working field. Replace *Firstname Lastname* in the closing with your first and last names.

c. Complete the merge of all records, producing a document containing three letters, each addressed to a recipient in the data source. Save the merged letters as **w03c1MergedWelcome_LastFirst** and close the document. Close *w03c1Welcome* without saving it.

Produce a Reminder Letter for Patients

Your second project for the day is the generation of a letter to remind patients of their appointment with therapists. For this project, you will use an Access database as the source because that is how your office stores patient information.

a. Begin a new document. You do not need to save the document at this time. Start a mail merge letter, using the current document, and pull your recipients from *w03c1Patients.accdb*. When you select the database file, use the Patients table.

b. Press **Enter** twice and insert today's date, aligned at the left margin. Press **Enter** three times and insert an Address Block, using default settings. Press **Enter** twice and type **RE: Upcoming Appointment**.

c. Press **Enter** twice and type **Please remember that you have an appointment at the Sports Medicine Clinic of Conway on *date*, at *time*. If you have paperwork to fill out, please arrive at our office 15 minutes prior to your appointment time stated above. Thank you!**

d. Press **Enter** twice and finish the letter by typing:
Sincerely,
The Sports Medicine Clinic of Conway
(501) 555-5555

e. Insert the fields for date and time in the first sentence and remove the markers. Change the formatting of the document so the letter is single spaced with no additional spacing before or after any paragraph. Insert three blank paragraphs between *Sincerely* and *The Sports Medicine Clinic of Conway*.

f. Merge all records from the data source into a new document. Save the document as **w03c1Appointments_LastFirst** and close it. Close the original mail merge document without saving it. Exit Word.

g. Submit *w03c1Welcome_LastFirst*, *w03c1MergedWelcome_LastFirst*, and *w03c1Appointments_LastFirst* based on your instructor's directions.

Collaboration and Research

Communicating and Producing Professional Papers

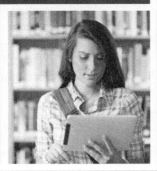

wavebreakmedia/Shutterstock

OBJECTIVES AFTER YOU READ THIS CHAPTER, YOU WILL BE ABLE TO:

1. Use a writing style and acknowledge sources p. 260
2. Create and modify footnotes and endnotes p. 266
3. Explore special features p. 268
4. Review a document p. 278

5. Track changes p. 281
6. Use OneDrive p. 286
7. Share and collaborate on documents p. 288

CASE STUDY | Literature Analysis

You are a college student enrolled in several classes in which you are required to write papers. One is a literature class, and the other is a business management class. Each class requires that you adhere to a specific writing style; each style differs with respect to writing guidelines and the use of citations. As a requirement for the literature class in which you are enrolled, you will prepare an analysis of *The White Heron*, a short story by Sarah Orne Jewett. The analysis is a group effort, completed by five students, including you. You are required to develop the paper based on a particular writing style, and you will include citations and a bibliography. Your instructor will provide feedback in the form of comments that the group will then incorporate into the paper. Because you are a commuting student with a part-time job, you are not always on campus and your time is very limited. As is typical of many college students, even those in your literature group, time and availability are in short supply. The group is quick to realize that much of the coordination on the project must be done from a distance. You will share the project in such a way that each student can contribute, although not in a group setting. Instead, the document will be available online, with each student reviewing, contributing, and reposting the project. Another project involves a short paper for your business management class in which you will include a cover page as well as footnotes.

Research Paper Basics

Researching a topic and preparing a research paper is a common component of most college degrees. The task of writing a research paper is often met with dread by many college students, and although Word cannot replace the researcher, it can provide a great deal of support for properly citing sources and adhering to specific style manuals. A *style manual*, or style guide, is a set of standards for designing documents. In addition, Word assists with preparing footnotes and endnotes and preparing a bibliography. Although the research and wording of a research paper are up to you, Word is an excellent tool in the production of an attractive, well-supported document.

In this section, you will explore the use of Word features that support the preparation of a research paper. Specifically, you will understand the use of style manuals, create source references and insert citations, develop a bibliography, and work with footnotes and endnotes.

Using a Writing Style and Acknowledging Sources

As you write a research paper, you will develop content that supports your topic. The wording you use and the way you present your argument are up to you; however, you will be expected to adhere to a prescribed set of rules regarding page design and the citing of sources. Those rules are spelled out in a style guide that you can refer to as you develop a research paper. A style guide prescribes such settings as margins, line and paragraph spacing, the use of footnotes and endnotes, the way sources are cited, and the preparation of a bibliography.

It is common practice to use a variety of *sources* to supplement your own thoughts when writing a paper, report, legal brief, or other type of document. In fact, the word *research* implies that you are seeking information from other sources to support or explore your topic when writing a research paper. Properly citing or giving credit to your sources of information ensures that you avoid plagiarizing. Merriam-Webster's Collegiate Dictionary's* definition of *plagiarizing* is "to steal and pass off (the ideas or words of another) as one's own." Not limited to failure to cite sources, plagiarism includes buying a paper that is already written and asking (or paying) someone else to write a paper for you. In addition to written words, plagiarism applies to spoken words, multimedia works, or graphics. Plagiarism has serious moral and ethical implications and is typically considered academic dishonesty in a college or university.

Select a Writing Style

When assigning a research paper, your instructor will identify the preferred *writing style*. Various writing styles are available and described in style manuals that are available both in print and online; however, the choice of writing style is often a matter of the academic discipline in which the research is conducted. For example, MLA style is often used in the humanities, while the field of social science typically prefers APA style. Those styles and others are described in this section.

A style manual does not require specific wording within a research paper. It will not assist with developing your topic or collecting research. However, it does provide a set of rules that results in standardized documents that present citations in the same manner and that include the same general page characteristics. In that way, research documents contain similar page features and settings so a reader can focus on the content of a paper without the distraction of varying page setups. Among the most commonly used style manuals are *MLA (Modern Language Association)*, *APA (American Psychological Association)*, and *Chicago*.

If you have recently been assigned the task of writing a research paper as a requirement for an English class, you most likely were instructed to use *MLA writing style*. The humanities

* By permission. From Merriam-Webster's Collegiate® Dictionary, 11th Edition ©2012 by Merriam-Webster, Inc. (www. Merriam-Webster.com).

disciplines, including English, foreign languages, philosophy, religion, art, architecture, and literature, favor the MLA style, which has been in existence for more than 50 years. Brief parenthetical citations throughout a paper identify sources of information, with those sources arranged alphabetically in a works cited page. MLA style is used in many countries around the world, including the United States, Brazil, China, India, and Japan. Current MLA guidelines are published in *MLA Handbook for Writers of Research Papers* and *MLA Style Manual and Guide to Scholarly Publishing*.

Such disciplines as business, economics, communication, and social sciences promote the use of *APA writing style*. Developed in 1929, APA attempts to simplify the expression of scientific ideas and experiment reports in a consistent manner. Its focus is on the communication of experiments, literature reviews, and statistics. The *Publication Manual of the American Psychological Association* provides current rules and guidelines associated with the writing style.

Chicago writing style is an excellent choice for those who are preparing papers and books for publication. In fact, it is one of the most trusted resources within the book publishing industry. True to its name, the Chicago writing style was developed at the University of Chicago in 1906. It is described in *The Chicago Manual of Style*, currently in its 16th edition. The style is often referred to as *CMS* or *CMOS*. Often associated with the Chicago writing style, the **Turabian** writing style originated as a subset of Chicago. The dissertation secretary at the University of Chicago, Kate Turabian, narrowed the Chicago writing style to focus on writing papers. To do so, she omitted much of the information that is relevant for publishing. Currently, Turabian style is used mainly for the development of papers in the field of history.

Regardless of the writing style used, most research papers share common formatting features, as described below. With minor tweaks, a research paper generated according to these suggestions will be well on the way to completion.

- Align text at the left.
- Double-space lines.
- Include no paragraph spacing before or after.
- Set all margins (top, bottom, left, and right) at 1".
- Indent the first line of all body paragraphs by 1/2".
- Separate sentences by only one space.
- Use a serif font, such as Times New Roman, at 12 pt size.
- Create a right-aligned header, including the page number, positioned 1/2" from the top of the page.

Create a Source and Include a Citation

By its very nature, a research paper is a collection of ideas and statements related to a topic. Many of those ideas are your own, summarizing your knowledge and conclusions. However, you will often include facts and results obtained from other sources. When you quote another person, glean ideas from others, or include information from another publication, you must give credit to the source by citing it in the body of your paper and/or including it in a bibliography. A **citation** is a brief, parenthetical reference placed at the end of a sentence or paragraph. Word 2013 enables you to select a writing style upon which all citations, sources, and bibliographic entries will be based. Before using Word to create a research paper, you should select a writing style:

STEP 1 ❯ 1. Click the REFERENCES tab.
2. Click the Style arrow in the Citations & Bibliography group (see Figure 4.1).
3. Click a writing style to use.

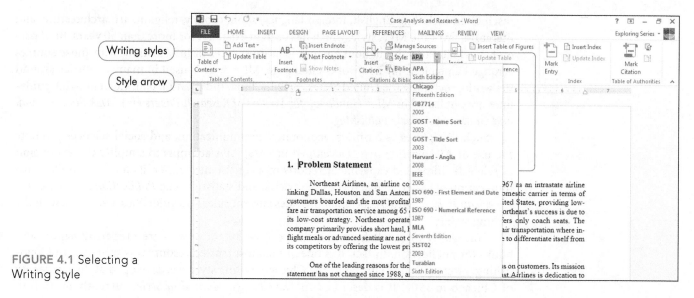

FIGURE 4.1 Selecting a Writing Style

Whenever you quote or paraphrase another person or publication, you should reference the source with a citation. Typically, a citation includes an author or publication name, with an optional page number. A citation directs a reader to a source of information you used. For more information, the reader can check the source on your bibliography or works cited page. Word 2013 formats sources and citations according to the writing style you specify, freeing you from the task of constantly checking a writing style for guidance. Even so, you should always compare citations and bibliographic entries created by Word with the most current writing style guidelines to ensure accuracy.

Proper placement of a citation within a research paper is critical. A citation should appear near a source of reference without interrupting the flow of a sentence. Use your judgment in placing a citation. For example, a long section of text that comes from one source should be cited at the end of the section—not after every sentence within the section. In other cases, a sentence that includes a quote or a direct reference to a particular source should be cited at the end of the sentence. Check a writing style manual for assistance with determining where to place a citation. Citations are typically placed before a punctuation mark that ends a sentence. As you create a citation, you will either add a new source or select a previously defined source as the reference. A cited reference includes the type of source (book, journal article, report, Web site, etc.), title, publisher, page number(s), and other items specific to the type of source. At the conclusion of a report, you can use Word to create a bibliography, listing all of the sources you have cited.

To insert a citation and source:

1. Click at the end of a sentence or phrase that you want to cite.
2. Click the REFERENCES tab.
3. Click Insert Citation in the Citations & Bibliography group.
4. If inserting a previously defined source, click the source. If creating a new source, click Add New Source and type the new source information (see Figure 4.2).

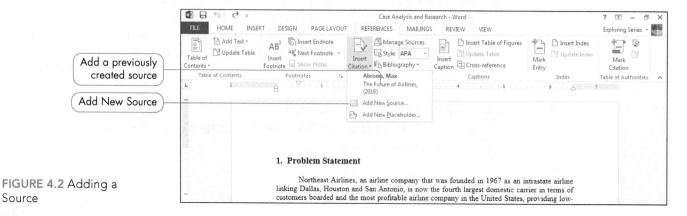

FIGURE 4.2 Adding a Source

Depending on the writing style in use, the way a citation is worded may vary. Although Word 2013 automatically formats citations, you might need to modify the wording or placement of items to accommodate the writing style. For example, if a sentence you are citing includes the author's name, most writing styles require only the page number in the citation, not the author's name. However, Word 2013 will place the author's name in the citation, so you must edit the citation to remove the name. A parenthetical citation is considered a field, which can be selected as a unit within a paper, with actions that can be taken after selecting (such as editing or removing). As such, you can simply click the citation to select it.

To edit a citation:

1. Click the parenthetical citation.
2. Click the Citation Options arrow.
3. Click Edit Citation.
4. Add a page reference and/or suppress the Author, Year, or Title by selecting the appropriate boxes.
5. Click OK.

 TIP Editing a Citation and Source

When you click a parenthetical citation and click the Citation Options arrow, you can do more than simply edit the citation. You can also choose Edit Source (updating the source citation wherever it appears in the document) or Convert citation to static text (removing the field designation from the citation so that you can treat it like normal text). When you convert the citation to text, however, it is no longer included in a bibliography generated by Word unless it also appears elsewhere in the paper.

Share and Search for a Source

When you create a source, it is available for use in the current document, saved in the document's *Current List*. It is also placed in a *Master List*, which is a database of all sources created in Word on a particular computer. Sources saved in the Master List can be shared in any Word document. This feature is helpful to those who use the same sources on multiple occasions. Suppose you are working with a research paper that addresses a topic similar to that of another paper you created on the same computer. To access a source from the Master List of previously defined sources:

1. Click the REFERENCES tab.
2. Click Manage Sources.
3. Select a source in the Master List that you intend to use in the current document (see Figure 4.3).
4. Click Copy to move it to the Current List.
5. Click Close.
6. Click in the location of the citation in the current document and click Insert Citation.
7. Select the source reference.

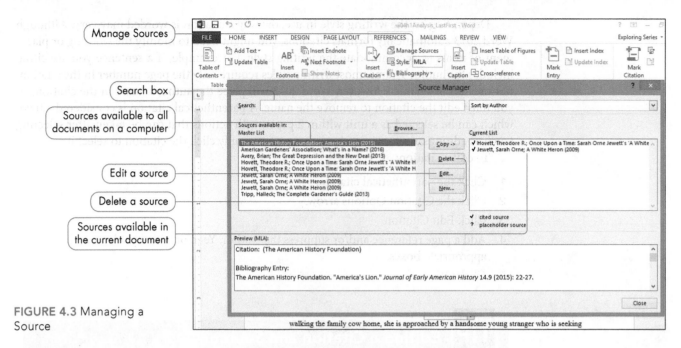

FIGURE 4.3 Managing a Source

The Source Manager not only enables you to share sources among several documents, but it also makes it easy to delete and edit sources. Click Manage Sources on the References tab, select a source from either the Master or Current List, and then click Delete or Edit (refer to Figure 4.3).

Especially if sources are numerous, you might appreciate a quick way to search for a particular source. You can search by author, title, or year. Type a search term in the Search box of the Source Manager dialog box (refer to Figure 4.3). As you type, Word narrows the results so you can more easily determine if a source exists that meets your search criteria.

Create a Bibliography

A *bibliography* is a list of documents or sources consulted by an author during research for a paper. It not only guides a reader to sources of your research for additional study, but it also provides a reader with an opportunity to validate your references for accuracy. In theory, a bibliography lists not only those references that were cited in parenthetical terms throughout the paper but also those that were not cited but were helpful as you prepared the paper. However, Word includes in a bibliography (or *works cited* page) only those sources that were cited in the paper, which is the way most research documents are expected to be prepared. Therefore, a bibliography and a works cited page (which is designed to contain only cited references) are considered synonymous terms when working with Word. After a bibliography is prepared, you can always edit it to add additional references if required. Figure 4.4 shows a bibliography developed in Word. The bibliography is formatted according to the MLA writing style, which requires the use of *Works Cited* as a title. Note that all sources include a hanging indent, which is typical of all writing style requirements. In addition, entries are listed in alphabetical order by last names of authors or editors, or by first words of titles.

> Works Cited
>
> Hovet, Theodore R. "Once Upon a Time: Sarah Orne Jewett's 'A White Heron' as a Fairy Tale."
>
> > *Studies in Short Fiction* 25 Sept. 2011: 63-68.
>
> Jewett, Sarah Orne. "A White Heron." *The American Tradition in Literature*. Ed. George Perkins
>
> > and Barbara Perkins. Vol. 2. New York: McGraw-Hill, 2009. 531-537.
>
> Propp, Vladimir. *Morphology of a Folk Tale*. New York: Anniston, 1994.

FIGURE 4.4 Bibliography

Depending on the writing style you are following, the term used for the list of references varies. MLA uses the term *Works Cited*, whereas APA requires *References*. Still others prefer *Bibliography*. You should be familiar with the preferred term and organization before using Word to develop the list of references. At that point, Word simplifies the addition of the reference page:

STEP 2 »

1. Insert a page break at the end of the research paper.
2. Click the REFERENCES tab.
3. Click Bibliography.
4. Select Bibliography, References, or Works Cited (depending on the particular writing style requirement). If you want no heading but simply the formatted references, click Insert Bibliography.

Regardless of which approach you take, you should always confirm that the resulting page meets all requirements of the particular style to which you are writing. Just as you would proofread a document instead of relying solely on Word's spelling checker, you should also consult a writing style manual to make sure your bibliography is correct.

When Word creates a bibliography page, it places all citations in a single field. As shown in Figure 4.5, when you click a bibliography list that Word has prepared, the entire list is shown as a unit, called a Citations field. The field can be updated; for example, if at a later time you include additional sources within the paper, click *Update Citations and Bibliography* (see Figure 4.5) to include the new sources in the bibliography. You can also choose to format the existing bibliography with a different title (perhaps changing from *Works Cited* to *References*), and you can convert the bibliography to static text, removing the field designation from the bibliography so that you can edit and delete references as you like. At that point, however, you cannot update the bibliography with additional sources.

Click to update the bibliography

Citations field

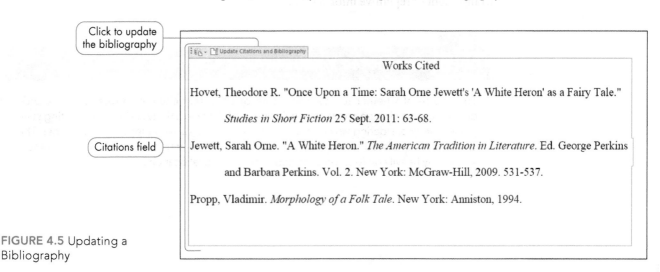

> | Update Citations and Bibliography
>
> Works Cited
>
> Hovet, Theodore R. "Once Upon a Time: Sarah Orne Jewett's 'A White Heron' as a Fairy Tale."
>
> > *Studies in Short Fiction* 25 Sept. 2011: 63-68.
>
> Jewett, Sarah Orne. "A White Heron." *The American Tradition in Literature*. Ed. George Perkins
>
> > and Barbara Perkins. Vol. 2. New York: McGraw-Hill, 2009. 531-537.
>
> Propp, Vladimir. *Morphology of a Folk Tale*. New York: Anniston, 1994.

FIGURE 4.5 Updating a Bibliography

Creating and Modifying Footnotes and Endnotes

A *footnote* is a citation or note that appears at the bottom of a page, while an *endnote* serves the same purpose but appears at the end of a document. Like in-text parenthetical citations, the purpose of a footnote and endnote is to draw a reader's attention to a specific source of information. In addition, footnotes and endnotes are often used to further describe a statistic or statement used in the report without including additional detail in the text. A footnote, providing clarification of a statistic, is shown in Figure 4.6. Note that the footnote is linked by superscript (elevated number) to the corresponding reference in the paper.

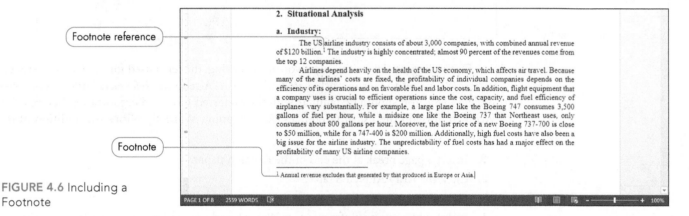

Footnote reference

Footnote

2. Situational Analysis

a. Industry:

The US airline industry consists of about 3,000 companies, with combined annual revenue of $120 billion.[1] The industry is highly concentrated; almost 90 percent of the revenues come from the top 12 companies.

Airlines depend heavily on the health of the US economy, which affects air travel. Because many of the airlines' costs are fixed, the profitability of individual companies depends on the efficiency of its operations and on favorable fuel and labor costs. In addition, flight equipment that a company uses is crucial to efficient operations since the cost, capacity, and fuel efficiency of airplanes vary substantially. For example, a large plane like the Boeing 747 consumes 3,500 gallons of fuel per hour, while a midsize one like the Boeing 737 that Northeast uses, only consumes about 800 gallons per hour. Moreover, the list price of a new Boeing 737-700 is close to $50 million, while for a 747-400 is $200 million. Additionally, high fuel costs have also been a big issue for the airline industry. The unpredictability of fuel costs has had a major effect on the profitability of many US airline companies.

[1] Annual revenue excludes that generated by that produced in Europe or Asia.

PAGE 1 OF 8   2559 WORDS   100%

FIGURE 4.6 Including a Footnote

You should never use both footnotes and endnotes in the same paper. Choosing whether to use footnotes or endnotes, if at all, depends in part on the number of citations included and the way you want your reader to process the report's information. Because endnotes are included as a list at the end of the document, they do not add clutter to the end of pages. In addition, they might make the report easier to read because a reader's gaze is not constantly shifting back and forth from the bottom of a page to the text. Conversely, a footnote provides immediate clarification of a source and enables the writer to make additional comments related to a statement on the same page as the footnote.

Although you might choose to include footnotes to provide additional information related to a statement on the same page, you will most likely use a bibliography or works cited page to provide a complete list of referenced sources in a paper. An advantage to using a bibliography for that task is that each source is listed only once. In contrast, a footnote or endnote appears each time a source is referenced, regardless of how many times the same source is cited in a paper. Although subsequent footnotes and endnotes referencing the same source are abbreviated, they are still listed, often resulting in a cluttered, possibly distracting, arrangement of repetitive information.

TIP Footnotes Versus In-Text Citations

The choice of whether to use a footnote or an in-text citation to reference a source depends somewhat on the writing style you are following. Always refer to the writing style guide when considering which to use, as each style tends to prefer one to the other. The choice is also related to the type of document. For example, legal documents almost always rely heavily on footnotes instead of parenthetical citations.

Including a bibliography does not mean that you cannot use footnotes to provide more detailed descriptions of statements or facts in the paper. You might use a footnote to provide an explanation of statistics. For example, a statistic on the number of victims in a natural disaster or the amount of money given through a government program could be further detailed in a footnote. You might also define or illustrate a concept included in the report, providing a personal comment. Much of business writing is actually persuasive text, in which you explain a situation or encourage others to take some action. Using a footnote is a great way to further describe a statistic used in your text without having to incorporate it into the written paragraph. That way, you do not risk cluttering the manuscript with overly explanatory text, perhaps losing or diverting the attention of the reader. You should be aware, however, that most writing styles limit a footnote to only one sentence. Therefore, any planned explanation of a report statement must be condensed to just one sentence.

Create Footnotes and Endnotes

Source information in a document that you reference with a footnote or endnote includes a number or symbol in superscript. The reference is then keyed to the same number or symbol at the end of the page (footnote) or at the end of the document (endnote).

The References tab includes the Insert Footnote and Insert Endnote options. To insert a footnote or endnote:

STEP 3》

1. Click beside the text to reference (or after ending punctuation, if referencing a sentence)
2. Click the REFERENCES tab.
3. Click Insert Footnote (or Insert Endnote) in the Footnotes group.
4. Type footnote text.

A footnote is automatically positioned at the end of the page, with the same superscript as that assigned to the in-text reference. An endnote is automatically positioned sequentially with other endnotes on a page at the end of the document. By default, Word sequentially numbers footnotes with Arabic numerals (1, 2, and 3). Endnotes are numbered with lower-case Roman numerals (i, ii, and iii). If you add or delete footnotes or endnotes, Word renumbers remaining notes automatically.

Although Word automatically assigns numbers to footnotes or endnotes, you can specify the use of a symbol instead. Click where the reference is to be placed and click the References tab. Click the Footnotes Dialog Box Launcher. Click Symbol in the *Footnote and Endnote* dialog box, select a symbol, click OK, and then click Insert.

Modify Footnotes and Endnotes

Occasionally, you will determine that different wording better suits a particular footnote or endnote. Or perhaps you want to remove a footnote or endnote completely. You can even change the format of a footnote or endnote, changing the font, font size, or character formatting. To modify a footnote or endnote, you can double-click the numeric reference in the body of the document. The insertion point will be placed to the left of the corresponding footnote or endnote text.

To insert a footnote or endnote while specifying settings other than those selected by default, use the *Footnote and Endnote* dialog box. Click the Footnotes Dialog Box Launcher to open the dialog box. As shown in Figure 4.7, you can modify the placement, number format, symbol, and initial number before you insert a new footnote or endnote.

Position in document

Number format

Start numbering

Select a symbol

FIGURE 4.7 *Footnote and Endnote* Dialog Box

You can remove note text and replace it with alternate wording, just as you would adjust wording in a document. If you plan to change the format of a single note, instead of affecting all footnotes or endnotes in a document, you can select text and apply different formatting—perhaps italicizing or bolding words.

More often, you might want to adjust the format of every footnote or endnote in a document. Footnotes are formatted in Footnote Text style, and endnotes are formatted in Endnote Text style. Those styles include a specific font and font size. To modify the style of either a footnote or endnote so that the formatting changes you make are applied to all notes in a document:

1. Right-click a footnote or endnote and click Style.
2. Click Modify (in the Style dialog box).
3. Adjust font and alignment settings or click Format for more selections.
4. Click OK (repeatedly, if necessary) to accept settings and return to the document.

TIP Deleting a Footnote or Endnote

To delete a footnote or endnote, select the numeric footnote or endnote indicator in the document. Press Delete.

Exploring Special Features

Although writing a research paper is a typical requirement of a college class, it is not the only type of paper you are likely to write. In the workplace, you might be asked to contribute to technical reports, grant proposals, and other types of business documents. Those reports are not likely to be as strictly bound to writing style rules as are reports written for academic purposes. In fact, you might find it necessary to include special features such as a table of contents, an index, and even a cover page to properly document a paper and make it easier to navigate. Such features are not usually included in a college research report or required by academic writing style guides, but they are common components of papers, chapters, and articles to be published or distributed.

Create a Table of Contents

A *table of contents* lists headings in the order they appear in a document, along with the page numbers on which the entries begin. The key to enabling Word to create a table of contents is to apply heading styles to headings in the document at appropriate levels. You can apply built-in styles, Heading 1 through Heading 9, or identify your own custom styles to use when generating the table of contents. For example, if you apply Heading 1 style to major headings, Heading 2 style to subordinate headings, and lesser numbered heading styles to remaining headings as appropriate, Word can create an accurate table of contents. At your request, Word will update the table of contents when you change heading text, sequence, or level.

STEP 4›

To insert a predefined table of contents, ensure that headings in the document are formatted with heading styles according to level. Then:

1. Click the REFERENCES tab.
2. Click *Table of Contents* in the *Table of Contents* group.
3. Select an Automatic table style to create a formatted table of contents that can be updated when heading text or positioning changes (or select Manual Table to create a table of contents that is not updated when changes occur).

For more flexibility as you design a table of contents, you can click *Table of Contents* (on the References tab) and then select *Custom Table of Contents*. From the *Table of Contents* dialog box, select options related to page numbering and alignment, general format, level of headings to show, and leader style (the characters that lead the reader's eye from a heading to its page number). The subsequent table of contents can be updated when changes occur in headings within the document.

A table of contents created by Word is inserted as a field. When you click a table of contents, the entire table is shown as an entity that you can update or remove. As shown in Figure 4.8, controls at the top of the selection enable you to update, modify, or remove a table of contents. As you make changes to a document, especially if those changes affect the number, positioning, or sequencing of headings, you will want to update any associated table of contents. You will indicate whether you want to update page numbers only or the entire table.

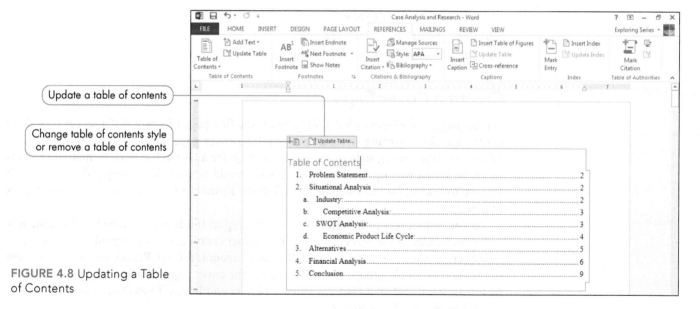

Update a table of contents

Change table of contents style or remove a table of contents

FIGURE 4.8 Updating a Table of Contents

Create an Index

No doubt you have used an *index* to locate a topic of interest in a book. In doing so, you were able to move quickly to the topic. Most books and many lengthy papers include an index. Typically located at the end of a book or document, an index provides an alphabetical listing of topics included in a document, along with related page numbers. Using Word 2013, you can mark items to include and then have them automatically formatted as an index.

To mark items to include in an index:

1. Select a word or phrase to include in an index.
2. Click the REFERENCES tab and click Mark Entry in the Index group.

3. Select or confirm settings in the Mark Index Entry dialog box.
   - Ensure that text in the Main entry box is stated exactly as it should appear in the index.
   - If only one occurrence of the selected text is to be noted in the index, click Mark. Otherwise, click Mark All to include all occurrences of the selected text.
   - Include a cross reference, if necessary. For example, an index entry for *appetizers* could be cross-referenced with *hors d'oeuvres*. Click Mark.

4. Repeat steps 1 and 3 for any additional terms to mark as index entries. Close the dialog box when all items have been marked.

As you mark entries for inclusion in the index, they will be coded in the document with a tag. After marking entries to include in an index, you are ready to create the index, typically among the last pages of a document. Word 2013 arranges the index entries in alphabetical order and supplies appropriate page references. To create an index:

1. Insert a blank page at the end of the document or at a location where the index is to display. Position the insertion point on the blank page.
2. Click the REFERENCES tab and click Insert Index in the Index group.
3. Adjust settings in the Index dialog box, including the format style, number of columns, language, and alignment.
4. Click OK.

Creating an index is usually among the last tasks related to preparing a paper, chapter, or book. However, even if an index has been created, you can still update the index with new entries. New entries are alphabetized along with the original entries in the index. To update an index so that newly marked entries are included:

1. Click in the index to select it.
2. Click the REFERENCES tab.
3. Click Update Index in the Index group.

Create a Cover Page

A *cover page*, sometimes called a *title page*, is the first page of a report if a report includes a cover page. Some writing styles do not require a cover page for a research report, whereas others do. APA writing style requires a cover page for a research report, formatted in a certain way. When writing a research paper, you should consult the writing guide of the style you are following for information related to the format of a cover page (if a cover page is required).

Because the cover page is the first page of a report but is not formatted in the same way as the remainder of the report, you might consider creating a cover page in its own section. Simply create the cover page and click the Page Layout tab. Click Breaks and click Next Page in the Section Breaks group. You will not want the cover page to include a page number, so be sure to select Different First Page on the Header and Footer Tools Design tab if you create a page number header or footer.

> **TIP Creating a Cover Page**
>
> If the writing style allows it or if you are not following a writing style, you can use Word 2013 to create a cover page in any of a variety of styles. Click the Insert tab and click Cover Page in the Pages group. Select from a number of designs, or click More Cover Pages from Office.com for even more choice. Personalize the cover page with your name, report title, and any other variable data.

1. What type of writing style would you expect to be required to use for a writing assignment in a business class? *p. 261*

2. How would you edit a citation to remove an author name and add a page number? *p. 263*

3. You find that you can use some of the same sources in the research paper you are currently working on were used in your previous research paper. How can you pull sources from the previous paper so that you do not have to recreate them? *p. 263*

4. You have developed a table of contents for a research paper. After having done that, you rearrange a few headings and add others. How can you make sure a table of contents is updated to reflect the current content of a document, especially if content has changed? *p. 269*

Hands-On Exercises

Watch the Video
for this Hands-
On Exercise!

MyITLab®
HOE1 Training

1 Research Paper Basics

You have completed a draft of an analysis of the short story *A White Heron*. As a requirement for the literature class in which you are enrolled, you must format the paper according to MLA style, including citations and a bibliography. In addition to the literature analysis, you have also completed a marketing plan for a fictional company, required for a business management class. The instructor of that class has asked that you consider submitting the paper for inclusion in a collection of sample papers produced by the School of Business at your university. For that project, you will include a cover page, table of contents, and an index.

Skills covered: Select a Writing Style and Create a Source • Share and Search for a Source and Create a Bibliography • Create and Update Footnotes • Create a Table of Contents and an Index • Create a Cover Page

---

STEP 1 ≫ SELECT A WRITING STYLE AND CREATE A SOURCE

You will format the analysis of *A White Heron* in MLA style and include citations where appropriate. Refer to Figure 4.9 as you complete Step 1.

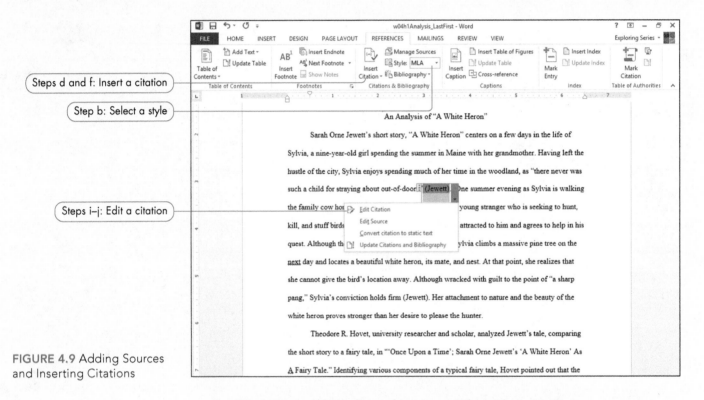

FIGURE 4.9 Adding Sources and Inserting Citations

a. Start Word. Open *w04h1Analysis* and save it as **w04h1Analysis_LastFirst**.

b. Click the **REFERENCES tab** and click the **Style arrow** in the Citations & Bibliography group. Select **MLA Seventh Edition**. Ensure that the following settings, required by the MLA writing style, are in place, adjusting any that may be missing or incorrect:

- Document is double-spaced.
- The font is Times New Roman 12 pt.
- There is no paragraph spacing before or after any paragraph.
- Margins are 1" at the top, bottom, left, and right.
- All body paragraphs are indented .5".
- The report title is centered.

c. Insert a right-aligned header that includes your last name, followed by a space and a plain page number. Make sure the page number is inserted as a field, not simply typed. The header should be formatted as Times New Roman 12 pt.

d. Place the insertion point after the ending quotation mark and before the ending period in the second sentence of the first body paragraph, ending in *straying about out-of-doors*. Click the **REFERENCES tab** and then click **Insert Citation** in the Citations & Bibliography group. Click **Add New Source**. Click the **Type of Source arrow** and click **Book Section**. Complete the citation as follows, but do not click OK after completing the source.

Author: **Jewett, Sarah Orne**

Title: **A White Heron**

Book Title: **The American Tradition in Literature**

Year: **2009**

Pages: **531–537**

City: **New York**

Publisher: **McGraw-Hill**

e. Click **Show All Bibliography Fields**. Click in the **Editor box** and type **Perkins, George**. Click **Edit** beside *Editor*. Type **Perkins** in the **Last box**. Click in the **First box** and type **Barbara**. Click **Add** and click **OK**. Click in the **Volume box** and type **2**. Click **OK**.

You have added a source related to a section of a book in which the short story is printed.

f. Click after the word *firm* and before the ending period in the sentence that ends in *Sylvia's conviction holds firm* in the same paragraph. Click **Insert Citation** in the Citations & Bibliography group and click **Jewett, Sarah Orne** to insert a citation to the same source as that created earlier.

g. Place the insertion point after the ending quotation mark and before the ending period in the sentence in the second body paragraph ending in *functions that are also present in "A White Heron"*. Add a new source, selecting **Article in a Periodical** as the source type:

Author: **Hovet, Theodore R.**

Title: **Once Upon a Time: Sarah Orne Jewett's 'A White Heron' as a Fairy Tale**

Periodical Title: **Studies in Short Fiction**

Year: **2011**

Month: **Sept.**

Day: **25**

Pages: **63–68**

h. Click **Show All Bibliography Fields**, complete the following, and then click **OK**.

Volume: **15**

Issue: **1**

i. Click the parenthetical citation in the first body paragraph beside the words *straying about out-of-doors*. Click the **Citation Options arrow** and click **Edit Citation**. Type **532** in the **Pages box**. Click **OK**.

You have added a page number to identify the source as required by MLA writing style.

j. Edit the next citation in the first body paragraph, following the sentence that ends in *Sylvia's conviction holds firm*, to include page number **537**. Click the only citation in the second body paragraph. Click the **Citation Options arrow** and click **Edit Citation**. Suppress the display of Author, Year, and Title, but include a Page Number of **63**. Click **OK**.

k. Save the document.

Now that sources are cited and stored in the document, you can quickly insert the bibliography at the end. You will also explore the sharing of sources. Refer to Figure 4.10 as you complete Step 2.

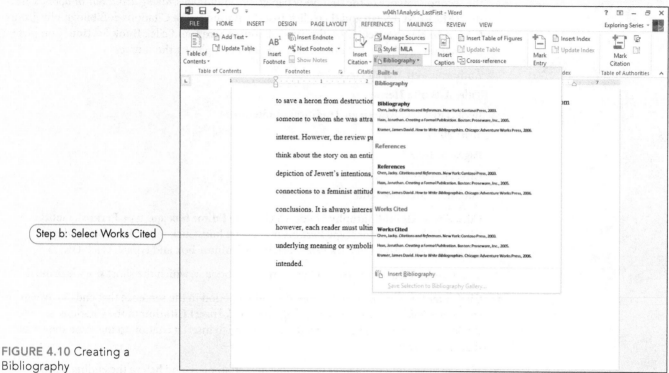

Step b: Select Works Cited

FIGURE 4.10 Creating a Bibliography

a. Click **Manage Sources**.

Note that the sources you created in the previous step are shown in the Master List as well as in the Current List. They are available for use in other documents, as well as in the current document.

> **TROUBLESHOOTING:** It is possible that sources other than those you just added are also shown in the Master List. The list includes all sources you have included in other documents as well as those in the current document.

b. Click **Close**. Press **Ctrl+End** to move to the end of the document. Press **Ctrl+Enter** to insert a page break. Click **Bibliography** in the Citations & Bibliography group and click **Works Cited.**

A bibliography is always included as a separate page at the end of the document. Therefore, you insert a page break before adding the bibliography. The bibliography includes the heading *Works Cited*. The two sources you used in your analysis are listed, although you may have to scroll up to see them.

c. Drag to select all text on the Works Cited page, including the heading *Works Cited* and all sources. Change the line spacing to **2.0** (or double), the paragraph spacing Before and After to **0**, and the font to **Times New Roman 12 pt**. Select the *Works Cited* heading, remove the bold format, and center the line.

The Works Cited page adheres to MLA writing style guidelines.

d. Save and close the document. Leave Word open for the next step.

STEP 3 >> CREATE AND UPDATE FOOTNOTES

You are a business major enrolled in a business management class. As a final project, you have prepared a case analysis of a fictional airline. Due to the large amount of statistical data included, you expect to use footnotes to provide additional clarification. Because footnotes and endnotes are mutually exclusive—you only use one or the other in a single paper—you will not use endnotes. However, you know that the way in which endnotes and footnotes are added is very similar. Refer to Figure 4.11 as you complete Step 3.

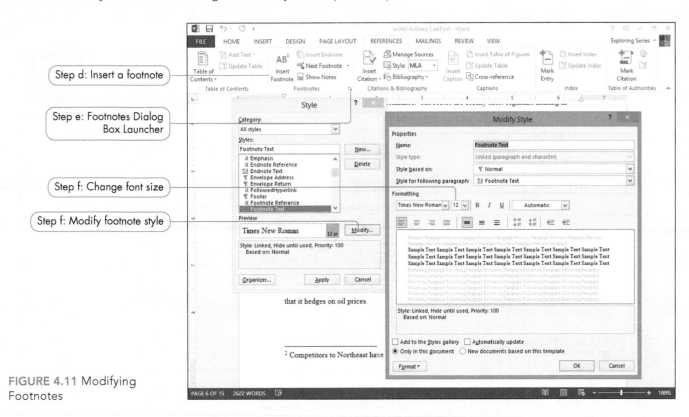

FIGURE 4.11 Modifying Footnotes

a. Open *w04h1Airlines* and save it as **w04h1Airlines_LastFirst**.

b. Click the **Select arrow** in the Editing group on the HOME tab, click **Select All**, and then apply the following formatting:

   - Line spacing is 2.0 (or double)
   - Paragraph spacing Before and After is 0
   - Font is Times New Roman at 12 pt size
   - Alignment is left aligned

c. Deselect the text.

d. Click **Find** in the Editing group. The Navigation Pane opens on the left. Type **200 million** in the Search box and press **Enter**. Click after the period ending the sentence that ends in *$200 million*, which is shown highlighted. Close the Navigation Pane. Click the **REFERENCES tab** and click **Insert Footnote** in the Footnotes group. Type **This statistic is obtained from the 2015 U.S. Air Transportation Log.** (include the period).

   You insert a footnote, numbered with a superscript, further clarifying the information stated.

e. Scroll to page 4 and place the insertion point after the period ending the first paragraph, ending in *34 years*. Click the **Footnotes Dialog Box Launcher** and click **Insert**. Type **Competitors to Northeast have proven slightly less profitable.** (include the period).

   You insert another footnote, numbered sequentially after the first footnote. Using the *Footnote and Endnote* dialog box, you have options to specify various choices, including numbering and formatting.

f. Right-click the footnote at the bottom of page 4 and click **Style**. Click **Modify**. Change the font size to **12**. Click **OK**. Click **Apply**.

You changed the footnote style for this document to include a font size of 12. The new format applies to all footnotes in the document.

g. Save the document.

STEP 4 ≫ CREATE A TABLE OF CONTENTS AND AN INDEX

The case study is almost complete, but your instructor requires a table of contents and an index. You will prepare a table of contents and will begin an index. Refer to Figure 4.12 as you complete Step 4.

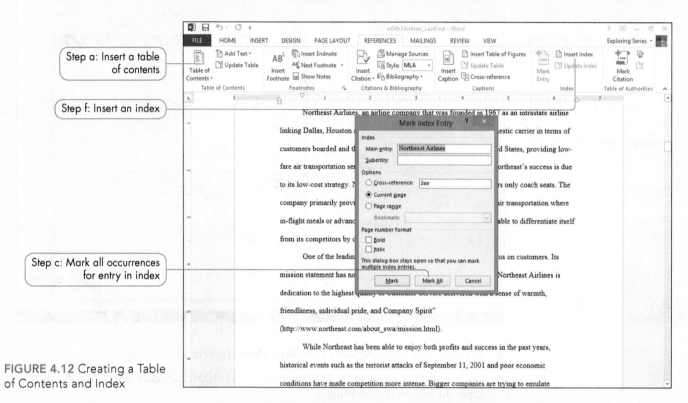

FIGURE 4.12 Creating a Table of Contents and Index

a. Press **Ctrl+Home** to move to the beginning of the document. Press **Ctrl+Enter** to insert a page break. Move to the beginning of the new page and press **Enter** twice. Click the **REFERENCES tab**, if necessary, and click **Table of Contents** in the Table of Contents group. Select **Automatic Table 2**.

You inserted a table of contents comprising headings and page numbers from the report.

b. Scroll to page 3 and change the heading *Situational Analysis* to **Data Analysis**. Press **Ctrl+Home** to move to the beginning of the document and ensure that the table of contents is selected. If not, click to select the table of contents. Click **Update Table** at the top-left corner of the table. Click **Update entire table**. Click **OK**.

You changed the wording of a heading in the report. After updating the table of contents, the new wording is also included there.

c. Click outside the table of contents to deselect it. Click the **REFERENCES tab**, if necessary. Scroll to page 2 and select **Northeast Airlines** in the first sentence of the first body paragraph. Click **Mark Entry** in the Index group, click **Mark All** in the Mark Index Entry dialog box, and then click **Close**.

You have marked the phrase *Northeast Airlines* for inclusion in the index. By selecting *Mark All*, you have instructed Word to include a page reference to the phrase wherever it occurs in the document.

d. Select the word **Northeast** in the sentence that begins *Northeast operates solely Boeing 737s* in the same paragraph. Click **Mark Entry** in the Index group. Select **Cross-reference** and type **Northeast Airlines** beside the word *See*. Click **Mark**. Click **Close**.

Because you refer to Northeast Airlines throughout the document as either *Northeast Airlines* or *Northeast*, you will cross-reference the term so that it appears appropriately in the index.

e. Scroll to page 4 and mark the first word on the page, **Code-sharing**, as an index entry, making sure to mark all occurrences. Place the insertion point at the end of the document and insert a page break. Ensure the insertion point is at the top of the new blank page.

f. Click **Insert Index** in the Index group. Click **OK** to accept all default settings and insert the index.

You inserted an index comprising the three terms you marked earlier. A complete index would most likely consist of many more terms, with all terms referenced to pages in the document.

g. Save the document.

STEP 5 ⟩⟩ CREATE A COVER PAGE

As a final touch, you will create a cover page with information related to the report title, your name, the course number, and the current date. Refer to Figure 4.13 as you complete Step 5.

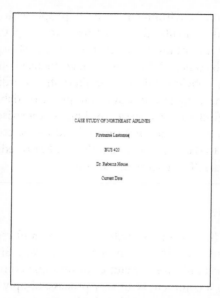

CASE STUDY OF NORTHEAST AIRLINES

Firstname Lastname

BUS 420

Dr. Rebecca House

Current Date

FIGURE 4.13 Creating a Cover Page

a. Insert a page break at the beginning of the document and place the insertion point at the top of the new blank page. Click the **HOME tab** and click **Center alignment**. Change the font size to **16 pt**. Change the font color to **Black, Text 1**. Toggle off **Italic**, if necessary.

b. Type **CASE STUDY OF NORTHEAST AIRLINES**. Press **Enter** three times. Type your first and last names. Press **Enter** three times. Type **BUS 420**. Press **Enter** three times. Type **Dr. Rebecca House**. Press **Enter** three times. Type the current date. Ensure that text on the cover page is neither bold nor italicized.

Although Word 2013 provides many more colorful choices of cover pages, you design a more conservative cover page to accompany this business report.

c. Click the **PAGE LAYOUT tab** and click the **Page Setup Dialog Box Launcher**. Click the **Layout tab**. Click the **Vertical Alignment arrow** and click **Center**. Click **OK**.

You centered the cover page vertically.

d. Click the **VIEW tab** and click **One Page**.

The cover page is centered vertically on the page.

e. Save the document and exit Word. Submit as directed by your instructor.

Document Tracking

Whether in a college class or in the workplace, it is likely that you will seek feedback from others or that you will collaborate with others on the completion of a project. Word 2013 provides a clutter-free way to make comments, reply to comments, and track changes that might have been made to a document by others during a review process. Called *Simple Markup*, Word 2013's approach to group editing makes it easy to track changes and review any comments that have been made. Documents are often saved in *PDF* format to share with others. PDF (portable document format) is a file format that captures all of the elements of a page and stores them in electronic format. Especially useful for documents like magazine articles, brochures, and flyers, PDF format accurately represents all page elements, including graphics and text effects. Using Word 2013, you can now convert a PDF document into a Word document and edit the content.

In this section, you will explore reviewing documents, adding and replying to comments in the process. As you track changes in a document, you will learn to control the level of detail that shows, and you can accept or reject changes made by others. Finally, you will explore ways that Word enables you to work with PDF documents.

Reviewing a Document

In today's organizational environment, teams of people with diverse backgrounds, skills, and knowledge prepare documents. Team members work together while planning, developing, writing, and editing important documents. A large part of that process is reviewing work begun or submitted by others. No doubt you have focused on a document so completely that you easily overlooked obvious mistakes or alternative wording. A reviewer can often catch mistakes, perhaps even suggesting ways to improve readability. In reviewing a document, you will most often find ways to change wording or otherwise edit the format, and you might find an opportunity to provide *comments* related to the content. Although comments are most often directed to the attention of another author or editor, you can even include comments to remind yourself of a necessary action.

Add a Comment

The Review tab includes options related to adding and replying to comments, as well as tracking changes and changing the markup view. Using Simple Markup, a feature new to Word 2013, you can minimize the clutter of multiple comments, viewing only those that you choose. Adding a comment is an easy process. Simply click in the document or select a word or phrase to comment on and click New Comment in the Comments group on the Review tab. In the subsequent *comment balloons*, type a comment. You will be identified as the author in the comment balloon. If you do not select anything prior to clicking New Comment, Word assigns the comment to the word or object closest to the insertion point. Figure 4.14 shows a document in the All Markup view with a few comments. All replies to original comments are indented beneath the original, which makes it easy to follow the progression of a comment through its replies, if any.

- All Markup view selected
- Track Changes
- Comment with a reply
- Edits to the document (revision marks)
- Bar indicating revisions

FIGURE 4.14 All Markup View

The document in Figure 4.14 is shown with All Markup selected in the Tracking group. Other options for markup views include Simple Markup, which is shown in Figure 4.15, as well as No Markup. The same document with the same comments, shown in Simple Markup, is much less cluttered. A small balloon on the right side of a paragraph in which a comment has been made provides access to the comment. A red vertical bar on the left side of a paragraph in which edits have been made alerts a reader to the existence of edits. Click a balloon to view a comment or click the red vertical bar to view edited text.

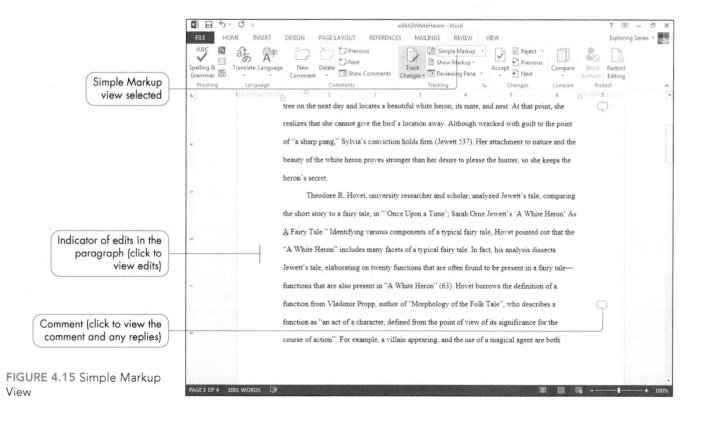

- Simple Markup view selected
- Indicator of edits in the paragraph (click to view edits)
- Comment (click to view the comment and any replies)

FIGURE 4.15 Simple Markup View

Before you use the Comments feature, make sure your name appears as you want it to in any comments. To do so, click the File tab and click Options. In the *General* section, confirm that your name and initials display as the user. Word uses that information to identify the person who uses collaboration tools, such as Comments. If you are in a lab environment, you might not have permission to modify settings or change the user name; however, you should be able to change those settings on a home computer.

View and Reply to Comments

With Simple Markup selected, comments are identified by comment balloons in Print Layout, Web Layout view, or Read Mode. Click a comment balloon to read the associated comment. Having viewed the comment, click Close in the comment to remove it from view. In Draft view, comments appear as tags embedded in the document; when you hover the cursor over the tag, the comment shows.

STEP 1 ❯❯   In any view, you can display the Reviewing Pane, which displays all comments and editorial changes made to the document, as well as statistics regarding the number of changes made. You will find the Reviewing Pane useful when contents of comments are too lengthy to display completely in a comment balloon. Figure 4.16 shows the Reviewing Pane on the left. To display the Reviewing Pane:

1. Click the Reviewing Pane arrow on the REVIEW tab.
2. Select Reviewing Pane Vertical or Reviewing Pane Horizontal.

FIGURE 4.16 Reviewing Pane

In previous versions of Word, the number of comments could become overwhelming. To reply to a comment, you would create yet another comment, complicating the display even more. Word 2013 addresses that problem with a new feature that enables you to reply to a comment within the original comment. Each comment has a Reply option. Click Reply (see Figure 4.17) and type a response. The response will be placed in the original comment's comment balloon, indented slightly, with the commenter identified by name.

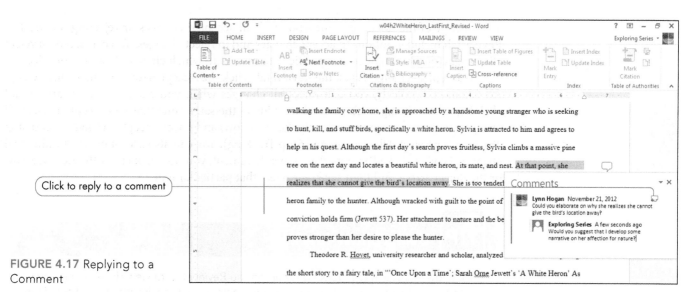

Click to reply to a comment

FIGURE 4.17 Replying to a Comment

When a comment has been addressed, it may no longer be relevant to the review process, and you might want to prohibit any further replies to the original comment. To deactivate a comment, right-click the open comment and select Mark Comment Done. Although the balloon remains in Simple Markup, the comment is grayed out when you click the balloon, so it is evident that it has been addressed. Further replies to the original comment are prohibited.

Tracking Changes

Whether you work individually or with a group, you can monitor any revisions you make to a document. The *Track Changes* feature keeps track of all additions, deletions, and formatting changes made to the document. Click Track Changes (refer to Figure 4.14) to track all changes made to a document. Click it again to toggle the feature off so that changes are no longer tracked. It is particularly useful in situations in which a document must be reviewed by several people—each of whom can offer suggestions or change parts of the document—and then returned to one person who will finalize the document.

Use Track Changes

When Track Changes is not active, any change you make to a document is untraceable, and no one will know what you change unless he or she compares your revised document with the previous version. When Track Changes is active, it applies *revision marks*, which indicate where a person added, deleted, or formatted text. In addition, a bar displays on the left side of any paragraph in which edits have occurred (refer to Figure 4.14).

STEP 3»

In Simple Markup, you will not see changes, even with Track Changes toggled on. Instead, a red bar on the left side of a modified paragraph will alert you to the fact that something is different. Click the red bar (refer to Figure 4.15) to show the changes. Click the bar again to remove them from view.

For a completely clean view of a document, temporarily hiding all comments and revisions, click the Markup arrow in the Tracking group on the Review tab and click No Markup. Although no revisions or comments show, keep in mind that they are only hidden. To remove them permanently, you have to accept or reject all changes.

Accept and Reject Changes

As you complete revision on a document, you will have reviewed all comments and acted on them or otherwise replied to the reviewer. You will also have had an opportunity to view all edits, including changes in wording and formatting. At that point, you will want to produce a clean copy of the document, incorporating all accepted changes or rejecting others. The Review tab includes options to accept changes and to reject changes. You can accept or reject all changes, or you can be more specific with respect to which changes to accept or reject.

To accept all changes, click the Review tab, click the Accept arrow, and then click Accept All Changes. Similarly, you can reject all changes when you click the Reject arrow and click Reject All Changes. To turn off tracking at the same time that you accept or reject all changes, click the Accept arrow (or the Reject arrow) and select Accept All Changes and Stop Tracking (or Reject All Changes and Stop Tracking). You can also accept or reject individual changes. Having clicked an edited area in a document, you can click either the Accept arrow or the Reject arrow, and then accept or reject that particular edit.

 Using Show Markup

Click Show Markup in the Tracking group on the Review tab to view document revisions organized by the type of revision (such as comments, formatting, insertions, and deletions) as well as by reviewer. You can toggle each selection on or off, so you can view several at the same time.

Work with PDF Documents

PDF Reflow is a feature that produces editable Word documents from PDF files—documents that retain the intended formatting and page flow of the original PDF document. PDF Reflow seeks to convert recognizable features of a PDF document into items that are native to Word. For example, a table in a PDF document is converted into a table in a Word document so you can use Word's table feature to modify and update the item. Similarly, bulleted lines in a PDF file become bulleted paragraphs in a Word document. Although using PDF Reflow does not always convert every feature flawlessly, the result is usually a close imitation of the original. PDF Reflow is more attuned to converting text than graphics.

STEP 2》 To convert a PDF document to Word 2013, start Word, click the File tab, click Open, and then browse for the PDF document to open. Within a few seconds, the PDF file opens as a Word document. At that point, you can edit it as you would any Word document. To save a Word document as a PDF file, click the File tab and click Export. Click Create PDF/XPS and click Publish.

Quick
Concepts

1. When you reply to a comment, where is your reply placed? *p. 280*

2. In Simple Markup, how can you tell that edits have been made to a paragraph? How can you see the changes that have been made? *p. 281*

3. As you complete a research paper that has been marked up by several reviewers (with Track Changes on), you now want to provide a clean copy. What steps might you follow to do that? *p. 282*

4. Briefly describe the Word feature that converts a PDF file into a Word document so that you can edit the document. *p. 282*

Hands-On Exercises

Watch the Video for this Hands-On Exercise!

MyITLab®
HOE2 Training

2 Document Tracking

Your literature group submitted a draft copy of the analysis of *A White Heron*. Your literature instructor will make comments and suggest any additional editing before the paper is considered complete. Even at this early stage, however, your instructor is very pleased with your group's initial analysis. In fact, she suggested that you prepare to submit the paper to the campus Phi Kappa Phi Honor Society for judging in a writing contest. She will provide a copy of the entry form in PDF format so you can have it on hand when you submit the paper. At this point, you will review her comments and changes and act on her suggestions.

Skills covered: Add, View, and Reply to Comments • Work with a PDF Document • Use Track Changes and Accept or Reject Changes

STEP 1 ≫ ADD, VIEW, AND REPLY TO COMMENTS

Your instructor has returned to you an electronic copy of the analysis with a few comments and edits. You will review the suggestions, make a few changes, and save the document for final review and group collaboration later. Refer to Figure 4.18 as you complete Step 1.

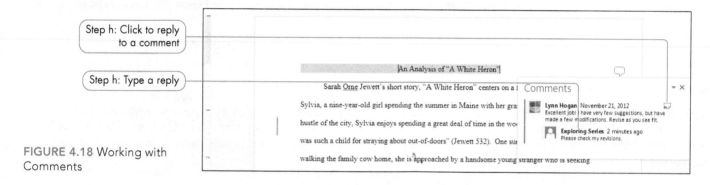

FIGURE 4.18 Working with Comments

a. Open *w04h2WhiteHeron* and save it as **w04h2WhiteHeron_LastFirst**.

b. Click the **REVIEW tab**, click the **Simple Markup arrow** in the Tracking group, and then click **All Markup**. Review the comments made by your instructor, as well as the tracked edits in the document. Click the **All Markup arrow** in the Tracking group and click **Simple Markup** to return to an uncluttered view.

> **TROUBLESHOOTING:** It is possible that All Markup is selected as the markup view before you begin this exercise. In that case, review the comments and edits, click the All Markup arrow, and then click Simple Markup. Continue to step c.

c. Click the **Reviewing Pane arrow** in the Tracking group and click **Reviewing Pane Vertical**. Scroll through the comments and edits shown in the Reviewing Pane. Close the Reviewing Pane (titled *Revisions*).

d. Click the vertical red bar on the left side of the first body paragraph to view all edits and comments. Click the bar again to hide the tracked changes. Point to the first comment balloon on the right of the report title and note the highlighted text. Click the comment balloon, if necessary, to view the comment. Click the comment balloon again to close the comment.

e. View the third comment on the first page and note that you need to add a citation. Click **Close** in the markup balloon to close it. Click after the quotation mark and before the period in the sentence in the last paragraph on the first page, ending with *for the course of action*. Add a new source for the following book:

Author: **Propp, Vladimir**

Title: **Morphology of a Folk Tale**

Year: **1994**

City: **New York**

Publisher: **Anniston**

f. Scroll to the end of the document and click to select the **Works Cited field**. Click **Update Citations and Bibliography**.

   You added a new source and updated the Works Cited page to include the newly added source.

g. Scroll to page 1 and click the second comment balloon to view the comment. Close the markup balloon. Click before the word *Although* in the sentence in the first body paragraph that begins with *Although wracked with guilt*. Type **She is too tenderhearted to give up the heron family to the hunter.** Press **spacebar**.

h. Click the first comment on page 1, point to the comment text, and then click **Reply** (see Figure 4.18) at the right side of the instructor name. Type **Please check my revisions.** Close the comment.

i. Save and close the document. Keep Word open for the next step.

STEP 2 ➤ WORK WITH A PDF DOCUMENT

You are ready to finalize the paper, and your instructor has let you know that you must include an entry form with the submission. You are not on campus, so your instructor has e-mailed the entry form as a PDF document. You will convert the form to Word and then complete it with your name and report information. You will then save it as a PDF document for later submission. Refer to Figure 4.19 as you complete Step 2.

FIGURE 4.19 Working with a PDF Document

a. Click the **FILE tab** and click **Open**. Open *w04h2Entry.pdf* from your student files. Click **OK** if warned that the conversion might take a while. Click after **Date** and type today's date. Complete the remaining information, including your name, instructor's name, college level, e-mail, and report title, **An Analysis of "A White Heron"**.

   PDF Reflow has converted the original PDF version of the entry form and opened it in Word so you can modify it.

> **TROUBLESHOOTING:** If the document opened as an Adobe PDF file instead of as a Word document, you opened the file from File Explorer. Instead, you should open the document from within Word when you click the File tab and click Open.

b. Click the **FILE tab** and click **Export**. Click **Create PDF/XPS**. Navigate to the location where you save your assignments and ensure that *Open file after publishing* is checked. Click **Publish**. After the PDF version of the completed entry form opens, close the document. Close the Word version of the entry form without saving it.

You saved the entry form you completed in Word as a PDF file for later submission with the entry.

STEP 3 >> USE TRACK CHANGES AND ACCEPT AND REJECT CHANGES

You are ready to submit the paper, but you must first accept or reject changes and remove all comments. Refer to Figure 4.20 as you complete Step 3.

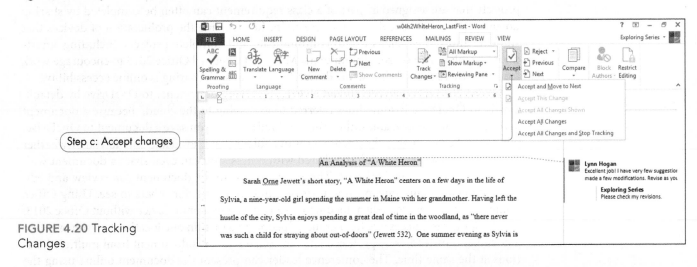

FIGURE 4.20 Tracking Changes

a. Open *w04h2WhiteHeron_LastFirst*. Click the **REVIEW tab** and click the **Simple Markup arrow**, unless All Markup is already selected. Click **All Markup**.

b. Click anywhere in the sentence you added on the first page, *She is too tenderhearted to give up the heron family to the hunter*. Click the **Reject arrow** in the Changes group and click **Reject Change**.

You decide the additional sentence is not necessary, so you reject the change you made earlier.

c. Click the **Accept arrow** and click **Accept All Changes and Stop Tracking**.

You have accepted all remaining changes and deleted all comments. The document is now ready for the group to finalize.

d. Click **Save** on the Quick Access Toolbar to save the document with the same name and in the same location. Save the document and submit based on your instructor's directions.

Online Document Collaboration

Word 2013 is changing the way education and the workforce expect projects to be completed. At one time, students primarily worked independently, completing projects on their own and being graded accordingly. Business professionals relied on their skills to produce projects that were often prepared at one site—typically by working independently in an office, coordinating efforts with others only occasionally. The global marketplace and the ease with which communication can occur worldwide have changed all that, creating a new dynamic in which collaboration on projects is the norm rather than the exception. Marketing proposals, company reports, and all sorts of other documents are often prepared by a group of people working with shared documents to which all can contribute at any time. Similarly, group projects that are assigned as part of a class requirement can often be completed by sharing documents online for review and completion. Recognizing the proliferation of devices that students and professionals use to communicate and complete projects, including smartphones, tablets, and personal computers, Microsoft designed Office 2013 to encourage work from anywhere and on almost any device. The key to such sharing is online accessibility.

Word 2013 facilitates document sharing by saving documents to OneDrive by default. Saving to OneDrive is sometimes referred to as "saving to the cloud," because a document saved in that way is available online (in the cloud). When you save a document to OneDrive, you can indicate whether the document is in a folder that is available only to you or whether the folder or document should be shared with others. You can even share a document with friends on Facebook or LinkedIn. Those with access to the document can review and edit the document at any time, posting revisions and comments for others to see. Using Office Online, contributors can edit a document even on a computer or device without Office 2013.

No longer is it necessary for a group of people to gather in one location to write or refine a document. Instead, busy professionals can collaborate on a document from multiple locations at the same time. The conference leader can present the document online using the Office Presentation service. At that point, users can comment, edit, and collaborate on the document although not simultaneously.

In this section, you will explore the use of Word Online, as it coordinates with OneDrive to facilitate the sharing and editing of documents. In addition, you will learn to present a document online.

Using OneDrive

Provided by Microsoft, **OneDrive** is an online storage system and sharing utility. More than a simple file storage location, OneDrive is an integral component of Microsoft's total solution to "anywhere computing." It is the backbone behind Microsoft's push for providing access to files from any location and from any mobile device, such as a laptop, tablet, or smartphone. You can use OneDrive to share documents with others, facilitating online collaboration in the production of documents and the completion of projects, or as a repository for backup copies of files. With 7GB of free storage made available to users, OneDrive is a viable storage alternative to a local drive. In fact, it is often used in lieu of a flash drive because it makes files available from any Internet-connected location.

When you save a Word document, you can indicate OneDrive as the storage location. In fact, OneDrive is the default storage location for Office 2013; documents are automatically saved there unless you specify otherwise (see Figure 4.21).

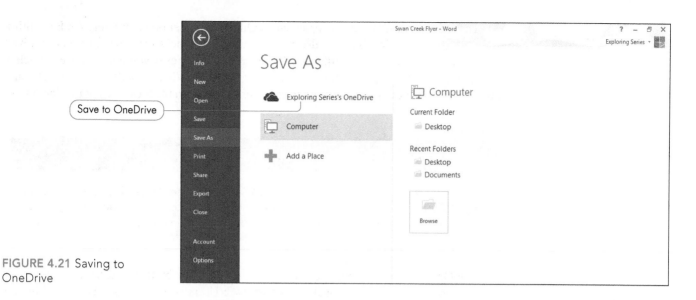

FIGURE 4.21 Saving to OneDrive

Understand OneDrive Apps

Word 2013 encourages the use of OneDrive as a storage location so that you can retrieve documents from any Internet-connected device and so that you can share documents with others. You are also likely to use OneDrive as a location for backing up documents. For example, you might save an important document on your hard drive and upload or save the document to OneDrive as a backup. If you grant access, others can view and edit the document. The inherent challenge in that scenario is that as you edit the local copy of the document or as co-authors edit the OneDrive copy, both copies of the document should be synchronized so that they are identical. Microsoft provides *apps* to simplify the process of organizing and managing OneDrive folders (and contents), as well as ensuring that files are synchronized.

Windows 8.1.1 includes a OneDrive app that displays OneDrive folders and files on your desktop. The *Windows 8.1.1 OneDrive app* enables you to access files from your OneDrive folders and upload others to OneDrive. However, it *does not include automatic synchronization of files* (maintaining up-to-date versions of files between OneDrive and copies of files saved on your computer). The purpose of the Windows 8.1.1 OneDrive app is to provide access to items you have saved to OneDrive and to facilitate uploading new files. In addition, the OneDrive app enables you to delete files and folders and create folders in OneDrive.

STEP 1 ≫   To ensure that OneDrive files are always up to date and that you can easily access them from your computer, you might consider downloading the *OneDrive for Windows app*. If you work with Windows 8.1.1, Windows 7, or Windows Vista, you can download the app (available at https://apps.live.com/onedrive), which *automatically synchronizes* files between your personal computer and your OneDrive account. The Windows 8.1.1 OneDrive app (described in the preceding paragraph) and the OneDrive for Windows app are separate entities with differing purposes.

The OneDrive for Windows app creates a OneDrive folder on your computer. Everything placed in the OneDrive folder is also made available in OneDrive, with files synchronized whenever changes are made either locally or online. Whenever you add, change, or delete files in one location, files in another location are updated. When co-authors collaborate on a shared OneDrive document, those edits are incorporated into the local copy of the document.

TIP OneDrive for Mobile Devices

You can download a OneDrive app on your Windows Phone, Android, iPhone, or iPad at http://windows.microsoft.com/is-IS/onedrive/mobile. The app enables you to easily access your OneDrive files from the mobile device and upload videos and pictures to OneDrive.

The OneDrive folder that is created on your computer by the OneDrive for Windows app is a subfolder of your personal Users folder (C:/Users/your name/OneDrive). Although you can navigate to the OneDrive folder through File Explorer, Windows provides easy access to the OneDrive folder in the Notification area on the taskbar. Click OneDrive to confirm that it is up to date and click Open your OneDrive folder for immediate access to files saved on OneDrive (and synced locally so they are also available on your computer). In the File Explorer interface, shown in Figure 4.22, you can simply drag and drop files between folders, including OneDrive.

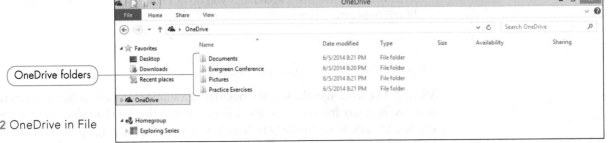

FIGURE 4.22 OneDrive in File Explorer

Regardless of whether you have downloaded the OneDrive for Windows app, you can save or upload documents to OneDrive. Simply save a Word file to OneDrive or upload it to http://onedrive.live.com.

To save a Word file to OneDrive:

1. Click the FILE tab and click Save As.
2. Confirm that OneDrive is selected in the Places section and navigate to the OneDrive folder to save to (or click Browse to create a new folder or select another storage location on OneDrive).
3. Click Save.

To upload a file (not restricted to Word 2013 files) to OneDrive:

1. Go to http://onedrive.live.com.
2. Sign in using your login information (or click Sign Up to create a new account).
3. Follow all prompts to upload the file, creating a new OneDrive folder if desired.

Sharing and Collaborating on Documents

For various reasons, you might want to share folders or files. In the educational environment and in the workplace, one of the most common reasons to share files is to facilitate collaborative projects. Because a document saved on OneDrive is available online, you can share the document with others who have access to the Internet. Although you are likely to use Word 2013 to share documents, you can also share a document that opens in Word Online (discussed later in this chapter). You might even find it convenient to share a file other than one created with a Microsoft Office application, such as a picture or a PDF file. You can access your files directly at http://onedrive.live.com.

Share Documents in Word 2013

After saving a document to OneDrive, you can share it with others in several ways and with varying levels of permission. You may be sharing a file for informational purposes only; you do not intend to ask others to edit or collaborate on the document. Other times, you will invite collaboration. You can share a document through a link, by posting to a social network, through e-mail, as a blog post, or even as an online presentation. As you share a document, you can indicate whether those you share with can edit the document or simply view it.

Invite Others to Share a Document or Share a Link

Perhaps the simplest way to share a document using Word 2013 is to *invite* others to edit or view the document. You can also share a link to a document that you have saved to OneDrive. To save a Word document to OneDrive while also inviting others to share the document (or sharing a link), create or open a document in Word 2013, then:

1. Click the FILE tab and click Share. As shown in Figure 4.23, you can invite people to access the document you will save to OneDrive.
2. Click Save to Cloud.
3. Navigate to the OneDrive folder in which to save the file and click Save.
4. Click Share
   - If you plan to invite others to share the document, type the e-mail addresses of invitees, include a message, and indicate whether the recipient can edit or only view the shared document. Select *Require user to sign-in before accessing document* if you want to provide the utmost privacy for your document. Click Share.
   - Instead of inviting others, you can create a sharing link when you click *Get a Sharing Link* and click *Create link* (indicating whether to limit a user to view or edit privileges). Copy the resulting link to share with others.

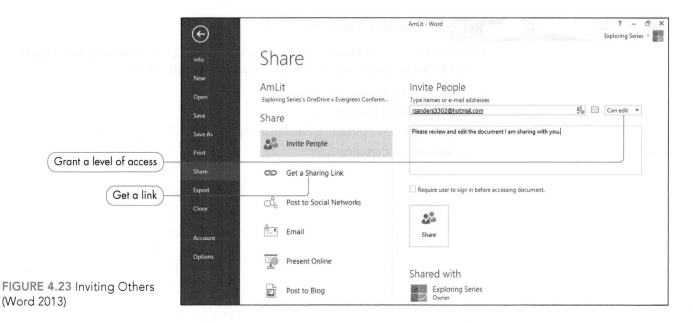

FIGURE 4.23 Inviting Others (Word 2013)

Post to a Social Network

You can post a Word document to a social network, including Facebook, LinkedIn, Flickr, Google+, and Twitter, indicating whether your contacts can only view the document or can also edit it. With a Word document open (that you have saved to OneDrive):

1. Click the FILE tab and then click Share.
2. Click Post to Social Networks (see Figure 4.24).
3. Click a link to connect to a social network, if necessary. You can share a document through a social network only if you have affiliated the network with your OneDrive account. You will connect the account by following Word prompts as you share the post.
4. Indicate a level of permission (*Can edit* or *Can view*) and include a brief message.
5. Click Post.

FIGURE 4.24 Posting to a Social Network (Word 2013)

Share a Document Through E-Mail

If you know the *e-mail* addresses of those you want to share a document with, open a Word document (that you have saved to OneDrive) and do the following:

1. Click the FILE tab and click Share.
2. Click Email (see Figure 4.25).
3. Select a method of including the document.
4. Follow any prompts presented.

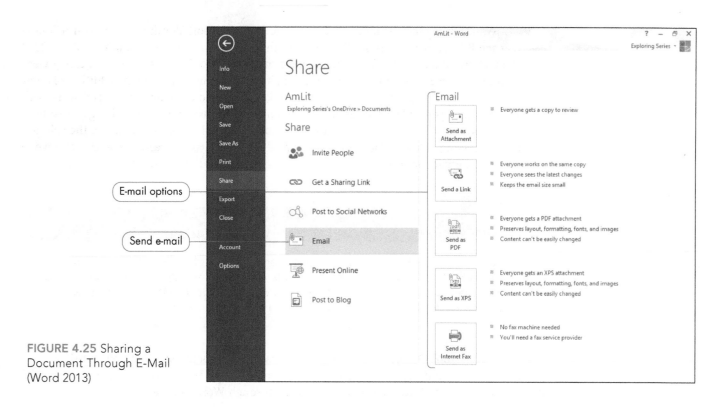

E-mail options

Send e-mail

FIGURE 4.25 Sharing a Document Through E-Mail (Word 2013)

Share Documents in Word Online

Word Online is a limited version of Word, enabling you to edit and format a document online. As a component of Office Online, which also includes Excel, PowerPoint, and OneNote, Word Online is free and accessible when you sign in to or create a OneDrive account. You are not required to install software to use Word Online. Neither are you required to have purchased a copy of Word 2013. That means that you can use Word Online, creating and editing Word documents, from any Internet-connected computer regardless of whether Word is installed on the computer. Although not as full-featured as Word 2013, Word Online enables you to create basic documents and share documents with others.

Word Online is available to you when you access a OneDrive account and either begin a new document or open a document previously saved in OneDrive and choose to use Word Online to edit the document. For example, when you sign in to your OneDrive account (http://onedrive.live.com), you can click a previously saved Word document to open it. As shown in Figure 4.26, the document opens in a browser window with a very limited selection of tabs. On the Edit Document tab, select Edit in Word (to open the document in a full Word version if installed on your computer) or Edit in Word Online (to open the document for editing in Word Online). You are not required to have Word 2013 installed on your computer in order to open a document using Word Online. In fact, that is an advantage of using Word Online—you can share and collaborate on Word documents with others, regardless of whether anyone has a version of Word installed.

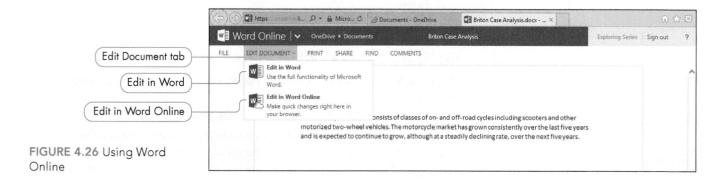

Edit Document tab

Edit in Word

Edit in Word Online

FIGURE 4.26 Using Word Online

Word Online has the familiar look and feel of Microsoft Word; however, you will note that the Ribbon is much more limited than the Ribbon included in a standard Word 2013 installation. In addition, Word Online views are limited to Reading view and Editing view, with Reading view showing the document as it will print and enabling the addition of comments, while Editing view enables you to make changes to a document. As you work with Word Online, you will find other differences and limitations; for example, dialog box launchers are not present, and certain features are not supported. However, it can be the solution to encouraging online collaboration on a Word document, as it is readily available to anyone with an Internet connection and facilitates simultaneous editing with others.

TIP | Creating a Document in Word Online

You can create a Word document using Word Online. At http://onedrive.live.com, click Create and select Word document. Provide a file name and click Create. Type a document, saving it to OneDrive. At any point, you can click *Open in Word* to take advantage of the more full-featured Word version if it is installed on your computer.

Using Word Online, you can open or create Word documents that you can share with others. In much the same way as documents are shared in Word 2013, through a link, social network, or e-mail, you can share documents through Word Online.

Share a Link

A very straightforward way to share access to a document is by providing a link. The link can be included in an e-mail or any other form of electronic or written communication. As you create a link, you can mark it as *View only*, *View and edit*, or *Public*, depending upon the level of access you want to grant. A *View only* link enables a recipient to view but not edit a shared document. A *View and edit* link enables a recipient to view the document and make changes to it. A *Public* link is the same as a *View and Edit* link, except that anyone can search for publicly shared files, whereas only those with whom you have shared a link can access those designated for viewing and editing.

TIP | Sharing a Link

A very straightforward way to share access to a document is by providing a link. The link can be included in an e-mail or any other form of electronic or written communication. As you create a link, you can mark it as *View only*, *Edit*, or *Public*, depending upon the level of access you want to grant. A *View only* link enables a recipient to view but not edit a shared document. An *Edit* link enables a recipient to view the document and make changes to it. A *Public* link is the same as an *Edit* link, except that anyone can search for publicly shared files, whereas only those with whom you have shared a link can access those designated for viewing and editing.

To use Word Online to create a link to a shared document:

STEP 3》
1. Open the document in Word Online. To do so, simply click the document in your OneDrive account.
2. Click the SHARE tab or click the FILE tab and click Share.
3. Click *Get a link* (see Figure 4.27). Click Create (selecting a level of permission). Click Shorten, if desired, to generate a shortened version of the link.
4. Copy the generated link for distribution to intended recipients.
5. Click Done.

Get a link

Varying levels of permission

FIGURE 4.27 Sharing a Link (Word Online)

TIP **Sharing with Embedded HTML**

You can embed a shared document in a blog or Web site that you manage. To do so, right-click the document in OneDrive and select Embed. Click Generate. OneDrive will create HTML code that you can copy and paste into your blog or Web page.

Post to a Social Network

Using Word Online, you can share documents with your contacts on several social networks, including Facebook, Twitter, Google+, and LinkedIn.

To share a document link to a social network:

1. Open the document in Word Online. To do so, click the document in your OneDrive account.
2. Click SHARE on the toolbar or click the FILE tab and click Share.
3. Click Get a link (see Figure 4.28).
4. Indicate whether recipients can edit the document. Click Create link.
5. Select the social network. Click Share Link. Type a short message, if you like, to accompany the posted document.

   A link to the document appears on the social media site, along with a message if you chose to include one. Follow the social network site's rules to advise intended recipients of the document's availability.

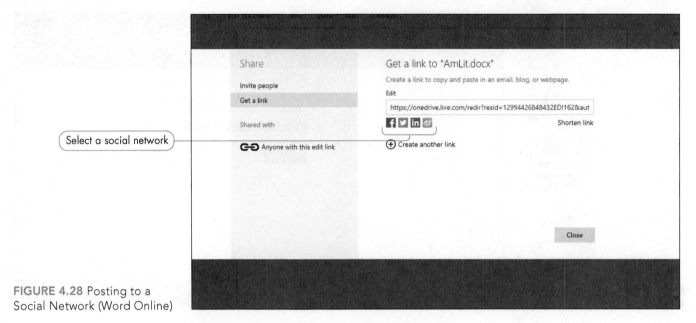

FIGURE 4.28 Posting to a
Social Network (Word Online)

Share a Document Through E-Mail

Word Online enables you to share a document with e-mail contacts:

1. Click SHARE on the toolbar or click the FILE tab and click Share.
2. Click Invite people (see Figure 4.29).
3. Type the e-mail addresses of those with whom you will share the document and a short note if desired.
4. Click the *Recipients can edit* link to display an additional option that enables you to limit recipients to viewing the document only. In addition, you can specify whether recipients need a Microsoft account to access the document.
5. Click Share to send invitations to all recipients with a link to the shared file.

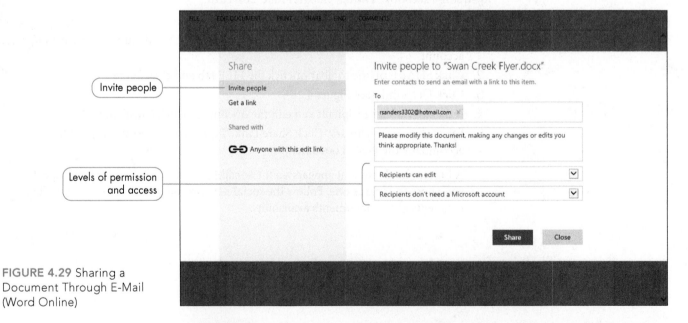

FIGURE 4.29 Sharing a
Document Through E-Mail
(Word Online)

TIP | Share a File on OneDrive

When viewing a list of files in OneDrive at http://onedrive.live.com, you can right-click a file and click Share to open a Share dialog box from which you can select a method of sharing.

Collaborate on a Document

Co-authoring a document is simple, with no specific commands required to begin editing. Simply open a shared document from OneDrive and use either Word Online or Word 2013 to modify the document. Of course, the document must be shared in such a way that editing by other authors is permitted.

STEP 4

When you save or post a Word document to OneDrive, anyone with whom you share the document (with editing privileges) can access and edit the document, even if you are also editing the document at the same time. The most straightforward approach to co-editing a document, especially if you will be doing so simultaneously, is to open the document in Word Online. Simply click a shared link or click a shared document in OneDrive to open it in Word Online. At that point, click Edit Document and select Edit in Word or Edit in Word Online (see Figure 4.30).

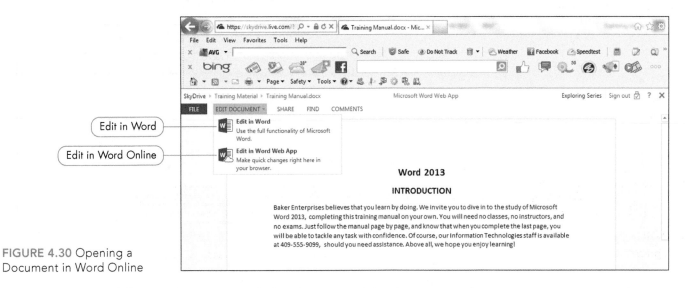

FIGURE 4.30 Opening a Document in Word Online

As you edit a shared document, you will be made aware of others who are editing the same document (see Figure 4.31). If using Word Online, you can edit a document simultaneously with other co-authors, with all changes occurring immediately. As you or others with whom the document is shared edit the document, the changes are immediately shown. In that way, it is possible for several people to work with the same document, each viewing changes made by others as those changes are being typed. You can check the right side of the toolbar for notification of others who might be editing the document at the same time (see Figure 4.32). As a co-author makes changes to a document, the area in which he or she is working will be identified with a colored flag (see Figure 4.33). When you point to the flag, the identity of the co-author is revealed.

Indicator that someone is currently editing the document

FIGURE 4.31 Notification of Co-Authors

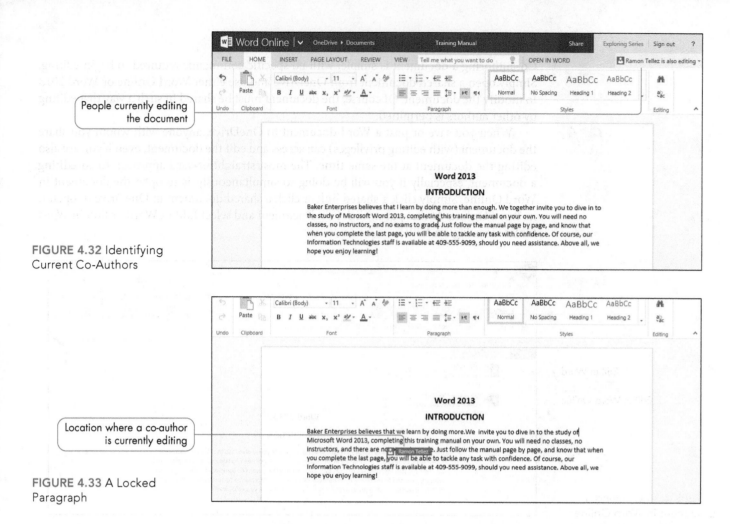

People currently editing the document

FIGURE 4.32 Identifying Current Co-Authors

Location where a co-author is currently editing

FIGURE 4.33 A Locked Paragraph

As you edit a document, even if others are editing the same document simultaneously, the document is being saved automatically. Therefore, you do not need to save the document periodically. The updated document is available to all co-authors in its most current form. If you like, you can download the document when you click the FILE tab, click Save As, and then click Download a Copy (see Figure 4.34). In that way, you can place a copy of the document on a form of local storage, such as your hard drive or a flash drive. The document is also saved on OneDrive so that it is available to everyone who collaborated on the document.

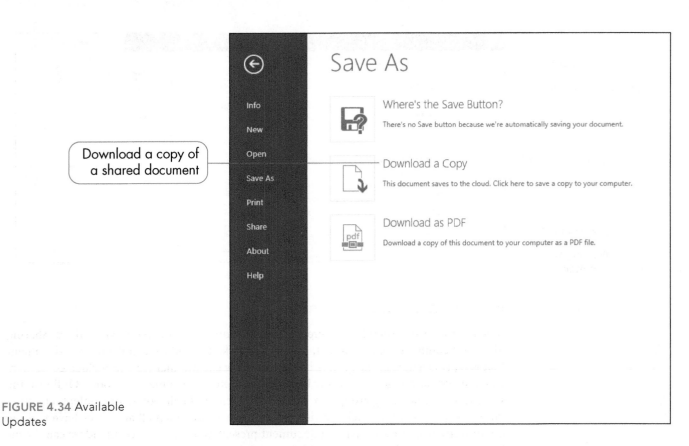

Download a copy of a shared document

FIGURE 4.34 Available Updates

At any point, you can switch to Word 2013 to continue working with a shared document. Because Word Online is somewhat limited, you might find that you need to edit a document in Word 2013 to access a feature not found in Word Online. For example, you might want to add a bibliography or check a document in Outline view. Even when working in Word 2013, you will be apprised of other editors.

When you work with a shared document, you will often want to make comments about the content or ask questions of co-authors. Often, the purpose of sharing a document is to seek feedback. Those with whom you share a document might not make any edits at all—they could simply comment on the document so that you can improve or validate the content. Using Word 2013 or Word Online, you can create comments as well as reply to comments others might include.

When using Word Online, you must be in Reading View to create or respond to comments. If in Editing View, click the View tab and click Reading View in the Document Views group. To create or reply to a comment:

1. Select a line of text (or double-click to select a paragraph).
2. Click COMMENTS (see Figure 4.35).
3. Click New Comment in the Comments pane on the right or click an existing comment and click Reply.
4. Type a comment and click Post.

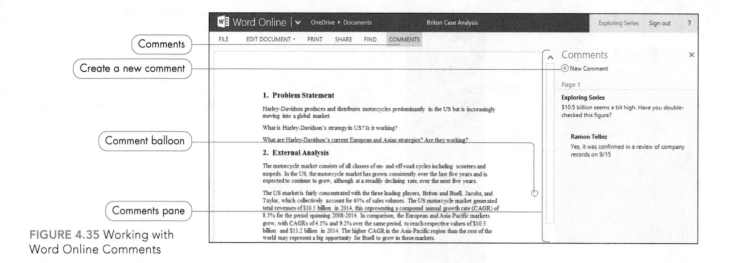

Comments

Create a new comment

Comment balloon

Comments pane

FIGURE 4.35 Working with Word Online Comments

Present a Document Online

Imagine gathering around a conference table to work on a document with others. Sharing ideas and commenting on content, the group works to produce a collaborative document that is representative of the group's best effort. Now expand that view to include co-authors who are widespread geographically instead of gathered in a conference room. Online at the same time, the far-flung group can view a document and collaborate on content, although *not simultaneously*, ultimately producing a document to which all attendees have had the opportunity to contribute. After a document presentation, conference attendees can download a copy of the document for additional editing if necessary. Word 2013 enables you to invite attendees and present a document online. Whether your goal is to present a document for discussion (but no editing) or to seek input from a group after the conference, you will appreciate the ease with which Word 2013 facilitates that task.

Begin an Online Presentation

During an online presentation, a conference leader will present a document. Although attendees can navigate the document independently during the presentation, they cannot edit the document. If an attendee independently navigates the document during the presentation, he or she will stop following the presenter but can rejoin the presentation at any time. As the conference leader, you can make a document available for download, inviting an audience to view the document as you work with it if desired. As the conference leader, you will open the document that you intend to share in Word 2013. Then complete the following steps:

STEP 2 »

1. Click the FILE tab, Share, Present Online, and then Present Online (see Figure 4.36). You will need a Microsoft account in order to begin the presentation.
2. Click Connect.
3. Click Copy Link (to copy and paste the meeting hyperlink, perhaps in a Skype chat window) or *Send in Email* (to e-mail the hyperlink in your e-mail client). If you have an IM chat client, you can click *Send in IM*.
4. Click Start Presentation. Your attendees can click the hyperlink or paste it in a browser window to view the document. Attendees can view the document even if they do not have a version of Word installed.

Enable viewers to download the document

Present Online

FIGURE 4.36 Presenting a Document Online

Figure 4.37 shows a presenter's view as well as an attendee's. If the presenter's goal is to inform an audience without inviting participation, he or she can simply navigate through the document as the audience follows along online. When the presentation is complete, the presenter will click End Online Presentation.

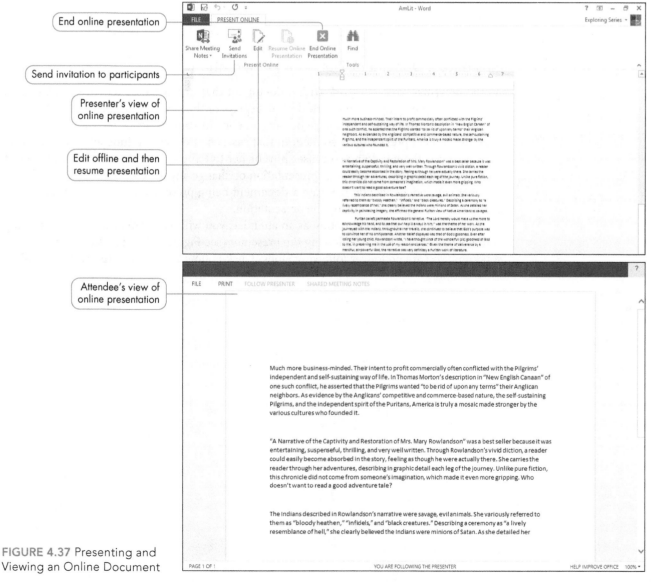

End online presentation

Send invitation to participants

Presenter's view of online presentation

Edit offline and then resume presentation

Attendee's view of online presentation

FIGURE 4.37 Presenting and Viewing an Online Document

Edit an Online Word Document During a Presentation

While presenting a document online, you might identify errors or modifications that you want to make. Perhaps a name is misspelled, or you see that a sentence could be reworded for better readability. Click Edit to temporarily move offline. After editing the document, click Resume, as shown in Figure 4.38, to return to the online presentation. Attendees will be informed that the presenter has made changes to the file.

Resume presentation

FIGURE 4.38 Editing a Document During a Presentation

Navigate a Document During a Presentation

As the presenter, you will work with a document that displays on each attendee's screen. As your screen displays changes, so do the displays of those watching the presentation. On occasion, you might move to a page before someone in your audience has had time to read all of the content previously presented. In that case, an attendee can independently navigate a document, although doing so causes him or her to temporarily leave the presentation. It does not, however, interrupt your presentation or change anyone else's display. An audience member can independently navigate a document being presented online but cannot make changes to the document during the presentation.

When you leave a presentation as an attendee, you will see a temporary alert informing you that you are no longer following the presenter (see Figure 4.39). The status bar also lets you know you are no longer following along. Click Follow Presenter to return to the online presentation.

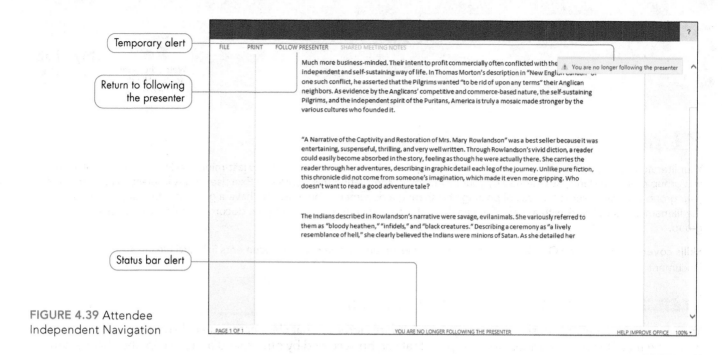

Temporary alert

Return to following the presenter

Status bar alert

FIGURE 4.39 Attendee Independent Navigation

Quick **Concepts** ✓

1. As you save a document to OneDrive, you will most likely want to also have a copy on your computer for backup purposes. How can you make sure that as you modify one copy, the other is also updated? *p. 288*

2. Both Word 2013 and Word Online enable you to create and edit a document. When might one be preferred over the other? *p. 292*

3. After editing a shared document online, you want to make your edits available to co-authors who might be editing the same file. How would you do that? *p. 295*

4. The Editing view and the Reading view of Word Online serve different purposes. Aside from enabling you to easily read a document, what purpose does the Reading view serve? *p. 297*

Hands-On Exercises

Watch the Video for this Hands-On Exercise!

MyITLab®
HOE3 Training

3 Online Document Collaboration

Your literature group will finalize the analysis of *A White Heron* by collaborating on a few last-minute edits online. You will work in a group of five students, as assigned by your instructor, in completing this Hands-On Exercise. You will select a chairperson of your group who will assume the task of posting and sharing a document. You must also have a group name that you will include in the filename. You will work with a draft of the analysis of the short story, co-authoring the document online with classmates in your group.

Skills covered: Understand OneDrive Apps • Present a Document Online • Share Documents in Word Online • Collaborate on a Document

STEP 1 ≫ UNDERSTAND ONEDRIVE APPS

You plan to use OneDrive to share the analysis of *A White Heron* so that classmates can collaborate on the project. You know that OneDrive provides storage space that can be accessed by others, and as a backup, the chairperson of your group will save a copy of the analysis on a hard drive. In doing so, you will want to make sure that edits made to the paper at either location are synchronized with the other location so that both copies remain current. You can use a OneDrive app to accomplish that goal, but first you will learn a bit more about the app. Because you are likely to be in a computer lab, you will not actually download the app, although you can do so on your home computer at http://apps.live.com/onedrive. Before beginning this exercise, you should have a Microsoft account. If you do not have a Microsoft account, create one at www.outlook.com. Refer to Figure 4.40 as you complete Step 1.

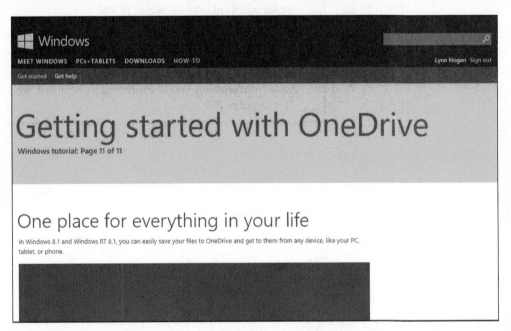

FIGURE 4.40 OneDrive for Windows App

a. Start Word and open a new blank document. Open an Internet browser window. Go to http://windows.microsoft.com/en-gb/windows-8/getting-started-onedrive-tutorial?ocid=onedrive_site_supportlink. Scroll through the Web page, learning more about OneDrive.

b. Having learned a bit more about the app, go to the new blank Word document and type **OneDrive Desktop App** for Windows. Press **Enter**. Type your first name and last name. Press Enter. Provide an example of when you might use OneDrive and how the OneDrive for Windows app would help with file coordination and organization. In your description, include system requirements for running the OneDrive Desktop App for Windows. Save the document as **w04h3OneDrive_LastFirst** and close the document.

c. Close the browser window.

Before collaborating on the analysis that is to be shared and edited by the group, the chairperson will present the document online to group members, highlighting areas to be edited in a later step. The group chairperson will make the presentation, sharing it with group members who will watch the presentation from their own Internet-connected computers. The group chairperson will use Word 2013 to prepare the online presentation, providing a link to attendees so they can watch. All group members must have a Microsoft account before beginning this exercise. You can create an account at http://www.outlook.com. Your instructor should assign your group a name. Refer to Figure 4.41 as you complete Step 2.

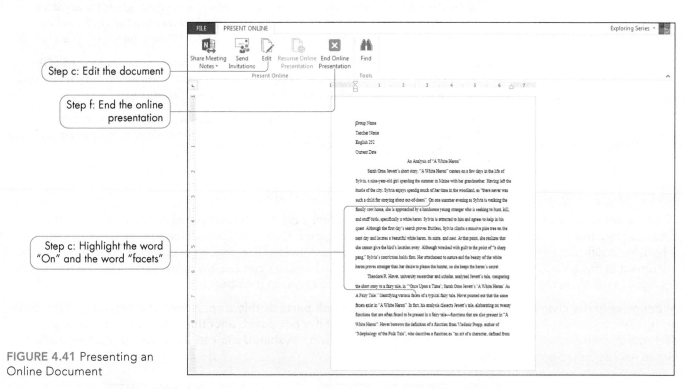

FIGURE 4.41 Presenting an Online Document

a. Start Word. Open *w04h3Analysis* and save it as **w04h3Analysis_GroupName,** replacing *GroupName* with the name assigned the group by your instructor. Keep the document open.

> **TROUBLESHOOTING:** To complete all steps of this exercise, every group member must have a Microsoft account. If you do not have a Microsoft account, create one at http://www.outlook.com.

b. Click the **FILE tab** and click **Share.** Click **Present Online** and click **Present Online** again. Log in to your Microsoft account if necessary and provide a copy of the link to all group members. Click **START PRESENTATION.**

> **TROUBLESHOOTING:** If you are unable to connect, proceed directly to Step 3, skipping all of the following parts of Step 2. However, you should check spelling first, correcting all mistakes (note that author names are not misspelled).

c. If you are the chairperson, scroll through the document, presenting it to the group. Each group member should see the document on individual computers as it is being presented. You will then click **Edit** to temporarily pause the presentation to make edits. Click the **HOME tab** and click **Text Highlight Color.** Highlight the following areas in the document, indicating that they are to be edited later (toggle off Text Highlight Color when highlighting is complete):

- Highlight the word *On* in the third sentence of the first paragraph.
- Highlight the word *facets* in the second paragraph.
- Highlight the words *by killing the white heron* after the word *nature* near the end of the paragraph that begins *On an even deeper level* on page 3.
- Highlight the word *helpful* in the last paragraph of the document.

d. Check the document for spelling errors. All authors' names are correctly spelled, so you should ignore flagged errors of names. The essay begins with a capital *A*, so ignore the apparent grammatical error. Correct any misspelled words. Click **Resume** to return to the online presentation. As a group member, you will see an onscreen message informing you of an edit.

e. If you are a group member, scroll the document independently, temporarily leaving the presentation. A temporary alert will display, letting you know you are no longer following the presentation. Click **Follow Presenter** to return to the presentation.

f. If you are the chairperson, click **End Online Presentation** to end the presentation. Click **End Online Presentation** again to disconnect all participants. Save the document and keep it open for the next step.

STEP 3 » SHARE DOCUMENTS IN WORD ONLINE

During a recent work session on campus, your group developed a draft of the analysis of *A White Heron*. In the previous step, the chairperson presented the analysis to the group, highlighting areas for editing. Coordinating schedules is difficult, so the group decides to edit the document online. That way, each group member can edit the document at any time from any location, while all other group members can see any edits made. The chairperson of your group will share the document through Word Online with all group members.

Although **only the chairperson of the group will complete all parts of this step**, it would be beneficial if the entire group were together to watch or participate in that process. If it is not possible for the entire group to be together, each group member will begin with Step 4, after the chairperson has shared a link to the shared document. Refer to Figure 4.42 as Step 3 is completed.

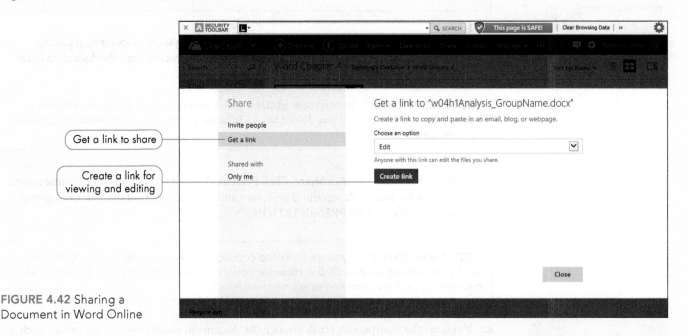

FIGURE 4.42 Sharing a Document in Word Online

a. If you are the chairperson, save *w04h3Analysis_GroupName* in a new folder on OneDrive. Open the document if it is not already open. To save the document to OneDrive, click the **FILE tab** and click **Save As**. Ensure that **OneDrive** is selected and click **Browse**. Click **New Folder**, type **Word Chapter 4**, and then press **Enter**. Double-click **Word Chapter 4** and click **Save**. Close the document.

> **TROUBLESHOOTING:** If you have difficulty saving the file to OneDrive, make sure the file is saved to a local drive and complete the following steps:
>
> 1. Go to http://onedrive.live.com and log in, if necessary.
> 2. Click Create, click Folder, type Word Chapter 4, and then press Enter. Click the new folder.
> 3. Click Upload and click *select them from your computer*. Navigate to the *w04h3Analysis_GroupName* file on your computer and double-click the file. After the file is uploaded, close the OneDrive information window at the bottom-right corner of the browser if necessary.
> 4. Click *w04h3Analysis_GroupName* to open it.
> 5. Proceed to step c.

b. Go to http://onedrive.live.com and sign in. Navigate to the Word Chapter 4 folder. Right-click **w04h3Analysis_GroupName** to open a shortcut menu.

> **TROUBLESHOOTING:** If you cannot find the document in OneDrive, click in the Search OneDrive box at the top left side of the display. Type w04h3Analysis_GroupName (replacing *GroupName* with your group's name, as you saved it in step a). Press Enter. Click the file name, if found, to open the document in Word Online.

c. Click **Share** and click **Get a link**. Click **Create Link**. Click **Shorten link** to display a shorter version of the link. Copy the link for distribution to team members, or have each team member (including the chairperson) make note of the link for later reference. You might include the link in an e-mail to group members or otherwise post it where group members can access it. Click **Done**.

d. Close the browser.

STEP 4 ≫ COLLABORATE ON A DOCUMENT

Each team member has a link to a shared document—*w04h3Analysis_GroupName*. Each person will access *w04h3Analysis_GroupName*, reviewing and editing the report individually. You do not have to access the report simultaneously, although that is an option. All team members will complete all parts of this step (with the exception of the last sentence of part b and all of part c). Refer to Figure 4.43 as you complete Step 4.

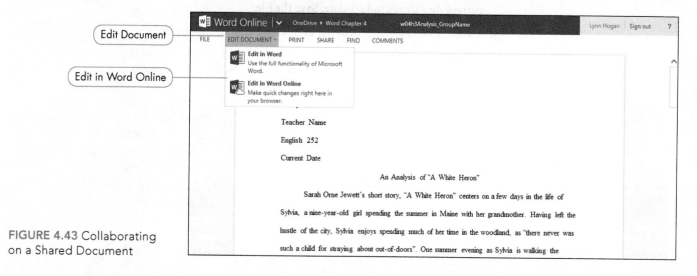

FIGURE 4.43 Collaborating on a Shared Document

a. Open a browser window and type or paste the link provided in part c of the previous step. Press **Enter**.

> **TROUBLESHOOTING:** If the link you use does not display the shared document, the chairperson can repeat Step 3 to produce another link.

b. Click **Edit Document**. Click **Edit in Word Online**. Provide login information related to your Windows account if required. As the chairperson, change the words *Group Name* in the first line of the document to the actual group name assigned by your instructor in Step 2 of this Hands-On Exercise.

c. Divide the following tasks among group members, excluding the chairperson, with each task completed by only one team member (unless there are fewer team members than tasks; in that case, assign the tasks as appropriate). As each group member completes a task, click Save in the upper left corner of the Word Online window. These tasks can be done simultaneously because they are in different paragraphs.

Task 1: Remove the word *On* from the third sentence of the first paragraph. The sentence should begin with the word *One*.

Task 2: Change the word *facets* in the second paragraph to *components*. Remove the text highlight if present.

Task 3: Change the words *by killing the white heron* to *by revealing the white heron* after the word *nature* near the end of the paragraph that begins *On an even deeper level*. Remove the text highlight if present.

Task 4: Change the word *helpful* to *interesting* in the last paragraph of the document. Remove the text highlight if present.

d. As you complete your edit, click **Save** in the upper left corner of the Word Online window.

e. When all edits are complete, click the **FILE tab**. Click **Save As** and click **Download**. Click the **Save arrow** and click **Save As**. Navigate to an offline storage location, change the file name to **w04h3Analysis_LastFirst**, replacing *LastFirst* with your name, and then click **Save**. Close the browser.

f. Start Word and open **w04h3Analysis_LastFirst**. Change the group name on the first page to your own first and last names and include a real or fictitious instructor name. Make sure the current date shows today's date. Save the file.

g. Submit *w04h3Analysis_LastFirst* as directed by your instructor.

Chapter Objectives Review

After reading this chapter, you have accomplished the following objectives:

1. **Use a writing style and acknowledge sources.**
   - Select a writing style: A research paper is typically written to adhere to a particular writing style, often dictated by the academic discipline.
   - Create a source and include a citation: Each source consulted for a paper must be cited, according to the rules of a writing style.
   - Share and search for a source: Sources are included in a Master List, available to all documents created on the same computer, and a Current List, available to the current document.
   - Create a bibliography: A bibliography, also known as *works cited* or *references*, lists all sources used in the preparation of a paper.

2. **Create and modify footnotes and endnotes.**
   - Create footnotes and endnotes: Footnotes (located at the end of a page) and endnotes (located at the end of a paper) enable you to expand on a statement or provide a citation.
   - Modify footnotes and endnotes: You can change the format or style of footnotes and endnotes, or delete them.

3. **Explore special features.**
   - Create a table of contents: If headings are formatted in a heading style, Word 2013 can prepare a table of contents listing headings and associated page numbers.
   - Create an index: Mark entries for inclusion in an index, which is an alphabetical listing of marked topics and associated page numbers.
   - Create a cover page: Some writing styles require a cover page, which you can create as the first page, listing a report title and other identifying information.

4. **Review a document.**
   - Add a comment: A comment is located in a comment balloon in the margin of a report, providing a note to the author.
   - View and reply to comments: Simple Markup enables you to view comments and reply to them in an unobtrusive manner.

5. **Track Changes.**
   - Use Track Changes: With Track Changes active, all edits in a document are traceable so you can see what has been changed.
   - Accept and reject changes: With Track Changes active, you can evaluate each edit made, accepting or rejecting it.
   - Work with PDF documents: PDF Reflow is a Word feature that converts a PDF document into an editable Word document.

6. **Use OneDrive.**
   - Understand OneDrive apps: Windows 8.1.1 OneDrive app and OneDrive for Windows app simplify the use of OneDrive for saving documents.

7. **Share and collaborate on documents.**
   - Share documents in Word 2013: Use Word 2013 to share documents through links, social media, or e-mail.
   - Share documents in Word Online: Use Word Online to share documents through links, social media, or e-mail.
   - Collaborate on a document: With an online document shared, multiple authors can collaborate on the document, editing it simultaneously.
   - Present a document online: Word 2013 enables you to present a document online, although those viewing the presentation cannot edit it at the same time as the presentation.

Key Terms Matching

Match the key terms with their definitions. Write the key term letter by the appropriate numbered definition.

a. Bibliography
b. Citation
c. Comment
d. Cover page
e. Endnote
f. Footnote
g. Index
h. MLA
i. PDF Reflow
j. Plagiarism

k. Revision mark
l. Simple Markup
m. OneDrive for Windows app
n. Source
o. Style manual
p. Table of contents
q. Track Changes
r. Windows 8.1.1 OneDrive app
s. Word Online
t. Works Cited

1. _____ Word feature that converts a PDF document into an editable Word document. **p. 282**

2. _____ A list of works cited or consulted by an author in his or her work; the listing preferred by MLA. **p. 264**

3. _____ A note recognizing a source of information or a quoted passage. **p. 278**

4. _____ A downloadable app that synchronizes documents between a computer and OneDrive storage so that documents in both locations remain up to date. **p. 287**

5. _____ An alphabetical listing of topics covered in a document along with the page numbers where the topic is discussed. **p. 269**

6. _____ Word feature that monitors all additions, deletions, and formatting changes you make in a document. **p. 281**

7. _____ A citation that appears at the end of a document. **p. 266**

8. _____ Word feature that simplifies the display of comments and revision marks, resulting in a clean, uncluttered look. **p. 278**

9. _____ Page that lists headings in the order they appear in a document and the page numbers where the entries begin. **p. 268**

10. _____ A note, annotation, or additional information to the author or another reader about the content of a document. **p. 278**

11. _____ A list of works cited or consulted by an author in his or her work. **p. 264**

12. _____ An online component of Office Online presenting a free, although limited, version of Word 2013. **p. 291**

13. _____ A guide to a particular writing style outlining required rules and conventions related to the preparation of papers. **p. 261**

14. _____ The act of using and documenting the works of another as one's own. **p. 260**

15. _____ A citation that appears at the bottom of a page. **p. 266**

16. _____ Writing style established by the Modern Language Association with rules and conventions for preparing research papers (used primarily in the area of humanities). **p. 261**

17. _____ App included in Windows 8.1.1 displaying in File Explorer all documents and folders saved to OneDrive. **p. 287**

18. _____ Indicates where text is added, deleted, or formatted while the Track Changes feature is active. **p. 281**

19. _____ The first page of a report, including the report title, author or student, and other identifying information. **p. 270**

20. _____ A publication, person, or media item that is consulted in the preparation of a paper and given credit. **p. 260**

Multiple Choice

1. What Word Online view is required when you are adding comments to a shared document?

   (a) Editing
   (b) Reading
   (c) Print Layout
   (d) Web Layout

2. A major difference between sharing a document through Word Online and sharing a document as an online presentation is that:

   (a) You cannot simultaneously edit a document shared through Word Online; you can simultaneously edit a document shared as an online presentation.
   (b) A document shared as an online presentation must be saved in PDF format; a document shared through Word Online must be a Word document.
   (c) A person viewing an online presentation of a document can edit the document; a document shared through Word Online is available for viewing only, not editing.
   (d) A document shared through Word Online is available for simultaneous editing and collaboration; viewers of an online document presentation cannot edit the document during the presentation.

3. The choice of whether to title a list of sources *bibliography*, *works cited*, or *references* is dependent upon:

   (a) The writing style in use.
   (b) The version of Word you are using.
   (c) Whether the sources are from academic publications or professional journals.
   (d) Your own preference.

4. When working with Word Online, how can you tell that someone is editing a shared document at the same time that you are?

   (a) A note displays on the right side of the status bar.
   (b) A comment balloon displays in the left margin.
   (c) The Reviewing Pane displays, providing the names of others who are editing the document.
   (d) There is no way to tell who is editing at the same time.

5. Which of the following is *not* an option on Word's Reference tab?

   (a) Update a Table of Contents
   (b) Create a Cover Page
   (c) Insert a Citation
   (d) Insert an Index

6. The writing style you are most likely to use in a college English composition class is:

   (a) APA.
   (b) Chicago.
   (c) Turabian.
   (d) MLA.

7. To ensure that documents you save on OneDrive are synchronized with copies of the same documents saved on your hard drive, you could use a(n):

   (a) Backup setting in Word Options.
   (b) Windows 8.1.1 OneDrive app.
   (c) OneDrive for Windows app.
   (d) AutoRecover option.

8. This feature ensures a simple, uncluttered, view of comments and tracked changes made to a document.

   (a) Track Changes
   (b) Show Markup
   (c) Show/Hide
   (d) Simple Markup

9. After you create and insert a table of contents into a document:

   (a) Any subsequent page changes arising from the insertion or deletion of text to existing paragraphs must be entered manually.
   (b) Any additions to the entries in the table arising due to the insertion of new paragraphs defined by a heading style must be entered manually.
   (c) An index cannot be added to the document.
   (d) You can select a table of contents and click Update Table to bring the table of contents up to date.

10. You are participating in a group project in which each member makes changes to the same document, although not simultaneously. Which feature should you suggest the members use so each can see the edits made by fellow group members?

    (a) Mark Index Entries
    (b) Track Changes
    (c) Accept Changes
    (d) Create Cross-References

Practice Exercises

1 Social Media and Marketing

As a graduate student, you are nearing completion of an M.B.A. degree. You and several friends plan to start a small business after graduation, offering business and Web design consulting services. Having been an active participant in all sorts of social networking and having studied the use of social media to promote businesses in several marketing classes, you are well aware of the benefits of using social media to help build a client base. You decide to conduct a bit of research to determine which social networks seem to be effective and how to incorporate them into a marketing strategy. The bonus is that you are involved in a group project to develop a research paper for a marketing class, so you will be able to use the paper to complete that objective as well. You will share the paper online so that others in your group can contribute and comment. This exercise follows the same set of skills as used in Hands-On Exercises 1–2 in the chapter. Refer to Figure 4.44 as you complete this exercise.

 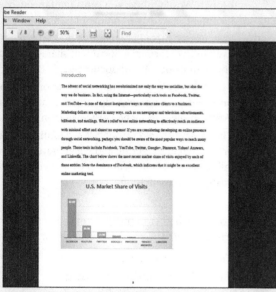

FIGURE 4.44 Social Media Documents

a. Open *w04p1Network* and save it as **w04p1Network_LastFirst**.

b. Press **Ctrl+Home**. Click the **INSERT tab**, click **Cover Page**, and then select **Austin**. Complete the cover page by completing the following:
   - Click **Document title** and type **Using Social Media**.
   - Click **Document subtitle** and type **Market Your Business**.
   - Remove the current author (unless the current author shows your first and last names) and type your first and last names.
   - Right-click the **Abstract paragraph** at the top of the page and click **Remove Content Control**.

c. Click the **REVIEW tab**. Click the **Track Changes arrow** and click **Track Changes**. All of your edits will be marked as you work. Change the view to **All Markup**, if necessary.

d. Make the following changes to the document:
   - Change the heading *Social Networking Sites* on page 2 (following the cover page) to **Social Media Sites**.
   - Select all text except the cover page. Change line spacing to **Double** (or **2.0**).
   - Click the **PAGE LAYOUT tab** and ensure that paragraph spacing Before and After is **0**.
   - Scroll to page 5 and select the heading *Maintain a blog*. Click the **REVIEW tab** and click **New Comment**. Type **Tricia – Would you please expand on this subject? It seems too short.**

e. Insert a page break at the beginning of the document and move to the beginning of the new page. Insert text from the file *w04p1Invitation*. Replace *Firstname Lastname* with your first and last names. Because Track Changes is on, the text you inserted is colored to indicate it is a new edit.

f. Scroll through the document, noting the edits that were tracked. On page 6, you should see the comment you made earlier. Press **Ctrl+Home** to move to the beginning of the document. Click the **REVIEW tab** and change the view to **No Markup**. Scroll through the document to note that revision marks (indicating edits) do not display. Move to the beginning of the document and select **Simple Markup**. Scroll through the document once more. Click a bar beside an edited paragraph to display the edits. Click the bar again to remove them from view.

g. Check the document for spelling errors. All names of people and Web sites are correctly spelled. Scroll to page 6 and click the comment balloon beside the *Maintain a blog* section. Click **Reply** in the expanded markup balloon. Type **I'll make my edits by Tuesday evening**. Close the comment balloon.

h. On page 4, click after the period at the end of the second sentence under *Social Media Sites*. The sentence ends in *growing audience of users*. Click the **REFERENCES tab** and click **Insert Footnote** in the Footnotes group. Type **See http://www.socialstats.org for current social media usage statistics.** (include the period). Right-click the hyperlink in the footnote and click **Remove Hyperlink**.

i. Click the **REVIEW tab**, if necessary, and change the view to **No Markup**. Right-click the footnote at the bottom of page 4 and click **Style**. Click **Modify**. Change the font to **Times New Roman**. The font size should be **10**. Click **OK** and click **Close**.

j. Move to the top of page 3 (beginning with *Introduction*) and insert a page break at the top of the page. Move to the top of the new page (page 3). Click the **REFERENCES tab**. Click **Table of Contents** in the *Table of Contents* group and click **Automatic Table 2**.

k. Scroll to page 7 and delete the *Downsides of Social Networking* section (removing the heading and the paragraph below the heading). Scroll to page 3 and click the **Table of Contents** to select the field. Click **Update Table** in the content control and select **Update entire table**. Click **OK**. Note that the *Downsides of Social Networking* section is no longer included in the table of contents.

l. Click the **REVIEW tab** and change the view to **Simple Markup**. Click the **Accept arrow** and click **Accept All Changes and Stop Tracking**. Click the **Delete arrow** in the Comments group and click **Delete All Comments in Document**. Scroll through the document and note that edits are no longer marked.

m. Click after the year *2010* and before the period in the sentence in the *Facebook* section that ends *$2 billion in 2010*. Click the **REFERENCES tab** and click the **Style arrow** in the Citations & Bibliography group. Select **APA Sixth Edition**. Click **Insert Citation** in the Citations & Bibliography group and click **Add New Source**. Add the following source from a *Journal Article* and click **OK**.

Author: **Amberley, Anna Leigh**

Title: **Growing More Social**

Journal Name: **Journal of Internet Studies**

Year: **2015**

Pages: **18–20**

Volume: **2**

Issue: **8**

(Hint: Click **Show All Bibliography Fields** to enter the volume and issue.)

n. Click the citation you just created, click the **Citation Options arrow**, and then click **Edit Citation**. Type **18** in the **Pages box**. Click **OK**.

o. Save the document as **w04p1Network_LastFirst**. Click the **FILE tab** and click **Export**. Ensure that *Create PDF/XPS Document* is selected and click **Create PDF/XPS**. Leave the file name as *w04p1Network_LastFirst* and ensure that the type is *PDF*. Click **Publish** to save the document as a PDF file. Close all open files, saving a file if prompted to do so.

p. Submit *w04p1Network_LastFirst.docx* and *w04p1Network_LastFirst.pdf* as directed by your instructor.

You are a partner in a law firm that deals with a large number of potential DREAM Act beneficiaries. The DREAM Act (Development, Relief, and Education for Alien Minors) provides conditional permanent residency to undocumented residents under certain conditions (good moral character, completion of U.S. high school degree, arrival in the United States as minors, etc.). Supporters of the Act contend that it provides social and economic benefits, whereas opponents label it as an amnesty program that rewards illegal immigration. Your law firm has partnered with leading law professors across the country to encourage the U.S. Executive Branch (Office of the President) to explore various options related to wise administration of the DREAM Act. In a letter to the president, you outline your position. Because it is of legal nature, the letter makes broad use of footnotes and in-text references. Because the letter is to be signed and supported by law professors across the country, you will share the letter online, making it possible for others to edit and approve of the wording. This exercise follows the same set of skills as used in Hands-On Exercises 1–3 in the chapter. Refer to Figure 4.45 as you complete this exercise.

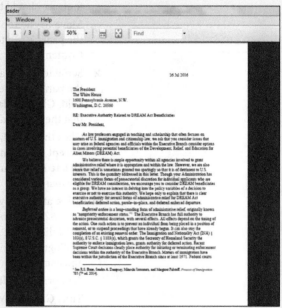

FIGURE 4.45 Dream Act Letter

a. Start Word and open a blank document. Click the **FILE tab** and click **Open**. Navigate to your data files and double-click the PDF file *w04p2Law.pdf*. Click **OK** when advised that Word will convert the document into an editable Word document. Save it as a Word document with the file name **w04p2Law_LastFirst**.

b. Scroll through the document and change *Firstname Lastname* in the closing to your first and last names. Check the document for spelling errors. All names are spelled correctly. The word *parol* should be spelled *parole*. The word *nonpriority* is not misspelled. Select text in the document from *As law professors engaged in teaching and scholarship* through *historically and recently*. Make sure paragraph spacing After is **6 pt**. Deselect the text.

c. Scroll down and select text from *Respectfully Yours* through the end of the document. Format the selected text in two columns. Deselect the text. Scroll to the last page and place the insertion point to the left of *Richard Hill*. Click **Breaks** in the Page Setup group on the PAGE LAYOUT tab. Click **Column**.

d. Place the insertion point after the ending quotation mark that ends the first sentence in the third body paragraph on page 1. Click the **REFERENCES tab** and click **Insert Footnote** in the Footnotes group. Type *See* **R.S. Bane, Sandra A. Dempsey, Minoshi Satomura, and Margaret Falstaff,** *Process of Immigration* **785 (7th ed. 2014).** (include the period).

e. Scroll to page 2 and place the insertion point after the quotation mark that ends the second sentence in the paragraph that begins *Parole-in-place is defined*. Click the **Footnotes Dialog Box Launcher** in the Footnotes group and click **Insert**. Type *See Lani Parosky, Comment, Congressional Policy, 64 U. Buffalo L. Rev. 578, 56–58 (2003).* (include the period).

f. Save the document. Next, save the document to a OneDrive account in a new folder called **Word Practice Exercises**. After saving the file to OneDrive, close the document and exit Word.

g. Go to http://onedrive.live.com and sign in to your Windows account if necessary. Navigate to the Word Practice Exercises folder and click **w04p2Law_LastFirst**. Click **EDIT DOCUMENT** and click **Edit in Word Online**. Scroll through the document and note that Word Online shows a placeholder for the footnotes you created. However, you cannot edit or work with footnotes in Word Online because it is limited in features. Point to a footnote placeholder to read a comment to the effect that you must open Word to work with footnotes.

h. Click **View** and select **Reading View**. Select the date at the top of the letter. Click **Comments** and click **New Comment**. Type **Please review this document in its entirety and make any edits you feel necessary.** Click **Post**. Close the Comments pane. Click **EDIT DOCUMENT** and click **Edit in Word Online**. Click **Save** in the top left corner.

i. Click the **FILE tab** and click **Open in Word**. Click **Yes** in the warning dialog box. When the document opens in Word, click the **REVIEW tab** and change the view to Simple Markup, if necessary.

j. Click the **Track Changes arrow** in the Tracking group and click **Track Changes**. Click **Reviewing Pane** (not the Reviewing Pane arrow). Reverse the words *to* and *not* in the second body paragraph on page 1. Note the changes in the Reviewing Pane as well as the vertical bar on the right side of the affected paragraph indicating that edits have been made. Click the vertical bar to view the changes. Click it again to return to Simple Markup. Close the Reviewing (Revisions) Pane.

k. Click the **FILE tab** and click **Save As**, saving the file to the location of your student files, not to OneDrive. Keep the file open. Click the **FILE tab** and click **Export**. Ensure that *Create PDF/XPS Document* is selected and click **Create PDF/XPS**. Leave the file name as *w04p2Law_LastFirst* and ensure that the type is *PDF*. Click **Publish** to save the document as a PDF file. Scroll through the PDF file and note that the edits and the comment were saved as part of the PDF document. Close the PDF document.

l. With *w04p2Law_LastFirst.docx* open, click the **REVIEW tab**, click the **Accept arrow** in the Changes group, and then click **Accept All Changes and Stop Tracking**. Right-click the comment and click **Delete Comment**.

m. Save the document. Close all open files.

n. Submit *w04p2Law_LastFirst.docx* and *w04p2Law_LastFirst.pdf* as directed by your instructor.

Mid-Level Exercises

1 WWW Web Services Agency

You work as a Web designer at WWW Web Services Agency and have been asked to provide some basic information to be used in a senior citizens' workshop. You want to provide the basic elements of good Web design and format the document professionally. Use the basic information you have already prepared in a Word document and revise it to include elements appropriate for a research-oriented paper.

a. Start Word and begin a blank document. Open the PDF file *w04m1Web*, agreeing that Word will enable the document as a Word document. Save the subsequent Word document as **w04m1Web_LastFirst**.

b. Change the author name to **Shannon Lee**.

c. Place the insertion point at the end of the *Proximity and Balance* paragraph (after the period) on the second page of the document. The paragraph ends with *indicates less proximity*. Insert the following footnote: **Max Rebaza, Effective Web Sites, Chicago: Windy City Publishing, Inc. (2014)**. Do not include the period.

d. Insert a table of contents on a new page after the cover page. Use a style of your choice.

e. You will add a bibliography to the document, inserting citation sources from the footnotes already in place. Because you will not use in-text citations, you will use the Source Manager to create the sources: To add new sources:
   - Click the **REFERENCES tab** and click **Manage Sources** in the Citations & Bibliography group.
   - Begin by adding a source for the footnote you created in step c (a Book). Click **New** in the Source Manager dialog box and add the source to both the Current and the Master list.
   - Create citation sources for the two additional sources identified in the document footnotes. The footnote on the fourth page is from an article in a periodical (issue 7), and the footnote on the fifth page cites a journal article.

f. Insert a bibliography at the end of the document on a separate page using the Chicago style. Select **Bibliography**. Apply **Heading 2 style** to the *Bibliography* heading and center the heading. Double space the bibliography and ensure that there is no paragraph spacing before or after.

g. Mark all occurrences of *Web*, *content*, and *site* as index entries. Create an index on a separate page after the bibliography using the **Formal** format.

h. Click the **FILE tab** and share the document, saving it to a folder of your choice on OneDrive in the process. After the document has been saved, click the **FILE tab** and get a sharing link that can be edited by anyone with whom you share the link. Copy the link and paste it as a footer in *w04m1Web_LastFirst*.

i. Begin to track changes. Select the heading *Proximity and Balance* on the third page. Add a new comment, typing **This section seems incomplete. Please check and add content.**

j. Add the following sentence as the second sentence in the *Contrast and Focus* section: **You are most likely familiar with the concept of contrast when working with pictures in an image editor.**

k. Save the document in the location of your student files (not OneDrive), replacing the existing file, and submit based on your instructor's directions.

2 New York City Trip

CREATIVE CASE

Your family is planning a seven-day trip to New York City next summer. Your responsibility is to research the city and develop a list of activities that your family will enjoy. You used the Internet to complete your research. Now you want to format the Word document to impress your family with your word-processing skills by incorporating different styles and formats and including a cover page, table of contents, and index.

a. Open *w04m2NYC* and save it as **w04m2NYC_LastFirst**.

b. Accept all formatting changes in the document. Turn on **Track Changes** so any further changes will be flagged.

c. Apply **Heading 1 style** to section headings that display in all capital letters. Apply **Heading 2 style** (scroll to locate the style) to section headings that display alone on a line in title case (the first letter of each word is capitalized).

⭐ d. Check all comments in the report, acting on them, if necessary. Reply to each comment after you have read and/or taken action on the item.

e. Create a footer for the document consisting of the title **Trip to New York City**, followed by a space and a page number. If the page number already appears as a footer, adjust it so that it follows *Trip to New York City*. Left align the footer in the footer area. Do not display the footer on the first page.

f. Create a page specifically for the table of contents and generate a table of contents.

g. Mark all occurrences of the following text for inclusion in the index: *New York City*, *Bronx Zoo*, and *Liberty Island*. Cross-reference *Big Apple* with *New York City*. On a separate page at the end of the document, create the index in **Classic format**.

h. Save and close the file, and submit based on your instructor's directions.

3   American History

COLLABORATION CASE

 FROM SCRATCH

You are working on a group project in an American history class. You and two other students will prepare an informal paper on favorite presidents, including a brief history of the United States and a summary of American government.

a. Determine a group name to be used throughout this project, or use one assigned by your instructor.

b. Allocate one of three tasks to each team member. One student will develop a paragraph describing a favorite president (along with a photo), another will compose a paragraph giving a very brief history of the United States, and a third will describe our system of government. All paragraphs will be included in one shared document that will be submitted to your instructor.

Student 1:

c. Begin a blank document, turn on Track Changes, and include three headings, formatted in Heading 1 style: **Favorite President, History,** and **American Government**. Save the document as **w04m3History_GroupName**, replacing Group Name with the name assigned by your instructor. In a paragraph beneath the *Favorite President* heading, format text as Times New Roman 12 pt. Type a paragraph about your favorite president, including a photo of the president. Type your name in the footer, save the document, and share it with the next student.

Student 2:

d. In a paragraph beneath the *History* heading, format text as Times New Roman 12 pt. Include a paragraph providing a brief description of American history. Type your name in the footer, save the document, and share it with the next student.

Student 3:

e. In a paragraph beneath the *American Government* heading, format text as Times New Roman 12 pt. Include a paragraph providing a brief description of American government. Type your name in the footer and save the document. Select the *Favorite President* heading and insert a new comment. In the comment, provide the names of group members and the date of submission. Turn Track Changes off, save, and submit the file based on your instructor's directions.

Beyond the Classroom

An Ethics Paper on Cheating

RESEARCH CASE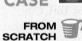

FROM SCRATCH

Cheating and the violation of schools' honor codes have become major problems in many school systems. We often hear stories of how high school and college students can easily cheat on tests or written papers without being caught. You will use the Internet to research the topic of plagiarism, honor codes, and the honor and judicial program at your university and several other universities in your state. You should use more than five sources, with at least one each from the Internet, a book, and a journal. After your research is complete, you will write a three-page, double-spaced report describing your findings. Include the definition of plagiarism, the penalty for violating the honor code at your school, and the statistics for cheating in high schools and colleges. Cite all the sources in your paper, insert at least one footnote, and develop a bibliography for your paper based on the APA Sixth Edition writing style. Save the report as **w04b2Cheating_LastFirst**. Also save the report on OneDrive and create a sharing link. Include the link as a footnote in the paper you will submit. Save and close the file, and submit based on your instructor's directions.

Computer History

DISASTER RECOVERY

You are preparing a brief history of computers for inclusion in a group project. Another student began the project, but ran completely out of time and needs your help. Open *w04b3Computers* and save it as **w04b3Computers_LastFirst**. Turn on Track Changes and respond to all comments left for you by the previous student. Save the document and submit based on your instructor's directions.

Making Ethical Choices

SOFT SKILLS CASE

FROM SCRATCH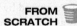

After watching the video on making ethical choices, prepare a two- to five-page research paper, using MLA style, on making ethical choices in the workplace or at school. Include at least three sources, cited in text and included in a bibliography. If directed by your instructor, you might work on the research paper with one or more fellow students, sharing the document online for co-editing. The document should be error-free. Save the document as **w04b4Ethics_LastFirst** (or **GroupName** if working in a group). Submit the document as directed by your instructor.

Capstone Exercise

You are a member of the Horticulture Society and have been asked to assist in the development of information packets about a variety of flowers and plants. A report about tulips has been started, and you are responsible for completing the document so that it is ready for the fall meeting.

Track Revisions

The document you receive has a few comments and shows the last few changes by the author. You will accept or reject the changes and then make a few of your own.

a. Open *w04c1Tulip* and save it as **w04c1Tulip_LastFirst**.

b. Ensure that the markup view is *All Markup*. Review the comments. Move to the third page and reject the insertion of a sentence about squirrels. (Hint: Click anywhere in the edited text. Click the **REVIEW tab**, click the **Reject arrow**, and click **Reject Change**.)

c. Accept all other tracked changes in the document and stop tracking. Keep all comments.

d. Change all headings that use Heading 3 style so they use **Heading 1 style**, as per the comment left by the author.

e. Click the first comment balloon and reply to the comment by typing **I have made the style replacement**.

f. Select the first tulip picture on the left on page 1, click the **REFERENCES tab**, and then click **Insert Caption** in the Captions group. Modify the caption text to read **Figure 1: Angelique**. Make sure the caption displays below the selected item. Assign captions below the remaining tulip photos using information in the comments. The photos are numbered from left to right, with the first row of pictures identified as *Figure 1, Figure 2,* and *Figure 3*. Delete all comments except the first one (to which you replied).

g. Add a caption below the image on page 3 showing *Figure 6: Planting Guide*.

Credit Sources

You are now ready to add the citations for resources that the author used when assembling this report.

a. Select **MLA Seventh Edition style**. Click before the period ending the second paragraph in the *Planting* section. The sentence ends in *5 to 6 inches apart*. Insert the following Book citation:

Author: **Tripp, Halleck**
Title: **The Complete Gardener's Guide**
Year: **2012**
City: **Houston**
Publisher: **Halpern**

b. Click before the period ending the first sentence in the document, ending in *turban*. Insert the following citation:

Corporate Author: **American Gardeners' Association**
Title: **What's in a Name?**
Journal Name: **Journal of American Gardeners**
Year: **2016**
Pages: **22–27**
Volume: **14**
Issue: **9**

c. Modify the book source (*The Complete Gardener's Guide*) to change the year to **2013**. To do so, click **Manage Sources** and edit the source in both the Current List and the Master List.

d. Click after the word *Tripp* in the last paragraph on page 2 (but before the period). Insert the Tripp citation you created in step a in this section. Edit the citation to include page 23 but no author, year, or title.

e. Insert a footnote on page 2 at the end of the third paragraph in the *Planting* section (after the period), which ends with *made by the planter*. Type the following for the footnote: **Stanley, Meredith Parelli, A Guide to Tulips (Sunrise, October 2009)**. (Do not include the period.) Change the number format for footnotes to **a, b, c** in the Footnotes dialog box. (Click **Apply**, not Insert.)

f. Insert a blank page at the end of the report and insert a bibliography in MLA style on the blank page with the title **Works Cited**. The bibliography should be double spaced, with no paragraph spacing and a font of Times New Roman 12 pt. The title *Works Cited* should be centered, 12 pt, and not bold. All text in the bibliography should be Black, Text 1 font color.

Finish with Table of Contents and Index

To put the finishing touches on your document, you add a table of contents and an index.

a. Automatically generate a table of contents and display it on a page between the cover page and page 2. The style is **Automatic Table 1**.

b. Mark the following words as index entries, selecting *Mark All* for each: *Holland, perennials, deadheading,* and *soil*. Create an index cross-reference entry using the word *dirt* in the index to indicate where the word *soil* is used.

c. Add an index on a blank page at the end of the document. Use the **Classic format**. Use all other default settings.

d. Display a centered page number, using **Plain Number 2** format, in the footer of the document. Do not display the page number footer on the first page. Numbering begins with page 2 on the Table of Contents page.

e. Save the file, then save it again as a PDF document with the file name **w04c1Tulip_LastFirst.pdf**. Close both files and submit them based on your instructor's directions.

Desktop Publishing and Graphic Design

Creating a Newsletter, Working with Graphics, and Linking Objects

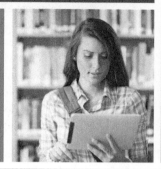

wavebreakmedia/Shutterstock

OBJECTIVES | AFTER YOU READ THIS CHAPTER, YOU WILL BE ABLE TO:

1. Construct a newsletter p. 320
2. Develop a document design p. 324
3. Insert graphic objects p. 334

4. Manipulate graphic objects p. 340
5. Use OLE to insert an object p. 352
6. Update a linked object p. 355

CASE STUDY | Along The Greenways

Kody Allen is director of The Greenways, a nonprofit organization. The organization was formed to generate interest in outdoor activities, as well as to provide support and funding for additional walking and biking trails in the city and surrounding counties. Maintaining positive public relations is key to generating support for the organization, and providing a quarterly newsletter is one way to do this. Director Allen hired you as the assistant director because you enjoy cycling, have been an outstanding volunteer for this organization, and demonstrate good computer skills.

Director Allen has asked you to create the newsletter in a format that is easy to read but also informative. Director Allen wants to limit the information to only what can be printed on a single page, even though there is much to convey. In addition to mailing the newsletter, it will also be posted on The Greenways' Web site.

Desktop Publishing

Desktop publishing evolved through a combination of technologies, including faster computers, laser and inkjet printers, and sophisticated page composition software that enables users to manipulate text and graphics to produce a professional-looking document. While there are separate applications available for desktop publishing needs, today's generation of word processors have matured to narrow the gap between word processing and desktop publishing. Microsoft Word, for all practical purposes, can offer powerful features that can be used to create all types of documents.

You can enjoy the challenge of creating a document that contains many graphic design techniques. Creating a document can be time consuming and can require an eye for detail, which is why documents such as brochures, newsletters, and flyers are often prepared by skilled professionals. Nevertheless, with a little practice and a basic knowledge of graphic design, you will be able to create effective and attractive documents like the newsletter shown in Figure 5.1.

In this section, you will learn how to develop a simple newsletter that includes a multi-column layout, images and other objects, and position those objects within a document.

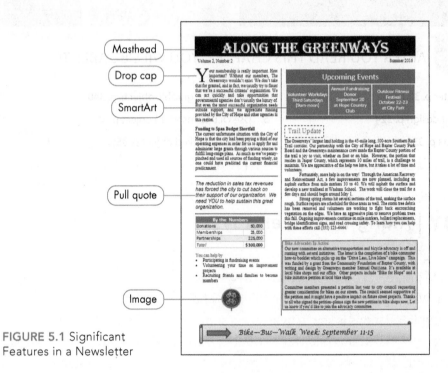

FIGURE 5.1 Significant Features in a Newsletter

Constructing a Newsletter

Microsoft Word can be used to create useful business documents. Documents such as flyers, event calendars, award certificates, and menus are usually one page long, but newsletters or brochures can be one or more pages long. In comparison, a newsletter usually consists of two or three columns, while a brochure is folded into two or three sections. When you use desktop publishing, or Microsoft Word, to create a document, such as a newsletter, there are several techniques to enhance readability and attractiveness. Many features used frequently in word processing are also very effective individually or in combination with one another to emphasize important information within the newsletter. These features include:

- **Images.** A graphic image or photograph can showcase people, events, or topics discussed in a newsletter. They are often reduced in size to take up only a small amount of space. The following are different types of images available in Microsoft Word:
    - **Bing Images.** When used in moderation, images will catch the reader's eye and enhance almost any newsletter. It is also used to break up text on a page so that the document does not bore the reader. Images can also help to direct the eye towards the text information. Be careful to have images face toward the text rather than away from the text.

- **WordArt.** WordArt uses some predefined styles to emphasize a major heading that can be placed anywhere in a document.
  - **SmartArt.** A SmartArt graphic can be used to represent a process or a hierarchy chart.
- **Shapes.** Microsoft has a set of built-in drawing tools that users can use to create simple shapes and objects to add another visual component to a document.
- **Tables.** Data values can be formally tabulated and presented in a professional-looking table.
- **Charts.** A variety of charts created in a spreadsheet application such as Excel can be inserted into a document to provide a graphical presentation of a data set.
- **Screenshots.** A screenshot is a graphical image captured by the user to show visible displays on the computer screen, such as an output or error message from a software program.
- **Borders.** A line border might surround a paragraph, or a page border might consist of a series of small graphics.
- **Shading.** When used as the background color of an element, such as a text box or as simple vertical and/or horizontal lines, shading is effective for attracting attention. Such techniques are especially useful in the absence of images or other graphics and are a favorite of desktop publishers to draw the reader's eye to a location on the document.
- **Lists.** Whether bulleted or numbered, lists help to organize information by emphasizing important topics.
- **Typography.** The arrangement and appearance of information is essential in adding personality to a newsletter. The selection of fonts, font styles, and font sizes that enhance the appearance of a document is a critical, often subtle, element in the success of a document. A good rule of thumb is to stick within one font family for headings, and another complimentary font family for body text that is easy to read. Indeed, good typography goes almost unnoticed, whereas poor typography stands out and detracts the user from a document.
- **Styles.** You can also use predefined styles in desktop publishing to add personality to your newsletter. Remember that a style is a set of formatting options you apply to characters or paragraphs. A style can store formats such as alignment, line spacing, indents, tabs, borders, and shading. You can use the same styles from one edition of your newsletter to the next to ensure consistency. Additionally, the use of styles in any document promotes uniformity and increases flexibility.

No hard and fast rules exist to dictate how many or which features you should include when designing a newsletter. Your objective should be to create a document that is easy to read and visually appealing. You will find that the design that worked so well in one document may not work at all in a different document. An effective presentation is often the result of trial and error, and you should experiment freely to find it.

You can create a newsletter using a newsletter document template or start from scratch. Microsoft provides several templates such as letters, resumes, faxes, newsletters, brochures, labels, cards, and more. To create a newsletter using a template, do the following:

1. Open Word.
2. Type Newsletter in the *Search online templates* search box and press Enter.
3. Scroll down the list of Newsletter templates to locate the design that you like.
4. Click a specific Newsletter selection to view more detailed information about the selection. Click Close to exit the view.
5. Click Create to accept the selected template.

TIP | Limit Use of Typography

Less is more—a rule that especially applies to typefaces and styles. Too many of either will produce cluttered documents. Try to limit the design to a maximum of two fonts per document, but choose multiple sizes or a variety of formatting treatments. Underlining for emphasis was reserved for typewriters, which didn't always offer variations beyond underlining text. However, professional typesetting relies more on boldface or italic for emphasis—not underlining—but always do so in moderation, because if there is an emphasis on too many elements, the effect is lost. A simple design is often the best design.

Change Page Setup Options and Column Layout

STEP 1 >> The margins of a document can be changed or adjusted from the Margins button in the Page Setup group found on the Page Layout tab. You can create a document with two columns of equal width by clicking the Page Layout tab and clicking Two under Columns in the Page Setup group. Notice that in Figure 5.1, the number of columns varies from one part of the newsletter to another. The masthead is displayed over a single column at the top of the page, whereas the remainder of the newsletter is formatted in two columns of different widths. The number of columns is specified at the section level. When you select one of the column preset designs, Microsoft Word will calculate the width of each column based on the number of columns, the left and right margins on the page, and the specified (default) space between columns. The newsletter shown in Figure 5.1, for example, uses a two-column layout with a wide and narrow column. This design may be preferred over columns of uniform width, as it adds interest to the document. Note, too, that once columns have been defined, text will flow continuously from the bottom of one column to the top of the next. To create columns of different sizes, do the following:

1. Position the insertion point anywhere in the document.
2. Click the PAGE LAYOUT tab.
3. Click Columns in the Page Setup group.
4. Click More Columns to display the dialog box as shown in Figure 5.2.
5. Choose the Left or Right Presets and/or uncheck the option *Equal column width*.
6. Enter the measurement for the column width and column spacing.

FIGURE 5.2 Columns Dialog Box

Insert Section Break

A section break is required whenever the column specification changes. Also, a section break is required at the end of the last column to balance the text within the columns. Insertion of the continuous section break, as shown in Figure 5.3, enables you to determine where columns start and end on a single page. To insert a continuous section break, do the following:

1. Position the insertion point at the desired location for inserting the section break.
2. Click the PAGE LAYOUT tab.
3. Click Breaks in the Page Setup group, as shown in Figure 5.3.
4. Under *Section Breaks*, click Continuous.

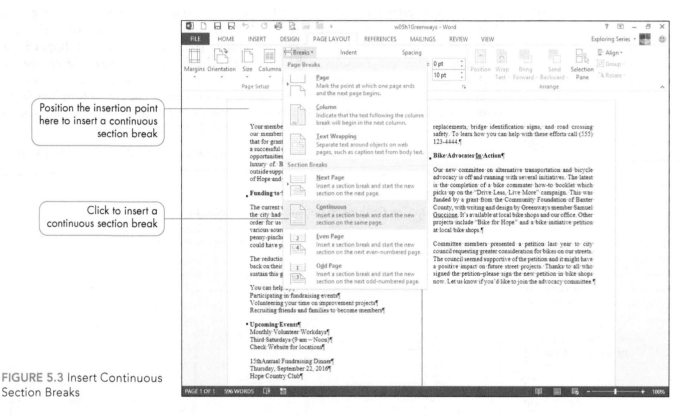

FIGURE 5.3 Insert Continuous Section Breaks

Insert a Column Break

A column break also plays an important role in the development of a newsletter. You use a column break to force paragraph text to start at the top of the next column. This provides control over where the bottom of one column ends before the text wraps to the top of the next column. To insert a column break, do the following:

1. Position the insertion point at the desired location for inserting the column break.
2. Click the PAGE LAYOUT tab.
3. Click Breaks in the Page Setup group.
4. Click Column Page Breaks to force a paragraph to start at the top of the next column.

Create a Masthead and a Reverse

STEP 3 ›› One technique desktop publishers use to emphasize text is called a *reverse*, and it consists of using light-colored text on a dark-colored background. It is often used in the ***masthead***, which is the identifying information at the top of the newsletter or other periodical.

It provides a distinctive look to the publication and often has the characteristics of a banner. The volume number of the newsletter and the date of publication also appear in the masthead in smaller letters. To create a masthead, do the following:

1. Position the pointer at the top of the page to insert a masthead.
2. Use WordArt to create a large text graphic across the top of the document.
3. Insert a one row by two column table under the masthead for information regarding the publication number and date.

Create a Drop Cap

STEP 4 ▶▶ Another way to catch the reader's eye and call attention to the associated text is a drop cap. A **drop cap**, or dropped-capital letter, is a capital letter formatted in a font size larger than the body text. The Drop Cap command in Word enables you to determine if the dropped cap will align with the text or display in the margin. The choice made will largely depend on the style and design of the newsletter. The size of a drop cap initial is also determined from the Drop Cap dialog box. Options for a drop cap include how many lines to drop, or how far to position the drop cap from the body text. A drop cap can be displayed in the margin or be turned off from this dialog box. To insert a Drop Cap, do the following:

1. Position the insertion point immediately before the letter intended to be a Drop Cap.
2. Click the INSERT tab.
3. Click Drop Cap in the Text group.
4. Click Drop Cap Options to display the dialog box, as shown in Figure 5.4.

FIGURE 5.4 Drop Cap Dialog Box

- Click to insert the drop cap
- Click None to remove a drop cap
- You can use formatting options in the text box, such as border and shading
- Select the size of the drop cap
- Set spacing between drop cap and text

Developing a Document Design

The most difficult aspect of creating a newsletter is to develop the design in the first place; the mere availability of a desktop publishing program does not guarantee an effective document any more than a word processor will turn its author into another Shakespeare. Other skills are necessary, and the following text provides a brief introduction to graphic design.

Much of the document layout is subjective, and what works in one situation will not necessarily work in another. Let your eye be the judge and follow your instincts. It also helps to seek inspiration from others by collecting samples of documents that succeed in capturing attention, and then using those document principles as the basic starting point for a design.

The design of a document is developed on a *grid*, an underlying, but invisible, set of horizontal and vertical lines that determine the placement of major elements. A grid establishes the overall structure of a document by indicating the number of columns; the space between columns; the size of the margins; and the placement of headlines, art, and so on. The grid does not appear in the printed document—draw or sketch it out on a piece of paper to solidify the layout prior to creating the newsletter in Word. Figures 5.5 through 5.7 show a document that was developed using different grid designs; the grid design displays on the right side of each completed newsletter document.

A grid may be simple or complex, but it is always distinguished by the number of columns it contains. The three-column grid of Figure 5.5 is one of the most common and utilitarian designs. Figure 5.6 shows an unequal two-column design for the same document. Figure 5.7 illustrates a three-column grid with unequal column widths to provide interest. Many other designs are possible as well. Use a one-column grid for term papers and letters. A two-column, wide-and-narrow format is appropriate for some textbooks and manuals. Two- and three-column formats are often used for newsletters and magazines.

The simple concept of a grid makes the underlying design of any document obvious, and it also helps to determine the page composition. Moreover, the conscious use of a grid will help organize the material and will result in a more polished and professional-looking publication. It will also help to achieve consistency from page to page within a document (or from issue to issue of a newsletter).

FIGURE 5.5 Three-Column Grid

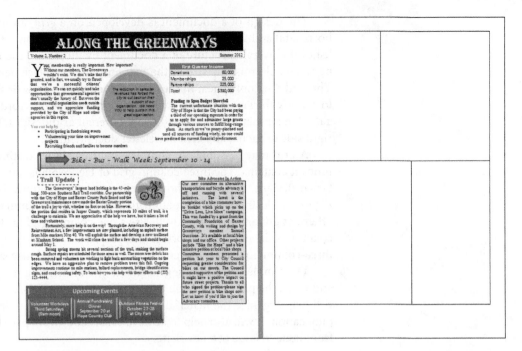

FIGURE 5.6 Two-Column Grid with Unequal Column Widths

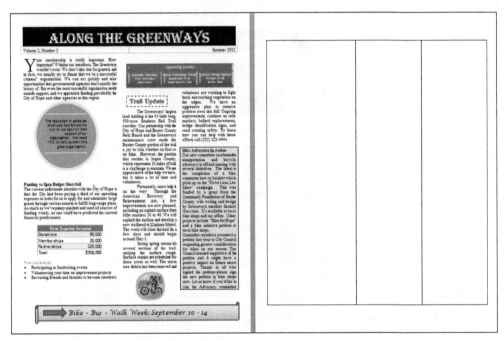

FIGURE 5.7 Three-Column Grid with Unequal Column Widths

Apply Borders and Shading

STEP 5 >>

Good design makes it easy for the reader to determine what is important. As indicated earlier, emphasis can be achieved in several ways, the easiest being variations in type size and/or type style. Headings should be set in type sizes at least two points larger than body copy. The use of bold and italic formatting is effective, but both should be done in moderation. UPPERCASE LETTERS and underlining are alternative techniques but are less effective. Uppercase letters are often associated with screaming because that is how you portray a raised voice in e-mail. Uppercase can also be harder to read because of the close spacing. Underlining is often associated with hyperlinks on a Web page, so it should be used on a limited basis, unless you are actually displaying a Web link.

Boxes and/or shading call attention to selected articles. Horizontal lines are effective to separate one topic from another or to call attention to a pull quote. Also recall that a reverse—light text on a dark background—can be striking for a small amount of text. Clip art, used in moderation, will catch the reader's eye and enhance almost any newsletter. Color is also effective, but it is more costly, so the budget allocated may be a factor to consider in designing a document.

All of the techniques and definitions discussed can be implemented with commands you already know, as you will see in Hands-On Exercise 1.

Quick Concepts ✓

1. Describe some of the techniques that can be used to enhance readability and attractiveness of a newsletter. *p. 320*

2. What is the purpose of creating a masthead and a reverse? *p. 323*

3. What is the difference between a continuous section break and a column break? *p. 323*

Hands-On Exercise

Watch the Video for this Hands-On Exercise!

MyITLab®
HOE1 Training

1 Desktop Publishing

Kody Allen, the director of The Greenways, forwarded you a document with short articles that he would like to include in the newsletter you are preparing. You must design a layout that will display the information in an easy-to-read and visually appealing manner. You will also consider how to display the masthead and other visual elements, then take steps to set up the document and add each feature.

Skills covered: Change Page Setup Options and Column Layout • Modify Column Layout • Create a Masthead and a Reverse • Create a Drop Cap • Apply Borders and Shading and Insert images

STEP 1 ❯❯ CHANGE PAGE SETUP OPTIONS AND COLUMN LAYOUT

After opening the file that Director Allen provides, consider the margins needed to display all the information and make appropriate changes to the document. You decide that the newsletter will display in two columns. Refer to Figure 5.8 as you complete Step 1.

FIGURE 5.8 Document Displaying Text in Two Columns

a. Start Word. Open *w05h1Greenways* and save it as **w05h1Greenways_LastFirst**. When you save your files, use your last and first names. For example, as the Word author, I would name my document *w05h1Greenways_LauLinda*.

> **TROUBLESHOOTING:** If you make any major mistakes in this exercise, you can close the file, open *w05h1Greenways* again, and then start this exercise over.

b. Click the **PAGE LAYOUT tab**, click **Margins** in the Page Setup group, and then click **Narrow**.

Because the newsletter contains many items, smaller margins are needed to allow for more working space within the document.

c. Click **Columns** in the Page Setup group and click **Two**.

The text of the newsletter displays in two columns. The column width for each column and the spacing between columns is determined automatically from the existing margins.

d. Click the **Zoom slider**, decrease the zoom to **50%**, and then view the whole page.

You can see both columns.

e. Save the document.

STEP 2 >> MODIFY COLUMN LAYOUT

In considering the best way to display the articles and information in the newsletter, you decide it would look better if you use unequal column widths for the two columns. You display the Columns dialog box so you can change the preset, set the width to your specifications, and then add a line to separate the columns. Refer to Figure 5.9 as you complete Step 2.

Step b: Select Left Preset

Step b: Click to display a line between columns

Step c: Change column width to 2.8"

Step c: Change spacing between columns to 0.25"

FIGURE 5.9 Modify Column Settings

a. Click the **Zoom slider** and increase the zoom to **80%**. Click the **PAGE LAYOUT tab**, click **Columns** in the Page Setup group, and then click **More Columns** to display the Columns dialog box.

b. Click **Left** under the *Presets* section and click the **Line between check box** to display a line between the columns.

c. Press **Tab** to select the Width list for the first column and type **2.8**. Press **Tab** and type **0.25** in the **Spacing list** for the first column. Uncheck *Equal column width*. Press **Tab** and notice that the width of the second column automatically changes to *4.45*. Click **OK**.

The columns are no longer the same width, and the vertical line displays as a separator.

d. Press **Ctrl+End** to move the insertion point to the end of the document. Click **Breaks** in the Page Setup group. Click **Continuous** under *Section Breaks*.

It is important to move the insertion point to the end of the document so that the continuous section break is inserted at the end of document. The columns are now balanced.

e. Save the document.

STEP 3 >> CREATE A MASTHEAD AND A REVERSE

The main title of your newsletter is important to design because it is most likely the first element the reader will view. You decide to insert a masthead and use a reverse technique so that it is very distinctive. To make it display properly as one column, you will first need to add a continuous section break at the top of the page. Refer to Figure 5.10 as you complete Step 3.

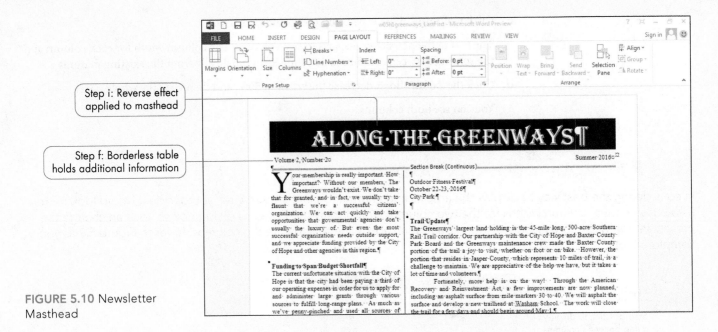

Step i: Reverse effect applied to masthead

Step f: Borderless table holds additional information

ALONG·THE·GREENWAYS¶

Volume 2, Number 2¤

Summer 2016¤

Your membership is really important. How important? Without our members, The Greenways wouldn't exist. We don't take that for granted, and in fact, we usually try to flaunt that we're a successful citizens' organization. We can act quickly and take opportunities that governmental agencies don't usually the luxury of. But even the most successful organization needs outside support, and we appreciate funding provided by the City of Hope and other agencies in this region.¶

Funding to Span Budget Shortfall¶
The current unfortunate situation with the City of Hope is that the city had been paying a third of our operating expenses in order for us to apply for and administer large grants through various sources to fulfill long-range plans. As much as we've penny-pinched and used all sources of

Section Break (Continuous)

¶
Outdoor Fitness Festival¶
October 22-23, 2016¶
City Park ¶

¶
Trail Update¶
The Greenways' largest land holding is the 45-mile long, 500-acre Southern Rail Trail corridor. Our partnership with the City of Hope and Baxter County Park Board and the Greenways maintenance crew made the Baxter County portion of the trail a joy to visit, whether on foot or on bike. However, the portion that resides in Jasper County, which represents 10 miles of trail, is a challenge to maintain. We are appreciative of the help we have, but it takes a lot of time and volunteers.¶

Fortunately, more help is on the way! Through the American Recovery and Reinvestment Act, a few improvements are now planned, including an asphalt surface from mile markers 30 to 40. We will asphalt the surface and develop a new trailhead at Washam School. The work will close the trail for a few days and should begin around May 1.¶

FIGURE 5.10 Newsletter Masthead

a. Click the **Zoom slider** and increase the zoom to **110%**.

b. Click the **HOME tab** and click **Show/Hide (¶)** in the Paragraph group, if necessary, to display formatting marks in the document.

c. Press **Ctrl+Home** to move the insertion point to the beginning of the document. Click the **PAGE LAYOUT tab**, click **Breaks** in the Page Setup group, and then click **Continuous** under *Section Breaks*.

   You should see a double dotted line, indicating a section break occurs at the top of the left column in the document. Adding this continuous section break enables you to format the area of the document that precedes the section break differently than the section that follows it.

d. Click **Ctrl+Home** to move the insertion point to the top of the page, click **Columns**, and then click **One**.

   The section break extends across the top of the document, creating one column at the top of the page. Information you type there will not be split into two columns like the text in the section below the break.

e. Type **Along The Greenways** and press **Enter** twice. Select the text you just typed, click the **HOME tab**, and then click **Center** in the Paragraph group. Click the **Font arrow** on the Mini toolbar, click **Algerian**, click the **Font Size arrow**, and then click **36**.

   This large heading is the masthead for the newsletter.

f. Click the left side of the section break, just below the masthead, to move the insertion point. Click the **INSERT tab**, click **Table**, and then drag the pointer over the cells to select two columns and one row (2 × 1 table). Click to insert the table.

   A table displays below the masthead and above the section break.

g. Make the following changes in the table:

   - Click in the left cell of the table, if necessary, and type **Volume 2, Number 2**.
   - Click in the right cell (or press **Tab**) and type **Summer 2016**.
   - Press **Ctrl+R** to right align text in the cell on the right.
   - Select the entire row, click the **PAGE LAYOUT tab**, and then click the **Spacing Before arrow** until **6 pt** displays.

h. Press **Ctrl+Home** to move the insertion point to the beginning of the masthead. Click the **HOME tab**, click the **Borders arrow** in the Paragraph group, and then click **Borders and Shading**.

The Borders and Shading dialog box displays. The Borders tab is active.

i. Click the **Shading tab**, click the **Style arrow**, click **Solid (100%)**, and then click **OK**. Click in the table to deselect the masthead.

The masthead displays white text on a black background.

j. Click the **Table Move handle** to select the entire table. Click the **Borders and Shading arrow** in the Paragraph group and click **No Border**.

k. Click outside the table and view the masthead.

l. Save the document.

STEP 4 ≫ CREATE A DROP CAP

You decide to pull the reader into the articles in your newsletter by adding features such as a drop cap, which is often applied to the very first paragraph of a document. Refer to Figure 5.11 as you complete Step 4.

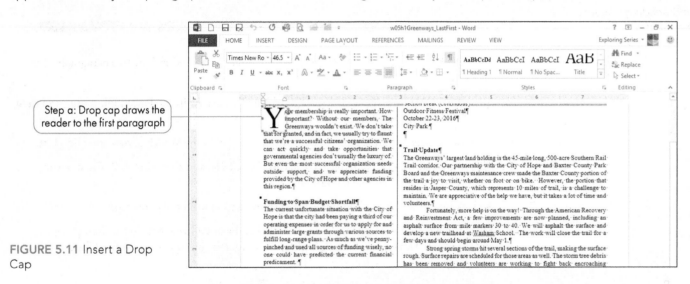

Step a: Drop cap draws the reader to the first paragraph

FIGURE 5.11 Insert a Drop Cap

a. Click to move the insertion point to the left of the first letter for the paragraph at the top left of the page, which reads *Your membership is really important*. Click the **INSERT tab**, click **Drop Cap** in the Text group, and then click **Dropped**.

b. Click anywhere outside the Drop Cap frame.

c. Select the first sentence of the fourth paragraph in the left column, *You can help by*. Click the **HOME tab**, click the **Font Color arrow** in the Font group, and then click **Orange, Accent 6, Darker 50%** (sixth row, tenth column).

d. Select the three paragraph items below the *You can help by* heading and click **Bullets** in the Paragraph group. Click **Decrease Indent** in the Paragraph group to align the bullets with the left edge of the heading.

e. Save the document.

Because some of the paragraphs look very similar, you decide to add distinction by using shading and placing a border around one of the paragraphs. You also add an image to add variety and a little interest to the page. Refer to Figure 5.12 as you complete Step 5.

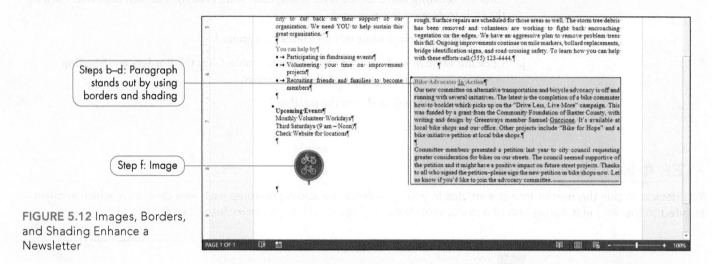

Steps b–d: Paragraph stands out by using borders and shading

Step f: Image

FIGURE 5.12 Images, Borders, and Shading Enhance a Newsletter

a. Select the heading in the right column, *Bike Advocates In Action*, and the two paragraphs that follow it.

b. Click the **HOME tab**, if necessary, click the **Borders arrow** in the Paragraph group, and then click **Borders and Shading**.

c. Click **Box** in the *Setting* section of the Borders tab. Click the **Width arrow** and click **1 pt**.

d. Click the **Shading tab**, click the **Style arrow**, click **15%**, and then click **OK**. Click in the article above to deselect the paragraph.

A black border and gray shading display around and behind the paragraph.

e. Select the heading *Bike Advocates In Action*, click **Font Color arrow** in the Font group, and then click **Dark Blue, Text 2, Lighter 40%** (fourth row, fourth column). Click in the paragraph below to deselect the heading.

f. Insert an image by completing the following steps:

- Position the insertion point at the bottom of the left column. Click the **INSERT tab**, click **Online Pictures** in the Illustrations group, and then type **bicycle** in the **Bing Image Search box**. Click the **Search icon** or press **Enter**.
- Click an image of a bicycle sign to select this image. Click **Insert** to insert the image into the document. If you do not find the same image displayed in Figure 5.12, substitute another appropriate image of your choice.

When the image is selected, a Layout Options icon appears next to the image. Click the icon to display the Layout Options dialog box.

- Click **Top and Bottom** (second row, first column) in the Layout Options dialog box.
- Click **See more** to display the Layout dialog box. Click the **Size tab**. Click the **Absolute arrow** in the *Height* section until **0.8** displays.
- Click **OK**.

To deselect the Layout Options dialog box, click **Close** or place the cursor anywhere outside of the dialog box.

- Drag the image to the bottom of the left column and center it under the paragraph text in that column.

- Select the image and click the **Layout Options** icon at the top-right corner of the clip art. Click **Fix position on page**.

> **TROUBLESHOOTING:** Use arrow keys to nudge the image, if needed, for more exact positioning.

g. Click the **HOME tab** and click **Show/Hide (¶)** in the Paragraph group to turn off the formatting marks. Drag the **Zoom Slider** to **50%**.

In viewing the whole document, notice how the changes already improve the look of the newsletter. More enhancements will be added in Hands-On Exercise 2.

h. Save the document. Keep it open if you plan to continue with Hands-On Exercise 2. If not, close the document and exit Word.

Decorative Text and Drawing Tools

Desktop publishing documents, and newsletters in particular, are more appealing to the reader when they display an appropriate level of variety of text and graphic objects. Word provides many graphic and drawing tools that enable you to enhance these documents. You can create text boxes containing text and format them to grab readers' attention, you can create professional-looking diagrams, and you can use predefined shapes or create your own. For each graphic object, you can choose from dozens of options, which you can customize and manipulate to create the effect you want. One thing you should keep in mind when adding graphics to your document—some objects may display better on the computer screen than in print, so view images with a critical eye before you finalize your document.

In this section, you will learn how to insert a variety of graphic objects found on the Insert tab and learn how to use tools to make adjustments such as changing colors, layering, and rotation.

Inserting Graphic Objects

Graphical elements—such as lines, arrows, diagrams, and text boxes—help enhance your documents by adding visual interest. Microsoft Word provides a variety of graphic objects you can use individually or combine to produce a one-of-a-kind drawing. For example, you can insert a shape, which is a geometric or non-geometric object, to represent balloons on strings and format these objects by applying different fill colors. You can position, size, and overlap shapes to achieve the visual effect you desire.

Insert SmartArt

STEP 1 ❯

Using shapes and text allows you to draw attention to your document; however, it is very time consuming to use these tools to create a complex and designer-quality illustration. Word includes *SmartArt*, which is a visual representation of information that can be created to effectively communicate a message or idea in one of many existing and visually appealing layouts. For example, you might insert a SmartArt diagram of an organizational chart, a list, or a process into your document to illustrate an important concept that is difficult to explain with simple text but easier to understand when viewed as an illustration. When you insert a SmartArt diagram in your document, you can select from several existing layouts, and SmartArt will conform to any theme you select for your document (see Figure 5.13). To insert SmartArt into your document, do the following:

1. Position the insertion point at the location where you want to insert the SmartArt.
2. Click the INSERT tab.
3. Click SmartArt in the Illustrations group to display the *Choose a SmartArt Graphic* dialog box as shown in Figure 5.14.
4. Click one of the diagram displays in the gallery. A short description displays in the right gallery pane when you click a diagram choice, as shown in Figure 5.14. After you select the type and subtype of the diagram, click OK.

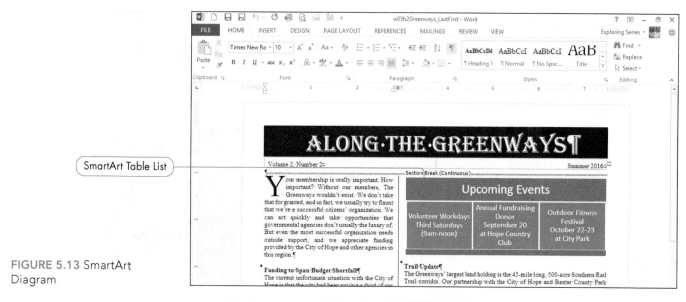

SmartArt Table List

FIGURE 5.13 SmartArt Diagram

Select type of SmartArt object

Preview and description of selected category

Click to insert SmartArt object

Select from category subtype

FIGURE 5.14 SmartArt Gallery

When a SmartArt diagram is inserted into your document, text placeholders display. You can click a placeholder and type text directly into the desired location in the diagram. Alternatively, you can click the arrow in the middle-left side of the diagram frame to view the Text pane if it is not already visible. The *Text pane* displays an outline view for typing the text items and enables you to type or to insert additional text into the SmartArt. The Design and Format tabs also display on the Ribbon when you select a SmartArt object. The Design tab also provides a toggle button for the Text pane, along with other tools to change the appearance of the diagram, such as adding shapes and changing the style, as shown in Figure 5.15. The Format tab provides tools to modify the appearance of the diagram text.

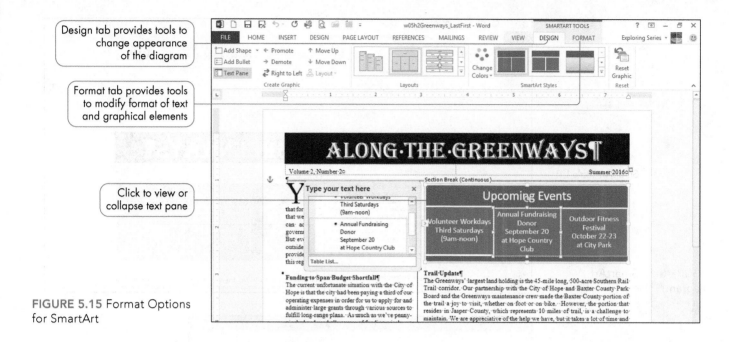

Design tab provides tools to change appearance of the diagram

Format tab provides tools to modify format of text and graphical elements

Click to view or collapse text pane

FIGURE 5.15 Format Options for SmartArt

Insert WordArt

STEP 2 >>

WordArt is a Microsoft Office feature that creates decorative text that can be used to add interest to the text you use in a document. The advantage of using WordArt is that you can rotate text in any direction, add three-dimensional effects, display the text vertically, slant it, arch it, or even display it upside down.

WordArt is intuitively easy to use. You choose a style from the gallery (see Figure 5.16), then enter the specific text in the WordArt text box, after which the results display (see Figure 5.17). The WordArt object can be moved and sized, just like any graphic object. A WordArt Format tab provides many formatting features that enable you to change alignment, add special effects, and change styles quickly. It is fun and easy to create some truly unique documents.

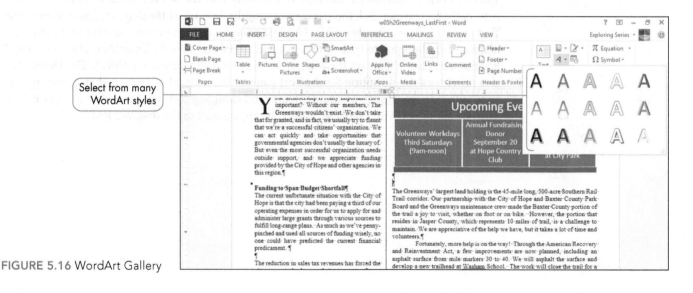

Select from many WordArt styles

FIGURE 5.16 WordArt Gallery

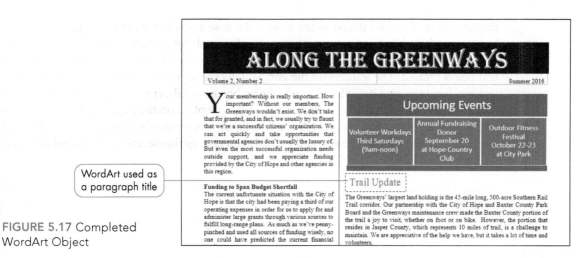

WordArt used as a paragraph title

FIGURE 5.17 Completed WordArt Object

Insert a Text Box

One way to combine the flexibility of a shape object with simple text is to create a text box. A *text box* is simply a graphic object that contains text. Magazine and newspaper articles often use text boxes to help control the placement of text as well as provide a visual tool to entice readers to focus on the contents of the text box. Text boxes can also be layered with other shapes or objects. For example, you can position a text box on a callout shape object and use it as a dialog bubble for a comic strip or illustration, as shown in Figure 5.18.

Click to insert a text box

Text box displays over shape object

FIGURE 5.18 Insert a Text Box

To insert a text box, click the Insert tab and click Text Box. A gallery of preformatted text boxes displays, or you can click Draw Text Box to create a custom text box. Several designs in the gallery are suitable for a sidebar or pull quote in a document, as shown in Figure 5.19, but you can also create your own. A *pull quote* is a phrase or sentence taken from an article to emphasize a key point. It is typically set in larger type, often in a different font or in italics, and may be offset with borders at the top, bottom, or on the sides. *Sidebars* also enable you to call attention to information in a document by displaying it in a space along the side of the featured information. Sidebars might display supplementary information, or they can simply display information of interest to the reader. Because a text box with a pull quote and sidebar are graphic objects, you can apply graphical formatting options such as wrapping style, horizontal alignment, outside borders, and font treatments. The Format tab displays when a text box is created. The features on the Format tab enable you to customize the border of the text box (you can give it a colored border or no border at all), apply shadow and 3-D effects, and position attributes, such as where the text box displays on the page and how text wraps around the text box. You can format the text using font properties you are already familiar with, such as size, type, and color, and you also can change the direction that the text displays within the text box.

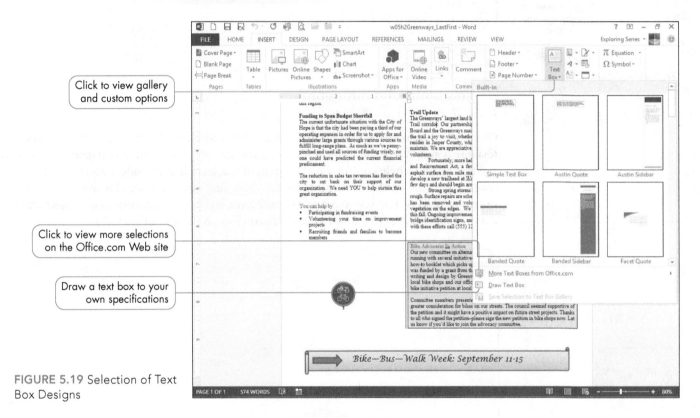

FIGURE 5.19 Selection of Text Box Designs

Create a Pull Quote

STEP 3 ▶▶ Pull quotes are frequently displayed in professional publications, such as company's monthly newsletters and annual reports, to draw attention to important topics. To create a pull quote, do the following:

1. Position the insertion point at the space where you want to insert the pull quote.
2. Click the INSERT tab and click Text Box in the Text group.
3. Click any of the text boxes given in the Built-in gallery options, as shown in Figure 5.19.
4. Type or copy and paste the desired text quote into the placeholder in the selected text box.
5. Move and position the pull quote text box in the exact location in the document.

Link Two Text Boxes

One text box can be linked to another text box so that when text runs out of space in one box it automatically flows into another box, as shown in Figure 5.20. The best use for linking text boxes is creating a booklet. Each page contains two text boxes that include the booklet text. Because booklets print on both sides of the paper, the text boxes link in such a way so that the text flows from the back of one page to the front of another. When you view the pages in Word, they appear out of order, but when assembled for the booklet, they display correctly.

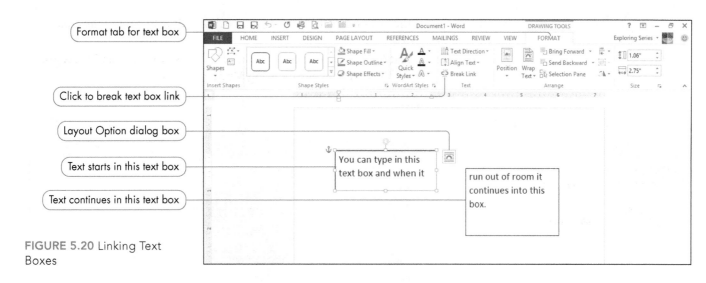

Format tab for text box

Click to break text box link

Layout Option dialog box

Text starts in this text box

Text continues in this text box

You can type in this text box and when it

run out of room it continues into this box.

FIGURE 5.20 Linking Text Boxes

Insert Drawing Shapes

STEP 4»

One tool that is especially useful is the Shapes tool located on the Insert tab in the Illustrations group. A shape is an object, such as a circle or an arrow, which you can use as a visual enhancement. Use one shape or combine multiple shapes to create a more complex image. When you click Shapes, the Shapes gallery displays the following categories of shapes:

- Lines
- Rectangles
- Basic Shapes
- Block Arrows
- Equation Shapes
- Flowchart
- Stars and Banners
- Callouts

To insert a shape, do the following:

1. Click the INSERT tab.
2. Click Shapes in the Illustrations group to show the shapes gallery options available.
3. Select the desired shape from the gallery.
4. The pointer changes to a cross-hair, which enables you to define the beginning and ending points of the shape. Click the location where you want to insert the shape and drag the pointer to create the default size for the shape or click and drag to control the desired shape size.

If you need to insert several instances of the same shape, do the following:

1. Click the INSERT tab.
2. Click Shapes in the Illustrations group to choose the desired shape from the gallery options.
3. Right-click the shape object in the gallery.
4. Click Lock Drawing Mode as shown in Figure 5.21.
5. The pointer changes to a cross-hair; position the cross-hair pointer at the desired location in the document for the shape.

6. Click to create the default size for the shape or click and drag to control the cross-desired shape size.
7. Repeat Steps 5 and 6 for as many desired instances of the same shape and press Esc when finished. To turn off the Lock Drawing Mode, press Esc.

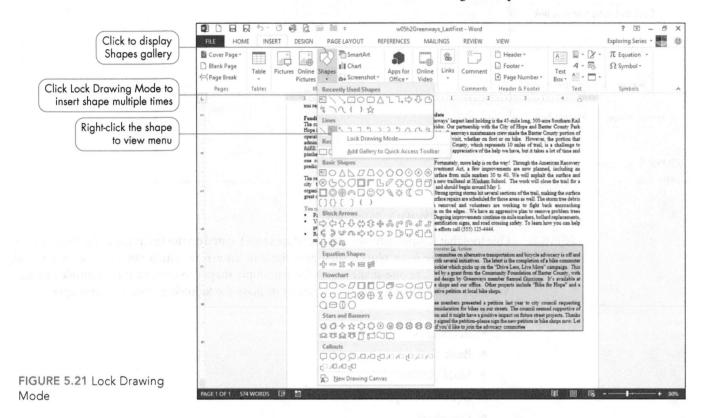

Click to display Shapes gallery

Click Lock Drawing Mode to insert shape multiple times

Right-click the shape to view menu

FIGURE 5.21 Lock Drawing Mode

Manipulating Graphic Objects

After you insert a shape, SmartArt, or text box, you can enhance its appearance by using one of the commands available on the Format tab for the object. Shapes display initially with a simple blue border and blue fill. But to capture the attention of the reader, you might want to change the border style, color, or fill effects.

Change Shape Fills and Borders

STEP 2

Shapes and text boxes have two main components that color can be applied to: the line or border of the object, and the *fill* or interior space of the object. Word provides the Quick Style gallery, which contains a selected list of styles that are predefined using a combination of colors, lines and other effects. On the other hand, you can also apply your personal preferences for the line using the Shape Outline option or adjust the fill colors using the Shape Fill option. Figure 5.22 shows the Shape Fill options you access from the Drawing Tools Format tab and gives examples of several fill and border options. Shapes such as a straight line obviously do not contain an interior area for applying a fill color, but you can change the color, width, and style of the line itself. You can also enhance the shape by adding visual effects such as shadow, reflection, glow, soft edges, bevel, and 3-D rotation listed under the Shape Effects option.

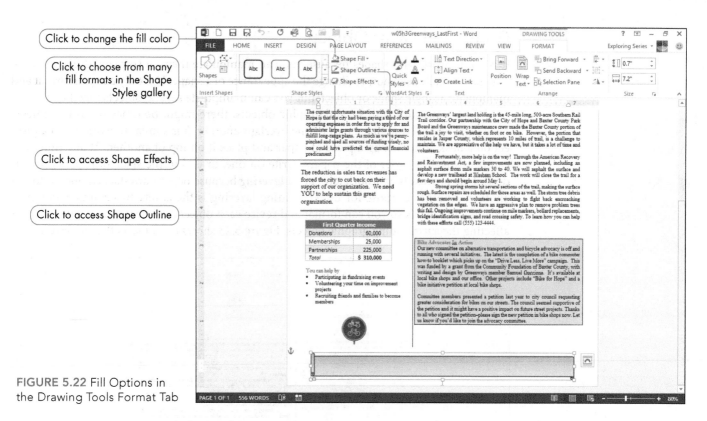

Click to change the fill color

Click to choose from many fill formats in the Shape Styles gallery

Click to access Shape Effects

Click to access Shape Outline

FIGURE 5.22 Fill Options in the Drawing Tools Format Tab

Resize an Object

Any object can be resized—such as a text box, WordArt, image, or shape—manually or precisely using the size group options. In addition, an object can be resized by cropping it. However, the primary purpose of cropping an object is usually to remove unwanted horizontal or vertical edges of the object. Cropping can also be used to hide or remove a part of the object that you do not want to display. Click the Crop tool in the Size group or the dialog box launcher to fine tune the cropping. You can also crop to a shape, use aspect ratio, and *Fill and Fit*. To resize an object manually, click the object to select it and increase or decrease the size by dragging the sizing handle. When you drag away from the object, you will increase the size of the object. Dragging towards the center of the object will decrease the object size. To resize the object precisely to a certain height and width, do the following:

1. Click the object to select it.
2. Click the FORMAT tab.
3. Click the Height and Width options in the Size group to adjust the height and width of the object to a specific measurement.

> ### TIP The Drawing Canvas
>
> When combining multiple shapes in one area, you should consider using the Drawing Canvas. The **Drawing Canvas** is a frame-like boundary object in the document to help you arrange parts of a drawing and to keep the parts together. The Drawing Canvas frame has no border or background fill color, but formatting can be applied to the drawing canvas as you would any object. To use the drawing canvas, click the Insert tab, click Shapes, and then click New Drawing Canvas. With the drawing canvas actively selected, insert shapes onto the canvas from the Insert Shapes group on the Drawing Tools Format tab. To delete the drawing canvas, click the frame border to select it and press Delete. The canvas and any shapes it contains are removed.

Group and Layer Objects

STEP 5 » It is fun to work with shapes because you can manipulate them in so many different ways. You have already seen how to change the appearance of a shape. Not only can you format and manipulate a single shape or object, but you can manipulate several objects together.

When you work with several graphic objects, there might be times when the objects need to be arranged so that a part of one overlaps another. It is similar to working on a project on a desk: You pick up a piece of paper and place it on top of another. At any time, you can rearrange the order of the papers, write on one, or add to the stack of papers on your desk. This process is appropriately called *layering* because objects are stacked one on top of another. Another purpose for understanding layering is the ability to separate a complex grouping of objects so you can format and revise each object (or layer) individually without affecting the surrounding graphic objects. Figure 5.23 shows two objects that are layered.

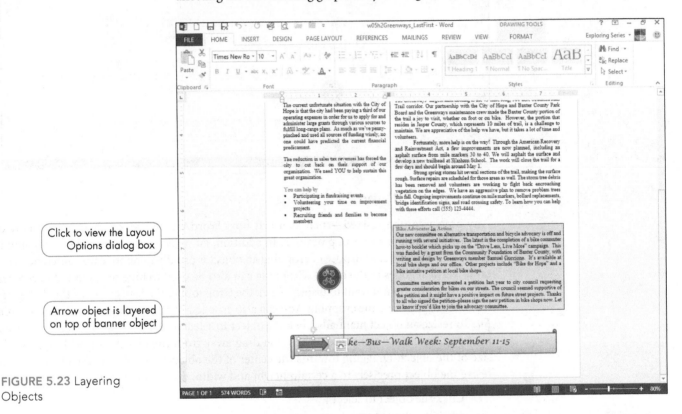

Click to view the Layout Options dialog box

Arrow object is layered on top of banner object

FIGURE 5.23 Layering Objects

When working with layered shapes in Microsoft Word, you can bring a shape to the front by one layer, push a shape back by one layer, move a shape to the front of all layers, or push a shape to the back of all layers. The commands in Table 5.1 are found in the Arrange group on the Format tab. To layer objects together, do the following:

1. Click the first object that you want to layer.
2. Click the FORMAT tab.
3. Click Bring Forward in the Arrange group to place the first object on top of the second object.

TABLE 5.1 Layering Options	
Bring to Front	Moves an object to the top of all other objects
Bring Forward	Moves an object on top of the object directly in front of it
Bring in Front of Text	Moves the object to display in front of text
Send to Back	Moves an object to the back of all other objects
Send Backward	Moves an object below the object directly in back of it
Send Behind Text	Moves the object to display behind text

After you layer objects, it might be useful to group them so they can be moved, resized, and adjusted together as one object. *Grouping* is the process of combining selected objects so that they appear as a single object. When objects are grouped, you can move them together or apply a style to all the grouped objects at one time. To select multiple objects for grouping, do one of the following:

1. Click one object, press and hold Shift, and then click the remaining objects.
2. After all the desired objects are selected, click Group on the FORMAT tab, as shown in Figure 5.24.

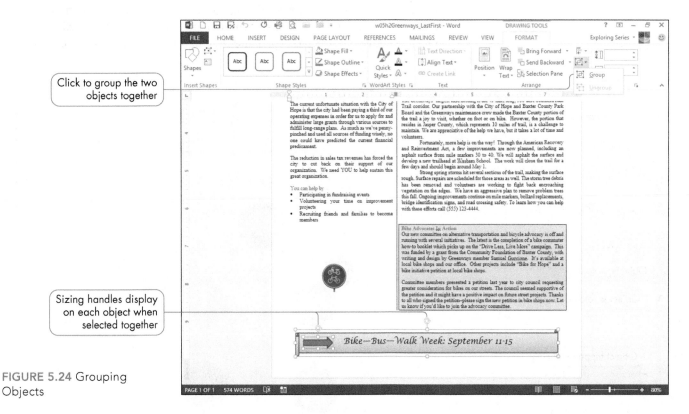

FIGURE 5.24 Grouping Objects

You can separate grouped objects by ungrouping them. *Ungrouping* breaks a grouped object into separate individual objects. You might ungroup objects because you need to make modifications to one individual part of the group rather than to the entire group, such as sizing or repositioning an individual object in the group. Ungrouping also makes it possible to delete an object or add another object to the group. To ungroup an object, click the grouped object to select it. On the Format tab, click Group Objects and click Ungroup in the Arrange group.

> **TIP** **Text Wrapping**
>
> If you encounter difficulties when working with graphic objects, you might need to change the text wrapping option applied to the object. The Wrap Text button can be found in the Arrange group on the Format tab. The Square or Tight text wrapping options are commonly applied settings. Or click Wrap Text and choose More Layout Options to view additional settings available in the Layout dialog box. The *Lock anchor* setting on the Position tab in the Layout dialog box is useful when you want to assign an absolute position to a graphic. In addition, Word 2013 has a new feature called Layout Options. This is an icon located at the top-right corner of the image, and it has an option for you to fix the image's position on the page.

Flip and Rotate Objects

The angle of an object can also be adjusted in several different directions by flipping or rotating the object at various angles. To flip and rotate an object, do the following:

1. Click the object to select it.
2. Click the FORMAT tab.
3. Click Rotate Objects in the Arrange group and select from several commands to rotate the object in a particular direction, or to flip horizontally or vertically.
4. Click More Rotate Options to display a dialog box and enter a precise Rotation measurement to modify the object, as shown in Figure 5.25. Alternatively, click the rotation handle above the selected object and drag to rotate the object to a desired angle.

FIGURE 5.25 Examples of Rotating an Object

Quick Concepts

1. Describe the purpose of using some of the graphic objects found on the Insert tab. *p. 334*
2. What is the purpose of creating a pull quote? *p. 337*
3. How can you enhance the appearance of a graphic object? *p. 340*

Hands-On Exercise

Watch the Video
for this Hands-
On Exercise!

MyITLab®
HOE2 Training

2 Decorative Text and Drawing Tools

The Greenways newsletter is coming together nicely. You decide to use graphical features in Microsoft Word to display information about upcoming events. You also decide to display article titles using a combination of graphics and text rather than simply changing the size and color of fonts.

Skills covered: Insert SmartArt • Insert WordArt • Create a Pull Quote • Insert Drawing Shapes and Apply Formatting • Group and Layer Objects

STEP 1 >> INSERT SMARTART

Members of The Greenways should be made aware of several upcoming events. You want to be sure these events stand out in the newsletter, so you decide to use SmartArt to display them. This will give this particular news item a unique look and will fit in the wider right column. Refer to Figure 5.26 as you complete Step 1.

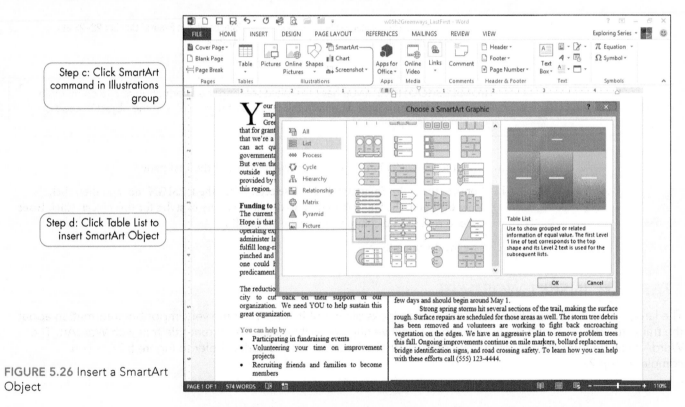

FIGURE 5.26 Insert a SmartArt Object

a. If necessary, open *w05h1Greenways_LastFirst* and save it as **w05h2Greenways_LastFirst**, changing *h1* to *h2*.

b. Drag the **Zoom slider** to increase the zoom to **80%**. Delete the heading *Upcoming Events* and the event information that follows, up to the blank line above the *Trail Update* heading. Click to position the insertion point on the blank line above the *Trail Update* heading.

> **TROUBLESHOOTING:** If there is no blank line above the *Trail Update* heading, position the insertion point on the left side of *Trail Update* and press **Enter**.

c. Click the **INSERT tab** and click **SmartArt** in the Illustrations group.

The *Choose a SmartArt Graphic* dialog box displays with a list of categories on the left pane of the box.

d. Click **List** on the left pane, scroll down to view the additional designs in the middle pane, and then click **Table List** (eighth row, first column, under *List category*). Click **OK** to close the dialog box.

A representation of the table list displays in your document.

e. Point to the bottom-right corner of the SmartArt shape until the two-headed arrow displays, drag to the right margin, and then release the mouse.

This increases the size of the SmartArt object to create additional space for the information you type next.

f. Click the **Text pane arrow** to expand the Text pane, if necessary, and type **Upcoming Events** in the top bullet.

This places text in the panel that displays at the top of the SmartArt object.

g. Populate the remaining text panels by completing the following steps:

- Click one time in the first sub-bullet, type **Volunteer Workdays**, press **Shift+Enter** to move the insertion point to the next line without a bullet, type **Third Saturdays**, press **Shift+Enter**, and then type **(9am–noon)**.
- Type the following text in the two remaining panels, pressing **Shift+Enter** as needed to move to a new line as shown for each panel.

Annual Fundraising Dinner September 20 at Hope Country Club

Outdoor Fitness Festival October 22–23 at City Park

> **TROUBLESHOOTING:** If you have trouble displaying the information above on multiple lines in each text box, type directly in the text boxes that display in the object instead of typing in the Text pane.

h. Click the **Close (X) button** in the top-right corner of the Text pane.

i. Confirm the entire SmartArt object is selected, click the **DESIGN tab**, and then click the **More button** in the SmartArt group to display a variety of styles for this object. Click **Inset** (second row, second column) under the *3D* heading.

j. Save the document.

STEP 2 ⟩ INSERT WORDART

The large article in the middle of the right column looks plain, but it contains some very important information about the trails. You decide that it deserves a more attractive title and will replace the current title text with WordArt. The WordArt can be formatted to coordinate better with the SmartArt added earlier. Refer to Figure 5.27 as you complete Step 2.

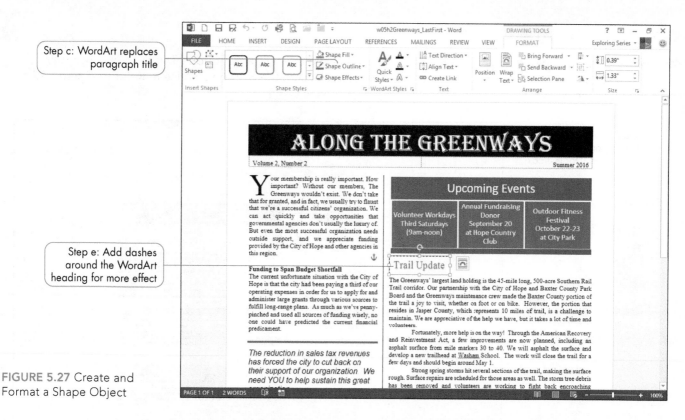

Step c: WordArt replaces paragraph title

Step e: Add dashes around the WordArt heading for more effect

FIGURE 5.27 Create and Format a Shape Object

a. Select the heading *Trail Update* and press **Enter** three times.

This removes the current title and makes room for the WordArt you will insert.

b. Click the **INSERT tab** and click **WordArt** in the Text group. Click **Fill - Blue, Accent 1, Shadow** (first row, second column).

The text box where you type the phrase displays on top of the paragraph. You will relocate the text box later.

c. Press **Backspace** once, type **Trail Update**, click the **Font size arrow**, and then click **16**.

The paragraph heading *Trail Update* displays in the text box in the WordArt style selected. You will move the WordArt heading into the proper position in the next step.

d. Click the **FORMAT tab**, click **Wrap Text** in the Arrange group, and then click **Top and Bottom**. Click the border to display the four-arrow pointer and drag the text box to the right column; position it under the SmartArt object and just above the paragraphs it describes.

> **TROUBLESHOOTING:** Use the arrow keys to nudge the object into exact positioning, if necessary.

e. Click **Shape Outline** in the Shape Styles group, click **Dashes**, and then click **Dash** (fourth item in the list). Click anywhere to deselect the WordArt object.

f. Click the **HOME tab** and click **Show/Hide (¶)**.

g. Save the document and keep it open if you plan to continue with Hands-On Exercise 3. If not, close the document and exit Word.

STEP 3 ➤➤ CREATE A PULL QUOTE

You decide to move one paragraph into a text box, which has the effect of a pull quote. This is an effective way to display a statement that is so important that you want to make sure the members notice it. Refer to Figure 5.28 as you complete Step 3.

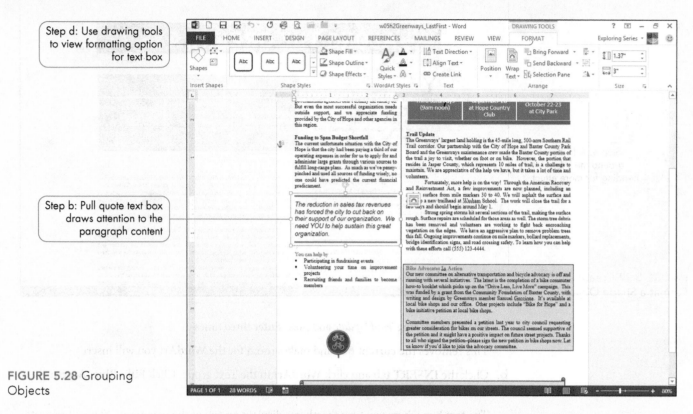

Step d: Use drawing tools to view formatting option for text box

Step b: Pull quote text box draws attention to the paragraph content

FIGURE 5.28 Grouping Objects

a. Click the **HOME tab** and click **Show/Hide (¶)**. Select the paragraph that begins with the text *The reduction in sales tax revenue has forced*, but do not select the paragraph symbol that displays at the end of the last sentence of this paragraph. To modify the format and prepare this text for a pull quote, complete the following steps:

- Click the **Font Size arrow** on the Mini toolbar and click **12**.
- Click the **Font arrow** and click **Arial**.
- Click **Italic**.
- Press **Ctrl+X** to cut the text from the document.
- Press **Backspace** two times to remove the paragraph marks that display between the two paragraphs.

Currently, there is one empty paragraph mark, which is normal, but no more large gaps of white space between the elements in this newsletter. This will enable you to position the pull quote more precisely.

b. Click the **INSERT tab**, click **Text Box** in the Text group, and then click **Austin Pull Quote** from the gallery.

The Text Box gallery includes building blocks that are preformatted for a variety of pull quote styles.

c. Press **Ctrl+V**.

The text you cut earlier displays in the text box.

d. Click the border of the pull quote to select it. To position it more precisely on the page, complete the following steps:

- Click the **FORMAT tab**, if necessary, click **Position** in the Arrange group, and then click **More Layout Options**.
- Click **Absolute position** in the *Horizontal* section and click the arrow until **–0.1** displays, or type in the measurement and be sure to include the negative sign. Click to the right of the arrow and click **Column**.
- Click **Absolute position** in the *Vertical* section and click the arrow until **1.4** displays. Click the **below arrow** and click **Paragraph**.
- Click **Lock anchor**.
- Click **OK** to save the settings.
- Click the **FORMAT tab** and use the Shape Width box in the Size group to resize the pull quote by typing **3.0** and pressing **Enter** so that the pull quote fits within the left column.

e. Save the document.

STEP 4 ≫ INSERT DRAWING SHAPES AND APPLY FORMATTING

You notice there is a significant amount of white space at the bottom of the newsletter and decide to use this space to add a shape object that will span the width of the newsletter and display text to remind readers of an upcoming event. Refer to Figure 5.29 as you complete Step 4.

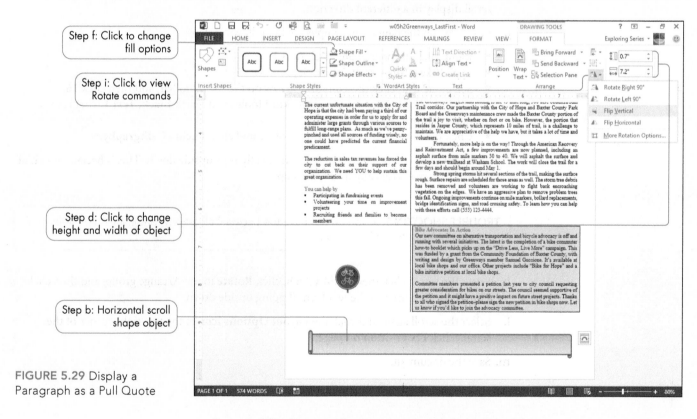

FIGURE 5.29 Display a Paragraph as a Pull Quote

a. Press **Ctrl+End** to move the insertion point to the bottom of the page.

b. Click the **INSERT tab**, click **Shapes** in the Illustrations group, and then click **Horizontal Scroll** (second row, sixth column) in the *Stars and Banners* set.

The insertion point is displayed as a cross-hair.

c. Drag the mouse across the bottom of the newsletter to create a scroll that extends across the width of the page.

The scroll remains selected after releasing the mouse, as indicated by the sizing handles. You can click and drag the yellow square near the top-left corner to change the size of the scroll.

d. Click the **Height arrow** in the Size group on the FORMAT tab until **0.7** displays (or, alternatively, type in the measurement and press **Enter**). Click the **Width arrow** until **7.2** displays.

The height and width can be adjusted more specifically using the sizing controls in the FORMAT tab.

e. Click **Wrap Text** in the Arrange group and click **More Layout Options**. Click the **Position tab** and click **Alignment** in the *Horizontal* section. Click the **Alignment arrow**, click **Centered**, click the **relative to arrow**, and then click **Margin**. Click **OK**.

f. Click the **Shape Fill arrow** in the Shape Styles group. Click the color **Blue, Accent 1, Darker 25%** (fifth row, fifth column).

g. Click the **Shape Fill arrow** again, point to *Gradient*, and then click **Linear Up** (third row, second column) under the *Light Variations* section.

The scroll color changes to display a lighter blue color that gradually lightens as it nears the top of the object.

h. Click the **Shape Outline arrow** in the Shape Styles group, click **Weight**, and then click **2 1/4 pt**.

i. Click **Rotate** in the Arrange group and click **Flip Vertical**.

The two previous steps enhance the outline of the object and flip it so that the edges of the scroll display in a different direction.

j. Insert text on the banner by completing the following steps:

- Right-click the banner and click **Add Text**.
- Type **Bike—Bus—Walk Week: September 11–15**.
- Select the text, click the **Font Size arrow** on the Mini toolbar, and then click **16**.
- Click the **Font Color arrow** on the Mini toolbar and click **Black, Text 1** (first row, second column).
- Click the **Font arrow** on the Mini toolbar and click **Lucida Calligraphy**.

Note that once you type the text, it automatically flips upside down. This is because you had flipped the scroll vertically in the last step.

TROUBLESHOOTING: If you do not have the Lucida Calligraphy font installed on your computer, substitute a different font.

---

k. Select the scroll, click the **FORMAT tab**, click **Rotate** in the Arrange group, and then click **Flip Vertical** to prevent the text from flipping upside down.

l. Select the scroll again and click the **Layout Options icon** at the top-right corner of the scroll. Click **Fix position on page**.

m. Save the document.

STEP 5 ≫ GROUP AND LAYER OBJECTS

Shape objects can be displayed together as layered objects, but moving multiple objects for precise placement can become a tedious process. You group the shapes so that, when necessary, you can move them together at the same time. Refer to Figure 5.30 as you complete Step 5.

Step e: Only one set of sizing handles displays after grouping items together

FIGURE 5.30 Using WordArt for a Paragraph Heading

a. Click the **INSERT tab**, click **Shapes** in the Illustrations group, and then click **Right Arrow** from the *Block Arrows* section. Drag the pointer to create the arrow on the left side of the scroll before the text that displays in the scroll object at the bottom of the page.

b. Click the **Height arrow** in the Size group on the FORMAT tab until **0.3** displays. Click the **Width arrow** until **0.8** displays or, alternatively, type in the measurements and press **Enter**.

c. Click the **arrow shape object** one time to select it, if necessary, and press the left or right arrow key to nudge the arrow shape into the middle of the scroll shape.

Using the left and right arrow keys will nudge the shape into a more precise position.

d. Press and hold **Shift** and click the banner.

Both objects, the banner and the arrow, are selected and sizing handles for both objects display.

e. Click **Group** in the Arrange group and click **Group**.

If a group object is selected, only one set of sizing handles will display. However, if you click again on one of the shapes in the grouped object, this will drill down to selecting the piece that was clicked and two sets of sizing handles will appear. The inner set of sizing handles belongs to the active shape selected within the group.

f. Save the document.

Object Linking and Embedding

Microsoft Office enables you to create documents that contain objects from other applications. For example, you might create a report in Word that explains the results of a survey. The survey data are saved in an Excel spreadsheet that also includes a chart to summarize the data. Rather than re-creating the data in a Word table, you can insert the spreadsheet and a chart can be inserted or linked into the Word document. The document in Figure 5.31 is a Microsoft Word document that contains objects (a worksheet and a chart) developed in Microsoft Excel. The technology that enables you to insert and link objects or information into different applications is called *Object Linking and Embedding* (abbreviated *OLE*; it is pronounced oh-lay).

In this section, you will learn about the many ways to embed and link an object, and then you will learn to update a linked object.

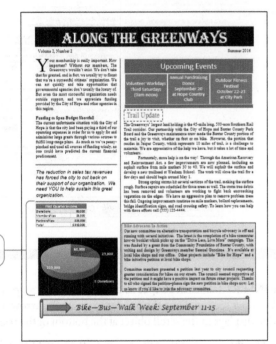

Linked or embedded from an Excel worksheet

FIGURE 5.31 Document Containing Linked and Embedded Objects

Using OLE to Insert an Object

When you insert objects into a document, there are two options for how the object can be imported into the document. The first option is embedding. *Embedding* imports an object into a document from its original source and allows editing directly in the document without changing the source data file. For example, if you embed a portion of an Excel worksheet, it becomes part of your document; you can make modifications to the copied data at any time, and those changes do not affect the original worksheet. Likewise, any changes to the original Excel file will not display in your document.

The second option for inserting an object or data into your document is by linking the data. *Linking* is the process of importing an object from another program, but the object retains a connection to the original data file. If you change the data in the original source file, the data in the destination file will reflect the changes, and vice versa. A data file used as a linked object may be linked to multiple documents. The same Excel chart, for example, can be linked to a Word document and a PowerPoint presentation. Any changes to the Excel chart are automatically reflected and updated in the document and the presentation to which it is linked.

The advantage of linking over embedding is that a linked object will reflect the most current information. This might be important, for example, when you insert the stock prices for your company into your weekly newsletter—you would always want the most current prices to display. On the other hand, an embedded object is a snapshot of the information at the time the data was embedded into the file; if the desired result is to keep the data constant and any updates are controlled within the document, then this would be a better option to use because you don't have to worry about having access to the source file at a later date. For example, if you want to display the previous year-ending sales figures in the January newsletter, you would embed the data because those numbers will not change.

You can link and embed data into a document using the *Copy and Paste* method in the Paste options.

Use the Copy and Paste Method

When using the *Copy and Paste* method, you first copy a selection from the source, such as an Excel spreadsheet or an object from a PowerPoint slide, and then do one of the following:

1. To Embed: Click Paste to insert the copied data into the destination document. When you paste Excel data into Word, the data is pasted into table cells and does not retain Excel spreadsheet capabilities. For example, all pasted formulas and functions convert to actual values; thus if you change one value it will not change any of the other pasted values that use that value. Additionally, the numbers will not align on the decimal points.

2. To Link: On the Home tab, click Paste in the Clipboard group, click Paste Special, and then click the *Paste link* option in the Paste Special dialog box, as shown in Figure 5.32, which creates the connection to the original file. Make sure the appropriate object from the *As list* box is selected; for example, if the data is from an Excel file, click the Microsoft Excel Worksheet Object in the listed items. Click OK. If you change a value in the Excel file, it will automatically update in the Word file and vice versa. When the object in the Word file is double-clicked, it opens the source data Excel file to allow editing.

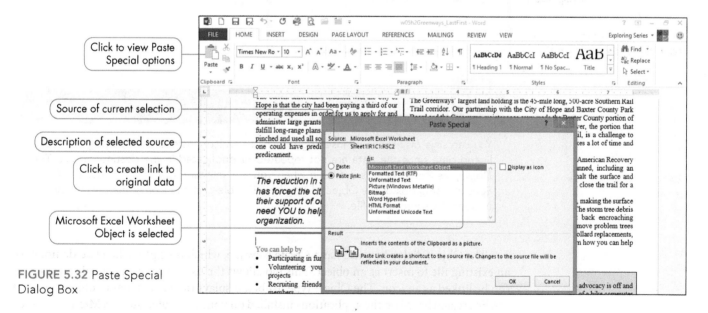

FIGURE 5.32 Paste Special Dialog Box

Use the Insert an Object Method

STEP 1 ≫ You can insert an object, such as an Excel workbook, within a Word document without displaying the data contents of the Excel workbook itself. The contents of the entire Excel workbook, which may contain several worksheets, appear as an icon in the document, and when you click the icon, the Excel workbook opens in a separate window. This allows you to associate the data or information with the document without using space to display the data. To use this method, do the following:

1. Click the INSERT tab and click Object in the Text group. The Object dialog box displays, as shown in Figure 5.33, with two tabs at the top.
2. Click the *Create from File* tab, click Browse to navigate to the location of the file, and then double-click the file name.
3. Click the *Link to file* option located on the right side of the dialog box to create a link to the file.
4. Click the *Display as icon* option located on the right to save disk space.
5. Click OK to insert the selected object into the Word document.

FIGURE 5.33 Create from File Tab in the Object Dialog Box

> **TIP** **Displaying a Link as an Icon**
>
> You can save disk space by inserting the link as an icon instead of displaying the actual linked data since the data are not repeated or duplicated in the destination file. The *Display as icon* option is available when you are selecting options in either the Paste Special dialog box or the Object dialog box. Double-click the icon in the destination file to open the source data file.

The Object dialog box also has a Create New tab, which is helpful when you do not have an existing file to insert as an object. This tab allows the user to create a new file source that can be linked as an icon. The Object type list box displays the many types of object files that can be created based on the applications installed on your computer, such as Microsoft Excel. When you click the Object type (without clicking the *Display as icon* option), a small window displays in the destination document (see Figure 5.34), and you can create the content for the object that will display in your document. After the object displays in the document, you can edit it by double-clicking the object. If the *Display as icon* option is checked on the Create New tab, the new file displays as an icon and double-clicking opens the object for adding or editing the data.

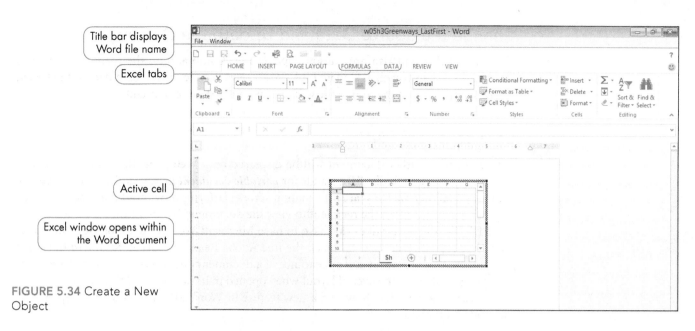

Title bar displays Word file name

Excel tabs

Active cell

Excel window opens within the Word document

FIGURE 5.34 Create a New Object

Updating a Linked Object

After you link an object to your document, you can still make modifications to the source file. At any time, you can open a source file in its native application—Excel, for example—to make modifications. You can also open the application by clicking the linked object in the Word document. To use this method, right-click the linked object, point to Linked Worksheet Object, and then click Edit Link or Open Link, as shown in Figure 5.35. Either option opens the source document to allow for editing or modifications made to the data within the source application.

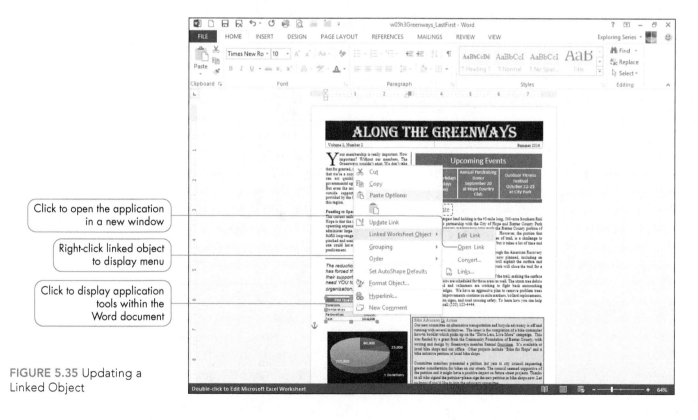

Click to open the application in a new window

Right-click linked object to display menu

Click to display application tools within the Word document

FIGURE 5.35 Updating a Linked Object

Change the Source Data and Update the Document

STEP 2 The right-click menu also provides an Update Link command on the menu, as shown in Figure 5.35. When you click Update Link, Word retrieves the most recent data to the linked object; any changes in the source file will display in the Word document.

Save as a PDF File

STEP 3 If a newsletter or other document will be displayed on a Web page, then you should consider saving it as a PDF file. *PDF* stands for *portable document format* and was developed by Adobe Systems as a way to share information across platforms or without the necessary fonts or programs installed for the recipient to view the document. By presenting the information as a PDF file, the reader does not have to have Microsoft Word to open or view the document; however, they do have to install the free Adobe Reader program. Saving in this form helps to preserve the layout and appearance of a document due to the fact that different font substitutes could alter the overall layout when opened in its native Word format. A PDF generally discourages editing; however, a new feature in Word 2013 allows users to open PDF files and edit the text.

Quick Concepts

1. What is the difference between embedding and linking an object? *p. 352*

2. What are some of the objects that can be pasted and then linked back to the source file? *p. 352*

3. Why would you want to link an object? *p. 352*

Hands-On Exercise

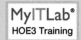

3 Object Linking and Embedding

The newsletter for The Greenways is nearly complete. Director Allen requests space to display first-quarter financial information and provides the information in an Excel worksheet. You will add this information by inserting a chart into the newsletter, then save the final copy as a PDF file before leaving for a bike ride!

Skills covered: Copy and Link a Worksheet • Change the Source Data and Update the Document • Save as a PDF File

STEP 1 >> COPY AND LINK A WORKSHEET

When Director Allen sends you the Excel worksheet that contains the first quarter income sources, he tells you that it should be added to the newsletter, but some changes to the worksheet might be necessary in the near future. You decide the proper course of action is to insert the information with a link to the original file so you have the option to update the data later. Refer to Figure 5.36 as you complete Step 1.

Step d: Click Copy

Step c: Border indicates cells A1:B5 are copied to the Clipboard

FIGURE 5.36 Copy Data from an Excel Worksheet

a. Start Word, and if necessary, open *w05h2Greenways_LastFirst* and save it as **w05h3Greenways_LastFirst**, changing *h2* to *h3*. Click the **HOME tab** and click **Show/Hide (¶)** to display formatting marks if they are not currently turned on.

   In the next step, you will open an Excel workbook. You might find it easier to work with the Excel spreadsheet if you minimize your Word document.

b. Start Excel. Open *w05h3Budget.xlsx* and save it as **w05h3Budget_LastFirst**.

   The file displays in an Excel window. The Windows taskbar now contains icons for both Word and Excel; click either icon to move back and forth between the applications.

c. Drag to select **cells A1 through B5** in the Excel worksheet.

d. Click **Copy** in the Clipboard group (or press **Ctrl+C**).

   A moving border displays around the selection, indicating it has been copied to the Clipboard.

e. Click the **Word icon** on the Windows taskbar to return to the Word document. Place the insertion point on the first blank line above the paragraph that begins *You can help by*. This is where you will insert the Excel worksheet.

> **TROUBLESHOOTING:** If necessary, press **Enter** to insert a blank line before the paragraph heading *You can help by*.

f. Click the **Paste arrow** in the Clipboard group on the HOME tab. Click **Paste Special** to display the Paste Special dialog box. In the As list, click **Microsoft Excel Worksheet Object**.

g. Click **Paste link** on the left side of the dialog box and click **OK**.

> **TROUBLESHOOTING:** If the Update Link option does not display on a right-click menu for the Excel object, that means the object is not linked to the source. Click **Undo** on the Quick Access Toolbar and repeat step g, making sure to click **Paste Special** and check the **Paste link option**.

h. Drag the image below the bullets, if necessary. Delete the two blank lines above the *Trail Update* heading.

i. Save the document.

STEP 2 ≫ CHANGE THE SOURCE DATA AND UPDATE THE DOCUMENT

As expected, Director Allen sends the changes you need to make in the budget worksheet, and thus on the newsletter. The changes will be applied to the Excel worksheet and updated in the newsletter table. Refer to Figure 5.37 as you complete Step 2.

Step e: Click to insert changes from Excel source file

FIGURE 5.37 Update Linked Data

a. Click the **Excel icon** on the Windows taskbar to return to the worksheet. Press **Esc** to deselect the cells.

b. Click **cell A1**, type **First Quarter Income**, and then press **Enter**.

The text typed automatically replaces the original text for cell A1.

c. Click **cell B2**, type **60000**, and then press **Enter**.

d. Save and close the workbook.

e. Click the **Word icon** on the Windows taskbar to return to the Word document. Right-click the **Excel worksheet object** and click **Update Link**.

The linked object reflects the changes you made in the Excel workbook.

> **TROUBLESHOOTING:** If your data table does not reflect the new changes, you need to check and make sure that your Excel workbook is closed.

f. Save the document.

STEP 3 ≫ SAVE AS A PDF FILE

Because you will post the newsletter on The Greenways Web site, you decide to save the document as a PDF file. As a result, anyone can view the newsletter, regardless of the type of computer they are using. You can also e-mail the PDF version to members and know they can read it even if they do not have Microsoft Word installed on their PC. Refer to Figure 5.38 as you complete Step 3.

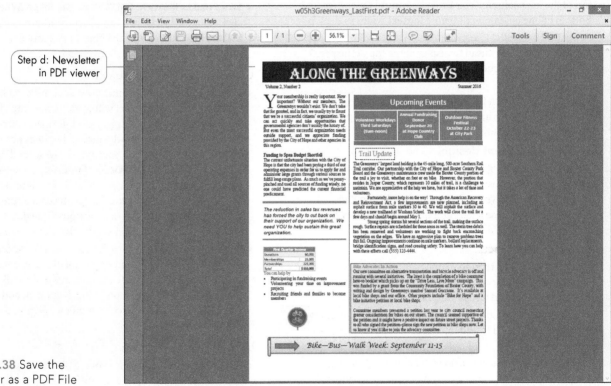

Step d: Newsletter in PDF viewer

FIGURE 5.38 Save the Newsletter as a PDF File

a. Click **File** and click **Save As**.

b. Click **Browse** and navigate to the folder where you want to save the PDF file.

c. Click the **Save as type arrow** and click **PDF (*.pdf)**.

d. Click **Save**.

An additional window displays the file in Adobe Reader. The file now exists in both Word and Adobe PDF formats.

e. Save and close the file, and submit based on your instructor's directions. Close the Adobe Reader (PDF) version of the file and submit it based on your instructor's directions.

Chapter Objectives Review

After reading this chapter, you have accomplished the following objectives:

1. Construct a newsletter.

- You can create a document with two or more columns of equal width. When you select one of the column preset designs, Microsoft Word will calculate the width of each column based on the number of columns, the left and right margins on the page, and the specified (default) space between columns. A two-column layout with a wide and narrow column design may be preferred over columns of uniform width, as it adds interest to the document.
- A section break is required whenever the column specification changes and at the end of the last column to balance the text within the columns.
- Use a column break to force paragraph text to start at the top of the next column. This provides control over where the bottom of one column ends before the text wraps to the top of the next column.
- You can create a masthead to display at the top of the page to introduce the document and use a reverse to enhance the appearance.
- Another way to catch the reader's eye and call attention to the associated text is a drop cap. A drop cap is a capital letter formatted in a font size larger than the body text.

2. Develop a document design.

- Good design makes it easier for the reader to determine what is important. Emphasis can be achieved using variations in type size and/or type style, headings, bold and italic formatting, uppercase letters and underlining, boxes and/or shading, pull quote, reverse, images, and color.

3. Insert graphic objects.

- SmartArt is a visual representation of information that can be created to effectively communicate a message or idea in one of many existing and visually appealing layouts.
- WordArt is a Microsoft Office feature that creates decorative text that can be used to add interest to the text you use in a document.
- One way to combine the flexibility of a shape object with simple text is to create a text box. A text box can control the placement of text and allow for layering with other objects and shapes.
- A pull quote is a phrase or sentence taken from an article to emphasize a key point. It is typically set in larger type, often in a different font or in italics, and may be offset with borders at the top, bottom, or on the sides. Pull quotes are frequently displayed in professional publications, such as company's monthly newsletters and annual reports, to draw attention to important topics.
- One text box can be linked to another text box so that when text runs out of space in one box it automatically flows into another box.
- A shape is an object, such as a circle or an arrow, which you can use as a visual enhancement. You can use one shape or combine multiple shapes to create a more complex image.

4. Manipulate graphic objects.

- After you insert a graphical object, you can enhance the appearance by using one of the commands available on the Format tab for the object, such as fill, outline, and effects.
- Any object can be resized—such as a text box, WordArt, image, or shape—manually or precisely using the size group options.
- Grouping is the process of combining selected objects so that they appear as a single object. When grouped, you can move objects simultaneously or apply a Style to all at one time. Layering is the process of placing one shape on top of another. After you layer objects, you might need to group them so you can manipulate them more easily.
- Word makes it easy to flip or rotate an object. When you click Rotate Objects, you can select from several commands that enable you to rotate the object in a particular direction or flip it along a horizontal or vertical axis.

5. Use OLE to insert an object.

- When you insert objects into your document, you have two options for how the object will work within your document. The first option, embedding, pulls information from its original source into your document, but does not change or maintain a link to that source file. The second option is linking, which is the process of inserting an object from another program, but the object retains a connection to the original data and file. If you change the data in the original source program, you can quickly update the data in the destination program to reflect the changes.
- You can insert an object, such as an Excel workbook, within a Word document without displaying the data contents of the Excel workbook itself. The contents of the entire Excel workbook appear as an icon in the document, and when you click the icon, the Excel workbook opens in a separate window.

6. Update a linked object.

- At any time, you can open a source file in its native application, for example, Microsoft Excel, to make modifications. You can also open the application by double-clicking the linked object in a Word document. When you click the Update Link option, Word retrieves the most updated form of the object from the source file and displays the changes in the Word document.
- If a newsletter or other document will be displayed on a Web page, then you should consider saving it as a portable document format (PDF) file. By presenting the information as a PDF file, the reader does not have to have Microsoft Word to open or view the document. A new feature in Word 2013 allows users to open PDF files and edit the text.

Key Terms Matching

Match the key terms with their definitions. Write the key term letter by the appropriate numbered definition.

a. SmartArt
b. Drop cap
c. Embedding
d. Grid
e. Text pane
f. Text box
g. Reverse
h. Pull quote
i. WordArt
j. Ungrouping

k. Linking
l. Drawing Canvas
m. Sidebar
n. Layering
o. Object Linking and Embedding (OLE)
p. Grouping
q. Masthead
r. Fill
s. Desktop publishing
t. PDF

1. _____ A feature that creates decorative text for a document. **p. 336**

2. _____ A frame-like area that helps you keep parts of your drawing together. **p. 341**

3. _____ Pulls an object into a document, where you can edit it without changing the source. **p. 352**

4. _____ A large capital letter at the beginning of a paragraph. **p. 324**

5. _____ The interior space of an object. **p. 340**

6. _____ An underlying, but invisible, set of horizontal and vertical lines that determine the placement of major elements. **p. 325**

7. _____ The process of combining objects so they appear as a single object. **p. 343**

8. _____ The process of placing one shape on top of another. **p. 342**

9. _____ Inserts an object from another program, but retains a connection to the original data. **p. 352**

10. _____ The identifying information at the top of a newsletter or other periodical. **p. 323**

11. _____ A technology that enables you to insert objects into a document regardless of the platform they use. **p. 352**

12. _____ A phrase or sentence taken from an article to emphasize a key point. **p. 337**

13. _____ The technique that uses light text on a dark background. **p. 323**

14. _____ Supplementary text that appears on the side of the featured information. **p. 337**

15. _____ Simply a graphical object that contains text. **p. 337**

16. _____ A special pane that opens up for entering text when a SmartArt diagram is selected. **p. 335**

17. _____ Breaks a combined single object into individual objects. **p. 343**

18. _____ A visual representation of information that can be created to effectively communicate a message or idea in one of many existing and visually appealing layouts. **p. 321**

19. _____ Stands for portable document format and was developed by Adobe Systems as a way to share information across platforms or without the necessary fonts or programs installed for the recipient to view the document. **p. 356**

20. _____ Evolved through a combination of technologies, including faster computers, laser and inkjet printers, and sophisticated page composition software that enables users to manipulate text and graphics to produce a professional-looking document. **p. 320**

Multiple Choice

1. What format do you see when you use a reverse effect on a masthead?

   (a) Light text on a clear background
   (b) Dark text on a clear background
   (c) Dark text on a light background
   (d) Light text on a dark background

2. How do you balance the columns in a newsletter so that each column contains the same amount of text?

   (a) Insert a section break at the end of the last column and use a column break in previous columns to control the flow.
   (b) Insert a page break at the end of the last column.
   (c) Manually set the column widths in the Columns dialog box.
   (d) Press Enter until the text lines up at the bottom of each column.

3. Which feature would not be used to add emphasis to a document?

   (a) Pull Quote
   (b) Borders and Shading
   (c) Paste Link
   (d) Bulleted and Numbered List

4. Which feature enables you to quickly insert an organizational chart, which you can modify and enhance as needed?

   (a) WordArt
   (b) SmartArt
   (c) Shapes
   (d) Clip art

5. You insert an arrow shape in the document that points left, but you need it to point right. You can use the Rotate Objects command under which group to change the direction of your arrow?

   (a) Page Setup
   (b) Paragraph
   (c) Arrange
   (d) Flip

6. To move several shapes as one object, you should:

   (a) Layer the shapes.
   (b) Anchor the shapes.
   (c) Position the shapes.
   (d) Group the shapes.

7. Which of the following processes inserts Excel data in a way that enables you to edit the values in Word, but without changing the source?

   (a) Embedding
   (b) Copying and Inserting
   (c) Linking
   (d) Find and Replace

8. Which process should you use to insert Excel data into Word so that any changes made to the original Excel worksheet can be automatically updated in Word?

   (a) Copying and Pasting
   (b) Linking
   (c) Embedding
   (d) Find and Replace

9. To quickly determine whether spreadsheet data displayed in a Word document is linked to the source file, you can:

   (a) Click the INSERT tab and click Object.
   (b) Single-click the object.
   (c) Click Paste Special.
   (d) Right-click the object and look for the Update Link option.

10. You just inserted two shape objects, a triangle and circle, into the document; the circle is larger and was inserted on top of the triangle, so the triangle cannot be seen. What can you do to display the triangle on top of the circle?

    (a) Click the circle and click *Bring to Front*.
    (b) Click the triangle and click *Bring to Back*.
    (c) Click the circle and click *Send to Back*.
    (d) Click the circle and click *Bring in Front of Text*.

1 Personal Computer Consulting

You are a local computer expert who operates a business named Personal Computer Consulting. You are often asked to give advice on purchasing a personal computer. Because the basic considerations are the same for everyone, you decide to create a simple shopping guide to explain those considerations. You want the guide to look professional, so you use several features in Word to develop an attractive document that is easy to read and that will make a good handout for anyone who asks how to buy a PC. This exercise follows the same set of skills as used in Hands-On Exercises 1–2 in the chapter. Refer to Figure 5.39 as you complete this exercise.

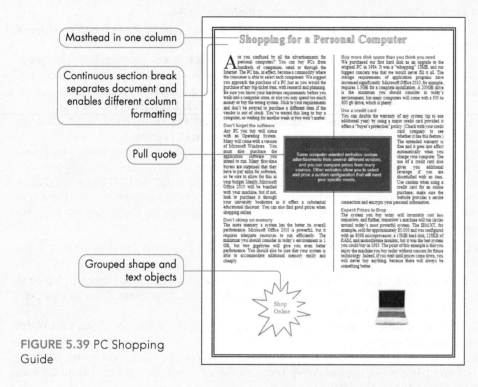

FIGURE 5.39 PC Shopping Guide

a. Open *w05p1PCHandout* and save it as **w05p1PCHandout_LastFirst**.

b. Click the **PAGE LAYOUT tab**, click **Columns** in the Page Setup group, and then click **More Columns**. Click **Two** in the *Presets* section, click the **Line between box**, and then click **OK**. Click **Breaks** in the Page Setup group and click **Continuous.**

c. Click the **HOME tab** and click **Show/Hide (¶)** in the Paragraph group to display formatting marks. Move the insertion point to the right side of the section break. Click the **PAGE LAYOUT tab**, click **Columns** in the Page Setup group, and then click **One**.

d. Create a masthead for this document by completing the following steps:

- Click **Enter** two times and press **Ctrl+Home** to move the insertion point to the beginning of the document.
- Click the **INSERT tab** and click **WordArt** in the Text group. Click the red-colored style named **Fill - Red, Accent 2, Outline - Accent 2** (first row, third column).
- Type **Shopping for a Personal Computer** and select the text. On the Mini toolbar, click **Font size** and click **26.**
- Click the **FORMAT tab** and click the **Size arrow**, if necessary. Click the **Height arrow** until **0.60"** displays and click the **Width arrow** until **6"** displays.
- Click the **Position arrow** and click **Position in Top Center with Square Text Wrapping.**
- Click the **Layout Options dialog box** and select **Fix position on page.**
- Drag the masthead to the space above the text.
- Place the insertion point on the left side of the blank line between the WordArt object and the section break and press **Delete**.

e. Click the **PAGE LAYOUT tab**, click **Margins**, and then click **Custom Margins**. Type **0.7** in each box for **Top**, **Bottom**, **Left**, and **Right**. In the *Apply to:* box, click **Whole document** and click **OK**. Click the **WordArt masthead** and use the arrow keys to nudge it higher on the page, if necessary.

f. Position the insertion point on the left side of the first paragraph in the left column of the page. Click the **INSERT tab**, click **Drop Cap** in Text group, and then click **Dropped**. Click anywhere outside the dropped cap to deselect it.

g. Press **Ctrl+End** to move the insertion point to the end of the document. Click the **PAGE LAYOUT tab**, click **Breaks** in the Page Setup group, and then click **Continuous** to display the content in two equally balanced columns.

h. Insert a text box to display a quote by completing the following steps:

- Select the heading and text in the paragraph titled *Let your fingers do the walking*. Press **Ctrl+X** to cut the paragraph.
- Click the **INSERT tab**, if necessary, click **Text Box** in the Text group, and then click **Grid Quote**. Click **Ctrl+V** to insert the paragraph you cut in this step. Click at the end of the paragraph pasted and press **Delete** to remove the extra empty paragraph mark if necessary.
- Click the **Bring Forward arrow** in the Arrange group and click **Bring in Front of Text**.
- Click the **Size arrow** and adjust the **Shape Height** to **1.69** and **Shape Width** to **3.4**. Click the paragraph heading and text in the pull quote and press **Ctrl+E** to center it.
- Omit the heading, but select the whole paragraph in the pull quote, click the **Font Color arrow**, and then click **White, Background 1** on the Mini toolbar.
- Click **Font** on the Mini toolbar and click **Arial**. Click the **PAGE LAYOUT tab** and click to change the Before spacing in the Paragraph group to **0**. Move the pull quote text box to the center and reposition it as seen in Figure 5.39. Click the **Layout Options dialog box** and select **Fix position on page**.

i. Press **Ctrl+End** to move the insertion point to the end of the document. Insert an image, a shape, and a text box by completing the following steps:

- Click the **INSERT tab**, click **Online Pictures** in the Illustrations group, and then type **laptop** in the **Bing Image Search box** in the Insert Pictures dialog box. Press **Enter**. Select an image of a laptop computer. Click **Insert**.
- Click the **Shape Height arrow** in the Size group until **1.5"** displays. If necessary, click the **Width arrow** until **1.5"** displays.
- Drag the object to the bottom of the right column, which displays on a second page. Click the **FORMAT tab**, if necessary, click **Wrap Text**, and then click **Square**. Click the **Layout Options dialog box** and select **Fix position on page**.
- Click the **INSERT tab**, click **Shapes** in the Illustrations group, and then click the **Explosion 1 shape** in the *Stars and Banners* section (first shape in that section). Click the left side of the bottom of the page to the left of the computer graphic to create a shape. Click the **More button** in the Shape Styles group to display the Quick Styles gallery. Click **Colored Outline—Blue, Accent 1** (first row, second column). Click **Rotate Objects** in the Arrange group and click **Rotate Left 90°**. In the Size group, adjust both the Shape Height and Width to **1.88**.
- Click the **INSERT tab**, if necessary. Click **Text Box** in the Text group and click **Draw Text Box**. Click near the shape to create a text box. Type **Shop**, press **Shift+Enter** to move to the next line, and then type **Online** in the text box. Select the text, click the **Font Color arrow** on the Mini toolbar, and then click **Dark Blue, Text 2, Lighter 40%** (fourth row, fourth column). Click the **Font Size arrow** and click **14**.
- Click the border of the text box. Click the **FORMAT tab**, if necessary, click **Shape Fill**, and then click **No Fill**. Click **Shape Outline** and click **No Outline**.
- Drag the box handles to resize as needed until the box is an appropriate size to fit and display all the text and drag it into a position where the text appears centered in the explosion shape.
- Click the text box, if necessary, press and hold **Shift**, and then click the explosion shape. Right-click, point to *Group*, and then click **Group**. Click the **Layout Options dialog box** and select **Fix position on page**. Click anywhere outside the explosion shape to deselect it.

j. Click the **DESIGN tab**, click **Page Borders**, drag the **Style scroll bar** down until a double line style displays, and then select the double line. Click the **Width arrow** and click **2 1/4 pt**. Click **Box** in the *Setting* section and click **OK**. Click the **HOME tab** and click **Show/Hide (¶)** to remove formatting marks.

k. Save and close the file, and submit based on your instructor's directions.

2 IBC Enterprises

You are the lead financial analyst for IBC Enterprises, a technology manufacturing organization. Each year, you are responsible for preparing a summary of the annual report. After you summarize the main points, you decide the report should include a chart and graph to emphasize certain points, as well as give a visual summary of the information. You begin this exercise by opening the general summary and add data from an Excel spreadsheet that contains the information you want to summarize. You also use SmartArt graphics to display an organization chart of the new administration. This exercise follows the same set of skills as used in Hands-On Exercises 1–3 in the chapter. Refer to Figure 5.40 as you complete this exercise.

Worksheet data inserted as an object

Worksheet data inserted as an object, but not linked

Chart is linked to Excel worksheet

SmartArt displays organization chart

FIGURE 5.40 Insert Excel Data and Graphs into a Financial Summary

a. Open *w05p2Report* and save it as **w05p2Report_LastFirst**. Open *w05p2Dividends.xlsx* and save it as **w05p2Dividends_LastFirst.xlsx**.

b. Insert an Excel object by completing the following steps:
- Place the insertion point on the empty paragraph mark just above the heading *Capital Expenditures* in the Word document. Press **Enter** one time.
- Click the **INSERT tab**, click the **Object arrow** in the Text group, click **Object**, and then click the **Create from File tab**.
- Click **Browse** and select *w05p2Dividends_LastFirst.xlsx*.
- Click **Insert** in the Browse dialog box. Click **OK** in the Object dialog box and scroll down to view the object, if necessary.
- Double-click the worksheet object and click **cell F5**.

- Type **10.00** and press **Enter**.
- Click anywhere outside the object to save the change.
- Right-click the object and click **Format Object**.
- Click the **LAYOUT tab** and click **Tight** under *Wrapping style*. Under *Horizontal alignment*, click **Center** and click **OK**.
- Click to position the insertion point on the left side of the *Capital Expenditures* heading, which has been separated by the object, and press **Enter** seven times to separate the object and the next paragraph.

c. Click one time on the worksheet object to select it. Right-click the object, click **Worksheet Object**, and then click **Open**. To insert and link a worksheet object into the document, complete the following steps:
- Click the **Expenses worksheet tab** at the bottom of the Excel window.
- Position the pointer over **cell A4** and drag down and over to **cell C8**, which contains the total $265.
- Click **Copy** in the Clipboard group on the HOME tab (or press **Ctrl+C**).
- Click the **Word icon** on the Windows taskbar to toggle back and view *w05p2report_LastFirst*. Click once on the empty paragraph mark above the *New Company Officers* paragraph.
- Click the **HOME tab**, if necessary, and click the **Paste arrow** in the Clipboard group.
- Click **Paste Special** to display the Paste Special dialog box. In the As list, click **Microsoft Excel Worksheet Object**. Click **Paste link** on the left side of the window and click **OK**.
- Right-click the object and click **Format Object**.
- Click the **LAYOUT tab** and click **Square** under *Wrapping style*. Under *Horizontal alignment*, click **Center** and click **OK**.
- Click to position the insertion point on the left side of the *New Company Officers* heading, which has been separated by the table, and press **Enter** five times to separate the object and the next paragraph.

d. Insert an Excel chart into the document by completing the following steps:
- Click once on the empty paragraph mark above the *Dividends* heading.
- Click the **Excel icon** on the Windows taskbar to toggle to the *w05p2Dividends_LastFirst* workbook.
- If the moving border remains on the range you copied earlier, press **Esc**.
- Click the **Earnings worksheet tab** at the bottom of the Excel window.
- Position the pointer on the border edge of the chart title *Earnings from Continuing Operations* and click one time to select the entire chart.
- Click the **HOME tab** and click **Copy** in the Clipboard group.
- Click the **Word icon** on the Windows taskbar to toggle back to *w05p2Report_LastFirst*.
- Click the **HOME tab**, if necessary, and click **Paste** in the Clipboard group. Click **Layout Options** (first icon on right of chart) and click **Fix position on page**. Click **Chart Elements** (second icon on right of chart), put your cursor over *Chart Title*, click the arrow, and then click **More options**. Make sure that *Title Options* on the right panel is selected. Click **Gradient Fill** under *Fill*. Click **Chart Styles** (third icon on right of chart) and change the style to the fourth choice on the list. Close the Format Chart dialog box.
- Click the **FORMAT tab**, if necessary, and click the **Shape Height arrow** in the Size group until **3.3"** displays.
- Click the chart below the *Dividends* paragraph and click the **Dividends tab** in the Excel file before closing the Excel file.

e. Create a document title using WordArt by completing the following steps:
- Press **Ctrl+Home** and select the title *Excerpts from the 2015 Annual Report*.
- Click the **INSERT tab** and click **WordArt** in the Text group. Click the style **Fill - Purple, Accent 4, Wireframe - Accent 4** (third row, fifth column). Drag the right middle sizing handle towards the right margin to resize to fit between the margins.
- Select the WordArt text and drag it across the top of the page. Click the **Font Size arrow** on the Mini toolbar and click **20**.
- Click the **FORMAT tab**, if necessary, click **Position** in the Arrange group, and then click **Position in Top Center with Square Text Wrapping**.

- Click **Shape Fill** in the Shape Styles group and click **Yellow**. Click **Shape Outline** in the Shape Styles group, click **Weight**, and then click **2 1/4 pt**.
- Click **Shape Effects** in the Shape Styles group, click **Bevel**, and then click **Cool Slant** (first row, fourth column).
- If necessary, delete additional empty paragraph marks at the heading and the first line of the subheading so that only one paragraph mark displays.

f. Create an organization chart with SmartArt by completing the following steps:

- Press **Ctrl+End** to move the insertion point to the end of the document. Press **Enter** one time.
- Click the **INSERT tab** and click **SmartArt** in the Illustrations group.
- Click **Hierarchy** in the left panel and click **Organization Chart**. Click **OK**.
- Type the following names and positions in the chart, starting from the top and then from left to right on the third level. Press **Enter** to put positions on a new line.

  Daniel Tovar
  CEO
  Rebecca Meinsen
  CFO
  Adam Barton
  VP - Sales
  Laurel Duncan
  VP - Finance
  Kyle Buckner
  VP - Manufacturing

- Click the **DESIGN tab**, click **Change Colors** in the SmartArt Styles group, and then click **Colorful Range - Accent Colors 4 to 5** (second row, fourth column).
- Click the **More button** in the SmartArt Styles and click **Intense Effect** (first row, fifth column).
- Click the **FORMAT tab**, click the **Size arrow**, and then click the **Height arrow** until **2.7** displays. Click the **Width arrow** until **5.5** displays. Click the **Layout Options dialog box** and select **Fix position on page**.

g. Drag the **Zoom slider** in the status bar to **50%**.

h. Save and close the file, and submit based on your instructor's directions.

Mid-Level Exercises

1 Computer Training Association, Inc.

You are preparing a report that announces the implementation of new technology for a computer training company. You need to include a chart that was created in Excel. Because you want the chart in Word to reflect changes in the original Excel workbook, you decide to link the chart.

a. Open *w05m1CTA* and save it as **w05m1CTA_LastFirst**.

b. Open the Excel workbook *w05m1Chart* and save it as **w05m1Chart_LastFirst**.

c. Select the **Projected Costs chart** in Excel and copy it to the Clipboard.

d. Link the Projected costs chart as a chart object to the bottom of the *w05m1CTA_LastFirst* document.

e. Make the following changes in the *w05m1Chart_LastFirst* worksheet:
   - Phase 1 Hardware value: **1.40**
   - Phase 2 Software value: **0.75**
   - Phase 3 Software value: **0.80**
   - Phase 4 Software value: **1.20**
   - Phase 3 Training value: **0.50**
   - Phase 4 Training value: **1.00**

 f. Update the linked chart object in the Word document. Center the chart horizontally on the page.

g. Select the heading *Computer Training Association, Inc.* and display the text as WordArt using **Gradient Fill - Blue, Accent 1, Shadow** (first row, second column). Modify the format of the WordArt by completing the following steps:
   - Change the font size to **24** and bold the text.
   - Use Help to learn how to create a custom fill color. Use the RGB values **196, 200, 234** as the custom color.
   - Apply a **10 pt Soft Edges Shape Effect**.
   - Increase width to **6"**.
   - Set the position to display the object in the top center with **square text wrapping**. Delete any blank lines if necessary.

h. Save and close the file, and submit based on your instructor's directions.

2 BRM Online Gift Baskets Sales Newsletter

You are the Web designer for BRM Online Gift Baskets, Inc., and you are in charge of developing the monthly sales newsletter. You have to advertise two sales items, announce the monthly lucky draw, and write a short Tips section, so the layout of the newsletter is important. The text you use for the newsletter is included in a file. Refer to Figure 5.41 as you complete this exercise.

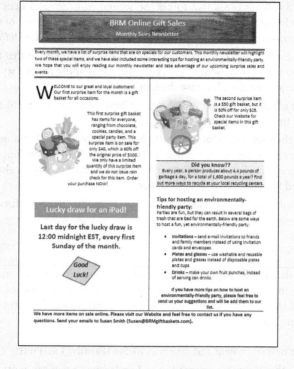

FIGURE 5.41 Online Gift Baskets Newsletter

a. Open *w05m2GiftBaskets* and save it as **w05m2GiftBaskets_LastFirst**. If you receive a message stating *Your document will be upgraded to the newest file format*, click **OK** to continue.

b. Set a **1.5" top margin** and a **0.18" bottom margin** for the whole document. Change **left and right margins** to **0.5"**. Increase the bottom margin as needed to comply with your printer's capability.

c. Create a two-column newsletter that displays a line between columns. Use a section break after the first paragraph to enable this paragraph and a masthead as a one-column section.

d. Create a masthead for the newsletter by completing the following steps:

- Insert a bevel shape (third row, first column in the Basic Shapes category) that spans the top of the page. Fill the bevel shape with the picture *w05m2Woods.jpg*.
- Add the text **BRM Online Gift Sales Monthly Sales Newsletter** to display on the shape. Change **Spacing after** to **0 pt**.
- Select the text *BRM Online Gift Sales* and change the font size to **20 pt** and have it display on the first line. The font size for *Monthly Sales Newsletter* should be **14 pt**, and it should display on the second line below.

e. Move the first paragraph, which starts *Every month, we have a list of surprise items* to the one-column section and display it just below the masthead. Justify the text and apply a top and bottom double line border to the paragraph. The border should be **3/4 pt** wide and colored **dark blue**.

f. Apply a **drop cap** to the first letter of the word *WELCOME*, which displays on the top of the left column.

g. Format the gift basket image to **Square Wrap Text**. Fix the image's position on the page.

h. Create a text box using the Ion Sidebar 1 style below *Order your purchase NOW!* to emphasize the lucky draw information. Insert **Lucky draw for an iPad!** as the sidebar title, center it, and increase the font size to **20**. Drag the sidebar to the bottom-left corner and change the height to **2.5"**. Increase the text size to **18** and fix the sidebar's position on the page.

i. Insert a diamond shape that is **1.2"** high and **1.5"** wide. Use the rotate handle to display it. Fill the shape using a **yellow color** and group the diamond shape with a text box containing the **16 pt** text **Good Luck!** Display the grouped item below the text in the sidebar.

j. Insert a column break that forces the second surprise sales item to display in the right column. Search for an image of a gift basket and display it on the left side of the paragraph. Insert at least one line return at the end of the paragraph to add space before the *Did you know??* heading that follows.

k. Select the heading *Did you know??* and the short paragraph that follows it. Apply a black single-line top and bottom border and also apply the shading pattern style **10%**. Bold and center the *Did you know??* heading. Increase the font size to **14**.

l. Create a bulleted list out of the tips for hosting an environment-friendly party. Increase the font size of the *Tips* heading to **14**.

m. Select the paragraph that begins *We have more items on sale online*. Apply a one-column format to the paragraph and apply a single-line top border. Increase the font size to **12 pt** and bold the text in this paragraph. Select the paragraph at the bottom of the right column that begins *If you have more tips* and bold the text and align center.

n. Save and close the file, and submit based on your instructor's directions.

3 Create a Family Tree

You have decided to begin charting your genealogy. You have a number of different methods for displaying the family tree, but you decide to use SmartArt graphics to show your immediate family. If directed by your instructor, substitute your own personal information and styles for those in the instructions below.

a. Open a new document and save it as **w05m3Family_LastFirst**.

b. Change the document orientation to **Landscape** so you can more easily view the complete family tree.

c. Insert the **Horizontal Hierarchy SmartArt graphic** from the Hierarchy group. Populate the family tree by completing the following steps:
- Click in the first element on the left and type **Michelle** in the first box.
- Type **Gary** and **Sandra** in the second-level boxes to represent Michelle's parents.
- Type **Lester** and **Verdene** in the boxes that represent Gary's parents.
- Type **Sidney** in the box to represent Sandra's father.
- Open the Text pane, add a box for Sandra's mother, and then type **Effie**.
- With the text box open, create sub-bullets so you can add Lester's parents, **Ralph** and **Emma**. Then add sub-bullets to represent Verdene's parents, **George** and **Mary**. Add sub-bullets for Sidney's parents, **Miles** and **Minnie**, and finally, add bullets for Effie's parents, **Jasper** and **Lou**.

d. Modify the chart by completing the following steps:
- Change the height of the chart to **6"** and the width to **9"**.
- Change the color set to your favorite colors.
- Change the Shape Fill to use an appropriate and coordinating color.
- Modify Shape Effects to use some visual effects of your choice.
- Change the position to **Middle Center with Square Text wrapping**.

e. Insert a text box at the top of the document to display the heading **My Family Tree**. Make the following enhancements to the text box:
- Change the size of the text to **28 pt** and center the text in the box.
- Change the font to use any **WordArt Quick Style**.
- Modify the Shape Style to use any style that you like.
- Set the height of the text box to **0.7"** and the width to **3"**.
- Modify Shape Effects to use some visual effects of your choice.
- Change the position so that the text box displays in the top-left corner of the SmartArt diagram.

f. Save and close the file, and submit based on your instructor's directions.

4 Travel Brochure

COLLABORATION CASE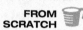

FROM SCRATCH

A local travel agency is conducting a contest for the best travel brochure. Your instructor wants the class to participate in this contest, and he has divided the students into groups of four. Your group project is to design a three-fold, professional-looking brochure with a country tour theme. Feel free to use any kind of graphical features that you have learned in this chapter to enhance your brochure.

a. Use an online collaboration tool such as Google groups or Skype to conduct a face-to-face meeting with your group members. During this online chat session, you will do the following:

- Choose a name for the group and select a group leader.
- Develop a list of tasks to complete.
- Assign tasks and responsibilities to each group member.

b. The list of tasks will include, but not be limited to, the following:

- Find a specific country to be the main focus of the brochure.
- Develop the tour itinerary and present the tour information in a table.
- Search for several pictures, either online or personal, to illustrate a concept or event.
- Design a masthead for the first page of the brochure.
- Insert a pull quote to highlight key components of the tour.
- Type the agency's contact information, Web site link, and e-mail address on the last page of the brochure.
- Format the final document with a border, narrow margins, and balanced columns.

c. Use the Snipping tool, SnagIt, or the PrtScn key to capture the chat session at several stages as a record of the contribution from team members. Copy and paste all the screenshots into a Word file and save it as **w05m4Travel1_GroupName**.

d. The team leader will create a OneDrive or Dropbox.com account, where each member can share and open the draft documents while designing the brochure.

e. Save the brochure as **w05m4Travel2_GroupName**.

f. Post the final version of the brochure and the screenshot files to the online storage location.

g. Inform your instructor that the documents are ready for grading and give directions to where they are located.

Beyond the Classroom

Astronomy Is Fun!

RESEARCH CASE

You are a member of the local astronomy club and have been asked to create a monthly newsletter for elementary schools and home-schooled children. Some information and a few short articles have already been provided to you, but it is not enough material for a whole newsletter. You can perform an Internet search to gather information so you can provide a chart of times when they might see shuttles or the ISS pass overhead. You will probably want to use an Excel file to keep track of times so it is easy to update for the next newsletter. Use the techniques from this chapter to organize your facts and present a professional-looking newsletter that children will enjoy reading. Open the Word document *w05b2Stars*, save your changes to **w05b2Stars_LastFirst**, and then submit based on your instructor's directions.

Car Financing Information

DISASTER RECOVERY

You work for a local automotive dealer, and your supervisor requests your help to fix a document he was unable to complete. He attempted to create a document that describes a vehicle, including a spreadsheet calculation for pricing that can be updated automatically. He thinks this will be a great resource for all sales associates, but his first attempt to create the document was not successful. He did not properly link the document with the source file, nor did his graphical enhancements provide the effects he desires. You have been assigned the task of repairing the document so the pricing information from the *w05b3Cooper.xlsx* spreadsheet can be updated easily and automatically. You must also modify the document to display the graphical elements correctly and make any other improvements that create a professional-looking document. Open the Word document your supervisor created, *w05b3Car*, save your changes to **w05b3Car_LastFirst**, and then submit based on your instructor's directions.

Job Fair

SOFT SKILLS CASE

FROM SCRATCH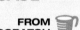

You will create a professional-looking newsletter describing (a) information of the job fair (date, time, place, and vendors) and (b) strategies for getting an interview. Use the features that you had learned to enhance your document. Some of the recommended features include, but art not limited to, masthead and a reverse, columns, SmartArt or Shapes graphic, and hyperlinks to the recruiters' Websites. Use any of the predefined styles in desktop publishing to add personality to your newsletter. After you have checked the spelling and grammar of your newsletter, save it as **w05b4JobFair_LastFirst**. Submit the document based on your instructor's directions.

Capstone Exercise

You are hired as a marketing manager for a small airline service that provides transportation from Denver to frequently requested locations and vacation cities such as Las Vegas, Orlando, and New York. Your first big assignment is to develop a marketing flyer that can be printed and mailed to potential customers in the Denver area and also in the cities serviced by the airline. From your previous marketing experience, you know that it is important to emphasize the positive attributes of the airline as well as provide information that will generate interest, and eventually revenue for, the company. In this exercise, you will recreate the newsletter as you see it in Figure 5.42.

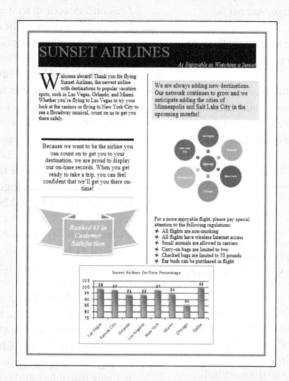

FIGURE 5.42 Sunset Airlines Flyer

Create the Masthead

You have a document with several important pieces of information that should be used in the marketing flyer. You must format the page so it can accommodate the amount of information you display, as well as any graphics you might add later.

a. Open the file named *w05c1Airline* and save it as **w05c1Airline_LastFirst**.

b. Change the margins to **0.7"** on all sides.

c. Set a **Continuous Section Break** at the beginning of the document. Use a single-column format for the masthead.

d. Create a masthead with the main heading **SUNSET AIRLINES**. Use a Reverse on the heading by changing the background to **100% solid black** and use the Text Effect **Gradient Fill - Orange, Accent 6, Inner Shadow** on *Sunset Airlines*. Increase font size to **36 pt**. Left-align the heading.

e. Create a second line for the masthead and type the subheading **As Nice as Riding into the Sunset**. Change the font size to **13 pt** and apply **Italics**. Change the color of the subheading to **Orange, Accent 6, Lighter 40%**. Right align the subheading.

Create Columns and Format Text

You now need to adjust the text to display in two columns below the masthead. You will also make several modifications to that text so that it is visually appealing and conveys all the important information the airline wants to promote to potential customers.

a. Set a two-column format to arrange the text below the masthead. Display a line between the columns and set equal column width. Insert another Continuous Section Break at the end of the text and set the area below to display in one column.

b. Set a dropped cap letter on the first letter of the word *Welcome* in the first paragraph.

c. Cut the paragraph that starts with the phrase *Because we want to be the airline* and display it in a text box in the same place using the Motion Quote design from the Text Box gallery. Add a row of 20 stars at both the top and bottom of the quote. Set the height to **1.9"**, set it to wrap on top and bottom, and then center the text. Adjust the position of the text box so it is centered horizontally in the column and fix on the page.

d. Insert a column break to force the paragraph that starts with the phrase *We are always adding* to display at the top of the second column. Apply a box border around the paragraph using the wavy line style, colored **Orange, Accent 6**, and with a **1 1/2 pt width**. Set shading for the fill of the box using the color **Orange, Accent 6, Lighter 60%**.

e. Insert a page border that uses the style found fourth from the bottom of the style list. Use the **Orange, Accent 6 color** and a **3 pt width**.

f. Use a bulleted list to organize the regulations listed under the paragraph that starts *For a more enjoyable flight*. Customize the bullets to use the airplane symbol, Webdings: 241. Decrease the indent of the bulleted list to display each item on one line.

g. Change the font of the paragraph and bulleted list to **Verdana** and set the size to **11 pt**.

Add Graphics for Visual Effects

You have several ways to make the flyer visually stimulating, but you know that it is easy to add too much and thus defeat the purpose of attracting customers. You decide to use SmartArt, WordArt, and a few shapes to complete the look.

a. Position the insertion point at the bottom of the document. Insert a SmartArt object; use the Diverging Radial from the *Cycle* section. Display the Text pane and type **Denver** on the first line to represent the circle in the middle. Press the down arrow to move to the next bullet and type the next city, **Las Vegas**. Continue to press the down arrow after each city to complete the graphic with the cities **Orlando**, **New York**, **Chicago**. Press **Enter** after you type *Chicago* and type **Minneapolis (Coming Soon!)**. Press **Enter** once again and type **Salt Lake City (Coming Soon!)**.

b. Change the Color scheme of the SmartArt to use **Colorful - Accent Colors**.

c. Format the SmartArt object with **Square Text wrapping** and change the size so the object is **2.5"** high and **3.5"** wide. Display the SmartArt below the shaded paragraph in the second column. Change the Layout properties to center the object horizontally in the column and use a *Lock anchor* setting so it will remain in position.

d. Place the insertion point at the end of the document. Open the Excel workbook *w05c1Flights.xlsx* and save it as **w05c1Flights_LastFirst.xlsx**. Copy the chart from the spreadsheet and link it into the Word document.

e. Reduce the chart size as needed so it fits centered on the bottom of the page, in the one-column section. If necessary, change the wrapping style and use the *Lock anchor* setting for precise placement. Edit the data in the Excel worksheet so the Los Angeles on-time percentage increases to **93%** in cell **D5** and update the chart in the flyer to reflect this change.

f. Insert a **Curved Up Ribbon shape** at the bottom of the first column. Change the shape style to **Light 1 Outline, Colored Fill - Orange, Accent 6**. Display the text **Ranked #1 in Customer Satisfaction** on the Ribbon. Increase the size of the text to **16 pt** and apply bold formatting and center the text. Use the yellow sizing handles on the top of the ribbon object to increase the size of the face of the ribbon so the text fits on it, if necessary.

g. Insert a Sun shape in the bottom-left corner of the flyer. The height and width of the object should be **1.2"**. Change the shape style to **Colored Fill - Orange, Accent 6**. Copy the object and paste it to create a second identical object. Drag the second object to the bottom-right corner of the flyer and use the Align Objects button to align so the two suns appear as bookends to the chart. Fix the position of the two suns on the page using the *Layout options* dialog box.

h. Make adjustments to spacing and line returns as necessary to display all text and objects without overlapping. Save and close all files, and submit based on your instructor's directions.

Time Saving Tools

Using Templates, Multiple Documents, and Themes

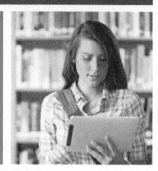

OBJECTIVES   AFTER YOU READ THIS CHAPTER, YOU WILL BE ABLE TO:

1. Select a template from the Backstage view p. 376
2. Create a Word template p. 379
3. Use Building Blocks p. 379
4. View documents side by side p. 387

5. Merge documents p. 388
6. Use navigational tools p. 393
7. Customize theme colors, fonts, and effects p. 405

CASE STUDY | Computer Training Concepts, Inc.

Alexandra Caselman is the director of marketing at Computer Training Concepts, Inc., a business that provides technical training on a variety of computer systems to other companies. Alexandra is responsible for collecting information about a potential training event, such as how much time the training will take, how many instructors will be needed, and how much the training event will cost. She collects this information from her staff, then spends a great deal of time copying and pasting the information into a few documents that she can package together and send to a potential client.

During a recent meeting, she mentions this cumbersome task to you, her assistant director, and you mention that Word 2013 has features that will make the process of assembling the information more efficient. Alexandra decides to split the job with you since her method of compiling the information is outdated and slow. She decides to set up some of the documents, then transfer all the files to you. At that point, you will take the information provided from a variety of sources and assemble into one very nice-looking document.

Document Templates

Word is useful for creating very interesting and complex documents because it provides a variety of formatting features that you can apply on your own. You can jump-start the formatting process by using professional designs provided in the form of templates. A **template** is a partially completed document that contains preformatted text and/or graphics. Word provides a variety of templates for common documents, and additional templates can be downloaded from Office.com. You can use Word templates to create letters, memos, reports, resumes, agendas, calendars, and brochures, as well as other documents. Each template contains the framework of formats and text to decrease the time it takes you to create a document. You can also develop your own templates to use when you create certain types of documents that are used frequently, such as specialized reports.

In this section, you will use a template to start a document. You save time using a template because you do not have to set fonts, bullets, or create a style for the document. You also can view and download more templates from Office.com.

TIP Document Template File Extensions

Document templates use the file extensions .dotx or .dotm (if it contains a macro) in Word 2013. Previous versions of Word (2007) use .dot as the extension for templates. When you search for a template on your computer, you must click the *Type of Files* arrow in the Open dialog box to display All Word Templates (*.dotx; *.dotm; *.dot).

Selecting a Template from the Backstage View

Each time you create a new blank document by clicking the New icon on the Quick Access Toolbar, you use the **Normal template**, the framework that defines the 1" left, right, top, and bottom margins, left horizontal alignment, 11 pt Calibri font, 8 pt After spacing, Multiple Line Spacing, and other settings. However, when you click the File tab on the Ribbon and click New, a menu of template options displays in the Backstage view from which you can select, as shown in Figure 6.1. To preview a template, you can click the particular template, click Create on the informational dialog box, and a new document will open with all the features, styles, and placeholders for information that you provide to complete the selected document. A **placeholder** is a field or block of text used to determine the position of objects in a document. If you insert text beside a placeholder instead of replacing it, you should be sure to delete the placeholder before you save the document.

Click to view category-specific templates available for download

Click to view templates installed on your computer

Click to view templates you created or downloaded

FIGURE 6.1 Selecting a Document Template

Select and Download a Resume Template

STEP 1 ➤

Templates often help provide assistance with layout for some documents, and Word provides several different templates for different types of documents, as shown in Figure 6.2, such as resumes, curriculum vitae, memos, letters, and faxes. Every person looking for a job should have a resume. A *curriculum vitae (CV)* is similar to a resume; it displays your skills, accomplishments, job history, or other employment information, and is often used by academics. A variety of different ways exist to lay out a resume, and using a template can be an easy way to determine which style best matches your needs. Many of these templates are preformatted using styles or themes such as Facet, Integral, Ion, Organic, Retrospect, Slice, and Whisp. By using templates with a similar style, you can coordinate documents. If the default resume templates do not meet your needs, you can review other choices on Office.com. To select a resume template, do the following:

1. Click the FILE tab.
2. Click New.
3. Click Resume in the *Suggested Searches* section of the Templates pane. A list of resume categories displays.
4. Click any of the resumes to preview it.

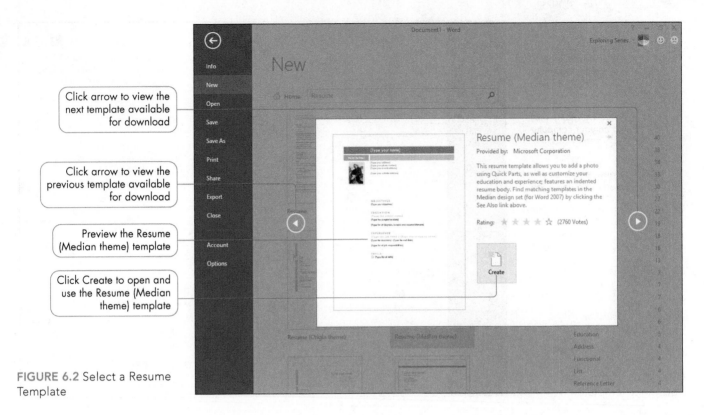

Click arrow to view the next template available for download

Click arrow to view the previous template available for download

Preview the Resume (Median theme) template

Click Create to open and use the Resume (Median theme) template

FIGURE 6.2 Select a Resume Template

After you select a resume template from the long list of choices, you may download the template to your computer. To transfer a selected template to your computer, do the following:

1. Click Create after you select a resume template of your choice from the gallery.
2. After the template downloads, it opens in a new document window to display placeholders and sample text as shown in Figure 6.3.
3. Replace the placeholders with your personal information.
4. Save the document; it will automatically save as a Word document. If you want to save the document as a template, change the *Save as type* to Word Template.

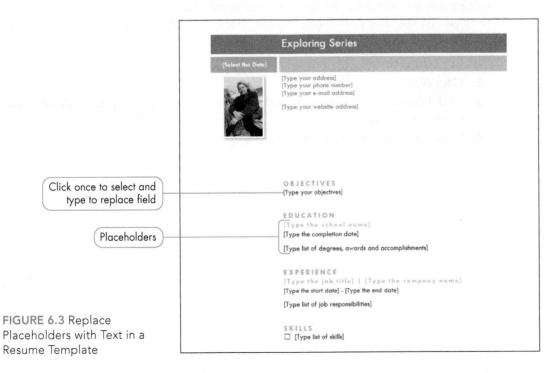

Click once to select and type to replace field

Placeholders

FIGURE 6.3 Replace Placeholders with Text in a Resume Template

After you use or rename a template, it will display in the *Featured* or *Personal* templates category in the Backstage view for a New File. But you can also view other templates installed on your PC or other templates you have created. If you cannot find a template that meets your immediate needs, you can view additional templates available for download from Office.com.

Creating a Word Template

If you create or use a particular document frequently, with only minor modifications each time, you should save the document as a template. When you create the template, you can insert placeholders for the information you change frequently. You can create a document template that contains a company letterhead, greeting, body, and salutation, thereby requiring you to replace only the information for the recipient. Or if you have a report that you update on a regular basis that is contained in a very structured and detailed table, you might consider making the report into a template.

Save a Document as a Template

STEP 2≫   To save a document as a template, you should note the location where the template is saved. Word will automatically save the template to a default location for templates. However, you can specify a location on your own hard drive, portable storage device, or OneDrive account by navigating through the folders of your choice. An appropriate location to store templates on the hard drive would be the Document Library folder. Be aware that templates saved in other locations will not display in the Templates dialog box. To save a document as a template, do the following:

1. Open the selected document.
2. Click the FILE tab.
3. Click Save As.
4. Click Browse.
5. Change the *Save as type* to Word template, as shown in Figure 6.4.
6. The file extension is added for you. Click Save.

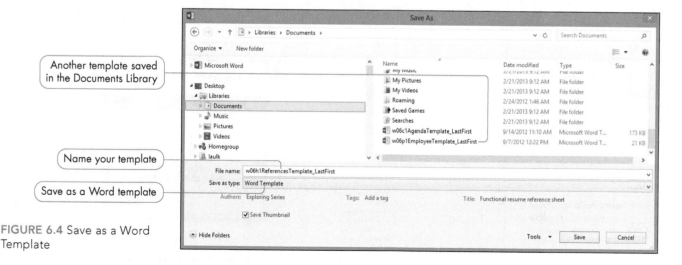

FIGURE 6.4 Save as a Word Template

Using Building Blocks

When you create templates or Word documents that frequently contain particular content or objects, you might want to save the content or objects so that you can use them again without recreating or retyping. Word enables you to create or save objects, called *Building*

Blocks, which are predefined and can be inserted quickly, easily, and frequently into any document. Building Blocks might include disclaimers that display at the bottom of a document, a company address or logo, a header, or a footer. Other objects that you can save as a Building Block include watermarks, tables, or larger objects such as a cover page to a report, or a whole page with specific tables and formatting. A predefined list of Building Blocks is available in the Building Block Organizer for you to quickly and easily insert into your own documents. A gallery of Building Blocks includes Bibliographies, Cover Pages, Equations, Footers, Headers, Page Numbers, Table of Contents, Tables, Text Boxes, and Watermarks. These Building Blocks can also be accessed from the Insert tab, Design tab, and References tab. You can also save information as AutoText, which is a type of Building Block, to store text or graphics that you want to use again, such as a standard contract clause or a long distribution list. You insert AutoText at a specific location indicated by the cursor, but you can insert building blocks anywhere in the document without having to indicate the specific location—for instance, a cover page or table of contents.

Create and Insert a Custom Building Block

STEP 2〉〉 Each selection of text or graphics that you add to the Quick Part Gallery is stored in the Building Blocks Organizer and is assigned a unique name that makes it easy for you to find the content when you want to use it. You can also assign a name you prefer. Figure 6.5 demonstrates the creation of the AutoText. To save an item as AutoText, which is also a customized Building Block, do the following:

1. Select the item.
2. Click the INSERT tab.
3. Click Quick Parts in the Text group.
4. Select Save Selection to Quick Part Gallery.
5. In the Create New Building Block dialog box, assign a name that reflects the object, select AutoText from the gallery, and then click OK.

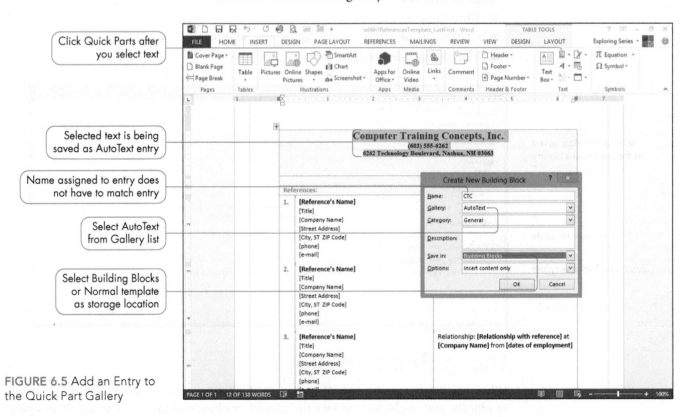

FIGURE 6.5 Add an Entry to the Quick Part Gallery

After you add text to the Quick Part Gallery, you can type the unique name that you assigned to the Quick Part and press F3 to insert the remainder text into your document. Word 2013 contains many Building Blocks already. You can also view and insert the building blocks into your document by doing the following:

1. Position the insertion point where you want to insert the Building Block.
2. Click the INSERT tab.
3. Click Quick Parts in the Text group and do one of the following:
   a. Click AutoText and select the specific AutoText entry.
   b. Click Building Blocks Organizer, as shown in Figure 6.6.
      • Click Name under *Building Blocks* to sort the Quick Parts alphabetically by name.
      • Scroll down the list to select the specific Quick Part that you want.
      • Click Insert.

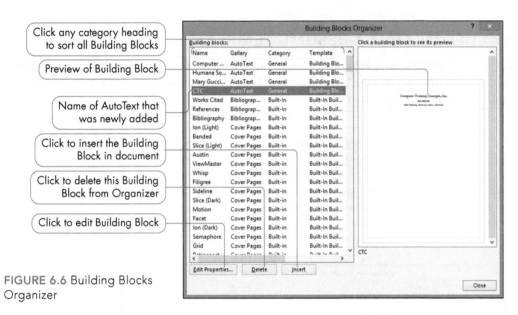

Click any category heading to sort all Building Blocks

Preview of Building Block

Name of AutoText that was newly added

Click to insert the Building Block in document

Click to delete this Building Block from Organizer

Click to edit Building Block

FIGURE 6.6 Building Blocks Organizer

Quick
Concepts

1. Why is it important to use the correct extension when saving a file? *p. 376*
2. What are the advantages of using a predefined template? *p. 376*
3. What are the benefits of using a building block? *p. 379*

1 Document Templates

When Alexandra Caselman assembles a quote for the cost of training, she always includes the instructor's resumes. She also creates a sheet of references—people who have used the services of Computer Training Concepts, Inc. She would like each resume and reference sheet to have a similar look, so she decides to use document templates instead of starting with blank documents each time.

Skills covered: Select and Download a Resume Template • Create and Insert a Custom Building Block • Modify a Template and Save as a Document

---

STEP 1 ≫ SELECT AND DOWNLOAD A RESUME TEMPLATE

Alexandra recently found the selection of resume templates that comes with Word and learned that she can search for more templates online at Office.com. She decides to select one style and fill in the information for the trainer whom she will send to the next job. Refer to Figure 6.7 as you complete Step 1.

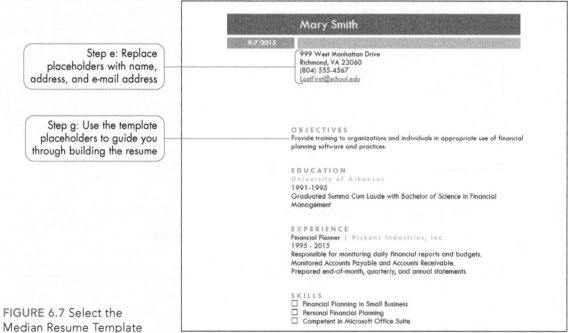

FIGURE 6.7 Select the Median Resume Template

a. Start Word.

   The Backstage view displays a list of templates available to users.

b. Click **Resume** in the Suggested Searches box of the Templates pane. In the Resume pane, scroll down and click the **Resume (Median theme) template**. Click **Create** to open the template.

   The Resume (Median theme) template opens as a new document, and the User Name specified in Word Options displays at the top.

c. Click one time in the brown bar that displays your name at the top of the resume and click the **Resume Name tab**. Click the **Quick Parts arrow** that displays on the right side of the tab and click **Name**.

   This template has two formats—*Name* and *Name with Photo*. When you click Name, you choose the template without a photograph.

> **TROUBLESHOOTING:** If your name does not display at the top of the resume, you can click the name placeholder and type to replace or modify it with your name. If it still does not display, place your cursor on the left side of the placeholder, type your name, and then delete the placeholder.

d. Click the **FILE tab** and click **Save As**. Click **Browse**. Type **w06h1Resume_LastFirst** in the **File name box**. Confirm the *Save as type* box displays *Word Document* and click **Save**.

> **TROUBLESHOOTING:** If the *Save as type* box displays *Word Template (*.dotx)*, click the *Save as type* arrow and click Word Document (*.docx) before you save.

> **TROUBLESHOOTING:** If you receive a message warning you that your document will be upgraded to the newest file format, click OK to accept the upgrade.

e. Replace the next three placeholders (address, phone, and e-mail) with the following information, right-click the **Web site address placeholder**, and then click **Remove Content Control** to delete the placeholder:

999 West Manhattan Drive
Richmond, VA 23060
(804) 555-4567
LastFirst@school.edu

 TIP **Change User Names**

To replace the current User Name with your own, click the File tab, click Options, click General, if necessary, and then type your name in the *User name* box in the *Personalize Your Copy of Microsoft Office* section.

f. Click **Select the Date** in the template to view an arrow control. Click the arrow and click **September 07, 2015**.

g. Type the following information in the resume for each category:

Objectives	[Type your objectives]	Provide training to organizations and individuals in appropriate use of financial planning software and practices.
Education	[Type the school name]	University of Arkansas
	[Type the completion date]	1991–1995
	[Type list of degrees, awards and accomplishments]	Graduated Summa Cum Laude with Bachelor of Science in Financial Management
Experience	[Type the job title]	Financial Planner
	[Type the company name]	Pickens Industries, Inc.
	[Type the start date]–[Type the end date]	1995–2015
	[Type list of job responsibilities]	Responsible for monitoring daily financial reports and budgets. Monitored Accounts Payable and Accounts Receivable. Prepared end-of-month, quarterly, and annual statements.
Skills	[Type list of skills]	Financial Planning in Small Business Personal Financial Planning Competent in Microsoft Office Suite

h. Save and close the file, and submit all files based on your instructor's directions.

STEP 2 ⟩⟩ CREATE AND INSERT A CUSTOM BUILDING BLOCK

The next step in compiling the proposal for a potential client is to generate a list of references. This information changes often, so Alexandra wants to use a template that she can update quickly. She also inserts the company letterhead frequently, so she decides to save that information as a custom Building Block, which can be inserted with only a few key strokes, instead of retyping the information each time. Refer to Figure 6.8 as you complete Step 2.

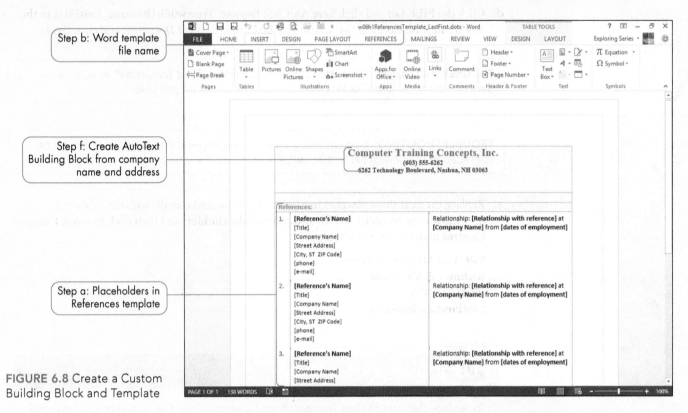

FIGURE 6.8 Create a Custom Building Block and Template

a. Click the **FILE tab** and click **New**. Type **References** in the **Search for online templates search box** and press. **Enter**. Scroll down until you see the Functional resume references sheet. Click to select it and click **Create**.

TROUBLESHOOTING: If a Microsoft Office Genuine Advantage dialog box displays, click *Do not show this message again* and click Continue. If you work in a lab environment, you may not have permission to download document templates from Office.com. If that is the case, read Steps 2 and 3 and continue to the next section.

A download window appears briefly, then the Functional resume reference sheet template displays with placeholders and sample text.

b. Click the **FILE tab** and click **Save As**. Click **Browse**. When the Save As dialog box displays, click the **Save as type arrow**. Click **Word Template**. Type **w06h1ReferencesTemplate_LastFirst** in the **File name box** and click **Save**.

If a Microsoft dialog box displays with a message about saving in a new file format, click OK. When you save this document as a template, you can open it later and make modifications without changing the original. Be sure to save the file as a template (.dotx) and not a document (.docx).

c. Replace the placeholders at the top of the page by completing the following steps:

- Click the **[Your Name] placeholder** and type **Computer Training Concepts, Inc.**
- Select the **[phone] placeholder** and type **(603) 555-6262**.
- Click one time in the **[Street Address] placeholder** and type **6262 Technology Boulevard**.
- Click the **[City, ST ZIP Code] placeholder** and type **Nashua, NH 03063**.
- Click the **[E-mail] placeholder**, right-click, and then click **Remove Content Control**. Repeat this step for the [Website] placeholder.

d. Select the three lines that contain the company name, phone, and address. Click the **LAYOUT tab** and click **Merge Cells** in the Merge group. Select **Times New Roman** and click **Center** on the Mini toolbar.

e. Select the three lines that display the company name, phone, and address. Click the **INSERT tab**, click **Quick Parts** in the Text group, and then select **Save Selection to Quick Part Gallery**.

f. Complete the following steps within the Create New Building Block dialog box:

- Type **CTC** in the **Name box**.
- Click the **Gallery arrow** and select **AutoText**.
- Click the **Save In arrow** and select **Building Blocks**.
- Click **OK**.

The entry is added to the Normal template and will be available for use in all documents.

> **TROUBLESHOOTING:** If you are in a lab environment, you might not have permission to add this item or save the changes to the Normal template. Consult with your instructor for alternate instructions, if necessary.

g. Test your Building Block by selecting the three lines and press **Delete**. On the INSERT tab, click **Quick Parts** in Text group, click **AutoText**, and click **CTC** at the top of the gallery list.

The entry displays just as you had formatted it. Now you can use this Building Block in other documents you design for the company.

h. Save the template.

STEP 3 ≫ MODIFY A TEMPLATE AND SAVE AS A DOCUMENT

Now that the template is set up, Alexandra forwards it to you so you can add the information about companies that will be used as references in this proposal. After adding the references, you save it as a document instead of a template. Refer to Figure 6.9 as you complete Step 3.

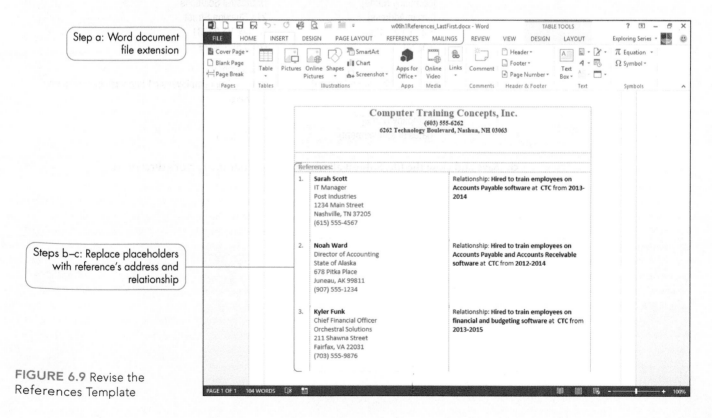

FIGURE 6.9 Revise the References Template

a. Click the **FILE tab** and click **Save As**. Click **Browse**. Click the **Save as type arrow** and select **Word Document**. Type in the file name **w06h1References_LastFirst**.

Be sure to save the file as a document (.docx) and not a template (.dotx).

b. Remove the e-mail placeholders for each reference because they are not used. Also, remove both rows containing the content for Reference #4 and Reference #5 since you only have three references. Select both rows, right-click, and click **Delete Rows**.

c. Type the following information into the respective reference placeholders:

Reference #1	[Reference's Name]	Sarah Scott
	[Title]	IT Manager
	[Company Name]	Post Industries
	[Street Address]	1234 Main Street
	[City, CT Zip Code]	Nashville, TN 37205
	[phone]	(615) 555-4567
	Relationship:	Relationship:
	[Relationship with reference]	Hired to train employees on Accounts Payable software
	[Company Name]	CTC
	[dates of employment]	2013–2014
Reference #2	[Reference's Name]	Noah Ward
	[Title]	Director of Accounting
	[Company Name]	State of Alaska
	[Street Address]	678 Pitka Place
	[City, CT Zip Code]	Juneau, AK 99811
	[phone]	(907) 555-1234
	Relationship:	Relationship:
	[Relationship with reference]	Hired to train employees on Accounts Payable and Accounts Receivable software
	[Company Name]	CTC
	[dates of employment]	2012–2014
Reference #3	[Reference's Name]	Kyler Funk
	[Title]	Chief Financial Officer
	[Company Name]	Orchestral Solutions
	[Street Address]	211 Shawna Street
	[City, CT Zip Code]	Fairfax, VA 22031
	[phone]	(703) 555-9876
	Relationship:	Relationship:
	[Relationship with reference]	Hired to train employees on financial and budgeting software
	[Company Name]	CTC
	[dates of employment]	2013–2015

d. Save and close the file. Submit all files based on your instructor's directions.

Multiple Documents

The collaboration features in Word facilitate an easy exchange of ideas and revisions to a document. But some users do not use the collaboration features, which causes the process of combining information into one document to be less efficient. Fortunately, other features in Word enable you to work with multiple documents simultaneously—you can view multiple documents at one time, as well as combine them into one.

In this section, you will view multiple documents side by side as well as compare and combine them. You will create a document that contains subdocuments and use tools to navigate within lengthy documents. Finally, you will create an electronic marker for a location in a document and use the Go To feature to find that marker.

Viewing Documents Side by Side

The *View Side by Side* feature enables you to display two documents on the same screen. This is a useful tool when you want to compare an original to a revised document or when you want to cut or copy a portion from one document to another.

View Two Documents Side by Side

STEP 1 >

To view two documents side by side, you must open both documents. The *View Side by Side* command is grayed out if only one document is open. When the documents are open, click *View Side by Side* in the Window group on the View tab and the Word window will split to display each document as shown in Figure 6.10. If you have more than two documents open, when you click *View Side by Side*, the *Compare Side by Side* dialog box will display and you may select which document you want to display beside the active document.

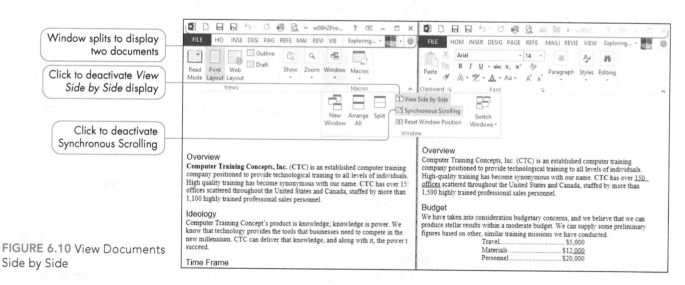

FIGURE 6.10 View Documents Side by Side

When the documents display side by side, synchronous scrolling is active by default. *Synchronous scrolling* enables you to scroll through both documents at the same time. If you want to scroll through each document independently, click Synchronous Scrolling on the View tab to toggle it off. If you are viewing two versions of the same document, synchronous scrolling enables you to view both documents using only one scroll bar. If you scroll through each document asynchronously, you must use the respective scroll bars to navigate through each document.

Resize Documents

While in *Side by Side* view, you can resize and reposition the two document windows. If you want to reset them to the original side-by-side viewing size, click Reset Window Position on the View tab. You can also switch the documents from left to right by clicking the Reset Windows position in the left document. To close *Side by Side* view, click *View Side by Side* to toggle it off. The document that contains the insertion point when you close *Side by Side* view will display as the active document.

Merging Documents

Besides enabling you to view two documents simultaneously, Word also provides different ways to combine multiple documents into one. The particular method you use depends on the purpose of the document. You might simply want to combine two documents, deciding which portions of each to keep and omit. You might need to add the entire contents of one document into another, or you might want to include the entire contents of several documents in one.

Ideally, when you have a document to submit to others for feedback, you want everyone to use the Track Changes feature in Word. However, sometimes it is necessary to have several people edit their own copy of the document simultaneously before they return it to you. When this occurs, you have several similar documents but with individual changes. Instead of compiling results from printed copies or viewing each one in *Side by Side* view to determine the differences, you can use the Compare and/or Combine features.

Compare Two Documents

The comparing of two documents and the displaying of the changes between the two documents using Word is known as *legal blacklining*. Legal blacklining allows attorneys to compare versions of documents or contracts, authors and editors to track progress of a manuscript, and financial managers to review changes in large tables. The *Compare* feature in Word automatically evaluates the contents of two or more documents and displays markup balloons that show the differences between the documents. You can display the differences in the original document, the revised document, or in a new document. You can also display the original and revised documents side by side with the changes in a new document as shown in Figure 6.11.

To compare the content of two documents, do the following:

1. Click the REVIEW tab.
2. Click Compare in the Compare group to display the *Compare and Combine Documents* dialog box.
3. Click Compare to display the Compare Documents dialog box.
4. Click the *Original document* arrow or the *Browse folder* icon to navigate to the first document that you want to compare.
5. Click the *Revised document* arrow or *Browse folder* icon to navigate to the second document that you want to compare.
6. Click the More button to display more options.
7. Click *New document* below *Show Changes in*. Click OK.
8. Click the document choice to keep formatting changes when a dialog box displays a message about keeping formatting changes.
9. Click *Continue with Merge*.
10. Click Compare in the Compare group and click Show Source Documents. You will have the following options regarding the two source documents: Hide Source Documents, Show Original, Show Revised, or Show Both.

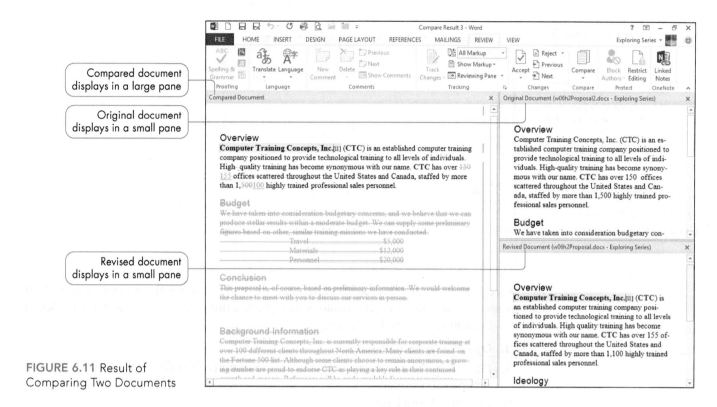

Compared document displays in a large pane

Original document displays in a small pane

Revised document displays in a small pane

FIGURE 6.11 Result of Comparing Two Documents

Combine Two Documents

STEP 2》 If you want to go a step further than just viewing the differences, you can use the *Combine* feature to integrate all changes from multiple authors or documents into one single document. To use the Combine feature, click Compare on the Review tab and select Combine. The Combine Documents dialog box contains a variety of options you can invoke, as shown in Figure 6.12; however, options only display after clicking the More button. The option you are most likely to change is in the *Show changes* section where you determine in which document the Combined documents will display—in the original document, the revised document, or in a new document. If you do not want to modify the original documents, you should combine the changes into a new document.

To combine the content of two documents to a blank new document, do the following:

1. Open the target document(s) or a blank new document.
2. Click the REVIEW tab.
3. Click Compare in the Compare group.
4. Click Combine to display the Combine Documents dialog box.
5. Click the *Original document* arrow or the *Browse folder* icon to navigate to the first document that you want to combine.
6. Click the *Revised document* arrow or *Browse folder* icon to navigate to the second document that you want to combine.
7. Click the More button to display more options.
8. Click *New document* below *Show Changes in*. Click OK.
9. Click the document choice to keep formatting changes when a dialog box displays a message about keeping formatting changes.
10. Click *Continue with Merge*.
11. Click anywhere in the left panel box to activate the Revisions tab.
12. Close the Revisions tab.
13. Click Compare in the Compare group and click Show Source Documents. You will have the following options regarding the two source documents: Hide Source Documents, Show Original, Show Revised, or Show Both.

Select first document to combine

Select second document to combine

Click to toggle More or Less settings

Click to switch the two documents

Select target document to display combined results

FIGURE 6.12 Combine Documents Dialog Box

Insert a File Object

STEP 3» You can quickly add the contents of one document to another without opening both documents by using the Object command. When you use this method to combine the content of two documents, you do the following:

1. Open the original document.
2. Place the insertion point where you want to insert the contents of the second (unopened) document.
3. Click the INSERT tab.
4. Click Object in the Text group.
5. Click the *Create from File* tab, as seen in Figure 6.13. You will be prompted to browse to the file that contains the text you want to insert. After you select the file, click Insert and the entire contents will be placed in the open document.

Click Object to view options

Click *Create from File* option to navigate to a document file

Navigate to the file to be inserted

Contents of the selected file will display in the current document at the insertion point location

FIGURE 6.13 Insert Text from an Unopened File into the Current Document

Create Master Documents and Subdocuments

STEP 3» Working with long documents can be cumbersome. If you are working with an older computer system, you may notice your computer slows down when you are working in a lengthy document—scrolling, finding and replacing, editing, and formatting may take longer to process. To improve this situation, you can create a ***master document***, a document that acts like a binder for managing smaller documents. A smaller document that is a part of a master document is called a *subdocument*. The advantage of the master document is that you can work with several smaller documents, as opposed to a single large document. Thus, you edit the subdocuments individually and more efficiently than if they were all part of the same document. You can create a master document to hold the chapters of a book, where each chapter is stored as a subdocument. You also can use a master document to hold multiple documents created by others, such as a group project, where each member of the group is responsible for a section of the document. The Outlining tab on the Ribbon contains the Show Document and Collapse and Expand Subdocuments buttons, as well as other tools associated with master documents. Figure 6.14 displays a master document with three subdocuments. The subdocuments are collapsed in Figure 6.14 and expanded in Figure 6.15. The collapsed structure enables you to see at a glance the subdocuments that comprise the master document. You can insert additional subdocuments or remove existing subdocuments from the master document. Deleting a subdocument from within a master document does not delete the actual subdocument file. Look carefully at the subdocuments in Figure 6.14. A padlock appears to the left of the first line in subdocuments. All subdocuments are locked when collapsed.

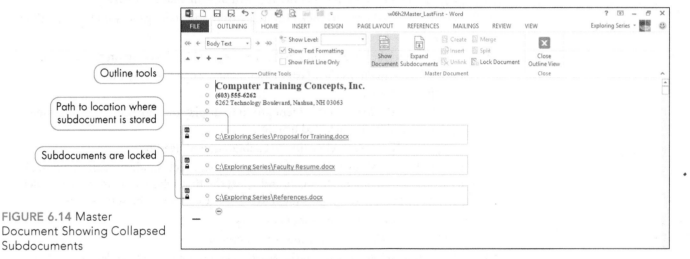

FIGURE 6.14 Master Document Showing Collapsed Subdocuments

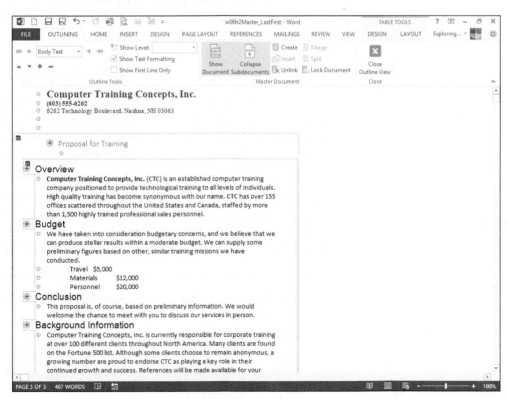

FIGURE 6.15 Master Document Showing Expanded Subdocuments

To work with master and subdocuments, do the following:

1. Open a blank new document.
2. Insert any Building Block if you like, such as a page title, company contact information, a masthead, or a page heading.

3. Type your headings on separate lines for each of your subdocuments.
4. Select all your headings and click Heading 2 from the Styles gallery on the HOME tab.
5. Click the VIEW tab.
6. Click Outline in the Views group to display the OUTLINING tab on the Ribbon.
7. Click Show Document in the Master Document group to display more master document commands.
8. Click Create in the Master Document group to display the individual subdocuments that were created for the selected headings.
9. Place the insertion point below the first subdocument heading.
10. Click Insert in the Master Document group to insert each subdocument individually into the master document. Navigate and select the first subdocument, and then click Open. Click *Yes to All* when prompted to rename the style in the subdocument.
11. Repeat Step 10 to insert more subdocuments.
12. Click OK to save changes to the master document.
13. Click Collapse Subdocuments in the Master Document group to collapse the subdocuments in the document, and to display the name and path of each saved subdocument.

Modify the Master and Subdocuments

The expanded structure enables you to view and edit the contents of the subdocuments. You can make changes to the master document at any time. However, you can make changes to the subdocuments only when the subdocument is unlocked. You have to issue locks to each subdocument individually. You can lock or unlock a document by doing the following:

1. Click Show Document in the Master Document group.
2. Click Lock Document in the Master Document group. The Lock Document command in the Master Document group is highlighted in a light orange color, and a padlock icon displays below the subdocument icon.
3. Click the Lock Document command again to unlock the subdocument.

Note, too, that you can make changes to a subdocument in one of the following two ways:

- When the subdocument is expanded (and unlocked) within a master document as in Figure 6.15.
- Open the subdocument as an independent document within Microsoft Word. You lock the subdocuments to prevent making changes to their content but also to prevent the subdocument from being deleted from the master document.

Regardless of how you edit the subdocuments, the attraction of a master document is the ability to work with multiple subdocuments simultaneously. The subdocuments are created independently of one another, with each subdocument stored in its own file. Then, when all of the subdocuments are finished, the master document is created, and the subdocuments are inserted into the master document, from where they are easily accessed. Inserting page numbers into the master document, for example, causes the numbers to run consecutively from one subdocument to the next. You also can create a table of contents or index for the master document that will reflect the entries in all of the subdocuments. And finally, you can print all of the subdocuments from within the master document with a single command.

Create Subdocuments from an Empty Master Document

Alternatively, you can reverse the process by starting with an empty master document and using it as the basis to create the subdocuments. This process is ideal for organizing a group project in school or at work, the chapters in a book, or the sections in a report. Start with a new document and type the topics assigned to each group member. Format each topic in a heading style within the master document and use the Create Subdocument command to create subdocuments based on those headings. Saving the master document will automatically save each subdocument in its own file.

Use Master Document and Subdocuments with Extreme Care

Creating a master document and subdocuments is a very useful feature if you want to combine several documents into one large document, for instance, when writing a manuscript. However, since this feature was introduced by Microsoft in Word 6, it had been problematic. Students using this feature must use the following precautions:

1. Backup the original files before creating the master document.
2. The newly created master document must be stored in the same directory as all the subdocuments.
3. If you move or rename a subdocument separately after you create the master document, you will break the link in the master document. You can only restore the link by deleting and recreating the link in the master file with the new file name.
4. If you want to move the master and subdocuments to a new location, you must first open the master file, then save all the subdocuments to the new location.
5. When you make changes to the links in the master document, you must delete all old subdocument files to avoid version confusion.
6. Do not attempt to recreate the master file. If you do, you must delete all the files previously created and used in your last attempt.

Using Navigational Tools

Without a reference source, such as a table of contents, it can be difficult to locate information in a long document. Even scrolling through a long document can be inefficient if you are uncertain of the exact location that you want to view. Fortunately, Word provides navigation tools that assist the author and reader in locating content quickly and easily.

Use the Navigation Pane

STEP 4 > You can use the Find and Go To features in Word to move through a document. Another helpful feature is the *Navigation Pane*, which enables you to navigate through the document by viewing headings, viewing pages, and browsing the results of your last search. The Navigation Pane setting is a toggle, enabling you to turn it on and off. When displayed, the Navigation Pane contains three tabs—one for each type of search.

You may navigate in a document using one of the following two ways:

- If you want to display the headings in a document, be sure the document is expanded to display the text of the whole document. The Navigation Pane will only display headings for a document that uses the styles feature to format headings. The best way to format headings is to apply the built-in title or heading styles from the Styles group on the Home tab. When you are working with long documents, this view provides a way to navigate quickly to a particular topic, as shown in Figure 6.16.

- In lieu of the document headings, you can display *thumbnails*—small pictures of each page in your document—in the Navigation Pane. Thumbnails display when you click the Pages tab in the Navigation Pane. As with the headings, you can click a thumbnail to move the insertion point to the top of that page. This is another method of navigating quickly through a document. Even though you cannot read the text on a thumbnail, you can see the layout of a page well enough to determine if that is a location you want to display (see Figure 6.17). And if you display revision marks and comments, the marks and comment balloons also display in the thumbnails.

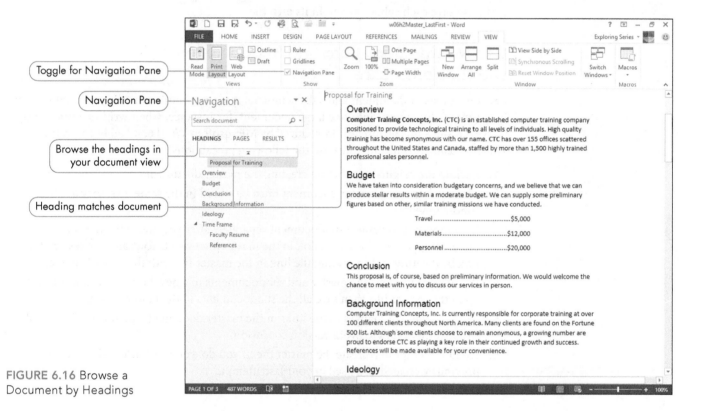

FIGURE 6.16 Browse a Document by Headings

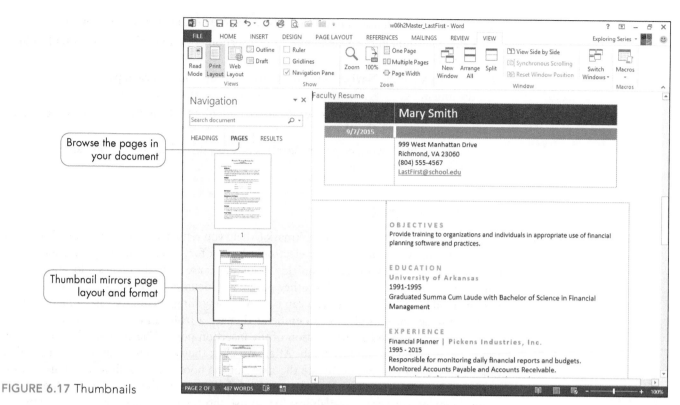

Browse the pages in your document

Thumbnail mirrors page layout and format

FIGURE 6.17 Thumbnails

The third panel in the Navigation Pane displays the results of a text search. When you type in a word or a string of text, each occurrence displays, as shown in Figure 6.18. You can click the occurrence and the text is highlighted in the document. This pane also enables you to search for other objects in the document, such as graphics and tables.

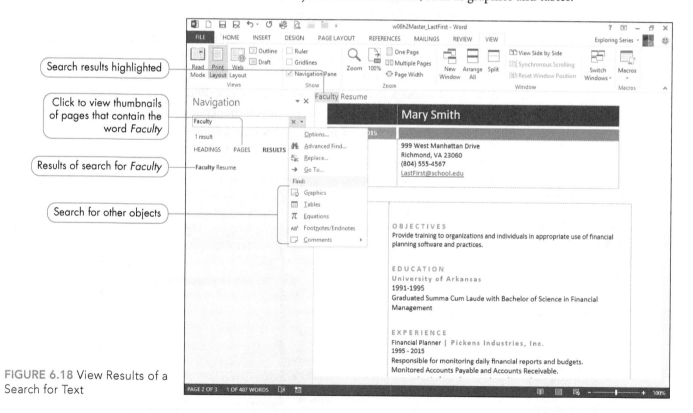

Search results highlighted

Click to view thumbnails of pages that contain the word *Faculty*

Results of search for *Faculty*

Search for other objects

FIGURE 6.18 View Results of a Search for Text

To view your document using the Navigation Pane, do the following:

1. Click the VIEW tab.
2. Click Navigation Pane in the Show group.

3. Click Headings in the Navigation Pane to display headings in the document.
4. Click a heading in the pane to move the insertion point to the location of that heading in the document.
5. Click Pages in the Navigation Pane to display thumbnails of each page in the document.
6. Click a page in the pane to move the insertion point to the location of that page in the document.
7. If you conduct a word or phrase search, click Results in the Navigation Pane to view the results of the search.

Create Bookmarks

STEP 4

When you read a book, you use a bookmark to help you return to that location quickly. Word provides the ***bookmark*** feature as an electronic marker for a specific location in a document, enabling you to find that location quickly. Bookmarks are helpful to mark a location where you are working. You can scroll to other parts of a document, then quickly go back to the bookmarked location. In Word, you can bookmark anything, including a heading or a paragraph, an image such as picture, an embedded chart, a table, an audio clip or a video file. Bookmarks are inserted at the location of the insertion point. The Bookmark command is in the Links group on the Insert tab. After you click the command, the Bookmark dialog box displays, and you can designate the name of the bookmark, as shown in Figure 6.19. Bookmark names cannot contain spaces or hyphens; however, they may contain the underscore character to improve readability. Try to use short, concise, and descriptive names to designate your bookmark. You may sort your bookmarks according to the bookmark name (in alphabetical order) or the bookmark location in the document. You may also delete any unwanted bookmarks by clicking the specified bookmark and clicking Delete in the Bookmark dialog box.

To create a bookmark, do the following:

1. Put the insertion point in front of the word or phrase that you want to add to the bookmark. Note: If you want to bookmark a whole paragraph, select the whole paragraph.
2. Click the INSERT tab.
3. Click Bookmark in the Links group to launch the Bookmark dialog box.
4. Type the word that you want to use for your bookmark and click Add.
5. Repeat the above steps to add all the bookmarks that you want.

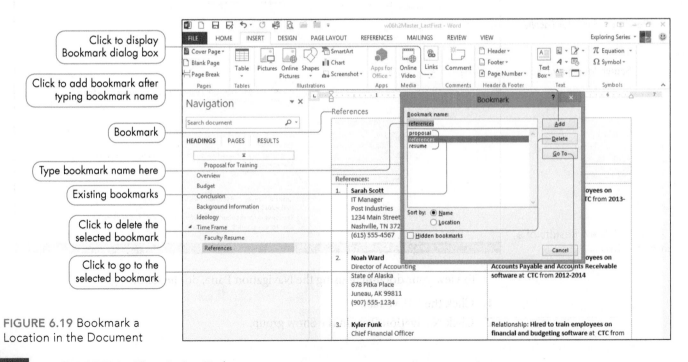

FIGURE 6.19 Bookmark a Location in the Document

Review the List of Bookmarks

STEP 4 ▶

At any time after creating your bookmarks, you may review the list of bookmarks and navigate to bookmarked content by doing the following:

1. Click the INSERT tab.
2. Click Bookmark in the Links group to launch the Bookmark dialog box.
3. Click a bookmark in the *Bookmark name* list.
4. Click Go To to move the insertion point to the bookmarked location.

Alternately, you may perform the above tasks by using the following method:

1. Press Ctrl+G to open the Go To tab of the *Find and Replace* dialog box.
2. Click Bookmark in the *Go to what* section.
3. Click the *Enter bookmark name* arrow to select the bookmark that you want to view.
4. Click the Go To button to go to the bookmarked location.
5. Click Close if you want to exit the bookmark dialog box without doing anything.

> **TIP** Using Numbers in Bookmark Names
>
> You can use numbers within bookmark names, such as Quarter1. However, you cannot start a bookmark name with a number.

Quick Concepts

1. What are the differences between comparing and combining two documents? *p. 389*
2. Why would you want to create a master and several subdocuments? *p. 390*
3. What is the purpose of creating a bookmark in a document? *p. 396*

Hands-On Exercises

Watch the Video for this Hands-On Exercise!

MyITLab®
HOE2 Training

2 Multiple Documents

When setting up a prospective job proposal, Alexandra collects information about the company, the trainers who might work with the clients, and references from previous clients. After collecting this information, she forwards it to you to combine into one or more different documents. The final proposal is created from several files, and it is time consuming to try to number each one so that it looks like they all came from a single document. But you know how to use the master document feature to make that task easier.

Skills covered: View Documents Side by Side • Combine Documents • Create Master Documents and Subdocuments • Use the Navigation Pane and Create Bookmarks

STEP 1 ≫ VIEW DOCUMENTS SIDE BY SIDE

Alexandra has forwarded documents to you which contain information that should be included in the multi-page proposal. Before you start the process of combining information, you decide to view the documents side by side so you can find any overlap in the content. Refer to Figure 6.20 as you complete Step 1.

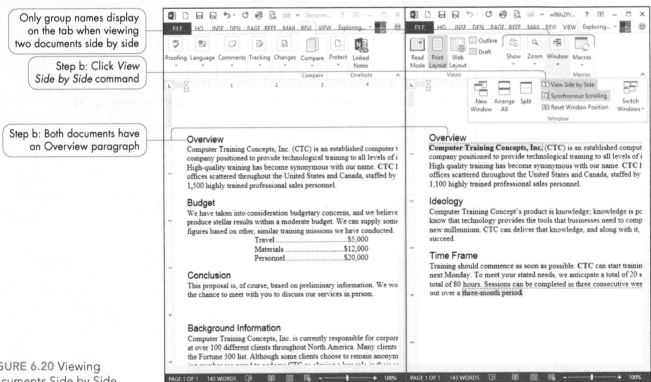

FIGURE 6.20 Viewing Documents Side by Side

a. Open the files *w06h2Proposal* and *w06h2Proposal2*.

If necessary, click **Enable Editing** on the yellow bar at the top so that you can edit the document.

b. Click the **VIEW tab** and click **View Side by Side** in the Window group.

Two windows display, containing the contents of each file. In the Window group, you see *Synchronous Scrolling* highlighted in light blue to indicate the setting is on. As you scroll in one document, the other will scroll also.

c. Click the document on the left to make it active and click the arrow at the bottom of the scroll bar in the window on the left to scroll to the bottom of the page.

Both documents scroll down evenly, and you can view the footer of each document.

d. Click **Synchronous Scrolling** in the Window group to turn the toggle off.

Notice that *Synchronous Scrolling* is no longer highlighted in light blue. Now you can scroll through a single document at a time.

e. Close both documents without saving. Do not exit Word.

STEP 2 ≫ COMBINE DOCUMENTS

Now that you know the two files you just viewed are not identical, you decide to use the Combine feature in Word to pull all content into one location. You then make some minor formatting changes, insert the entire contents of another document, and then save the file so that it is ready to accompany the other files in the proposal. Refer to Figure 6.21 as you complete Step 2.

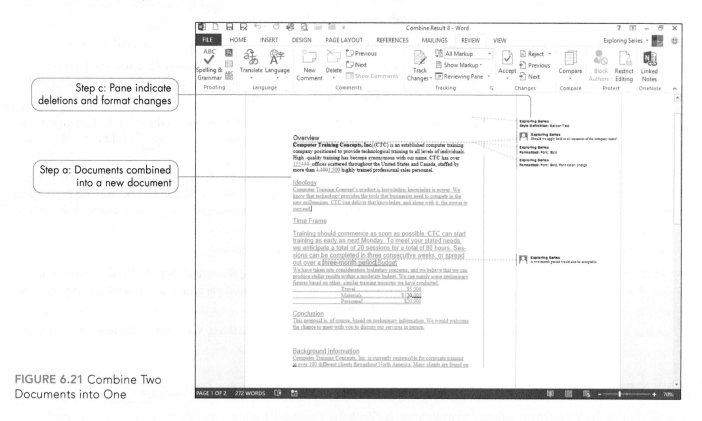

FIGURE 6.21 Combine Two Documents into One

a. Combine the two documents you viewed in the last step by completing the following steps:

- Click the **REVIEW tab**, click **Compare** in the Compare group, and then select **Combine** to display the Combine Documents dialog box.
- Click the **Original document arrow** and select *w06h2Proposal*. If necessary, click **Browse**, navigate to *w06h2Proposal*, and then click **Open**.
- Click the **Revised Document arrow** and select *w06h2Proposal2*. If necessary, click **Browse**, navigate to *w06h2Proposal2*, and then click **Open**.
- Click the **More button**, if necessary, and click **New document** below *Show changes in*, if necessary. Click **OK**. Click **Continue with Merge** to accept the default choice if a Microsoft Word dialog box displays with a message about accepting the tracked changes from both documents.

> **TROUBLESHOOTING:** If the two documents you just merged display in small windows on the screen, select Show Source Documents in the Compare group on the Review tab and click Hide Source Documents to close them.

The document opens in a new window and contains markup balloons to indicate each difference in the two documents. Depending on your Track Changes settings, the balloons might display on either the left or right side of your document.

> **TROUBLESHOOTING:** If the paragraphs in your document do not display in the same order as those in Figure 6.21, close the document and begin the process again. Make sure you select *w06h2Proposal* as the Original document.

b. Click the **Display for Review arrow** in the Tracking group and select **Simple Markup**, if necessary.

   The document in this view appears to include information from both files and is what you need to present to the customers. Notice the level of detail in the markup balloons when you switch between Simple Markup and All Markup. After some minor edits, it will be ready for use.

c. Click **Track Changes** in the Tracking group to turn off Track Changes, if necessary.

   This prevents future changes from being recorded.

d. Click the **Display for Review arrow** in the Tracking group and select **All Markup**.

e. Click the **Accept arrow** in the Changes group and click **Accept All Changes**. Place the insertion point in the first comment, click the **Delete arrow** in the Comments group, and then click **Delete All Comments in Document**.

f. Press **Ctrl+End** and press **Enter**. Click the **INSERT tab**, click **Object** in the Text group, and then click the **Create from File tab**. Navigate to *w06h2Faculty* and click **Insert**. Click **OK**.

   You insert the entire contents of the *w06h2Faculty* document at the bottom of the page because it contains information that you want to display with the rest of the proposal. You will revise the order of the paragraphs later. This feature does not work on PDFs that contain text that was created as an image, however, but the majority of forms and other PDFs that you would want to type on will be supported.

g. Make the following format changes to the document:

   • Right-click anywhere in the *Ideology* paragraph text and click the **Format Painter** in the Mini toolbar. Click anywhere in the *Time Frame* paragraph to change the font from Arial to Times New Roman, if necessary.

h. Save the document as **w06h2FinalProposal_LastFirst**. Close the document but leave Word open for the next step.

STEP 3 ❯❯ CREATE MASTER DOCUMENTS AND SUBDOCUMENTS

You now have the three main pieces of information (*w06h2FinalProposal_LastFirst*, *w06h1Resume_LastFirst*, and *w06h1References_LastFirst*) that you will send to the potential client. You decide to create a master document so that you can insert each piece and make formatting modifications to the subdocuments. Refer to Figure 6.22 as you complete Step 3.

> **TIP** | **Backing Up Your Files**
>
> Before you create a master document, you should back up all data files you will insert into the master document. Any changes made to the content in the master will alter the originals.

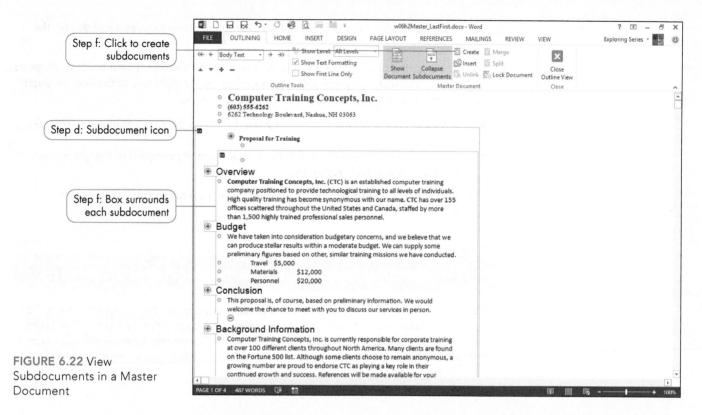

Step f: Click to create subdocuments

Step d: Subdocument icon

Step f: Box surrounds each subdocument

FIGURE 6.22 View Subdocuments in a Master Document

a. Press **Ctrl+N** to open a new document and save it as **w06h2Master_LastFirst**.

b. Type **ctc** and press **F3** to insert the Building Block that contains the company name and address.

c. Press **Enter** one time. Right-align the insertion point. Type the following headings, each on a separate line, for the subdocuments: **Proposal for Training**, **Faculty Resume**, and **References**.

d. Select the three headings you just typed and click **Heading 2** from the Styles group on the HOME tab.

e. Click the **VIEW tab** and click **Outline** in the View group.

> **TROUBLESHOOTING:** If the Heading 2 style does not display in the Styles group, click the Styles dialog box launcher to display the Styles pane, select the Heading 2 style, and then close the Styles pane.

The OUTLINING tab displays and the document text displays in Outline view. Be sure all three headings are still selected before you perform the next step.

f. Click **Show Document** in the Master Document group to display more master document commands. Click **Create** in the Master Document group.

Note that when the Show Document command is selected, it is shaded in light blue.

Individual subdocuments are created for the selected headings. A box surrounds each subdocument, and you see a subdocument icon in the top-left corner of each subdocument box. You also will see section breaks and other formatting marks if the Show/Hide ¶ feature is turned on.

g. Click **Collapse Subdocuments** in the Master Document group to collapse the subdocuments in the document. Click **OK** if prompted to save changes to the master document.

Note that when you click Collapse Subdocuments, it will display the name and path where each subdocument is saved.

h. Click **Expand Subdocuments** in the Master Document group to reopen and display the subdocuments.

i. Place the insertion point on the line directly below the first subdocument heading, *Proposal for Training*. The insertion point will appear to align on the right side of the line. To insert the appropriate subdocument complete the following steps:

- Click **Insert** in the Master Document group to display the Insert Subdocument dialog box.
- Select *w06h2FinalProposal_LastFirst* and click **Open**. If prompted to rename the style in the subdocument, click **Yes to All**.

The entire document displays under the *Proposal for Training* section of the master document.

 Inserting Subdocuments in a Master Document

You need to insert the subdocument in a precise location on the master document. To insert the subdocument into the master document, you need to place the insertion point on the line directly below the subdocument heading. Sometimes it can be difficult to get to the line below. Another way to do this is to click the subdocument heading and press the down arrow to get to the line below.

j. Place the insertion point on the line below the subheading *Faculty Resume*. Repeat the steps above to insert the file *w06h1Resume_LastFirst*. Click **OK** when the Microsoft Word information window displays indicating the subdocument has a different template than its master document. Click **Yes to All** when prompted to rename styles because there are several used in this document.

k. Place the insertion point on the line below the subheading *References*. Repeat the steps above to insert the file *w06h1References_LastFirst*. Click **OK** when the Microsoft Word information window displays indicating the subdocument has a different template than its master document. Click **Yes to All** when prompted to rename styles because several are used in this document.

> **TROUBLESHOOTING:** Be sure to insert the *w06h1References_LastFirst* document, ending in *.docx*, and not the template, which ends in *.dotx*.

 Displaying Subdocuments in a Master Document

After you create subdocuments, the link or path to the location where the subdocument is stored displays in the master document. If you move or rename the subdocument from that original location, the content will no longer display in the master document.

l. Place the insertion point to the right of *Faculty Resume* on page 2 and click **Delete**. Place the insertion point to the right of *References* on the bottom of page 3 and click **Delete**.

m. Save the document.

You remember that inserting bookmarks is a quick way to get to different pages in a document, so you decide to insert one at the top of each section of the document. You decide to display the Navigation Pane so you can move quickly from one page to another to add those bookmarks. Refer to Figure 6.23 as you complete Step 4.

a. Click the **VIEW tab** and click **Navigation Pane** in the Show group to display the Navigation Pane on the left side of the window. Click **HEADINGS** in the Navigation Pane to display all the headings in the document.

The headings from the master document appear in the pane. A light blue shade appears around the heading of the paragraph where the insertion point displays.

b. Click the **Proposal for Training heading** in the Navigation Pane, if necessary.

Word positions the insertion point at the CTC heading on the first page. Position the insertion point on the first heading.

c. Click the **INSERT tab** and click **Bookmark** in the Links group. Type **proposal** in the **Bookmark name box** and click **Add**.

Word inserts a bookmark with the name you entered. A large, gray I-beam indicates the location of the bookmark.

> **TROUBLESHOOTING:** If you do not see the bookmark indicator, you can change a setting that enables it. Click the File tab and click Options. Click Advanced, scroll down, and then click the *Show bookmarks* check box in the *Show document content* section. Click OK to save the settings and return to the document.

d. Click **PAGES** in the Navigation Pane to display thumbnails of each page in the Navigation Pane. Click the thumbnail of page 3, the resume, to display the page and move the insertion point to the top of that page.

e. Click **Bookmark** in the Links group. Type **resume** in the **Bookmark name box** and click **Add**.

f. Type **reference** in the **Search Document box** and press **Enter**. Click **RESULTS** to view the results of the search. Click the second item listed, which is the label *References* that displays at the top of page four.

g. Click **Bookmark** in the Links group. Type **reference** in the **Bookmark name box** and click **Add**.

Notice the brackets that display to show the location of the bookmark. When a block of text is selected at the time you insert a bookmark, brackets display around the text to locate the bookmark instead of a single I-beam, which displays at the location of the cursor.

h. Click the **HOME tab** and click **Replace** in the Editing group. Click the **Go To tab** in the *Find and Replace* dialog box. Click **Bookmark**, if necessary, in the *Go to what* list.

Word displays the *research* bookmark in the *Enter bookmark name* box because it was the last bookmark that you added. If you click the *Enter bookmark name* arrow, the *proposal* and *resume* bookmarks also display in the list.

 TIP Command to Search for Bookmarks

You can also access the list of bookmarks by pressing Crl+G to display the Go To tab of the *Find and Replace* dialog box. Click Bookmark, if necessary, in the *Go to what* list.

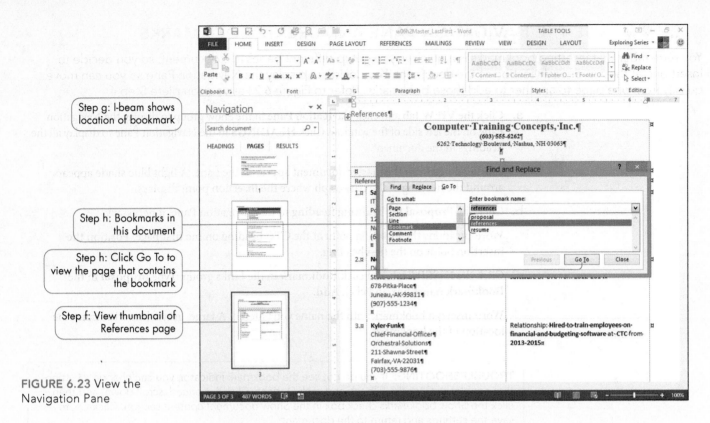

Step g: I-beam shows location of bookmark

Step h: Bookmarks in this document

Step h: Click Go To to view the page that contains the bookmark

Step f: View thumbnail of References page

FIGURE 6.23 View the Navigation Pane

i. Click **Go To**.

The insertion point moves to the bookmark's location and the Bookmark dialog box remains onscreen in case you want to go to another bookmark.

j. Click **Close** to remove the Bookmark dialog box. Click the **Close (X) button** in the top-right corner of the Navigation Pane.

k. Save and close the file. Submit all files based on your instructor's directions.

Document Themes

To create a professional-looking document, you want to select features and styles that coordinate, but creating and managing document design is very time consuming. Word 2013 contains several document themes that enable you to focus on the content of your document instead of spending time creating a design for it. A **document theme** is a set of coordinating fonts, colors, and special effects, such as shadowing or glows that are combined into a package to provide a stylish appearance. Microsoft provides consistent document themes across all the Office applications. Therefore, you can use the same theme on different types of files that are used in a project, such as a report created in Word, a worksheet and chart created in Excel, and a slide presentation created using PowerPoint, and even e-mail the files to other users using the same theme in Outlook.

In this section, you will apply themes to a document. You will also create your own theme by customizing the theme elements.

Customizing Theme Colors, Fonts, and Effects

Document themes are formatted with matching color schemes, fonts, and special effects. Currently, ten document themes are available in Word 2013. More themes are available for download at Office.com. Once you download a theme from Office.com, it is saved to your computer, ready to use another time.

When you create a document, it is automatically given a default document theme. If you want to change the document theme, you might want to try several themes before deciding on the best choice for your document. At any time, you may switch back to the original default document theme by clicking the Design tab, clicking the More arrow in the Document Formatting group, and selecting the *Reset to the Default Style Set* selection.

Apply a Theme to a Document

STEP 1 ⟩ Everyone has his/her own preferences, so picking the right theme can be a difficult task. But when you are ready to apply a theme to a Word document, do the following:

1. Open the document.
2. Click the DESIGN tab.
3. Click Themes in the Document Formatting group to view a gallery of available themes.
4. You may apply a particular theme to your document by:
   a. Clicking one of the available themes.
   b. Clicking *Browse for Themes* to see themes previously saved to your computer.
5. Click the Themes arrow and click *Reset to Theme from Template* if you decide to revert back to your original theme.
6. Click Page Color in the Page Background group to change the document background to a different color, if you want to use a background color other than white.
7. You can also add the document theme to the Quick Access Toolbar by right-clicking a theme's thumbnail.

Apply a Style Set

STEP 2 ⟩ In Word 2013, Microsoft introduces several new features in the Document Formatting group. For instance, a new Style Sets visual gallery allows users to preview a new font style in a title, heading, and text body of a document before applying it. The Style Set also changes the paragraph properties of the document. You may pick a new Style Set as often as you like from one of the nearly twenty style sets available in Word 2013. You can review the full effect of changing each Style Set by clicking the Design tab, clicking the More button to view the

Style Set gallery in the Document Formatting group, and then picking the Style Set selection. The Paragraph Spacing command allows you to quickly change the line and paragraph spacing of your entire document by selecting from a predefined set of values or customizing your own values. Also, the *Set as Default* button will save your current customized theme and will apply the saved settings to all your new documents. This is very helpful to users who have a preferred font type or specified paragraph styling.

To quickly and easily change the look of your document by applying a selected style set, do the following:

1. Click the DESIGN tab.
2. Click Style Set in the Document Formatting group.
3. Click any of the available built-in choices to apply the selected style set.

Revise Theme Colors

STEP 3 >>

If you wish to make changes to any part of the design, you can modify and customize the theme elements individually. Microsoft Word has more than twenty color schemes and font combinations, in addition to fifteen special effects, resulting in hundreds of combinations available to you. *Theme colors* include four text/background colors, six accent colors, and two hyperlink colors. To create a custom color theme, do the following:

1. Click the DESIGN tab.
2. Click Colors in the Document Formatting group and click Customize Colors. Two text/background colors and four accent colors display, as shown in Figure 6.24.
3. Click any of the available predefined color schemes or the Customize Colors option at the bottom of the gallery to modify the colors in the current theme.
4. Make your color selection for text/background, accents, and hyperlinks.
5. Type a new name for your custom theme in the Name text box.
6. Click Save to save the custom theme with a new name.

The new color theme will then display at the top of the theme color gallery. You may click the Reset button to undo any color changes or the Cancel button to exit the Create New Theme Colors dialog box without saving any changes.

FIGURE 6.24 View Theme Colors

Revise Theme Fonts

STEP 4 ▶

The *theme fonts* contain a coordinating heading and body text font for each different theme. You can view the fonts used in the theme when you click Fonts in the Document Formatting group on the Design tab, as shown in Figure 6.25. Theme fonts display at the top of the font list when you click the Font arrow on the Home tab or on the Mini toolbar. As with theme colors, you can quickly change the text in your document by picking a new font set with a predefined font type. You can also create a new theme font set. Each theme font has the font type for the headings and the body text.

- Click to display font type
- Fonts for the Office default theme
- Fonts for the Office 2007–2010 theme
- Click to customize your own font theme

FIGURE 6.25 View Theme Fonts

Customize Theme Effects

Theme effects are another feature that you can incorporate into a document theme. *Theme effects* include lines, fill, and 3-D effects, such as shadowing, glows, and borders. When you apply a theme effect, the theme effects will affect objects such as shapes, SmartArt, and borders around graphics. Unlike theme colors and theme fonts, you cannot create your own set of theme effects, but you can choose from the built-in sets when compiling your own document theme. When a shape or object is created, the theme effects chosen will be reflected in the Shape Styles gallery on the Format tab for the object. When you click Effects in the Document Formatting group found on the Design tab, you will see that the lines, fills and special effects are represented in combinations of three shapes.

A circle represents a line effect applied that includes the width or weight of the line, a rectangle represents the effects applied to an object such as bevels or shadows, and the arrow displays the fill effects that might include gradients, as shown in Figure 6.26.

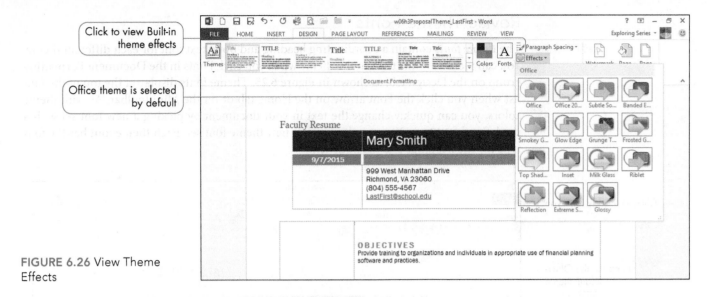

Click to view Built-in theme effects

Office theme is selected by default

FIGURE 6.26 View Theme Effects

Save a Custom Theme

STEP 5

You can save a customized theme color or font separately, and you can also save a theme with both customized color and font. Once you have chosen the theme colors and fonts, you can save these to a custom theme for future use by doing the following:

1. Click the DESIGN tab.
2. Click Themes in the Document Formatting group.
3. Click Save Current Theme at the bottom of the gallery to save a theme.
4. Navigate to the directory to save the custom theme.
5. Click Open to apply the selected theme to the document.

TIP Delete Custom Theme Colors and Fonts

You can easily delete a custom theme, a custom theme color set, or custom theme fonts. To remove these custom sets, click Themes (or Colors, or Fonts) on the Design tab, right-click the custom set that displays in the top of the gallery, and then click Delete. You will see a confirmation dialog box before the .thmx theme file is removed permanently. You cannot delete the themes, color themes, or font themes that are included in Word.

Quick Concepts

1. What are the advantages of using document themes? *p. 405*
2. Why would you want to create your own custom themes? *p. 406*
3. Is it difficult to customize theme effects? *p. 407*

Hands-On Exercises

3 Document Themes

You are almost ready to print the proposal and send it to the potential client. But each document that you inserted into the master is formatted a bit differently, and you want this document to have a very consistent look. You remember that Microsoft Word enables you to apply a theme to documents so they use the same style of fonts and colors—which is exactly what you need to put the finishing touches on this proposal!

Skills covered: Apply a Theme to a Document • Apply a Style Set • Revise Theme Color • Revise Theme Fonts • Save a Custom Theme

---

STEP 1 ≫ APPLY A THEME TO A DOCUMENT

Your proposal should have a very professional look to it, so you decide to apply one of the built-in themes in Word. By using the theme, all colors in the resume template and colors used for headings in the other documents will coordinate. The colors in the Organic theme closely match the colors of your business, so you select that theme. Refer to Figure 6.27 as you complete Step 1.

Step e: Shaded box indicates Office theme is in use until you click a new theme

Step e: Hold your pointer over the Organic theme to preview effects of theme

Step e: Resume displays Organic theme colors and fonts

FIGURE 6.27 Select a New Theme

a. Open the *w06h2Master_LastFirst* document and save it as **w06h3ProposalTheme_LastFirst**.

b. Click the **HOME tab** and click **Show/Hide (¶)** in the Paragraph group to turn off formatting marks, if necessary. Click the **VIEW tab** and click **Outline** in the Views group to view the OUTLINING tab and commands. Click **Show Document** in the Master Document group on the OUTLINING tab and click **Expand Subdocuments**, if necessary, to view all of the content in the subdocuments. Click **Close Outline View** to return to Print Layout view.

When you close the document in the last step, the subdocuments in the master document will be collapsed. Step b will expand the subdocuments so that the whole document will be visible for you to review or modify.

c. Press **Ctrl+G** and click **Bookmark** in the *Go to what* box. Click the **Enter bookmark name arrow** and select **resume**. Click **Go To** and the resume displays. Close the *Find and Replace* dialog box.

d. Click the first **DESIGN tab** and click **Themes** in the Document Formatting group.

The gallery of themes displays and a shaded box surrounds the Office theme. It is active because that is the theme applied to the master document when it was created.

> **TROUBLESHOOTING:** If you see two Design tabs, you will click the first Design tab to format the document themes. The second Design tab is the Table Tools Design tab, which is used to format tables.

e. Click the **Organic theme** to apply the Organic theme to all pages in the master document. Notice how the resume features change to reflect that theme. Also, the content for the *Proposal for Training* section is now on page one only.

f. Save the document.

 TIP **Using Themes in Compatibility Mode**

If you click the Design tab and notice *Theme* is grayed out, and thus unavailable, your current document is probably open in Compatibility Mode. To use Themes, you must save your document in Word 2013 format (.docx). If you save a Word 2013 document in a compatible format, such as Word 97-2003, any theme previously applied to the document will be removed.

STEP 2 ≫ APPLY A STYLE SET

The Organic theme looks great on the master document, but you want to change the font style and paragraph properties of the document. You decide to take steps to change the font style for the title, heading, and text body of the document. Refer to Figure 6.28 as you complete Step 2.

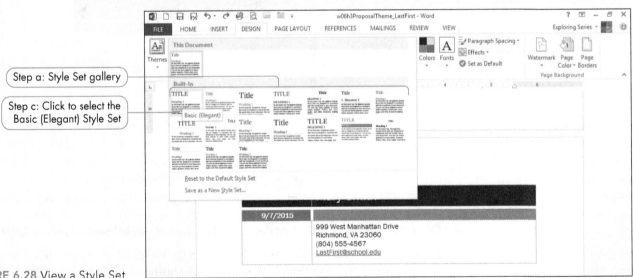

FIGURE 6.28 View a Style Set

a. Click the **DESIGN tab**. Click **Style Set** in the Document Formatting group.

The Style Set gallery appears, with the current Style Set listed at the top and the built-in Style Sets created by Microsoft in the section below. You can select one of the Style Sets from this gallery.

b. Move the insertion point over each of the thumbnail images of the Style Set gallery to reveal the name of the individual Style Set.

c. Click the **Basic (Elegant) Style Set**.

d. Save the document.

STEP 3 ≫ REVISE THEME COLOR

The Organic theme looks great on the master document; however, you would like to change a color that you do not particularly like. You take steps to make a color change in the theme, and you save the changes as a custom theme so you can use it again in other documents. Refer to Figure 6.29 as you complete Step 3.

Step c: Click to select different color

Step d: Name of modified color scheme

FIGURE 6.29 Revise Theme Colors

a. Click **Colors** in the Document Formatting group.

The color gallery appears, with the Custom colors at the top and the Office selections in the section below. You can select the colors for other built-in themes from this gallery.

b. Click **Customize Colors** at the bottom of the gallery.

The Create New Theme Colors dialog box displays. Now you can customize the colors used in the theme that is currently applied to your document.

c. Click the **Text/Background - Dark 2 arrow** and click **Blue-Gray, Accent 3, Lighter 40%** (fourth row, seventh column).

d. Type **w06h3Proposal_LastFirst** in the **File name box**. Click **Save** to save this color scheme.

The *w06h3Proposal_LastFirst* color theme is automatically applied to your document. When you click Theme Colors, *w06h3Proposal_LastFirst* displays at the top of the gallery with a box around it.

e. Press **Ctrl+Home** to view the first page of the document. Select the title *Computer Training Concepts, Inc.* and click the **Font Color arrow** on the Mini toolbar.

Notice the top of the box displays *Theme Colors*, so you know any color you select will coordinate with the document theme.

f. Click **Orange, Accent 5** from the first row.

g. Save the document.

STEP 4 ≫ REVISE THEME FONTS

You notice the same font is used for headings and body text in the theme applied to this document. You would like to make a change so a different, yet coordinating, font is used for the headings. And then the proposal is ready for the printer! Refer to Figure 6.30 as you complete Step 4.

Step d: Name your new custom font theme

Step c: New font for heading

Step c: New font for body

FIGURE 6.30 Select Custom Fonts for a Theme

a. Click the **DESIGN tab**. Click **Fonts** in the Document Formatting group.

The fonts for each theme display. The font style in use for the Organic theme is Garamond.

b. Click **Customize Fonts** at the bottom of the gallery.

c. Click the **Heading font arrow** and select **Calisto MT**. Click the **Body font arrow** and select **Franklin Gothic Book**.

d. Type **w06h3Proposal_LastFirst** in the **File name box**. Click **Save** to save this font scheme.

The headings *Proposal for Training*, *Resume*, and *Resources* change to reflect the new font.

e. Click **Fonts** in the Document Formatting group. Notice *w06h3Proposal_LastFirst* displays at the top of the list with blue shading to indicate it is in use. Press **Esc** to return to the document.

f. Save the document.

STEP 5 ⟩⟩ SAVE A CUSTOM THEME

Since you made changes to both colors and fonts for this theme, you decide to take one more step and save the whole theme with a new name so you can use it again without modifying the individual features. Refer to Figure 6.31 as you complete Step 5.

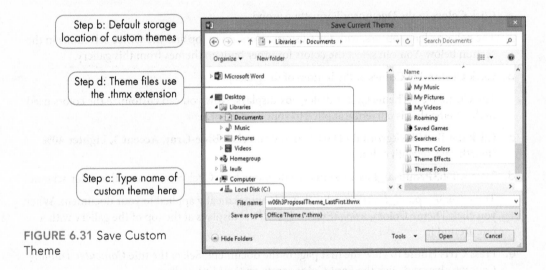

FIGURE 6.31 Save Custom Theme

a. Click the **DESIGN tab**, if necessary, and click **Themes** in the Document Formatting group.

b. Click **Save Current Theme** at the bottom of the gallery.

The Save Current Theme dialog box displays. By default, the new themes are saved in the Document Themes folder for the current user. They are not stored in a folder with the themes that install with Word 2013.

c. Type **w06h3ProposalTheme_LastFirst** in the **File name box**.

d. Click **Save** to save the theme file with the .thmx extension.

> **TROUBLESHOOTING:** If your lab environment does not enable you to save the template to the default folder, or if instructed by your teacher, save the theme file to your own storage media.

e. Save and close the document, and submit it based on your instructor's directions.

Chapter Objectives Review

After reading this chapter, you have accomplished the following objectives:

1. **Select a template from the Backstage view.**
   - Each time you create a new blank document, you use the Normal template. When you use a template, it will display under Blank and Recent documents, but you can also view other templates installed on your PC or templates you have created. Many people will take advantage of the resume templates. By default, resume templates are installed in Word, and they contain placeholders, a field or block of text, to determine the position of objects in a document.

2. **Create a Word template.**
   - If you create or use a particular document frequently, with only minor modifications each time, you should save the document as a template. When you create the template, you can insert placeholders for the information you change frequently.

3. **Use Building Blocks.**
   - Building Blocks are document components you use frequently such as disclaimers, company addresses or logos, or your name and address. Word enables you to create Building Blocks in such a way that they are easy to insert as document parts. Each selection of text or graphics that you add to the Quick Part Gallery is stored in the Building Blocks Organizer and is assigned a unique name that makes it easy for you to find the content when you want to use it.

4. **View documents side by side.**
   - This feature enables you to view two documents on the same screen. It is useful when you want to compare the contents of two documents or if you want to cut or copy and paste text from one document to another. To view two documents side by side, they must both be open in Word.
   - While in *Side by Side* view, you can resize and reset the two document windows.

5. **Merge documents.**
   - When you have several copies of the same document submitted from different people, you can use the compare and combine features. The compare feature evaluates the contents of two or more documents and displays markup balloons that show the differences between the documents. You can determine if the differences display in the original document, a revised document, or a new document.
   - The combine feature goes a step further and integrates all changes from multiple documents into one.
   - Another way to work with multiple documents, especially those that will be combined into one long document, is to create a master document that acts like a binder for managing smaller documents. The smaller document is called a subdocument and can be edited individually at any time.

   - You can quickly add the contents of a document to an opened document by using the Object command on the Insert tab.
   - You can make changes to the master document at any time but you can make changes to the subdocuments only when they are unlocked.
   - If necessary, you can create subdocuments from an empty master document.
   - Creating a master document and subdocuments can be very helpful, but they can also be very problematic. Students using this feature must following several precautions.

6. **Use navigational tools.**
   - When you use the Navigation Pane feature *Browse the headings in your document*, only the headings display. You can click a heading in the Navigation Pane to move the insertion point to that heading in the document. The feature is only available when headings are formatted using the Styles feature. You also can use thumbnails to navigate quickly through a document. Thumbnails are small pictures of each page that display in the Navigation Pane when the feature is toggled on. When you click a thumbnail, the insertion point moves to the top of that page. You can also navigate through a document using search keywords or phrases.
   - The Bookmark feature is an electronic marker for a specific location in a document. You can designate a bookmark in a particular location in a document and use the Find and Replace dialog box to return to that bookmark.
   - At any time after creating your bookmarks, you may review the list of bookmarks and navigate to a bookmarked content.

7. **Customize theme colors, fonts, and effects.**
   - You can select a document theme from the Themes group on the Page Layout tab. When you select a document theme, formatting occurs immediately.
   - Style Set allows you to change the font type and paragraph properties of the whole document.
   - Theme colors represent the current text and background, accents, and hyperlinks. To create a custom color theme, you can modify the colors in the current theme and save the set with a new name.
   - The theme fonts contain a coordinating heading and body text font for each theme. Theme fonts display at the top of the font list when you click the Font arrow on the Home tab or on the Mini toolbar.
   - The theme effects include lines and fill effects, such as shadowing, glows, and borders. You cannot create your own set of theme effects, but you can choose from the built-in sets.

Key Terms Matching

Match the key terms with their definitions. Write the key term letter by the appropriate numbered definition.

a. Bookmark
b. Building Block
c. Combine
d. Compare
e. Curriculum vitae (CV)
f. Document theme
g. Legal blacklining
h. Master document
i. Navigation Pane
j. Normal template

k. Placeholder
l. Subdocument
m. Synchronous scrolling
n. Template
o. Theme color
p. Theme effect
q. Theme font
r. Thumbnail
s. View Side by Side

1. _____ A document component used frequently, such as a disclaimer, company address, or cover page. **p. 379**

2. _____ Enables you to display two documents on the same screen. **p. 387**

3. _____ Enables you to simultaneously scroll through documents in side by side view. **p. 387**

4. _____ Evaluates the contents of two or more documents and displays markup balloons showing the differences. **p. 387**

5. _____ Incorporates all changes from multiple documents into a new document. **p. 389**

6. _____ The comparing of two documents and the displaying of the changes between the two documents. **p. 388**

7. _____ A document that acts like a binder for managing smaller documents. **p. 390**

8. _____ A smaller document that is a part of a master document. **p. 390**

9. _____ Enables you to quickly move through documents using text, headings, or pages. **p. 390**

10. _____ A small picture of each page in your document that displays in the navigation pane. **p. 394**

11. _____ An electronic marker for a specific location in a document. **p. 396**

12. _____ A partially completed document containing preformatted text or graphics. **p. 376**

13. _____ The framework that defines the default page settings. **p. 376**

14. _____ A field or block of text used to determine the position of objects in a document. **p. 376**

15. _____ Like a resume, displays your skills, accomplishments, and job history. **p. 377**

16. _____ A set of coordinating fonts, colors, and special effects that give a stylish and professional look. **p. 405**

17. _____ Represents the current text and background, accent, and hyperlinks. **p. 406**

18. _____ Contains a heading and body text font. **p. 407**

19. _____ Includes lines or fill effects. **p. 407**

Multiple Choice

1. If you create new documents every day that contain your company letterhead, which productivity tool would best fit your need?

   (a) Mail merge

   (b) Building Blocks

   (c) Document themes

   (d) Document templates

2. Which of the following is not a way you can obtain a document template?

   (a) Select it from the Styles gallery.

   (b) Download from Office.com.

   (c) Select an installed template on your computer.

   (d) Create a document yourself and save it as a template.

3. What file extension is given to a template?

   (a) .dotx

   (b) .docx

   (c) .xlsx

   (d) .accdb

4. What is another name for the text or fields that display in a document template so you will know where to insert your own information?

   (a) Flag

   (b) Extension

   (c) CV

   (d) Placeholder

5. Why would you use a document theme?

   (a) So you can restrict the use of color in the document

   (b) To merge information from a data source into a document

   (c) To color coordinate elements used in the document and give a professional appearance

   (d) To easily locate bookmarks

6. Which of the following theme elements cannot be customized and saved?

   (a) Theme color

   (b) Theme font

   (c) Theme effect

   (d) Document theme

7. Which of the document elements listed below can you find using the Go To command?

   (a) Hyperlink

   (b) Bookmark

   (c) Table of Contents

   (d) Cross-reference notation

8. After you use the styles feature to format headings, which of the following features can be used to view small pictures of each page in your document?

   (a) Bookmarks

   (b) Navigation Pane—headings

   (c) Navigation Pane—thumbnails

   (d) Navigation Pane—search

9. What comprises a master document?

   (a) Subdocuments

   (b) Templates

   (c) Outline documents

   (d) Combined documents

10. Which feature enables you to evaluate the differences in two documents?

    (a) Side by side view

    (b) Compare documents

    (c) Master documents

    (d) Subdocuments

Practice Exercises

1 My Home Town Cable Services

You work in the Employee Benefits Department of the local cable provider, My Home Town Cable Services. You want to set up a form that all new and existing employees can use to document personal information and emergency contact numbers. Before you create a new form, you decide to look for an existing form in the Word templates gallery. You find just the right form and need to make only minor modifications, adding the company name and logo. You also insert the contents of another document to add insurance information, and the form is ready to be distributed to all employees. This exercise follows the same set of skills as used in Hands-On Exercises 1 and 2 in the chapter. Refer to Figure 6.32 as you complete this exercise.

Document template file name

Company name as a Building Block

Second page content was inserted from another file

FIGURE 6.32 Download and Save an Employee Information Document Template

FROM SCRATCH

a. Start Word. Type **Employee Information Form** in the **Search online templates box** and hit **Enter**. Click the first form to preview it and click **Create**. Close the Navigation Pane if it displays.

b. Click the **FILE tab**, click Save As, click **Browse**, click the **Save as type arrow**, and then select **Word Template**. Type **w06p1EmployeeTemplate_LastFirst** in the **File name box** and click **Save**.

c. Select the border of the text box that displays *Your Logo Here* and press **Delete**.

d. Select the text **Company Name** to display the text box. Select the text *Company Name* and type the following:
   My Home Town Cable Services
   1234 Sutton Place
   Richmond, VA 23060

e. Insert a blank line after the zip code. Select the two lines that contain the address and press **Decrease Font Size** in the Font group once to decrease the font size.

f. Select the company name and address and click the **INSERT tab**. Click **Quick Parts** in the Text group and select **Save Selection to Quick Part gallery**.

g. Click the **Gallery arrow** in the Create New Building Block dialog box and select **Text Boxes**. Click the **Save In arrow** and select **Building Blocks**, if necessary. Click **OK**.

h. Press **Delete** to remove the text box. Click **Quick Parts** in the Text group, click the **Building Blocks Organizer**, click **Name** to sort the entries by name, scroll down to the *My Home Town Cable Services* entry, click it, and then click **Insert**.

i. Select the whole document. Click the **Paragraph dialog box launcher** in the Paragraph group on the HOME tab and change the Before and After Spacing to **0**. Click **OK**.

j. Press **Ctrl+End** to move to the end of the document. Click the **INSERT tab**, click **Object** in the Text group, and then click the **Create from File tab**. Browse to the location where data files are stored, select *w06p1Insurance.docx*, and then click **Insert**.

k. Position the insertion point on the *Full Name:* line under *Employee Information*, type your last name, press **Tab**, and then type your first name.

l. Save and close the file, and submit it based on your instructor's directions.

2 Anderson High School

You volunteer at the Anderson High School Computer Club and have the opportunity to observe the computer skill level of many students. You decide to create a document that contains new features of Microsoft Word and Excel 2013 that the students can use as a reference. You found two sources of information and want to combine them into one document. You are familiar with the compare and combine features in Word, so you are going to use them to combine the two documents into one document and make modifications so that it is easy to read. This exercise follows the same set of skills as used in Hands-On Exercises 2 and 3 in the chapter. Refer to Figure 6.33 as you complete this exercise.

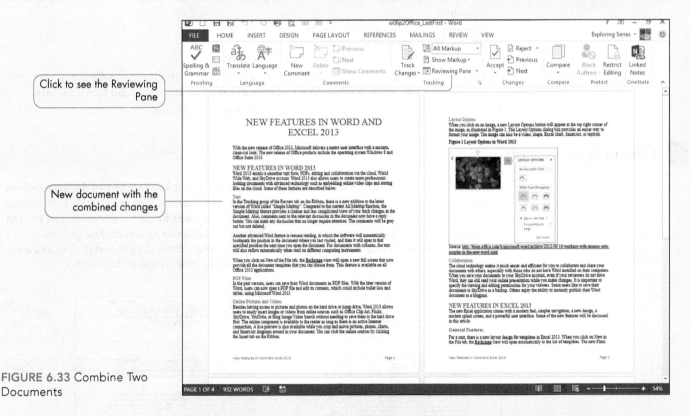

Click to see the Reviewing Pane

New document with the combined changes

FIGURE 6.33 Combine Two Documents

a. Open both *w06p2Office1* and *w06p2Office2*. Click the **VIEW tab** and click **View Side by Side** in the Windows group. Use Synchronous Scrolling to scroll down to view the contents of each and click **View Side by Side** again to turn off the feature.

b. Click the **REVIEW tab**, click **Compare** in the Compare group, and then click **Combine.**

- Click the **Original document arrow** and select *w06p2Office1.docx*. If necessary, click **Browse** and navigate to the document. Click **Open**.
- Click the **Revised document arrow** and select *w06p2Office2.docx*. If necessary, click **Browse** and navigate to the document. Click **Open**.
- Click the **More button** if necessary and click **New document** below *Show changes in* to select, if necessary. Click **OK**.

    c. Save the new document as **w06p2Office_LastFirst**.

    d. Click the **REVIEW tab**. If necessary, click **Reviewing Pane** in the Tracking group to show all the changes to your document in a list. Review each of the following tracked changes and accept all of them:

- Two changes in Style Definition for Headings 1 and 2.
- Two changes for the title.
- Four changes for the Layout Options.
- One change for the *NEW FEATURES IN EXCEL 2013* heading.
- Two changes for the FORMULA tab and figure.
- Two changes for the blank line at the end of the document.
- One change for the footnote.

    e. Change the first heading *New Features in Word 2013* to all caps and bold it.

    f. Click the **DESIGN tab** and format the document as follows:

- Click **Themes** in the Document Formatting group. Click **Retrospect** to apply colors from that theme to the text.
- Click **Colors** in the Document Formatting group and click **Customize Colors** at the bottom of the gallery.
- Click the **Accent 1 arrow** and select **Red** from the Standard Colors group.
- Click in the **Name box**, type **Office colors**, and then click **Save**.
- Click **Fonts** in the Document Formatting group and click **Customize Fonts** at the bottom of the gallery.
- Click the **Heading font arrow** and select **Broadway**.
- Click the **Body font arrow** and select **Arial**.
- Type **Office fonts** in the **Name box** and click **Save**.

    g. Click **Themes** and click **Save Current Theme**. Navigate to the location where you save your solution files, type **w06p2OfficeTheme_LastFirst** in the **File name box**, and then click **Save**.

    h. Save and close the file. Submit it based on your instructor's directions.

3   Cancer Information

You are a health care professional working at a local hospital, and you receive two documents from co-workers who searched for information about cancer on the Internet. The information is interesting and could be valuable to your patients, so you decide to create a well-formatted document that you can distribute to anyone who expresses an interest in basic information about cancer. And you also apply a document theme so it will look more professional. This exercise follows the same set of skills as used in Hands-On Exercises 1–3 in the chapter. Refer to Figure 6.34 as you complete this exercise.

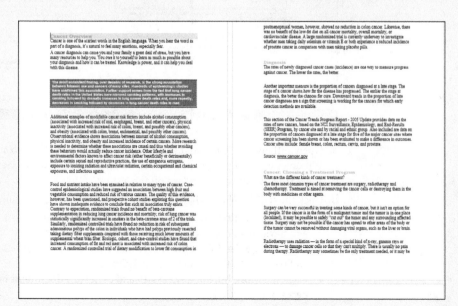

FIGURE 6.34 Theme Applied to Combined Document

a. Open *w06p3Cancer1* and open *w06p3Cancer2*. Click the **VIEW tab** and click **View Side by Side** in the Window group. Use Synchronous Scrolling to scroll down to view the contents of each and click **View Side by Side** again to turn off the feature.

b. Click the **REVIEW tab**, click the **Compare arrow** in the Compare group, and then select **Combine**.

- Click the **Original document arrow** and select *w06p3Cancer1*. If necessary, click **Browse**, navigate to the document, and then click **Open**.
- Click the **Revised document arrow** and select *w06p3Cancer2*. If necessary, click **Browse**, navigate to the document, and then click **Open**.
- Click the **More button** and click **New document** below *Show changes in*, if necessary. Click **OK**.

c. Save the document as **w06p3Cancer_LastFirst**. To accept and reject the tracked changes, complete the following steps:

- The first three track changes describe the changes in Style Definition - Normal; Heading 1: Font color: Accent 1; and text pattern: Clear (Accent 1). Click **Accept** in the Changes group to accept all three changes.
- Click **Reject** to remove the extra space below the first paragraph.
- Click **Accept** to keep the paragraphs with shading.
- Scroll down until you see a large amount of deleted text, starting with the *What is cancer?* heading. Right-click the selected text and click **Reject Deletion**.

d. Press **Ctrl+Home** to view the first page. Close the Reviewing Pane, if necessary.

e. Click the **DESIGN tab** and click **Themes** in the Document Formatting group. Click **Facet** to apply colors from that theme on the text. Modify theme features by completing the following steps:

- Click **Colors** in the Document Formatting group and click **Customize Colors** at the bottom of the gallery.
- Click the **Accent 1 arrow** and click **Dark Green, Accent 2, Lighter 40%** (fourth row, sixth column).
- Type **Cancer colors** in the **Name box** and click **Save**.
- Click **Fonts** in the Document Formatting group and click **Customize Fonts** at the bottom of the gallery.
- Click the **Heading font arrow** and select **Bookman Old Style**.
- Type **Cancer fonts** in the **Name box** and click **Save**.
- Click **Themes** and click **Save Current Theme**. Navigate to the location where you save your solution files, type **w06p3CancerTheme_LastFirst** in the **File name box**, and then click **Save**.

f. Save and close the file, and submit it based on your instructor's directions.

Mid-Level Exercises

1 Sidewalk Café

Your friend, Mary Guccione, just purchased the Sidewalk Café restaurant. She prepared an information sheet to distribute to several office buildings within the neighborhood, and she asked you to look at it and offer suggestions. Before you start reviewing the information sheet, she sends another version with new changes. With two different documents, you use the Compare and Combine features to view them, consolidate the documents into one final copy, add your suggested changes, and return it to Mary. Refer to Figure 6.35 as you complete this exercise.

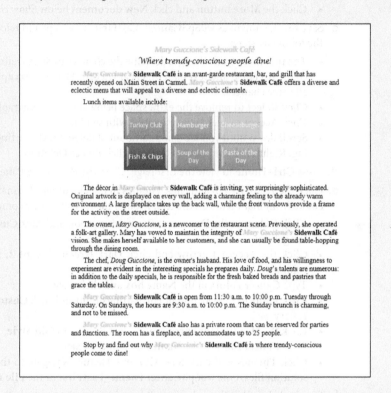

FIGURE 6.35 Information Sheet for Sidewalk Café

a. Use the Compare feature to open the two documents Mary sends, *w06m1Cafe* and *w06m1CafeRevision*, and display the results in a new document. View the differences, save the new document as **w06m1CafeCompare_LastFirst**, and then close the document.

b. Use the Combine feature to combine *w06m1Cafe* (hint: open this as an original document) and *w06m1CafeRevision*. Save the newly combined file as **w06m1CafeCombined_LastFirst**.

c. Accept and reject the following changes that display in the document:

- Accept the tracked change *Formatted: Space Before: 0 pt.*
- Reject the tracked change *Formatted: Font: 10 pt.*
- Reject the addition of text *on a daily basis* that displays above the SmartArt.
- Reject the insertion of the SmartArt object that includes *Fresh Seafood, Homemade Soup, etc.*
- Reject the tracked change that displays in the text *is homey and* in the third paragraph.
- Accept the inclusion of the text *trendy-conscience people.*
- Accept the tracked change *Deleted: those in the know.*
- Accept all remaining changes in the document.

d. Apply the **Office theme** to the document.

e. Type **Mary Guccione's** on the title line, so that the title reads *Mary Guccione's Sidewalk Café.* Apply the **Intense Emphasis style** from the style gallery to this text. Change the font color to **Gold, Accent 4**. Select the name, *Mary Guccione's,* and add it as an AutoText entry in the Building Block Organizer.

f. Display the Building Block in front of each occurrence of the *Sidewalk Café* title throughout the document, replacing *The*, where necessary. Bold the AutoText entry, if necessary.

g. Italicize all other instances of Mary Guccione and Doug Guccione, or any variation of their names.

h. Save and close the file, and submit based on your instructor's directions.

2 Creating Themes

CREATIVE CASE

Because you learned about the themes that Word 2013 provides, you decide that you need to use them more often and also create your own custom theme. You download a letter that incorporates a theme already, add a custom Building Block, and then make modifications to create your own custom theme that you can use in other documents.

a. Start Word. Search for and download the Urban Letter template. Save the file as a document template named **w06m2CustomTemplate_LastFirst**. Make certain the *Save as type* box displays *Word Template*.

★ b. Delete the image placeholder at the top of the page.

c. Create a Building Block that contains your name and address. Use a style from the Styles group on the HOME tab to format the name and/or address.

d. Delete the placeholders for *[Type the sender name]*, *[Type the sender company name]*, and *[Type the sender company address]*. Insert your new Building Block entry here.

e. Pick today's date in the *[Pick the date]* placeholder.

DISCOVER

f. Display the Theme gallery and select a theme of your choice.

g. Display the Theme Colors gallery and change the color of any two objects. Save the new color theme as **Custom colors**.

h. Create a new font theme. Change the body font to **Arial font**. Save the font theme as **Custom fonts**.

i. Save the Current Document Theme as **w06m2MyTheme_LastFirst**, since you have personalized several pieces of the theme.

j. Save and close the document template. Submit it based on your instructor's directions.

3 Research on Templates

COLLABORATION CASE

Group collaboration among team members has become more common and easier with the advent of several collaboration tools. There are collaboration tools available in MyITLab, in your campus's course management software, and for free download from the Internet such as Google Docs, Microsoft 365 Online, SharePoint, Sky Drive, Dropbox, OpenOffice, Facebook, Twitter, blogs, chat, and Skype. In this exercise, your group will collaborate on a research paper to describe the various templates available in Word 2013 and at the Microsoft.com Web site. Some of the popular templates are resumes, letters, labels, cards, calendars, award certificates, and announcements.

a. The team will use an online collaboration tool, such as Google groups or Skype, to conduct a face-to-face meeting. During this online chat session, you will do the following:
   • Choose a name for the group and select a group leader.
   • Develop a list of tasks to complete.
   • Assign tasks and responsibilities to each group member.

b. After the initial face-to-face meeting, the team may continue with the discussion using any communication tool, such as Twitter, blogs, Google Docs, or Facebook chat.

c. The team leader will create a OneDrive or Dropbox.com account where team members can post and share their documents.

d. Each member will review one category of the available templates and will save the individual template as **w06m3Template_LastFirst.dotx**. The team member will then populate the template with the necessary information before saving it as **w06m3Template_LastFirst.docx**, a Word document.

The team member will post his/her own individual template and Word document to the online storage location.

e. The group leader will combine members' files into one master file. The final research report will describe each template in detail.

f. Each team member will be responsible for inserting his/her own Word document as a file object into the research report.

g. Each team member will also take turns to enhance the research report with an appropriate document theme, theme colors, fonts, or effects.

h. Save the research report as **w06m3TemplatesResearch_GroupName**.

i. Inform your instructor that the documents are ready for grading, and also give directions to where they are located.

Beyond the Classroom

Use the Calendar Wizard

RESEARCH CASE

You want to create a monthly calendar for the current year. However, you do not want to manually create and populate 12 tables, one for each month, typing in dates within cells. You know many calendar templates are available on Office.com and decide to find one there. Find and download the Calendar Wizard, and after you complete the steps you can apply Document Themes and modify colors and fonts for a very personalized and custom calendar. Save the calendar as a template, which you can share with others, naming it **w06b2CalendarTemplate_LastFirst.dotx**. For your personal calendar, insert information for important dates such as birthdays and anniversaries; create Building Blocks for frequently used names. Save the calendar as **w06b2Calendar_LastFirst.docx** and submit it based on your instructor's directions.

Repairing Bookmarks

DISASTER RECOVERY

You work in the city's Planning and Zoning department as an analyst. You begin to prepare the *Guide to Planned Developments* document for posting on the city's intranet. The administrative clerk who typed the document attempted to use bookmarks for navigation purposes, but he did not test the bookmarks after inserting them. You must review the document and repair the bookmarks. Additionally, several cross-reference statements are embedded in the document, but appear to be erroneous. The cross-references are highlighted in the document so you can locate them; the highlights should be removed when you have corrected the references. Open *w06b3Bookmarks* and save your revised document as **w06b3Bookmarks_LastFirst**. Close the document and submit it based on your instructor's directions.

Resume and Cover Letter Tips

SOFT SKILLS CASE

You will create a professional-looking resume and cover letter using templates from Microsoft Word to apply for a summer internship. Your resume will display the various types of skills you have, accomplishments you achieved, your job history, or other employment information. Choose a cover letter using a template with a similar style to coordinate your documents. You may also coordinate the appearance of your resume and cover letter by customizing them with an appropriate theme, theme colors, fonts, and effects. After you have checked the spelling and grammar of your documents, save them as **w06b4Resume_LastFirst** and **w06b4CoverLetter_LastFirst**. Submit the documents as directed by your instructor.

You have recently been elected secretary of the local professional chapter of Information Technologist Professionals (ITPs). You decide to send professional-looking documents to the other officers so they can prepare for meetings, as well as collect and distribute information. Your next meeting occurs in one week, so you begin the process of assembling your information. Refer to Figure 6.36 as you complete the exercise.

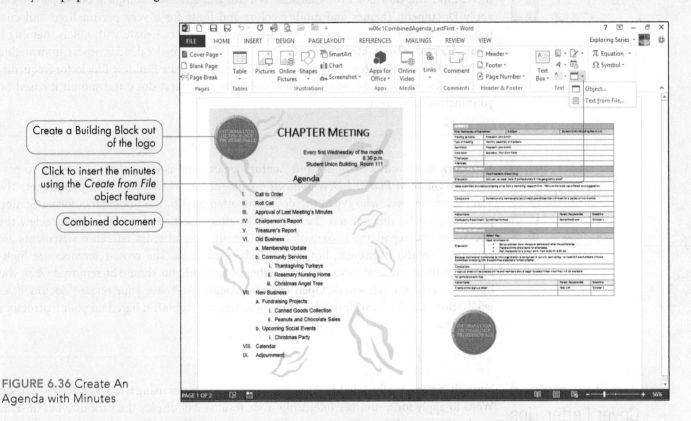

FIGURE 6.36 Create An Agenda with Minutes

Download a Word Template

You want to prepare a meeting agenda that is comprehensive, yet looks attractive and is easy to read. Instead of creating one from scratch, you download a meeting agenda document template from Office.com. Once you personalize these templates with the organization name and logo, you save them as templates so you can use them for each monthly meeting.

a. Open a new document. Conduct a search on online templates using the key term **Agenda** and download the **Community meeting agenda template**.

b. Save the file as a Word template named **w06c1AgendaTemplate_LastFirst**.

c. Replace the word *COMMUNITY* with **CHAPTER**. On the left of this text, insert the graphic *w06c1Logo.png*, which is stored with other data files for this chapter. Position the image so that it is aligned with the upper left corner of the template background color borders and change the wrapping to tight.

d. Remove the bullet points under *Chairperson's Report* and *Treasurer's Report*.

e. Replace the following text in the document template:

Replace This Text	With This Text
[Click to select date]	Every first Tuesday of the month
[Time]	7:00 p.m.
[Location]	Student Union Building, Room 111
VI. a. [Item]	Membership Update
VI. b. [Item]	Community Services
VII. a. [Item]	Fundraising Projects
VII. b. [Item]	Upcoming Social Events

f. Create a Building Block out of the meeting date, time, and place, name it **Meeting_Info**, and then save it to the Quick Part Gallery.

g. Save and close the template.

Combine Documents to Create an Agenda with Minutes

After you create the agenda template, you send it to the president and vice president and ask them to revise it and add their topics for the meeting. When they each return their version to you, you combine them into one final agenda for the upcoming meeting. You also attach the minutes from the last meeting to the end of the agenda.

a. Use the Combine feature to view the returned agendas named *w06c1EileenAgendaTemplate* and *w06c1JohnAgendaTemplate*. Save the combined file as a Word document named **w06c1CombinedAgenda_LastFirst**.

b. Accept all changes to the agenda after the files are combined.

c. Change the date to **Wednesday**. Change the time to **6:30 p.m.**

d. Insert a blank page after the agenda. Use the *Create from File object* feature to add the minutes of the meeting, stored in *w06c1Minutes*, to the end of the agenda.

e. Type your name as Note taker/Secretary for the First Wednesday of September minutes.

f. Insert the logo Building Block at the bottom of the page where you just inserted the minutes. Position the logo so that it is 0.5" from the left margin and 0.2" below the last line.

g. Save and close the file.

Apply a Document Theme to the Meeting Agenda and Minutes

After you combine the agendas and insert the minutes, you decide to customize the document to reflect the national organization's colors. You begin by selecting a theme, but decide to modify it so your colors match and fonts are easier to read. You save your custom settings so that you can use them again on other documents.

a. Change the document theme to **Retrospect**.

b. Modify the colors used in this theme by changing the Accent 1 color to **Orange, Accent 2, Lighter 60%** (third row, sixth column) and changing the Text/Background - Light 1 color to **Black, Background 1** (first row, first column). Save the font colors as **w06c1AgendaColors_LastFirst**.

c. Create new theme fonts by replacing the heading font with **Arial Black** and the body font with **Arial Narrow**. Save the font theme as **w06c1AgendaFonts_LastFirst**.

d. Save the current theme, which includes the revisions you just made, as **w06c1AgendaTheme_LastFirst**.

e. Click the **dark blue-colored logo graphic** on the page where the agenda displays. Change the fill color of that object to **Orange, Accent color 1 Light** (third row, second column under *Recolor*) and apply the **Cement Artistic Effects** (fourth row, first column).

f. Save and close the document.

Add Bookmarks to a Document

After the minutes for each meeting are approved, you are responsible for adding them to a document that holds the minutes for a whole year. The document becomes so lengthy that it is easier to navigate when bookmarks are applied to each month. You will add the minutes from the last meeting and add missing bookmarks.

a. Open *w06c1YearlyMinutes*. Save the document as **w06c1YearlyMinutes_LastFirst**.

b. Add a page break at the beginning of the document and use the *Create from File* object to add the minutes of the September meeting, *w06c1Minutes*.

c. Insert a bookmark named **September** at the left edge of the date *First Wednesday of September*, which displays in the second line of the table holding the minutes.

d. Insert a bookmark named **August** at the left edge of the date *First Wednesday of August*, which displays on the next page. Continue to insert bookmarks for July and June.

e. Press **Ctrl+G** and go to the bookmark named *June*. Close the *Find and Replace* dialog box.

f. Type your name as the Timekeeper. Apply the **w06c1AgendaTheme_LastFirst**.

g. Save and close the document. Submit all files based on your instructor's directions.

Document Automation

Forms, Macros, and Security

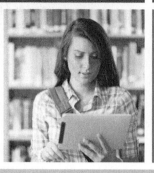

wavebreakmedia/Shutterstock

OBJECTIVES | AFTER YOU READ THIS CHAPTER, YOU WILL BE ABLE TO:

1. Create an electronic form p. 428
2. Insert form controls p. 430
3. Protect a form p. 432
4. Create a macro p. 442

5. Run a macro p. 445
6. Apply document restrictions p. 452
7. Set passwords to open a document p. 455
8. Use digital signatures to authenticate documents p. 458

CASE STUDY | Oak Grove Products, Inc.

Cassie Artman has purchased Oak Grove Products, Inc., a company that sells tulip, hyacinth, and crocus bulbs. Cassie wants to take the company to the next level by automating some of the resources they use. One of the first projects she assigns to you, her technology coordinator, is to create a sales invoice that can be filled out quickly by salespeople who take phone or online orders. The invoice will include check boxes, drop-down menus, and fields that calculate prices automatically. She also wants you to incorporate an informational document about the products sold. She has created a document that she considers complete, so she wants you to password-protect it to prevent any accidental editing. But she also wants you to get feedback from staff before you consider it final and stamp it with a digital certificate.

In the Hands-On Exercises, you will create the invoice form, work with macros, and practice protecting documents.

Forms

Forms are quite common in our society. A form is a document designed for collecting data for a specific situation. For example, you complete a medical history form when you visit a doctor's office; you complete an account application form when you open a bank account; you complete a registration form when you register software and hardware; and you fill out a job application form when you apply for a job. Forms are also used for class registrations, purchase orders, and invoices. The form may be electronic and completed online, or it may exist as a printed document. Figure 7.1 displays a completed form that is an invoice for goods or services.

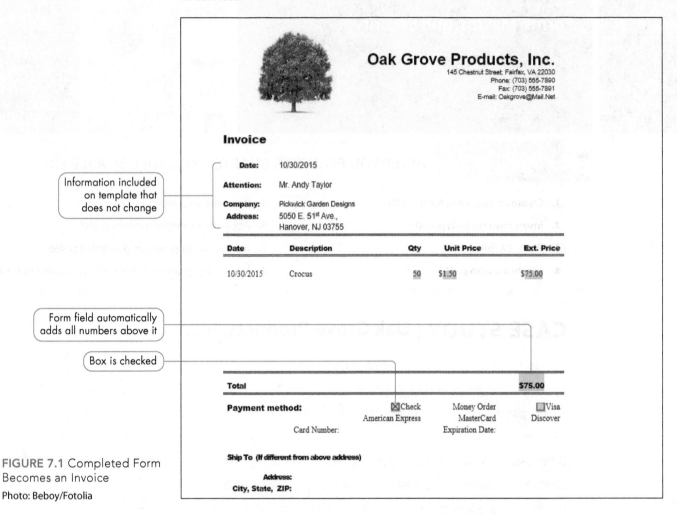

FIGURE 7.1 Completed Form Becomes an Invoice
Photo: Beboy/Fotolia

In this section, you will create and use a simple form that can be printed and filled in or completed onscreen. You will learn how to create and customize form controls, perform calculations in a table form, and then protect the document so you can use the form.

Creating an Electronic Form

In Word, you can create a *form template*, a document that defines the standard layout, structure, and formatting of a form. You save the document as a Word template and establish settings to enable the user to enter data in specific places, but prevent editing it in any other way. The process requires you to create the form and save it to disk, where it serves as an original template for future documents. Then, when you need to enter data for a specific situation, you open the template form, enter the data, and save the completed form as a document. This process is more efficient than removing old information from a standard document so you can replace it with current data for the new situation. It also minimizes errors that sometimes occur when you intend to replace old information with updated data but overlook some portion of the older data. Using a form enables you to maintain the integrity of an original document or template while also allowing you to customize it.

Figure 7.2 displays a blank form. The shaded fields indicate where a user enters information into a form. To complete the form, the user presses Tab to move from one field to the next and enters data as appropriate. Then, when all fields have been filled in, the form is printed to produce the finished document (an invoice). The data entered into the various fields appear as regular text when printed.

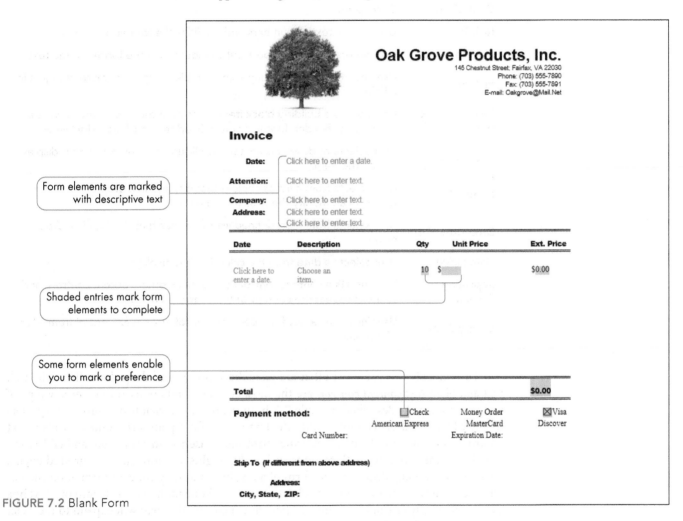

FIGURE 7.2 Blank Form

Create a Document Template

STEP 1 » Before you can create a document template, the Developer tab must be visible on the Ribbon. This tab does not display automatically but is easy to activate. If the Developer tab is not shown on the Ribbon, you may display it by doing the following:

1. Click the FILE tab.
2. Click Options on the left panel.
3. Click Customize Ribbon.
4. Click the Developer (Custom) check box in the *Customize the Ribbon* column.
5. Click OK.

Before you can use the document, you need to save it as a Word template file. This file will have the .dotx instead of the .docx extension. Then, you will add form controls to create a blank form as shown in Figure 7.2.

Inserting Form Controls

You can design forms that will be printed and also forms that will be completed electronically. If you want users to fill out a form electronically, you must insert *form controls*, also called form fields, into the form template. Form controls help the user complete a form by displaying prompts such as drop-down lists and text boxes. Table 7.1 describes the most common types of content controls, located in the Controls group under the Developer tab.

TABLE 7.1	Content Controls
Control Type	**Description**
Rich Text	User enters text or numbers and modifies the format of the text.
Plain Text	User enters text or numbers but cannot modify the format of the text.
Picture	User inserts a drawing, shape, chart, table, image, or SmartArt object in a field.
Building Block Gallery	User selects a building block item to insert in the document, such as a cover page, header, footer, or predefined text, such as a disclaimer.
Check Box	User selects or deselects an item by clicking the check box that displays beside the item.
Combo Box	User selects from a list of choices that displays in a drop-down box, but the user can modify the choices in the list.
Drop-Down List	User selects from a predefined list of choices that displays in a drop-down box.
Date Picker	User selects a date from the calendar that displays.
Repeating Section	User inserts a content control that contains other content controls, and user can repeat the content of the control as needed.
Legacy Tools	User inserts a legacy form content control or ActiveX control from a list of options.

The controls you use most often are text, check boxes, and drop-down lists. The rich text and plain *text content controls* are the most common and are used to enter any type of text into a form. As described in Table 7.1, both the plain and rich text controls allow users to enter text, but users cannot modify the text format for a plain text control. A plain text control is often preferred, but a rich text control allows users to insert images and tables, and to enhance the text entry with features such as highlights and fore and background colors. Text controls usually display in the form of a text box, and they collect information such as name and address and even numerical data such as a phone number. The length of a text box can be set exactly or can be left unspecified, in which case the field will expand to the exact number of positions that are required as the data are entered.

When you have a form that uses numerical information, you can use a text content control to perform calculations. You can use basic formulas, such as those that add or multiply the numbers that display in text form fields. The properties for the text form content control enable you to select the form fields you include in the calculation. You can adjust the format of the numbers; for example, you can use currency format that displays dollar signs and decimal points for a price field.

A *check box form field*, as the name implies, consists of a box that is checked or unchecked. A check box might include the responses *Yes* or *No*, or *Male* or *Female*, for example. You can customize check box form fields so they display checked by default, or not checked. You can also specify the size of the check box.

A *drop-down list* enables the user to choose from one of several existing entries. This type of control should only be used on electronic forms because the list of options will not display on a printed form. A drop-down list enables users to click an arrow and then click one option from the list; the option they click will then display on the form. A list of cities or states is appropriate to display in a drop-down list.

Many forms require a date. The *Date Picker* displays a calendar that the user can navigate on an electronic form and click rather than typing in a date. If the user wants to select the current date, the Date Picker calendar has a Today button. The Properties dialog box for the Date Picker enables you to select from several date formats, such as 3/2/2016 or 2-Mar-16.

If you create forms that might be used by people who are not yet using Word 2013, you should remember to use only legacy controls and save the document or template in Compatibility Mode. The Legacy Tools include a list of options for Legacy Forms and ActiveX controls. As the word *legacy* implies, the legacy controls, also called *legacy form fields*, are created and/or used in Word 2003 or earlier versions. Legacy forms are created using form fields that will only work when the document is in protected mode; that is, all parts of the document are locked and only the form fields can be edited. The legacy form fields can be used in the newer versions of Word documents or templates when you open the files in Compatibility Mode. The controls created for Word 2007 and later versions are called content controls. These controls do not need form protection or macros to work. Unfortunately, content controls cannot be used in Word 2003 or earlier versions. *ActiveX controls* are form elements designed for use in Office 2007 and later versions. These controls can be easily inserted into a Word document or template, and especially a Web page. ActiveX controls require macros to work. Figure 7.3 shows the Developer tab and available controls.

Click Legacy Tools to display ActiveX Controls and Legacy Form fields

Legacy Form fields can be used in all Word documents and templates

ActiveX controls can only be used in Word 2007 and newer documents and templates

Click Design Mode prior to inserting controls

FIGURE 7.3 Controls on the Developer Tab

Insert Form Controls in a Document

STEP 2 On the Developer tab, you see the form controls as well as other commands you use while creating the form. Before you insert the controls in your document, you must enter Design Mode. *Design Mode* enables you to view and select the control fields so you can make any necessary modifications to their layout or options. Design Mode is a toggle; click it once to activate Design Mode and click it again to deactivate it. To insert form controls into a form template, do the following:

1. Click the DEVELOPER tab.
2. Click Design Mode in the Controls group. The Properties icon is activated when Design Mode is active.
3. Position the insertion point at the location where you want to insert the form control.
4. Click the specific form control icon in the Controls group to insert it into the document.

Insert Form Controls in a Table

STEP 3 Besides inserting form controls directly into a document, sometimes it is easier to insert form controls using a table to help you align information and to make the form easier for users to fill out. For instance, you can insert a two-column table. You can insert the appropriate content controls in the right column and the label for the corresponding content controls in the left column. Labels for content controls in a form can include Last Name, First Name, Street Address, State, Zip Code, Cell Phone, E-mail Address, Date, and so on. In the right column, you can insert a Drop-Down List content control for the user to select from a list of states, a Date Picker content control for the date, and several plain text content controls for the other labels. All controls already have default settings, but you can redefine the characteristics of any control by clicking Properties in the Controls group. You can also copy and paste a control after you create it.

In addition, you can use the Table feature to format and manipulate the fields and data to improve the form. For example, you can right-align the labels in the left column, such as Last Name and First Name, and then you can left-align the content controls in the right column of the table. This alignment clarifies the instructional information that accompanies the control.

Perform Calculations with Form Control Data

STEP 4

Forms can be created to automatically calculate data values or update calculations by clicking a certain button or when exiting from Word. For instance, you can design a form to automatically calculate the sales tax or total price when the user types in the quantity or cost of an item. After you have designed the calculating form, the next step is to determine the data values that will be stored in the form, followed by constructing the formula(s) needed for the calculation. Finally, you will type the formula into the appropriate content control, either directly or using the Formula button in the Data group of the Layout tab. It is important to note that formulas can only be used in tables.

TIP Planning the Order of Fields

When a user completes an electronic form, Word moves through fields in the order in which you inserted them. Once a form has been completed, the tab order is very difficult to change or modify. Therefore, it is very important that you plan carefully how you want users to fill out the form before you insert the form fields. If you want users to move from left to right across the page, insert form fields from left to right. If you want users to move down the page, insert form fields down the page. You should also keep labels close to the form controls because programs that are used by the visually impaired cannot distinguish which label matches a particular field when they are not positioned closely.

Protecting a Form

STEP 5

After the form is created and ready to be distributed to other users to input data, it should be protected to prevent any modification other than data entry. After you have inserted all the necessary content controls into your form, you can protect the form by doing the following:

1. Click the DEVELOPER tab, if it is not selected.
2. Click Design Mode in the Controls group to deactivate it, if necessary.
3. Click Restrict Editing in the Protect group to display the Restrict Editing pane. The Restrict Editing pane displays, as shown in Figure 7.4.
4. Click *Allow only this type of editing in the document* in the Editing restrictions section.
5. Click the arrow and select *Filling in forms* to enable the user to type in, click, or select only the form fields in the form.
6. Click the Yes, Start Enforcing Protection button to activate protection of the form.

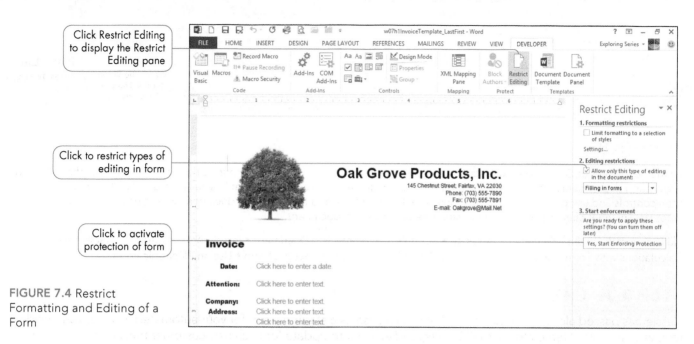

Click Restrict Editing to display the Restrict Editing pane

Click to restrict types of editing in form

Click to activate protection of form

FIGURE 7.4 Restrict Formatting and Editing of a Form

After you enforce the protection of a form, you are prompted for a password. You can create a password for the form to serve as another layer of protection and to prevent unauthorized users from deactivating the protection. Without a password, anyone can deactivate the protection. However, if you forget the password, it cannot be recovered. You can skip the password protection by omitting a password in the *Enter new password* box and clicking OK. If you want to revise the form, click Stop Protection in the Restrict Editing pane.

You can protect specific controls on a form without restricting access to the entire document by using the Group command in the Controls group on the Developer tab. When you select a range and apply the Group command, the range is protected from editing. This feature is useful when you want to be able to make modifications to a document that contains form controls, but you do not want to allow any changes to the form controls within that document. After you apply the Group command to the range, click Properties and set one of the two locking options. The first option—*Content control cannot be deleted*—enables you to edit the content of a control but does not enable you to remove the control. The second option—*Contents cannot be edited*—enables you to delete the control, but you cannot edit the content in the control.

Use an Electronic Form

STEP 6 >> After an electronic form is created and protected, you may e-mail it to the user or upload it to a Web site. The user will open the form like any other Word document and navigate through the form controls by pressing Tab or the arrow keys, depending on the control types. For instance, the user must use the arrow keys when navigating to the next text box. To insert dates, the user may click the Date Picker arrow to select a date with the date format stipulated in the Properties dialog box. After all the data are entered, the user will save and close the document. If necessary, the user may print the electronic form as a hard copy.

Quick Concepts

1. Describe the reasons for creating a form document. ***p. 428***

2. Describe the three most common content controls. ***p. 430***

3. What is the main purpose of protecting a form? ***p. 432***

Hands-On Exercises

Watch the Video
for this Hands-
On Exercise!

MyITLab®
HOE1 Training

1 Forms

As the new owner of Oak Grove Products, Inc., Cassie Artman wants to improve the resources used by employees in the sales and accounting departments. She asks you to update and automate the invoice form so that it is easier to use. You begin by inserting form controls and using automated calculations from those controls. You then save the document so that employees can open and enter data without affecting the content or structure of the invoice document.

Skills covered: Create a Document Template • Insert Form Controls in a Document • Insert Form Controls in a Table • Perform Calculations with Form Control Data • Add Check Box Controls and Protect the Form • Use an Electronic Form

STEP 1 ≫ CREATE A DOCUMENT TEMPLATE

Cassie has passed along an invoice form that you can use as a starting point for your automated invoice. You decide to save it as a Word template so it will be easy and efficient to update for each new customer transaction. Refer to Figure 7.5 as you complete Step 1.

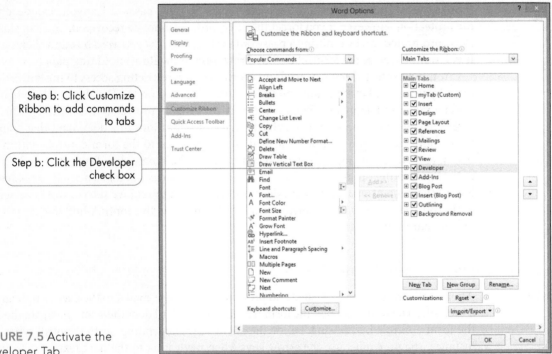

FIGURE 7.5 Activate the Developer Tab

a. Open *w07h1Invoice*. Click **Enable Content** when you see the warning message *Macros have been disabled.*

This file is saved as a Word 97-2003 document and will open in Compatibility Mode.

TROUBLESHOOTING: If you make any major mistakes in this exercise, you can close the file, open *w07h1Invoice* again, and then start this exercise over.

b. Click the **FILE tab**, if necessary, click **Options**, click **Customize Ribbon**, and then click the **Developer (Custom) check box**, which displays in the *Customize the Ribbon* column on the right. Click **OK**.

This step is necessary to display the Developer tab, which contains all form controls.

c. Click the **DEVELOPER tab** and locate the Controls group.

Notice that most of the controls in the Controls group are grayed out. These ActiveX controls cannot be used in a document that opens in Compatibility Mode.

d. Click the **FILE tab** and click **Save As**. Click **Browse**. Type **w07h1InvoiceTemplate_LastFirst** in the **File name box**. Click the **Save as type arrow** and select **Word Template**. Navigate to the folder where your student files are stored, uncheck the *Maintain compatibility with previous versions of Word* checkbox, and then click **Save**.

Make sure that you uncheck the *Maintain compatibility with previous versions of Word* checkbox or else the content controls will not be available to you.

TIP Saving a Template Document

When saving a template, the Save As dialog box will open to a default file folder on the hard drive. Therefore, if needed, you may have to adjust the path by navigating to your preference location to save the template. When saving as a template file type, you will adjust the file type and navigate to the appropriate file directory. You can also change the default directory by clicking Save Options on the Tools drop-down list in the Save As dialog box.

e. Click **OK** to the Microsoft Word dialog box displaying a warning that your document will be upgraded to the newest file format.

f. Click **Yes** to the Microsoft Word dialog box asking if you want to continue to save as a macro-free template.

STEP 2 » INSERT FORM CONTROLS IN A DOCUMENT

Now that the document is saved as a template, you insert form controls for the customer's name, address, and date of the sale. You especially appreciate the Date Picker control, which enables you to click the date from a calendar; this process prevents mistyped dates and should reflect more accurate record keeping. Refer to Figure 7.6 as you complete Step 2.

FIGURE 7.6 Insert Form Controls in the Invoice

a. Click the **HOME tab** and click **Show/Hide (¶)** in the Paragraph group, if necessary, to display formatting marks.

b. Click the left side of the paragraph mark that displays at the end of the line for *Date*, which is just below the text *Invoice*.

You are positioning the insertion point prior to inserting a date control.

c. Click the **DEVELOPER tab**, click **Design Mode** in the Controls group, and then click **Date Picker Content Control** in the Controls group.

The control for choosing a date displays with a light blue border and the text *Click here to enter a date.*

> **TROUBLESHOOTING:** If the Date Picker Content Control is grayed out and not available to you, you should repeat Step 1d and make sure that you uncheck the *Maintain compatibility with previous versions of Word* checkbox.

d. Press ↓ one time to move the insertion point to the end of the line for *Attention* and click **Rich Text Content Control** in the Controls group.

The control for entering text displays with a light blue border and the text *Click here to enter text.*

e. Repeat the process from step d to insert Rich Text Content Controls at the end of the *Company* and *Address* lines.

f. Click the left side of the paragraph mark that displays on the line just below the *Address* line. Click **Rich Text Content Control** in the Controls group.

You must insert a second text control for the city, state, and Zip code portions of the address. The text controls do not align text properly when you press Enter when typing within them, so a second box is necessary to align all the address information.

g. Save the template.

STEP 3 ≫ INSERT FORM CONTROLS IN A TABLE

Customer purchases are recorded in an area of the invoice that is formatted in a Word table. By using a table, you have more control over the placement and alignment of the controls and text that display in the invoice. Because this invoice will be used in digital form, you insert form controls that enable the salesperson to select the product purchased—another way to reduce the possibility of error that occurs when information is typed into a form. Refer to Figure 7.7 as you complete Step 3.

Step b: Click to change properties and insert content that displays in the drop-down list

Step d: Click for each item you want to display in the drop-down list

FIGURE 7.7 Insert Form Controls to Display Transaction Details

a. Click the left side of the first blank row in the table, just below the text *Date*. Click **Date Picker Content Control** from the Controls group. Click the left side of the next cell, below the text *Description*.

> **TROUBLESHOOTING:** If you have difficulty positioning the insertion point in the table, click the View tab and click Gridlines in the Show group so you can view each cell border. This border does not display when printed.

b. Click **Drop-Down List Content Control** in the Controls group. Click **Properties** in the Controls group to display the Content Control Properties dialog box.

Users will select from a predefined list of products when they click this control in the form.

c. Type **Spring Bulbs** in the **Title box**. Type **Bulbs** in the **Tag box**.

d. Click **Add** in the *Drop-Down List Properties* section to display the Add Choice dialog box. Type **Tulip** in the **Display Name box** and click **OK**.

e. Repeat the process in step d to add two more types of bulbs: **Hyacinth** and **Crocus**.

f. Click **OK** to close the dialog box. Save the template.

STEP 4 ≫ PERFORM CALCULATIONS WITH FORM CONTROL DATA

The next few pieces of information entered into the invoice will reflect the quantity and amount paid for the products. Because these fields work with numbers, you use form controls that enable you to format the price entered using currency symbols. The controls also perform calculations using formulas resembling those used in table cell calculations. By using these form controls, you increase the frequency of very accurate sales figures that display on the invoices. Refer to Figure 7.8 as you complete Step 4.

FIGURE 7.8 Create a Calculation in the Text Form Field Options Dialog Box

a. Click in the cell below *Qty*. Click **Legacy Tools** in the Controls group and click **Text Form Field** below the heading *Legacy Forms*.

A series of small circles displays with a gray background.

> **TROUBLESHOOTING:** If the gray background does not display behind the circles, click Legacy Tools and click Form Field Shading below the heading *Legacy Forms*.

b. Set up the form field by completing the following steps:

- Click **Properties** in the Controls group to display the Text Form Field Options dialog box.
- Click the **Type arrow** and select **Number**.
- Type **10** in the **Default number text box**.
- Press **Tab** four times and replace the contents of the **Bookmark box** with **Qty1**.

Make sure that there is no space between Qty and 1 in the bookmark name.

> **TROUBLESHOOTING:** No spaces or special characters are allowed in the bookmark names. Use only characters and numbers when you name the bookmark.

- Click to enable the **Calculate on exit check box**, confirm *Fill-in enabled* is checked, and click **OK**.

By naming the bookmark *Qty1*, you will be able to add more product items to the invoice. The next row can contain a bookmark named Qty2, and eventually, you can use the bookmark names to create formulas to perform calculations within the form. Checking *Calculate on exit* ensures that calculations are updated after users enter numbers.

c. Click in the cell below *Unit Price*, placing your cursor on the right side of the dollar sign, and complete the following steps:

- Click **Legacy Tools** in the Controls group and click **Text Form Field** below the heading *Legacy Forms*.
- Click **Properties** in the Controls group.
- Replace the contents of the **Bookmark box** with **UnitPrice1**.
- Click to enable the **Calculate on exit check box** and confirm *Fill-in enabled* is checked.
- Click **OK** to close the Text Form Field Options dialog box.

d. Click in the cell below *Ext. Price*, placing your cursor on the right side of the dollar sign, and complete the following steps:

- Click **Legacy Tools** in the Controls group and click **Text Form Field**.
- Click **Properties**.
- Click the **Type arrow** and select **Calculation**.
- Type **Qty1*UnitPrice1** after the equal sign in the **Expression box**.
  The equal sign in the Expression box specifies that you are creating a mathematical formula. This formula multiplies the value in the Qty1 field by the value of the UnitPrice1 field. Because you assigned bookmark names to the fields, you can use the bookmark names in the formula.
- Select **#,##0.00** in the Number Format list.

e. Click **OK** to close the dialog box.

The Ext. Price field immediately displays *$0.00*, which is the result of multiplying the default value of 10 in the Qty field by the empty value in the Unit Price field.

f. Click in the cell at the right end of the Total row, below *Ext. Price*, and complete the following steps:

- Click **Legacy Tools** in the Controls group and click **Text Form Field**.
- Right-click the shaded field that displays on the invoice and click **Properties**.
- Click the **Type arrow** and select **Calculation**.
- Click in the **Expression box** and type **sum(above)** after the equal sign.

You do not need to type the formula in all caps; either lowercase or all caps will work.

- Select **$#,##0.00;($#,##0.00)** in the Number Format list.
- Click **OK**.

You want to add all the values in as many fields as appear in the Ext. Price column. You use the SUM function to add values in all fields in this column. You will add more rows to the invoice later. The results display as a dollar value.

g. Save the template.

Your changes to the invoice are almost complete. You decide to add only one more form control, a check box for the type of payment, which displays at the bottom of the invoice. You use the document protection tools to prevent editing of the document, allowing only edits that serve to fill out the form. Refer to Figure 7.9 as you complete Step 5.

Step c: Click here to display a checked mark in this control field automatically

FIGURE 7.9 Change Check Box Properties

a. Click the left side of the cell containing *Check* in the *Payment method* section of the form. Click **Legacy Tools** in the Controls group and select **Check Box Form Field** below *Legacy Forms*.

This action inserts a check box form field in the cell to the left of the Check payment method. Users can mark the check box next to the payment method they prefer. You use the Legacy form field instead of the ActiveX form field because it enables you to set custom properties for that field, which you complete in a future step.

b. Click the left side of the cell containing *Visa*, click **Legacy Tools** in the Controls group, and then select **Check Box Form Field**.

You do not yet display check boxes next to all the payment methods, but you will add them in a future Hands-On Exercise. However, you do have enough controls to test your form in the next step.

c. Right-click the **Visa check box** and click **Properties**. Click **Checked** in the *Default value* section. Click **OK**.

Because the majority of purchases are charged to the Visa credit card, you decide to check this option automatically. If customers use a different type of payment, they can click the option, but this saves time if they use a Visa card for payment.

d. Click **Design Mode** to turn off Design Mode. Save the document. Click **Restrict Editing** in the Protect group to display the pane.

The Restrict Editing pane displays.

e. Click **Allow only this type of editing in the document**, which displays in the *Editing restrictions* section. Click the down arrow in the box below this option and select **Filling in forms**, if necessary. Click **Yes, Start Enforcing Protection** in the *Start enforcement* section.

> **TROUBLESHOOTING:** If *Yes, Start Enforcing Protection* is grayed out, make sure you are not in Design Mode.

f. Click **OK** when the Start Enforcing Protection dialog box displays.

If you want to password-protect a document, you can insert and confirm the password in this dialog box. Remember that if you forget the password, you cannot recover it and your document cannot be opened. You are going to remove the password so that anyone can open the file to read and edit.

g. Click the **Close button** in the top-right corner of the Restrict Editing pane. Click the **HOME tab** and click **Show/Hide** (¶) to turn off formatting marks.

h. Save and close the template.

STEP 6 >> USE AN ELECTRONIC FORM

It is now time to test the electronic invoice. You will open the document template and save it as a Word document prior to entering sales information on the invoice. You will also view the automatic calculations that display to show the full amount of a purchase. If this works as designed, you will update the invoice later and add rows to the table for entering more sales. Refer to Figure 7.10 as you complete Step 6.

Step e: Date selected from Date Picker

Step c: Text form fields filled in

Step f: Drop-down control enables you to choose product

Step g: Legacy text fields display with gray shading

Step g: Calculating fields

FIGURE 7.10 Completed Form

a. Open the template *w07h1InvoiceTemplate_LastFirst.dotx*. Save it as a Word document and name it **w07h1InvoiceTest_LastFirst**.

Word creates the new Word Document file based on the template. By default, the first form control is selected. Notice the Ribbon is grayed out, preventing you from using the formatting commands, because the document is protected from editing. You will only be able to click and use the form controls.

b. Click the **Date Picker arrow** in the first control. Click **Today**.

c. Click the words **Click here to enter text**, which display next to *Attention*, and type **Mr. Andy Taylor**. Press ↓.

Word enters the name in the field. You must press the directional arrows to move to the next field for text boxes.

d. Type **Pickwick Garden Designs**, press ↓, type **5050 E. 51st Ave.**, press ↓, type **Hanover, NH 03755**, and then press ↓.

e. Click the **Date Picker arrow** for the date of the first purchase and click **October 30** of the current year. Press **Tab**.

f. Press **Tab** or click one time on the Description field and click the **Description arrow** to display the list of bulbs. Select **Crocus** from the list.

You will click or press Tab to get to the Description field first before the Description arrow will display.

g. Double-click the **Qty control field**, type **50**, and then press **Tab**. Type **1.50** and press **Tab**.

As soon as you press Tab to move out of the Unit Price control field, the Ext. Price and Total fields calculate, and the insertion point moves forward in the form to the check box for the Check method of payment.

h. Press the **Spacebar** to select *Check*. Press **Tab** one time and press **Spacebar** to deselect *Visa*. Press **Tab** two times to cycle through the text fields and update the calculations.

You can also use your mouse to select or deselect a check box.

i. Save and close the file, and submit it based on your instructor's directions.

 Creating Hard Copy Forms

Many offices still use hard copy forms instead of electronic forms. For example, some job application forms are printed, and the job applicants must write or type on the hard copy form. These types of forms contain labels, text boxes, and check boxes. To create a hard copy form, open a document from the form template and print as many copies as you need.

Introduction to Macros

Have you ever pulled down the same menus and clicked the same sequence of commands over and over? If you find yourself performing repetitive tasks, whether in one document or in a series of documents, you should consider using macros. A *macro* is a set of instructions (that is, a program) that executes a series of keystrokes, often to complete a repetitive task, using only a button click or keyboard shortcut. Using a macro in Word is like recording your favorite television show: You turn on the DVR, record the show, and play the show over and over again as often as you want. Examples of useful macros include designating actions to change paragraph format and font styles; insert a page number, header, footer, or watermark such as "Confidential" into a document; change page layout; and format printing procedures.

Office 2013 allows you to save documents with macros automatically enabled or disabled. By default, Word documents with the .docx extension automatically disable any macros the file might contain. If you store a macro in a document, save it as a *Macro-Enabled Document*, which adds the extension .docm to the file and stores VBA macro code in the document to enable execution of a macro.

In this section, you will record a macro that enables you to update and make repetitive modifications to the invoice you are updating for the Oak Grove Products Company. Specifically, you will place additional form controls in the payment section you started in Hands-On Exercise 1. You will run the macro, and you will modify the macro using the editor.

Creating a Macro

Before creating a macro, you should decide what you want to accomplish (such as formatting a letter) and plan exactly which commands and tasks to include (such as margins, alignment, tabs, and so on). Furthermore, you should practice completing the tasks and commands, and make notes of the sequence of steps to perform. Doing so helps you create (record) the macro successfully the first time.

Record a Macro

STEP 1 ▶ The process of creating a macro is called *record macro*. When you record a macro, Word records a series of keystrokes and command selections, and converts the tasks into coded statements. The macro commands are located on two tabs—the Developer tab and the View tab—and also in the status bar. You can start recording a macro by clicking Record Macro in the Code group of the Developer tab. You can also perform the same action by clicking the Macros arrow in the Macros group and clicking Record Macro on the View tab. The Record Macro dialog box opens so that you can name the macro, as shown in Figure 7.11. The macro name can consist of up to 80 characters, but no spaces. You have the option of assigning the macro to a button, which can be placed on the Quick Access Toolbar so that it is readily available, or you can assign a keystroke combination that runs the macro. If you do not choose either option, the macro is only available in the Macros dialog box. You also have the choice of storing a macro in a particular file, so that it can only be executed when that file is open, or you can store macros in the normal template so that they can run in all files. To record a macro, do the following:

1. Click the DEVELOPER tab.
2. Click Record Macro in the Code group to activate the Record Macro dialog box.
3. To name or assign a macro, do one or more of the following:

   - Type the selected name of the Macro in the *Macro name* box.
   - If desired, click the Keyboard icon under the *Assign macro to* option to assign a hotkey to this macro.
     i. Place the cursor in the *Press new shortcut key* box and assign a hotkey by pressing the selected key combination.
     ii. Click Assign to assign a hotkey to the macro.

4. Click OK and a recorder-like image with a pointer appears, indicating that the macro is being recorded.
5. Perform the designated tasks for the macro.
6. Click Stop Recording or Pause Recording in the Code group to stop or pause (respectively) the recording at any time.

When you close the Record Macro dialog box, Word records everything—every keystroke and click of the mouse (including any errors and corrections to errors). For this reason, you do not want to perform any unnecessary actions while recording a macro. For example, if you press Ctrl+Home to correct a mistake while recording the macro, Word records the command to move the insertion point to the beginning of the document. This is problematic if you run the macro in an existing document and the macro inserts or formats text in the wrong location. Therefore, it is very important that you take great care in planning the order of the fields on the form. Keep in mind that it is easy to delete a macro that does not function as you intend and record it again.

You may review a macro by clicking the Macros arrow in the Macros group of the View tab. When the Macros dialog box appears, you will see commands for you to run, edit, create, or delete a macro.

FIGURE 7.11 Record Macro Dialog Box

Type Text in a Macro

You can type text to include in a macro. If you want the macro text to contain character attributes, such as bold or font color, you should turn on the attribute before typing that particular text, type the text, and turn off that attribute. While recording a macro, Word does not let you click and drag to select text to be able to apply formatting. If you already have typed text and want to add an attribute while recording, you can select the text by pressing Shift + ➡. You can apply the attribute you want to the selected text.

Modify a Macro

STEP 3›› Macro instructions are written in *Visual Basic for Applications (VBA)*, a programming language that is built into Microsoft Office. Fortunately, however, you don't have to be a programmer to use VBA. Instead, the macro recorder within Word records your actions, which are translated automatically into VBA. If you need to edit a macro, you can edit the statements after they have been recorded by opening the Visual Basic editor. The Developer tab includes the Visual Basic command in the Code group, which opens the Visual Basic editor and displays the macro contents as programming statements, a set of code written in a specific syntax created by a particular programming language, such as Visual Basic. When editing a macro, it is helpful to have some knowledge of the Visual Basic programming language and how it works. When necessary, you can make minor adjustments to the code to improve the speed and efficiency of the macro. Another way to open the Visual Basic editor is to perform the following steps:

1. Click the VIEW tab.
2. Click Macros in the Macros group to display the Macros dialog box.

3. Click the specific macro that you want to edit in the *Macro name* list.
4. Click the Edit button to open the Microsoft Visual Basic for Applications window to display the programming statements for the macro.
5. Locate the specific task that you want to edit and revise the programming statement accordingly.
6. Click the Save Normal icon to save the change.
7. Close the window.

Each programming statement performs a specific task, such as setting a margin. Every time you choose a dialog box option for a macro, the macro recorder records all dialog box settings, even those you do not change, such as the default font size. Figure 7.12 displays the macro you will create in Hands-On Exercise 2.

Macro displays in a Visual Basic editor window

Macro name

Programming statements

FIGURE 7.12 Programming Statements of a Macro

Copy a Macro

When you record macros, Word saves them in the Normal template by default and stores them in a macro project called NewMacros. Instead of recreating the same macro in multiple documents, you can copy a macro project to another template or document. To copy the NewMacros project to another template or document, do the following:

1. Click the DEVELOPER tab.
2. Click Macros in the Code group.
3. Click Organizer in the Macros dialog box.
4. Specify the destination document or template in the list box on the left side of the dialog box.
5. Click NewMacros in the *In Normal.dotm* list box.
6. Click Copy to copy the macro from the open Word document to the global template named Normal.dotm.
7. Use Help for more specific information on using the Organizer dialog box.

If you no longer need the macros, you can delete them from the Macros dialog box. Select the name of the macro you want to delete and click Delete. Follow the onscreen prompts.

Running a Macro

STEP 2 >> The process of playing back or using a macro is called ***run macro***. When you run a macro, Word processes the series of commands and keystrokes saved in the macro. Running a macro is faster than manually choosing each command when you need to use a series of commands frequently. You can run a macro by clicking on an object that contains the macro or by pressing the specified hotkey assigned to the macro. You can run, edit, or delete a macro using the Macros dialog box, as shown in Figure 7.13. To open the Macros dialog box, you can use one of the following three options:

- Display the DEVELOPER tab and click Macros in the Code group.
- Display the VIEW tab, click Macros in the Macros group, and then click View Macros.
- Press Alt+F8.

FIGURE 7.13 Run a Macro

If your macro includes a command that types text, that text takes on the current document's format when you run the macro. If you specially formatted the text while recording a macro, that special format is retained when you run the macro, regardless of the document's other formats.

Understand the Security Risks of Macros

Because macros are coded in a Visual Basic application, they are essentially programs. As a program that executes commands, a macro has the potential to include code that imposes harmful viruses onto your computer. Microsoft Office includes a Trust Center to help protect users from unsafe macros. The Trust Center checks for the following scenarios before enabling a macro:

- The macro is signed by the developer using a digital signature.
- The digital signature is valid.
- The digital signature is not expired.
- The certificate associated with the digital signature was issued by a known certificate authority.
- The person who signed the macro is a trusted publisher.

If the Trust Center does not find any of these scenarios, the macro is automatically disabled and a message displays to inform you of the potential risk. You can edit the settings on your computer according to your preference for security. Table 7.2 describes the settings from the Trust Center in the Options dialog box.

Change Macro Security Settings

You can change the macro security settings using the Developer tab. Click Macro Security in the Code group to display the Trust Center dialog box and view the settings. When you change the settings in the Trust Center, they are only valid for the program you are currently using, such as Word 2013. Alternately, you can change the macro security settings in the Trust Center by doing the following:

1. Click the FILE tab.
2. Click Options.
3. Click Trust Center.
4. Click Trust Center Settings.
5. Click Macro Settings, if necessary.
6. Select the Macro Settings that you want, as displayed in Table 7.2.

TABLE 7.2 Macro Security Settings

Macro Setting	Description
Disable all macros without notification	If you do not trust macros, click this option. All macros and security alerts about macros are disabled.
Disable all macros with notification	This is the default setting. All macros are disabled, but it alerts you when a document contains a macro.
Disable all macros except digitally signed macros	This setting works similarly to Disable all macros with notification; however, it enables macros to run if they are digitally signed by a trusted publisher. If you have not included the publisher in your trusted list, you will be alerted about the macro. The alert enables you to allow a macro or to include a publisher in your trusted list. All unsigned macros are disabled and you will not see an alert.
Enable all macros (not recommended; potentially dangerous code can run)	This setting enables all macros to run regardless of their authenticity or signature. This option is not recommended because it exposes your computer to potential attacks by viruses.
Trust access to the VBA project object model	This setting is for use by developers only.

When you open a document that contains macros and you see a *Macros have been disabled* security warning, click the File tab, click Options to display the Microsoft Office Security Options dialog box, click *Enable this content,* and then click OK to return to the document and to use any macros that were stored in the document.

Quick
Concepts

1. Explain the reasons for using a macro. **p. 442**
2. Under what circumstances would you want to copy a macro? **p. 444**
3. Why is it important to understand the security risk of macros? **p. 445**

Hands-On Exercises

Watch the Video
for this Hands-
On Exercise!

MyITLab®
HOE2 Training

2 Introduction to Macros

After modifying the invoice, you realize it can take several minutes to insert form fields one by one; if a field property needs changing, the time increases even more. But knowing that using a macro can shorten the time it takes for repetitive tasks, you decide to create a macro to update the invoice. After playing the macro to confirm how it works, you might make modifications using the Visual Basic editor, which is faster than re-creating the macro. Finally, you will run it one last time to finish revisions to the invoice.

Skills covered: Record a Macro • Run a Macro • Modify a Macro • Run an Edited Macro

STEP 1 ❯❯ RECORD A MACRO

After a successful test of the electronic invoice you created, you want to insert additional check boxes in the payment options section of the invoice. Instead of inserting each check box individually, you create a macro to insert them and change the property settings for that form control. Refer to Figure 7.14 as you complete Step 1.

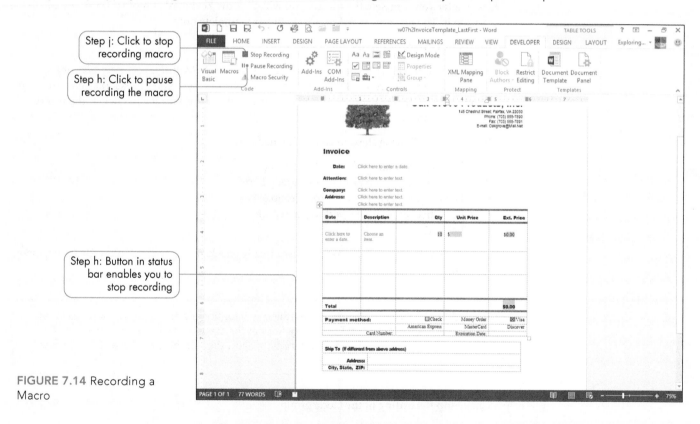

FIGURE 7.14 Recording a Macro

a. Open *w07h1InvoiceTemplate_LastFirst.dotx* and save it as a Word template with the new name **w07h2InvoiceTemplate_LastFirst.dotx**, changing *h1* to *h2*.

b. Click the **DEVELOPER tab** and click **Restrict Editing** to display the Restrict Editing pane. Click **Stop Protection** and close the Restrict Editing pane.

   You must remove the form protection so you can edit the invoice.

c. Click **Design Mode** in the Controls group. Click to position the insertion point on the left side of the Money Order payment method.

d. Click **Record Macro** in the Code group.

The Record Macro dialog box displays so that you can name the macro before you record it. The macro name can consist of up to 80 characters, but no spaces.

> **TROUBLESHOOTING:** If the Developer tab does not display, click the File tab, click Options, click Customize Ribbon, and then click Developer below the *Customize the Ribbon* pane on the right side of the window. Click OK to return to the document.

e. Type **PaymentCheckBox** in the **Macro name box**.

f. Click the **Description box** and type **Inserts a Check Box form field**.

g. Assign a keyboard shortcut to run the macro by completing the following steps:

- Click **Keyboard** to display the Customize Keyboard dialog box.
- Press **Alt+B**.

The dialog box indicates whether the keyboard shortcut is already assigned or not; pay attention to this visual clue of information.

- Click **Assign** and click **Close**.

Later, after you complete the macro, you will click the keyboard combination Alt+B to execute it. The macro is saved in this document template only.

h. Click **OK** to start recording, if necessary.

Word assigns the macro name you entered. You see *Stop Recording* and *Pause Recording* display in the Code group of the Developer tab. The mouse pointer looks like an arrow with an attached recorder. A square button displays on the status bar; if you click it, the macro will stop recording.

i. Perform the following steps to create the macro:

- Click **Legacy tools** in the Controls group.
- Click **Check Box Form Field** in Legacy Forms.
- Click **Properties** in the Controls group.
- Click **Checked** in the *Default value* section.
- Click **OK**.

You insert a check box field that displays already checked next to the Money Order payment method.

> **TROUBLESHOOTING:** If you click something unintentionally or decide you are too far off track for the macro, click Stop Recording. Repeat the steps to begin recording again. You can use the same macro name and description; allow the new macro to overwrite the first attempt when prompted to replace it.

j. Click **Stop Recording** in the Code group.

You can also click the square button in the status bar to stop recording a macro.

k. Save the template.

STEP 2 》 RUN A MACRO

Now that you have a macro that inserts the box to check when indicating the form of payment, you want to run the macro to display the box by other forms of payment. Refer to Figure 7.15 as you complete Step 2.

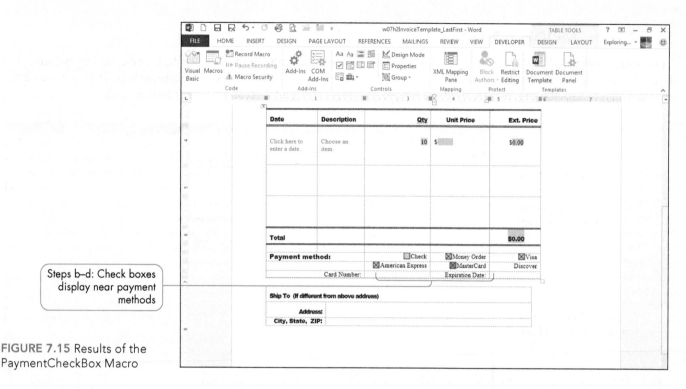

Steps b–d: Check boxes display near payment methods

FIGURE 7.15 Results of the PaymentCheckBox Macro

a. Click to position the insertion point on the left side of the payment method *American Express*.

TIP Make a Backup

To avoid destroying a document due to macro problems, you should save the document prior to running a macro. If the macro does not provide the desired results, you can close the document and open the original document again.

b. Click **Macros** in the Code group.

The macros dialog box displays, and the PaymentCheckBox macro is the only macro available to run.

c. Click **PaymentCheckBox**, if necessary, and click **Run**.

Word runs the macro and inserts a checked box next to the American Express payment method.

TROUBLESHOOTING: The macro security level is too high if you receive a message stating that macros are disabled. A high security level protects you from running a macro that contains a virus. To disable this security so the macro can run, click Macro Security on the Developer tab, click *Enable all macros (not recommended; potentially dangerous code can run)*, and then click OK. Be sure to reset the security to *Disable all macros with notification* after completing this exercise.

d. Click to position the insertion point on the left side of the payment method *MasterCard* and click **Alt+B**.

Word runs the macro again and inserts a checked box next to the MasterCard payment method.

e. Save the template.

STEP 3 ≫ MODIFY A MACRO

The macro works well, but you realize that you only want one of the payment methods to be checked by default. Rather than delete each one and start all over, you modify the macro using the Visual Basic editor. Then you run the macro again to replace the incorrectly checked boxes. Refer to Figure 7.16 as you complete Step 3.

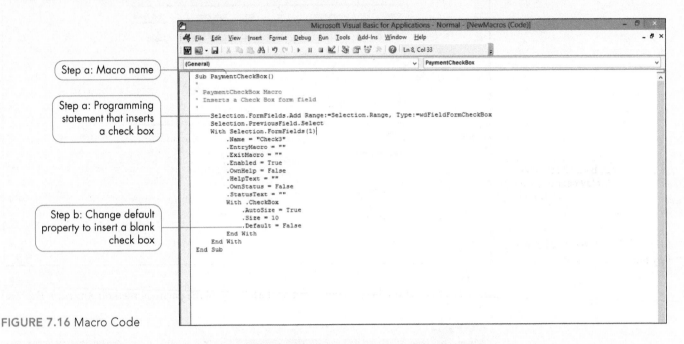

FIGURE 7.16 Macro Code

Labels on figure:
- Step a: Macro name
- Step a: Programming statement that inserts a check box
- Step b: Change default property to insert a blank check box

Code shown:
```
Sub PaymentCheckBox()
'
' PaymentCheckBox Macro
' Inserts a Check Box form field
'
    Selection.FormFields.Add Range:=Selection.Range, Type:=wdFieldFormCheckBox
    Selection.PreviousField.Select
    With Selection.FormFields(1)
        .Name = "Check3"
        .EntryMacro = ""
        .ExitMacro = ""
        .Enabled = True
        .OwnHelp = False
        .HelpText = ""
        .OwnStatus = False
        .StatusText = ""
        With .CheckBox
            .AutoSize = True
            .Size = 10
            .Default = False
        End With
    End With
End Sub
```

a. Press **Alt+F8** to display the Macros dialog box. Select **PaymentCheckBox** in the **Macro name list** if necessary and click **Edit**.

The Visual Basic Editor opens so that you can edit the programming statements. You will modify the Default statement near the end of the code, which shows a *True* value; this causes the box to display as checked.

b. Delete the word *True* at the end of the statement .*Default = True* and replace it with the word **False**.

> **TROUBLESHOOTING:** Do not delete any other part of the Default statement or any other statements. If you do, the macro may not run correctly. If you accidentally delete programming statements, refer to Figure 7.16 to retype them and edit the Default statement again.

c. Click the **FILE tab** and click **Close and Return to Microsoft Word**.

You are ready to run the macro again to replace the checked boxes with boxes that are not checked.

d. Save the template.

STEP 4 ≫ RUN AN EDITED MACRO

Now that your macro is revised, you can replace the checked boxes for each payment method on the invoice. You want to leave only one box checked—the one that displays beside the Visa payment method. You select each one individually and run the macro to replace the form field check boxes. Refer to Figure 7.17 as you complete Step 4.

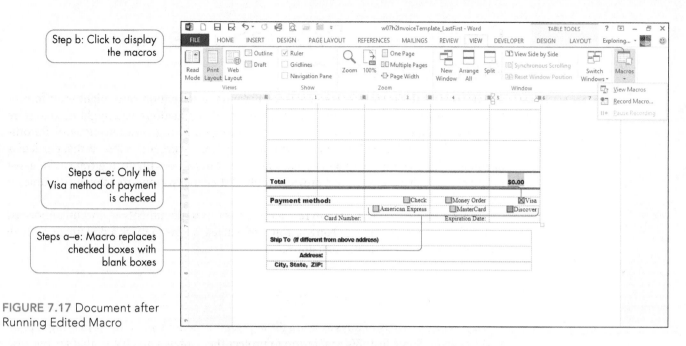

Step b: Click to display the macros

Steps a–e: Only the Visa method of payment is checked

Steps a–e: Macro replaces checked boxes with blank boxes

FIGURE 7.17 Document after Running Edited Macro

a. Select the checked box that displays beside *Money Order*.

> **TROUBLESHOOTING:** If you do not properly select the original check box, the macro will insert a second check box beside the Money Order payment method. Use Shift+→ to select the check box, if necessary.

b. Click the **VIEW tab**, click the **Macros arrow**, and then click **View Macros**.

The Macros dialog box displays so that you can run a macro.

c. Click **PaymentCheckBox** in the *Macro name* box and click **Run**.

The checked box is replaced by a box that does not display as checked.

d. Select the checked box that displays beside *American Express* and press **Alt+B**.

e. Press **Alt+B** to replace the checked box beside *MasterCard*, position the insertion point beside *Discover*, and then run the macro again.

After you run the macro, all payment types display beside a box and only the Visa payment displays beside a checked box.

f. Click the **FILE tab** and click **Save As**. Click **Browse**, click the **Save as type arrow**, and then select **Word Macro-Enabled Template**. If necessary, navigate to the folder where your student files are stored and click **Save** to save the template as **w07h2InvoiceTemplate_LastFirst**.

g. Save and close the file, and submit it based on your instructor's directions.

Document Protection and Authentication

As you work with documents containing confidential information, you might want to protect those documents from unauthorized access. In other situations, you might need to store reference documents, such as policies and procedures, on an organization's network for others to read but not change. You might also want to assure document recipients that particular documents have come from you and have not been tampered with during transit. To assist in situations such as these, Word provides tools that enable you to protect your documents on many levels.

In this section, you will learn to restrict permissions to documents against unauthorized access, formatting, or content changes. You also will learn how to mark a document as final, set passwords, and add digital signatures.

Applying Document Restrictions

Word provides a variety of ways to save a file to preserve the content or the formatting applied to the content. Some features enable you to protect the contents of a file so that anyone else who opens it cannot change the contents in any way. Other features allow the content to be altered, but restrict the use of formatting tools such as the bold feature or predefined styles. You can use these restrictive features independently or in combination with others.

Mark a Document as Final

STEP 1 ❯❯ You may have the occasion to share a file with other people, but before you send it you want to make it a read-only file, which prevents others from changing the document. The *Mark as Final* command enables you to create a read-only file and sets the property to Final on the status bar. To alert the reader to this status, it displays an icon in the status bar to indicate the file is in its final form, as shown in Figure 7.18. This is a helpful command for communicating with other people that the document is not a draft but a completed and final version. It also prevents unintentional changes to the document. When marked as final, typing, editing, and proofing marks do not display; all commands in the Ribbon are grayed out; and the document cannot be modified. To use this command, do the following:

1. Click the FILE tab.
2. Click Protect Document.
3. Select *Mark as Final*.

Even though this feature provides a way to communicate the status of the document and enables you to set it as read-only, it does not completely secure the document. *Mark as Final* is a toggle setting and anyone can remove the status from the document as easily as it is set. Additionally, if you use the *Mark as Final* command on a Word 2013 document, it will not retain the read-only status if opened in an earlier version of Word. Therefore, Restricting Editing is a more permanent way of preventing changes from being made to a document.

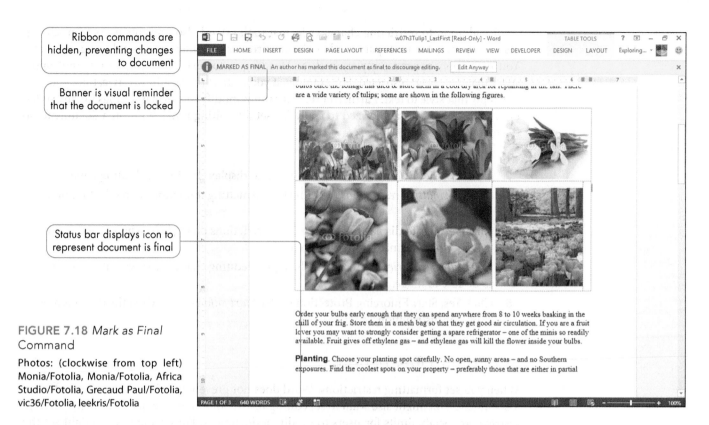

FIGURE 7.18 *Mark as Final* Command

Photos: (clockwise from top left) Monia/Fotolia, Monia/Fotolia, Africa Studio/Fotolia, Grecaud Paul/Fotolia, vic36/Fotolia, leekris/Fotolia

Set Formatting Restrictions

STEP 2>>

Organizations often use specific styles and formatting to ensure consistency among documents. The person who oversees document formatting might create or modify styles that should not be changed by other users. To ensure that others do not modify formatting or styles, you can set *formatting restrictions* on documents. When you set formatting restrictions, character formatting tools, such as bold and font size, are unavailable, as shown in Figure 7.19.

FIGURE 7.19 Formatting Restrictions Disable Commands on the Home Tab

In addition to restricting character format tools, Word also prevents users from changing the formats for font, paragraph, column, drop caps, bullets and numbering, and tabs. You may apply approved styles, such as Heading 1, to text. However, you cannot apply styles that have been restricted. For example, if you restrict the Heading 3 style, then you cannot apply that style to text. Furthermore, you cannot modify the format settings for any styles, even those the user is authorized to apply. To set formatting restrictions on a document, do the following:

1. Click the DEVELOPER tab.
2. Click Restrict Editing in the Protect group to display the Restrict Editing pane.
3. Click *Formatting restrictions* to define the formatting limitations to a selection of styles.
4. Click Settings to display the Formatting Restrictions dialog box, where you can specify exactly which formatting options to disable.
5. Click *Editing restrictions* to define the type of editing changes that you allow the users to be able to make.
6. Click Yes, Start Enforcing Protection under *Start enforcement* when the document is ready for distribution.

Set Editing Restrictions

STEP 3 » When you set formatting restrictions, Word does not prevent you from changing content in a document. You might also want to set editing restrictions on particular documents. ***Editing restrictions*** specify limits for users to modify a document. For example, you might set the Tracked changes editing restriction to make sure the Track Changes feature is active when users make any changes to the document. Doing so lets you know what edits are made to collaborative documents, even if the users forget to activate Track Changes themselves. Other types of editing restrictions include limiting users to inserting comments without changing document content, restricting data entry to fields or unprotected areas within a form, and preventing users from making any changes to a letterhead template.

To set editing restrictions on a document, do the following:

1. Click the DEVELOPER tab.
2. Click Restrict Editing in the Protect group to display the Restrict Editing pane.
3. Click the *Allow only this type of editing in the document* checkbox under *Editing restrictions* to show the four editing restrictions, as outlined in Table 7.3.
4. Select one of the four restrictions.
5. Click Yes, Start Enforcing Protection under *Start enforcement* to activate the protection.

TABLE 7.3 Editing Restrictions

Restriction Type	Description
Tracked changes	Enables the track changes feature automatically and marks document with any changes made.
Comments	Users can add comments to the document but cannot make any other changes.
Filling in forms	Users can insert information into form controls or fields but cannot modify other content.
No changes (Read only)	Users cannot make any changes to the document; they can only view it.

Set Exceptions for Restricted Documents

STEP 4> If you apply the editing restriction *Comments* or *No changes (Read only)*, you can specify user exceptions. A **user exception** is an individual or group of individuals who are allowed to edit all or specific parts of a restricted document. For example, you might want all team members to edit only a particular section of a collaborative document. You can create an exception by enabling users to edit that section only. You can create various user exceptions throughout a document by enabling some individuals to edit particular text, while enforcing the editing restrictions for other individuals. Word color-codes text for which you create different user exceptions.

The default check box in the Exceptions list is *Everyone*. You can add individual users or groups to the list of exceptions by doing the following:

1. Click *More users* to open the Add Users dialog box, as shown in Figure 7.20.
2. Type user names, domains, or e-mail addresses for individuals you want to add, separated by semicolons.
3. Click OK. After you add users, you can continue selecting text and clicking the appropriate user name to create a user exception for editing text.

Type name or ID in this area

FIGURE 7.20 Add Users Who Are Exceptions to Editing Restrictions

You must install a special service to add users in the Add Users dialog box. **Information Rights Management (IRM)** services are designed to help you control who can access documents containing sensitive or confidential information. By using an IRM, you can specify different users and the types of permissions you grant to them. If the IRM Services Client is not installed on your computer, a prompt to download it will display when you try to open files that have been rights-managed. Follow the prompts to download and install the software. If you work in a network lab, you might not be able to install it. Use Help to learn more about permissions, IRM, and adding users as exceptions.

Remove Editing Restrictions

If, for whatever reason, you want to remove the editing restrictions, do the following:

1. Click the DEVELOPER tab.
2. Click Restrict Editing in the Protect group to display the Restrict Editing pane.
3. Click Stop Protection at the bottom of the Restrict Editing pane.
4. If the formatting restrictions are password-protected, you must enter the correct password.
5. Click OK. If you did not assign a password, the restrictions are automatically removed. If you applied both formatting and editing restrictions, clicking Stop Protection removes both types of restrictions.
6. If you want to remove only one type of restriction, you must reset the restriction you want to continue to enforce in the Restrict Editing pane.

Setting Passwords to Open a Document

STEP 1> When creating the form in Hands-On Exercise 1, you had the opportunity to set a password for the document. Setting passwords is one way to secure a document. For example, you might want to password-protect highly confidential documents from being opened by unauthorized users. This is helpful when you need to store a document on a network drive but do not want everyone to be able to open the document. When you assign a password to the document, only those who know the password can open the document. Passwords are case-sensitive, meaning they must match upper- and lowercase letters perfectly. They may consist of letters, numbers, and symbols; a good password will use a combination of all three. You may even use a combination of upper- and lowercase characters, such as EW7_proj_2.

To set a password that must be entered before a document will open, do the following:

1. Click the FILE tab.
2. Click Save As.
3. Click Browse.
4. Click Tools.
5. Click General Options, as shown in Figure 7.21.
6. Type your password in the *Password to open* box.
7. Click OK. The Confirm Password dialog box will prompt you to reenter the password.
8. Retype the password.
9. Click OK to close the dialog box.
10. Save the document.

FIGURE 7.21 Open the General Options Dialog Box to Set a Password

Set a Password to Modify a Document

STEP 1 >> You may want to allow others to open a document but not be able to modify the content. To restrict users from modifying a document, do the following:

1. Click the FILE tab.
2. Click Save As.
3. Click Browse.
4. Click Tools.
5. Click General Options.
6. Type the password in the *Password to modify* box. You can set a password containing up to 15 characters.

7. Click OK.

8. Retype the password into the Confirm Password dialog box.

9. Click OK and you will return to the Save As dialog box.

10. Click Save to save the document. Other users can now open the document, but they must know the password to modify the document.

11. When users attempt to open a document protected against unauthorized modifications, the Password dialog box opens (see Figure 7.22).

Type correct password to modify and click OK...

...or click to open the document in Read Only mode

FIGURE 7.22 General Options Dialog Box

Authorized users can type the password in the Password box and click OK. They are able to make changes and save the document with those changes. In Read Only mode, users can make changes; however, they cannot save those changes to the original file. They must choose a different folder or specify a different file name for saving the document through the Save As dialog box.

TIP Set Passwords to Open and Modify a Document

You can assign two passwords to a document—one to open it and another to modify the content. If you choose to use both types, you might prefer to use different passwords for each restriction so that you have the option to authorize another person to open the document but not to modify it by giving them the first password.

Modify a Password to Open or Modify a Document

STEP 2» If you want to change a password, you must know the current password to open or modify the document. With the document open, do the following:

1. Click the FILE tab.

2. Click Save As.

3. Click Browse.

4. Click Tools.

5. Click General Options.

6. Type the replacement password in the *Password to open* or the *Password to modify* box.

7. Click OK.

8. Retype the replacement password into the Confirm Password dialog box.

9. Click OK to close the dialog box.

10. Click Save to save the document.

Delete a Password to Open or Modify a Document

You can remove a password for opening or modifying a document if you decide you no longer want to protect the document with a password. To remove the password, do the following:

1. Open the document using the current password for opening or modifying the document.
2. Click the FILE tab.
3. Click Save As.
4. Click Browse.
5. Click Tools.
6. Click General Options.
7. Select the password in the *Password to open* or the *Password to modify* box.
8. Press Delete on the keyboard to remove it.
9. Click OK to close the dialog box.
10. Click Save to save the document.

Using Digital Signatures to Authenticate Documents

Word uses Microsoft Authenticode technology to enable you to digitally sign a file by using a *digital certificate*—an attachment to a file or e-mail that guarantees the authenticity of the file, provides a verifiable signature, or enables encryption. This authentication is important because as you share files with others, you increase your risk of having files tampered with or infected with a virus. By adding a digital signature to your documents, you confirm through electronic encryption that the information comes from you, is valid, and has not been changed after you signed it. You can use one of the following two ways to use digital signatures to sign Office documents:

- Add an invisible digital signature to a document or
- Add visible signature lines to a document to capture one or more digital signatures.

Attach a Digital Signature to a Document

STEP 5》 When you need to confirm the authenticity of a document, you can attach a digital signature. *Digital signatures* are electronic stamps that display information about the person or organization that obtained the certification. You can obtain a digital certificate from a certification authority such as VeriSign by completing an application and paying a fee. Some companies have in-house security administrators who issue their own digital signatures by using tools such as Microsoft Certificate Server.

If you want to create your own digital certificate for personal use, you need to install the *Digital Certificate for VBA Projects* from Microsoft Office. This program allows you to create a self-signed digital signature that you can use for personal macros on the specific machine that you use to create the digital signature. When you sign your document, you are validating its contents, and the document remains signed until it is modified. Therefore, signing a document and attaching the signature should be the last action you take before you distribute it. Adding a digital signature causes the document to be marked as final, so it also becomes a read-only document.

To install the *Digital Certificate for VBA Projects* from Microsoft Office to your computer, do the following:

1. Open File Explorer.
2. Type SELFCERT.EXE in the *Search Programs and Files* box. You do not have to type the file name in all caps.

3. When File Explorer opens and displays the location of the file, double-click it. The SELFCERT.EXE file should be located in the C:\Program Files\Microsoft Office\ Office15 folder.

4. The Create Digital Certificate dialog box opens and provides information about the self-certification program.

5. Type your name in the Your Certificate's Name box.

6. Click OK. A message box appears, stating that you successfully created a certificate. If a system message indicates that your certificate is unauthorized, you can still use it to practice working with digital certificates.

7. Click OK to close the message box.

To use the built-in digital signature feature, you must first save the document and do the following:

1. Click the FILE tab.

2. Click Protect Document.

3. Select *Add a Digital Signature*.

4. Click OK to the Microsoft Word dialog box that explains the feature if this is the first time you use this feature. After that, your signature stamp will attach automatically, as shown in Figure 7.23, but you can change the stamp if more than one certificate is available.

5. Type in the purpose for signing the document, although it is not required.

FIGURE 7.23 Add a Digital Signature

If you decide that a digital signature is not needed for a document, you can view and remove the digital signature from a signed document by doing the following:

1. Click the FILE tab.

2. Click View Signatures to display the Signatures pane, which lists all signatures attached to the document.

3. In the Signatures pane, you can click a particular signature to view a menu that includes Signature Details and Remove Signature.

4. When all signatures are removed, the document is no longer marked as final and all formatting commands are available.

Add a Signature Line in a Document

STEP 6 ▶ Word allows you to insert a signature line into a document. The *signature line* enables individuals and companies to distribute and collect signatures, and then process forms or documents electronically without the need to print and fax or mail. The digital signatures, especially if verified by a certifying authority, provide an authentic record of the signer and enable the document to be verified in the future.

When the document opens and the signature line displays, users can type a signature, select a digital image of a signature, or write a signature if they use a tablet PC. After the user inserts his or her signature using one of the options listed above, a digital signature tag is attached to the document to authenticate the identity of the signer and the document becomes read-only to prevent modifications to the content. To insert a signature line, do the following:

1. Click the INSERT tab.
2. Click the Signature Line arrow in the Text group.
3. Click Microsoft Office Signature Line.
4. Click OK to the Microsoft Word dialog box, if it displays.
5. Enter information about the signer when the Signature Setup dialog box displays, as shown in Figure 7.24.
6. Enter the expected signer's name, title, e-mail address, and any additional instructions you want to display near the signature line.
7. Enable signers to add comments to the document and attach the current date to the document when they sign if you prefer.

FIGURE 7.24 Insert a
Signature Line

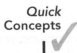

Quick Concepts

1. What are the reasons for using editing restrictions on certain documents? *p. 454*
2. Why do you want to set a password to open a document? *p. 455*
3. Explain the reason for using a digital signature. *p. 458*

Hands-On Exercises

Watch the Video
for this Hands-
On Exercise!

MyITLab®
HOE3 Training

3 Document Protection and Authentication

When people purchase tulips, Cassie Artman wants to include information about tulip bulbs in their packages. You have put together a document about tulips, but you want staff members to review it for accuracy. After they return the document to you, edits will be incorporated, a final version will be saved, and you can then mark it with a digital signature. You also want to add a signature line to the invoice so that when it is delivered to a customer he or she will know it has come from the company and is a valid document.

Skills covered: Set a Password to Open a Document and Mark as Final • Set Formatting Restrictions and Modify a Document Password • Set Editing Restrictions • Set Exceptions for Restricted Documents • Attach a Digital Signature to a Document • Insert a Signature Line in a Document

STEP 1 ≫ SET A PASSWORD TO OPEN A DOCUMENT AND MARK AS FINAL

The tulip information document that will accompany all purchases has been created, and you believe it to be in final form. To prevent anyone from opening it, you password-protect the file. Additionally, to prevent any accidental changes to the document when it is open, you mark it as final. Refer to Figure 7.25 as you complete Step 1.

Step d: Set password to open document

Step c: Click Tools to display General Options dialog box

FIGURE 7.25 Display the General Options Dialog Box to Set a Password

    a. Open the document *w07h3Tulip*.

        This is a draft of the document, and you want to password-protect it until all modifications have been finalized.

    b. Click the **FILE tab** and click **Save As**. Click **Browse** and replace the file name with **w07h3Tulip1_LastFirst**. Navigate to the folder where your student files are stored, but do not close the Save As dialog box.

    c. Click **Tools** and click **General Options**.

        The General Options dialog box displays; this is where you set passwords to open and modify a document.

> **TROUBLESHOOTING:** The Tools menu is located in the Save As dialog box. If you closed that dialog box, click the File tab, click Save As, and then repeat step c.

d. Type **W7h3a** in the **Password to open box**.

Security experts recommend you use a combination of upper- and lowercase letters, numbers, and special characters when you create passwords. Passwords are case-sensitive, meaning they must match upper- and lowercase letters perfectly. For that reason, you must pay special attention to capitalization when setting and using passwords to protect a document.

e. Click **OK**. In the Confirm Password dialog box, type **W7h3a** in the **Reenter password to open box**, click **OK**, and then click **Save** in the Save As dialog box.

> **TROUBLESHOOTING:** If you do not type the same password using the same capitalization, an error message appears stating you have not typed the same password. Click OK to close the message box, delete the passwords in the General Options dialog box, and then type the passwords again.

f. Click the **FILE tab**, click **Protect Document**, and then click **Mark as Final** to avoid accidental editing. Click **OK** in all Microsoft Word dialog boxes. Click the **back arrow** to display the document.

Dialog boxes might display after you mark the document as final. The first informs you the document will be marked as final and saved. The second dialog box informs you that the document has been marked final and all editing marks are disabled. After these dialog boxes close and you return to the document, the banner displays at the top to indicate the document is *Marked as Final*.

g. Close the document.

 TIP **Don't Show This Message Again**

If a Microsoft Word dialog box displays *Don't show this message again*, you can click the option so the dialog box will not display in the future. However, if you work in a lab environment, you should ask for instructor permission before changing this type of setting.

STEP 2 ≫ SET FORMATTING RESTRICTIONS AND MODIFY A DOCUMENT PASSWORD

You are now ready to send the tulip information to a marketing manager so she can look over the document. She can make suggestions for changing the format because she will know how best to present the information. However, you do not want her to change any of the content of the document because that is not her area of expertise. You apply restrictions that only enable the marketing manager to change formatting, and you secure the restrictions with a password. Refer to Figure 7.26 as you complete Step 2.

Step f: Information about format restrictions

Step f: Check mark indicates that you may apply style

Step f: Indicates styles selected if you click Recommended Minimum

Step f: Click to enable AutoFormat changes, such as changing straight quotation marks to curly quotation marks

FIGURE 7.26 Formatting Restrictions Dialog Box

a. Open *w07h3Tulip1_LastFirst*, enter the password **W7h3a** when prompted, and then click **OK**. Click **Edit Anyway** in the yellow bar across the top of the page to release the read-only status.

b. Click the **FILE tab** and click **Save As**. Click **Browse**. Type **w07h3Tulip2_LastFirst** in the **File name box** and click **Tools**, and then click **General Options**. Remove the existing password. Click **OK** and click **Save** to return to the document.

If a Microsoft Word dialog box displays with a warning that your document will be upgraded to the newest file format, click OK.

c. Click the **REVIEW tab** and click **Restrict Editing** in the Protect group to display the Restrict Editing pane.

d. Click **Limit formatting to a selection of styles** on the pane. Click **Settings** to display the Formatting Restrictions dialog box.

In this dialog box, you can enable users to apply styles of your choice.

e. Click **None**.

Notice that the check marks beside each style disappear. If you click OK, none of the styles can be used in this document. Next, you reselect the styles.

f. Click **All** and click **OK**. Click **No** in the Microsoft Word dialog box that asks if you want to remove styles that are not allowed.

The user can now apply any style. However, they cannot modify the styles. This option is useful when you want to be sure anyone who edits the document uses a style that is included in Office 2013.

g. Click **Yes, Start Enforcing Protection** on the Restrict Editing pane.

The Start Enforcing Protection dialog box opens. You can use this dialog box to set a password required to remove formatting restrictions.

h. Type **W7h3b** in the **Enter new password (optional) box**. Retype the password in the **Reenter password to confirm box** and click **OK**.

i. Click the **HOME tab**.

Most commands on the Home tab are dimmed, indicating that the document is restricted against formatting changes.

j. Position the insertion point in the title *Tulip Basics* and click **Title** from the Styles gallery.

Word enables you to apply a different style; however, you cannot change character or font attributes or paragraph alignment.

k. Save the document.

You want the company botanist to review the tulip information for accuracy. The botanist has only basic computer skills, and you want to make sure he does not make any major changes to the document which would alter placement of information or graphics. You use features to restrict the document so that the botanist can only insert comments, and you add a password so he will not be able to remove the restrictions. Refer to Figure 7.27 as you complete Step 3.

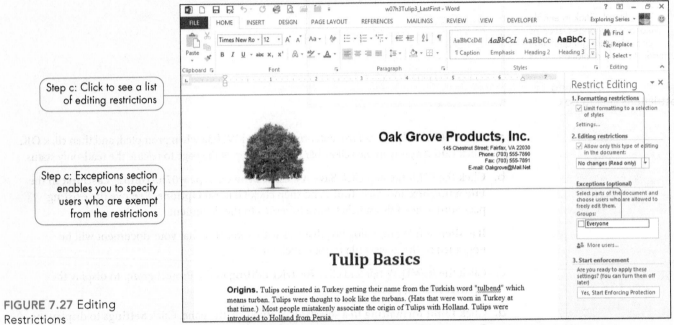

FIGURE 7.27 Editing Restrictions

a. Save the document as **w07h3Tulip3_LastFirst.**

b. Click **Stop Protection**, which displays at the bottom of the Restrict Editing pane, type **W7h3b** in the **Unprotect Document dialog box**, and then click **OK**.

The formatting restriction is removed so that users may use any format features on the document.

> **TROUBLESHOOTING:** If the Restrict Editing pane does not display, click the Review tab and click Restrict Editing.

c. Click **Allow only this type of editing in the document** in the *Editing restrictions* section.

The *Editing restrictions* arrow is available so that you can specify the type of editing to restrict. Additionally, an *Exceptions (optional)* section appears on the pane so that you can apply exceptions to the editing restrictions, as shown in Figure 7.27.

d. Click the **Editing restrictions arrow** and click **Comments**.

e. Click **Yes, Start Enforcing Protection**. Type **W7h3c** in the **Enter new password (optional) box**. Retype the password in the **Reenter password to confirm box**. Click **OK**.

Users are now restricted from editing the document content. They can only insert comments. The formatting restrictions are also still in place.

f. Press **Ctrl+Home** to move the insertion point to the beginning of the document. Select the title *Tulip Basics* and press **Delete**.

You cannot delete the text. The status bar displays the message *This modification is not allowed because the selection is locked*. The Restrict Editing pane now displays buttons to show document regions you can edit. However, because you restricted editing to comments only, no regions are available for editing.

g. Click the **REVIEW tab**, click **New Comment**, and then type **Should we call this "Bulb Basics"?**

Because of the type of editing restrictions on the document you can insert a comment. The comment balloon appears on the side of the text.

h. Save the document.

STEP 4 ›› SET EXCEPTIONS FOR RESTRICTED DOCUMENTS

After reflecting on the situation, you notice one section of the document where you should allow the botanist to modify content. You change the editing restrictions for the document to allow access to that one section, and you reinforce the restrictions for the rest of the document again. Refer to Figure 7.28 as you complete Step 4.

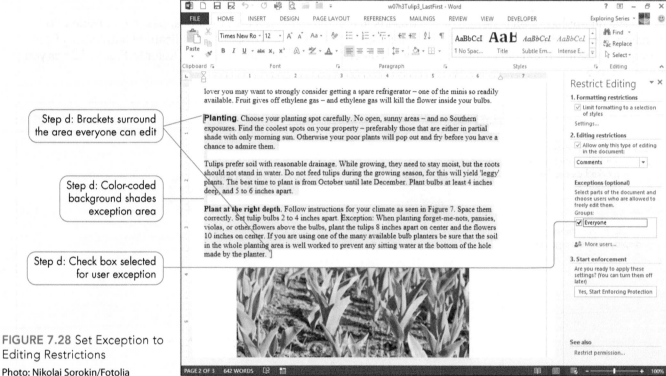

Step d: Brackets surround the area everyone can edit

Step d: Color-coded background shades exception area

Step d: Check box selected for user exception

FIGURE 7.28 Set Exception to Editing Restrictions
Photo: Nikolai Sorokin/Fotolia

a. Display the Restrict Editing pane, if necessary. Click **Stop Protection**. Type **W7h3c** in the **Password box** and click **OK**.

b. Confirm the first two boxes on the pane contain check marks. If they do not, click to mark those boxes.

c. Scroll to the top of page 2 and select the paragraph title *Planting*. Press **Shift+↓** to select the three paragraphs that follow it. Do not select the graphic titled *Figure 7 Planting Tulip Bulbs*.

You want to set a user exception to allow all users to edit this section of the document. You do not want to include the graphic in your selection.

d. Click **Everyone** in the *Exceptions (optional)* section of the Restrict Editing pane. Deselect the text.

The paragraphs you selected display with a light gray background, indicating that the user exception is applied to them.

> **TROUBLESHOOTING:** If you are unable to click the check box for *Everyone* in the *Exception* section of the Restrict Editing pane, make sure you have first selected text in the document.

e. Click **Yes, Start Enforcing Protection**. Type **W7h3d** in the **Enter new password (option) box**. Retype the password in the **Reenter password to confirm box**. Click **OK**.

f. Select the graphic titled *Figure 7 Planting Tulip Bulbs* and press **Delete**.

You cannot delete the graphic because it is protected against editing.

g. Click the paragraph heading *Planting*, click the **HOME tab**, and then click **Book Title** from the Styles gallery.

Word enables this editing because you are a part of *Everyone* included in the user exception for the heading.

h. Save the document.

STEP 5 » ATTACH A DIGITAL SIGNATURE TO A DOCUMENT

After the document has been reviewed by the experts in the company, you take their changes into consideration and finalize it for distribution. When sent in a digital format, you want it to display a certificate of authenticity from the company; you insert a digital signature in the document, which also marks it as final. Refer to Figure 7.29 as you complete Step 5.

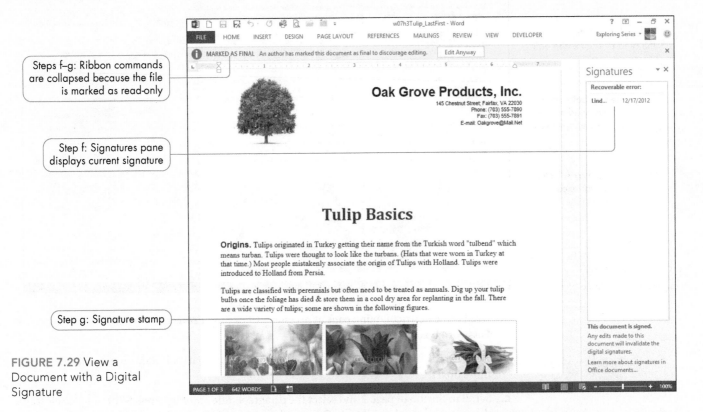

Steps f–g: Ribbon commands are collapsed because the file is marked as read-only

Step f: Signatures pane displays current signature

Step g: Signature stamp

FIGURE 7.29 View a Document with a Digital Signature

a. Open File Explorer. Type **SELFCERT.EXE** in the **Search Programs and Files box**. When Windows Explorer opens and displays the location of the file, double-click it.

You do not have to type the file name in all caps. The *SELFCERT.EXE* file should be located in the C:\Program Files\Microsoft Office\Office15 folder. The Create Digital Certificate dialog box opens and provides information about the self-certification program.

> **TROUBLESHOOTING:** If you cannot find the *SELFCERT.EXE* file, or if your lab computer will not allow you to install the program, continue to read over the steps in this activity so that you can see how digital signatures work.

b. Type your name in the **Your Certificate's Name box** and click **OK**.

A message box appears, stating that you successfully created a certificate. Although your certificate is unauthorized, you can still use it to practice working with digital certificates.

c. Click **OK** to close the message box.

d. Remove all restrictions and prepare the final version of the document by completing the following steps:

- Click **Stop Protection** in the Restrict Editing pane, enter the password **W7h3d** when prompted, and then click **OK**.
- Remove all check marks from the Restrict Editing pane. When the Microsoft Word dialog box displays and asks if you want to remove the ignored exceptions, click **No**.
- Close the Restrict Editing pane.
- Scroll to the top of page 1. Right-click the **comment balloon** and click **Delete Comment**.

e. Save the document.

f. Click the **FILE tab**, click **Protect Document**, and then click **Add a Digital Signature**. Click **OK** in the Microsoft Word dialog box, if necessary.

The Sign dialog box displays. Your name displays at the bottom of the window because you recently created a digital signature.

> **TROUBLESHOOTING:** If your name does not display in the Sign dialog box, click Change to display the Select Certificate dialog box. Click your name from the *Issued to* column and click OK.

g. Type **To validate contents** in the **Purpose for signing this document box**. Click **Sign** to close the Sign dialog box. Click **OK** to close the Signature Confirmation dialog box and click the back arrow to return to the document.

A yellow information bar displays *MARKED AS FINAL An author has marked this document as final to discourage editing. Edit Anyway* below the ribbon. The Ribbon commands are hidden because the document has been marked as read-only. The signature stamp displays in the status bar.

h. Click once on the signature stamp in the status bar.

The Signatures pane displays on the right side of the document. If you click a signature, a menu arrow displays enabling you to click an option to view details about the signature or to delete the signature.

i. Save and close the file, and submit it based on your instructor's directions.

STEP 6 ≫ INSERT A SIGNATURE LINE IN A DOCUMENT

You decide to add a signature line to the invoice, which will be signed by the person who completes the order. When the invoice is printed, the customer service representative can sign his or her name on the signature line. When he or she sends the invoice in digital format, the representative can type in his or her name or insert a graphic representation of his or her signature. Refer to Figure 7.30 as you complete Step 6.

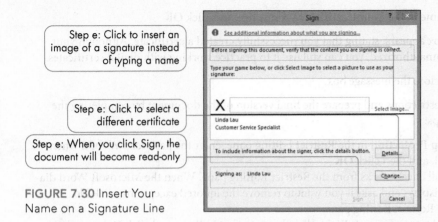

Step e: Click to insert an image of a signature instead of typing a name

Step e: Click to select a different certificate

Step e: When you click Sign, the document will become read-only

FIGURE 7.30 Insert Your Name on a Signature Line

a. Open the document *w07h2InvoiceTemplate_LastFirst.dotm* and save it as a Word Document, **w07h3Invoice_LastFirst**, changing the *h2* to *h3* and removing the word *Template*.

You are opening a template document but saving it as a Word document file.

b. Press **Ctrl+End** to move the insertion point to the end of the document.

c. Click the **INSERT tab** and click **Signature Line**. The Signature Setup dialog box displays.

d. Type your name in the **Suggested signer box**. Type **Customer Service Specialist** in the **Suggested signer's title box**. Type **oakgrove@mail.net** in the **Suggested signer's e-mail address box**. Click **OK**.

The signature line displays in the document, as well as the signer's information that you entered in the Signature Setup dialog box.

e. Insert a signature by completing the following steps:

- Double-click the signature line to display the Sign dialog box. Click **OK** in the Microsoft Word dialog box if necessary.

  If you did not set up the signature ID in the previous step, you will see a dialog box that says *Get a Digital ID*. You need to repeat Steps 5a–c before you can continue with this step.

- Type your own name in the **Type your name below box** or click **Select Image . . .** to select a picture to use as your signature box.
- Click **Sign**.
- Click **OK** in the Signature Confirmation dialog box, if necessary.

The name displays above the signature line, and the date displays in the top-right corner of the *signature line* box. The document is marked as read-only, and formatting features are grayed out.

f. Close the document, exit Word, and then submit it based on your instructor's directions.

Chapter Objectives Review

After reading this chapter, you have accomplished the following objectives:

1. Create an electronic form.

- Before you can create a document template, the Developer tab must be visible on the Ribbon. Then, you need to save the document as a Word template file.

2. Insert form controls.

- If you want users to fill out a form electronically, you must insert form controls, also called form fields, into the form template.
- Forms can be created to automatically calculate data values or update calculations by clicking a certain button or when exiting from Word.

3. Protect a form.

- After you create a form, you can apply protection that prevents any modification except data entry.
- After an electronic form is created and protected, you may e-mail it to the user or upload it to a Web site.

4. Create a macro.

- When you record a macro, Word records a series of keystrokes and command selections and converts the tasks into specifically coded statements.
- Before recording a macro, you should decide what you want to accomplish with your macro, and then you should plan exactly which commands and tasks to include.
- When you start the macro, you can save it in the current document only or you can save it to the Normal template, where it will be available in all documents.

5. Run a macro.

- The process of playing back or using a macro is called running a macro.
- A macro has the potential to include code that imposes harmful viruses onto your computer. Fortunately, you can edit the security settings in the Trust Center.
- You can change the macro security settings using the Developer tab.

6. Apply document restrictions.

- The *Mark as Final* command enables you to create a read-only file, and the status property is set to Final. This is a helpful command for communicating with other people that the document is not a draft but a completed and final version.
- When you set formatting restrictions, Word does not prevent users from changing content in a document. You might also want to set editing restrictions on particular documents.
- Editing restrictions specify conditions for users to modify a document. If you set the editing restriction to Comments or *No changes (Read only)*, you can specify user exceptions.
- A user exception is an individual or group of individuals who is allowed to edit all or specific parts of a restricted document.
- You can remove all or any type of restrictions from the document any time.

7. Set passwords to open a document.

- Setting passwords is one way to secure a document. When you assign a password to modify the document, only those who know the password can open the document.
- If you want to change a password, you must know the current password to open or modify the document.
- You can remove a password to open or modify a document if you decide you no longer want to protect the document with a password.

8. Use digital signatures to authenticate documents.

- When you need to confirm the authenticity of a document, you can attach a digital signature. Digital signatures are electronic stamps that display information about the person or organization that obtained the certification.
- The signature line enables individuals and companies to distribute and collect signatures, and then process forms or documents electronically without the need to print and fax.

Key Terms Matching

Match the key terms with their definitions. Write the key term letter by the appropriate numbered definition.

a. ActiveX control
b. Check box form field
c. Date Picker
d. Design Mode
e. Digital certificate
f. Digital signature
g. Drop-down list
h. Editing restriction
i. Form control
j. Form template

k. Formatting restriction
l. Information Rights Management (IRM)
m. Legacy form field
n. Macro
o. Macro-Enabled Document
p. Record macro
q. Signature line
r. Text content control
s. User exception
t. Visual Basic for Applications (VBA)

1. _____ A document that defines the standard layout, structure, and formatting of a form. **p. 428**

2. _____ Enables you to view and select the control fields to allow for modifications to the control field layout or options. **p. 431**

3. _____ Helps a user complete a form by displaying prompts such as text boxes and drop-down lists. **p. 430**

4. _____ Used to enter any type of text into a form. **p. 430**

5. _____ Consists of a box that can be checked or unchecked. **p. 430**

6. _____ Enables the user to choose from one of several existing entries. **p. 430**

7. _____ Displays a calendar that the user can click rather than typing in a date. **p. 431**

8. _____ A form element that is created or used in Word 2003 and later. When used in a later version of Word, the document must be opened in Compatibility Mode. **p. 431**

9. _____ A form element designed for use in Office 2007 or later versions that requires a macro to work. **p. 431**

10. _____ A set of instructions that executes a specific task or series of keystrokes that complete a repetitive task. **p. 442**

11. _____ Adds the extension.docm to the file and stores VBA macro code in the document to enable execution of a macro. **p. 442**

12. _____ The process of creating a macro. **p. 442**

13. _____ A programming language that is built into Microsoft Office. **p. 443**

14. _____ Ensures that others do not modify formatting or styles in a document. **p. 453**

15. _____ Specifies limits for users to modify a document. **p. 454**

16. _____ An individual or group that is allowed to edit all or specific parts of a restricted document. **p. 455**

17. _____ Services designed to help control who can access documents containing sensitive or confidential information. **p. 455**

18. _____ An attachment to a file that guarantees the authenticity of the file, provides a verifiable signature, or enables encryption. **p. 458**

19. _____ An electronic stamp that displays information about a person or organization. **p. 458**

20. _____ Enables the user of the document to digitally sign the document. **p. 459**

Multiple Choice

1. Which of the following is true about password protection?

   (a) All documents are automatically saved with a default password.

   (b) The password assigned to a document should use a combination of upper- and lowercase letters, numbers, and special characters.

   (c) A password must be set on a document that is restricted from editing.

   (d) A password cannot be changed after it has been established.

2. When you create a form template that will be broadly distributed outside your organization, you should do all of the following except:

   (a) Insert form controls where needed.

   (b) Protect the template using *Restrict Formatting and Editing* features.

   (c) Save the template with a .dotx extension.

   (d) Set a password to protect the template.

3. Which form control will enable a user to choose from a list of options?

   (a) Drop-Down Box

   (b) Check Box

   (c) Date Picker

   (d) Text

4. Which of the following statements about protecting a form is true?

   (a) The Formatting restrictions of the Restrict Editing pane enable you to prevent users from modifying the content of and the styles used in a form.

   (b) The Formatting restrictions of the Restrict Editing pane enable you to prevent users from adding comments to the document.

   (c) If you forget the password that protects a form, you can recover it by running a macro.

   (d) You cannot specify certain individuals who are exempt from the formatting and editing restrictions placed on a form.

5. Which of the following can you use to authenticate the contents of a document?

   (a) Password

   (b) Digital signature

   (c) Macro

   (d) Form control

6. How can you tell if a document has been digitally signed?

   (a) An icon that looks like a certificate displays on the status bar.

   (b) You must open the Add Digital Signature dialog box.

   (c) A message appears when you open the document.

   (d) A signature line displays at the bottom of the document.

7. When you create a macro in Microsoft Word, where is it stored automatically?

   (a) In the document in which it was created, where it is available only to that document

   (b) In the Normal template, where it is available to every Word document

   (c) In the Macros folder on your OneDrive account

   (d) In the folder on your hard drive that you are using right now

8. Which of the following is the least appropriate advice to give to someone who wants to learn how to create and run macros?

   (a) Decide what you want the macro to accomplish.

   (b) Make a list of the sequence of tasks you want to perform prior to recording the macro.

   (c) Change your macro security settings to enable all macros all the time.

   (d) Practice completing the steps before actually recording the macro.

9. Before you can insert form controls into a form or display the Visual Basic editor to modify macros, what tab must you display in the Ribbon?

   (a) Add-Ins

   (b) Review

   (c) View

   (d) Developer

10. Which statement about a signature line is false?

    (a) If you specify a name and e-mail address of the signer, they do not display with the signature line.

    (b) You can insert a digital image of a signature on the line.

    (c) If you specify instructions for the signer, they display in the document along with the signature line.

    (d) You can have the date inserted automatically when a signature is inserted on the line.

Practice Exercises

1 White Glove Cleaners

You are the marketing manager for White Glove Cleaners, a small but growing company that offers residential and commercial cleaning services. When potential customers are contacted, they receive a printed document that highlights the cleaning services. You recently decided to update the document so it looks more professional and draws attention to key services. Reversing the shading of the headings will enhance important features of the document. So you create a macro to quickly apply the reverse shading to all the appropriate headings. You also want to include a signature line where clients can sign before they return it and set an appointment for a free estimate. After you make the changes, you mark the document as final to prevent further changes. This exercise follows the same set of skills as used in Hands-On Exercises 2 and 3 in the chapter. Refer to Figure 7.31 as you complete this exercise.

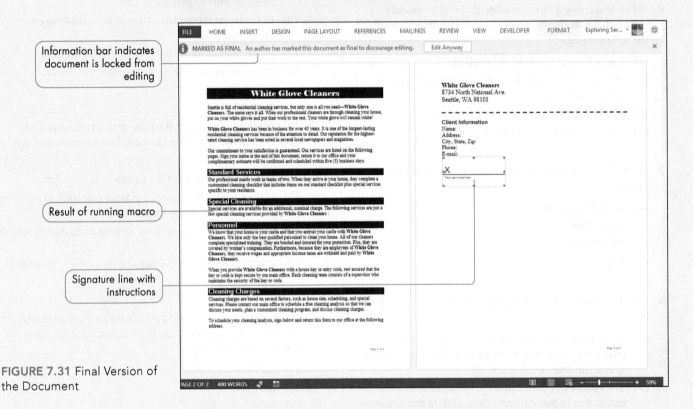

FIGURE 7.31 Final Version of the Document

a. Open the document *w07p1Cleaners*. Click the **FILE tab** and click **Save As**. Click **Browse**. Click the **Save as type arrow** and click **Word Macro-Enabled Document**. Type **w07p1Cleaners_LastFirst** in the **File name box**, navigate to the folder where your student files are stored, uncheck the *Maintain compatibility with previous versions of Word* checkbox, and then click **Save**.

b. Display the **DEVELOPER tab**, if necessary. Click the **FILE tab**, click **Options**, click **Customize Ribbon**, and then check **Developer**, which displays on the right side under the *Customize the Ribbon* section. Click **OK**.

c. Record a macro by completing the following steps:
- Click the left side of the heading *Standard Services* on the first page.
- Click the **DEVELOPER tab**, if necessary, and click **Record Macro** in the Code group.
- Type **reverse** in the **Macro name box**.
- Click **Keyboard** to display the Customize Keyboard dialog box.
- Press **Alt+R** to assign the keystroke combination to the macro.
- Click the **Save changes in arrow**, click **w07p1Cleaners_LastFirst**, and then click **Assign**.
- Click **Close** to return to the document, where the macro recording symbol displays with the pointer. You are now recording the macro.

- Click the **HOME tab**, click the **Border arrow**, and then click **Borders and Shading**.
- Click the **Shading tab**, click the **Style arrow**, click **Solid (100%)**, and then click **OK**.
- Click **Stop Recording** on the status bar.

d. Click the left side of the heading *Special Cleaning* on the first page. Press **Alt+R** to run the macro and apply the reverse effect to the heading. Run the macro on the headings *Personnel* and *Cleaning Charges*.

e. Press **Ctrl+End** to move the insertion point to the bottom of the document. Click the **INSERT tab** and click **Signature Line** in the Text group.

f. Type **Type your name here** in the **Suggested signer box** in the Signature Setup dialog box and click **OK** to insert the signature line in the document.

g. Click the **FILE tab**, click **Protect Document**, and then click **Mark as Final**. Click **OK** in all Microsoft Word dialog boxes that explain the document will be marked as final and saved. Click the back arrow to return to the document.

h. Select the address for White Glove Cleaners and press **Delete**. Because the document is marked as final, it is also protected from any changes and you cannot delete the address.

i. Close the document and submit it based on your instructor's directions.

2 White Glove Cleaners Service Plan

The sales representative for White Glove Cleaners informs you that he would like to use a document that offers more details of the services offered to customers, but he would like it modified as a form. He would like to be able to check off the services that a customer is most interested in contracting from your company. In addition to using a printed form, he indicates that he also communicates with several clients electronically, so he needs an electronic version of the document as well. And he wants it certified to assure the clients that the document is authentic. You make the necessary modifications by replacing bullets with check boxes and adding form controls at the bottom where clients can type their name and address. You protect the form so the clients can only enter their information in the form, and you finish up by adding a digital signature. This exercise follows the same set of skills as used in Hands-On Exercises 1–3 in the chapter. Refer to Figure 7.32 as you complete this exercise.

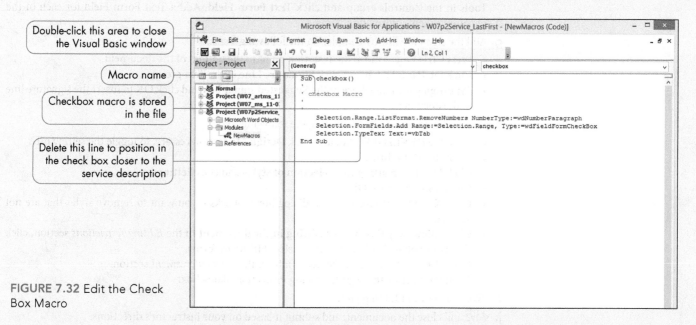

FIGURE 7.32 Edit the Check Box Macro

a. Open *w07p2Service*, click **Edit Anyway**, which displays in yellow at the top of the document, and then save it as a Macro-Enabled document with the name **w07p2Service_LastFirst**.

b. Position the insertion point on the left side of the word *Sweep* that displays in the first bulleted list under the *Entryway* paragraph. Record a macro by completing the following steps:

- Click the **DEVELOPER tab** and click **Record Macro** in the Code group.
- Type **checkbox** in the **Macro name box**.
- Click the **Store macro in arrow**.
- Click **w07p2Service_LastFirst** (document).
- Click **Keyboard**.
- Press **Alt+C**.
- Click the **Save changes in arrow**, click **w07p2Service_LastFirst**, click **Assign**, and then click **Close**.
- Click the **HOME tab**, click the **Bullets arrow**, and then click **None**.
- Click the **DEVELOPER tab**, click **Legacy Tools** in the Controls group, and then click **Check Box Form Field**.
- Press **Tab** and click **Stop Recording** in the Code group.

c. Press ⬇ to move the insertion point to the next bulleted list item that starts *Shine both sides*. Press **Alt+C** to run the macro and replace the bullet with a check box. You adjust the alignment of the check box in the next step.

d. Edit the macro by completing the following steps:

- Click **Macros** in the Code group.
- Click **Checkbox** and click **Edit**.
- Press **Ctrl+End** to move to the bottom of the window and view the programming statements for the checkbox macro.
- Select the third statement, *Selection.TypeText Text:=vbTab*, and press **Delete**.
- Press **Alt+Q** or double-click the top-left corner to close the window.

e. Select the check box and white tab space that follows the first bulleted item (*Sweep*) and press **Delete**. Press **Alt+C** to replay the macro, which removes the space between the check box and the service description. Run the macro and remove any white tab space that follows the bulleted list item on the page (those on the latter pages are completed for you).

f. Move the insertion point to the right side of *Name:* in the *Client Information* section on the last page. Click the **DEVELOPER tab** and click **Design Mode** in the Controls group. Click **Legacy Tools** in the Controls group and click **Text Form Field**. Add a Text Form Field for each of the remaining client information items.

g. Add the signature line by completing the following steps:

- Press **Ctrl+End** to move the insertion point to the bottom of the document.
- Click the **INSERT tab** and click **Signature Line** in the Text group.
- Type **Sign your name here** in the **Suggested signer box** and click **OK** to insert the signature line in the document.

h. Protect the document by completing the following steps:

- Click the **DEVELOPER tab** and click **Design Mode**, if necessary, to toggle the setting off.
- Click **Restrict Editing**.
- Click **Limit formatting to a selection of styles** and click **Settings**.
- Click **None** and click **OK**.
- Click **No** in the Microsoft Word dialog box that asks if you want to remove styles that are not allowed.
- Click **Allow only this type of editing in the document** in the *Editing restrictions* section, click the arrow below that line, and then select **Filling in forms**.
- Click **Yes, Start Enforcing Protection** from the *Start enforcement* section.
- Click **OK** to close the Start Enforcing Protection dialog box.

i. Close the Restrict Editing pane.

j. Save and close the document, and submit it based on your instructor's directions.

1 Real Estate Appraisal Report

You are a real estate appraiser who estimates the value of residential homes. At the end of each week, you must submit a report to your supervisor of the properties you appraised during the past seven days. You decide to create a form that you can fill out quickly, even while you are on location with your laptop. You have a document containing a table for the information, but you decide to automate it using form fields; then you will use features to protect the form and create a digital signature prior to submitting it to your boss. Refer to Figure 7.33 as you complete this exercise.

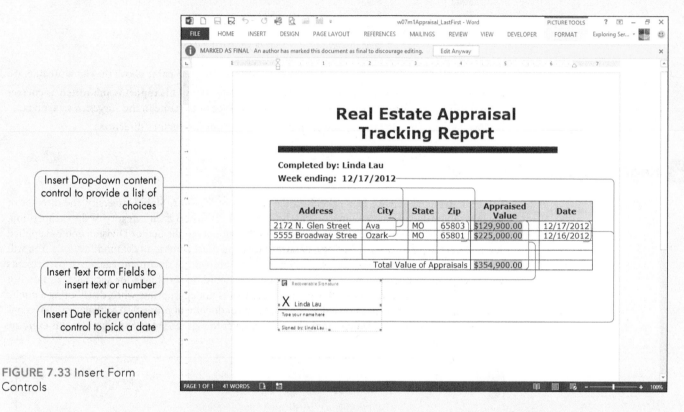

Insert Drop-down content control to provide a list of choices

Insert Text Form Fields to insert text or number

Insert Date Picker content control to pick a date

FIGURE 7.33 Insert Form Controls

a. Open *w07m1Appraisal.dotx* and save it as **w07m1AppraisalTemplate_LastFirst.dotx** (a Word template).

b. Insert a Rich Text Content control on the right side of *Completed by*. This is where you enter your full name.

c. Insert the Date Picker Content control on the right side of *Week ending* and in each cell in the Date column in the table (except for the last Total Value row).

d. Insert Rich Text Content controls in each cell in the Address column (excluding the Total Value row).

DISCOVER

e. Add Drop-Down List Content controls in each cell for City and Zip Code. Since you only assess homes in four cities, populate the *City drop-down list* box with **Ava**, **Salem**, **Ozark**, and **Nixa**. Create a Drop-Down List Content control in the Zip cells for Zip codes using **65800**, **65801**, **65802**, and **65803**. Insert the state abbreviation **MO** in each cell in the state column. *Hint:* You can create one drop-down list control for each category and copy it into other cells in the column.

f. Enter a Text Form Field in each cell of the Appraised Value column. Format the Text Form Field in the last row to calculate the total of the Appraised Value column with dollar formatting. *Hint:* Select the **Calculate on exit property**.

g. Protect the document; allow users to fill in form controls only. Save and close the template.

h. Open the template you just created and save it as **w07m1Appraisal_LastFirst.docx** (a Word document).

i. Fill out the form by entering the following information:
- Type your name in the **Completed by text form control**.
- Select **Today** in the date picker control.
- Type the address and appraised value information below into the table for the first two rows. Select specified dates from the date picker controls.

Address	1387 E. Main Street	8977 N. Fremont Ave.
City	Ava	Ozark
State	MO	MO
Zip	65803	65801
Appraised Value	129,900	225,000
Date	*select* Today	*select yesterday's date*

j. Insert a signature line at the end of the document and type your name above the signature line.

k. Add a digital signature to the document when complete. Type **This report is submitted as correct and valid** as the purpose for signing the document. Type your name in the *Suggested signer* box.

l. Save and close the document, and submit it based on your instructor's directions.

2 Regional Science Fair Results

CREATIVE CASE

After the Regional Science Fair is held on the campus of Missouri State University, the director of the event must document the winners and distribute the awards in each category of the competition. The director's assistant has created an initial list of the winners in the Senior Division and has applied several layers of protection, including a password that you must enter to make modifications. You will open the document, make any necessary changes, and protect the document again. All participants will receive the results via e-mail, and the document should be certifiable for accuracy. You do not want to assign a password to open the document, as that is not appropriate when distributing a public record, but you can use your knowledge of other forms of document protection so that it will be recognized as the official results, which cannot be altered. Refer to Figure 7.34 as you complete this exercise.

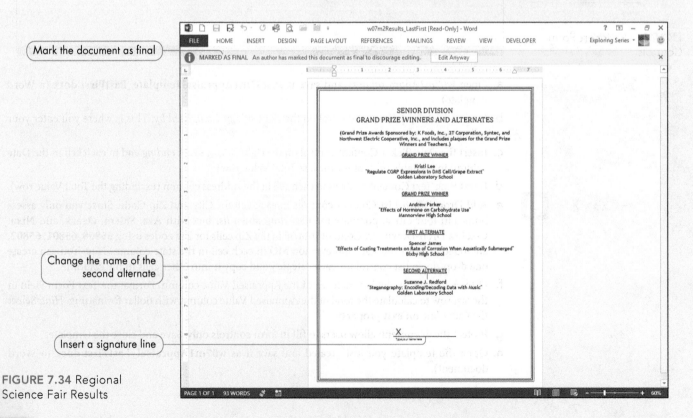

FIGURE 7.34 Regional Science Fair Results

a. Open the *w07m2Results* document and type **Chap7_mid2** as the password to modify the document. Save it as **w07m2Results_LastFirst**.

b. Remove any formatting and editing protection that is applied to the document so you can make the following changes.

c. Change the name of the *Second Alternate*, which is incorrect, to display **Suzanne J. Redford**.

d. Change the main heading of the document to use the **Title style**. Decrease the font size to **20**, center the heading, and then insert a line break so *Senior Division* appears on the first line and the remaining title displays below it.

e. Insert a signature line at the bottom of the page, two lines below *Golden Laboratory School*.

f. Set editing restrictions so the document is read-only and no changes are allowed.

g. Remove the password necessary to open the document.

h. Mark the document as final.

i. Save and close the document, and submit it based on your instructor's directions.

3 | Computer Training Concepts

Your company, Computer Training Concepts, was recently purchased, and the new owner is considering a new name for the organization. His first choice for a new name is *Computer Training Solutions*. The new CEO asked you to automate the process of changing the name of the company on all documentation and correspondence. As company documents are used, modifications to reflect the new name should take place. You decide to create a macro that will quickly search each document and replace the old name with the new name. You are also directed to change the appearance of the new name so it is more distinguishable in the documents. Refer to Figure 7.35 as you complete this exercise.

FIGURE 7.35 Use a Macro to Change Company Name

a. Open *w07m3Training* and save it as a Macro-Enabled document named **w07m3Training_LastFirst**.

b. Create a macro named **ReplaceName**. Save it in the *w07m3Training_LastFirst* file. Press **Alt+R** to run the macro and save changes to the macro in the *w07m3Training_LastFirst* Macro-Enabled document.

   c. Perform the following steps in the ReplaceName macro:
- Activate the **Find and Replace command**.
- Find occurrences of *Computer Training Concepts* and replace them with **Computer Training Solutions**.
- Change the font attributes of Computer Training Solutions to bold and italic from the *Find and Replace* dialog box.
- Replace all occurrences and close the *Find and Replace* dialog box. Stop recording the macro.

   d. Edit the header in each section by replacing *Student's Name* with your name.

   e. Restrict formatting of the document to a selection of styles. When you enforce that protection, use a password to secure it. Set the password to modify as **Chap7_mid3**.

   f. Edit the macro to reflect the CEO's latest decision to name the company **Digital Training Solutions**. Change the *.Text* statement in the macro to find **Computer Training Solutions** and change the *.Replacement. Text* statement to use **Digital Training Solutions**. Save and close the macro, and run it to make the new corrections. Pay special attention to all the locations in the document where the company name displays, including headers and footers.

   g. Insert a Signature Line at the end of the document. The name that displays beneath the line is *Tyler Batten* and his title is *CEO*. Insert **Tyler Batten** in the signature line so that it displays on the document.

   h. Save and close the document, and submit it based on your instructor's directions.

4   Electronic Sales Forms

You are a member of the university's chess club, and your club organizes several fund-raising events throughout the year to raise money for field trips and community projects. One of the popular fund-raising activities is to sell chocolate bars and cookie dough. It has occurred to you that it would be more efficient to use a standardized form to keep track of the sales items. Several club members volunteered to work together to create and test an electronic fund-raising form with macros.

   a. You may use any kind of collaboration tools available to you on the Internet, such as Facebook, Twitter, blogs, Skype, and Google Chat, or the collaboration tools available in your campus's course management content software or the MyITLab, to chat. During the first online chat session, you will do the following:
- Choose a name for the group and select a group leader.
- Develop a list of tasks to complete.
- Assign tasks and responsibilities to each group member.

   b. The team leader will create a OneDrive or Dropbox.com account, where each member can share, upload, view, and open all the documents posted online.

   c. Each member will design the form layout by hand, scan it as a PDF file, and then submit it to the online storage location.

   d. The group will work together to select an appropriate design for the chess club and also decide on the text labels for the form.

   e. The team leader will create the selected form layout.

   f. Team members will take turns working on the corresponding form controls, which may include, but are not limited to, the following:
- Text boxes for contact information such as last and first name, street address, city, state, Zip code, and dates.
- Drop-down lists for item selection.
- Text boxes for quantity sold, unit price, and total sales for each buyer.
- Calculating fields to sum the total sales.

   g. Each member will also create a macro for a specific activity in the form.

   h. The team leader will apply document restrictions by adding the team members to the list of user exceptions to editing restrictions.

   i. The team leader will insert a Signature Line at the bottom of the document. Below the line, display the text *Salesperson*.

j. Save the form template as **w07m4FormTemplate_GroupName.dotx**. Then, populate the form with some test data and save it as a form document with the name **w07m4Form_GroupName.docx**.

k. Post all the individual documents and the final version of the research report to the online storage location.

l. Inform your instructor that the documents are ready for grading, and also give directions to where they are located.

Beyond the Classroom

So Many Features to Choose From

RESEARCH CASE

In this chapter, you learned the benefit of using macros to perform a repetitive task. Other features in Word also help you with a repetitive task. Which feature should you use for a particular task? Take this opportunity to create a chart that lists the features and tools in Word such as macros, Format Painter, and Building Blocks, and compare each feature. Consider a scenario that would require the use of each feature and why you would use one instead of the other. Use Microsoft Word Help to learn more about each feature, if necessary. Save your work as **w07b2Features_LastFirst**, close the document, and then submit it based on your instructor's directions.

Calculating Form Fields

DISASTER RECOVERY

A colleague wants to use a form as a purchase order for his small company. He created the form, but it does not work as he expected. The calculating fields do not function properly, the customer information does not appear as a form field, and to top it off, he's no longer able to type anything into his form. His frustration has forced him to call you and ask for advice on solving his problems. Your task is to troubleshoot the form and make corrections or additions that will turn it into a functioning and professional-looking electronic form that is suitable for use. Open the file *w07b3Problem.dotx* and save it as **w07b3Problem_LastFirst. dotx**. Determine the reason why the form fields are not calculating, make corrections to fix the problem, add any other form features that would make this a true digital form, and then save and test the form. When complete, save and close the document, and submit it based on your instructor's directions.

Performance Evaluations

SOFT SKILLS CASE

Students will work as a group to create an employee performance evaluation form that discusses the key points from the video. The electronic form will consist of form controls, document restrictions to protect the form from editing by users, several useful macros, and a digital signature to authenticate the document. Save the form as **w07b4EvaluationForm_ GroupName**. Then, each group will conduct mock performance evaluations and record the work performance discussion on the created forms. Save the evaluated performance as **w07b4PerformanceEvaluations_GroupName**. Submit the documents as directed by your instructor.

Many professionals have a job that requires travel. In most organizations, individuals must pay for all travel-related expenses and submit a form in order to receive reimbursement. The form details every expense—from food to hotel to airfare—and at the end of the form the total of all expenses is calculated. The company you work for has a travel reimbursement form that all employees must print, fill out, and submit via interoffice mail. You are responsible for converting that form so that it can be completed online and e-mailed to the accounting office. Refer to Figure 7.36 as you complete this exercise.

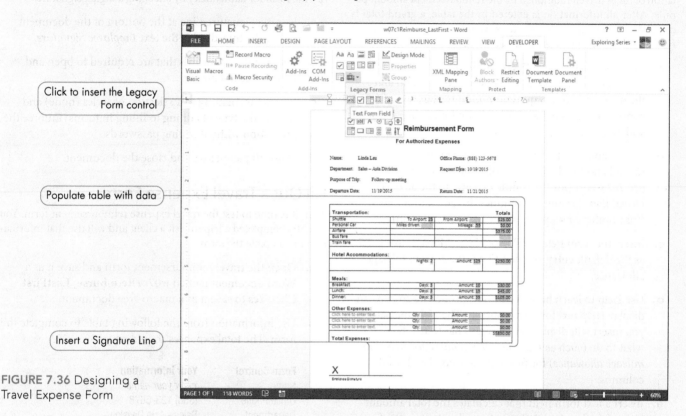

FIGURE 7.36 Designing a Travel Expense Form

Create a Macro That Inserts Text Controls

The travel expense form will require several text controls to enter information such as name, department, and phone number. To expedite the process of inserting text controls, you create a macro that inserts the field as soon as you press a keyboard combination.

a. Open the file *w07c1Travel*. The password to open is *Chap7_cap* and the password to modify is *2Travel*.

b. Save the file as a Macro-Enabled Document named **w07c1Travel_LastFirst**.

c. Display the DEVELOPER tab, if necessary. Switch to Design Mode. Record a macro named **TextControl**. Store it in the *w07c1Travel_LastFirst* document. Assign the macro to the keyboard combination Alt+L and save changes to the macro in *w07c1Travel_LastFirst*.

d. Click anywhere in the document and perform the following commands in the macro: Click the **DEVELOPER tab** and click the **Rich Text Content Control**. Click **Properties** and select the **Content control cannot be deleted option**. Close the Content Control Properties dialog box and stop the macro.

e. Deselect the control and press **Alt+L** to confirm that the macro runs correctly. Delete all text controls added while recording and testing the macro.

Insert Text and Date Controls on a Form

The Word document you opened in the last steps is the basis for the printed travel reimbursement form. You decide to keep the basic outline of the document and add form controls for users to enter their personal information. The document contains asterisks to mark the location where you want to enter the personal information, so you will delete the asterisks before you insert form controls.

a. Select the asterisks and use the TextControl macro to insert text controls to the right side of *Name*, *Office Phone*, *Department*, and *Purpose of Trip*.

b. Insert Date Picker controls on the right side of *Request Date*, *Departure Date*, and *Return Date*.

c. Save the document.

Insert Controls That Compute Totals

The actual expenses are entered in a table in the document that sorts by category such as transportation, accommodations, and meals. Some expenses, such as Personal Car, might require a calculation of miles driven multiplied by the reimbursement amount per mile. After all information is entered in the table, a grand total is calculated by adding all the expenses. You decide to use legacy text fields in the table, which allow calculations.

a. Insert *legacy text form* fields within the table and apply **Number formats** for each expense in the second and third columns that requires a number to be entered (no controls in second and third column for *Airfare, Bus fare,* and *Train fare*).

b. Assign bookmark names to all fields you insert in the second and third columns. For example, you might use *ToAirport* (for the shuttle expense to the airport), *DriveMiles* (for number of miles driven), and *Brkdays* (for number of days you ate breakfast on the trip).

c. Insert the form field for Personal Car Mileage, using **.55** as the default entry, because this is the current mileage allowance.

d. Use Help to learn how to edit field properties so you can display Help text for form controls. The Help message you insert will display on the status bar to tell the user what to do (such as *Enter number of miles driven* or *Enter mileage allowance*) for fields in the second and third columns.

e. Insert a text form field that calculates the total amount in the fourth column. Create formulas that use the form field bookmark names from fields in columns two and three. For example, use *=Brkdays*Brkamt* to calculate the total amount spent for breakfasts during a trip. Notice that some fields will add the results from columns 2 and 3, and others will multiply them. Format calculating fields in the last column with **Currency format** and set them to **calculate on exit**.

f. Insert text form fields in the first column below the Other Expenses category.

g. Insert a calculation field in the last cell with this formula: **=SUM(D2:D16)**. Format the field to display the results as **Currency** to **calculate on exit**.

h. Set right alignment on the text and fields in the second, third, and fourth columns.

i. Save the document.

Protect the Form

To make a true digital form, you wisely decide to add a line for a signature and protect the document so users can only enter information in the control field areas. You remove all passwords and certify the form for authenticity by attaching a digital signature.

a. Insert a Signature Line at the bottom of the document. Below the line, display the text *Employee Signature*.

b. Remove the passwords that are required to open and modify the document.

c. Restrict formatting to a selection of styles (none) and restrict the type of editing to filling in forms. Enforce the protection without setting passwords.

d. Close all panes; save and close the document.

Fill Out a Travel Expense Form

Now, it is time to test the travel expense reimbursement form. You recently completed a trip to visit a client and will use that information to complete the form.

a. Open the travel reimbursement form and save it as a Word document named **w07c1Reimburse_LastFirst**. Click **Yes** to save it as a macro-free document.

b. Use information from the following table to complete the form. The total expenses should equal $830.00.

Form Control	Your information
Name	*enter your name*
Office Phone	(888) 123-5678
Department	Sales - Asia Division
Request Date	October 19, 2015
Purpose of Trip	Follow-up meeting
Departure Date	November 19, 2015
Return Date	November 21, 2015
Shuttle to Airport	25
Airfare	375
Hotel	2 nights @ 125
Breakfast	3 days @ 10
Lunch	3 days @ 15
Dinner	3 days @ 35

c. Sign your name on the digital signature line after you complete the form.

d. Save and close the document, and submit it based on your instructor's directions.

Word and the Internet

Web Page Creation and Enhancement, and Blogs

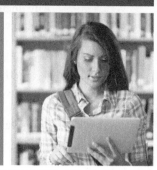

wavebreakmedia/Shutterstock

CASE STUDY | A Math Tutoring Club

You are working on your bachelor's degree to become a middle school teacher. You know that there is a need for math tutors, so you want to create a Web site to provide online resources to students who want to improve their math skills. It could be just a simple Web site to provide information about your new endeavor, information on how to request tutoring services, sample worksheets for students to practice, and other resources for students to consult. By keeping it simple, you can maintain and update it yourself using tools such as Word 2013.

Your knowledge of the Office suite enables you to set up the Web pages to be multifunctional and to format information about your services in a way that displays well on a Web site. You will use these tools to get started and create a blog where you post more personal notes and links about updates on your Web site.

Web Page Creation

For most students, the Internet is as much a part of their education as books and teachers. The *Internet* is a network of networks that connects computers anywhere in the world. It is easy to connect your computer to the Internet, and that connection enables you to view an abundance of information about every imaginable topic.

The *World Wide Web (WWW)* or, simply, the Web, is a very large subset of the Internet, consisting of those computers that store a special type of document known as a *Web page*. Any document that displays on the World Wide Web is a Web page. Web pages may be self-contained and might provide all the information you need about a topic, or they may offer links to other Web pages. And therein lies the fascination of the Web—you simply click link after link to move effortlessly from one document or resource to the next.

In this section, you will learn to create a Web page using Microsoft Word. However, like any other Microsoft word processors such as WordPad or Publisher, the Web page is best displayed using a Web browser, such as Internet Explorer. You will first customize the Ribbon to display commands you will use for Web page development, then you will format the page, add hyperlinks and bookmarks, and finally save the document as a Web page.

Customizing the Ribbon

The features in Word enable you to create just about any kind of document you could want, and the Ribbon makes it easy to find the commands that you use when creating those documents. But did you know you can create a custom tab for the Ribbon that contains just the commands you want to use? Ribbon customization enables you to include features that you use most frequently or features that are not available on the standard Ribbon. By creating a custom tab, you have access to these features. In addition to creating a new tab, you can change the order of the tabs, change the order of the groups that appear within the tabs, and create new groups within a tab.

To customize the Ribbon, right-click an empty area of the Ribbon and click *Customize the Ribbon*, or do the following:

1. Click the FILE tab to open the Backstage view.
2. Click Options.
3. Click Customize Ribbon.

Figure 8.1 shows the Customize Ribbon options displaying the current arrangement of the Ribbon in the right pane. To expand the view to display the groups within a tab click the plus icon (+), and to collapse the view to hide the groups click the minus icon (–). To change the order of the existing tabs or groups, drag and drop a selected tab and group to a new position.

Click to expand a group or tab

Click to collapse a group or tab

Existing tabs and groups on Ribbon

Click to add selected command

Click command to select

FIGURE 8.1 Customize Ribbon Options

Restore the Ribbon

You can restore the Ribbon to its original arrangement by clicking *Reset* at the bottom of the *Customize the Ribbon* view and clicking *Reset all customizations*. Reset also enables you to reset individual tabs.

Create a Custom Tab

STEP 1 To have access to the commands you use most, you can add a new tab to the Ribbon and add the frequently used commands. Below the *Customize the Ribbon* pane, click New Tab. The new tab displays immediately below the tab in the pane that is also the active tab in your document and is named *New Tab (Custom)*. The new tab contains a new group named *New Group (Custom)*. To add additional groups, click New Group below the pane. You can rename tabs or groups by selecting the desired tab or group and clicking Rename. When you rename a group, you can select a colorful symbol to represent the contents of the group. You can reorder the tab in the Ribbon by selecting the desired tab and clicking the Move Up and Move Down arrows on the right side of the pane. Figure 8.2 displays a new tab containing a new group. You may create the new custom tab by doing the following:

1. Click the FILE tab to open the Backstage view.
2. Click Options.
3. Click Customize Ribbon in the left pane.
4. Click New Tab, below the *Customize the Ribbon* pane on the right side of the window.
5. Click to select the New Tab (Custom) and click Rename, which displays below the pane.
6. In the Rename dialog box, give the new tab a name in the *Display name* box.
7. Click OK.
8. Click New Group (Custom) and click Rename.
9. In the Rename dialog box, click a symbol of your choice in the *symbol* section, if one is desired.
10. Give the new group a name in the *Display name* box.

11. Click OK.
12. Click OK again to close the Word Options dialog box.

FIGURE 8.2 New Tab and Group Options

Add Commands to a Group

To add commands to an existing tab or group or to a newly created tab, make sure that the tab or group under the *Customize the Ribbon* pane is selected, click a command from the *Choose commands from* pane, and then click Add. Popular commands that you can add are displayed in the default view, but you can also click the *Choose commands from* arrow to choose from additional commands and macros. You will also find a category named *Commands Not in the Ribbon*. For example, you can add commands that are not on the default tabs, such as Web Page Preview, to a group in a personalized tab. Figure 8.3 displays a customized tab with commands you use while creating Web pages.

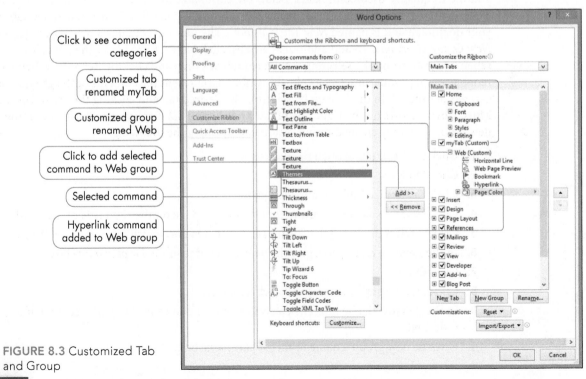

FIGURE 8.3 Customized Tab and Group

You may also add commands not in the Ribbon, such as Horizontal Line and Web Page Preview, to the new tab. If your Web page is relatively long, you may want to insert horizontal lines to separate sections of the document content for easier reading. Add new commands to the custom tab by doing the following:

1. Click to select the desired group below the *Customize the Ribbon* pane on the right.
2. Click the *Choose commands from* arrow and click *Commands Not in the Ribbon*. If you prefer, you may click the All Commands option instead.
3. Scroll down the list of commands, find the desired command, and then click Add.
4. Repeat step 3 to add more desired commands.
5. Confirm that the new tab is checked and click OK to close the Word Options dialog box.

 TIP Export and Import a Custom Tab

If you customize a tab or the Quick Access Toolbar (QAT), that customization will only be applied to the Word application that is installed on that particular computer. You can export the customized tab or the QAT to a file that can be imported to a different computer. Click Import/Export at the bottom of the Word Options dialog box to save your customizations. Copy the file you save onto a different computer and click Import/Export again on the new computer to import your custom tab or QAT.

Building and Publishing a Web Page

Sooner or later, anyone who surfs the World Wide Web wonders if he or she can create a home page or a Web site of his or her own. Word provides all the tools necessary to create a basic Web page. You can use tables and SmartArt graphics to organize and lay out the page elements, add online images and your own pictures to enhance the page with visual elements, use bulleted and numbered lists to organize information on the page, create WordArt for text, and so on. If your Web page design is complex, you will want to use a Web authoring tool such as Microsoft Expression.

Web pages are developed in a special language called *HyperText Markup Language (HTML)*. In the early years of Internet development, the only way to create a Web page was to learn HTML, which is a programming language consisting of a set of codes (or tags) that are assigned to the content and which describe how the document is to appear when viewed in a Web browser.

Office 2013 simplifies the Web page development process because you can create the document in Word from scratch or a template and simply save it as a Web page. Word converts the document and generates the HTML code for you. You can continue to type text or change the formatting just as you can with an ordinary document. Figure 8.4 shows a Web page you will create in the next Hands-On Exercise, and Figure 8.5 displays the HTML code for that page.

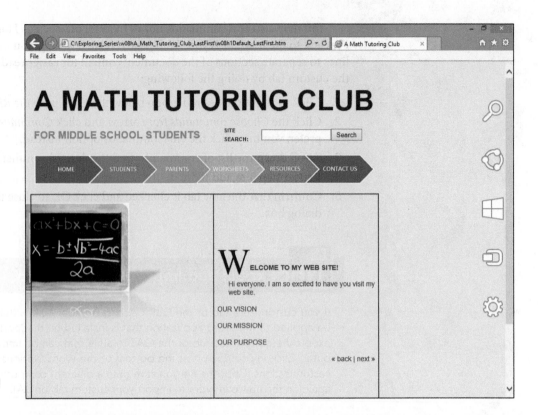

FIGURE 8.4 A Math Tutoring Club Web Page

Code specifies how to format the contents

FIGURE 8.5 HTML Code for A Math Tutoring Club Web Page

Save Document as a Web Page

STEP 2>>
When you create a document in Word, you can display it in Web Layout view. This particular view enables you to continue using regular Word formatting features while displaying the document as it will appear in a Web browser. After you create and format documents, you can save them as Web pages. From within the Save As dialog box, click the *Save as type* arrow and choose an appropriate Web format. Table 8.1 lists and describes the three Web file types. When you save your file as a regular Web page, the file will contain all the Word tags

and HTML tags, thereby increasing the size of the file. When you save your file as a single file Web page, it will increase the file size because all the images will be embedded and saved in the file. Care must be taken to ensure that the file size does not exceed the maximum size imposed by the e-mail server and that the Web browser used can display this type of file properly. If large file size is a major concern to you, you could save your file as a Web Page, Filtered. All the Word tags are removed, and only the HTML tags remain in the file. Images will be saved in an accompanying folder, which must be located in the same directory as the Web page. This format is often used for Web sites presented on Amazon's Kindle tablet. The downside is that you cannot edit a filtered Web page in Word.

TABLE 8.1	Options for Saving Web Pages
File Type	**Description**
Web Page (*.htm; *.html)	Create and edit Web page documents and use regular Word editing tools. Keep saving in this format until you are done.
Single File Web Page (*.mht; *.mhtml)	Save all Web site files, including graphics, into one file so that you can send it to someone.
Web Page, Filtered (*.htm; *.html)	Save the final Web page in this format to reduce file size and reduce Word editing options. Upload this file to a Web server.

For a quicker reference, it is a good idea to change the title of each page to reflect the content of the document. You also need to save all the Word documents as individual Web pages in one folder. For instance, to create a Web folder and save the home page for the Web site, do the following:

1. Open the document that will be the designated home page.
2. Click the FILE tab.
3. Click Save As. You can save your Web pages to the following locations:
   a. OneDrive
   b. Other Web Locations
   c. Computer
   d. Add a Place
   e. Recent Folders
4. If you save your document to your computer, you will click Browse, and in the Save As dialog box, navigate to the drive and folder in which you want to create a folder.
5. Click New folder on the Save As dialog box toolbar or right-click for the shortcut menu and click New.
6. Type a new folder name and click Open.
7. Type Default in the *File name* box. The default name for the home page is either *default* or *index*.
8. Click the *Save as type* arrow and click Web Page (*.htm; *.html).
9. Click Change Title to display the Enter Text dialog box.
10. Type the title of the Web page in the *Page title* text.
11. Click OK.
12. Click Save.

 TIP **Folder and File Names**

Many Web servers do not handle spaces well in folder and file names; they might replace each space with the %20 combination. Therefore, it is a good habit to avoid using spaces when naming folders and files by substituting the spaces with underscores. Other options include using the CamelCase notation (a combination of capital and lowercase letters) or hyphens to replace the spaces.

Apply a Theme and Background Color to a Web Page

STEP 3 > Web pages are more interesting when you add design elements such as background images, bullets, numbering, lines, and other graphical features. They also display better when colors and fonts are coordinated among the design elements. You can use the Word themes while developing a Web page, which enables you to coordinate colors and fonts, as shown in Figure 8.6. To make sure themes are as effective as possible, you should format your document by using Word heading styles, such as Heading 1, Heading 2, and so on. You may add a theme by doing the following:

1. Click the DESIGN tab. You may also click the customized new tab/group if you have added selected commands to the customized new tab.
2. Click Themes in the Document Formatting group.
3. Hover the mouse over the theme choices to display a live preview of the individual theme.
4. Click the selected theme to apply the theme features to the Web page.

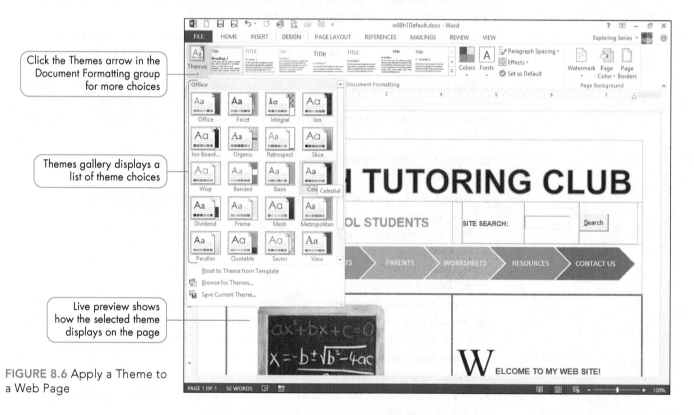

Click the Themes arrow in the Document Formatting group for more choices

Themes gallery displays a list of theme choices

Live preview shows how the selected theme displays on the page

FIGURE 8.6 Apply a Theme to a Web Page

Themes assign colors to the elements on the Web page, such as fonts, numbers, and horizontal lines, which enable you to emphasize key information. However, the theme does not automatically add a background to the Web page. A *background* is a color, design, image, or watermark that appears behind text in a document or on a Web page. A colored background adds visual enhancement to the Web page. You can quickly add a background color to a Web page by clicking the Design tab. If a theme has been selected, the Page Color palette automatically displays colors that coordinate with the theme. To add a background color to a Web page, do the following:

1. Click the DESIGN tab.
2. Click Page Color in the Page Background group.
3. Hover the mouse over any of the theme colors to see a live preview of the selected color.
4. Click the selected color to apply the new color to the Web page.

If you prefer to customize the background color, design, or image, you can click the Page Color command in the Page Background group on the Design tab and select from the commands that display below the Theme Color gallery. The More Colors command displays the Colors dialog box, which enables you to choose from the standard colors or to mix a custom color. The Fill Effects command enables you to apply a gradient, texture, pattern, or picture background. Figure 8.7 shows the Gradient tab of the Fill Effects dialog box, where you can select a gradient design to display on the background of your Web page.

Click to change colors used for gradient

Gradient tab selected

Theme color is selected

Preview selected gradient pattern

Click to select the Shading styles options which affect the angle for the Variants

Select the direction Variants for gradient pattern

FIGURE 8.7 Apply a Color Gradient Background to a Web Page

TIP Web Page Background

The size of a Web page is not the same as a Word document; Web pages are wider than a typical 8 1/2" × 11" document using portrait orientation. Therefore, any color, pattern, or image you use as a background will repeat so that it covers the entire Web page. You want to carefully select a background color, pattern, or image so that it is not distracting and does not affect the readability of the contents on the page.

Insert Bookmarks in a Web Page

STEP 4 ▶ Some Web pages are very lengthy and require the viewer to scroll a great deal to view all the contents on the page. You can help the viewer to return to the top, bottom, or other location in that page by inserting bookmarks. A *bookmark* is an electronic marker for a specific location in a document, enabling the user to go to that location quickly. A hyperlink takes you to a different page and can even take you to a specific location on a page, but the location must be identified somehow so the hyperlink knows exactly where to go; a bookmark provides that identification. Bookmarks are helpful in long documents because they enable you to move easily from one place to another within that document, without having to manually scroll. They are often used on FAQ (frequently asked questions) Web pages, which help the user to navigate quickly between a question and the respective answer. Another example for the use of bookmarks is shown in Figure 8.8. A bookmark was created for each math category, so that when you click any of the categories at the top of the page, you immediately move to that category and subject topics further down the page. Additionally, the placement of a bookmark at the top of the page enables the user to click a link at the end of each category to return the user to the top of the page to view the list of categories.

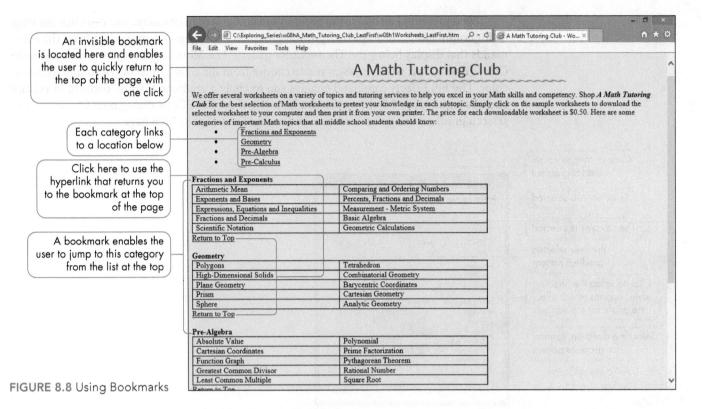

An invisible bookmark is located here and enables the user to quickly return to the top of the page with one click

Each category links to a location below

Click here to use the hyperlink that returns you to the bookmark at the top of the page

A bookmark enables the user to jump to this category from the list at the top

FIGURE 8.8 Using Bookmarks

Creating a bookmark and linking to it is a two-step process. You first create the bookmark(s) throughout the document, and you insert a hyperlink that links to that bookmark. A bookmark for the top of the page is created automatically, so you do not have to create that one manually. To create a bookmark on a Web page, do the following:

1. Click the INSERT tab.
2. Place the insertion point on the left side of the word that you want to use as a bookmark.
3. Click Bookmark in the Links group.
4. Give the bookmark a name in the *Bookmark name* box.
5. Click Add.

TIP | Bookmark Names

Spaces and special characters, including hyphens, are not allowed in bookmark names. You can use a combination of capital and lowercase letters, numbers, and the underscore character, but cannot begin the name of a bookmark with a number. You should create descriptive names so you can identify the bookmark easily when you create a hyperlink to it. For example, a bookmark to question #1 in a FAQ listing might be FAQ1.

Insert Hyperlinks in a Web Page

STEP 5 ›› One benefit of a Web page is that it contains references, called hyperlinks, to other Web pages. *Hyperlinks* are electronic markers that, when clicked, do one of several actions: move the insertion point to a different location within the same document, open another document, or display a different Web page in a Web browser. Hyperlinks can lead you to Web pages stored on different computers that may be located anywhere in the world.

Hyperlinks can be assigned to text or graphics. For example, consider a Web page you might create to document your visit to several national parks. You display several pictures of the beautiful scenery and provide a summary of the trip. In your summary, you might mention a particular lodge where you spent a few nights, so you create a hyperlink from your Web page to the home page of the lodge. Anyone who reads your page can click the name of the lodge and be directed to the Web site, where they can inquire about reservations for themselves. Additionally, you might want to create a link to a particular park from a picture that was taken there. You can select the picture and assign a hyperlink that, when the picture is clicked, will direct the reader to the Web site for that national park.

To create a hyperlink on your Web page, do the following:

1. Select the text or picture.
2. Click the INSERT tab and click Hyperlink in the Links group.
3. In the Insert Hyperlink dialog box, as shown in Figure 8.9, you have the following options to specify several types of hyperlinks in the *Link to* box:

   - Existing File or Web Page: Links to another Web page by inserting the address (or URL).
   - Place in This Document: Links to another place within the same document. If necessary, click the plus sign (+) next to Bookmarks and select the desired bookmark.
   - Create New Document: Links to a new document that you can edit now or later.
   - E-mail Address: Links to an e-mail address, which opens a new e-mail message when clicked.

4. Click OK.

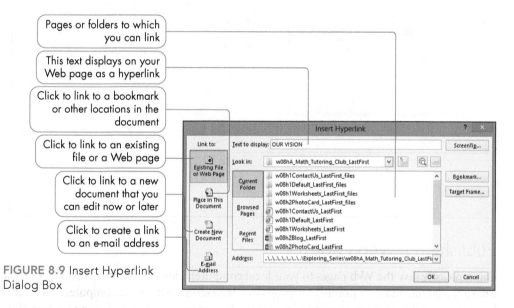

FIGURE 8.9 Insert Hyperlink Dialog Box

When you point to a hyperlink in a Word document, you will see a ScreenTip that directs you to press Ctrl+Click to follow the link, which is not the way you use hyperlinks in a Web page. However, this gives you more control over the link from a developmental standpoint because you are able to select the link and make changes without it automatically opening a new page. If you right-click a hyperlink in a Word document, you will see several options for working with the hyperlink, including Edit Hyperlink (which opens the Edit Hyperlink dialog box), Copy Hyperlink, and Remove Hyperlink (which removes the link but does not remove the text or graphic).

TIP Hyperlink Colors

When you apply a hyperlink to text in a Web page, the text displays in a color that coordinates with the theme in use. After you click the hyperlink, the color of the text changes to the theme or default color for a followed link.

Preview a Web Page

STEP 6 »
After finalizing pages for a Web site, you save the document(s) as described earlier. The Web Layout view gives you a very accurate representation of how the page will look when published. You can also preview the page in an actual Web browser before you upload and publish it so that you can confirm it contains the content and is formatted to your specifications. Word contains a Web Page Preview command that you can add to a tab on the Ribbon or to the Quick Access Toolbar before you use it.

You can also open the page from within Internet Explorer, or the browser of your choice, when Word is not active. To view a Web page in Internet Explorer, do the following:

1. Open a Web browser window. Click the File menu.
2. Click Open (or press Ctrl+O if the menu bar does not display), and the Open dialog box displays as shown in Figure 8.10.
3. Click Browse.
4. Navigate and open the folder where the page is stored.
5. Select the file name of your Web page.
6. Click Open.
7. Click OK. The document opens in an Internet Explorer window.

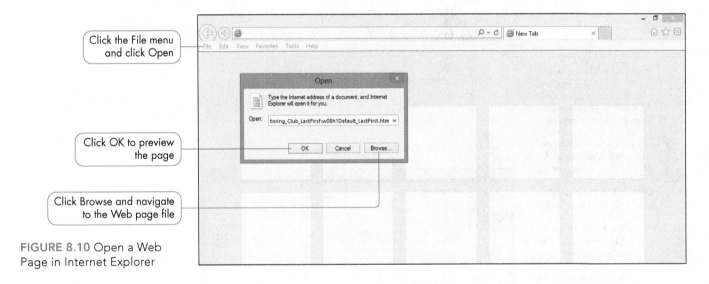

Click the File menu and click Open

Click OK to preview the page

Click Browse and navigate to the Web page file

FIGURE 8.10 Open a Web Page in Internet Explorer

Publishing a Web Page

You can easily save the Web pages to your local computer. However, to view the pages on the Internet, you must save or publish the pages to a *Web server*, which is a computer system that hosts pages so that they are available for viewing by anyone who has an Internet connection. You will need additional information from your instructor about how to obtain an account on a Web server at your school, if available, as well as how to upload the pages from your PC to the server. The most common method of uploading Web pages to the server is by using *File Transfer Protocol (FTP)*, a process that uploads files from a PC to a server or from a server to a PC.

Quick Concepts

1. What are the advantages of using Microsoft Word to create a Web page? *p. 484*
2. What are the benefits of using a Word theme in a Web page? *p. 490*
3. What are the benefits of inserting hyperlinks in a Web page? *p. 492*

Hands-On Exercises

Watch the Video
for this Hands-
On Exercise!

MyITLab®
HOE1 Training

1 Web Page Creation

You are designing a Web site for your own math tutoring club. You want a simple design that provides basic information about your service. You have a few documents started but need to refine each one to use a common theme, add color, and add general Web components such as hyperlinks and bookmarks. When complete, you will preview the results to make sure it is ready to go live on the Web.

Skills covered: Create a Custom Tab • Save Document as a Web Page • Apply a Theme and Background • Insert and Hyperlink to Bookmarks • Insert Hyperlinks and a Horizontal Line • Preview a Web Page

---

STEP 1 ❯❯ CREATE A CUSTOM TAB

Before you begin designing a Web page, you want to organize the tools that will enable you to work quickly and efficiently. You decide to create a custom Tab to display the commands you will use most frequently while designing the Web site. Refer to Figure 8.11 as you complete Step 1.

Step d: New tab named myTab

Step f: New group named Web

Steps h and i: Commands added to the new custom tab

FIGURE 8.11 Custom Tab Containing Web Development Commands

a. Start Word and open a new document.

You can create a custom tab or group in any open document, and it can be used in all documents on the computer on which the software is installed.

b. Click the **FILE tab**, click **Options**, and then click **Customize Ribbon**.

The Word commands available display in the pane on the left side. On the right side, you customize the tabs and groups with the available commands.

> **TROUBLESHOOTING**: If you work in a lab environment where you are unable to customize the applications on your PC, read through the remainder of Step 1.

c. Click **New Tab**, which displays below the *Customize the Ribbon* pane on the right side of the window.

A new tab is created in the Main Tabs list and positioned between the Home tab and the Insert tab. The tab is named *New Tab* (*Custom*) and contains a new group named *New Group* (*Custom*).

d. Click **New Tab (Custom)** and click **Rename**, which displays below that pane. Type **myTab** in the **Display name box** and click **OK**.

The new tab displays as *myTab* (*Custom*).

e. Click **New Group (Custom)** and click **Rename**.

The Rename dialog box opens.

f. Type **Web** in the **Display name box** and click **OK**.

The group displays as *Web (Custom)*. You may select a symbol of your choice from the Symbol gallery if you want.

g. Click the **Choose commands from arrow** and click **Commands Not in the Ribbon**.

All the commands that are not on the Ribbon display in the left panel.

h. Scroll down the list of commands, click **Web Page Preview**, and then click **Add**.

Web Page Preview is added to myTab (Custom) in the Web (Custom) group.

i. Click the **Choose commands from arrow** and click **All Commands**. Select each of the following commands and click **Add** to display them in the Web (Custom) group on the myTab (Custom) tab:

- **Bookmark**
- **Horizontal Line** [Note: Make sure that you select the Horizontal Line, NOT the Horizontal Line…(followed by ellipsis) command]
- **Hyperlink**
- **Page Color**
- **Themes**
- **Web Layout**

j. Confirm that the myTab tab is checked so that it will display on the Ribbon and click **OK** to close the Options dialog box.

k. Click the **myTab tab** and notice the Web group contains seven commands. Right-click an empty area of the Ribbon and click **Customize the Ribbon**.

The Word Options dialog box opens.

l. Click the **plus sign (+)** to display all commands in the Web group under the myTab tab.

m. Click to select **Hyperlink** and drag and drop it above *Horizontal Line*. Click **Web Layout** and click **Remove**. Click **OK** to close the Options dialog box.

This removes the Web Layout command, which you can access from the status bar. It also changes the order in which the commands display on the tab.

n. Leave the blank document open for the next step.

STEP 2 ≫ SAVE DOCUMENT AS A WEB PAGE

You have a few documents prepared as a foundation for the Web site, but before you get started, you first create a folder for storing Web page files. You open each one and save it as a Web page, which places it in the proper format for viewing in a Web browser. You recognize that the name of the page displays in the task bar in Windows and Internet Explorer, so you are careful to change the title for each page. Refer to Figure 8.12 as you complete Step 2.

Steps f–g: Text typed here displays in the title bar of the Web browser when viewing the Web page

Step f: Click to change the page title

Step f: Current page title

FIGURE 8.12 Change the Page Title from the Enter Text Dialog Box

a. Open *w08h1Default*.

This document is designed to be the home page for the *A Math Tutoring Club* Web site. In the next step, you create a folder and save the document in that folder.

b. Click the **FILE tab**, click **Save As**, and then click **Browse**. In the Save As dialog box, navigate to the drive and folder in which you want to create a folder.

Before you start creating Web documents, you need to create a folder to store all Web documents for a specific Web site.

c. Click **New folder** on the Save As dialog box toolbar, type **w08hA_Math_Tutoring_Club_ LastFirst**, and then press **Enter**. Click **Open** or double-click the new folder to open it.

Be aware that the folder name does not have a *1* after the letter *h*. This is because we will use the same folder name for both Hands-On Exercises 1 and 2. Usually, you will have many files when you create Web pages, so it is a good idea to put all the files and subfolders in the same folder.

 Naming a Web Site Home Page

A Web site's home page is typically saved as default.html or index.html so that it loads automatically when you type the main URL in a Web browser address box.

d. Make sure that the same file name [*w08h1Default*] is in the *File name* box and add an underscore, follow by your last name and first name.

e. Click the **Save as type arrow** and click **Web Page (*.htm; *.html)**.

When you save as a Web page, the Save As dialog box displays the *Page title* text area and the Change Title button.

f. Click **Change Title** to display the Enter Text dialog box.

In this dialog box, you can edit the Web page title—the text that appears on the Web browser's title bar when the Web page displays.

g. Place the insertion point before the word *Club*, type **Tutoring**, and then press the **Spacebar** to add a space between words as appropriate in the *Page title* box. Click **OK** and click **Save**.

The page displays in Web Layout view.

h. Open the Word documents listed in the table below. Save each document as a Web page in the w08hA_Math_Tutoring_Club_LastFirst folder. Assign new file names and Web page titles using the information in the following table.

Open This File	Save As Web Page (.htm)	Web Page Title
w08h1Worksheets	w08h1Worksheets_LastFirst.htm	A Math Tutoring Club - Worksheets
w08h1Contact	w08h1ContactUs_LastFirst.htm	A Math Tutoring Club - Contact Us

The *w08hA_Math_Tutoring_Club_LastFirst* folder now contains three Web pages that you use to complete your Web site.

i. Leave each document open for the next step.

 Naming Pages in Your Web Site

When you save a folder or page that you plan to use on a Web site, you should refrain from using spaces in the folder or file name. Even though it is possible to include spaces, it forces the Web browser to insert codes in place of the spaces when it displays the file name and path in the Address bar. For example, if you name a Web page *contact info*, it displays as *contact%20info* when viewed in a Web browser. If you need to use a long name, consider using dashes or underscores in place of spaces.

STEP 3 >> APPLY A THEME AND BACKGROUND

Now that your Web pages are in the proper form, you select a common theme to use on each one. The theme affects the fonts but not the background. So you also select a background color that gives a dramatic look to your simple pages. Refer to Figure 8.13 as you complete Step 3.

Steps b–c: Page Color and Themes commands display on the custom tab

Step c: Page Color palette displays Celestial Theme Colors

Step c: Live preview shows how background color displays on the page

FIGURE 8.13 Select a Background Color for a Web Page

a. Click the **VIEW tab**, click **Switch Windows** in the Window group, and then click *w08h1Default_LastFirst.htm* from the list of open files.

b. Click the **myTab tab**, click **Themes** in the Web group, and then click **Celestial**.

The *A Math Tutoring Club* title and text below it display in colors represented in the Celestial theme.

c. Click **Page Color** in the Web group. Click **Blue, Accent 2, Lighter 80%** (second row, sixth column).

You applied a light blue background color that covers the entire page.

d. Click **Save** in the Quick Access Toolbar to save the changes to the default.htm document.

e. Press **Alt+Tab** repeatedly until the *w08h1ContactUs_LastFirst.htm* document displays. Repeat steps b and c to apply the same theme and background color to the page. Click **Save** on the Quick Access Toolbar to save the changes.

When you press Alt+Tab, you will move from one open Web page to another.

> **TROUBLESHOOTING**: If you accidentally closed a document, you may open it again by clicking the File tab, clicking Open, and then clicking the document, which should be displayed under *Recent Documents*.

f. Press **Alt+Tab** repeatedly until the *w08h1Worksheets_LastFirst.htm* document displays. Repeat steps b and c to apply the theme and background color to the page. Click **Save** on the Quick Access Toolbar to save the changes.

STEP 4 ❯❯ INSERT AND HYPERLINK TO BOOKMARKS

The Web page that describes the worksheets is quite lengthy. You know that a good Web design will assist the viewer in navigating up and down the page without having to scroll. With that in mind, you incorporate bookmarks, which are a type of hyperlink, to help the reader move from section to section on the page. Refer to Figure 8.14 as you complete Step 4.

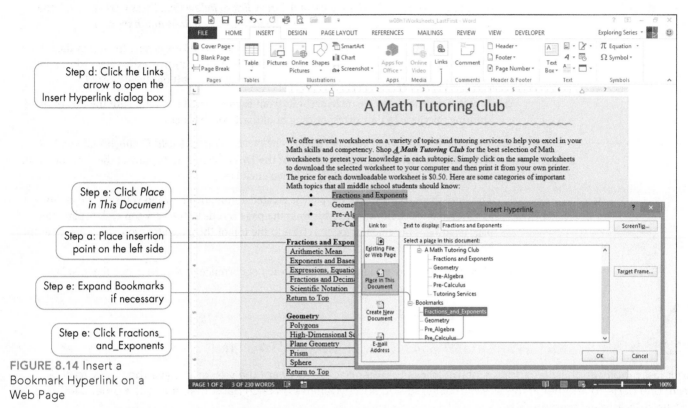

Step d: Click the Links arrow to open the Insert Hyperlink dialog box

Step e: Click *Place in This Document*

Step a: Place insertion point on the left side

Step e: Expand Bookmarks if necessary

Step e: Click *Fractions_ and_Exponents*

FIGURE 8.14 Insert a Bookmark Hyperlink on a Web Page

a. Display the Worksheets page, if necessary. Place the insertion point on the left side of the first table heading, *Fractions and Exponents*.

This table describes the variety of worksheets that are available on the A Math Tutoring Club Web site. Make sure that you do not select *Fractions and Exponents* in the bulleted list.

b. Click **Bookmark** in the Web group, type **Fractions_and_Exponents** in the **Bookmark name box**, and then click **Add**.

> **TROUBLESHOOTING**: If you did not type the underscores, the Add button will not display and you cannot add this bookmark to the Web page. Remember that special characters such as hyphens are not allowed in bookmarks. If you forgot to type the underscore for *Fractions and Exponents*, you will need to recreate the bookmark to meet your specifications, if necessary. Besides underscore, you may choose to use CamelCase notation to replace the hyphenated terms. For instance, you may type PreCalculus to replace Pre-Calculus and PreAlgebra to replace Pre-Algebra.

c. Repeat step b to create bookmarks at the beginning of the table headings that display down the page for *Geometry*, *Pre-Algebra*, and *Pre-Calculus*. The bookmarks should be named to match table heading names. Remember to use the underscore to replace the hyphen (-) sign in Pre-Calculus and Pre-Algebra.

d. Press **Ctrl+Home** to view the top of the page. Select **Fractions and Exponents** in the bulleted list and click **Hyperlink** from the Web group on the myTab tab.

The Insert Hyperlink dialog box displays. You will select the bookmark to create a link from the words *Fractions and Exponents* to the location in the document where the subtopics for Fractions and Exponents display.

e. Click **Place in This Document** in the *Link to* panel of the Insert Hyperlink dialog box. If necessary, click the **plus sign (+)** next to *Bookmarks*. Click **Fractions_and_Exponents** and click **OK**.

Fractions and Exponents displays as a hyperlink and the text color changes to blue.

f. Hover your mouse over the *Fractions and Exponents* hyperlink and view the ScreenTip that displays the name of the bookmark and *Ctrl+Click to follow link*. Press **Ctrl** and click the hyperlink to move the insertion point to the listing of *Fractions and Exponents*.

The page scrolls so the heading Fractions and Exponents displays near the top of the screen, and the insertion point moves as well. This simplifies navigation on the page. Additionally, the color of the hyperlink changes as a visual indication that it has been clicked.

g. Repeat steps d and e to create hyperlinks from each bulleted list item, with the exception of Tutoring Services, to the corresponding bookmark for that item.

h. Select the text *Return to Top* that displays below the *Fractions and Exponents* table. Click **Hyperlink** in the Web group, click **Top of the Document** that displays at the very top of the *Select a place in this document* list, and then click **OK**.

This bookmark to the top of the page is created automatically when you save the document as a Web page. When you click this link, the page scrolls to the very top and displays the page heading. This enables you to return to the top of the page after you view content at the bottom of the page.

i. Repeat step h to create a hyperlink from each occurrence of *Return to Top* that displays below each skill table.

j. Save the Web page.

STEP 5 » INSERT HYPERLINKS AND A HORIZONTAL LINE

Your last modification is the addition of hyperlinks to other pages. You want the viewer to have the ability to click from one page to another in this site with ease, so you add hyperlinks on each page that link to the others. Refer to Figure 8.15 as you complete Step 5.

FIGURE 8.15 Insert a Hyperlink to the Worksheets Web Page

a. Click **w08h1Default_LastFirst.htm** on the task bar to display the default Web page. Scroll to the bottom, select **Worksheets** (fourth column in the 1-row table), right-click to display the shortcut menu, and then click **Hyperlink** to display the Insert Hyperlink dialog box.

b. Click **Existing File or Web Page** in the *Link to* panel of the Insert Hyperlink dialog box. Scroll, if necessary, and click the *w08h1Worksheets_LastFirst.htm* file. Click **OK**.

By creating this link, the Worksheets page displays when you click Worksheets on the home page.

> **TROUBLESHOOTING**: If you select the w08h1Worksheets_LastFirst folder instead of the Worksheet Web page, your hyperlink will not work. You need to repeat this step and make sure that you select the Worksheet Web page this time.

c. Repeat step b to create a hyperlink from *Contact Us* on the default page to the w08h1ContactUs_LastFirst.htm Web page. Click **Save** in the Quick Access Toolbar.

   You will create a link for *Resources* using the Web page to be created in a future exercise.

> **TROUBLESHOOTING**: If your link does not work properly, right-click the hyperlink and select Edit Hyperlink, which displays the Edit Hyperlink dialog box and enables you to revise the link. Remove Hyperlink also displays when you right-click a hyperlink, and this enables you to remove the hyperlink completely.

d. Click **w08h1ContactUs_LastFirst.htm** on the task bar to display the ContactUs Web page. Complete the following steps to create a link to the default page:

   - Press **Ctrl+End** and press **Enter**.
   - Type **Return to the Home Page**
   - Select the text *Return to the Home Page* and click **Hyperlink** in the Web group on the myTab tab.
   - Select *w08h1Default_LastFirst.htm* and click **OK**.

e. Press **Enter** two times to move the insertion point below the hyperlink. Click **Horizontal Line** in the Web group and an orange-colored wavy line displays right below the *Return to the Home Page* link.

   Now you have a second wavy line in the document that matches the graphic that displays below the heading.

f. Click **Save** on the Quick Access Toolbar.

g. Click **w08h1Worksheets_LastFirst.htm** on the task bar to display the Worksheets Web page. Press **Ctrl+End** and press **Enter** one time. Type **Return to the Home Page**, select the text you just typed, and then click **Hyperlink**. Select *w08h1Default_LastFirst.htm* and click **OK**.

   The ContactUs and Worksheets pages now include a link back to the home page of the Web site.

h. Click **Save** on the Quick Access Toolbar. Minimize all documents.

STEP 6 » PREVIEW A WEB PAGE

With your changes and edits complete, you decide to take a look at the final Web pages. All files are saved in the w08hA_Math_Tutoring_Club_LastFirst folder, so you can open and preview them from within a Web browser. If everything looks acceptable, you will later send them to the company that will host the Web site. Refer to Figure 8.16 as you complete Step 6.

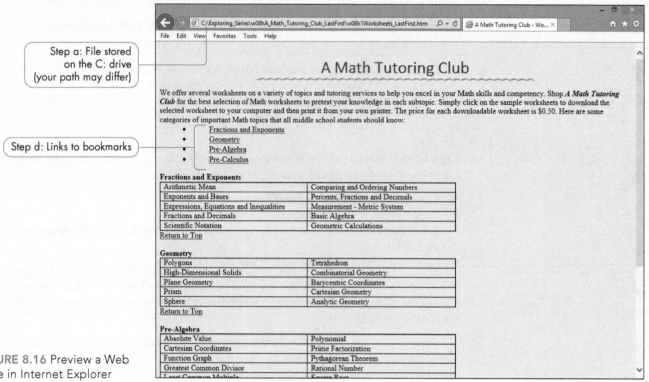

Step a: File stored on the C: drive (your path may differ)

Step d: Links to bookmarks

FIGURE 8.16 Preview a Web Page in Internet Explorer

a. Click the **w08h1Default_LastFirst.htm Web page** on the task bar. Click the **myTab tab** and click **Web Page Preview** in the Web group.

The Web browser window opens and the page displays. Look closely at the components of the URL in the Address bar, reading from right to left. You are viewing the *w08h1Default_LastFirst.htm* document, which is stored in the w08hA_Math_Tutoring_Club_LastFirst folder, which, in turn, is probably stored in one or more folders that are stored on the hard drive (C:). That means you are viewing the site locally, as opposed to seeing it on the Web. Next, you will open and view a page from within the Web browser. If your default Web browser is not Internet Explorer, you can adjust the instructions as needed for your preferred browser.

b. Press **Ctrl+O** with the Web browser open to display the Open dialog box of your Web browser. Click **Browse**, navigate to the w08hA_Math_Tutoring_Club_LastFirst folder, and then double-click *w08h1ContactUs_LastFirst.htm*. Click **OK** in the Open dialog box to display the page.

> **TROUBLESHOOTING:** If the menu bar does not display in Internet Explorer, right-click anywhere in the toolbar area and click Menu Bar. You can also use this same procedure to remove the toolbar. If you do not want to display the menu bar, press Alt+F to display the menu on a temporary basis.

c. Click the **Return to Home Page link** to make sure it works properly.

The home page, *w08h1Default_LastFirst.htm*, displays.

d. Click the **Worksheets page hyperlink** at the bottom on the home page. Once the Worksheets page displays, click the hyperlinks to navigate from top to bottom and back to top.

You are now in the Worksheets page. When you click each of the hyperlinks in this page, the hyperlinks will bring you to the place where you inserted the bookmarks.

e. Click **Return to the Home Page** to verify the link to the default page works.

You are now back to your home page, *w08h1Default_LastFirst.htm*.

f. Exit your Web browser.

All your opened Web pages in the Web browser will be closed automatically.

g. Click any of the Word documents. Close all the documents (*w08h1Default_LastFirst.htm*, *w08h1Worksheets_LastFirst.htm*, and *w08h1ContactUs_LastFirst.htm*) and exit Word.

h. Open File Explorer and navigate to the w08hA_Math_Tutoring_Club_LastFirst folder. Select all the files and subfolders in this folder, right-click to display the shortcut menu, click **Send to**, and then select **Compressed (zipped) folder**.

All the selected files and subfolders in the w08hA_Math_Tutoring_Club_LastFirst folder are now contained in a zipped file.

i. Select the zipped file name and rename it **w08h1A_Math_Tutoring_Club_LastFirst**. Submit your zipped file based on your instructor's directions.

Notice that you rename the folder with *h1* instead of *h*. This way, your instructor will know that this solution file is for Hands-On Exercise 1. When your instructor downloads the zipped file onto his or her computer, he or she can view all the Web pages that you have created for this exercise using a Web browser.

Web Page Enhancement

Electronic communication and data sharing are common, if not critical, today. People create electronic documents and Web pages and distribute them all over the world using many types of devices such as smartphones, tablets, and computers. The latest release of the Microsoft Office suite was accompanied by a variety of online tools that allow you to work on your own computer or on the cloud via Microsoft's OneDrive cloud integration technology. Besides the traditional Office 2013 installed on desktop or laptop computers, its online counterpart—Office 365—is available for business or home use via Microsoft cloud services, based on a user subscription. Social media services are made easier when you can quickly post your blog or tweet directly from Word. You can also share and collaborate on your work with anyone, including friends, family, and co-workers, in real time, from wherever you are. By posting any of your Office documents to a virtual storage location, such as Microsoft's OneDrive account, or to your office's SharePoint work site, you have easy and quick access to them using smartphones, desktop computers, or tablets, across platforms, and without losing any of the Office features or formats. You can even link your non-Microsoft accounts, such as Flickr and YouTube, to your OneDrive account. When you save your document to OneDrive, it will also automatically save a copy to your hard drive. If you do not have network access at that point, all changes are automatically synced back to OneDrive once you are online again.

In this section, you will learn how to create online blogs using the Word blog template, collaborate online with your teammates, save a blank design Word template as a Web page, and embed online pictures and video clips to enhance your Web page.

Creating a Blog Post

Everyone has the ability to post information on the Internet about themselves, their thoughts, their interests, or simply whatever they want to make public. The chronological publication of personal thoughts and Web links is called a *blog*. The term *blog* is derived from the phrase *Web log*, which refers to publishing personal information on the Web. Blogs can provide a vehicle to display the works of current or future journalists and authors, or they can simply reflect the emotions and ideas of an individual at a particular point in time.

Download a Blog Template

STEP 1 One exciting feature of Word is the Blog post template. These templates benefit users who are accustomed to working in Word, but who also publish blogs on a frequent basis. To download a blog template, do the following:

1. Click the FILE tab.
2. Click New.
3. Type blog in the *Search online templates* search box and press Enter.
4. Click the *Blog post* template.
5. Click Create to download the blog template.
6. Click Register Later in the *Register a Blog Account* dialog box. You will be prompted for this information again the first time you post.

When you open the blog post template, the window looks different because the seven tabs on the Ribbon that you are accustomed to viewing are replaced with only tabs that will provide commands you need to complete the blog post. The Blog Post tab contains commands you use to format text, but also commands that enable you to publish your blog directly to the host server for your blog, as shown in Figure 8.17. The Insert tab displays commands for items you might include in your blog, such as tables, illustrations, hyperlinks, WordArt, and symbols.

Only display tabs with commands for creating and publishing a blog post

Click to upload blog to your blog service provider

FIGURE 8.17 New Blog Post Window

Create and Set Up a Blog Account

Before you can publish your blog posts, you must have a blog account with one of the several blog service providers. To learn about and find service providers, visit the Microsoft Office Marketplace, perform an Internet search, or ask your friends which service they use. Word supports several blogging sites, including, but not limited to, the following:

- SharePoint Blog
- WordPress
- Blogger
- Telligent Community
- TypePad

Once you have an established blog account with a blog service provider, you can register and publish blogs directly from Word. Click Manage Accounts in the Blog group on the Blog Post tab, and click New in the Blog Accounts dialog box to view the New Blog Account dialog box. From this dialog box, the blog registration wizard prompts you for the service provider information and configures Word to enable you to post your blog directly from Word. If you use a service not listed, you can click Manage Accounts, click New, click Other in the Blog list, click Next, and then type the account information, your user name, and your password. You can register several blog accounts in Word. After they are registered, you can use the Manage Accounts command to change, delete, and set one account as your default blog location.

Include Pictures in a Blog Posting

Some blogs include pictures. Even though they display with the blog post, pictures are stored in a file separate from the blog text. The file that stores the blog text includes a link to the path where the picture is stored. Your blog service provider might supply storage space for images, or you might have a completely different service provider for images. In the New Account dialog box, you can click Picture Options and specify the picture provider location where you store your images that display with the blog.

TIP **Image Provider Considerations**

If you sign up for an account with an image provider, pay special attention to the terms and conditions for using the service. Some free services might impose a limit on the maximum size of files, total amount of storage, or the types of files you are allowed to store.

Publish a Blog Post

STEP 3 > After you have created a blog account and are ready to publish your blog post, do the following:

1. Click the FILE tab.
2. Click Share.
3. Click *Post to Blog*.
4. Click *Post to Blog* again.

Presenting a Word Document Online

How does a group of students with different class schedules find the time to work together on a school project? What is the best way for a big group of consultants who are stationed in different locations or countries to work together on a request for proposal? What is an effective way that small business owners can present their products or services to potential clients? The Share feature in the Backstage view of Word 2013 enables users to present their Word document online to their target audience. You can use any interactive communication channel, such as Instant Messaging and Skype, to conduct a real-time collaboration with other people. If you have a Microsoft account and Microsoft Office 2013, you can use the Office Presentation Service for free.

Collaborate on a Word Document Online

After you work on your document and you are ready to submit and present it online, do the following:

1. Click the FILE tab.
2. Click Share and you will see the following four options:
   a. Invite People—click to invite and add colleagues, team members, and friends to view and/or work with you online.
   b. Email—click to e-mail your Word document to other people.
   c. Present Online—click to share the link with remote viewers and to start your online presentation.
   d. Post to Blog—click to post your document to a blog service.
3. Click Present Online to open the Present Online dialog box, as shown in Figure 8.18.
4. Click Copy Link to copy and paste the meeting invitation's hyperlink so that your selected viewers can have access to it, or click *Send in Email* if you prefer to send the meeting hyperlink instead.
5. Click Start Presentation when you are ready to start your online presentation. When your audience is ready to watch the presentation, he or she will click the hyperlink and the attached document will display in a Web browser or Skype chat window. Microsoft Office applications are not needed to view the presentation.

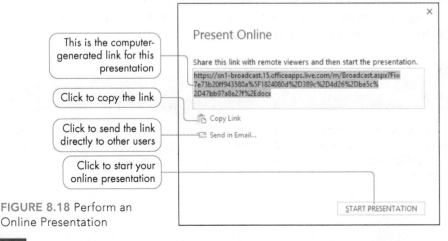

FIGURE 8.18 Perform an Online Presentation

Edit a Word Document Online

During the online presentation, you can quickly and easily make any editorial changes to the document without ending the presentation. When you click Edit in the Present Online group, you will switch into the edit mode as shown in Figure 8.19. You will resume the presentation after you have completed your editing by clicking the Resume Online Presentation button. The attendees can also receive the updated document instantly. If you want to allow attendees to download the document, simply select the *Enable remote viewers to download the document* check box when you start the presentation. You can also share meeting notes with an audience, which can be a particular page or a section of a whole document. You can also create a new document.

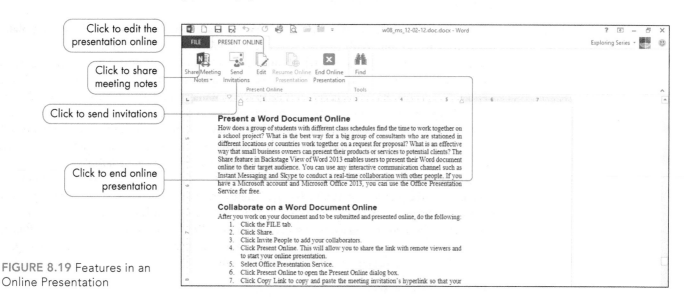

Click to edit the presentation online

Click to share meeting notes

Click to send invitations

Click to end online presentation

FIGURE 8.19 Features in an Online Presentation

The targeted audience can review the document independently on any electronic devices and at their own time and own pace. A temporary alert and the status bar located at the bottom of the Word document indicate that the reader is no longer following the presenter. The reader can go back to the same place that the presenter is presenting by clicking the Follow Presenter button, as shown in Figure 8.20.

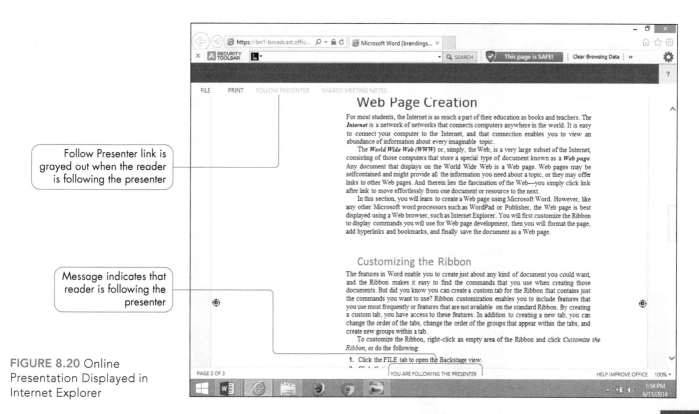

Follow Presenter link is grayed out when the reader is following the presenter

Message indicates that reader is following the presenter

FIGURE 8.20 Online Presentation Displayed in Internet Explorer

Enhancing a Web Page

Besides the professional-looking templates, Microsoft has also provided blank design templates in Word. While Office applications have always made it easy to insert graphics and other assets into documents, Office 2013 is the first version to allow online sources of photos and videos to be embedded into the documents. This is a time saver, and it also allows you to find the items that you need in the places that you often search.

Download a Design Template and Save as a Document or Web Page

STEP 4 ≫ In the past, Microsoft has provided many creative and attractive looking Word templates with built-in content. With the latest version of Word 2013, Microsoft has also provided blank design templates to users, which are empty documents preformatted with frequently used styles. Common examples of blank design templates include the Single spaced (blank), Report design (blank), and Classic double spaced (blank) templates. After you pick a design, you will type your content into the blank template and not have to worry about formatting the document. The predefined heading styles are saved in the Style gallery on the Home tab and can be easily applied to the content of the document. You can search for additional blank design templates by clicking Blank located under the *Search for online templates* box.

Any of the professionally created or blank design templates can be downloaded and saved as a regular Word document or as a Web page. Therefore, instead of creating your Web page from scratch, you have the option of downloading a template that is nearly completed, or a blank template that has been formatted to some specific standards. Both options make it more time efficient to download a predefined template from Office.com, modify it, and then save it as a Web page.

To download a design template, do the following:

1. Click the FILE tab.
2. Click New.
3. Click Blank under the *Search online templates* box to see results as shown in Figure 8.21.
4. Click the thumbnail of the template you want to download.
5. Click Create to download the template.
6. Save the template as a Word document or Web page.

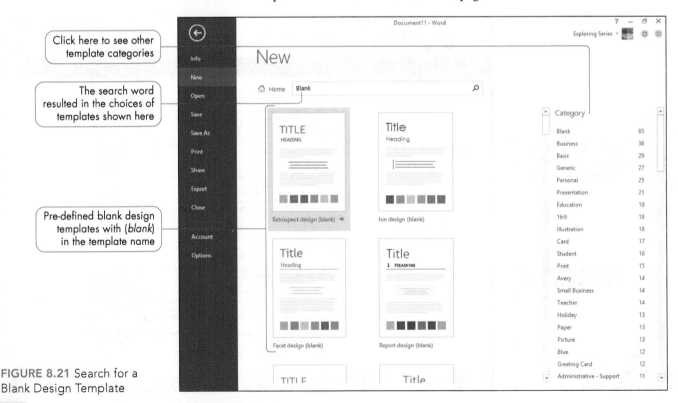

FIGURE 8.21 Search for a Blank Design Template

Insert Online Photos onto a Web Page

STEP 5 >> For many years, users have been storing their photo albums and video clips on hard drives, CD-ROM, or portable drives. Office 2013 now allows users to insert photos and pictures into a document directly from an online service without having to first download and save the files to a hard drive. Some of the popular online sites where you can obtain or store photos include, but are not limited to, Office.com, Bing Image Search, Flickr, OneDrive, and Facebook. Sign in to your OneDrive account to add other accounts and upload photos. You can see a live preview while you resize and move photos and images in your document. The new alignment guides make it easier for you to arrange images such as tables, charts, photos, and diagrams with your text. The Object zoom feature will enlarge the image when you double-click it to zoom in, making sure that the selected image displays in full screen. Click the image to zoom back to the regular size. If you want to add your photos from other sources to your OneDrive account so that you can access the photos online, do the following:

1. Click the INSERT tab.
2. Click Online Pictures in the Illustrations group.
3. Click the *Also insert from* button in the bottom-left corner of the Insert Pictures dialog box.
4. Click Connect in the *All your photos in one place* dialog box.
5. Sign in to any of your online accounts, such as Flickr or Yahoo.
6. Click Done. You will be connected to your online account.
7. Check to make sure that your selected online account is added to the Insert Pictures dialog box, as shown in Figure 8.22.
8. Click your newly added account to access your photos.
9. Click Insert after you have selected the photos that you want.

FIGURE 8.22 The Bing Image Search Dialog Box

When you access photos from public sites such as Flickr or Bing Image Search, most of the online photos are subject to Creative Commons licensing, as shown in Figure 8.23. It is very important that you review the specific license for any image to ensure that you comply with the copyright guidelines. Creative Commons is a nonprofit organization located in Mountain View, California, that allows users to share the use of creativity and knowledge through free legal tools. By signing a simple, standardized, copyright license, you give the public the permission to use your creative work under conditions stipulated by you. You can also easily change your copyright terms at any time. Usually, you can use the images for free if it is for personal use. However, you should review the specific license for any image if you want to use it for business or commercial purposes.

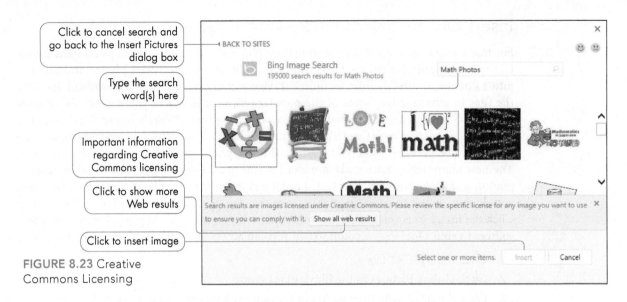

Click to cancel search and
go back to the Insert Pictures
dialog box

Type the search
word(s) here

Important information
regarding Creative
Commons licensing

Click to show more
Web results

Click to insert image

FIGURE 8.23 Creative
Commons Licensing

Insert Online Videos onto a Web Page

STEP 6》 One of the most exciting features in Word 2013 is the ability to search and embed online video clips from Web sources, such as YouTube and Bing Video Search, into Office documents and to view the video directly within the context of the document itself. When you do not have to leave your open document to go to another window, you can stay focused on the content itself. From the Insert tab, click Online Video in the Media group. The Insert Video dialog box will appear, and you will have instant access to online video sources such as Bing Video Search, OneDrive, or YouTube, or you can embed video HTML code manually into the document. You can enlarge the video easily by clicking the embedded item. Figure 8.24 shows a video clip embedded in this Word document. To search for and insert a video into a Web page, do the following:

1. Click the INSERT tab.
2. Click Online Video in the Media group.
3. In the Insert Video dialog box, you may do one of the following:
   a. Type the key search word(s) in the Bing Video Search box and press Enter.
   b. Type the embed code in the *From a Video Embed Code* box and press Enter.
4. Click Insert to insert the video into the document.

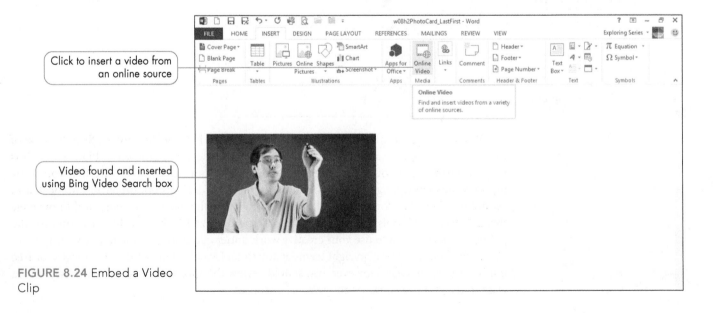

Click to insert a video from
an online source

Video found and inserted
using Bing Video Search box

FIGURE 8.24 Embed a Video
Clip

TIP | Watching an Online Video in a Word Document

Although an online video clip is embedded into the document, it is not stored on your hard drive. Therefore, you still need to have Internet access to watch the video. Certain Web browsers work better with online videos than others, so you might need to change your default Web browser.

Quick
Concepts

1. What is the purpose of writing a blog? *p. 504*
2. What are the advantages of presenting a Word document online? *p. 506*
3. Describe the reasons for using a blank design Word template. *p. 508*
4. Why do you want to store your photos online? *p. 509*
5. What are the advantages of embedding a video into a Word document? *p. 510*

Hands-On Exercises

Watch the Video
for this Hands-
On Exercise!

MyITLab®
HOE2 Training

2 Web Page Enhancement

The Web pages for *A Math Tutoring Club* are businesslike, and their purpose is to display information about the math worksheets and online resources that you provide. However, you enjoy a personal relationship with your students and often chat with them about their learning process. You want to start a blog to post some of the conversations and ideas you share with your students, hoping that your students can enjoy them as well. Also, you were very happy with the simple Web site that you built, and you want to present your math tutoring services to a larger group of participants. One of the things you had considered to enhance the Web page is to include a photo page, as well as conceptual and instructional videos that show students how to think critically and solve math problems. You will download a photo template to insert an online photo and to embed an online video. Then you will save the design template, first as a Word document and then as a Web page. Don't forget to link your PhotoCard page back to the home page and also to put the PhotoCard link on the home page. Once the process is complete, you will preview your Web pages using a Web browser.

Skills covered: Create and Set Up a Blog Account • Write a Blog Entry • Publish a Blog Post • Download a Design Template and Save as a Word Document • Insert an Online Photo • Insert an Online Video Clip • Save as a Single File Web Page and Preview Web Page

---

STEP 1 ≫ CREATE AND SET UP A BLOG ACCOUNT

In order to create a blog for the business, you must first set up an account with a service provider. You decide to use Blogger because it is one of the biggest blog providers on the Internet. Refer to Figure 8.25 as you complete Step 1.

FIGURE 8.25 New Blog Account Dialog Box

a. Start Word. Type **blog** in the *Search online templates* box and press **Enter**. Click the **Blog post template**. Click **Create** to download the blog template. If a *Register a Blog Account* dialog box appears, click **Register Later**.

A new document opens and the Ribbon contains only three tabs: File, Blog Post, and Insert. You might see more tabs if you install programs that create their own tabs or if you created your own custom tabs such as the myTab created in Hands-On Exercise 1. A placeholder prompts you to type the title of your post, and the insertion point is below the horizontal line, ready for you to create your post.

b. Click **Manage Accounts** in the Blog group on the BLOG POST tab. Click **New**.

c. Click the **Blog arrow** in the New Blog Account dialog box. Click **Blogger** and click **Next**.

If you have a different blog service provider, you should click the arrow, select that provider, and then type your personal identification and password in the next step. If you do not have an account with a blog service provider, you can create an account and return to this exercise or read through these steps and continue with Step 2. If you have a Gmail account, you can use the same logon and password to log on to Blogger.

d. Type your blog service user name in the **User Name box**. Type your blog service password in the **Password box**. Click **OK**.

If you have a Google account, you can use the same user name and password for your Google account to log on to your Blogger account.

e. Click **OK** when the Picture Options dialog box displays.

If you have a picture provider, you can click the Picture Provider arrow and select *My own server*. After you choose that option, boxes display where you type the Web address (URL) for the location where you upload your pictures and where the pictures are stored. In this exercise, we will not specify a picture provider.

f. Click **Yes** to the Microsoft Office Word dialog box that tells you a possibility exists that the information you send to your blog service provider could be seen by other people.

The information that passes from Word to your blog service provider is not encrypted, and this does provide the possibility of information being intercepted; however, this possibility is very small.

g. Select your blog in the *Choose a Blog* dialog box and click **OK**. Click **OK** to the Microsoft Office Word dialog box that indicates your account registration was successful.

When you register a blog service successfully, the service will display in the Blog Accounts dialog box.

h. Click **Close** in the Blog Accounts dialog box.

STEP 2 ≫ WRITE A BLOG ENTRY

Now it is time for you to start posting information that your students will enjoy viewing. You are going to write about the How to Learn Algebra I video clip presented by Mr. Jimmy Chang. You remember to use the Spell Check tool, which is an important resource to use before posting information publicly. Refer to Figure 8.26 as you complete Step 2.

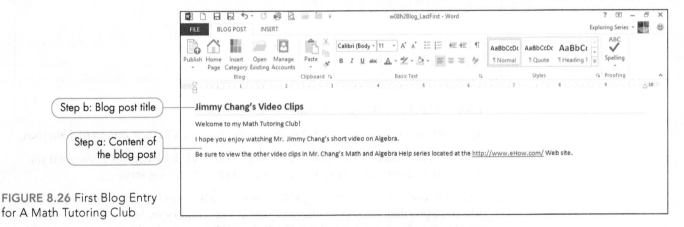

Step b: Blog post title

Step a: Content of the blog post

FIGURE 8.26 First Blog Entry for A Math Tutoring Club

a. Type the following text at the insertion point (below the title):

Welcome to my Math Tutoring Club!

I hope you enjoy watching Mr. Jimmy Chang's short video on Algebra.

Be sure to view the other video clips in Mr. Chang's Math and Algebra Help series located at the http://www.ehow.com/ Web site.

After you type the Web site address, notice that it will automatically turned into a hyperlink.

b. Click the placeholder *Enter Post Title Here* and type **Jimmy Chang's Video Clips**. Click anywhere in the document to deselect the post title you just typed.

c. Click **Spelling** in the Proofing group on the Blog Post tab. When spell check is complete, click **OK**.

d. Click the **FILE tab**, click **Save As**, click **Browse** to navigate to the w08hA_Math_Tutoring_ Club_LastFirst folder, and then type **w08h2Blog_LastFirst** in the **File name box**. Click **Save** to keep a copy of the post until you are ready to publish.

STEP 3 ›› PUBLISH A BLOG POST

Now that you have completed the post, it is time to upload it to the Blogger site. You can publish the blog posts right from Word with only a few clicks! Once complete, you display your blog in an Internet Explorer window so you can see the final product. Refer to Figure 8.27 as you complete Step 3.

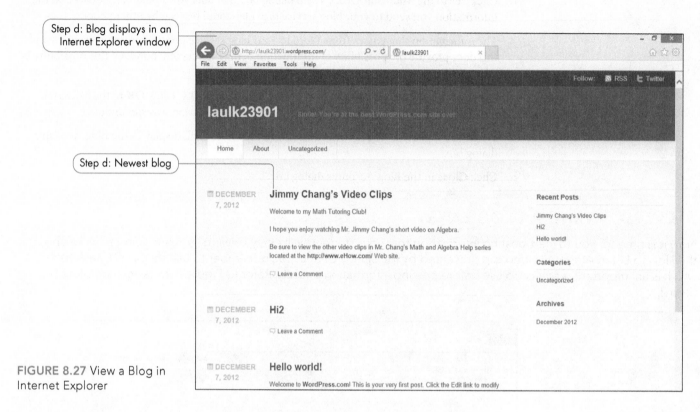

FIGURE 8.27 View a Blog in Internet Explorer

a. Click **Publish** in the Blog group on the BLOG POST tab.

b. Type your user name and password in the appropriate boxes in the Connect to dialog box.

The dialog box displays the name of your blog. You can click Remember Password if you want to avoid typing the password each time you post to the blog server.

c. Click **OK** to save and post the blog. Click **Yes** in the Microsoft Office Word dialog box that tells you a possibility exists that the information you send to your blog service provider could be seen by other people. Click **Don't show this message again** if you want to avoid clicking Yes at this dialog box each time you post a blog entry.

d. Click **Home Page** on the BLOG POST tab to display your blog in a separate Internet Explorer window.

e. Save and close the document. Exit Word. Submit based on your instructor's directions.

Instead of creating a Web page from scratch, you want to take advantage of the design templates available to you. The blank templates, along with other sorted template categories, are available for easy retrieval. For this exercise, you will search Office.com for a photo template, and you will insert an online picture, a text box, and an online video clip. Refer to Figure 8.28 as you complete Step 4.

Step b: Click to download the template

Step b: Click to view the previous template

Step b: Click to view other pages included with the template

FIGURE 8.28 Download a Blank Photo Greeting Card Template

a. Start Word. Click the **FILE tab**, click **New**, click in the **Search online templates box**, and then type **Photo**.

You have already created several pages for your A Math Tutoring Club Web site. You will now search for a template to use to insert and display your photo instead of creating the Web page from scratch. In the next few steps, you will select and download a photo template, and save the document as a Web page in the Web folder.

b. Scroll down the middle pane template options, click **Photo greeting card (tree design, half-fold)**, and then click **Create** to download the template.

c. Click the **FILE tab**, click **Save As**, and then click **Browse**. Navigate to the w08hA_Math_Tutoring_Club_LastFirst folder.

This is the same folder where you had saved all the other Web pages in Hands-On Exercise 1. You need to save all your documents together in the same folder to keep yourself organized. It would also be easier if you need to upload or email all the Web pages to someone else in a zipped file.

d. Double-click the **w08hA_Math_Tutoring_Club_LastFirst folder** to open it.

TIP **Pin a Design Template**

If you find a design template that you would like to use often, you can pin it to the Backstage view by clicking the *Pin to list* button so that it is always at the top portion of your template selection.

e. Type **w08h2PhotoCard_LastFirst** in the **File name box**. Make sure that it is saved as a Word document (.docx) file.

You want to save this file as a Word document file, and you will save it as a Web page later.

f. Click **Save** and click **OK** if a Microsoft Word message box appears to upgrade to the newest file format.

g. Leave the document open for the next step.

STEP 5 ≫ INSERT AN ONLINE PHOTO

With a photo template page, you will replace the photo with one of your choice. You will delete the current photo, search for another photo online that is more appropriate for your Web page, and then insert it into the same placeholder. This process is made easy by the design layout that was predefined for you as a template. Refer to Figure 8.29 as you complete Step 5.

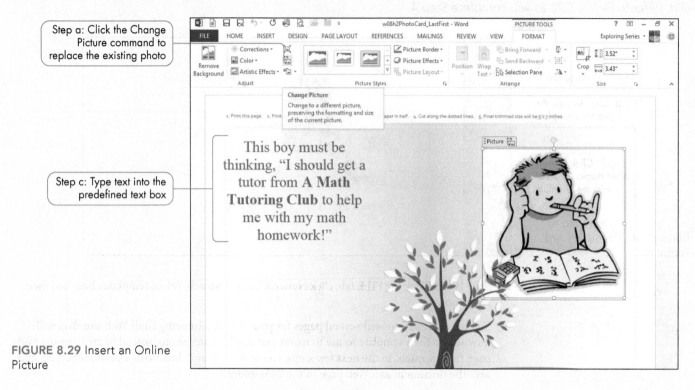

FIGURE 8.29 Insert an Online Picture

a. Insert a picture by completing the following steps:

- Click the photo located on the right side of the first page.
- Click the **FORMAT Tab** and click **Change Picture** in the Adjust group. Type **Math photo** in the **Bing Image Search box**. Press **Enter**.
- Review the list of photos and click the image of the little boy, as seen in Figure 8.29, to insert it into the document. If you do not find the same image that displays in Figure 8.29, you may substitute something different.
- Click **Insert** to insert the image into your document.

You searched for a photo from the Bing Image Search Web site. You can also search other online service photos, which include your own Flickr account.

b. Adjust the size of the image in the Size group of the FORMAT tab, if necessary.

c. Move the *thank you* box and insert your own text by doing the following:

- Select the text box on the second page. Right-click to display the shortcut menu and click **Cut**.
- Move up to the left side of the first page of the document. Press **Ctrl+V** to paste.
- Select the text in the text box and type: **This boy must be thinking, "I should get a tutor from A Math Tutoring Club to help me with my math homework!"**
- Select the text that you just typed and click **Times New Roman** and **26** on the mini toolbar. Select the text *A Math Tutoring Club* and click **Bold** from the mini toolbar.
- Click the **FORMAT tab** and click the **Shape Height arrow** in the Size group until *3.45"* displays.

d. Save the document.

STEP 6 ⟩⟩ INSERT AN ONLINE VIDEO CLIP

You know that many kids learn their math by watching someone teach them. So you want to insert an online instructional video on learning algebra in the PhotoCard Web page. You will search online for a video clip on algebra and insert the video onto the second page of the PhotoCard Web page. Refer to Figure 8.30 as you complete Step 6.

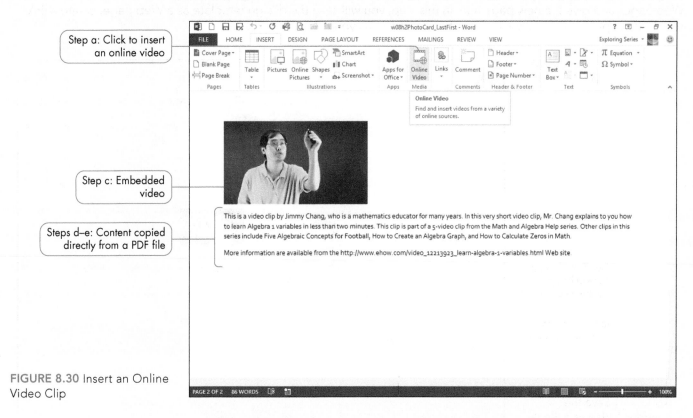

FIGURE 8.30 Insert an Online Video Clip

a. Delete the text box with a green gradient located at the top-left side on the second page. Click the **INSERT tab** and click **Online Video** in the Media group.

b. Type **How to Learn Algebra 1** in the **Bing Video Search box** and press **Enter**.

c. Click the first video, as illustrated in Figure 8.30, and click **Insert**.

   You inserted the video from Bing Video Search into your document, but you could also insert a video clip that you created on your own. If you cannot find the same video as that illustrated in Figure 8.30, you may substitute a similar one.

d. Navigate to your student files and open the *w08h2JimmyChang.pdf* file. Press **Ctrl+A** to select all of the text, press **Ctrl+C** or right-click the selected text, and then click **Copy**. Close the PDF file without saving changes if prompted.

   You are opening a PDF file in Word 2013, which allows you to open a PDF file without losing any of its formats. If you see a warning sign indicating that the PDF will be converting to an editable Word document, click **OK**.

e. Click **Word** on the task bar to display all the open documents. Click **w08h2PhotoCard_LastFirst**, press **Ctrl+End**, and then press **Enter**. Press **Ctrl+V** to paste.

   You are copying the text from the PDF file to Word. If needed, format the text and image layout so that it is more presentable.

f. Save the document.

STEP 7 >> SAVE AS A SINGLE FILE WEB PAGE AND PREVIEW WEB PAGE

After the video clip is embedded into your Word document, you are ready to save the document as a Web page so that viewers can watch the How to Learn Algebra I video clip from the Web page itself. Besides saving the design template as a Web page, you also want to put it in the w08hA_Math_Tutoring_Club folder together with the other Web pages and give it a new page title. In this step, you will save the design template as a Web page, create a link to the home page, and vice versa. Refer to Figure 8.31 as you complete Step 7.

Step b: Single File Web Page file extension

Step f: Web page showing the online photo and embedded video

Step h: *Return to Home Page* hyperlink

FIGURE 8.31 Save the Embedded Video as a Single File Web Page

a. Click the **FILE tab**, click **Save As**, and then click **Browse**.

b. Navigate to the drive and the w08hA_Math_Tutoring_Club_LastFirst folder in the Save As dialog box to save the file. You will save the document with the same name. Click the **Save as type arrow** and click **Single File Web Page (*.mht; *.mhtml)**.

    When you save as a Web page, the Save As dialog box displays the *Page title* text area and the Change Title button.

c. Click **Change Title** to display the Enter Text dialog box and change the title to **A Math Tutoring Club - Photo Card**. Click **OK**.

    In this dialog box, you can edit the Web page title, which will also appear on the Web browser's title bar when the Web page displays.

d. Click **Save**. If necessary, click **Continue** when you see a dialog box telling you that each video will be converted to an image with a link.

    The page displays in Web Layout view.

TIP | **Saving an Embedded Video document as a Web Page**

If you intend to embed an online video to a Word document or template, you must insert the video *before* you save it as a Web page. Once you save a document or template as a Web page, this immediately disables the Online Video button.

e. Open the *w08h1Default_LastFirst* Web page and save it as **w08h2Default_LastFirst** by changing *h1* to *h2*.

f. Create a link to the home page by completing the following steps:

- Press **Ctrl+End**, press **Enter**, and then type **Return to the Home Page**.

  Pressing Ctrl+End brings you to the end of the image, and pressing Enter inserts a blank line for you to type text.

- Select the **Return to the Home Page text**, click the **INSERT tab**, click **Hyperlink** in the Links group to display the Insert Hyperlink dialog box.
- Click **Existing File or Web Page** in the *Link to* panel of the Insert Hyperlink dialog box. Scroll, if necessary, and click the **w08h2Default_LastFirst.htm file**. Click **OK**.

  By creating this link, the home page displays when you click *Return to the Home Page* on the PhotoCard page.

g. Create a link to the Photo Card page from the home page by completing the following steps:

- Click the *w08h2Default_LastFirst.htm* file on the task bar.
- Scroll to the bottom of the page, select **Resources** in the 1-row table, right-click, and then click **Hyperlink**.
- Click the *w08h2PhotoCard_LastFirst* Web page and press **OK**.

  You will see two *w08h2PhotoCard_LastFirst* files in this folder. One is a Word document and the other is a Web page. Make sure that you select the Web page file.

- Save the document.

  Now the home page has a link to the page that contains the photo and the embedded video clip.

h. Click the **myTab tab** and click **Web Page Preview** in the Web group to view the PhotoCard page in an Internet Explorer window. Click the **Return to Home Page hyperlink page** to navigate back to the home page. Close Internet Explorer.

> **TROUBLESHOOTING**: If you are using a Web Browser other than Internet Explorer, you might notice that the Position Object and Wrap Text features are disabled because they are not compatible with your Web browser. You may want to switch to Internet Explorer instead, which is more user-friendly with Word Web pages.

i. Go back to Word. Click the **FILE tab**, click **Options**, and then click **Customize Ribbon**. Uncheck **myTab tab** to reset the ribbon back to the default ribbon setting. Close all files and exit Word.

j. Open File Explorer and navigate to the w08hA_Math_Tutoring_Club_LastFirst folder. Select ALL of the files and subfolders in this folder, right-click to display the shortcut menu, click **Send to**, and then select **Compressed (zipped) folder**.

  Make sure that all the selected files and subfolders in the w08hA_Math_Tutoring_Club_LastFirst folder are now contained in a zipped file. These files and folders include those that you created in Hands-on Exercise 1.

k. Highlight the zipped file name and rename it **w08h2A_Math_Tutoring_Club_LastFirst**. Submit your zipped file based on your instructor's directions.

  Notice that you rename the file with *h2* instead of *h1*. This way your instructor will know that this solution file is for Hands-On Exercise 2. When your instructor downloads the zipped file onto his or her computer, he or she can view all the Web pages that you have created for this exercise using a Web browser.

Chapter Objectives Review

After reading this chapter, you have accomplished the following objectives:

1. Customize the Ribbon.

- Create a custom tab: Create a custom tab for the Ribbon that contains only the features that you use most frequently or features that are not available on the standard Ribbon. You can also create new groups within the tab.
- Add commands to a group: Besides changing the order of the tabs or the groups that appear within the tabs, you can also add commands that are not on the default tabs to a group in your personalized tab, and export and import custom tabs.

2. Build and publish a Web page.

- Save as a Web page: Word provides all the tools necessary to create a basic Web page, converts the document, and generates the HTML (HyperText Markup Language) code for you. You can easily save a Word document as a Web Page to be published to the Internet to be accessed by anyone online.
- Apply a theme and background color to a Web Page: A colored background adds visual enhancement to the Web page. Use the Word themes to coordinate colors and fonts.
- Insert bookmarks in a Web page: A bookmark is an electronic marker for a specific location in a document, enabling the user to go to that location quickly. Bookmarks are helpful in long documents because they enable you to move easily from one place to another within that document, without having to manually scroll through the document.
- Insert hyperlinks in a Web page: Hyperlinks are electronic markers that, when clicked, move the insertion point to a different location within the same document, open another document, or display a different Web page in a Web browser.
- Preview a Web page: As you prepare a Web page, the Web Layout view gives you a very accurate representation of how the page will look when published. You can preview the page in an actual Web browser before you upload and publish it so that you can confirm it contains the correct content and is formatted to your specifications.
- Publish a Web page: To view the pages on the Internet, you must save or publish them to a Web server, which is a computer system that hosts pages so that they are available for viewing by anyone who has an Internet connection.

3. Create a blog post.

- Download a blog post template: A blog post template downloaded from Microsoft would be very beneficial to you if you are accustomed to working in Word and also publish blogs on a frequent basis.
- Create and set up a Blog Account: You must establish a blog account with one of several blog service providers before you can register and publish blogs directly from Word.
- Include pictures in a blog posting: Word 2013 allows you to post pictures with your blog. However, the pictures are stored in a separate file and can be accessed via a link on the blog text.
- Publish a blog post: When you are ready, you can publish your blog post from Word by clicking the File tab, Share, and then *Post to Blog*.

4. Present a Word document online.

- Collaborate on a Word document online: After you work on a document, you may collaborate on the work by uploading and sharing the document with others online.
- Edit a Word document online: Besides sharing your document online with others, you can also make changes to the document instantly and in real time during your presentation.

5. Enhance a Web page.

- Save a blank design Word template as a Web page: Blank design templates are empty documents preformatted with frequently used styles. It is more time efficient to use a predefined template and save it as a Web page.
- Insert online photos onto a Web page: After you create your Web site, you can go a step further by enhancing it using features such as online photos from any of the online sources or from your own Flickr account.
- Insert online videos onto a Web page: One of the new features in Word 2013 is the ability to insert and embed an online video into your Word or Web page so that your audience can view the video clips without having to leave the document page.

Key Terms Matching

Match the key terms with their definitions. Write the key term letter by the appropriate numbered definition.

a. Internet
b. World Wide Web (WWW)
c. Web page
d. HyperText Markup Language (HTML)
e. Background

f. Hyperlink
g. Web server
h. File Transfer Protocol (FTP)
i. Blog
j. Bookmark

1. _____ An electronic marker that points to a different location or displays a different Web page. **p. 492**

2. _____ A network of networks that connects computers anywhere in the world. **p. 484**

3. _____ Any document that displays on the World Wide Web. **p. 484**

4. _____ The chronological publication of personal thoughts. **p. 504**

5. _____ A process that uploads files from a PC to a server or from a server to a PC. **p. 494**

6. _____ An electronic marker for a specific location in a document. **p. 491**

7. _____ A color, design, image, or watermark that appears behind text in a document or on a Web page. **p. 490**

8. _____ A very large subset of the Internet that stores Web page documents. **p. 484**

9. _____ Uses codes to describe how a document appears when viewed in a Web browser. **p. 487**

10. _____ A computer system that hosts pages for viewing by anyone with an Internet connection. **p. 494**

Multiple Choice

1. While you are creating and editing documents that will be part of a Web site, you should save them in which format?

    (a) XML
    (b) HTML
    (c) Compatibility Mode
    (d) Text

2. Which of the following is not a legitimate object to use in a hyperlink?

    (a) Schema
    (b) E-mail address
    (c) Web page
    (d) Bookmark

3. What is the advantage of applying a theme to a Web page?

    (a) It adds a background color automatically.
    (b) It cannot be removed after you apply it.
    (c) It applies a uniform design to the links and other objects in a document.
    (d) It is automatically applied to each additional Web page you create.

4. If you view a Web page and hyperlinks display in two different colors, what is the most likely explanation?

    (a) A different theme was applied to each hyperlink.
    (b) One of the hyperlinks is invalid.
    (c) One of the hyperlinks was previously visited.
    (d) One of the hyperlinks is a bookmark.

5. Which of the following is not a format used to save documents as Web pages?

    (a) Web Template
    (b) Single File Web Page
    (c) Web Page
    (d) Web Page, Filtered

6. What information is relayed to the Web browser by HTML tags?

    (a) How to categorize the data on the Web page
    (b) How to save the information on the Web page
    (c) How to transfer the data to a Web server
    (d) How to format the information on the Web page

7. Which of the following statements about online video is not true?

    (a) Once it is embedded into a Web page, it can be viewed without Internet access.
    (b) To insert an online video, click Online Video in the Media group.
    (c) You can insert videos from YouTube.com directly onto your Word document.
    (d) You can manually insert the video HTML code into the Insert Video dialog box.

8. Which of the following statements about online presentations is not true?

    (a) The presenter can share notes with the audience.
    (b) The presenter can start or pause the online presentation at any time.
    (c) The audience must complete the viewing of the whole online presentation at one sitting.
    (d) The audience can retrieve updated documents instantly from the presenter.

9. What type of Web site enables you to view the frequent, chronological publication of personal thoughts?

    (a) Search engine
    (b) FTP
    (c) Web server
    (d) Blog

10. What feature should you change in order to display information about your Web site at the top of the Internet Explorer window?

    (a) XML element
    (b) File name
    (c) Page title
    (d) Document theme

Practice Exercises

1 Dave Meinert Realtors

Dave Meinert owns a large real estate company in New Orleans. The company offers a comprehensive list of services beyond the standard commercial and residential real estate sales and listings, including management of retirement community properties and commercial properties. Although the company is profitable, Dave realizes he should post information about the organization and its services on a Web site. He prefers to establish a very simple Web site in the beginning, and contract a Web site development professional to enhance the site if it generates a lot of business. Dave takes the following steps to turn a few basic Word documents into Web pages. This exercise follows the same set of skills as used in Hands-On Exercise 1 in the chapter. Refer to Figure 8.32 as you complete this exercise.

HTM extension indicates the file is saved as a Web page

Web Page Preview command added to View tab

Hyperlink takes you to a paragraph below

Click this link to return to the very top of the page

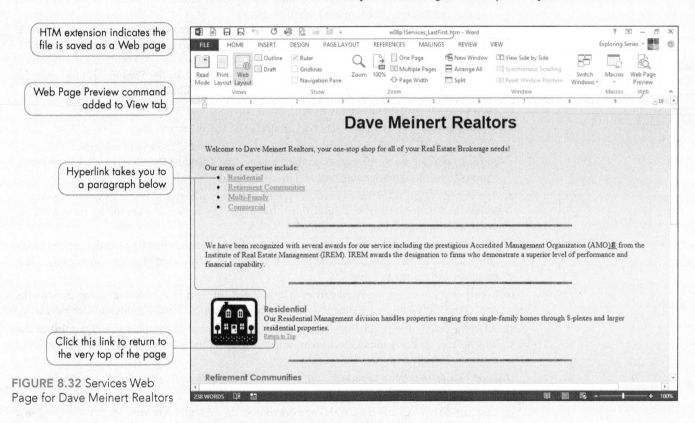

FIGURE 8.32 Services Web Page for Dave Meinert Realtors

a. Start Word and open *w08p1Default*.

b. Customize the Ribbon by completing the following steps:
   - Click the **FILE tab**, click **Options**, and then click **Customize Ribbon**.
   - Click the **VIEW tab** in the Main Tabs list on the right. Click **New Group** and click **Rename**. Type **Web** in the **Display name box** and click **OK**.
   - Click the **Choose commands from arrow** and select **Commands Not in the Ribbon**.
   - Scroll down and click **Web Page Preview**. Click **Add** to add the command to the Web group in the VIEW tab.
   - Click **OK** to close the Word Options dialog box.

c. Click the **FILE tab**, click **Save As**, and then click **Browse**. In the Save As dialog box, navigate to the drive and folder in which you want to create a Web folder.

d. Create a folder and save the file as a Web page by completing the following steps:
   - Click **New Folder** on the Save As dialog box toolbar, type **w08p1Realtor_LastFirst**, and then press **Enter**. Click **Open**.
   - Type **w08p1Default_LastFirst** in the **File name box**. Click the **Save as type arrow** and click **Web Page (*.htm; *.html)**.
   - Click **Change Title** to display the Enter Text dialog box. Type **Dave Meinert Real Estate** in the **Page title box** and click **OK**. Click **Save**.

e. Open *w08p1Services* and save it as a Web page named **w08p1Services_LastFirst** in the w08p1Realtor_LastFirst folder. Click **Change Title**, type **Dave Meinert Real Estate Services**, click **OK**, and then click **Save**.

f. Press **Alt+Tab** as needed to display the *w08p1Default_LastFirst* file. Select **Real Estate Services** and click **Hyperlink** in the Links group on the INSERT tab. Click **Existing File or Web Page** in the *Link to* panel of the Insert Hyperlink dialog box. Double-click the **w08p1Realtor_LastFirst folder**, if necessary, click the *w08p1Services_LastFirst.htm* file, and then click **OK**.

g. Apply themes and color to the pages by completing the following steps:
   - Click the **DESIGN tab**, click **Themes** in the Document Formatting group, and then click **Wisp**.
   - Click **Page Color** in the Page Background group. Click **Fill Effects** to display the Fill Effects dialog box and click the **Gradient tab**, if necessary.
   - Click **Two colors** in the *Colors* section. Click the **Color 1 arrow** and select **Orange, Accent 2, Lighter 80%** (second row, sixth column). Click the **Color 2 arrow** and select **Orange, Accent 2, Lighter 60%** (third row, sixth column).
   - Click **Horizontal** in the *Shading styles* section, if necessary. In the *Variants* section, click the square in the top-right corner. Click **OK** to apply the background.

h. Press **Ctrl+S** to save the changes to *w08p1Default_LastFirst.htm*.

i. Repeat step g to apply the theme and background color to the Services page.

j. Place the insertion point on the left side of the second instance of the word *Residential*, which displays as a heading for the paragraph on the Services page. Click the **INSERT tab**, click **Bookmark**, type **res** in the **Bookmark name box**, and then click **Add**.

k. Repeat step j to create bookmarks at the beginning of the headings *Retirement Communities*, *Multi-Family*, and *Commercial* that display down the page. The bookmarks should be named **retire**, **multi**, and **com** respectively.

l. Select **Residential** in the bulleted list near the top of the page and click **Hyperlink** from the Links group. Click **Place in This Document** in the *Link to* panel of the Insert Hyperlink dialog box. Click **res** under *Bookmarks* and click **OK**.

m. Repeat step l to create hyperlinks from each bulleted list item to the corresponding bookmarks retire, multi, and com for bulleted text *Retirement Communities*, *Multi-Family*, and *Commercial*.

n. Select the text *Return to Top* that displays below the *Residential* paragraph. Click **Hyperlink** in the Links group, click **Top of the Document**, which displays at the very top of the *Select a place in this document* list, and then click **OK**.

o. Repeat step n to create a hyperlink from each occurrence of *Return to Top* that displays throughout the Services page.

p. Click the **VIEW tab** and click **Web Page Preview** in the Web group to view the Services page in a Web browser window. Click the hyperlinks in the Services page to navigate up and down the page. Close your Web browser.

q. Save and close all pages. Open File Explorer and navigate to the w08p1Realtor_LastFirst folder. Select all the files and subfolders in this folder, right-click to display the shortcut menu, click **Send to**, and then select **Compressed (zipped) folder**.

r. Select the zipped file name and rename the zipped file **w08p1Realtor_LastFirst**. Submit your zipped file based on your instructor's directions.

2 Create a Blog Post

Jane Stone is participating in a study abroad program at Illinois State University this fall and will spend the semester in China. She is excited about the opportunities to learn about a different country, the people, the language, and the culture. She is also very happy that they do not have classes on Friday, so she can travel and see as much of the country as possible. Her parents are nervous about her time away and want her to write home as much as possible. Her friends are also eager to hear about her experiences. Jane decides the most convenient and efficient way to communicate with everyone is to post blog entries frequently. She can use Word 2013 on her laptop, which she will have with her most of the time, to quickly write and post the blog entries to Blogger—the blog she set up using her Google account. Jane will follow these steps to connect to her blog account and prepare the first entry. Jane can also post photos to her blog. This exercise follows the same set of skills as used in Hands-On Exercise 2 in the chapter. Refer to Figure 8.33 as you complete this exercise.

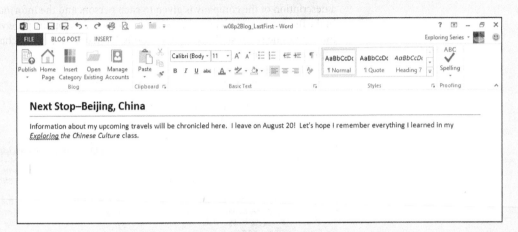

FIGURE 8.33 Blog Post for China Trip

FROM SCRATCH

a. Start Word. Type **blog** in the *Search online templates* box and press **Enter**. Click the **Blog post template**. Click **Create** to download the blog template. If the *Register a Blog Account* dialog box displays, click **Register Later**. If you do not have an account with a blog service provider, you can create an account and return to this exercise. If you have a blog account, continue with step b.

b. Click **Manage Accounts** in the Blog group on the BLOG POST tab. Click **New**. Click the **Blog arrow** in the New Blog Account dialog box. Click **Blogger** and click **Next**.

c. Type your blog service user name in the **User Name box**. Type your blog service password in the **Password box**. Click **OK**. Click **OK** when the Picture Options dialog box displays.

d. Click **Yes** in the Microsoft Office Word dialog box that tells you a possibility exists that the information you send to your blog service provider could be seen by other people.

e. Click **OK** in the Microsoft Office Word dialog box that indicates your account registration was successful. Click **Close** in the Blog Accounts dialog box.

f. Type the following text at the insertion point: **Information about my upcoming travels will be chronicled here. I leave on August 20! Let's hope I remember everything I learned in my Exploring the Chinese Culture class.** Select the text *Exploring the Chinese Culture* in the last sentence typed and click **Italic** from the mini toolbar.

g. Click the placeholder *Enter Post Title Here* and insert the text **Next Stop–Beijing, China**.

h. Click the **Spelling arrow** in the Proofing group on the BLOG POST tab.

i. Click the **FILE tab**, click **Save As**, and then navigate to the folder where you store solution files. Type **w08p2Blog_LastFirst** in the **File name box**. Click **Save** to keep a copy of the post until you are ready to publish.

j. Click **Publish** in the Blog group on the BLOG POST tab to publish this blog to your account, if you previously created one. Type your user name and password in the appropriate boxes in the Connect to dialog box.

k. Click **OK** to save and post the blog. Click **Yes** in the Microsoft Office Word dialog box that tells you a possibility exists the information you send to your blog service provider could be seen by other people. Click **Don't show this message again** if you want to avoid clicking Yes at this dialog box each time you post a blog entry.

l. Click **Home Page** on the BLOG POST tab to display the blog in a separate Web browser window.

m. Close the document. Submit it based on your instructor's directions.

1 FlyRight Airways Web Site

The marketing manager at a fledgling airline company is hosting a competition that awards a prize to the employee who designs the best home page for the company's Web site. A document that provides a description of the company is given to each person, and the information on that page should display in the final version. You take the following steps to develop the page you will submit. This exercise follows the same set of skills as used in Hands-On Exercise 1 in the chapter. Refer to Figure 8.34 as you complete this exercise.

FlyRight Airways
Contact us

The mission of FlyRight Airways is to provide courteous, on-time charter services to our customers in well-maintained aircraft flown by highly trained, professional flight crews. Our fleet of 15 Boeing 737 aircraft and 5 Boeing 767 is among the most reliable and safest in the industry. Each plane has been outfitted with modern, state-of-the-art equipment – including Global Positioning Systems, radar, auto-pilot systems and smoke detectors in all cargo and luggage compartments. Every FAA safety inspection conducted has been passed with excellent evaluations. In addition, our passenger safety record is, and always has been, a perfect one.
Our 737 aircraft are outfitted for 146 passengers and have a range of 2,200 miles non-stop. The 767 aircraft are outfitted for 220 passengers and have a range of 4,000 miles non-stop. Catering services from snacks to full meal service is available, depending on your particular needs. In-flight entertainment, including radio, TV, and movies, is also available. Whatever your needs, we will do our best to meet them and more.
For more information on Boeing aircraft, visit the Boeing site and click on the link to Products & Services. Once you have booked your flight, you may follow it from take-off to landing at FlyteComm.

Fleet Information Courtesy of Boeing.com
The Boeing 737 is the world's most popular commercial jet transport. The 737 family has won orders for more than 6,000 airplanes, which is more airplanes than The Boeing Company's biggest competitor has won for its entire product line since it began business. The 737 is a short-to-medium-range airplane, based on a key Boeing philosophy of delivering value to airlines with reliability, simplicity and reduced operating and maintenance costs.

The Boeing 767 family of airplanes provides maximum market versatility in the 200- to 300-seat market. The Boeing Signature Interior uses state-of-the-art lighting and design concepts to amplify the feeling of spaciousness on an airplane already prized for long-range comfort. They include deeper stowage bins, and offer increased flexibility in positioning and maintaining lavatories. They also feature an improved in-flight entertainment interface.

FIGURE 8.34 FlyRight Airways Web site

a. Open *w08m1Airline* and save the document as a Single File Web page (*.mht; *.mhtml) using the name **w08m1Airline_LastFirst**.

b. Change the Page title to **Take off with FlyRight Airways**.

c. Customize the Ribbon to put the buttons you use most on one custom tab with groups. You can modify the myTab tab you created in Hands-On Exercise 1 or reset the Ribbon to its original state and create a new tab with groups.

d. Apply any theme to the page. Apply the **Intense Emphasis style** to the company name that displays at the top of the document and increase the font size to **20**. Use a different style if you do not find Intense Emphasis on your list of styles.

e. Apply a background color to the page. Use a Gradient Fill Effect that uses two colors. Use a Diagonal down shading style and select **variant effect** in the top-left corner.

DISCOVER

f. Select the text *Contact us* that displays near the top of the document. Insert a hyperlink that links to the e-mail address *help@flyrightairways.org* and that contains the subject *Request for Information*.

g. Perform a Web search to find Web site addresses for the two companies mentioned—Boeing and FlyteComm—in the second paragraph. Create hyperlinks to those companies after you find their Web site addresses. The FlyteComm site enables you to track a flight from takeoff to landing.

h. Create bookmarks named **b737** and **b767** at the beginning of the paragraphs at the bottom of the page that describe the two types of aircraft. Create hyperlinks to these bookmarks from the text *Boeing 737* and *Boeing 767* that display in the first paragraph.

i. Save and close the document. Start File Explorer, navigate to the folder containing your Web page, and double-click the file you just created. A Web browser will start automatically because your document was saved as a Web page. Look carefully at the Address bar and note the local address, as opposed to a Web address. Test all links.

j. Close the Web browser. Submit the document based on your instructor's directions.

2 Introduce Myself Blog

CREATIVE CASE

FROM SCRATCH

You are enrolled in a social media marketing class at the local university. Companies often use popular social media tools such as Twitter, Facebook, MySpace, LinkedIn, apps, Youtube, Google+, and blogs to advertise products. Therefore, the first assignment in this marketing course is to "sell" yourself to your instructor and your classmates. Your instructor suggests that you use a blog to advertise your first product. You may write about your hobbies, interests, strengths, classes you are taking, and your career goals. Also, to put a face to a name, you need to insert a reasonably sized photo of yourself on a blog post. Since this is a marketing class, feel free to use any kind of Word features to spice up your blog posting. However, you need to remember that you are treading a very fine line in this assignment. On one hand, you want to present enough information to "sell" yourself, but on the other hand, you need to be careful not to reveal information that may be considered private. After all the blogs are posted, students will evaluate the blog postings and will vote on them using "likes" or "dislikes." Your grade for this assignment will be determined by the number of "likes" that you receive from the class.

a. Download the blog post template and save it as **w08m2Blog_LastFirst**. If you do not have an account with a blog service provider, you can create an account and return to this exercise. If you have a blog account, continue with step b.

b. Write several paragraphs about yourself in your blog that you want others to know about you.

c. Use graphics or a table to tabulate data or information to present your case, if desired.

d. Insert a picture of yourself at the bottom of the blog page. Resize the picture to roughly 2" in height.

e. Type your last name and first name as the Post Title.

f. Proofread your blog entry by clicking the **Spelling arrow** in the Proofing group on the BLOG POST tab.

g. Publish your blog entry online.

h. Close the document. Submit it based on your instructor's directions.

3 A Politician Web Site

COLLABORATION CASE

FROM SCRATCH

One of the local politicians is a friend of the instructor of your Web Design class. He was looking for someone to create a Web site for him in order to convey pertinent information to the constituents. This Web site can also help to address important issues, collect suggestions and constructive feedback from citizens, provide local construction updates, and publicize social events. Your instructor divides the class into groups of several students and assigns this request as a class project to replace the final exam. Each group will design a Web site from scratch and will use all the Web design features described in this chapter. For instance, one of the appointed team members will customize the Ribbon to include a new tab and group with commands that the team will use frequently for this project. The Web site will include, but will not be limited to, the following pages:

- Home page with a welcome message from the politician and links to all the other pages
- *Important Issues* page to address pertinent concerns of the constituents
- *Local Updates* page
- *Social Events* page
- *Local Resources Available to Citizens* page
- *Contact Information* page

a. Use an online collaboration tool such as Google Chat or Skype to conduct an online meeting with your group members. During this online chat session, the group will do the following:

- Choose a name for the group and select a group leader.
- Develop a list of tasks to complete, which will include designing a story board and deciding on the number of Web pages.
- Assign tasks and responsibilities to each group member.

b. The team leader will create a OneDrive or Dropbox.com account, where each member can share, download, and open the submitted documents.

c. Hand draw several Web pages, scan them, and save them as one image file with the name **w08m3WebDesign_LastFirst**. All the students' individual image files will be assembled into one zipped file and posted to the online storage location.

d. Meet online as a group to review all the designs and will decide on the final choice. Each group member, except the team leader, will be responsible for developing one or more Web pages.

e. The group leader will use tools such as Snipping tool, SnagIt, or the PRT SC button on your keyboard to capture the chat session at several stages and to record the contributions from team members. Copy and paste all the screenshots into a Word document and save it as **w08m3WebDiscussion_GroupName**. Make sure to add a caption to your screenshots.

f. After all the individual Web pages are uploaded to the virtual storage location, the group leader will assemble all the Web pages and test all the hyperlinks and bookmarks.

g. Save the Web page as a Single File Web page (*.mht; *.mhtml), using the name **w08m3Default_GroupName**.

h. Post all your files to the online storage location.

i. Inform your instructor that the documents are ready for grading, and also give directions to where they are located.

j. Present your proposed Web site to the client via the Present Online option in Word 2013 since your client is a very busy person and is frequently out of town.

Beyond the Classroom

Track Your Investments

You are enrolled in a personal finance class this semester. One of the major semester projects for this class is to develop your own retirement plan. The Internet is a great resource for you to research and make a short list of companies in which you would like to invest. You will track stock prices, sales performances, profit margins, and other financial indicators and tabulate the results in a table. Copy and paste several performance charts to your Word document. Save the document as **w08b2Stocks_LastFirst.docx** and submit it based on your instructor's directions. A portion of your course grade requires that you present your proposed retirement plan online to your classmates during the last week of class using the Share option in Microsoft Word 2013. Finally, you will create a blog online to solicit feedback and comments from your classmates on your proposed retirement plan.

Modify a Video Clip

You are a member of the Web Design team for the Christmas Candle Web site. One of the junior Web designers had embedded a video clip from youtube.com that has since been removed from the Web site. Create a folder named **w08b3ChristmasCandle_LastFirst**. Open the *w08b3Default.mht* file, rename it **w08b3Default_LastFirst.mht**, and then save it to the newly created folder. Search the Internet using a search engine such as Bing or Google for a video clip that emphasizes safety when lighting candles at home. Locate the nonworking video on your Web page and replace it with the new video clip. Test your Web page and the new video. Save and close all files, and submit them based on your instructor's directions.

E-Mail Etiquette

You will review your own online postings and blogs to see if you adhere to the standards of email etiquette. Also, evaluate your own postings on Facebook and Twitter, the photos that you have attached, and your understanding of the Creative Commons licensing. Summarize your findings in a three-page paper on the etiquette of using social media tools. After you have checked the spelling and grammar of your three-page paper, save it as **w08b4EmailEtiquette_LastFirst**. Submit the document as directed by your instructor.

Capstone Exercise

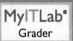
MyITLab®
Grader

Joyful Scents Candle Company is a family-owned business that manufactures and sells candles. So far, this company has relied on telephone and fax orders. Because of your extensive experience with Word 2013, the company president hired you to create a Web site. Refer to Figure 8.35 as you redesign the home page.

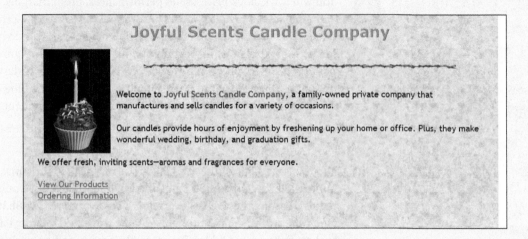

FIGURE 8.35 Joyful Scents Candle Company Web Site

Save a PDF File as a Word Document

The Order page is in PDF format, but you want to save it as a Word document before you link it to the home page.

a. Create a folder named **w08c1Candles_LastFirst** and download the student files to this folder.

b. Start Word. Open the file named *w08c1Order.pdf* and save it as a Word document named **w08c1Order_LastFirst** in the w08c1Candles_LastFirst folder.

Design a Set of Web Pages

You need to convert existing documents to Web pages for Joyful Scents, but before you save them as Web pages, you redesign the pages to incorporate visual enhancements, such as color and graphics.

a. Open the documents *w08c1Default* and *w08c1Products*.

b. Customize the Ribbon to put the buttons you use most on one custom tab with groups. You can modify the myTab tab you created in Hands-On Exercise 1 or reset the Ribbon to its original state and create a new tab with groups.

c. Display the default document, which will become the home page of the Web site. Create a background color with the **Bouquet Texture Fill Effects** (fifth row, fourth column). Apply the **Frame theme**. Increase font sizes of headings to **22 pt** and apply the text effect **Fill - Orange, Accent 4, Soft Bevel** (first row, fifth column).

d. Insert an image of a candle and display it on the right side of the home page. Use picture format tools to resize the picture to **2"** tall and apply the **Soft Edge Oval effect**. If you do not have access to the Internet, use your judgment

on the image you use and use the picture format tools that would be most appropriate for that image.

e. Save this document in the w08c1CandlesLast_First folder as a Web Page named **w08c1Default_LastFirst**.

f. Display the Products document. Apply the **Frame theme** and **Bouquet Texture Fill Effects** to the document. Apply the same text effect and **22-pt font size** used on the default page to the products page heading. Save this document in the w08c1Candles_LastFirst folder as a Web page (*.htm, *.html) named **w08c1Products_LastFirst**.

g. Display the Order document. Apply the **Frame theme** and **Bouquet Texture Fill Effects** to the document. Apply the same text effect and **22-pt font size** used on the default page to the order page heading. Center the text that is currently left justified. Save this document as a Web page in the w08c1Candles_LastFirst folder and change the page title to **Joyful Scents Ordering Information**.

Add Navigation Elements to Web Pages

Your pages are looking good. Now you want to add the ability to navigate within a long page and also to navigate easily between the pages.

a. Display the Default page. Type **View Our Products** and **Ordering Information** on the bottom of the default page. Create hyperlinks to the Products and Order Web pages from these lines of text.

b. Display the Products page. Create the following bookmarks in the appropriate heading location that correspond with the information on the page: **standard**, **exotic**, **sizes**, and **descriptions**.

c. Create a list near the top of the page under the paragraph beginning with *Joyful Scents Candle Company provides* for the categories that display down the page. Center the list and create a hyperlink from each item on the list to the appropriate bookmark.

d. Create a **Back to Top hyperlink** at the end of each category that will use a bookmark to navigate back to the top of the document.

e. Type **HOME** at the bottom of the page and create a hyperlink to the default page. Save the page.

f. Display the Order page. Create a hyperlink from *HOME* to the default page. Save the page.

Replace the Photo on the Default Page

You want to replace the photo on the default page with a photo showing a candle on a cupcake.

a. Select the *w08c1Default_LastFirst* document.

b. Select the candle photo on the first page.

c. Conduct a search on Bing Image Search using the key words *a single candle on a chocolate cupcake*. You may substitute the photo with a similar one.

d. Replace the original photo with this new photo.

Add an Online Video to the Order Page

You want to include a video on the safety of burning candles at home on the last page.

a. Go to the last page of the document.

b. Position the insertion point in the paragraph above *HOME*.

c. Conduct a search on youtube.com using the key words *Candle Burning Safety Tips*. You may substitute with a similar video.

d. Insert the video into the document.

Document Progress in a Blog Post

The president of Joyful Scents Candle Company is a strong proponent of documentation. She would like to know how much time you spent on this project and what resources you used. She advocates a casual workplace, so she recommended you just post a blog on the company server so she can read it later. You start the blog and then find the server is down for maintenance, so you save your work and post it at a later time.

a. Open a new blog post document.

b. Note that the title of the blog post is *Preparing the Company Web Site*. Type the following sentence for the post: **I used Word 2013 to design the Web site. Features such as background color, themes, hyperlinks, and bookmarks made the process easy.**

c. Save the blog post in the w08c1Candles_LastFirst folder as **w08c1Blog_LastFirst**.

d. Save and close all files. Preview all your Web pages and test all links. Open File Explorer and send all the files in this folder to a zipped file named **w08c1Candles_LastFirst**. Submit it based on your instructor's directions.

You are an employee of Calypso Travel Club, which is a timesharing resort management company. Your position requires that you encourage owner participation and promote travel programs. You are also involved with providing new owners with all the information they need to begin planning vacations and taking advantage of club ownership. One of the first things you send each new owner is a Quick Start Guide. You typically create a mailing once each month, with a welcome letter and the Quick Start Guide. You have prepared that material and are ready to merge the document with a database table of new owners. You will format the letter and the Quick Start Guide to produce a mailing that is both attractive and informative.

Review Comments

You will review and respond to comments left by your supervisor.

a. Start Word. Open *w00ac1Travel*. Note: You may notice some spelling errors; you will fix these later in this exercise.

b. Ensure that all of the markup is shown. Track Changes should not be on. You will find three comments on page 2 of the document. Read and act on each comment. There is no need to reply to the comments; just take the action required.

c. Delete all comments in the document.

Format Characters and Paragraphs

You will improve the appearance of the document by adjusting line and paragraph spacing and modifying the font. In addition, bullets will draw attention to selected paragraphs.

a. Select all text from *Welcome to the Club!* on page 2 to the end of the document. (Because the WordArt object is anchored to the first paragraph, it will be selected as well.) Change the line spacing to **1.5** and ensure that paragraph spacing before and after is **0**.

b. With all document text selected, change the font to **Georgia** with a font size of **12 pt**.

c. Add solid round bullets to the following paragraphs:

- The three paragraphs under the *Flexibility* heading near the end of page 2, beginning with *Experience exotic destinations* and ending with *Bonus Time*.
- The three paragraphs under the *Convenience* heading at the bottom of page 2 and the top of page 3, beginning with *Automatically receive* and ending with *vacation planning*.
- The three paragraphs under the *Affordability* heading on page 3, beginning with *Enjoy vacations* and ending with *from your taxes*.

d. Add checkmark bullets to the following paragraphs:

- The three paragraphs in the *Purchase Points* section on page 3, beginning with *Determine your family's vacation needs* and ending with *A Calypso resort is never far away*.
- The two paragraphs in the *Plan Your Vacation* section on page 3, beginning with *Choose when, where, and for how long* and ending with *make and cancel reservations*.
- The two paragraphs near the top of page 4, beginning with *With each reservation* and ending with *as your vacation needs change*.
- The two paragraphs in the *Take Off!* section on page 4, beginning with *Not only are you entitled* and ending with *Take your pick!*.

e. Apply a hollow round bullet to the first five paragraphs on page 4, beginning with *Make points reservations* and ending with *Access frequently questions*. Indent the five paragraphs with hollow round bullets so they appear as a sublevel of the checkmarked bullets on the previous page.

Review Word Usage

You will check for spelling and grammatical errors, correcting any that are identified. You will also use the thesaurus to identify an alternate word.

a. Use Word's Spelling & Grammar feature to check for spelling and grammatical errors, making any necessary corrections. The word *Your* is used correctly in the document, as is the word *later*.

b. Use Word's Thesaurus to identify an alternate word for *globally* in the fourth paragraph on page 2. Replace *globally* with *worldwide*.

Apply and Modify Styles

Headings are used in the document but are not clearly delineated. You will apply heading styles to the headings and modify a heading style.

a. Apply **Heading 1** style to the following headings, beginning on page 2:
Explore the World with the Leader in Vacation Club Ownership
Vacation Club Points
The Points System
Ready to Begin Your Experience?

b. Apply **Heading 2** style to the following headings, beginning on page 2:
Flexibility
Convenience
Affordability
Purchase Points
Plan Your Vacation
Take Off!

c. Modify the Heading 1 style to include an underline and a font color of **Orange, Accent 2, Darker 25%**. Modify the Heading 2 style to include a font color of **Orange, Accent 2, Darker 25%**.

Insert Features that Improve Readability

You will insert symbols to improve readability. You will also include a page number, adjust margins, and insert a page break.

a. Place the insertion point to the left of the heading *Purchase Points* on page 3. Insert a number 1 symbol from the (normal text) font, character code **2776**. Similarly, insert a number 2 symbol (character code **2777**) at the left of the heading *Plan Your Vacation* heading, and a number 3 symbol (character code **2778**) at the left of the heading *Take Off!*.

b. Replace the hyphen between the words *program* and *Calypso* in the third multiline paragraph on page 2 with an **em dash symbol**.

c. Insert a page number footer, using a center-aligned **Plain Number 2 selection**.

d. Change the margins on all sides to **1"**. Insert a page break before the *The Points System* heading on page 4.

Work with Columns and Section Breaks

You will format sections of the document differently, including a two-column format for some areas and a one-column format for others. In addition, you will add a page border to one section of the document. You will insert section breaks appropriately so that formatting can differ.

a. Place the insertion point after the word *Team* (before the Page Break) at the end of the text on page 1. Add a **Continuous section break** at the location of the insertion point.

b. Click anywhere on page 2 and add a page border. Select a **Box border** with a color of **Orange, Accent 2, Darker 25%**. Apply the border to **This section**. Accept all other default border settings.

c. Select text on pages 5 and 6, beginning with *Destinations Plus* and ending with *Calypso Vacation Services* (before the final line in the document). Format the selection in two columns.

d. Center the final paragraph in the document, beginning with *For more information*.

Insert and Format Graphics

You will modify the WordArt object at the beginning of page 2 so that it coordinates with other elements of the document. You will also insert a graphic in the two-columned section near the end of the document.

a. Select the WordArt object at the top of page 2. Change the font size of the second line in the WordArt object, *Relax with Us*, to **24 pt**. Change the WordArt style to **Fill – Orange, Accent 2, Outline – Accent 2**. Change the WordArt Shape Style to **Colored Fill – Orange, Accent 2**. Apply a Shape Effect of **Bevel, Riblet**. Visually center the WordArt object horizontally, using the green alignment guides to assist.

b. Click to the left of the *Explorer* heading on page 5. Insert an online picture, using **Airplane** as a search term and selecting the picture of a jet in flight titled *Airplane in sunny sky* (also included in your data files). Change the height to **0.8"** and wrap text as **Tight**. Remove the background from the picture, keeping the suggested changes. Drag to position the graphic at the top right corner of the left column, using the green alignment guides to position it in the top-right corner of the column.

Insert Tables

You will create two tables to describe the vacation club points system.

a. Insert a blank paragraph after the *The Points System* section (not the heading, but the paragraph following, ending in *Calypso Points ownership levels*). Insert a 4 × 6 table and populate it as follows:

Calypso Club Points	Purchase Price (one-time)	Maintenance Fees	Annual Club Dues
1,500 points	$11,700	$325	$175
2,500 points	$19,250	$575	$175
3,500 points	$25,300	$785	$175
5,000 points	$30,250	$1,015	$175
6,500 points	$34,890	$1,500	$215

b. Select a table style of **Grid Table 4 – Accent 2**. AutoFit the contents of the table. Center align all dollar amounts in the last three columns.

c. Select the second, third, and fourth columns. Change the properties of the selected columns to include a width of **1.3"**. Insert a column at the right of the Annual Club Dues column and add the column heading **Total Fees and Dues**. Include a formula in the new column for each points level, adding Maintenance Fees and Annual Club Dues. Delete the extra paragraph mark below the table.

d. Click before the last line in the document, beginning with *For More Information*, and press **Enter**. Click before the new blank paragraph, clear all formatting, and then insert a 3 × 4 table. Create the following table, merging all cells in the first row. Bold entries in rows 1 and 2 and center items in columns 2 and 3 (and row 1).

Bonus Time Reservation Window		
	La Sonora and Wailaki	All Other Resorts
Book Online	83 days	36 days
Call Vacation Services	80 days	32 days

e. Shade row 1 with **Orange, Accent 2, Darker 25%**. Shade remaining rows with **Orange, Accent 2, Lighter 40%**. Select the entire table. Select a Pen Color of **Orange, Accent 2, Darker 50%** and apply the color to **Outside Borders**. Select a **double-underline Line Style** and apply it to the border dividing row 1 and row 2. Press **Esc**.

Insert Captions and a Footnote

You will add captions to the two tables and provide additional information in a footnote.

a. Click anywhere in the first table and insert a caption below the table: **Table 1: Calypso Points System**. Insert a caption below the second table: **Table 2: Bonus Time Reservations**.

b. Modify the Caption style to include a font color of **Orange, Accent 2, Darker 25%**.

c. Click after the words *Calypso Club Points* in the top-left cell of Table 1. Insert a footnote: **The examples in this table are for illustrative purposes only. The number of points required for club rentals may change from time to time**. Save as **w00ac1Travel_LastFirst**.

Complete a Mail Merge

You will prepare a mailing to new owners, merging the document you have prepared with a data source.

a. Move to the beginning of the document. Begin a new mail merge, creating letters using the current document. The data source is the *NewOwners* workbook, using the Sheet1 worksheet.

b. Insert an Address Block, using default settings, in the identified area on page 1. Include the number of points (Points Purchased) in place of the bracketed area on page 2. Insert or type the current date at the top of the letter on page 1.

c. Merge all records, resulting in an 18-page document, with letters and a Quick Start Guide going to each of the three new owners. Save the new document as **w00ac1MergedTravel_LastFirst**.

d. Submit *w00ac1MergedTravel_LastFirst* according to your instructor's directions. Close *w00ac1Travel_LastFirst* without saving it.

You are an intern with the Hospitality Industry Professionals Association (HIPA), which hosts a conference for its members every year at different locations in this country. This year, the conference will be held July 20–22 in Miami, Florida. One of your responsibilities is to create a document that provides a description of HIPA and the conference, the conference agenda, and a form for members to calculate conference expenses. You will apply several Word features to make the document look more professional. Then, you will insert several form controls into the Calculate Your Expenses table and create a macro to align the document. After you create the Agenda bookmark, you will create hyperlinks to this bookmark, the About HIPA bookmarks, and also to a Web site. Restrict the editing to allow filling in forms so that members can only type in description and expense into the Expenses table. Finally, you will create and insert a digital signature into the document.

Save a Template as a Word Document and Combine Two Documents

You will open a Word template and save it as a Word document. Then you will combine this saved document with the content from another Word file to create the Conference document.

a. Start Word. Open the Word template file named *w00c2ConferenceTemplate.dotx*.

b. Save a copy of the template as a Word document with the file name **w00c2Original.docx**.

c. Combine the contents of the *w00c2Original.docx* and the *w00c2Revised.docx* documents into a new document.

d. Accept all changes in the combined document.

e. Save the combined document as **w00c2Conference_LastFirst.docx**.

f. Close all documents except for *w00c2Conference_LastFirst.docx*.

Insert a Continuous Section Break and a Column Break

You want to format the document to have two columns below the masthead. Therefore, you will insert a continuous section break near the beginning of the document and change the column layout. Also, you want the column content to look balanced on the page, so you will insert a column break on the first page.

a. Position the insertion point immediately to the left of the *Description* heading and insert a Continuous section break.

b. Change the layout of the section starting with the *Description* heading to two equal columns, with a line between.

c. Change the left and right margins to **0.75"**.

d. Position your insertion point immediately to the left of the paragraph that begins *In addition to* and insert a column break.

Copy and Paste a Link to a Spreadsheet File

You will copy and paste the content of a spreadsheet file to the Word document. But you also want to maintain the link so that the data in the Word document can be updated when you make changes to the spreadsheet file.

a. Open the *w00c2Fields.xlsx* spreadsheet file.

b. Copy the **range A1:B8** to the Clipboard.

c. Click the Word document on the taskbar.

d. Paste the copied Excel data as a linked Microsoft Office Excel Worksheet Object in the first blank paragraph of the Word document, below the paragraph that begins *The Hospitality Industry*.

e. Center the object in the left column.

f. Close the spreadsheet file.

Insert a WordArt Object and Format a Paragraph

You will improve the appearance of the document with a masthead created using WordArt, format a selected paragraph, and use shading.

a. Insert a WordArt object at the beginning of the document by doing the following steps:

- Position the insertion point to the left of the text *About HIPA* and insert a Gradient Fill - Aqua, Accent 1, Reflection WordArt.
- Type **HIPA 2016 Conference** as the text for the WordArt.
- Change the width of the WordArt to **6.47"** and the height to **1.6"**.
- Change the font size to **48 pt**.
- Change the wrapping style of the WordArt object to **Top and Bottom**.

b. Format a paragraph with shading and a border by following the steps below:

- Select the paragraph beginning *In addition to*.
- Apply a **Blue, Accent 1, Lighter 80% shading** to the selected paragraph.
- Set the border width to **1 pt**.
- Set the border color to **Blue, Accent 1, Darker 50%**.

Insert a Logo, a SmartArt Graphic, and Group Objects

A logo will help to improve the visibility of the association, so you want to insert a logo below the first heading of the document. You will continue to improve the appearance of the document by using a SmartArt graphic and by grouping four stars together.

a. Insert a logo for HIPA by implementing the following steps:

- Position the insertion point immediately to the left of the text *The Hospitality Industry* under the *Description* heading.
- Insert the *w00c2Logo.png* file.
- Resize the logo's height to **1.5"**. The width will automatically change to 1.05".
- Apply the **Tight wrapping style** to the picture.

b. Insert a Vertical Curved List SmartArt graphic by doing the following steps:

- Position your insertion point in the first blank paragraph below the paragraph that begins *A few of the main reasons.*
- Insert a Vertical Curved List SmartArt graphic.
- Type the following text into the three shapes (from top to bottom):

  Educational Opportunities

  In-person Networking

  Inspiration and Innovation
- Change the height of the three shapes in the SmartArt graphic to **0.5"**.

c. Select the four star shapes immediately below the newly created SmartArt graphic and group them together.

Create and Insert Subdocuments

You will highlight a portion of the text in the Conference document and convert the selected text into a subdocument. The conference agenda is in another file so you will insert the content of the conference agenda into the document that you are currently working on.

a. Switch to Outline view to create and insert subdocuments.

b. Select the heading *Calculate Your Expenses* and the table that follows it.

c. Click **Show Document** and click **Create** to create a subdocument.

d. Select the **Agenda heading** and insert the subdocument *w00c2Agenda.docx* into the current document.

e. Agree to rename the style in the subdocument, when prompted. Note: The original *Agenda* heading will be replaced when the subdocument is inserted.

f. Unlink all subdocuments since you prefer to have the files' content in the document that you are currently working on.

g. Close Outline view.

Insert a Header, and Apply a Document and a Font Theme

You want to include a header, which will display the title of the document and the date that you are preparing the document. You will then apply a document theme and a font theme to the document so that all the features in the Word document are color-coordinated.

a. Insert the header building block named *Retrospect*.

b. Type **Conference Information** in the **Title field**.

c. Type **1/1/2016** in the **Date field**.

d. Apply the **Retrospect theme** to the document.

e. Apply the **Office font theme** to the document.

f. Apply a page background color that uses the **Newsprint texture fill effect**.

Insert Form Fields

You want to insert several form fields into the document. For instance, you want to use a Date Picker content control for date, a Drop-Down List content control to list item choices available to members, a Text Form field to display the individual amount, and another Text Form field to calculate the Total Expenses incurred for the conference.

a. Show the Developer tab on the Ribbon.

b. Turn on Design Mode.

c. Insert a Date Picker Content Control in the table on page 3, in the cell immediately below *Date*.

d. Insert a Drop-Down List content control in the same table, in the cell immediately below *Type of Expense*.

e. Set the properties for the drop-down list to display **Type of Expense** as the title. Enter **Type** in the **Tag box**.

f. Add the following items to the list in the order given:

Transportation

Lodging

Meals

Misc.

a. Insert the Legacy control, Text Form Field in the table, in the cell below *Amount*.

b. Set the properties of the text form field to be a number, the default number to **0**, and the format to **#,##0**. Replace the contents of the Bookmark box with **Amt1** and select the option to **Calculate on exit**.

c. Insert the Legacy control, Text Form Field in the cell to the right of *Total Expenses*.

d. Set the properties of the text form field to be a calculation, the expression to **=SUM(ABOVE)**, and the format to **$#,##0.00;($#,##0.00)**.

e. Turn off Design Mode.

Create a Macro

A macro can be very useful if you need to repeat a certain set of specified tasks regularly. You will practice your macro skills by creating a macro to align the adjustment of the document and then editing the macro using the Visual Basic editor.

a. Create a new macro by doing the following steps:

- Select **Record Macro**.
- Name the macro **Alignment**.
- Type the description of the macro as **Change document alignment** (no period). While recording the macro, be sure to follow the steps exactly as specified. Do not switch between windows in between steps.
- Press **Ctrl+A** to select the entire document.
- Press **Ctrl+E** to change the alignment of the entire document to center.
- Stop recording the macro.

b. Edit the macro by completing the following steps:

- Open the Alignment macro in the Visual Basic Editor.
- Edit the text *Selection.ParagraphFormat.Alignment = wdAlignParagraphCenter* to read **Selection.ParagraphFormat.Alignment = wdAlignParagraphLeft**.
- Save the macro.

c. Copy the entire Alignment macro from the Sub statement to the End Sub statement inclusive to the Clipboard.

d. Click the Word document and paste the code into the last line of this Word document.

e. Run the Alignment macro.

Insert Bookmarks and Hyperlink

Bookmarks and hyperlinks will help members to move quickly from one part of the document to another. You want to create a new bookmark and then hyperlink the newly created bookmark and an existing bookmark to the right place. You will also add a Web site link to the document for easier access to the conference Web site.

a. Create a bookmark to the left of the *Conference Agenda* heading on page 2, using **Agenda** for the name of the bookmark.

b. Create a hyperlink from the word *Agenda*, at the top of page 1, to the Agenda bookmark.

c. Create a hyperlink from the text *About HIPA* to the About bookmark.

d. Select the text *Web site* on page 1, at the bottom of the paragraph that begins *The Hospitality Industry*, and create a hyperlink to the Web page http://www.hipa .conference.net. (Note: This link does not actually open a live Web site.)

Restrict Editing

You do not want the members to make any editorial changes to the document, but at the same time, you want them to be able to enter the data pertaining to their conference expenses.

a. Click the **REVIEW tab** and restrict editing in the document by checking the **Limit formatting to a selection of styles check box**.

b. Allow filling in forms as the only type of editing in the document.

c. Start enforcing protection, leaving the password boxes blank.

Create a Digital Certificate and Add a Digital Signature

Finally, you will create a digital certificate using the name Conner Lee and add a digital signature to the document before you send it out to the members as an e-mail attachment.

a. Create a digital certificate for **Conner Lee**. (Hint: Search for the *SELFCERT.EXE* file in File Explorer.)

b. Add a digital signature to the document for Conner Lee. Note that you may have to change the signature to select Conner Lee.

c. Type **verify integrity of contents** (no period) in the **Purpose for signing this document box**.

d. Click **Yes** to use the certificate if a warning that the certificate cannot be verified is displayed.

e. Ignore any references to Invalid Signatures that may be displayed in the Backstage view after this step is completed.

f. Save and close the document, and exit Word.

g. Submit the *w00c2Conference_LastFirst.docx* document as directed.

Glossary

Access Relational database management software that enables you to record and link data, query databases, and create forms and reports.

ActiveX control A form element designed for use in Office 2007 or later versions and that requires a macro to work.

Alignment guide A horizontal or vertical green bar that appears as you move an object, assisting with aligning the object with text or with another object.

APA (American Psychological Association) Writing style established by the American Psychological Association with rules and conventions for documenting sources and organizing a research paper (used primarily in business and the social sciences).

Argument A positional reference, contained in parentheses within a function.

AutoRecover A feature that enables Word to recover a previous version of a document.

Background A color, design, image, or watermark that appears behind text in a document or on a Web page.

Backstage view A component of Office 2013 that provides a concise collection of commands related to common file activities and provides information on an open file.

Backup A copy of a file or folder on another drive.

Bibliography A list of works cited or consulted by an author in his or her work.

Blog The chronological publication of personal thoughts and Web links.

Bookmark A feature that provides an electronic marker for a specific location in a document, enabling you to find that location quickly.

Border A line that surrounds a paragraph, page, or a table or table element.

Border Painter A feature that enables you to choose border formatting and click on any table border to apply the formatting.

Building Block A predefined object to insert quickly and easily for frequently used document components, such as a disclaimer, company address, logo, or cover page.

Bulleted list A graphic element that itemizes and separates paragraph text to increase readability; often used to identify lists.

CAPTCHA A scrambled code used with online forms to prevent mass sign-ups. It helps to ensure that an actual person is requesting the account.

Caption A descriptive title for a table.

Cell The intersection of a column and row in a table.

Center alignment Positions text horizontally in the center of a line, an equal distance from both the left and right margins.

Charms A toolbar for Windows 8.1.1 made up of five icons (Search, Share, Start, Devices, and Settings) that enables you to search for files and applications, share information with others within an application that is running, return to the Start screen, control devices that are connected to your computer, or modify various settings depending on which application is running when accessing the Setting icon.

Check box form field Consists of a box that can be checked or unchecked.

Chicago Writing style established by the University of Chicago with rules and conventions for preparing an academic paper for publication.

Citation A note recognizing a source of information or a quoted passage.

Clip art An electronic illustration that can be inserted into an Office project.

Clipboard An Office feature that temporarily holds selections that have been cut or copied and allows you to paste the selections.

Cloud storage A technology used to store files and to work with programs that are stored in a central location on the Internet.

Column A format that separates document text into side-by-side vertical blocks, often used in newsletters.

Combine A feature that integrates all changes from multiple authors or documents into one single document.

Command A button or area within a group that you click to perform tasks.

Comment balloon A note, annotation, or additional information to the author or another reader about the content of a document.

Compare A Word feature that evaluates the contents of two or more documents and displays markup balloons showing the differences between the two documents.

Contextual tab A Ribbon tab that displays when an object, such as a picture or table, is selected. A contextual tab contains groups and commands specific to the selected object.

Copy To duplicate an item from the original location and place the copy in the Office Clipboard.

Cover page The first page of a report, including the report title, author or student, and other identifying information.

Crop The process of reducing an image size by eliminating unwanted portions of an image or other graphical object.

CSE (Council of Science Editors) Writing style providing rules and conventions for preparing reports in the sciences.

Current List Includes all citation sources you use in the current document.

Curriculum Vitae (CV) Similar to a resume, displays your skills, accomplishments, job history, or other employment information, and is often used by academics.

Cut To remove an item from the original location and place it in the Office Clipboard.

Data source A list of information that is merged with a main document during a mail merge procedure.

Date Picker Displays a calendar that the user can navigate on an electronic form and click rather than typing in a date.

Default Office settings that remain in effect unless you specify otherwise.

Design Mode Enables you to view and select the control fields to allow for modifications to the control field layout or options.

Desktop publishing The merger of text with graphics to produce a professional-looking document.

Dialog box A window that displays when a program requires interaction with you, such as inputting information, before completing a procedure. This window typically provides access to more precise, but less frequently used, commands.

Dialog Box Launcher An icon in a Ribbon group that you can click to open a related dialog box. It is not found in all groups.

Digital certificate An attachment to a file that guarantees the authenticity of the file, provides a verifiable signature, or enables encryption.

Digital signature An electronic stamp that displays information about a person or organization that obtained the certification.

Document Inspector Checks for and removes certain hidden and personal information from a document.

Document Panel Provides descriptive information about a document, such as a title, subject, author, keywords, and comments.

Document theme A set of coordinating fonts, colors, and special effects that gives a stylish and professional look.

Draft view View that shows a great deal of document space, but no margins, headers, footers, or other special features.

Drawing canvas A frame-like area that helps you keep parts of your drawing together.

Drop cap A large capital letter at the beginning of a paragraph.

Drop-down list Enables the user to choose from one of several existing entries.

Editing restriction Specifies limits for users to modify a document.

Embedding Imports an object into a document from its original source and allows editing directly in the document without changing the source data file.

Endnote A citation that appears at the end of a document.

Enhanced ScreenTip A feature that provides a brief summary of a command when you point to the command button.

Excel A software application used to organize records, financial transactions, and business information in the form of worksheets.

Field The smallest data element in a table, such as first name, last name, address, or phone number.

File Electronic data such as documents, databases, slide shows, worksheets, digital photographs, music, videos, and Web pages.

File Explorer A component of the Windows operating system that can be used to create and manage folders.

File Transfer Protocol (FTP) A process that uploads files from a PC to a server or from a server to a PC.

Fill The interior space of an object.

Find An Office feature that locates a word or phrase that you indicate in a document.

First line indent Marks the location to indent only the first line in a paragraph.

Folder A directory into which you place data files in order to organize them for easier retrieval.

Font A combination of typeface and type style.

Footer Information that generally displays at the bottom of a document page, worksheet, slide or database report.

Footnote A citation that appears at the bottom of a page.

Form control Helps a user complete a form by displaying prompts such as drop-down lists and text boxes.

Form letter A letter with standard information that you personalize with recipient information, which you might print or e-mail to many people.

Form template A document that defines the standard layout, structure, and formatting of a form.

Format Painter A command that copies the formatting of text from one location to another.

Formatting The process of modifying text by changing font and paragraph characteristics.

Formatting restriction Ensures that others do not modify formatting or styles in a document.

Formula A combination of cell references, operators, values, and/or functions used to perform a calculation.

Full Screen Mode Provides a completely clear document space in which to edit a document.

Function A predefined computation that simplifies creating a complex calculation and produces a result based on inputs known as arguments.

Gallery A set of selections that displays when you click a More button, or in some cases when you click a command, in a Ribbon group.

Grid An underlying, but invisible, set of horizontal and vertical lines that determine the placement of major elements.

Group A subset of a tab that organizes similar tasks together; to combine two or more objects.

Grouping The process of combining selected objects so they appear as a single object.

Hanging indent Aligns the first line of a paragraph at the left margin, indenting remaining lines in the paragraph.

Header Information that generally displays at the top of a document page, worksheet, slide or database report.

Header row The first row in a data source that contains labels describing the data in rows beneath.

Homegroup A Windows 8.1.1 feature that enables you to share resources on a home network.

Hyperlink An electronic marker that points to a different location within the same document, another document, or displays a different Web page.

HyperText Markup Language (HTML) Uses codes to describe how a document appears when viewed in a Web browser.

Indent A setting associated with the way a paragraph is distanced from one or more margins.

Index An alphabetical listing of topics covered in a document, along with the page numbers on which the topic is discussed.

Information Rights Management (IRM) Services designed to help control who can access documents containing sensitive or confidential information.

Insert control An indicator that displays between rows or columns in a table; click the indicator to insert one or more rows or columns.

Insertion point Blinking bar that indicates where text that you next type will appear.

Internet A network of networks that connects computers anywhere in the world.

Justified alignment Spreads text evenly between the left and right margins, so that text begins at the left margin and ends uniformly at the right margin.

Key Tip The letter or number for the associated keyboard shortcut that displays over features on the Ribbon or Quick Access Toolbar.

Landscape orientation An orientation for a displayed page or worksheet that is wider than it is tall.

Layering The process of placing one object on top of another.

Left alignment Begins text evenly at the left margin, with a ragged right edge.

Left indent A setting that positions all text in a paragraph an equal distance from the left margin.

Legacy form field A form element that is created or used in Word 2003 and later. When used in a later version of Word, the document must be opened in Compatibility Mode.

Legal blacklining The comparing of two documents and the displaying of the changes between the two documents using Word.

Library A collection of files from different locations that is displayed as a single unit.

Line spacing The vertical spacing between lines in a paragraph.

Linking The process of importing an object from another program, but the object retains a connection to the original data file.

Live Preview An Office feature that provides a preview of the results of a selection when you point to an option in a list or gallery. Using Live Preview, you can experiment with settings before making a final choice.

Macro A set of instructions that executes a specific task or series of keystrokes that complete a repetitive task using only a button click or keyboard shortcut.

Macro-Enabled Document Adds the extension .docm to the file and stores VBA macro code in the document to enable execution of a macro.

Mail Merge A process that combines content from a main document and a data source.

Main document Contains the information that stays the same for all recipients in a mail merge.

Margin The area of blank space that displays to the left, right, top, and bottom of a document or worksheet.

Mark as Final Creates a read-only file and also sets the property to Final on the status bar.

Markup balloon A bordered area in the margin of a report that contains a comment and any replies to the comment.

Master document A document that acts like a binder for managing smaller documents.

Master List A database of all citation sources created in Word on a particular computer.

Masthead The identifying information at the top of a newsletter or other periodical.

Merge field Serves as a placeholder for the variable data that will be inserted into the main document during a mail merge procedure.

Microsoft Office A productivity software suite including four primary software components, each one specializing in a particular type of output.

Mini Toolbar The feature that provides access to common formatting commands, displayed when text is selected.

MLA (Modern Language Association) Writing style established by the Modern Language Association, with rules and conventions for preparing research papers (used primarily in the area of humanities).

Navigation Pane Enables you to navigate through a document by viewing headings, viewing pages, and browsing the results of your last search.

Normal template The framework that defines the default page settings for all new blank Word documents.

Numbered list Sequences items in a list by displaying a successive number beside each item.

Object An item, such as a picture or text box, that can be individually selected and manipulated in a document.

Object Linking and Embedding (OLE) A technology that enables you to insert and link objects or information into different applications.

OneDrive An application used to store, access, and share files and folders.

OneDrive for Windows app A downloadable app that synchronizes documents between a computer and OneDrive storage so that documents in both locations remain up to date.

Operating system Software that directs computer activities such as checking all components, managing system resources, and communicating with application software.

Order of operations (order of precedence) Determines the sequence by which operations are calculated in an expression.

Outline view A structural view of a document that can be collapsed or expanded as necessary.

Paragraph spacing The amount of space before or after a paragraph.

Paste To place a cut or copied item in another location.

PDF Reflow Word feature that converts a PDF document into an editable Word document.

Picture A graphic file that is retrieved from storage media or the Internet and placed in an Office project.

Placeholder A field or block of text used to determine the position of objects in a document.

Plagiarizing The act of using and documenting the works of another as one's own.

Portable Document Format (PDF) A file type that was created for exchanging documents independent of software applications and operating system environment.

Portrait orientation An orientation for a displayed page or worksheet that is taller than it is wide.

PowerPoint A software application used to create dynamic presentations to inform groups and persuade audiences.

Print Layout view View that closely resembles the way a document will look when printed.

Pull quote A phrase or sentence taken from an article to emphasize a key point.

Quick Access Toolbar A component of Office 2013, located at the top-left corner of the Office window, that provides handy access to commonly executed tasks such as saving a file and undoing recent actions.

Range A group of adjacent or contiguous cells in an Excel worksheet.

Read Mode View in which text reflows automatically between columns to make it easier to read.

Record A group of related fields representing one entity, such as data for one person, place, event, or concept.

Record macro The process of creating a macro.

References A list of works cited or consulted by an author in his or her work; the list is titled *References*.

Replace An Office feature that finds text and replaces it with a word or phrase that you indicate.

Reverse A technique that uses light text on a dark background.

Revision mark Indicates where text is added, deleted, or formatted while the Track Changes feature is active.

Ribbon The long bar of tabs, groups, and commands located just beneath the Title bar.

Right alignment Begins text evenly at the right margin, with a ragged left edge.

Right indent A setting that positions all text in a paragraph an equal distance from the right margin.

Run macro The process of playing back or using a macro.

Sans serif font A font that does not contain a thin line or extension at the top and bottom of the primary strokes on characters.

Section break An indicator that divides a document into parts, enabling different formatting for each section.

Serif font A font that contains a thin line or extension at the top and bottom of the primary strokes on characters.

Shading A background color that appears behind text in a paragraph, page, or table element.

Shortcut menu Provides choices related to the selection or area at which you right-click.

Sidebar Supplementary text that appears along side the featured information.

Signature line Enables the user of the document to digitally sign the document.

Simple Markup Word feature that simplifies the display of comments and revision marks, resulting in a clean, uncluttered look.

Sizing handle A series of faint dots on the outside border of a selected chart or object; enables the user to adjust the height and width of the chart or object.

SmartArt A visual representation of information that can be created to effectively communicate a message or idea in one of many existing and visually appealing layout.

Snip The output of using the Snipping Tool.

Snipping Tool A Windows 8.1.1 accessory program that provides users the ability to capture an image of all (or part of) their computer's screen.

Source A publication, person, or media item that is consulted in the preparation of a paper and given credit.

Start screen The display that you see after you turn on your computer and respond to any username and password prompts.

Status bar A horizontal bar found at the bottom of the program window that contains information relative to the open file.

Style A named collection of formatting characteristics that can be applied to text or paragraphs.

Style manual A guide to a particular writing style outlining required rules and conventions related to the preparation of papers.

Style set A combination of title, heading, and paragraph styles that can be used to format all of those elements in a document at one time.

Subdocument A smaller document that is a part of a master document.

Subfolder A folder that is housed within another folder.

Symbol A character or graphic not normally included on a keyboard.

Synchronous scrolling Enables you to simultaneously scroll through both documents in Side by Side view at the same time.

Tab (Office Fundamentals) A component of the Ribbon that is designed to appear much like a tab on a file folder, with the active tab highlighted, that is used to organize groups by function. (Word) A marker that specifies the position for aligning text in a column arrangement, often including a dot leader.

Table A grid of columns and rows that organizes data.

Table alignment The position of a table between the left and right document margins.

Table of Contents Page that lists headings in the order in which they appear in a document and the page numbers on which the entries begin.

Table style A named collection of color, font, and border design that can be applied to a table.

Template A partially completed document containing preformatted text or graphics.

Text box A graphical object that contains text.

Text content control Used to enter any type of text into a form.

Text pane A special pane that opens up for entering text when a SmartArt diagram is selected.

Theme A collection of design choices that includes colors, fonts, and special effects used to give a consistent look to a document, workbook, database form or report, or presentation.

Theme color Represents coordinated colors for the current text and background, accents, and hyperlinks.

Theme effect Includes lines, fill effects, and 3-D effects such as shadowing, glows, and borders to incorporate into a document theme.

Theme font Contains a coordinating heading and body text font for each different theme.

Thesaurus A tool used to quickly find a synonym (a word with the same meaning as another).

Thumbnail A small picture of each page in your document that displays in the Navigation Pane.

Tile A colorful block on the Start screen that when clicked will launch a program, file, folder, or other Windows 8.1.1 app.

Title bar A component of Microsoft Office that identifies the current file name and the application in which you are working and includes control buttons that enable you to minimize, maximize, restore down, or close the application window.

Toggle The action of switching from one setting to another. Several Home tab tasks, such as Bold and Italic, are actually toggle commands.

Track Changes Word feature that monitors all additions, deletions, and formatting changes you make in a document.

Turabian Writing style that originated with the Chicago style but omits much of the information that is relevant for publishing.

Ungrouping Breaks a grouped object into separate individual objects.

User exception An individual or group that is allowed to edit all or specific parts of a restricted document.

User interface The screen display through which you communicate with the software.

View The way a file appears onscreen.

View Side by Side Enables you to display two documents on the same screen.

Visual Basic for Applications (VBA) A programming language that is built into Microsoft Office.

Watermark Text or graphic that displays behind text.

Web Layout view View that displays how a document will look when posted on the Internet.

Web page Any document that displays on the World Wide Web.

Web server A computer system that hosts pages for viewing by anyone with an Internet connection.

Windows 8.1.1 A Microsoft operating system released in 2012 that can operate on touch-screen devices as well as laptops and desktops because it has been designed to accept multiple methods of input.

Windows 8.1.1 OneDrive app An application specifically designed to run in the Start screen interface of Windows 8.1.1 that is either already installed and ready to use or can be downloaded from the Windows Store.

Wizard A tool that makes a process easier by asking a series of questions, then creating a structure based on your answers.

Word A word processing software application used to produce all sorts of documents, including memos, newsletters, forms, tables, and brochures.

Word processing software A computer application, such as Microsoft Word, used primarily with text to create, edit, and format documents.

Word Online An online component of Office Online presenting a free, although limited, version of Word 2013.

Word wrap The feature that automatically moves words to the next line if they do not fit on the current line.

WordArt A Microsoft Office feature that creates decorative text that can be used to add interest to the text used in a document.

Works cited A list of works cited or consulted by an author in his or her work; the list is titled *Works Cited*.

World Wide Web (WWW) A very large subset of the Internet that stores Web page documents.

Writing style Writing a paper as directed by a style manual such as MLA or APA.

Zoom slider A horizontal bar on the far right side of the status bar that enables you to increase or decrease the size of file contents onscreen.

Index

Insert Video dialog box, 510
inserting
    Building Blocks, 379–381
    columns/rows, in Word tables, 208–209
    file object, combining two
        documents, 390
    form controls, 431–432
    headers and footers, 103–105
    hyperlinks, in Web pages, 492–493
    merge fields, 235, 239–240
    objects, 60–62
    OLE and, 352–355
    photos, in Web pages, 509–510
    pictures, 61, 177–179
    rows/columns, in Word tables, 208–209
    screenshots, 178
    shapes, 339–340
    SmartArt, 334–336
    symbols, 105–106
    table captions, 227–228
    text boxes, 337–338
    watermarks, 103, 108
    Word tables, 206–211
    WordArt, 183–184, 336–337
    workbooks, in documents, 354–355
    worksheets, in documents, 207
insertion point, 91
interface. *See also* Start screen; user
        interface
    File Explorer, 10–11
Internet, 484
Internet Explorer, 4, 5, 484
in-text citations, 266
invite others to share documents, 289
invoice, forms, 428–429
IRM (Information Rights Management),
    455
italic, 322, 326
Italic command, 48, 147

less is more, 322
libraries, 11–12
ligature, 148
line spacing, 151
Link to file option, Object dialog box, 354
Linked Worksheet Object, 355
LinkedIn, 286, 290, 293
linking
    defined, 352
    OLE, 352–356
    text boxes, 338–339
    updating linked objects, 355–356
lists
    bulleted/numbered, 155–156
    Current List, 263
    defined, 321
    drop-down, 430–431
    Master List, 263
    recipient list, Mail Merge, 236–237
Live Preview, 26, 144
Lock anchor setting, 343
Lock Drawing Mode, 339–340
locked document, 453
locked paragraphs, 295, 296
locked subdocuments, 391, 392
logging in, Microsoft account, 2–3
long documents, 387–397
    combining two documents, 389–390
    compare two documents, 388–389
    inserting file object, 390
    master documents, 390–393
    merging, 388–393
    resizing, 388
    subdocuments, 390–393
    view two documents side by side, 387–388

M

Macro-Enabled Document, 442
macros, 442–446
    ActiveX controls, 430, 431
    digital signatures, 458–459
    security settings, 446
Macros dialog box, 443–444, 445
Mail, Outlook Inbox, 3, 4
Mail Merge
    completing, 239–240
    data sources, 235–240
    defined, 235
    form letters, 235, 236
    goal of, 239
    main document, 235, 240
    merge fields, 235, 239–240
    recipient list, 236–237
    sort and filter records in data source,
        238–239
    wizard, 235–236
main document, Mail Merge, 235, 240
manipulating graphic objects, 340–344
margins
    Cell Margins command, 213
    defined, 65, 106
    documents, 65–66, 106–107
    worksheet data, 65–66, 106–107

Mark as Final command, 452–453
markup
    All Markup, 278, 279
    No Markup, 279, 281
    Show Markup, 282
    Simple Markup, 278–282
master documents, 390–393
Master List, 263
masthead, 323–324
Math Tutoring Club Web page, 488
mathematical order of precedence, 222
mathematics and formulas. *See also*
        functions
    defined, 220
    in documents, 223
    order of precedence, 222
    Word tables, 220–223
MAX function, 223
merge and split, Word table cells,
    209–210
merge fields, 235, 239–240
merging multiple documents, 388–393
metadata, 124
Microsoft account, 2–3, 287
Microsoft Authenticode technology, 458
Microsoft Certificate Center, 458
Microsoft Excel Worksheet Object, 353
Microsoft Office (Office 2013). *See also*
        Access 2013; Excel 2013; PowerPoint
        2013; Word 2013
    applications, characteristics, 22
    common interface components, 22–29
    defined, 22
    Help, 28–29
Microsoft Office Security Options dialog
        box, 446
Microsoft Word dialog box, 459, 460
MIN function, 223
Mini toolbar, 46–47, 146
minus (–) sign, on Start screen, 4
MLA (Modern Language Association)
        writing style, 260–261, 264, 265
Modern Language Association (MLA)
        writing style, 260–261, 264, 265
modify and select styles, 166–167
Modify Style dialog box, 167, 228
modifying
    footnotes and endnotes, 267–268
    macros, 443–444
    master and subdocuments, 392–393
    passwords, 457
    pictures, 181
    text boxes, 183
monospaced font, 146
move to beginning (Ctrl+Home), 27
move to end (Ctrl+End), 27
moving
    files and folders, 16
    pictures, 179–180
    ranges, 407
    text, Clipboard group commands,
        50–51
    text boxes, 183
multilevel lists, 156

Wrap Text button, 343
wrapping
    text wrap feature, Word, 179–180
    word wrap feature, 88
writing styles, 260–261, 262, 264, 265.
    See also research papers
WWW (Web, World Wide Web), 484

XPS files, Create PDF/XPS, 282

YouTube, 504, 510

Z

Zoom slider, 28, 86, 111
Zoom to Page, 39
Zune, 287